International Relations

CONFLICT AND COOPERATION AT THE TURN OF THE 21ST CENTURY

Conway W. Henderson
University of South Carolina—Spartanburg

Boston   Burr Ridge, IL   Dubuque, IA   Madison, WI   New York   San Francisco   St. Louis
Bangkok   Bogotá   Caracas   Lisbon   London   Madrid
Mexico City   Milan   New Delhi   Seoul   Singapore   Sydney   Taipei   Toronto

McGraw-Hill
*A Division of The **McGraw·Hill** Companies*

INTERNATIONAL RELATIONS: CONFLICT AND COOPERATION AT THE TURN OF THE 21st CENTURY

Copyright © 1998 by The McGraw-Hill Companies, Inc. All rights reserved. Printed in the United States of America. Except as permitted under the United States Copyright Act of 1976, no part of this publication may be reproduced or distributed in any form or by any means, or stored in a data base or retrieval system, without the prior written permission of the publisher.

This book is printed on acid-free paper.

1 2 3 4 5 7 8 9 0 DOC/DOC 9 0 9 8 7

ISBN 0-07-028255-2

Editorial director: Phillip A. Butcher/Jane Vaicunas
Sponsoring editor: Leslye Jackson
Editorial coordinator: Stephanie Cappiello
Marketing manager: Annie Mitchell
Project manager: Jim Labeots
Production supervisor: Melonie Salvati
Designer: Kiera Cunningham
Compositor: Shepard Poorman Communications
Typeface: 10/12 Times Roman
Printer: R. R. Donnelley & Sons Company

Henderson, Conway W.
    International relations : conflict and cooperation at the turn of the 21st century / Conway W. Henderson.
     p.   cm.
    ISBN   0-07-028255-2   (acid-free paper)
    Includes bibliographical references.
    1. International relations.   2. International cooperation.   I. Title.
JZ1305.H46 1997
327--dc21   97-20932

http://www.mhhe.com

This book is for two outstanding parents who have given unconditional support and encouragement throughout my life:

Adeline T. Henderson
Lester C. Henderson (1906–1996)

Author's Background

CONWAY W. HENDERSON was born and grew up in Franklin, NC, in the Blue Ridge Mountains. After graduating from Franklin High School in 1961, the author attended and graduated *cum laude* from Wake Forest University in 1965. He then earned his M.A. (1967) and Ph.D. (1971) at the University of Iowa. Since 1971, Professor Henderson has taught a wide range of political science courses at the University of South Carolina at Spartanburg with an emphasis on the international relations field. Although very busy with teaching and various writing projects, the author finds time to be an amateur woodworker and mechanic as well as to spend time with two beautiful grandchildren.

Preface

This textbook is a distinctly post–Cold War learning tool that will help make sense of the rapid changes now taking place in international relations. *International Relations: Conflict and Cooperation at the Turn of the 21st Century* contributes to an understanding of a world more willing to abide by rules and norms, especially as expressed in international law and a world shifting to an emphasis on the "soft power" of economic influence rather than relying on the "hard power" of military force.

This textbook can help students to develop an appreciation for a world of multiple actors where international organizations, international business corporations, churches, terrorist organizations, and many private groups and individuals join the 200 states on the world stage. Many of these varied kinds of actors are interacting with each other in patterns that are increasingly cooperative and designed to deal with the common problems of an interdependent world. Among these problems are the widespread abuse of human rights, environmental concerns, drug smuggling, health problems such as AIDS, economic needs, and weapons proliferation. While this text is cautiously optimistic about humankind's future as we enter the 21st century, the text warns about the continuing turbulence caused by terrorism, rogue states, intense trade competition, ethnic conflict, and the antagonism between rich and poor states.

For students, this text ties the chapters together with an overarching theme that argues the world is moving from an *international anarchy* based on fear and military power to the early stages of an *international society* comprised of multiple actors cooperating to solve problems they cannot handle on their own. Also, this book has a useful set of pedagogical aids that include a set of color maps and numerous pictures and political cartoons. Then, for each chapter, there is a glossary, a section of quotations to stimulate discussion, review questions, and a list of suggested readings. Moreover, the author believes he has written the textbook in a crisp but interesting style that makes the complexities of international relations accessible to a wide range of students, but without neglecting the substance of the field of international relations.

And for professors, this textbook is concisely written and packed into a 15-chapter format, allowing professors on both the semester and quarter system to complete the book within one term. This text will permit professors in the field of international relations to prepare students for a broad range of upper-level international courses, and, yet, non-majors can comfortably read the text as part of a survey course. Additionally, professors can stimulate class discussion not only with quotes and review questions but also with a theoretical section in each chapter. The positions of realists, neorealists, and transnationalists (liberals or Wilsonians) are made clear for each chapter's subject, encouraging teachers and students to discuss which theoretical position best matches the world.

As an added ancillary for instructors, this text has an instructor's manual test bank as well as a computerized test bank. Prepared by Marijke Breuning of Truman State University, the instructor's manual/test bank will include general teaching suggestions such as additional readings and paper topics. It will also include a lecture outline, teaching tips, ideas for activities, simulation exercises, resources for further information in books and on the Internet, glossaries and review questions, and multiple choice and essay text questions for each chapter.

Students and instructors should also make use of the information and resources available on McGraw-Hill's web page for international relations (http://www.mhhe.com/socscience/i</).

The ambition of writing a book begins with the author alone, but the completion of a book only happens with the help and cooperation of many. The able staff at McGraw-Hill first offered the services of Lyn Uhl as editor backed up by the capable assistance of Monica Friedman and Katy Redmond. Then, as McGraw-Hill expanded and became more specialized in its editorial staff, the capable team of Leslye Jackson, as political science editor, and her assistant editor, Stephanie Cappiello, took over my project about two-thirds of the way through. The talents and patience of all the McGraw-Hill staff that have guided this project are deeply appreciated.

I owe much thanks as well to some of my colleagues at USC-Spartanburg whose expertise I did not hesitate to exploit. Richard Combes, in philosophy, read and critiqued my rendition of several philosophers' views in Chapter One, and he frequently offered encouragement throughout the project. Alice Henderson, in history, helped me improve Chapter Two substantially. Joyce Wiley, in political science, offered considerable help on Chapter Three about actors and on the section in Chapter Fourteen dealing with Islamic fundamentalism. Page Sicora, as Interlibrary Loan Specialist, has been indispensable to the effort of moving this project along. Of the works cited in this book, she brought half of them into my hands from other libraries. Also, at USC-Spartanburg, a faculty committee and Vice-Chancellor Jane Stephens granted a one semester sabbatical leave at the mid-point of writing that gave my book project a significant boost. I would also like to thank the many reviewers who did their job well by offering numerous criticisms and suggestions, most of which are reflected in some form in this textbook: Marijke Breuning, Truman State University; Gerald Bridgeman, Moorpark College; William E. Carroll, Sam Houston State University; Cindy Courville, Occidental College; Michael Gold-Biss, St. Cloud State University; Douglas Griffith, Inver Hills Communty College; Siba N. Grovogui, Eastern Michigan University; Paul Haber, University of Montana; Ross Miller, Santa Clara University; Robert A. Poirier, Northern Arizona University; John Queen, Glendale Community College; Gholam H. Razi, University of

Houston; John M. Rothgeb, Jr., Miami University; Karrin Scapple, Southwest Missouri State University; Valerie Schwebach, University of Nebraska-Lincoln; Henry A. Shockley, Boston University; John R. Soares, Butte College; Okbazghi Yohannes, University of Louisville.

On a more personal note, I thank my wife, Victoria A. Smith, who, most assuredly, has broken a spousal record for both patience and encouragement. Writing this project with a lesser life-partner would have doomed this undertaking from the beginning. Also, I would be remiss if I did not reach back in my educational history and remember the important influence of Vernon Van Dyke, Carver Professor of Political Science Emeritus at the University of Iowa. Not only did he construct the foundation of my international relations knowledge but, almost as importantly, he taught me the value of clarity in writing. He has been a teacher, mentor, and friend for over 30 years.

Titles of Related Interest from Duskhin/McGraw-Hill

Taking Sides: Clashing Views on Controversial Issues in World Politics, 8/e, 1998, John T. Rourke, ISBN 0-697-39107-8

Taking Sides: Clashing Views on Controversial Political Issues, 10/e, 1996, George McKenna and Stanley Feingold, ISBN 0-697-35718-X

Student Atlas of World Politics, 2/e, 1996, John Allen, ISBN 1-56134-384-6

Annual Editions: World Politics 97/98, 18/e, Helen E. Purkitt, ISBN 0-697-37371-1

Annual Editions: Global Issues 97/98, 13/e, Robert M. Jackson, ISBN 0-697-37276-6

Annual Editions: Developing World 97/98, 7/e, Robert J. Griffiths, ISBN 0-679-36333-3

Annual Editions: Comparative Politics 97/98, 15/e, Christian Soe, ISBN 0-697-37226-X

Annual Editions: American Foreign Policy 97/98, 3/e, Glenn P. Hastedt, ISBN 0-697-36338-4

Analyzing Controversy: An Introductory Guide, 1997, Gary K. Clabaugh and Edward G. Rozycki, ISBN 0-697-34335-9

Please contact your local McGraw-Hill representative for information on packaging these titles with Henderson, *International Relations: Conflict and Cooperation at the Turn of the 21st Century.*

Brief Contents

PART ONE

Understanding International Relations 1

1. The Study of International Relations 3
2. The Historical Setting of International Relations 33
3. Actors on the International Stage 61

PART TWO

The Instruments of International Relations 97

4. Defining Power in a New Era 99
5. War and Lesser Conflict: Force in Decline? 129
6. Penetration Operations: Intelligence, Covert Acts, and Propaganda 165
7. The Role of Diplomacy: A Traditional Tool in Changing Times 201
8. The International Political Economy: Instruments of Competition and Conflict 237
9. The International Political Economy: The Institutions of Cooperation and Integration 275

PART THREE

The Struggle for World Order 309

10. Arms Limitations: Passage Into the Post-Cold War Era 311

11. International Law As the Framework for International Society 351

12. International Organizations for Security and Progress 385

PART FOUR

Sharing a Planet and Planetary Experiences 427

13. Environment of Humankind: A Future in Jeopardy 429

14. Shared Experiences of Humankind 465

PART FIVE

Conclusion 491

15. Conditions and Trends at the Turn of the 21st Century 493

INDEX 505

Contents

PART ONE

Understanding International Relations 1

1. The Study of International Relations 3
   - Why Study International Relations? 3
   - How Do We Study International Relations 10
   - What Is the Study of International Relations? 20
   - Chapter Summary 26

2. The Historical Setting of International Relations 33
   - The Origins of the Modern State 33
   - The Classical State System, 1648–1914 37
   - The Twentieth Century 42
   - The Post–Cold War Era 51
   - Globalization as a Stage of History 52
   - History and International Society 55
   - Chapter Summary 56

3. Actors on the International Stage 61
   - The State 61
   - Substate Actors 66
   - International Government Organizations 74
   - International Nongovernment Organizations 77
   - Multiple Actors and International Society 87
   - Chapter Summary 89

PART TWO

The Instruments of International Relations 97

4. Defining Power in a New Era 99
   - The Meaning of Power 99
   - Special Dimensions of Power 100
   - The Measurement of Power 102
   - The International Power Structure 112
   - The Changing Faces of Power 118

xiii

Power and International Society 121
Chapter Summary 123

5. War and Lesser Conflict: Force in Decline? 129
   The Traditional Role of War 129
   Patterns of War 131
   Causes of War 132
   Types of War 140
   The Just War Concept 143
   To Purge War 144
   Lesser Conflicts 149
   War and International Society 155
   Chapter Summary 157

6. Penetration Operations: Intelligence, Covert Acts, and Propaganda 165
   The Intelligence Process 166
   Counterintelligence 166
   Covert and Overt Intelligence 167
   The Usefulness of Intelligence 167
   The Techniques of Intelligence 168
   Covert Acts 176
   National Intelligence Agencies 178
   Propaganda 184
   Penetration Operations and Nonstate Actors 189
   Secrecy and Democracy 190
   Penetration Operations in the Post–Cold War Era 191
   Intelligence Activities and International Society 194
   Chapter Summary 195

7. The Role of Diplomacy: A Traditional Tool in Changing Times 201
   A Brief History of Diplomacy 202
   Functions of Diplomacy 202
   Negotiation and Bargaining 210
   The Legal Setting of Diplomacy 212
   Diplomatic Styles 218
   Operating Conditions of Diplomacy 219
   Nonstate Actors and Diplomacy 227
   Multilateral Diplomacy 229
   Diplomacy and International Society 230
   Chapter Summary 232

8. The International Political Economy: Instruments of Competition and Conflict 237
   Contending Perspectives on the International Economy 238
   Major Trade States: Liberal Order or Adversarial Competition? 241
   Economic Healing in the Post–Cold War Era 247
   The North-South Relation: A Diminishing Conflict? 249
   Economic Instruments: Positive and Negative Tools 260
   Economic Instruments and International Society 265
   Chapter Summary 268

9. The International Political Economy: The Institutions of Cooperation and Integration 275

Postwar Economic Cooperation 276

Globalism Versus Regionalism 283

European Economic Integration 284

The Emergence of NAFTA 293

Prospects for Regionalism in the Asian-Pacific Area 297

Economic Cooperation and International Society 301

Chapter Summary 302

PART THREE

The Struggle for World Order 309

10. Arms Limitations: Passage Into the Post–Cold War Era 311

The Objectives of Arms Limitations 312

Obstacles to Arms Limitation 315

Types of Arms Limitations 319

A Proliferation of Arms 327

The Status of Weapons Regimes 337

The Role of Nonstate Actors 340

Arms Limitations and International Society 343

Chapter Summary 344

11. International Law As the Framework for International Society 351

The Sources of International Law 352

The Subjects of International Law 355

The Scope of International Law 361

The Effectiveness of International Law 365

International Law in a Multicultural World 372

International Law and International Society 376

Chapter Summary 379

12. International Organizations for Security and Progress 385

Types of International Organizations 386

A Brief History of International Organizations 387

The Pursuit of Peace 394

Efforts at Economic Progress 405

Efforts at Social Progress 407

IGO Cooperation in Technical Areas 416

United Nations Vitality 417

International Organizations and International Society 419

Chapter Summary 421

PART FOUR

Sharing a Planet and Planetary Experiences   427

13. Environment of Humankind: A Future in Jeopardy   429

    Human Ecology   430

    The Core Variables   434

    Elements of the Environment   439

    Protecting the Environment Through a Global Civil Society   447

    The Environment and International Society   455

    Chapter Summary   457

14. Shared Experiences of Humankind   465

    The Global Communications Network   465

    English as a Global *Lingua Franca*   468

    A Cosmopolitan World?   470

    Prospects for A Democratic World   471

    The Reputed "Clash of Civilizations": The Case of Islamic Fundamentalism   475

    International Health Threats   477

    International Organized Crime   479

    Shared Experiences and International Society   483

    Chapter Summary   485

PART FIVE

Conclusion   491

15. Conditions and Trends at the Turn of the 21st Century   493

    Authority   493

    Actors   494

    Orientation   496

    Force   497

    Interaction   498

    Issues   499

    Problem-Solving Level   500

    Consensus   501

    A Parting Word   502

INDEX   505

North America

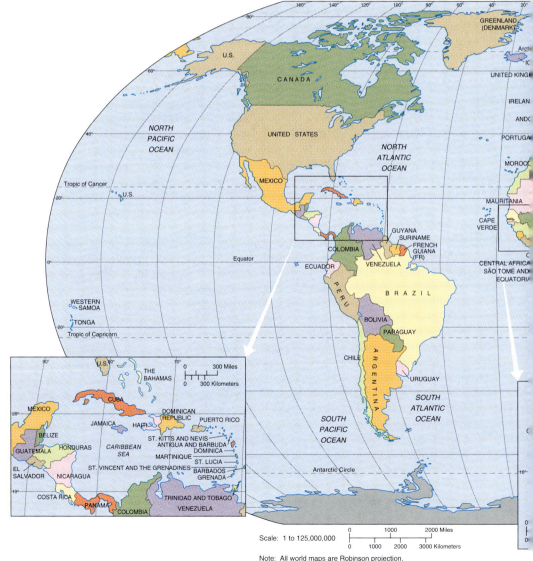

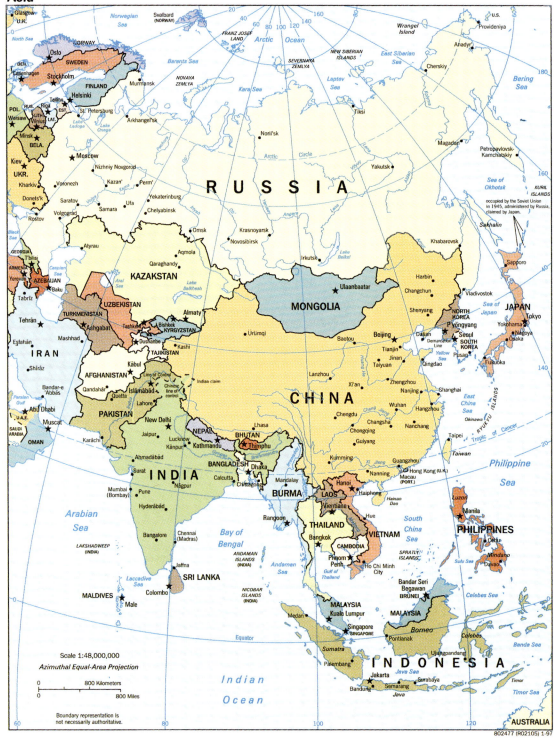

Africa

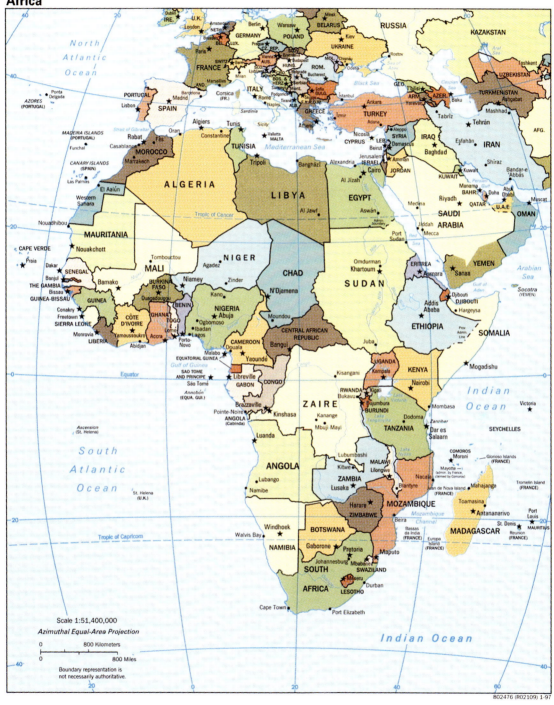

PART ONE

UNDERSTANDING INTERNATIONAL RELATIONS

CHAPTER 1

THE STUDY OF INTERNATIONAL RELATIONS

We are embarking on an intellectual journey to study **international relations,** a subject as interesting as it is challenging. International relations is not an esoteric subject of interest for only a few but a sweepingly broad and complex phenomenon that produces manifold effects on almost all of us. Specialists in international relations pursue their field as an academic discipline, but increasingly ordinary citizens are realizing the relevance of international events to their own lives. A high-tech, global communication system brings international awareness to millions of people daily, and college students in particular are finding that the educational mission of their schools includes making students more globally aware. An introductory course in the international relations field offers the most direct way to fulfill such a mission.

In this chapter, we attempt to answer several important questions. First, we address the question of why one should study international relations by examining a survey of current and relevant conditions operating in the world. Next, we take up the question of how to study international relations using a special approach designed for this textbook. Finally, we address the question of what is the field of international relations as an academic discipline. Although new concepts appear in every chapter, those presented in this introductory chapter form a conceptual toolbox for investigating and understanding international relations.

WHY STUDY INTERNATIONAL RELATIONS?

The world today is in an exciting time for the study of international relations because of the dramatic changes brought about by the collapse of European communism and the end of the Cold War. We now must take into account the turbulence of the post–Cold War era and make sense out of it. The "new world order" of peace and cooperation proclaimed at the end of the Persian Gulf War has lost some of its promise. Policy analyst and former Secretary of State Henry Kissinger recently said we are facing not a new world order but the remnants of the old system based on the power structure that predominated during the Cold War.

The world is experiencing negative, disintegrating forces as well as positive, integrating forces. Such negative forces as the threat of Russian nationalism to Russian democracy, terrorism, nuclear proliferation in North Korea, and ethnic turmoil in Bosnia and sub-Sahara Africa run counter to positive forces including the spread of democracy, a growing world zone of peaceful states, significant steps toward disarmament, and greater cooperation in an integrating world. Replacing a simplistic focus on a worldwide struggle between two alliance systems of communist and democratic states is a growing recognition of a world facing diverse issues that concern not only states but nonstate entities, including international organizations such as the United Nations.

The world is in transition from the system of the Cold War to a new arrangement as yet undefined. The interesting question is whether negative and conflictive or positive and cooperative forces will gain primacy in the new structure that is forming. Is the world to be dominated by many lesser threats and conflicts as the threat of a nuclear holocaust continues to recede? Or is the world experiencing and expanding on a new awareness of the benefits of cooperation in areas ranging from the deterrence of aggression to the protection of the global environment?

In this textbook, we will examine the direction and the extent of the transition from the Cold War system to a new structure. We will explore whether the world is truly experiencing receding conflict and increasing cooperation, thus enhancing the chances for global peace and prosperity.

For now, however, let us consider how our lives take place not only in local communities and in national societies but also in a global context. The relevance of international relations is evident along several dimensions that make people around the globe "world citizens." The dimensions many people commonly share are security, economic prosperity, health and human rights, and a global communications network.

Security

Almost everyone wants a sense of security, a feeling of well-being and freedom from harm. For this reason, war has been one of the most dreaded human experiences. In the twentieth century alone, numerous wars have cost millions of lives. This century has witnessed more battle casualties and collateral loss of civilian lives than any other century in history, and the prospects for another war have always loomed over the horizon. During the four decades of the Cold War, populations on both sides lived from crisis to crisis, with the threat of a nuclear holocaust ever present. Had one of these crises erupted into war, the Soviet Union and the United States probably would have destroyed much of the world in a matter of minutes through an exchange of nuclear missiles.

The tearing down of the Berlin Wall in 1989 symbolically marked the demise of the communist states in Europe. With the implosion of the Soviet Union in 1991, the Cold War came to an end. The fear of nuclear war among the great powers subsided as the hostile polarization between two alliance systems came to a close. However, the euphoric pronouncements of a new world order by Western leaders, notably by President George Bush in the early 1990s, were premature.

An immediate danger to an improved world security situation concerns the future of Russia, the largest and most powerful republic of the former Soviet Union. Russia may achieve the goals of democracy and a market economy, or it may fall to hard-line communism or extreme nationalism. If an aggressive government should come to power in Russia, the specter of a Europe dominated by one state would reappear. The historical pattern of European alliances, counteralliances, and the threat of war could reemerge as well.

Russia's prospects for democracy may not be particularly good.[1] President Boris Yeltsin used troops to oust rebel lawmakers from the Russian parliament, an action that took 140 lives. He has banned public rallies, implemented curfews, and increased police powers of search and seizure. Ethnic unrest among the 100 minorities in Russia could lead to more instances similar to that in Chechnya, where the Russian army struggled to put down a revolt in the 1995–1996 period. Organized crime, which now operates at an outrageous level, further tempts the authoritarian tendencies within the Russian culture. Double-digit inflation and low incomes batter the Russian people further. Only a few economic entrepreneurs and crime bosses enjoy prosperity. As for Russia's role in Europe, Henry Kissinger observes that Russia is redefining its identity and worries that it will return to its historical imperial pretentions.[2] Already Russia has demonstrated a tendency toward intrigue in the "Near Abroad," the former Soviet republics where Russian minorities have remained after the Soviet empire receded.

A threat from Germany is far less likely to occur. Germany is a secure, prosperous democracy, and the transformation of Germany from a warlike, authoritarian state to a peaceful, democratic one may be complete. Yet, given Germany's potential military strength, problems associated with reuniting East and West Germany, the rise of neo-Nazism, negative economic forces such as high unemployment, and a large immigrant and refugee influx, it is justifiable to raise some doubts about Germany's future course. Today, journalists and political scientists are asking if there will be a European Germany or a German Europe.[3]

Security threats today are not wars among great powers but numerous smaller conflicts operating mostly inside countries and scattered about the globe. These smaller conflicts not only undermine the internal security of many countries but threaten to spill over into neighboring countries. Ethnic warfare in the now fragmented Yugoslavia and in the former Georgian republic of the Soviet Union, civil war in the Sudan, turmoil in Somalia, a wave of genocide in Rwanda, and desperate hunger and widespread political killings in Haiti are among the recent conflicts that have brought misery to millions. These smaller conflicts have created great numbers of casualties and refugees and drawn the compassion of world opinion, leading sometimes to humanitarian intervention by the United Nations. Unfortunately, the marginal success of the United Nations at making peace inside strife-torn countries stands in marked contrast to the UN coalition forces' spectacular foiling of Iraq's takeover of Kuwait in 1990.

International war among several regional powers remains a concern, however. Arms races between Iraq and Iran and among several Asian states are especially worrisome. Some of these states already have or may develop the dreaded weapons known as the "ABCs" or atomic, biological, and chemical instruments of war. Combined with a growing missile capability, these weapons allow states to pose a horrendous danger for their regions. Attempting to dissuade North Korea from developing an atomic weapon has been a high priority for President Bill Clinton's administration. On a lesser scale, the brief border clash in 1995 between Ecuador and Peru dispels any notion that internal warfare has completely displaced international conflict.

A final example of a global security threat is terrorism. Angry over what they perceive as injustices, bands of terrorists have tried to thrust their grievances before governments and world opinion. Innocent bystanders are as frequently the victims of terrorists' acts as are

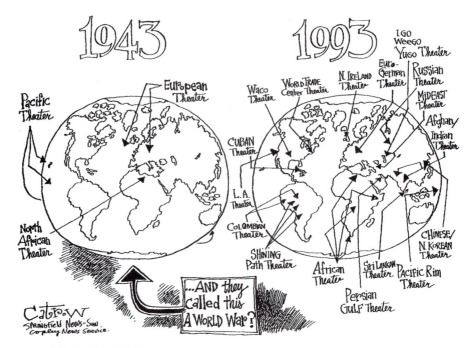

Catrow and Copley News Service.

government officials. Although the numbers of people worldwide killed or wounded by terrorists are very small, the random killing of a few has instilled fear among masses of people. Terrorist activity began to decline somewhat by the late 1980s, but the bombing of New York's World Trade Center by a radical Islamic group in 1993 and the lethal gas attack in a Tokyo subway by a fanatical Japanese religious cult in 1995 are vivid reminders of continued terrorist danger. The acquisition of weapons of mass destruction, such as lethal gas or nuclear devices, by terrorists concerns security experts perhaps more than any other threat.

The world is still a dangerous place, and no one has a complete guarantee of security. Yet people are not doomed to life-threatening conflict. Peace among the major nuclear states is especially promising and encourages hope that other kinds of conflict will prove controllable without bloodshed. After all, the ongoing nuclear disarmament process between Russia and the United States is unprecedented, and few observers, if any, predicted the end of the Cold War. Imagining a world with less conflict and finding practical ways to make that world a reality are not necessarily vain efforts.

A Global Economy

We can identify a local or a national economy in an analytical sense, but realistically economic activity is a global phenomenon. Today extensive global trade patterns enmesh the world's population in ways that provide more goods in greater variety and quality than ever before in history. Countries around the world count on one another for the functioning of their respective economies. In America and other manufacturing countries, many jobs are dependent on selling high-tech products such as computers, medical technology, and oil-drilling equipment to countries that cannot make their own. Most states must import one or more critical resources such as food, finance capital, oil, and raw materials of all kinds to serve their industries. Just as local economies once integrated with national economies, so have national economies interlocked with regional and global trade patterns, thus reducing the independence and effectiveness of national economic policymaking.

Since national authorities can no longer manage their economies within national jurisdictions alone, important economic policy decisions commonly take place in international conferences organized for regulating and promoting global trade. An excellent example of such a conference is the latest round of the General Agreement on Tariffs and Trade (GATT), completed at the end of 1993. This agreement called for further reductions in the remaining trade barriers among more than 120 countries. A major focus of this agreement concerns reducing protectionist policies on agricultural products, an area of trade especially resistant to free trade principles. Billions of dollars in additional international trade will likely result from GATT's more liberal trade rules of 1993. The current trend is to move deeper into international economic policy planning. Major trading states are leading the effort by creating the World Trade Organization, which will have greater powers than GATT to encourage even higher levels of trade.

The global economy highlights the **interdependence** of today's world. Interdependence has several dimensions, but economic interdependence is especially striking. Interdependence simply refers to the widely recognized fact that the countries of the world are experiencing mutual dependence.[4] This mutual dependence, however, is not always equally shared. Some trading partners may enjoy a balance of trade tilted in their favor and more economic power than others. Interruption of the mutual dependence can produce negative results ranging from some loss of sales and jobs to a devastating impact on a national economy if vital oil supplies come to a halt. We will return to the subject of interdependence in more detail later in this chapter.

The global economy has become increasingly integrated over time, but not without the persistence of some important fissures. While the division of the world between capitalist and communist economies has largely disappeared, the People's Republic of China and a few other communist holdouts remain, namely Cuba, North Korea, and Vietnam. At least the rapidly growing economy of China, a potential world-class economic power, reflects some capitalist characteristics and is cautiously integrating with the global economy. A downside of communism's collapse in Europe is that these former communist states now present a new problem. In a "beggar-thy-neighbor" fashion, they absorb valuable economic resources in the form of loans and foreign aid that could go to the Third World,* and they hungrily insist on more help from Western countries. Western countries dare not refuse help if the former communist states are to become prosperous, stable democracies rather than threats to European peace.

---

*The classification scheme of First World (Western democracies), Second World (communist states), and Third World countries probably has less meaning nowadays since the European communist governments have fallen. Nonetheless, the label "Third World" remains in vogue.

A more enduring fissure involves the wide void between the wealthier industrial states and the poorer Third World states. The Third World states are mostly in Africa, Asia, and Latin America, though some are in the Middle East. Many leaders from these less developed countries and sympathetic intellectuals from other countries accuse the wealthier states of exploiting the weaker ones.

Some of these leaders and intellectuals embrace an interpretation of the world economy known as *globalism*. According to this theoretical view, the countries of the world belong either to the North (the richer industrial states generally above the equator) or to the South (the poorer Third World countries, usually below the equator). The North-South categories form a global class structure, with the North exploiting the South. This exploitation supposedly derives from an unfair trade structure based on high prices for the finished products of the wealthier countries and low prices for the raw materials of the poorer countries. The capitalist world economy thus perpetuates an injustice of great magnitude. Globalism is a prescriptive calling for revolutionary change by replacing world capitalism with world socialism.[5] The huge economic gap between North and South is a fact, but the globalist interpretation of this fact adds antagonism and conflict to the North-South relationship. Chapter Eight provides a more complete account of globalism.

Still another fissure is the long-term slowed economic growth that has aggravated the trade competition among the three economic titans of the world: the European Union, Japan, and the United States. Unless these economic powers can successfully negotiate their trade problems and avert trade wars, they may retreat more deeply into regional trade arrangements at the expense of global trade patterns. Overcoming these economic fissures and promoting a prosperous world economy will have a direct effect on how many people in the world will have jobs and how well they can live.

Health and Human Rights Concerns

A variety of conditions in the world can harm people's health, including illegal drugs, AIDS, and environmental abuse. These conditions pay little heed to borders and are clearly international in scope. The raw materials of illicit drugs (opium poppies, coca shrubs, and hemp) originate as crops in various Third World countries. Internationally connected crime organizations process the raw materials into illegal drugs and then sell these drugs in the well-to-do countries of Europe and North America. Opium, morphine, heroin, cocaine, and marijuana wreck the lives of millions of people and result in expenditures of billions of dollars for health care and law enforcement.

AIDS is a pandemic disease that begins as a virus and leaves its victims highly vulnerable to opportunistic diseases such as pneumonia and tuberculosis. In only a few years, thousands of people have become ill and died, and millions more will suffer the same fate from AIDS unless recent medical developments can save them. In modern times, a significant portion of the world's population travels from country to country as diplomats, tourists, exchange students, businesspeople, and in other capacities. The result has been a rapid transmission of AIDS worldwide.

People everywhere are becoming more cognizant that they live in an era of environmental interdependence. Environmental abuse in one place can mean harm elsewhere. Damage to the ozone layer through chemical pollution in richer countries can result in skin cancer among people in rich and poor countries. Dumping garbage on one coast of an ocean can contaminate the food chain and make people ill on the other coast. When the meltdown of the Chernobyl nuclear reactor occurred in the Ukraine in 1986, not only were local citizens harmed, but some degree of radiation threatened most of northern Europe. Many environmental hazards await solutions that can happen only through international cooperation.

Human rights concerns also have drawn the attention of many people to the importance of international relations. Considering governments' historical jealous control over their territories and peoples, the modern human rights movement that began after the Second World War was an unlikely but momentous development. Government leaders have traditionally maintained that the way they treated their citizens was not the business of outsiders. Nonetheless, acting through international organizations ranging from the globally based United Nations, with its concern for the full scope of human rights, to Amnesty International, which represents political prisoners, people in one part of the world demonstrate their concern for the welfare of people in other places around the globe. Unfortunately, the extant harsh lives of millions of people testify that the human rights movement has much work to do before everyone can enjoy a broad set of rights.

Global Communication

Electronic technology has created today's "information age" by transmitting voluminous amounts of information around the world. Through satellites, fiber optic technology, and cable hookups, the world maintains close contact via the "information highway." The printed word, radio, the telephone, fax, E-mail, the Internet, and, most important, television reach all parts of the world. A remote area such as the Amazonian rain forests of Brazil, which years ago received a newspaper once a week, can now capture television news every day with a satellite dish antenna.

The effects of the information age have been dramatic. The dissatisfaction of "have-not" populations has intensified due to television depictions of better lives elsewhere. Western television broadcasts reaching into communist societies may have stimulated the rapid change of communist Europe into fledgling capitalist and democratic countries. Vivid pictures on color television also can set priorities in a given country's foreign policy. Televised scenes of starving children in Somalia induced the American people to push President George Bush toward humanitarian intervention in that country; scenes of Somalians dragging dead American soldiers along the dirt streets of Mogadishu produced President Bill Clinton's promise to withdraw American forces.

The ability to transmit information and interpret that information for others has become a source of political power. Western countries have a strong advantage over other parts of the world in terms of influence through information flows. These countries are the producers of communication technology, and they host the headquarters of the global news services.

It is easy to understand that international relations today are no longer the preserve of leaders, diplomats, and soldiers. Ordinary citizens have many reasons to become globally aware, including security, economic, and health concerns, all brought to the attention of a global public through a high-tech communication system. This awareness includes the realization that people around the world experience similar problems and depend on one another to meet a variety of human needs. Since they can relate world forces and distant events to their own lives, citizens are engaging in international collective action to promote their interests. Private citizens working through international human rights and environmental organizations are a common occurrence today.

HOW DO WE STUDY INTERNATIONAL RELATIONS?

This textbook employs an overarching theme concerning the balance between conflict and cooperation in the world. The nature of politics in international relations obviously involves both conflict and cooperation. Usually the two intermingle in all human affairs, including the international context. A need for cooperation only makes sense when some form of conflict stands in the way of meeting complementary, shared interests. Since failure to cooperate can result in warfare or economic depression, more cooperation rather than less is the preferred outcome.[6]

Basic to our query about conflict/cooperation patterns is the notion of a *continuum,* a continuous dimension of reality that, for our purposes, varies in the degree of cooperation. Hypothetically, at one extreme point of this dimension is total conflict and the exercise of power in a war-prone environment. At the opposite point, also hypothetical, is a complete harmony of interests and cooperation among actors.[7] Although neither of these extremes has existed in history as an enduring pattern, we can still place any era of history at some point on this continuum as a particular mix of conflict and cooperation. Much of this book evaluates the present conflict/cooperation mix to determine if a post–Cold War world is a more cooperative and thus better one.

Our inquiry about cooperation is worthwhile because it concerns the emerging world conditions of the post–Cold War era. The end of the Cold War encouraged euphoric expectations about the extent of cooperation and the peaceful resolution of many problems. Some international specialists have cautioned against the rosy optimism about a world headed toward new levels of cooperation. Toward what kind of world are we moving? In what kind of world will the children of today's college students grow up during the early part of the 21st century? The normative preference of the author is for a peaceful, cooperative world as opposed to a conflictive one, but the degree of cooperation, now and in the future, is a subject that deserves analysis and constructive argumentation. The professors and students who use this book, whether or not they agree with the author that cooperation is pulling ahead of conflict, will have a full opportunity for lively discussion and critical analysis as they move from chapter to chapter.

Will the changes the world is undergoing be extensive enough to amount to a new order? An **order** involves enduring patterns of behavior that give a society structure and establish the relationships among the society's constituent parts. A given order depends on the division of power, who is in control, and what rules and norms the controlling power(s) want respected. Traditionally, a global order is based on the states and how they interact with one another. The recently ended Cold War, for instance, was a simple global order based on two nuclear-armed, ideological camps. This order has now passed into history. What kind of order will replace the Cold War structure?[8]

Because of post–Cold War turbulence, the new global order taking form is difficult to predict. There is both sharp conflict, as in Bosnia, and promising cooperation, as in the completed round of the General Agreement on Tariffs and Trade at the end of 1993. Are the changes in the post-Cold War era sufficiently profound to constitute "new world order"?[9] Probably not, but the changes so far in evidence may presage a formative order of a new kind. First, the world no longer faces the immense threat of strategic nuclear warfare, nor do hostile ideological differences polarize the world.

Second, something else clearly new about the emerging world order is that for the first time, the United States can neither dominate the world nor withdraw from it.[10] U.S. leadership at first seemed ready to fill the vacuum left by the Cold War's end, but now appears more timid. This leadership felt vindicated with the collapse of the Soviet Union and then experienced frustration over an increasingly complex international system.[11] Gradually, leaders in the United States are choosing to work with other Western democracies in the management of global problems.

Third, the world is now experiencing unprecedented military dominance by democracies accustomed to working together as an alliance. Though they may squabble, the democracies will not likely divide into competing military alliances. The peace and wealth associated with their democratic status can now radiate influence to the rest of the world, perhaps reducing some of the world's disorder.[12] Other countries, freed from the grip of the Cold War and desirous of a better life, are receptive to the ideals of democracy and capitalism.[13] In the years to come, the democracies may craft a stable global system, a world order made in their own image. A better world order than what went before is not a certainty, however.

Added to the continuum concept, the analytical strategy of the author is to focus on three models of possible world orders that can fit somewhere on the cooperation continuum. These models are alternative "pictures" of how international relations may work. While these models do not have absolute lines of distinction among them, we can nevertheless assess which one offers the best fit for the world of today. These models will sharpen our analytical ability as we evaluate how cooperative the world is becoming.

The three models that will guide our evaluation of the emerging order are inspired by the writings of English philosopher Thomas Hobbes (1588–1679), the work of Dutch legal writer Hugo Grotius (1583–1645), and some of the thinking of philosopher Immanuel Kant (1724–1804). For our purposes, Kant's essay "Perpetual Peace," written in 1795, is the most important of his many works. Other writers have successfully used the models of *anarchy, society,* and *community* drawn from these philosophers, respectively, to analyze international relations.[14]

The concern of Thomas Hobbes in *Leviathan* (1651) was with humankind's natural bent toward chaos and violence. Hobbes was cynical and pessimistic about human nature. In a state of nature, the selfish conduct of people would create a war of all against all. The only hope for peace and a modicum of happiness would occur if humankind gave up their natural rights to enter a "social contract" under a leviathan, that is, a strong king who would establish a peaceful and safe civil society. In this arrangement, people could avoid the death and mayhem of **anarchy.**[15] Although Hobbes saw the anarchy of his imagined state of nature as brutal, anarchy actually means the absence of government. Violent disorder may or may not occur with anarchy.

Hobbes was among the first theorists to make an explicit analogy between international relations and the state of nature.[16] Although Hobbes's main concern was with domestic societies, he was sure that international relations would remain in a state of nature characterized by conflict and war.[17] Not only was Hobbes negative about human nature, but his view of history calls for repetitive cycles of international anarchical conditions. In a Hobbesian world, states possess power and use their power much as they please. Constant violence may not always be present, but it is an ongoing threat. Without a global leviathan, the potential for a war of all against all exists in the Hobbesian world. A Hobbesian model holds a point on our continuum involving considerable conflict; it is a model of *international anarchy*.

The views of Hugo Grotius about what can happen in international relations are much more positive. The importance of Grotius rests on the contribution he made to the idea of an international society.[18] Martin Wight, known for helping to crystallize thinking about the three models presented here, once claimed the most important question you can ask in international relations theory is: What is international society?[19] Grotius provides a fundamental answer to this question by observing that states form a society among themselves by sharing the institutions of commerce, diplomacy, and especially international law. He imagined states leaving a state of nature to embrace this international society.[20] In fact, Grotius's writings contributed significantly to the body of international law, particularly the laws of commerce, of the sea, and of war. In some quarters, Grotius receives recognition as the "father of international law." For Grotius, laws applied in wartime as well as in peacetime, and so the world can never be totally lawless or anarchical.[21]

Living in the seventeenth century, Grotius envisioned a society based on legally equal states but extending to include nonstate entities, even individuals, within a framework of rules and shared values. He insisted on the universality of international society, a society encompassing the world rather than focusing on Europe. By the mid-eighteenth century, international society had diminished in practice because international law emphasized only the state as an actor, providing rights and duties for states and leaving individuals and groups as mere objects of law. Then, in the eighteenth and nineteenth centuries, the growth of European power and dominance reduced the universality of international society as much of the world fell to the conquest of European colonial expansion. In the twentieth century, nonstate entities and non-European areas reembraced the Grotian conception of international society.[22]

Supporters of the Grotian model believe the world holds a greater potential for more cooperation and less conflict than do supporters of the Hobbesian model. Grotians are hopeful about a more cooperative future, though they recognize much about the world is unpredictable and uncertain.[23] The Grotian model holds an intermediate point in the cooperation continuum and is the model of *international society*.

A model of the world derived from the influence of Immanuel Kant is a forward-looking, optimistic picture of what international relations can be. Whereas Grotius saw international conditions of law and cooperation as mitigating conflict within a livable international society, Kant envisioned peace reigning in an economically prosperous international community devoted to the welfare of individuals.

Although Kant's religious writing was once censored by a Prussian king and Kant lived to see the Napoleonic wars begin, he believed a pacific union of republican states (representative democracies) eventually would form and produce conditions for a "perpetual peace." These states would cohabit in a "civil society," as would individuals in their own respective countries.[24] Kant had a radically different view of human nature than did Hobbes. He thought individuals deserve to be independent and free in the face of authority.[25] People can use reason to find ways to cooperate over their common interests instead of bogging down in conflict. Then, if individuals are citizens of republics, these republics will act on behalf of their citizens by carrying a cooperative approach into the international arena.

For Kant, a republican citizenry will prefer peace and growth in commerce, while a monarch's intrigue and ambition will cultivate war. Kant did not expect international anarchy to disappear easily or altogether in any specific period of time. While great and sad experiences would eventually teach all states the lessons of peace, war would take place for an unknown time. Kant believed republics, at peace among themselves, would war with monarchies until the latter disappeared.[26] As a result of republics vanquishing monarchies, the welfare of general human society would displace the constant bickering and warfare of kings.

Kant was content with a world of separate states because he thought this arrangement would prevent a global despotism. The evolution toward a pacific union of republics did not require a central government for the republics. Unity in the pacific union would depend on the moral integration of people embracing the same principles; people living in separate states would become "citizens of the world" through shared values.[27] A cosmopolitan community would emerge with people free of national biases and comfortably at home in any country. An extensive amount of trade would further enhance people's sense of community, hence reducing the importance of national borders. How did Kant think this remarkable development might occur?

Kant's view of history was linear. History would unfold as a progression, setbacks and all, moving inevitably in a cosmopolitan direction. Progress toward a peaceful, cosmopolitan community would come about through a historical process, according to Kant, guided by "no less an authority than the great artist *Nature* herself."[28] Does Kant mean a desirable, future community is inevitable? On a closer examination of his writing, we find that *Nature* provides the opportunity for people to act, and they have a moral obligation to do so.[29] A Kantian order, then, is a liberal one based on republican states interacting in peace and inhabited by citizens who interact easily with one another across national boundaries and share moral values and commerce. The Kantian model falls on our continuum at a point involving a high degree of cooperation, suggesting an *international community*.

Parts of the real world resemble each of our models. Border conflicts, ethnic civil war, and terrorism exemplify the Hobbesian anarchic model. The trade negotiations of the three economic giants of the world—the European Union, Japan, and the United States—represent the Grotian model because cooperation is sought in the face of some conflict, and the three giants usually work out trade agreements they place under rules. Are there signs of a future community that emphasizes the welfare of individuals? The Kantian model is found in the European Union, where republics prevail and encourage extensive free trade and the free movement of citizens across their borders. As we take our intellectual journey through the chapters that follow, we will try to acquire a sense of the world and which model overall best fits the world and its future direction. Now we will elaborate on these models further and see how the thinking of modern theorists in the field of international relations relate to the models.

International Anarchy

For a time after the First World War, specialists in the study of international relations downgraded the extent of the world's anarchy. Scholars with Grotian and even Kantian views about international relations held sway in the interwar years (1919–1939). Dubbed idealists by a later generation of scholars, they focused on "what ought to be" and hoped to banish the role of power by channeling international affairs through the League of Nations. Through the function of the League, idealists believed a framework of law and morality could determine international outcomes rather than armies. War would be no more. A harmony of interests would develop from a collective, international interest that would surmount the interests of separate states. States would become republics, democratic and peaceful. They would use reason, debate in parliamentary fashion, and act reasonably within the framework of the League.

Idealists held a highly optimistic view of humankind. By setting up new standards and institutions, the natural perfectability, or at least improvability, of humans would progress. President Woodrow Wilson, who led the formation of the League and had once been a professor of political science at Princeton University, embraced idealists' views as well. It would be safe to say that President Wilson was the intellectual scion of Immanuel Kant.

After the Second World War, a group of scholars called *realists* challenged the idealists with a different theoretical outlook, one that recognized the prominence of power within an international context of anarchy. Generally, these scholars considered power to be the capacity of one state to coerce or persuade another state to do what it otherwise would not do. The realists redirected scholarly thinking to power, the "life's blood" of international politics from their view.[30]

Realists, in turn, have been the targets of criticism, but they have come closer to producing a true theory of politics than any other school of thought. Professors James E. Dougherty and Robert L. Pfaltzgraff, after a careful review of a number of theoretical proposals, have said, "Despite its critics, realism ranks as the most important attempt thus far to isolate and to focus on a key variable in political behavior—namely power—and to develop a theory of international relations."[31] While many scholars today look past a focus on power for the theoretical development of their field, the theoretical accomplishment of the realists deserves appreciation.

Although realism is traceable back to Thucydides in the fourth century B.C., to Machiavelli in the early sixteenth century, and to Hobbes in the seventeenth century, we will emphasize modern thinkers here. Before the Second World War, the British scholar E. H. Carr, in *The Twenty Years' Crisis,* criticized the lack of a marriage between fact and theory where idealism was concerned and recommended a more realistic view of international politics.[32] Yet it is Hans Morgenthau whom American political scientists regard as the "father of realism." Professor Morgenthau had a tremendous impact on the international relations field with his classic *Politics Among Nations,* published in 1948.[33]

Realists start with the assumption that international relations take place within an anarchy in which sovereign, independent states interact with one another in a competitive and conflictive world unregulated by a central authority. For Morgenthau, politics is a struggle for power with states seeking to maximize their power. States rationally seek power to protect their national interests, the chief interest being national security in a war-prone world. Realists also give much emphasis to immutable laws of history associated with power. Wise statesmen do not try to escape power but learn the proper guiding principles from history and conduct foreign policy accordingly. History is a repetitious cycle of wars because human nature never changes. People are self-centered and act accordingly through states to pursue more power and wealth, and at the expense of others if necessary.[34]

While an international anarchy is not necessarily chaotic or even disordered, if leaders follow power principles, realists see a pattern of repetitious war with the strong doing as they please and the weak bearing what they must.[35] When states do cooperate in the conflict-prone world, they do so to form alliances as a way to dissuade one or more other states from attacking. As other states form a counteralliance, a balance of power may form and result in a period of temporary peace, according to the realists.

As a conflict-oriented approach, realism has serious trouble accounting for peaceful change and cooperation, although Morgenthau did put some hope in the use of diplomacy for avoiding war.[36] Realists, for example, cannot explain why leaders in the Soviet Union willingly gave up power in eastern Europe in 1989 and voluntarily dissolved the Soviet state in 1991, thus ending the Cold War. The European Union is an anomaly for the realists as well, since these states are not at war but live amicably with one another and enjoy enviable wealth through economic integration and free trade.[37] Realists, after all, believe power is an end-all. States are supposed to make war among their own kind and increase and even maximize their power, not surrender it.[38]

Neorealists (also known as *structural realists*) made significant adjustments to realism. Professor Kenneth N. Waltz, the most systematic spokesperson for the neorealists, inspired this new realism of the 1980s. He expressed his views through his 1979 book *Theory of International Politics*.[39] As one adjustment, Waltz sees a world structure as the principal determinant of outcomes at the international level. This structure is based on the configuration of power distributed among the major states. While Waltz sees this structure as operating under anarchy, states can still make rational choices about their interests within a framework of incentives and constraints imposed by the world power structure.[40]

A second adjustment to earlier views of realism is that an incessant drive for power is not always the main concern, even if states do at least seek self-preservation and may sometimes strive to increase their power. In spite of Professor Waltz's general view of the world as an anarchic system populated by self-help- and conflict-oriented states, Waltz observes adjustment and accommodation by states that on occasion choose to bargain rather than fight. Sometimes cooperation stems from the more powerful states avoiding the high costs of conflict, preferring to preserve peace and to manage economic problems.[41] The views of neorealists, led by Waltz, allow a little more room in the world for cooperation than the earlier realists guided by Morgenthau's thinking.

However, when cooperation does occur, according to the neorealists, power relationships are at work within the cooperative arrangement. The more powerful states take larger shares of any joint gain that flows from cooperation.[42] Professor Stephen Krasner, for example, has observed that although a large group of states may agree to share global communications, such as through the International Telecommunications Union, the states possessing the highest level of technology and those first acquiring such valued resources as the lion's share of broadcast bands and geostationary positions for communication satellites will maintain their advantages into the future.[43] For a neorealist, cooperation means relative gains based on the amount of power a state possesses.

International Society

Other writers observe an even more cooperative world than the neorealists do and move us closer to a Grotian model of the world. Although not rejecting the realist view outright, by the 1970s a number of scholars believed realism did not account for visible changes in the international scene. Reality began to appear in the world that neither realism nor neorealism could adequately explain. Instances of this reality are the decline in international warfare, the shift to economic sources of power for influence over military means for coercion, and intensified efforts to integrate global trade patterns through international cooperative ventures.

A major feature of international relations is the growth in **transnational activities.** These are private activities that take place across national boundary lines, such as when Mazda executives from Japan meet with Ford executives from the United States to make a business deal. Realists, of course, have tended to focus on state-to-state dealings.

Another important, closely related feature is the emergence of various kinds of **actors** on the international stage. The dominance of the state has declined (though states remain as the primary actors), making room on the international stage for numerous kinds of nonstate actors such as churches, multinational corporations, environmental and human rights groups, and other private individuals and groups that are increasingly pursuing interests and goals in an international context. In general, actors can be individuals, groups, and states that behave—that is, act with a purpose—internationally. International activities by growing numbers of state and nonstate actors concerning an increasing range of issues have drawn the world into a tighter frame of interaction that calls for more cooperation to secure multiple actors' needs.

The major work that stimulated a new focus on developments that realists could not explain was the 1972 publication of *Transnational Relations and World Politics,* edited by Robert O. Keohane and Joseph Nye, Jr. Almost as important is their 1977 publication of *Power and Interdependence.*[44] These *transnationalists* (also known as *international liberals, neoliberals,* and *globalists*) largely focus on interdependence. As mentioned earlier, this concept refers to mutual dependence among two or more actors, although the actors involved may not share the dependence evenly. One or more actors may enjoy advantages, even if they remain needful of one another and realize they should coordinate plans and actions.

Japan and the United States, for example, negotiate their trade ties almost continuously, though sometimes with ruffled feelings. Both these state actors know a serious disruption in trade would become a shared calamity. Perhaps Japan holds the advantaged position in the trade relationship, with the United States more dependent on Japan than the reverse. Japan enjoys a more than $60 billion trade surplus at the United States' expense and loans billions of these dollars back to the U.S. government with interest. Most of the negotiating leverage the United States has rests on its unusually large consumer-oriented population, that is, its capacity to buy huge amounts of goods from Japan.

Interdependence has existed in the world throughout history in some form and degree. At the turn of the last century, scholars produced a flurry of academic activity over growing trade interdependence that the First World War and then the Great Depression disrupted. Today's economic interdependence exists not only because of trade but also due to capital investment, currency speculations and exchanges, and the role of multinational corporations. Multiple economic ties now knit the world tightly together. Indeed, the present generation of scholars has recognized a growing sensitivity in the world's interdependence. We ask not only how regular interdependence patterns are but how rapidly they occur and how much impact they have. Also, both costs and benefits result from the bonds of mutual dependence. Certainly not all effects of interdependence are benign. Interdependence can be negative due to global environmental decay, the spread of AIDS, international terrorism, and internationally organized drug trafficking. Or it can be positive because of joint economic growth through mutual trade.[45] Overall, since interdependence means shared problems and needs, it produces the potential for mutual help. Thus, states tend to move toward cooperation as well as continuing to engage in some degree of conflict.

Transnationalists frequently refer to *complex interdependence* because of the many diverse kinds of actors mentioned earlier that have arisen in recent decades, changing the world from one of domination by a few powerful states to a mixed-actor world.[46] Individuals worldwide are entering into associations of all sorts at the local, national, and international levels for goal satisfaction.[47] These private actors contribute to networks of interdependence because their goals and activities become inextricably linked to one another across borders.[48] In addition, states today regularly interact in important ways with nonstate actors such as multinational corporations, which control a large portion of world trade; Amnesty International, which lobbies governments for better human rights practices; and terrorist organizations that target government officials and private citizens.

Most transnationalists, however, do not go as far as John Burton in his book *World Society,* published in 1972.[49] He observed a "cobweb" of many fine lines of private transactions crossing borders, with nonstate actors acting irrespective of those borders. In Burton's view, relations among private actors had become the core of international relations, reducing and even displacing the state's importance. Transnationalists can see an interrelated international society but view the state as primary. States possess force, regulate international economic relations of all kinds, and represent their populations diplomatically. Clearly, states continue to have greater impact than any other actor.[50]

Transnationalists also recognize complex interdependence because of multiple modern issues that do not lend themselves to simplistic settlement by force. Conquest for territory, a classic motive for the use of force, has rarely happened in recent years and has not been successful when it has occurred, as in the case of Iraq's aggression against Kuwait in 1990. The dust-up between Ecuador and Peru in 1995 over rich mineral deposits in a disputed border area produced first a military stalemate and then negotiations. The large majority of state leaders probably would prefer to have more influence in the global economy than to have more territory. Trade issues and wealth accumulation have replaced power drives as the chief concerns, at least among the major states.

In addition to trade, other issues largely unmanageable by force include AIDS, human rights, environmental decay, illegal drugs, and economic development. National governments are unable to cope with such issues alone because they arise in multiple national jurisdictions. These issues basically relate to human welfare needs, and meeting these needs is having a dynamic, international effect. People and governments are establishing networks of cooperation to meet needs that are, in turn, helping to create an international society.[51]

Not only are widely shared needs contributing to an emerging international society, but so are values. The world is increasingly embracing values rooted in democracy, principles of human rights, and capitalism. These Western values are making at least slow headway toward worldwide acceptance, though they are not the preferences of surviving communists, dictators, hypernationalists, and Islamic fundamentalists.

In addition, the rules and norms of international law, the United Nations, and other international institutions underpin the emerging order of an international society.[52] Professor

James Rosenau thinks a broad set of rules and norms, widely adhered to at the global level, amounts to **governance** without (world) government. This "governance" provides guidance for cooperation and collective benefits in world politics. Actors usually comply with these rules and norms because it is in the common interest to do so.[53]

An international society need not be harmonious, but it should reflect some degree of consensus. The emerging society is not without significant dissension, however. Perhaps the chief obstacle in the path of the established order of an international society is the sense of injustice felt by leaders and peoples in Third World states over their role in the world economy. Nevertheless, these states use the important institutions of international society, namely diplomacy, international law, and international organizations, to render the world economy fairer to them. As a result, the Third World, in spite of its grievances, has become a part of the emerging international society.[54]

International Community

The Kantian model of international relations involves a potential community of humankind. Over time, such a community has remained appealing even if fairly idealistic. A number of modern proposals for world order have called for humanity to be viewed as a single community.[55] Although a global-level community is mostly an imaginary one, Professor Richard Falk, writing over a decade ago, believed humankind is drawing closer with a sense of oneness. This "oneness," he thinks, derives from mutually shared dependence and shared stewardship of the same spinning island in space that we call earth. Falk asserts that although the planet is divided by political boundaries and bloodshed, the unity of humankind is at least sinking into our political imagination.[56] We may be slowly progressing, in Kantian fashion, toward cosmopolitanism with a view of ourselves as "citizens of the world." According to Professor Seyom Brown, however, further progress along the cooperation continuum to an international community will not happen unless conscious choices and skilled leadership occur.[57]

Only a shadowy outline of a future international community appears today, but we can project some developments that might encourage such a community. The pursuit of human welfare might be a rallying point for consciously restructuring the global order. Cultural consensus over democracy and capitalism may grow because these can help to promote human welfare; responsive governments with more wealth can do a great deal for people. Democracies, republics to Kant, are on the rise and dominate militarily in the world, though they do not war among themselves. These states appear dedicated to increasing the world's wealth through greater levels of trade.

Governance at the international level may guide cooperation as the common good is more clearly understood and pursued. Governance may even lead to some political integration under *supranational* institutions, institutions that can exercise a degree of authority over states that are declining somewhat in importance. Achieving cooperation around shared norms and rules, that is, governance, may be enough for an international community. After all, Kant wanted to avoid central authority over republics out of a fear of world despotism.

Moreover, cooperation over multiple issues, healthy developments in trade, and a reluctance to use military means may be the forerunners of forces shaping a Kantian perpetual

TABLE 1.1
Three Abstract Models of International Relations

	International anarchy	International society	International community
Authority	No central authority, weak international law	Respect for international law	Extensive use of rules and norms
Actor(s)	State is dominant	Multiple actors, state is primary	Multiple actors, state declines
Orientation	Conflict	Cooperation/conflict	Cooperation/competition
Force	Coercion common	Persuasion/some coercion	Persuasion for the common interest
Interaction	Minimal, mostly allies	Interdependence	Some political integration
Issues	National security	National security, global trade, global ecology, human rights	Justice in human welfare, especially redistribution of the earth's wealth
Problem-solving level	Unilateral, occasional conference for ad hoc issues	Multilateral problem solving in UN and conferences	Supranational institutions
Consensus	Strong sense of nationalism, focus on national interest	Multiple ideologies, but in decline; English grows as a world *lingua franca*	World is increasingly democratic and capitalistic; emerging world culture

peace. If lasting peace is to come about, a sense of justice for all, rather than the "rules of the strong," must pervade the order of the community. For example, future economic growth must include the poorer countries in such a way that they are gradually brought up to speed economically with the better-off countries.

In spite of Kant's linear view of history, no "law of progress" actually exists to carry the world along the continuum toward greater cooperation. Any cooperative changes could reverse and move us back toward greater anarchy. Nothing is assured. International anarchy still characterizes much of the Middle East with its arms races and threat of war, and anarchy may engulf Russia and eastern Europe if democracy and capitalism fail there.

In contrast, western Europe is well ahead of most of the world as an economically successful and democratic region concerned with human rights and human welfare. True, racial clashes due to the arrival of nonwhite immigrants in Britain, France, and Germany somewhat mar a positive European picture. Guided by supranational institutions, western Europe is entering into deepening patterns of cooperation and integration. The chances of a war among these European countries is remote, and they seem to enjoy a perpetual peace. Western Europe is at least a regional international society, if not an international community, and may be a harbinger of the world's future as a community. Chapter Nine discusses Europe's integration more fully.

Overall, the world appears to be in an inchoate stage as an emerging international society. At least, the transnationalists observe realities that fit closely the international society model and detect a world struggling, setbacks and all, to become more cooperative in its nature. Unlike the realists, transnationalists also hold the liberal, or Kantian, view that people are basically good and that a peaceful social order is possible. Kant's idea of a pacific union of democratic republics, once thought utopian, is not so far-fetched in the post–Cold War period with democracies on the increase.[58] The idealists of the post–First World War era, able to look at today's world, might feel gratified that "what ought to be" is becoming.

This assessment is, of course, arguable. Realists and neorealists would certainly take exception, and some transnationalists would claim the "picture" of the world, as described here, is too sanguine. Nevertheless, our cooperation continuum touches on the whole scope of international relations and can guide our analytical perspective throughout this textbook as well as stimulate constructive argument and discussion. We will remain alert as to whether the subject matter of each chapter best supports the model of international anarchy, international society, or international community.

Finally, one might well ask: Why is world government not serving as the most cooperative point on our continuum? World government, after all, has appeared in many schemes of world order idealists. Frankly, it is so far removed from anything resembling a visible future that it would not help our analysis. Without an integrated world culture and a strong sense of global community, world government is unsustainable. Then too, world government is not necessarily a solution to global problems. World government could be at the center of global revolution and civil war just as national governments are often the central issue of domestic conflict.

WHAT IS THE STUDY OF INTERNATIONAL RELATIONS?

Every academic discipline tries to develop its literature and history, scope and methods, and theoretical way of thinking to produce and organize a body of knowledge. Understanding how specialists in the field of international relations think and work will provide additional conceptual tools to deal with the subject matter of international relations. Thus, offering a profile of the international relations discipline will be useful.

International relations is the study of who gets what, when, and how in matters external to states or in matters crossing national boundary lines. For example, imagine two governments negotiating over a fishery in international waters for their respective fishers. Or think about two governments sharing a common border and working out agreements on the travel of tourists, the migration of animals, or the transborder drift of acid rain. Multitudinous activities are transnational, with private citizens and organizations creating far more international behavior than state-to-state business, although private impact may not always be as great as public impact. Trade and other commercial exchanges are the most common type of transnational activity today.

The *who* of international relations are primarily states or the countries of the world. In addition, nonstate actors, including terrorists, churches, international organizations, and associations representing ethnic groups, are increasingly being recognized as important in international relations. The goals of actors are the *what* of international relations, and these goals can be of a political, economic, social, or cultural kind. The *when* of international relations can range from continuous activity by states providing for the security of their populations to the episodic activity of a private international organization. The *how* of international relations refers to the instruments actors use to achieve goals. A wide range of instruments are available, including military force, propaganda, foreign aid, diplomacy, and numerous others.

Traditionally, the distinctive character of international relations has been the condition of anarchy—that is, the absence of a government, a legal and coercive center that can control the actors in a given political arena. Without the presence of government, some scholars view the use of force and the occurrence of war as normal outcomes. In fact, some scholars in the international relations field have treated the problem of war as the central concern of their discipline. These scholars often contrast international relations with the domestic politics of states. They see the central government of a country as regulating domestic politics and producing more stable and peaceful conditions than are possible in international politics.

In modern reality, lines between domestic and international politics have blurred, bringing the two kinds of politics closer together. Some scholars question whether a specialized international relations field, one within the broader discipline of political science, is even necessary. However, the continuation of many specialized courses and journals under the rubric of international relations demonstrates that this field is alive and robust. Although the distinction between international and domestic politics is not always sharp, international specialists operate on the assumption that they have a definable field of study.

Actually, international relations are not nearly as anarchic as some might suppose. World anarchy, in essence the absence of world government, does not necessarily lead to disorder and violence. Countries frequently choose to avoid war and follow the norms and rules of international law. Also, the many civil wars and revolutions taking place within countries prove that the presence of governments inside states is no guarantee of stable and peaceful domestic conditions. Sometimes the internal affairs of states turn into anarchy involving both the collapse of central government and chaotic violence. Ironically, it is the United Nations that must come to the rescue of internally disturbed states. The international level, supposedly without order, sends help down to the state level, presumably where order and peace reign almost by definition.

The History of the Study of International Relations

The study of international relations as a discipline is ancient if we bear in mind that writers centuries ago performed analyses of the wars of Greek city-states, the relations of Italian city-states, and the ties of tribute states to the Chinese empire. The modern study of international relations began in the early twentieth century as an interest of diplomatic historians and a specialty of international lawyers.

While American political science began in the 1880s, political scientists specializing in the subject of international relations appeared in the United States with the advent of the First World War (1914–1918) and the formation of the League of Nations (1919–1939). These events heightened attention on international affairs in the English-speaking countries.[59] The First World War involved American troops in Europe for the first time, and the League, in a bold departure from historical practice, became an institutional effort to prevent war. New scholarly fields come into being in response to either a social or a technical need. Hence, after the First World War, the desire to avoid war in the future determined the initial direction of the international relations field.[60]

European immigrant scholars helped the field to emerge in the United States, and some of the early, important American scholars also studied in Europe. Today associations of international specialists continue to communicate and influence one another on a transnational basis. For example, the International Studies Association (ISA), founded in 1959, has made considerable effort to increase transnational contacts. The ISA, though basically a U.S. association, has held annual meetings in foreign cities and has attracted a membership of foreign scholars.[61]

Although many political scientists view international relations as a subfield of political science, the study of international relations took clearer form with the development of specialized journals. Some of the primary journals that focus on international relations are *Foreign Affairs* (1922), *International Organization* (1947), *World Politics* (1948), the *Journal of Conflict Resolution* (1956), *Orbis* (1957), *International Studies Quarterly* (1963), and the *Journal of Peace Research* (1964).

The Scope of International Relations

The **scope** of an academic field is the range of subject matter that falls within its boundaries. Traditionally, international specialists have given much attention to the state as an actor and the state's interests, chiefly national security and power. A concern with arms races, crises, wars, and the causes of wars became logical extensions of these interests. Then, understandably, as a response to the anarchical nature of international relations, some scholars began to focus on diplomacy, international law, world order, and even proposals for a world government.

Other scholars have taken a special interest in human welfare subjects at the global level. They investigate how to improve the human condition in a decentralized world with limited resources. What can be done for refugees fleeing war and famine across national boundary lines? In a multicultural world, what human rights standards can apply globally? How can the economic conditions of poor countries improve as they confront the problem of overpopulation? These questions and many others occupy the teaching and research of international specialists with a concern for human welfare.

Newer subjects that have arisen recently in international relations are gender perspectives, environmental issues, and ethnicity. A feminist perspective has shed light on several international subjects, in particular drawing attention to male-controlled culture as a cause of war. Both publics and their leaders have come to realize that various parts of the earth interconnect through environmental interdependence. Ethnicity, once thought by scholars to be in decline, has raised its head anew. Ethnic division threatens many countries' political integrity and has already caused the dissolution of Czechoslovakia and Yugoslavia.

One of the most prominent subjects in the field in recent years has been the international political economy. This subject involves the interaction of political and economic phenomena and how the two affect each other. In particular, scholars have observed a tendency on the part of states to rely increasingly on economic rather than military power. Specialists in the international political economy look closely at the political effects of economic phenomena such as international monetary exchange rates, international loans and debts, intellectual property rights, and foreign direct investment.

International specialists have drawn on other social sciences as well as economics. They have enriched the subject matter of international relations as a discipline by borrowing knowledge and theoretical ideas from anthropology, demography, history, psychology, and sociology. These scholars are said to be **interdisciplinary** in their teaching and research because they draw on other fields of study.

International relations has become a robust, developing academic study that is highly eclectic in nature. As a burgeoning enterprise, the study of international relations has ever-expanding boundaries. New subject matter is frequently added to the old as scholars attempt to satisfy intellectual curiosity and improve the human condition.

The Methods of International Relations

In addition to discussing the subject matter of international relations, we wish to know about the **methods** of the field, the means international specialists use to conduct research and reach conclusions. By the 1960s, many scholars in the international relations field sought to apply scientism in their field of study. **Scientism** is the belief that the academic rigor and methods of the physical sciences, such as biology and chemistry, are usable in all fields. Scholars who hold this belief stress objective observations, empirical analysis, hypotheses for testing, quantified data, the use of computers, and theory building aimed at explanation and prediction.

More traditional scholars in the international relations field believe people are too complex and unpredictable to apply scientific rigor to the study of international relations. These scholars prefer to use the insights of classical philosophers, refer to documents such as treaties, and accumulate empirical evidence through historical anecdotes and case studies. Recently debate among international specialists over scientism has largely subsided. The newest generation of graduate students trains both in the sophisticated methods of the social sciences and in more traditional methods. These broadly trained students can first ask their questions and then choose whatever method is suitable for the question at hand.

Regardless of scholarly differences regarding scientism, most international specialists desire a theory to guide their work as they explore the field of international relations. A **theory** is a set of logically connected propositions that propose to explain and predict the relationships among variables in a given field of study. A theory can exist in either proven or unproven form. Proven theories are usually associated with the physical sciences, such as the law of gravity. Some philosophers of science do not view a theory as something that can be proven completely; rather, a theory stands until it is disproven. When enough anomalies appear surrounding a set of propositions standing as theory, scholars will move on to new propositions that they find more effective in pursuing their subject of interest.

When scholars fail to produce a theory, they frequently have to make do with an approach. An **approach** provides the criteria for asking questions about the subject of concern. The answers to the questions may suggest a picture of how the real world, or some part of it, works. An approach guides research but is too undeveloped to offer a convincing propositional framework for thorough explanation and prediction. The use of approaches rather than theories is the usual situation for scholars in the international relations field.

Several approaches may rival one another in a given field until one approach is so widely accepted by scholars that it finally dominates as the standard framework for research and explanation in the field. Such an approach, in other words, becomes the **paradigm** of the field. As we mentioned earlier, a focus on power by realists became the paradigm of international relations during the 1950s and 1960s. Realism has come closer than any other effort to achieve the vaunted status of theory, although enthusiasm for developing a theory around the power concept eventually waned. Anomalies involving substantial cooperation that the conflict-oriented realists could not explain began to appear on the international scene. Later other approaches appeared as serious challenges from scholars who held grave doubts about a focus on power as the field's paradigm.

Scholars try to produce a paradigm to move beyond the status of an approach that offers only criteria for asking questions. A paradigm will add concepts and a set of hypothesized relationships about those concepts to ongoing research in the field. Ideally, a deductively related set of propositions that invite testing will emerge that allows the paradigm's supporters to claim theoretical standing for their ideas, such as in the physical sciences. *Paradigmatic revolutions* sometimes take place, at least in the physical sciences, when a new paradigm challenges and replaces an older one.[62] For instance, in astronomy, Nicolaus Copernicus (1473–1543) challenged the earth-centered Ptolemaic system and produced a paradigmatic revolution when he claimed the solar system is sun centered.

So far, the field of international relations struggles along with competing approaches or models, except for the brief paradigmatic rise of realism. In this field, the model of international anarchy, supported by realists, is slipping in status as a would-be paradigm before the challenge of the international society model, championed by the transnationalists. Regarding the European Union, some scholars might even think the international community model is a good fit. Clear and decisive paradigmatic choices over the subject of international relations are not likely, however. Our subject is incredibly complex, involving as it does patterns of human behavior, and so marshaling evidence for firm conclusions that will satisfy all scholars is rarely possible. Also, the reality we study is always changing and does not wait patiently for scholars to adjust their theoretical gunsights. In general, the shift by some scholars to the transnational approach merely reflects their belief that the world has changed in nature and become a world less conflictive and more cooperative.

Finally, many international relations scholars believe, whatever the approach in use, there is no value-free inquiry, and if there were, their subject might then hold little interest for them.[63] To apply values as we study is to make **normative choices,** that is, make judgments about *what ought to be* as well as recognize *what is*.[64] Scholars often direct their research according to normative choices to improve the human condition, for instance, by looking for ways to reduce warfare and hunger.

Levels of Analysis

We can conceptualize international phenomena as occurring on several levels of human activity. Although different schemes of these levels exist on the part of international specialists, most scholars recognize at least the *individual,* the *state,* and the *system* levels. Inquiry about international phenomena, and explanations for them, on these vertically distinct planes is an analytical tool known as *levels of analysis*. Each level offers a different perspective by suggesting special questions for researchers to answer. With these different perspectives, we can learn much about an international subject that might otherwise go unanswered. A scholar may choose to focus on one level, two levels, or all three. Kenneth N. Waltz, in his classic work *Man, the State and War,* found all three levels useful to organize research about the causes of war.[65] The discussion of the causes of war in Chapter Five of this book follows Professor Waltz's good lead.

The *individual level* invites questions of all sorts. Are there special political personalities? Do power seekers or belligerent personality types appear who, once positioned as leaders, are more likely to lead countries to war? Do people have innate biological characteristics that induce them, through herdlike instincts, to follow an authoritarian leader, or are people individualistic by nature and resist authority altogether? How do individual decision makers process information and make decisions? Are the biographies of "great leaders" worthy of study? Can they shape an age as Napoleon perhaps did at the turn of the eighteenth century?

The *state level* exists between the individual and international system levels. Are the foreign policies of the most powerful states the core of international relations? What difference does it make that varied kinds of governments, such as democratic and authoritarian, lead national societies? What patterns in group decision making occur in governments and international organizations, and with what effects? What are the types of national cultures in the world, and are they relevant to international affairs? One of the most pronounced observations about states is that democratic states do not fight wars among themselves but will fight nondemocratic states. Will the present trend toward more democratic states result in a more peaceful world?

A focus on the *international system* sensitizes scholars to think about a whole divided into subparts and how those components relate to one another. The system level can be either global or regional in span, meaning countries collected together geographically and perhaps culturally, as in Africa and Latin America. Are the states of the world interacting with growing interdependence? Are trade patterns intensifying more at the regional level than at the global level? Is global military power more or less centralized with the collapse of the Soviet Union? Does the global context shape the future of states more than their respective leaders do? Can the global economy affect a country more than the initiatives of its national government?

In addition to producing different sets of questions with a range of insights, the levels-of-analysis tool helps us account for the rise of multiple actors and what they do. International activity can begin from the bottom up, such as when *substate actors* carry their interests to their national governments and then on to the international system level. For example, for years organizations of Native Americans have focused efforts on the Indian Bureau in Washington, D.C., before joining other indigenous peoples, such as the Maori from New Zealand or the Sami (Lapps) from Scandinavia, in a globally coordinated movement to produce a United Nations–sponsored treaty protecting indigenous populations.

Alternatively, international activity can start from the top down. At the system level, the International Monetary Fund (IMF), associated with the World Bank, has required austere policies by Third World national governments before loaning them money to bolster sagging national currencies. The austere policies call for national belt tightening that further impoverishes Third World peoples. The good intentions of the IMF are to put a given country on a sounder economic basis, such as by strengthening its currency, to improve its prospects for more international trade. The bad effects, according to some specialists on the international political economy, include the destabilization of the national governments following these austere policies. Masses experiencing hardscrabble lives offer even less support to their governments as austerity tightens its hold. As a result of IMF and other system-level effects, new actors form, such as the UN Conference on Trade and Development to represent the interests of the poorer states to the richer states. Inside countries, peasant unions or rebel armies form to demand relief or reform from national governments.

In studying the complex phenomenon of international relations, many scholars rely on one, two, or all three levels of analysis as they try to describe and explain events. Frequently the strategy of scholars is to search for linkages among the three levels, and, ideally, research will lead to a general theory that will encompass all three.

CHAPTER SUMMARY

Over time, the international context has become increasingly important to greater numbers of people. The possibility is real that anyone can experience the threats of war or terrorism. The global interdependence of the world economy can determine whether we have jobs and how well we will live. Borders cannot stop the spread of diseases such as AIDS, and many people believe borders should not restrain worldwide concern over human rights violations. Finally, the high-tech communication grid encompassing the world has produced a citizenry with a global awareness unmatched in history.

Although a wide variety of approaches are available to guide the writing of a textbook, the one this book employs involves the theme of conflict and cooperation. In spite of the frequency of conflict, a rough, historical progression toward a more desirable world order based on cooperation may be taking place. We can think in terms of three models—international anarchy, international society, and international community—as we determine which model, as a plausible "picture" of the world, best fits the world today and its foreseeable future.

The field of international relations has developed throughout the twentieth century and is now a robust, eclectic subject taught on most college campuses. The scope of the study of international relations is continually expanding and involves many specialties. While the methods used in the study of international relations have not become as sophisticated as those in the physical sciences, international specialists can use a variety of techniques to accumulate evidence and reach conclusions. We can use much of the international relations conceptual toolbox to aid us in our quest to place the emerging world order somewhere on the cooperation continuum. This quest begins in the next chapter, where we look at the history of international relations.

POINTS OF VIEW

We may . . . wake up one day lamenting the loss of the order that the Cold War gave to the anarchy of international relations.

—JOHN J. MEARSHEIMER
PROFESSOR OF POLITICAL
SCIENCE AT THE UNIVERSITY
OF CHICAGO

What is new about the emerging world order is that for the first time, the United States can neither withdraw from the world nor dominate it.

—HENRY KISSINGER,
DIPLOMACY, p. 19

In short the new world order has begun. It is messy, evolving, and not susceptible to simple formulation or manipulation.

—JOSEPH S. NYE, JR.
PROFESSOR OF POLITICAL SCIENCE AT HARVARD UNIVERSITY

A planet no longer held in thrall to superpower conflict or a nuclear arms race now has a chance to craft a stable global system.

—PAUL BOYER,
PROMISES TO KEEP, P. 520

Ours is not the only opinion that matters. World Press Review *reminds me of that. It causes me to think globally. It reminds me that we are all very similar, no matter what continent we call home.*

—THOMAS MEGA
PRIVATE CITIZEN IN MIDDLETON, CT

. . . the study of politics is, in every sense of the word, a science. In fact we've had a science of politics since Aristotle.

—CHARLES W. KEGLEY, JR.
1993 PRESIDENT OF THE INTERNATIONAL STUDIES ASSOCIATION

REVIEW QUESTIONS

1. What is the study of international relations? How can it be distinguished from the study of domestic politics?
2. In what ways do international events affect average citizens? In what ways has your life been affected by international developments not covered in this chapter?
3. What changes will occur if the world transforms from international anarchy to international society?
4. What advantages for the world can we expect from the end of the Cold War?
5. Do you think we have a new world order in the 1990s? Why or why not?
6. How scientific is the study of international relations?
7. What do we mean when we say that the international relations field is interdisciplinary?
8. What are the "levels of analysis," and how do we seek explanation through them?
9. What distinction can be made between an approach and a paradigm?
10. To what extent does the international relations field belong to American scholars and to scholars in other countries?

GLOSSARY

actors An individual or a collective entity, such as the state or an international organization, that plays a role in international relations.
anarchy The absence of government and control in a given order, sometimes but not necessarily leading to disorder.
approach A researcher's strategy for giving direction in a field of study by offering a set of questions that need answering.
governance A framework of accepted rules, norms, and institutions on the global level that provides a basis for cooperation without the involvement of a strong, central authority.
interdependence Mutual dependence among actors, such as states; this dependence may not be evenly distributed among the actors.
interdisciplinary Enriching a given academic field by drawing theoretical ideas from other fields.
international relations The study of who gets what, when, and how in the transborder context involving both states and nonstate actors.
methods The means scholars have available to conduct research and reach conclusions in a given academic field.
normative choice A value choice as to what ought to be.
order An enduring pattern of relationships among the members of a society.
paradigm An approach that holds primacy in a given academic field and shows promise of theoretical development.
scientism The belief that methods used to investigate the natural sciences should be used in all fields, even those involving human behavior, such as in the social sciences.
scope The subject matter of a given field that falls within known academic boundaries.
theory A set of logically coherent propositions about a set of variables that offer explanation and prediction. A theory may be proven or unproven.
transnational activities Activities and occurrences that cross national borders. Sometimes thought of as private in nature as opposed to governmental or public.

RECOMMENDED READINGS

David A. Baldwin, ed. *Neorealism and Neoliberalism: The Contemporary Debate.* New York: Columbia University Press, 1993.

Seyom Brown. *International Relations in a Changing Global System: Toward a Theory of the World Polity.* Boulder, CO: Westview Press, 1992.

Barry Buzan, Charles Jones, and Richard Little. *The Logic of Anarchy.* New York: Columbia University Press, 1993.

Hedley Bull. *The Anarchical Society: A Study of Order in World Politics.* New York: Columbia University Press, 1977.

Ian Clark and Iver B. Neumann, eds. *Classical Theories of International Relations.* New York: Macmillan, 1996.

Richard Falk. *Explorations at the Edge of Time.* Philadelphia: Temple University Press, 1992.

Michael J. Hogan, ed. *The End of the Cold War.* New York: Cambridge University Press, 1992.

Charles W. Kegley, Jr., ed. *Controversies in International Relations Theory: Realism and the Neorealism Challenge.* New York: St. Martin's Press, 1995.

Robert O. Keohane and Joseph S. Nye, Jr., *Power and Interdependence.* 2nd ed. Boston: Scott, Foresman, 1989.

Robert O. Keohane and Joseph S. Nye, Jr., eds. *Transnational Relations and World Politics.* Cambridge, MA: Harvard University Press, 1972.

Richard W. Mansbach and John A. Vasquez. *In Search of Theory.* New York: Columbia University Press, 1981. See especially Chapter 1, "The Decay of an Old Paradigm," pp. 3–27.

J. D. B. Miller and R. J. Vincent. *Order and Violence: Hedley Bull and International Relations.* Oxford: Clarendon Press, 1990.

Joseph S. Nye, Jr. *Understanding International Conflicts: An Introduction to Theory and History.* New York: HarperCollins, 1993.

James N. Rosenau and Ernst-Otto Czempiel, eds. *Governance Without Government: Order and Change in World Politics.* New York: Cambridge University Press, 1992.

Max Singer and Aaron Wildavsky. *The Real World Order: Zones of Peace/Zones of Turmoil.* Chatham, NJ: Chatham House, 1993.

Paul R. Viotti and Mark V. Kauppi. *International Relations Theory: Realism, Pluralism, Globalism.* 2nd ed. New York: Macmillan, 1993.

Martin Wight. *International Theory: The Three Traditions,* edited by Gabriele Wight and Brian Porter. New York: Holmes & Meier, 1992.

Frank W. Wayman and Paul F. Diehl, eds. *Reconstructing Realpolitik.* Ann Arbor, MI: University of Michigan Press, 1994.

ENDNOTES

1. Max Singer and Aaron Wildavsky. *The Real World Order: Zones of Peace/Zones of Turmoil* (Chatham, NJ: Chatham House, 1993), p. 96.
2. Henry Kissinger, *Diplomacy* (New York: Simon & Schuster, 1994), p. 25.
3. David Fromkin, "The Coming Millennium: World Politics in the Twenty-First Century," *World Policy Journal,* Spring 1993, p. 5. See also Josef Janning, "A German Europe—A European Germany? On the Debate over Germany's Foreign Policy," *International Affairs,* January 1996, pp. 33–41.
4. Robert O. Keohane and Joseph S. Nye, Jr., *Power and Interdependence.* 2nd ed. (Boston: Scott, Foresman, 1989).
5. Torbjorn L. Knutsen, *A History of International Relations Theory* (New York: Manchester University Press, 1992), pp. 236–38, 260–62.
6. David A. Baldwin, "Neoliberalism, Neorealism, and World Politics," in *Neorealism and Neoliberalism: The Contemporary Debate,* ed. David A. Baldwin (New York: Columbia University Press, 1993), p. 9; Robert Axelrod and Robert O. Keohane, "Achieving Cooperation under Anarchy: Strategies and Institutions," in *Neorealism and Neoliberalism,* pp. 85, 114.
7. Lynn H. Miller, *Global Order: Values and Power in International Politics* (Boulder, CO: Westview Press, 1990), p. 80; James N. Rosenau, "Governance, Order, and Change in World Politics," in *Governance Without Government: Order and Change in World Politics,* ed. James N. Rosenau and Ernst-Otto Czempiel (New York: Cambridge University Press, 1992), p. 11.
8. Michael N. Nagler, "Ideas of World Order and the Map of Peace," in *Approaches to Peace: An Intellectual Map,* ed. W. Scott Thompson and Kenneth M. Jensen (Washington, D.C.: U.S. Institute of Peace, 1991), p. 383; R. D. McKinlay and R. Little, *Global Problems and World Order* (Madison: University of Wisconsin Press, 1986), p. 15.
9. Rosenau, "Governance, Order, and Change in World Politics," p. 24; James N. Rosenau, *Turbulence in World Politics* (Princeton, NJ: Princeton University Press, 1990), pp. 439–40.
10. Kissinger, *Diplomacy,* p. 19.
11. Adam Roberts, "Thinking about International Relations: A New Age in International Relations?" *International Relations,* July 1991, p. 523.
12. Singer and Wildavsky, *The Real World Order,* pp. 189–202.
13. Knutsen, *A History of International Relations Theory,* pp. 243–44, 256.
14. Martin Wight, *International Theory: The Three Traditions* (New York: Holmes & Meier, 1992); Hedley Bull, *The Anarchical Society: A Study of Order in World Politics* (New York: Columbia

University Press, 1977); David S. Yost, "Wight and the 'Three Traditions': Political Philosophy and the Theory of International Relations," *International Affairs,* April 1994, pp. 263–90; Pierre Hassner, "Beyond the Three Traditions: The Philosophy of War and Peace in Historical Perspective," *International Affairs,* October 1994, pp. 737–56; Chris Brown, "International Theory and International Society: The Viability of the Middle Way?" *Review of International Studies,* April 1995, pp. 183–96.
15. Norberto Bobbio, *Thomas Hobbes and the Natural Law Tradition* (Chicago: University of Chicago Press, 1993), p. 199.
16. Knutsen, *A History of International Relations Theory,* p. 236.
17. Bobbio, *Thomas Hobbes,* p. 199.
18. Hedley Bull, "The Importance of Grotius in the Study of International Relations," in *Hugo Grotius and International Relations,* ed. Hedley Bull, Benedict Kingsbury, and Adam Roberts (Oxford: Clarendon Press, 1992), p. 93.
19. Benedict Kingsbury and Adam Roberts, "Introduction: Grotian Thought in International Relations," in *Hugo Grotius and International Relations,* p. 6.
20. Knutsen, *A History of International Relations Theory,* p. 237.
21. Yost, "Wight and the 'Three Traditions'," p. 272.
22. Bull, "The Importance of Grotius," pp. 65–93.
23. Yost, "Wight and the 'Three Traditions'," p. 274.
24. Evan Luard, *Basic Texts in International Relations: The Evolution of Ideas about International Society* (New York: St. Martin's Press, 1992), pp. 421–22. See also Wade L. Huntley, "Kant's Third Image: Systemic Sources of the Liberal Peace," *International Studies Quarterly,* March 1996, pp. 45–76.
25. Hans Reiss, *Kant's Political Writings* (Cambridge, England: Cambridge University Press, 1970), pp. 3–4, 10–11.
26. Michael W. Doyle, "Liberalism and International Relations," in *Kant and Political Philosophy: The Contemporary Legacy,* ed. Ronald Beiner and William James Booth (New Haven, CT: Yale University Press, 1993), pp. 187–89; Michael W. Doyle, "An International Liberal Community," in *Rethinking America's Security: Beyond Cold War to New World Order,* ed. Graham Allison and Gregory F. Treverton (New York: W. W. Norton, 1992), pp. 307–33; Jurg Martin Gabriel, *Worldviews and Theories of International Relations* (New York: St. Martin's Press, 1994), p. 56.
27. Gabriel, *Worldviews,* p. 57; Doyle, "An International Liberal Community," in *Kant and Political Philosophy,* p. 313.
28. Joseph M. Knippenberg, "The Politics of Kant's Philosophy," in *Kant and Political Philosophy,* p. 161.
29. Ibid., pp. 160–65.
30. Richard Falk, *Explorations at the Edge of Time: The Prospects for World Order* (Philadelphia: Temple University Press, 1992), pp. 218–19; Miller, *Global Order,* p. 75.
31. James E. Dougherty and Robert L. Pfaltzgraff, Jr., *Contending Theories of International Relations,* 3rd ed. (New York: Harper & Row, 1990), pp. 126–27.
32. Edward Hallet Carr, *The Twenty Years' Crisis* (New York: St. Martin's Press, 1966; first published in 1939).
33. Hans J. Morgenthau, *Politics Among Nations: The Struggle for Power and Peace,* 5th ed. (New York: Alfred A. Knopf, 1978). For a critical assessment of Morgenthau's thinking, see Jaap W. Nobel, "Morgenthau's Struggle with Power: The Theory of Power Politics and the Cold War," *Review of International Studies,* January 1995, pp. 61–85.
34. Some of these points are influenced by Ole R. Holsti, "Models of International Relations: Perspectives on Conflict and Cooperation," in *The Global Agenda: Issues and Perspectives,* 3rd ed., ed. Charles W. Kegley, Jr., and Eugene R. Wittkopf (New York: McGraw-Hill, 1992), pp. 140–41.
35. A good, concise summary of realism is found in Paul R. Viotti and Mark V. Kauppi, *International Relations Theory: Realism, Pluralism, Globalism,* 2nd ed. (New York: Macmillan, 1993), pp. 61–66.
36. Morgenthau, *Politics Among Nations,* Chapters 31, 32.
37. Robert O. Keohane, "Institutional Theory and the Realist Challenge after the Cold War," in *Neorealism and Neoliberalism,* p. 291.
38. John Lewis Gaddis, "The Cold War, the Long Peace, and the Future," in *The End of the Cold War: Its Meaning and Implications,* ed. Michael J.

Hogan (New York: Cambridge University Press, 1992), p. 31.
39. Kenneth N. Waltz, *Theory of International Politics* (Reading, MA: Addison-Wesley, 1979).
40. Ibid., pp. 104–11. See also Steven Forde, "International Realism and the Science of Politics," *International Studies Quarterly,* June 1995, pp. 141–60.
41. Waltz, *Theory of International Politics,* pp. 111–14, 194–99.
42. Robert Powell, "Anarchy in International Relations Theory: The Neorealist-Neoliberal Debate," *International Organization,* Spring 1994, pp. 338–40.
43. Stephen D. Krasner, "Global Communications and National Power: Life on the Pareto Frontier," *World Politics,* April 1991, pp. 336–66.
44. Robert O. Keohane and Joseph S. Nye, Jr., eds., *Transnational Relations and World Politics* (Cambridge, MA: Harvard University Press, 1972); Robert O. Keohane and Joseph S. Nye, Jr., *Power and Interdependence* (Boston: Little, Brown, 1977). Published as a second edition in 1989 (see note 4).
45. Helen Milner, "The Assumption of Anarchy in International Relations Theory: A Critique," in *Neorealism and Neoliberalism,* pp. 163–64.
46. Holsti, "Models of International Relations," pp. 139–50.
47. Roger A. Coate and Jerel A. Rosati, "Human Needs in World Society," in *The Power of Human Needs in World Society,* ed. Roger A. Coate and Jerel A. Rosati (Boulder, CO: Lynne Rienner Publishers, 1988), pp. 1–20.
48. Rosenau, *Governance Without Government,* p. 439.
49. John Burton, *World Society* (Cambridge, England: Cambridge University Press, 1972). For an evaluation of Burton's influence, see David J. Dunn, "Articulating an Alternative: The Contribution of John Burton," *Review of International Studies,* April 1995, pp. 197–208.
50. Luard, *Basic Texts in International Relations,* pp. 575–76.
51. The emergence of interests besides security issues is covered in James N. Rosenau, "Turbulence Change," in Viotti and Kauppi, *International Relations Theory,* p. 443; Seyom Brown, *International Relations in a Changing Global System: Toward a Theory of the World Polity* (Boulder, CO: Westview Press, 1992), pp. 132–38; Coate and Rosati, *The Power of Human Needs in World Society,* pp. 5–8.
52. Joseph S. Nye, Jr., *Understanding International Conflicts: An Introduction to Theory and History* (New York: HarperCollins, 1993), p. 273.
53. Rosenau, "Governance, Order, and Changes in World Politics," pp. 2–3, 28–29.
54. Hedley Bull and Adam Watson, *The Expansion of International Society* (Oxford: Clarendon Press, 1984), pp. 429–35. See also Nicholas J. Wheeler and Timothy Dunne, "Hedley Bull's Pluralism of the Intellect and Solidarism of the Will," *International Affairs,* January 1996, pp. 91–107.
55. Nagler, "Ideas of World Order," p. 374.
56. Richard A. Falk, "Unraveling the Future of World Order," in *The War System: An Interdisciplinary Approach,* ed. Richard A. Falk and Samuel S. Kim (Boulder, CO: Westview Press, 1980), p. 636.
57. Brown, *International Relations,* p. 168.
58. Knutsen, *A History of International Relations Theory,* p. 238; Joseph S. Nye, Jr., "What New World Order?" in *The Theory and Practice of International Relations,* 9th ed., ed. William Clinton Olson (Englewood Cliffs, NJ: Prentice Hall, 1994), p. 75.
59. Carr, *The Twenty Years' Crisis,* pp. 1–2.
60. Knutsen, *A History of International Relations Theory,* p. 193.
61. For a brief history of the field, see Norman D. Palmer, "The Study of International Relations in the United States: Perspectives of Half a Century," *International Studies Quarterly,* September 1980, p. 346; John Spanier, *Games Nations Play,* 7th ed. (Washington, DC: Congressional Quarterly Press, 1990), p. 9; Frederick H. Gareau, "The Discipline of International Relations: A Multinational Perspective," *Journal of Politics,* August 1981, p. 802; Gene M. Lyons, "Expanding the Study of International Relations: The French Connection," *World Politics,* October 1982, p. 149; Fred Halliday, "International Relations and Its Discontents," *International Affairs,* October 1995, pp. 733–46.
62. Thomas Kuhn, *The Structure of Scientific Revolutions,* 2nd edition (Chicago: University of Chicago Press, 1970).

63. For example, see Stanley Hoffmann's views of Hedley Bull's views in "International Society," in *Order and Violence: Hedley Bull and International Relations,* ed. J. D. B. Miller and R. J. Vincent (Oxford: Clarendon Press, 1990), p. 20.
64. Viotti and Kauppi, *International Relations Theory,* p. 532.
65. Kenneth N. Waltz, *Man, the State and War* (New York: Columbia University Press, 1959).

CHAPTER 2

THE HISTORICAL SETTING OF INTERNATIONAL RELATIONS

For thousands of years, people have lived scattered over the earth in myriad cultures, frequently unaware of one another's existence. People also have experienced the rule of varied types of government including tribes, city-states, empires, and the nation-state or modern state that evolved in Europe from the seventeenth century and is now the prevailing form of government in the world.

Much of the interaction of cultures and governments across the centuries has been conflictual in nature, since contact frequently meant conquest for slaves, wealth, territory, and enhanced security. In fact, until recent history, the European domination and influence over other continents occurred largely through conquest. Barbara Ward once wrote, "conquest has been the greatest lever of change in human history."[1] Conflictual interactions do not have to monopolize contacts among distinct societies, however. While people have often fought wars, they also have learned patterns of cooperative behavior whenever they share problems they cannot solve alone. The human effort to constrain conflict and promote cooperation is a major theme of history and a central concern of this textbook. Remarkably, after a century dominated by world wars, a pattern of cooperation now appears in ascendancy as we move into the 21st century, at least among the major states.

In this chapter, we cover the formation of the modern state from its beginnings in the feudal system of Europe to its status as the foremost political entity in the world. Next, we examine the interactions of the various states in the classical state system that prevailed between 1648 and 1914. Then we look at the three world wars—the First and Second World Wars and the Cold War—as the dominating events of the twentieth century. We will see how the end of the Cold War served as a breaking point in history, clearing the way for more widespread cooperation, a pattern that is becoming increasingly global as countries around the world realize they share many of the same concerns. Finally, we look at how historical changes have shaped the beginnings of an international society.

THE ORIGINS OF THE MODERN STATE

Much of the history that will help us understand current international relations deals with the modern state. A **state** is a central government, ruling over a population and a territory, that represents and protects that population in international politics. A modern state expects the population to share a sense of identity and to offer loyalty to the state, although numerous exceptions occur. Many scholars in the international relations field commonly use the term "nation-state," but this is an awkward construct. *Nation* refers to a particular cultural or ethnic group, such as the Cherokee nation or the Persian majority living in Iran. A political entity governing within known boundaries is a *state*. In the large majority of modern states are found two or more "nations" in the cultural sense. Not uncommon today, some of these nations aspire to create their own states. In this book, we will refer to the nearly 200 entities ranging from Australia to Zimbabwe simply as states or countries. The subject of "nations" and "states" appears again in the next chapter on actors.

Antiquity

An outline of the state began to take form in the seventeenth century, but some influences originated in antiquity. From the Greek city-states (800 B.C.–168 B.C.) came antecedents of modern diplomacy and arbitration to settle disputes that states and international organizations, such as the United Nations, would later use. Athens in particular created and practiced democracy, which later revived in Europe as a challenge to European monarchies. A legacy of Rome in the West (27 B.C.–A.D. 476) was the rudiments of international law that Rome created to conduct relations with barbarian tribes living on the borders of its empire. Another legacy of the Roman Empire, in its Byzantine days, was the Justinian Code, developed in the sixth century A.D., that has influenced modern code law states.

Feudalism

The collapse of Roman rule left western Europe in the *Dark Ages* (A.D. 476–800), a period marked by a decline in law and order, trade, and learning and a decrease in population. Power and authority, once concentrated, became fragmented among many petty kings and warlords who provided a modicum of security from local lawlessness and barbarian raids.[2] Protection improved as **feudalism** evolved, reaching its full form between the eleventh and thirteenth centuries of the *Middle Ages* (A.D. 801–1400). Feudalism called for lords to distribute land to vassals and to offer them protection. In return, the vassals contributed money and soldiers to their lords. Over the centuries, a pattern of consolidation of the fragmented feudal units gradually developed to provide the territorial bases for larger states.

Attempts at a Universal State

Before large, independent states began to emerge, however, there were two related attempts to create a "universal state" to end the disorder of Europe following the collapse of the Roman Empire. Charlemagne (A.D. 742–814), king of the Franks, established a Christian kingdom over the former Roman Empire in western Europe, and Pope Leo III anointed him as the "Roman Emperor." Unfortunately for Europe's unity, Charlemagne's three grandsons divided his empire after his death.

After Charlemagne, the Holy Roman Empire (A.D. 962–1806) took shape, usually under the rule of a German emperor approved by the Roman Catholic pope. The Holy Roman Empire existed on territory presently shared by Austria, Belgium, the republics of Czech and Slovakia, Germany, the Netherlands, and northern Italy. This empire was a weak governmental system with territorial boundaries that tended to recede rather than expand. Napoleon dissolved the Holy Roman Empire in 1806. Voltaire (1694–1778), a famous French philosopher, supposedly said that this empire was "neither Holy, Roman, nor an Empire." The dream of a united Europe lived on, mostly as the ambition of conquerors, first for Napoleon in the early nineteenth century and later for Hitler before the mid-twentieth century. Today Europe has considerable unity in economic and security arrangements, but a unity based on voluntary cooperation, not the coerced cooperation of conquerors.

Strong Kings

An important step in the formation of the state was the emergence of strong kings. A king usually began as a lord but, over time, came to rule over other lords and large territories. Not only did kings have to gain control over the feudal lords within their domains; these rulers also had to wrest themselves free of the control of the Roman Catholic pope at the same time. The Roman Catholic Church was a cultural unifier for centuries in Europe, and the pope had considerable powers. He could excommunicate recalcitrant kings, withhold annulments of royal marriages, and had the standing to render judgments in disputes between kings.

Fortunately for kings and the evolution of the modern state, the pope's powers declined. The Protestant Reformation of the sixteenth century severely shook the Roman Catholic Church. In fact, several different Protestant churches appeared during the *Renaissance* (1400–1600). This period was an era of enlightenment and reform that marked the end of the Middle Ages, an era that helped to create the cultural atmosphere that made the Protestant Reformation possible.

In some cases, Protestant faiths became national churches in several countries. The most important was the creation of the Church of England during the reign of King Henry VIII (1509–1547). As head of the Church of England, Henry seized all Catholic lands and wealth. Other kings followed suit in the Netherlands, Scandinavia, and Scotland. In the 1600s, some kings even asserted they ruled by **Divine Right** and were directly answerable only to God, not to the governed or to the pope.

Between 1400 and 1600, territorial units began to appear that would foreshadow some of the modern states of today. Primarily these territorial states were England, France, Holland, Portugal, Russia, Spain, Sweden, and the small principalities known collectively as the Germanies. Divided along Catholic and Protestant lines, some of these states fought intense, bloody wars over whether the Catholic or the Protestant faith would prevail in Europe. Religious warfare finally culminated in the Thirty Years' War (1618–1648). The accord ending this war, known as the *Peace of Westphalia* of 1648, ended religious warfare by recognizing the **sovereignty** of each king. This legal status meant that no authority operated above the king, and states were not to interfere with one another because they were legal equals. Sovereignty is the cornerstone of the modern state, and many scholars use the date 1648 to mark the beginning of the modern international system.

Some kings of Europe came to view their sovereignty as completely unbridled authority. They took seriously the views of French philosopher Jean Bodin (1530–1596), who claimed the monarch had supreme power over his citizens, and English philosopher

Thomas Hobbes (1588–1679), who maintained that without a monarch's firm control, life would be "poor, nasty, brutish, and short." Subjects usually addressed a king as "His Sovereign Majesty." Louis XIV of France (1643–1715), a particularly powerful and successful French king, supposedly uttered the words "L'etat, c'est moi" ("I am the state").

The American Revolution of 1776 and the French Revolution of 1789 jolted the monarch's powerful position, since these revolutions rejected the entire concept of monarchical rule. The latter revolution had the most impact on Europe because Europeans genuinely admired the French court and French culture, and the nobility of Europe experienced shock when Louis XVI went to the guillotine in 1793. Following its revolution, France, like the United States, became a **republic,** a government conducted by representatives of the people. The French people became the first to embrace a sense of national will and to give intense loyalty to their state rather than leave government to elites. The state absorbed the sovereign status once held by a king, and the interests of the state and the French people intertwined as one.

In time, sovereignty passed from the state to the people, meaning the people were the ultimate source of all legitimate political authority. This locus of authority in the people became known as **popular sovereignty,** and the people exercised this authority mainly through elections to choose those who were to govern. Popular sovereignty spread as an ideal, with some European states turning to democracy in the nineteenth century.

The Role of Nationalism

Not only did authority finally transfer to the people, but passion sprang from them that empowered the state as well. Although Napoleon Bonaparte (1769–1821) disrupted French republicanism when he crowned himself emperor of France in 1804, he still encouraged the fervor of French **nationalism.** This set of beliefs involves a special sense of identity and pride among a group of people that distinguishes them from other groups. Napoleon employed nationalism to raise an army of hundreds of thousands of men and marched them to far-flung places, including Egypt and Russia, all for the greater glory of France and, of course, Napoleon.

Nationalism today is not the fierce political force that it was in the Second World War or during the colonial independence movement following this war, but it remains an important political force in the world. A major concern of the Western democracies is that Russia could veer toward an extreme form of nationalism and try to rebuild the territorial base of the old Soviet Union. Although strong nationalistic feelings can engender hostility among countries, at the same time the sense of unity and loyalty nationalism brings to countries has become essential to hold states together as viable political units.

A viable state may have to have what French historian Ernest Renan (1823–1892) called a "spiritual principle." Renan examined, one by one, geography, religion, race, military needs, and language before he concluded that none of these are sufficient to unite a people within a state. He found that a population sharing a state's territory must have a strong sense of a shared past and must expect to share a future, regardless of whether these experiences bring glory or grief.[3] A sense of unity such as that nationalism brings, then, is often the psychological "glue" that holds an ethnically divided people together. Nationalism does not always succeed in this task, however.

TABLE 2.1
Relevant History of the Origins of the State

800 B.C.–168 B.C.	Greek city-states
27 B.C.–A.D. 476	Roman Empire in the West
A.D. 395–1453	Roman Empire in the East
A.D. 527–565	Justinian Codes from Justinian I's reign
A.D. 476–800	Dark Ages
A.D. 800–1400	Middle Ages
A.D. 800–843	Charlemagne's empire
A.D. 843	Charlemagne's three grandsons divide his empire
A.D. 962–1806	Holy Roman Empire
1400–1600	Renaissance
1517	Protestant Reformation
1618–1648	Thirty Years' War
1648	The beginning of the international system of states

The major concern over nationalism today involves ethnic nationalism. Most states have ethnic divisions of race, language, religion, and other cultural differences that can tear at country-level nationalism. The recent histories of the now defunct Soviet Union and fragmented Yugoslavia clearly demonstrate that ethnic-level nationalism is a source of much conflict today, a topic covered in the next chapter.

To summarize, the state began its formation under the leadership of strong kings in the Middle Ages, and over time kings had to controls lords and free themselves from the pope. Republicanism challenged monarchical rule in the eighteenth century, although some important European monarchs would remain on their thrones until the First World War. An important step in the state's development occurred when a sense of nationalism, which first emerged in France at the turn of the eighteenth century, enlivened mass participation in the state's purposes.

THE CLASSICAL STATE SYSTEM, 1648–1914

Until well into the twentieth century, the pattern of interaction among states, the *state system,* was largely a European experience. Europe contained the most important states in terms of military and economic power and their ability to project power to other areas of the world. When contact occurred with other peoples on other continents, Europe usually dominated.

The War System

Scholars sometimes cite the number of wars European states have fought as evidence that the state system is anarchic and war prone. This observation contains an element of truth, but war by European states was mostly an instrument of foreign policy to achieve limited objectives. After the religious wars of the sixteenth and seventeenth centuries, Europeans fought wars not to completely destroy an opponent but to take a piece of territory in

Europe, grab a colony from another state, or check the advances of an opposing state. War was never inevitable, and gradually the prosecution of war fell under the regulation of international law, although an effort to outlaw war altogether was not made until well into the twentieth century.

The most important concern of states was to avoid domination by others, especially the unification of Europe into an empire. A *balance of power* system helped to preserve the independence of states. Ideally, under this system, a powerful state or alliance always faced a counteralliance marshaling about equal power. The balance of power system of the eighteenth and nineteenth centuries could work only because a diffusion of power prevented one state from possessing overwhelming power. Also, because these centuries were without serious religious divisions or political ideologies, states had the flexibility to switch alliances as needed to prevent a dangerous concentration of power in one state or alliance.[4] The balance of power concept is a subject of more thorough discussion in Chapter Four.

The most serious challenge to the balance of power system was Napoleon's military skills and empire ambitions between 1804 and 1815. For a decade, Napoleon kept Europe embroiled in war, taking the French army into Austria, Prussia, and Russia. Napoleon ruled much of continental Europe until his defeat at the Battle of Leipzig in 1813. Although exiled to Elba Island, located between Corsica and Italy, Napoleon escaped and rallied another French army. This time an alliance of states, led by Great Britain, decisively defeated his army at the Battle of Waterloo in 1815. So concerned were Europeans that Napoleon had nearly forced Europe into a French empire and might try again that the British shipped him off to St. Helena Island in the South Atlantic, where he died in exile. At the Congress of Vienna in 1815, following Napoleon's defeat, the European allies reestablished the traditional French monarchy and wisely brought France back into their system of states to establish a new and more stable balance of power in Europe.

Warfare during the remainder of the nineteenth century was fairly limited. The Crimean War (1853–1856) was significant because over half a million men died, due mostly to bungled decisions and disease. Great Britain and France had the limited goal of preventing Russia from closing the Black Sea to international trade, and they were successful. Then Prussia waged several wars in rapid succession against Denmark, Austria, and France between 1864 and 1871, with Prussia achieving spectacular successes. Prussian victory led to the creation of the German Empire in 1871, moving Germany from a second-rank to a front-rank power position in the European hierarchy of states. Compared to the ideologically driven, bloody wars of the twentieth century, fought with sophisticated weapons, the classical state system was almost a peaceful era. Scholars often credit this achievement to skilled diplomacy and the balance of power system.

The Economic System

The history of the classical state system experienced two economic systems, *mercantilism* and *free trade*. Mercantilism stressed the accumulation of gold and silver by the state and state control over manufacturing and trade to enhance state power and prestige. This economic system stressed protection for home markets and, consequently, greatly restricted trade among countries. States were prone to fight wars to secure colonies for resources and markets. Mercantilism was the predominant economic system from approximately the sixteenth century through the eighteenth century and extended to some degree into the nineteenth century.

Free trade, or *laissez-faire,* is an alternative economic system proposed in *The Wealth of Nations* by Adam Smith during the mercantile period in 1776. Smith advocated that countries sell their best products without trade restrictions such as tariffs and quotas so that everyone would have quality goods at cheaper prices and enjoy a higher standard of living. Free trade among countries was a spin-off of the practice of *capitalism* inside countries. Capitalism called for the private ownership of property and for market forces of supply and demand to manage the economy instead of the government.

The *Industrial Revolution* (1750–1850) helped to prepare Europe for a free trade system by providing the technological means to produce great amounts of goods for sale. Developing first in Great Britain, the Industrial Revolution reached various countries at different times and evolved at varied paces. Factories with complex machines became the basis of wealth instead of agriculture. Urbanization occurred at a rapid rate, and transportation and communication improved through new technology. Also, banking and finance became major industries. In the latter part of the nineteenth century, the effects of the Industrial Revolution encouraged partial acceptance of Smith's ideas. By this time, Europe had an excess of goods and the means to carry those goods around the world to non-European markets. However, states continued to restrict much foreign trade and to maintain their own near-monopolies in trade in colonies. We will return to the subjects of mercantilism and free trade in Chapter Eight.

The Colonial System

The acquisition of colonies had many motives. A primary objective was to enhance the wealth of the colonizing state in a different way. The first European colonial period, from the late sixteenth century to the middle nineteenth century, accompanied and served the policy of mercantilism. Even before the state system formed, Europeans had discovered the Americas, circumnavigated the African coast, and encountered several Asian empires. Spain exercised mercantilism in the 1500s by mining gold and silver from the Americas, while in the 1600s and 1700s, other European countries placed settler colonies along the Atlantic seaboard of North America to generate a rich variety of resources. Europeans were able to dominate other lands and civilizations so far from their own continent in part because they had superior ships and cannons.[5] The major European accomplishments in the first colonial period were the settler colonies in the Americas, the opening of important trade routes to Asia, and the sweeping conquest of Asia, beginning with the British opening of China to trade during the Opium War (1839–1842) and the French seizure of Indo-China starting in the 1860s.[6]

The second colonial period, known as the *age of imperialism,* principally involved the "scramble for Africa" (1870–1900), although Europeans tightened their grip on Asian societies as well. Particularly important was the carving up of China into European "spheres of influence" that gave Europeans near-monopolies in trade in their respective spheres by 1900. Interestingly, in the second colonial period, Europeans wanted more than to achieve wealth and power. A spirit of "manifest destiny" animated Europeans and convinced them they had a mission to rule over nonwhite races. With cultural hubris, they felt a "white man's burden" to better the conditions of nonwhites by exposing them to European civilization.

During the second colonial period, Europeans were able to establish far-flung empires through two important technological developments. With the combination of the steamship and the steam locomotive, Europeans projected their power across oceans and penetrated deeply into continents, including the almost unexplored Africa. European states moved cargo, soldiers, and settlers with logistical ease. The opening of the Suez Canal in Egypt in 1869 by the French especially encouraged imperialism in eastern Africa and in Asia. With the additional inventions of the telegraph and, a few decades later, the wireless radio, writers of the period began to speak of the "shrinkage of the earth." By 1900, Britain and France had built world empires, and Germany was trying to do the same.[7]

For the first time, the planet had become a single geopolitical unit involving European competition over trade and colonies and, perhaps equally important, producing global competition for the sake of pride and prestige. This competition did not veer into serious conflict and war, however, because of successful negotiations among states that were mostly in concert about the conditions of the system they shared. For example, negotiations in the Conference of Berlin (1884–1885), held over disputed colonial claims in Africa, set the boundaries of the various African empires and forestalled disputes among European states that might have led to war.

The Political System

The classic era of the state system in Europe also bore witness to the emergence of democratic self-rule as the prevalent form of government. Despite the restoration of the French monarch following Napoleon's defeat and exile, the American and French revolutions' liberal force of republicanism still hurled a future challenge to European monarchies. Monarchies held on for years, but by the mid-nineteenth century, European parliaments were beginning to wrest power from kings. Also accompanying parliamentary ascendance were voting reforms and the emergence of mass political parties. In Europe, only Austria-Hungary, Germany, and Russia retained powerful monarchies by the time of the First World War. The defeat of these three states in this war appeared to confirm that imperial autocracies were less adaptable and capable than the democracies of Britain, France, and the United States that won the war.[8] Although many governments became more democratic, they also developed bureaucracies with higher capacities to regulate, tax, and mobilize people in the service of state policy.[9]

In addition to the internal development of popular self-rule, a European international society emerged during the classical state system. These states interacted with some regularity because they shared common rules and institutions. A growing body of international law governed diplomacy, the prosecution of war, and many other aspects of states' relationships. Less formally, norms concerning the role and importance of the balance of power system guided policymakers as they protected the independence of European states. Another norm held leadership in the most powerful states responsible for preserving an acceptable European order, as major states did at the Congress of Vienna in 1815.[10] The institution of conference diplomacy became well established in the nineteenth century,

TABLE 2.2
Relevant History of the Classical State System, 1648–1914

1648–1763	Colonial wars among European states
1750–1850	Industrial Revolution in Great Britain
1776	American Revolution
1789	French Revolution
1804–1815	Napoleonic threat to Europe
1815	Congress of Vienna
1853–1856	Crimean War
1869	Opening of the Suez Canal
1864–1871	Prussian wars
1870–1900	Scramble for Africa
1871	Creation of the German Empire
1884–1885	Conference of Berlin
1899 and 1907	Hague conferences
1914	First World War begins

leading to the important Hague conferences of 1899 and 1907 and setting the stage for the creation of the League of Nations in 1919.

By the First World War, the European society of states was regularly interacting with some states from other continents. Non-European states as diverse as China, Japan, Mexico, Persia (Iran), Siam (Thailand), and the United States attended the Conference of 1899, while the Conference of 1907 also included 16 Latin American states. Still, the global society before the First World War was clearly *Eurocentric* in the sense that the Europeans played a dominating role and non-Europeans accepted European rules of order. Weaker states sometimes chafed under the European order and wanted secure national integrity for themselves and reform of the European-dominated order.

At minimum, the non-European states wanted independence and equality that came with sovereignty and the protection of international law, all of which developed with European international society. The weaker, non-Western states came to realize, however, that sharing an international society does not necessarily mean participation in a just international order. The European states, possessing military superiority and perceiving themselves as culturally superior, often wanted privileges within the widening international society. The Europeans frequently exploited other states in trade, imposed unequal treaties, denied racial equality to non-Europeans, and applied their legal justice to their own citizens on the territories of some of the weaker states.[11]

To summarize, the classical state system began by establishing sovereignty through the Peace of Westphalia of 1648. This period of history allowed kings to go to war as they saw fit, and yet the balance of power system and diplomacy restricted a reliance on war. Economically, early in the history of the state system, mercantilism was the policy of choice, but after the Industrial Revolution, states began to contemplate the free trade ideas of Adam Smith. Politically, many European states were making significant strides toward democratic government in the nineteenth century, and their colonizing of other continents prepared the way for spreading their state system to the rest of the world. By the turn of the nineteenth century, enough non-European states were in place to form a dim outline of a world society of states.

THE TWENTIETH CENTURY

If the nineteenth century featured stability through diplomacy and the balance of power, the twentieth century has experienced sharp ideological divisions and, in its second half, the potential for nuclear war. An **ideology** is a fundamental belief system concerned with the nature of society's political, social, and economic arrangements and the role of individuals and groups within these arrangements. An ideology can be a guide and call to action for its believers and a political "blueprint" for organizing society and even for conducting foreign policy.

Different visions of world order, bound up in ideological perspectives, have contributed to three long, intense wars: the First World War, the Second World War, and the Cold War. Although the Cold War was not a shooting war between the superpowers of the Soviet Union and the United States, it was an intractable, bitter conflict that had historical impact equal to a major shooting war. With the implosion of the Soviet Union as the protagonist of the communist world, a post–Cold War era began with a new opportunity to build consensus about a new world order.

Mass Ideologies and World Wars

The First World War (1914–1918), like most wars, had multiple causes that included the rise and challenge of German industrial and military power, the ethnic conflicts between Germanic and Slavic peoples, and the existence of secret alliances. After the United States entered the First World War in 1917 and Russia left it in the same year, the war became a conflict between democracies and monarchies. President Woodrow Wilson expressed America's war mission as "making the world safe for democracy." He went further to elaborate an idealistic world order through his "Fourteen Points." One "point," in particular, **self-determination** for cultural nationalities living in the remaining European empires of that day, has resounded up to the present as a major democratic principle for various minorities wanting autonomy or independent statehood.

President Wilson argued that democracies were peace loving and that the Great War, as everyone once called the First World War, would not have happened if the peoples under the monarchies of Germany, Austro-Hungary, and Ottoman Turkey had played a role in the decision about war. As noted earlier, the victory of the major democracies over the monarchies appeared to prove the inherent worth of democracy. For a time after the war, many leaders enshrined democracy as the "touchstone" of good government, but democracy would soon encounter serious challenges by **totalitarian dictatorships** formed in Germany, Italy, and the Soviet Union between the world wars. A totalitarian government is a severe form of authoritarianism and is fairly rare, with the chief examples being Nazi Germany and the communist Soviet Union.

There are six classic characteristics of totalitarianism: an ideology of unquestioned truth, a single political party to implement and protect this ideology, a secret police that uses terror, centralized operation of the economy, state-owned mass media, and the use, when needed, of preponderant force by the state. These characteristics are a twentieth-century mix that could not exist without modern technology and techniques of population control. Totalitarianism, once established, can seem permanent and irreversible.

By the 1930s, several dictatorships had emerged in Europe with territorial ambitions that portended war. Germany wanted an empire based on the European continent, Italy desired an empire in East Africa, and the Soviet Union held ambitions for the Baltic Republics and Poland. Stirring the recipe for war more vigorously was the ambition of Japan to conquer much of Asia and the Pacific regions. Regrettably for peace, the leading great powers of the day that were democratic, France and Great Britain, were unable to act early and effectively enough through the League of Nations to stop the aggressions of the 1930s.

Compounding the territorial ambitions of major states in the 1930s was the presence of three powerful ideologies that clashed with one another: democracy, communism, and fascism. Robert Gilpin has called these ideologies "parochial conceptions of world order."[12] Ideologies are powerful because in addition to a state's taxing and bureaucratic capabilities, they provide a state with passionate followers, "true believers" who are easy to mobilize for grand purposes and will make great sacrifices. Ideologies divide states deeply, making negotiation and compromise difficult, if not impossible. When war does erupt between ideologically opposed states, it is more fierce, and participants may fight to the finish, such as when the Allies demanded an unconditional surrender of Germany in the Second World War. Some awareness of the content of the three ideologies will help us to understand the sharp conflicts ideological differences produce among states, sometimes bringing states to war or the brink of war.

Democracy as an ideology calls for a population to select its government and hold that government accountable to the people through elections. Scholars sometimes disagree over the institutional prerequisites that will activate this definition of democracy, but most modern scholars would agree that two or more competing political parties must be present allowing the voting public a choice. The practice of democracy is traceable to Greek antiquity, to American independence in 1776 and the French Revolution of 1789, and to much of Europe since the latter half of the nineteenth century. Through the extension of British culture and people to other areas, democracy also took deep roots in Australia, Canada, and New Zealand. In its modern form, democracy has stressed the values of individual liberty, equality, and the rule of law. Well before the Second World War, democratic values also included support for peace, international law, and the League of Nations. Finally, France, Great Britain, and the United States were the principal democratic states participating in both world wars. We will explore the concept of democracy more fully in Chapter Fourteen.

Communism emanated from the writings of Karl Marx (1818–1883), a nineteenth-century socialist. Marx thought history moved forward propelled by economic forces involving class exploitation and conflict. At each stage of history, class exploitation took place through masters exploiting slaves, lords their serfs, and finally capitalist factory owners their workers. Marx believed it was historically inevitable that the workers in the industrial age would revolt and destroy capitalism and the governments of the states that protected the rich capitalists and factory owners. Although critical of socialists that focused on utopian notions, eventually he expected an international brotherhood to form that would be free of the greed of private ownership and wealth accumulation.

Marx's prediction did not come true, but an important intellectual disciple, Vladimir Lenin (1870–1924), seized control of the Russian Revolution of 1917, nationalized factories, and protected the Russian state from the danger of the "capitalist encirclement" of enemy states. In this instance, believers of an ideology took a state out of war instead of pushing it toward one. Lenin pulled Russia from the First World War to deal with the internal instability that his October Revolution of 1917 and the Russian civil war had caused. In 1922, victorious in the Russian civil war, Lenin formed the Russian Soviet Socialist Republic. This Russian republic later became the core of the Union of Soviet Socialist Republics (USSR) as the Soviets added other republics.

Lenin's successor, Joseph Stalin (1879–1953), transformed Lenin's venture in government into a more extreme communism by turning the Soviet Union into a totalitarian dictatorship. Instead of a paradise for workers, a harsh, draconian system of life emerged as Stalin atomized society into millions of easily controlled individuals whom he envisioned becoming examples of the ideal "Soviet Man." In theory and in practice, communists always put the group interest of Soviet society ahead of individual rights. Soviet citizens had almost no means of resistance, yet Marxist-Leninist theorists claimed the communist leadership was "democratic" because they "represented" the people, albeit in their own way and on their own terms.

Regarding foreign policy, the Soviet Union promoted communism internationally and instigated communist activities in other states. Soviet leaders assigned themselves the moral mission of eliminating the evils of capitalism from the world. Communists viewed Western capitalist societies, such as Great Britain and the United States, as completely incompatible with their own. Soviet leaders felt no compulsion to rush into war with the powerful capitalist states because history was on the side of communism, and Soviet leaders thought they could wait until the internal decay of capitalism brought the downfall of their enemies. Although communist parties, operating in other states, served the Soviet cause, the Soviet Union was alone in the world as a communist state until after the Second World War.

Fascism is another major ideology that emerged between the two world wars. Fascism has a totalitarian structure, but its content in values is entirely different from that of communism. Fascism is mystical in nature and does not have the intellectual heritage and sophistication that Karl Marx and others gave to communism. In fact, supporters of the two ideologies are "blood enemies," and each regards the values of the other group as heinous. Fascists worship the state and treat it as having an organic existence, a life of its own, that is greater and more important than those who serve it. For fascists, the individual has worth only to the degree to which he or she serves the state.

Fascists also are usually militaristic and ready to follow a charismatic leader who offers a clear vision of the future that promises imagined glory. Fascism is the only modern ideology that extols the virtues of war, and fascists have eagerly sought victory in war to prove their superiority. Fascism typically arises out of conditions of instability and economic hardship and subverts democratic institutions that are failing to meet economic needs and maintain order. Fascists leave property in private hands as long as corporations and businesses are willing to serve the state. Benito Mussolini (1883–1945) created the prototype of the fascist state in Italy after 1922. Fascist regimes of various hues cropped up in the 1930s in Argentina, Germany, Japan, and Spain, as well as in several eastern European states.

The most significant case of fascism was Adolf Hitler's Nazi Germany. Hitler's infamy and Germany's power exceeded those of Mussolini and fascist Italy by far. *Nazism* differed from fascism primarily in the Nazi emphasis on race in addition to the state. Nazis believed that Germans were a superior race of *Übermenschen* ("supermen"), that Germany had a mission to destroy "inferior peoples" such as the Roma (gypsies), Jews, handicapped individuals, and homosexuals, and that Germany, because of its superior people, had a right to rule over other Europeans within a new German empire.

What Italian fascism and German Nazism shared above all was an extreme form of nationalism. Not only did Italians and Germans see themselves as special and different as peoples, but they insisted they were culturally and even physically superior to other peoples.

Although these three mutually antagonistic ideologies contributed to the Second World War and affected the selection of friend and foe, nationalism, perhaps the strongest ideology of all, came to intensify each country's participation in the war. For example, Stalin, who incorrectly interpreted Nazism as an extreme form of capitalism, tried to rally Russians to throw back the German invaders with appeals based on communist jargon. He called the war with Germany the "Great Proletarian War," or workers' war. Only when Stalin changed to the "Great Patriotic War" and made appeals to defend "Mother Russia" did the Russian people rise to fight hard at great sacrifice.

Nor were these ideological states that warred with one another entirely immune to the practical considerations of power politics. Germany and the Soviet Union, unprepared to fight each other, drew up the Non-Aggression Pact of 1939–1941 and calmly divided Poland between them before engaging in war in 1941. In addition, the democracies of Great Britain and the United States allied with the communist Soviet Union, thus creating an ideologically incongruous alliance forged by necessity. U.S. propagandists tried to make this affiliation more palatable to the American people by calling Stalin "Papa Joe" and referring to the cadre of the Communist Party of the Soviet Union as "agrarian democrats." The United States was simply following the old maxim of power politics that "the enemy of my enemy is my friend."

The Second World War began with Germany's and Russia's attack on Poland in 1939 and ended in 1945 with the unconditional surrender of the German and Japanese leaders, a total surrender made possible by the complete victory of the Allies. After the Allies invaded Italy in 1943, Mussolini's fascist government also fell, and Italy switched sides to join the Allies. Although Hitler's strategic blunders greatly contributed to the Allied victory, the Allies fought hard to win because fascism threatened not only the independence of many states but their way of life as well. Such high priorities are always at stake when ideologically opposed states make war.

After the Second World War, the Western allies brought democratic reforms to West Germany, and the United States did the same in Japan. These Western states wisely assisted the conquered states in their economic renewal and in their return to the state system. The society of Western states did not make the mistake they made with Germany after the First World War when they punished Germany with war reparations and took some of its territory. This unfavorable treatment of Germany contributed to the outbreak of the Second World War. The treatment of Germany and Japan after the Second World War was closer to the reclamation of France for the society of states after the defeat of Napoleon. Both states also soon became allies of the United States in a new balance of power arrangement.

Meanwhile, the Soviet Union moved energetically to spread its ideological system to eastern Europe and to East Germany and to lead their own alliance in this region to counter Western power. Unknowingly, both sides had laid the groundwork for the decades-long Cold War.

The Cold War (1947–1989)

The United States and the Soviet Union had a cool relationship long before 1917, when Lenin's communists took control. As the communist era began, the American-Soviet relationship became antagonistic, with the United States strongly opposed to Lenin's Bolsheviks who took charge of Russia in the midst of the First World War. The United States and its allies in the First World War intervened on Soviet soil from 1918 to 1919, ostensibly to prevent war material from falling into German hands. In reality, the Allies probably hoped their presence would encourage the counterrevolutionary forces to overthrow the communists. The United States and the Soviet Union did not recognize each other diplomatically until 1933.

Although allies in the Second World War, Josef Stalin of the Soviet Union frequently accused Great Britain and the United States of failing to send enough supplies and deliberately delaying the allied invasion of Europe, a step that would take pressure off the Soviet Union on the eastern front. The destruction wrought by the Second World War left the Soviet Union and the United States standing as the major states of the day, but ideologically opposed and with the United States armed with atomic weapons in 1945 and the Soviet Union similarly armed in 1949.

The Cold War, following closely on the heels of the Second World War, created an atmosphere of extreme tension and hostility. A move by either side caused fear and suspicion on the part of the other. Crises that could easily turn the Cold War into a "hot" or shooting war frequently punctuated the basic ideological clash over competing world orders. The danger that a small conflict somewhere in the world would escalate into a full-scale nuclear war was ever present. The threat of a nuclear holocaust finally forced the two antagonists to co-exist, though within an atmosphere of mutual hostility.

However, the nuclear stand-off between the two superpowers resulted in more than four decades of peace in the sense that these states did not fight each other directly. In lieu of fighting a "hot war," superpower competition and conflict occurred in almost every other form. Each side sought to outdo the other in the arms race, the space race, the Olympics, the recruitment of client-states in the Third World, and the waging of propaganda and intelligence operations. No arena of activity was too minor for the Soviet Union and the United States to ignore.

The Cold War began because of opposing ideological world views but also because of the usual power struggle among major states to establish a new balance of power after a war. Scholars will argue whether great power competition or ideological differences was the main driving force that divided the Soviet Union and the United States. Since the two forces intertwined and both pushed this relationship into a pattern of conflict, it is difficult to evaluate which was the more important. In a few short years, these two states led competing alliances, creating a *bipolar* power structure enforced with nuclear weapons. By the 1950s, most states had affiliated in some way with one of the two sides.

With wartime cooperation having failed, the United States began to implement the now famous **containment policy** in 1947. Attributed to George F. Kennan, a State Department official and past ambassador to Moscow, this policy focused on the nature of Soviet intentions and what the United States should do. This policy idea began in 1946 when Kennan sent a lengthy telegram outlining his views from Moscow to Washington, views later published anonymously in the widely read policy journal *Foreign Affairs*.[13] Kennan thought a long, protracted struggle lay ahead between the United States and an expansionistic Soviet Union. He wanted the United States to contain the Soviet Union with patience and diplomacy and to wait until the Soviets wore down, leading to their eventual acceptance of a traditional place in the state system.

Gradually, American leaders came to see containment in military terms as the Soviet Union loomed more and more as a military threat rather than a political challenge. Paul Nitze, Kennan's successor on the State Department's planning staff, came up with a policy recommendation, known as *National Security Council Memorandum No. 68*, that was closer to the actual policy used.[14] This policy called for, first, a strong military system to counter the Soviet military threat and second, the use of political, economic, and psychological warfare by the West to wear down the Soviet Union. Perhaps the central difference was that Kennan's recommendation stressed a defensive strategy while Nitze's emphasized a policy closer to an offensive strategy.

The Cold War was a series of tense and dangerous crises over a four-decade period. A **crisis** is a sudden, unexpected threat that portends serious consequences. Because of multiple crises, careful calculations were necessary by both sides since they had their fingers on nuclear triggers. Crisis management in the Cold War received top priority and put a premium on statecraft skill. The history of Cold War crises is a long one, but the two most important crises described here help to capture the nature of the Cold War. Ultimately the outcomes of these two crises were intertwined.

The Soviet Union created a crisis in 1948 by closing off Allied routes for ground access to West Berlin. The Allies had divided Germany and its capital, Berlin, into sectors for occupation purposes at the end of the war. Berlin was an enclave entirely within the Soviet sector that would later become East Germany (the Democratic Republic of Germany). While there were agreements on American-British air access to West Berlin, no formal agreement on ground access existed, though the Soviets had customarily permitted access by land.

It appeared the Western allies might have to give up their claims to West Berlin or risk a shooting confrontation with the powerful Soviet ground forces. The showdown over Berlin was a test of strength between two great powers that might determine the fate of Europe. The Soviet Union, if successful in this crisis, could take the first step in "Finlandizing" all of Europe, meaning reducing Europe to a nearly disarmed, neutral status compliant with Soviet wishes.

The United States and Britain found a clever way out of the crisis with the now famous Berlin airlift. Between 1948 and 1949, American and British planes flew around the clock for months, supplying West Berliners with everything they needed, from coal to food. The Soviet Union finally relented and removed the barriers on the land routes to Berlin. However, the Berlin crisis was renewed from 1958 to 1962. The issues were essentially the same, only this time the Soviet Union threatened to make a separate peace with East

Germany and thus force the Allies to deal with a communist East German government over Western allied rights of access to Berlin. This second Berlin crisis did not appear solvable until another crisis halfway around the world ended.

The Soviets, realizing they were not on the same strategic power scale as the United States, decided to improve their position by placing intermediate-range missiles in communist Cuba, just 90 miles from U.S. territory. After discovering these missiles in October 1962, President John F. Kennedy wisely chose to blockade Cuba with America's superior navy rather than attack the missile sites. Confronting a stronger military power, the Soviet Union removed the missiles, thus averting the possibility of escalation to nuclear annihilation for both sides. The missile crisis was a shock therapy that led to better-managed competition and conflict during the remainder of the Cold War. Facing the close call of nuclear war, the Soviets let the Berlin controversy drop from discussion.[15]

Accompanying the crises of the Cold War were pendulumlike swings from high tension to co-existence and then back again. The Berlin crisis (1948–1949) and the Korean War (1950–1953) preceded Nikita Khrushchev's promise of a "thaw" in the latter 1950s. A good-faith act by Khrushchev was the withdrawal of Soviet troops from Austria, followed by the independence and neutralization of Austria in 1955. Later the shooting down of an American spy plane in 1960 destroyed a summit conference planned for that year. Then, during the 1960s, the shock therapy of the Cuban missile crisis generated a series of important arms control agreements. By the early 1970s, the Richard Nixon administration was referring to the Soviet-American relationship as one of *détente,* a period of relaxed tensions, and was vigorously pursuing several trade agreements and political understandings.

However, by the Jimmy Carter administration (1976–1980), human rights issues and the Soviet intervention in Afghanistan in 1979 had soured the United States' relationship with the Soviet Union. In 1981, President Ronald Reagan came into office voicing the rhetoric of a "Cold War warrior" and even referring to the Soviet Union as the "Evil Empire."

In Reagan's second term, the pendulum swung a final time when Mikhail Gorbachev came to power in the Soviet Union in 1985. Reagan and Gorbachev resumed summit conferences and signed the Intermediate Nuclear Force Treaty of 1987. In 1988, Gorbachev began downsizing the Soviet military and withdrawing the Soviet Army from Afghanistan. The pattern of pendulum swings might have continued indefinitely had communism not collapsed in Europe between 1989 and 1991.

The Collapse of Communism

One well-established tenet of politics is that a totalitarian government could last forever unless destroyed by outside forces, as was the fate of Nazi Germany. Dedicated ideologues, using the secret police and other means, can make internal control seem complete and indisputable. Yet, in Soviet totalitarianism, control proved more difficult and resistance more resilient than notions about totalitarianism would have predicted.

In the 1980s, the communist system in Europe began to implode with a swiftness that caught almost all Western leaders and scholars by surprise. The Solidarity Movement in Poland first challenged Poland's Community Party in 1981 and later Poland's military regime after it took control. No intervention by the Soviet Army occurred to protect a client-state as had happened on previous occasions, and demands for reforms in Poland

Gary Brookins © 1991, *Richmond Times-Dispatch*

escalated. Pressures for change spread across eastern Europe as more people became frustrated with the bungled attempts of their communist governments to deliver the long-promised material goods enjoyed in western Europe. By 1989, mass demonstrations across eastern Europe had brought down communist governments while Soviet troops remained in their barracks. The "Iron Curtain," in its physical form of electric fences, came down, and in Berlin, people on both sides broke through the infamous Berlin Wall.

Conditions in the Soviet Union were probably the worst of the European communist countries. Since the late 1960s, the Soviet economy had experienced a downward spiral of decay with widespread corruption, rampant alcoholism and absenteeism, and black marketeers operating openly. The bureaucratized, centrally planned economy simply did not work. Even for the downtrodden, patient Soviet people, to whom democracy and sufficient material goods were unknown, the stagnant economy was acceptable only when forced on them by state terror.

In 1985, when the Politburo, the top decision-making body of the Communist Party in the Soviet Union, chose Mikhail Gorbachev to lead, they were clearly choosing the path of reform and were rejecting Stalinist-type terror. Gorbachev undertook reforms in 1985 within a communist framework, first trying *perestroika,* or a restructuring of the economy, and then *glasnost,* political reform permitting criticism and ideas for change. Demand for more revolutionary change quickly escalated.[16]

The sharpest critics, such as Boris Yeltsin, soon to become president of Russia in 1991, wanted radical movement toward a free market economy and a full political democracy. Had Gorbachev read Crane Brinton's *Anatomy of a Revolution,*[17] he would have known that when

Gary Brookins © 1992, *Richmond Times-Dispatch*

an authoritarian regime attempts to pace the reform of long-neglected problems, that regime may lose control of events. Revolutionaries may overthrow such a regime or simply push it aside, as happened to Gorbachev's reform-minded but weak communist state.

In a desperate move to counter Gorbachev's unsettling reforms, the Soviet Army attempted a *coup d'état* in August 1991. Top generals ordered the arrest of Gorbachev and his family and held them prisoner for 73 hours. Boris Yeltsin led a popular movement and, aided by friendly elements of the Soviet Army, was able to secure the release of Gorbachev and the arrest of the coup leaders. Gorbachev did not have much longer as president of the Soviet Union. In 1991, a new but weak Commonwealth of Independent States (CIS) came into existence and was all that remained for Gorbachev to oversee. Yeltsin seized Communist Party offices in Moscow, and Gorbachev resigned as president of the defunct Soviet Union in December 1991.

No longer did a communist government rule any state in Europe, and only a few significant communist states remain elsewhere. The People's Republic of China may be with us for a while if the massacre at Tiananmen Square in 1989 is any indication of the Chinese leaders' determination to stay in power. Cuba's economy is staggering toward collapse under the dual burden of poor management and a United States–led trade embargo. North Korea has a failed economy and a population facing hunger, while Vietnam seeks to adopt some capitalist methods and build trade ties with Japan and the Western states.

To sum up, the twentieth century is one of ideologies and three great wars. The First World War pitted monarchies against the democracies, with the latter coming out on top. In the Second World War, the democracies, in an alliance of convenience with communist

Soviet Union, eliminated the fascist regimes in Germany and Italy, along with the militarists in Japan. A Cold War, fraught with crises and the dangers of nuclear holocaust, replaced these "hot" wars. The Cold War was a multidimensional conflict but came up short of all-out war. The Soviet Union, leading the communist states, and the United States, championing the cause of democracy, were the chief antagonists. Without the superpowers warring directly against each other for over 40 years, the Cold War ended with the collapse of European communism. This collapse resulted mainly from serious economic woes and the internal strife of ethnic discontent.

THE POST–COLD WAR ERA

Although the Cold War did not involve direct fighting between the two superpowers, communism's defeat was as resounding as if the West had won a Third World War. As in other postwar periods, matters in the post–Cold War era are in a state of flux before a new balance of power and a new order of values and rules can take clear form. A period of this kind is a "defining movement," an opportune time for victorious leaders to shape conditions that will serve the common interests of the international society if they choose to do so.

If history is a guide, this pattern must include reintegrating the vanquished into the state system by the victors. We can note that the victorious took such a step after Napoleon's defeat in 1815 and Germany's defeat in 1945 but failed to do so after the Allied victory over Germany in 1918. Germany, geographically close to eastern Europe and fearful of the anarchy that might develop there, has taken the lead in making loans and investments and offering food aid to stabilize the area. German Chancellor Helmut Kohl has pressed the Group of Seven economic powers for billions of dollars in loans for Russia and the other ex-communist states. Since a dramatic military victory did not end the Cold War, the United States has probably focused less on reintegrating Russia and eastern Europe into the state system than should be the case.[18]

At least, in 1990, after leading the Western coalition that defeated Iraq's aggression against Iraq in 1990–1991, President George Bush spoke of a "new world order" that could form with the end of competing ideological visions for the world. Although a vague concept, the West's goals of stopping aggression, respecting international law, promoting human rights, and expanding the world economy through free trade now had a clearer field for advancement. Importantly, President Bush indicated that although the United States was the sole remaining superpower, it must lead from within a group of major states and not try to dictate. After 1992, President Bill Clinton continued the leadership strategy of acting from a coalition of cooperating states. Largely at President Clinton's initiative, Western states belatedly entered Bosnia in 1996 to halt four years of terrible acts involving "ethnic cleansing" and war crimes.

The post–Cold War era is still new, and its pattern of cooperation is not entirely clear, though it holds promise. In spite of unprecedented agreement among major states, these states still do not know just when and how to act. They may have to muddle along from one threat or problem to another, sometimes helping one another out and sometimes not. Beleaguering the world are internal conflicts and acts of terrorism, often spawned from ethnic discontent; regional arms races among Third World states that may soon include intermediate-range missiles with nuclear warheads; a vast economic gap between rich and

Rob Rogers, reprinted by permission of United Feature Syndicate, Inc.

poor states, creating a chafing sense of injustice; and an array of lesser but still vexing issues such as pandemic diseases and international crime. Obviously, the end of most ideological division did not remove all problems from the international scene.

A coalition of major states, even if acting in concert, cannot closely govern the world, but it has a better chance than in decades past to act cooperatively and creatively to reduce problems and advance worthy goals such as peace, human rights, and economic progress. In the post–Cold War era's state of flux, the basic question is whether or not the major states, perhaps led by the United States, will establish a consistent pattern of cooperation to deal with a wide range of scattered threats and problems.

The most important conclusion about the post–Cold War era is that although its exact nature is uncertain, a window of opportunity exists for the major states to work together for a better international society. The apparent end of major ideological struggles more than any other single factor provides this opportunity. Democracy is left standing almost alone as a significant ideology, thus removing a critical line of conflict from world affairs.

GLOBALIZATION AS A STAGE OF HISTORY

We have seen that much of history's core involves the evolution and interaction of states. Although states prevailed for several centuries as the *dominant* actor, they would over time drop in status somewhat to become the *primary* actor among multiple actors. The rise of the state resulted from its efficiency in providing security and meeting people's economic

TABLE 2.3
Relevant History of the Twentieth Century

1914–1918	First World War
1918–1920	Allied intervention into the Soviet Union
1933	Mutual recognition between the United States and the Soviet Union
1939–1945	Second World War
1946	Winston Churchill's "Iron Curtain" speech
1947	Truman Doctrine
	Marshall Plan to rebuild Europe
	George Kennan's "X" article published
1947–1989	Cold War
1948–1949	First Berlin crisis and airlift
1949	Chinese communists rule in China
	NATO formed
	Soviet Union acquires the atomic bomb
1950	NSC issues memorandum no. 68
1950–1953	Korean War
1956	Hungarian Revolution suppressed by the Soviet Union
1958	Second Berlin crisis begins
1959	Castro leads communists to power in Cuba
1961	The United States breaks off relations with Cuba
	Bay of Pigs invasion of Cuba by Cuban exiles fails
	Berlin Wall goes up
1962	Cuban missile crisis
	Second Berlin crisis ends
1963–1975	Vietnam War
1970	Two independent Germanies affirmed
1972	Normalization of relations with China begins
1979	Mutual recognition between the United States and China
	Soviet Union intervenes in Afghanistan
1981	Solidarity movement begins in Poland
1983	Ronald Reagan denounces the Soviet Union as "Evil Empire"
1985	Mikhail Gorbachev comes to power in the Soviet Union
1989	Multicandidate elections are held in the Soviet Union
	Communist governments fall throughout Europe
	Berlin Wall dismantled
	Chinese government represses democracy movement
1990	Soviet Union Community party votes to end its power monopoly
	Gorbachev elected to more powerful presidency
	United States and Soviet Union agree to troop reductions in Europe
	Iraq invades Kuwait
	United States sends troops to Saudi Arabia
	Bush announces "new world order" justifying war with Iraq

(continued)

TABLE 2.3
Relevant History of the Twentieth Century
(concluded)

1991	Boris Yeltsin first freely elected president of Russia
	Gorbachev resigns as president of the Soviet Union
	Creation of the Commonwealth of Independent States
	UN Coalition attacks Iraqi forces in Kuwait
1993	Communist rebellion against Russian democracy quashed
1996	NATO forces enter Bosnia
1996	Boris Yeltsin wins a second term as president of Russia

needs. Its decline derived from its inability to handle an array of issues arising across state borders, often with global sweep. Drawing on our *levels of analysis* from the first chapter, we can better appreciate that just as people came to accept the higher authority of a king and a state, they now look to an even higher level for some solutions.

According to James N. Rosenau, the state has proven unable to provide solutions to many problems that originate outside the territory and beyond the authority of a single state. The result has been an authority crisis that has pushed states to find ways to compensate. States have reached new levels of cooperation and have worked out a new form of authority to make up for what they cannot do alone. *Governance,* discussed in the first chapter, allows sovereign states to converge around rules and norms guiding cooperation when dealing with problems in common.[19] Far short of the true authority that we find in a well-organized state, governance enjoys an uneven success according to issue areas and circumstances.

Although a new type of global authority, one above the state level, may be tenuous, the shift to new policymaking arenas is more certain. States still conduct their individual *foreign policies* toward other countries, but they also frequently plan *international policies* with one or more other states. Sometimes this planning is at a regional level, such as when American states work within the Organization of American States (OAS) or African states plan joint policies through the Organization of African Unity (OAU).

Increasingly, *global policies* are taking shape as most states identify many of the same problems and recognize they must work together in a world of growing interdependence.[20] Much of the history of the twentieth century teaches that war can be global, and today more countries can fight with weapons of mass destruction at greater distances than ever before in history. World efforts to defuse conflicts and halt the proliferation of weapons have become critical. People now widely accept interdependence in the world's economy as common knowledge, but developing a global consensus on expanding and sharing that economy is an ongoing process. Setting and promoting standards in such issue areas as human rights, health, and the environment is a flourishing global business, often supported by the United Nations.

Documenting globalization within a neat set of dates is a challenging task of history. Unquestionably, globalization could not occur before humankind had a modern travel and communication system that would provide regular interaction. Nor could it take place before leaders and their populations recognized that events and conditions in one part of the world could have impact elsewhere, as happened during and after the Second World

War. During this war, millions of people traveled farther and experienced more than at any time in history. After the war, governments and private organizations tackled a broader range of human needs and with an intensity previously unknown. The United States and the United Nations led efforts to cope with the aftermath of war in most regions of the world, including problems of refugees, hunger, disease, the exchange of POWs, repairing communication and travel infrastructures, rebuilding economies, and many other tasks.

Therefore, we can say that globalization, in the form of global awareness by leaders and citizens, was waxing into place at least by the mid-twentieth century, and the process has strengthened ever since. Today, citizens around the world commonly speak of a "global village" or use similar metaphors. With the Cold War's division of the world now at an end, more states and peoples can join the globalized effort to create a better international society.

HISTORY AND INTERNATIONAL SOCIETY

A fundamental question of this textbook is whether basic historical changes are under way that are moving humankind from a conflictual anarchy to a more peaceful, cooperative world society that focuses on the common interest. Hans Morgenthau, in his classic study *Politics Among Nations,* would almost certainly tell us such a development is not happening. Morgenthau believes social laws govern politics. Since these laws have roots in human nature, including the drive for power, we should not expect much to change about international relations. These laws, according to Morgenthau, are impervious to human preferences, so people can do little to alter their international destiny.

Morgenthau calls his thinking *realism* because he takes human nature for what it is and historical processes for what they are. Although Morgenthau does not completely rule out the improvement of human society, he believes the pursuit of power by states and the resulting conflict are durable.[21] For realists, power lessons from history have proven themselves over the centuries and should apply in the future.

After realism's dominance in international relations in the 1950s and 1960s, neorealists began to hold theoretical sway with a new version of realism in the 1960s and 1970s. Led by Kenneth N. Waltz, whose views culminated in his *Theory of International Politics,* neorealists focus on "structural realism." This form of realism concerns the distribution of power among a given number of major states bounded within the same system. Neorealists think historical change is significant when that change brings power reconfigurations among the states. They might ask: Are there two important centers of power, a *bipolar* system, or is power dispersed in a *multipolar* system, meaning several or more centers of power? Further, neorealists wish to know if historical change is bringing a more peaceful system with fewer wars or the absence of wars.

For Waltz, structural transformation sufficiently radical to alter the anarchical nature of the international system is unfathomable. He believed the world is fortunate, at the time of his writing late in the Cold War, to have arrived at a simple bipolar system in which the two sides rationally collaborate to avoid a nuclear holocaust.[22]

Robert Gilpin offers a different twist to neorealist theory. He thinks international relations operate by the rules of a strong, dominating state until a challenging state arises to replace the first. For Gilpin, power relations are the central, perennial force of history. Also, history is cyclical in the sense of repeated patterns of rising powers to challenge the lead state.[23]

Transnationalists such as Robert O. Keohane and Joseph S. Nye, Jr., with their work *Power and Interdependence,* represent a group of scholars who regard realism as less adequate today to account for significant changes in international relations. By the 1970s, according to these writers, history had undeniedly brought into play new, important actors besides the state and had created new issues and policy areas in addition to national security. Also, the world was becoming more interdependent, requiring emphasis on cooperation instead of conflict.[24]

We can restate these historical changes through our abstract models from Chapter One. In only the last 20 years or so, a model of *international anarchy,* which focuses on the states and their conflicts, no longer accounts for important changes. An embryonic *international society* complies with too many rules and offers too extensive a pattern of cooperation to prevent us from claiming that a new, rudimentary order is in place.[25] And, disputing the claims of some realists that only world government can end anarchy and bring basic system change, a central government is not part of this new society. Instead, states are learning to cooperate by adjusting their behavior to the anticipated preferences of others through a policy coordination.[26]

Even a cursory glance shows that history has brought us to a time when many kinds of *actors,* including private groups with global membership, such as Amnesty International and Greenpeace, are working to improve global conditions. Nonsecurity *issues* such as health, human rights, drug smuggling, and the environment are new concerns attracting the attention not only of governments but of citizens around the world. An *orientation* of conflict has declined sharply, with major states no longer pursuing opposing ideological crusades. Cooperation is now at a premium since the *interaction* of states is interdependent. Without regular meetings and extensive negotiations, for instance, the world economy might unravel, leading to spiraling trade wars and depression.

Authority is not as complete as it is inside tightly cohered states, but states and other actors that break the rules of international society do so at their peril. The world often can deal effectively with harmful, scofflaw behavior. Iraq should understand this point after invading Kuwait. Serbian leaders in Bosnia face the possibility of extradition to the Netherlands since the International War Crimes Tribunal, holding court there, has issued warrants for their arrest. China faces losing billions of dollars in trade when its trade partners sanction China for copying the music tapes and computer software of other countries without paying the required licensing fees.

An *international community,* composed of democratic states living in peace and pursuing justice for all the peoples of the world, would be preferable to the progress we have now. Yet the world has moved dramatically forward, especially since the end of the Cold War, and humankind may truly be setting out in a new and positive direction. At least many scholars, leaders, and private citizens share a vision, though a rough-hewn and uncertain one, that an improvable world order is possible.

CHAPTER SUMMARY

The international relations of today largely began with the emergence of the state and the interaction of states in a state system by the seventeenth century. Some precedents for the state system are traceable to antiquity, but states of today most clearly trace their heritage through European history. The comingling over several centuries of strong kings, sovereign independence, and a vibrant sense of nationalism helped mold the modern state. The patterned interaction of the state system came to include wars and efforts to control them; increasing free trade that replaced mercantilism, due largely to the advent of the Industrial Revolution; colonial empires that carved up much of the world for European use but also opened the way for the spread of international society; and the sharing of democracy and international law among other features of an expanding international society. By the end of the nineteenth century, a growing list of non-European as well as European states had attended international conferences.

The twentieth century gave the world three world wars driven in large part by ideological divisions. The First and Second World Wars were the largest shooting wars in history, while the Cold War was a protracted conflict between two antagonistic nuclear powers that dared not fight for fear they would both perish. With a suddenness almost unforeseen, the Cold War ended between 1989 and 1991 with the collapse of European communism. Left standing, after a long ideological struggle, was democracy, the form of government of the triumphant Western states. Other states, including ex-communist ones, began to embrace democracy along with capitalism. Although the post–Cold War era has not taken a definite direction, it ushered in a period of hope and the promise of deepening cooperation among the major states and most lesser states as well.

Before the Cold War ended, states, peoples, and a growing list of international organizations realized many problems existed beyond state boundaries and required policy coordination by multiple states and, increasingly, at the global level. Extensive patterns of cooperation began in Europe, but a formative international society is now encompassing the world. Historical change has taken us past the views of the realists with their focus on state power and security. Today states deal with many issues, including human rights, the environment, health, and much more. And nonstate actors, such as private human rights and environmental groups, are joining the efforts of these states to improve the human situation. The international relations of today include a world of multiple actors, the subject of the next chapter.

POINTS OF VIEW

What's past is prologue.
—WILLIAM SHAKESPEARE

We have it in our power to begin the world over again.
—THOMAS PAINE

What is history but a fable agreed upon?
—NAPOLEON

Everything changes but change.
—ISRAEL ZANGWILL

Our duty is to preserve what the past has had to say for itself, and to say ourselves what shall be true for the future.
—ATTRIBUTED TO JOHN RUSKIN (UNVERIFIED)

Human history is in essence a history of ideas.
—H. G. WELLS

Those who cannot remember the past are condemned to repeat it.
—GEORGE SANTAYANA

In a time of drastic change, it is the learners who inherit the future. The learned usually find themselves equipped to live in a world that no longer exists.
—ERIC HOFFER

History is not, of course, a cookbook offering pretested recipes. It teaches by analogy, not by maxims. It can illuminate the consequences of actions in comparable situations, yet each generation must discover for itself what situations are in fact comparable.
—HENRY KISSINGER

REVIEW QUESTIONS

1. What are some of the influences from antiquity that have contributed to the state system?
2. What changes allowed strong kings to emerge as rulers over large territories?
3. What is nationalism, and what was its role in the formation of the state?
4. Contrast the handling of France at the Congress of Vienna in 1815 with the handling of Germany at the end of the First World War in 1919.
5. How did the role of ideology in the twentieth century influence war and alliances?
6. How do fascism and Nazism differ from each other?
7. How did the containment policy of George Kennan differ from the actual containment policy that evolved?
8. How did the Cuban missile crisis end the second Berlin crisis?
9. Why is it surprising that the totalitarian Soviet Union collapsed?
10. Why is the end of the Cold War an opportunity for the nascent international society?
11. Why are states being pulled into patterns of cooperation and away from the conflict-prone anarchy that realists stress?
12. What do you think are some of the threats that may confront the international society in the post–Cold War period?

GLOSSARY

communism An ideology stressing that economic and historical forces will bring the working class to power, ending an exploitative class system, and property will come under common ownership.

containment policy A policy of the United States and its allies to block the advancement of communism during the Cold War.

crisis A sudden, unexpected danger that must be handled with skill to be defused.

democracy An ideology that calls for a population to select its government and hold that government accountable for what it does.

Divine Right The belief once held in Europe that kings are the choices and agents of God and answer only to God, thus significantly enhancing a king's power.

fascism An ideology based on the intense nationalist belief that a given people are superior and have a special destiny, and should give the state their complete loyalty.

feudalism A social and political hierarchy in western Europe during the Middle Ages that called for mutual services between lords offering land and security and vassals reciprocating with military service to the lords.

ideology A belief system that concerns the organization of society and can serve as a guide and call to action for those who embrace the beliefs.

nationalism A sense of identity among a population that leads them to believe that they are special and different from others and be proud of what makes them different.

popular sovereignty The natural rights belief that the highest authority belongs to the people, who usually loan this authority to elected representatives for fixed terms.

republic A democracy of representatives chosen by the general population.

self-determination A highly sanctified right of a population to rule themselves, which led many colonial subjects and ethnic groups to demand and sometimes receive independence.

state A central government that rules over a population and territory and represents and protects that population in international politics.

sovereignty The supreme authority possessed by a king or state; this concept implies equality among states in a legal sense.

totalitarian dictatorship A dictatorship that draws on twentieth-century advances and technology to completely control the lives of its citizens.

RECOMMENDED READINGS

Ian Adams. *Political Ideology Today.* New York: Manchester University Press, 1993.

Hedley Bull and Adam Watson, eds. *The Expansion of International Society.* Oxford: Clarendon Press, 1984.

James A. Caporaso, ed. *The Elusive State: International and Comparative Perspectives.* Newbury Park, CA: Sage Publications, 1989.

Nazli Choucri and Robert C. North. *Nations in Conflict: National Growth and International Violence.* San Francisco: W. H. Freeman, 1975.

Yale H. Ferguson and Richard W. Mansbach. *The State, Conceptual Chaos, and the Future of International Relations Theory.* Boulder, CO: Lynne Rienner Publishers, 1989.

John Lewis Gaddis. *Russia, the Soviet Union, and the United States: An Interpretive History.* 2nd ed. New York: McGraw-Hill, 1990.

John Lewis Gaddis. *Strategies of Containment: A Critical Appraisal of Postwar American National Security Policy.* New York: Oxford University Press, 1982.

Michael J. Hogan, ed. *The End of the Cold War: Its Meaning and Implications.* New York: Cambridge University Press, 1992.

Robert H. Jackson and Alan James. *States in a Changing World: A Contemporary Analysis.* Oxford: Clarendon Press, 1993.

William R. Keylor. *The Twentieth-Century World: An International History.* 3rd ed. New York: Oxford University Press, 1996.

Evan Luard. *The Globalization of Politics: The Changed Focus of Political Action in the Modern World.* Washington Square, NY: New York University Press, 1990.

William H. McNeill. *The Rise of the West.* Chicago: The University of Chicago Press, 1991.

William Pfaff. *The Wrath of Nations: Civilization and the Furies of Nations.* New York: Simon & Schuster, 1993.

Bruce D. Porter. *War and the Rise of the State.* New York: The Free Press, 1994.

Thomas M. Poulsen. *Nations and States: A Geographic Background to World Affairs.* Englewood Cliffs, NJ: Prentice Hall, 1995.

Marvin S. Soroos. *Beyond Sovereignty: The Challenge of Global Policy.* Columbia, SC: University of South Carolina Press, 1986.

Hendrik Spruyt. *The Sovereign State and Its Competitors.* Princeton, NJ: Princeton University Press, 1994.

Vernon Van Dyke. *Ideology and Political Choice: The Search for Freedom, Justice, and Virtue.* Chatnam, NJ: Chatnam House Publishers, 1995.

Barbara Ward. *Five Ideas That Changed the World.* New York: W. W. Norton, 1959.

ENDNOTES

1. Barbara Ward. *Five Ideas That Changed the World* (New York: W. W. Norton, 1959), pp. 17–18.
2. Robert C. North, *War, Peace, Survival: Global Politics and Conceptual Synthesis* (Boulder, CO: Westview Press, 1990), pp. 66–67.
3. Ernest Renan, "What Is a Nation?" in *World Politics,* ed. Arend Lijphart (Boston: Allyn & Bacon, 1971), pp. 82–90.
4. Robert Gilpin, "The Global Political System," in *Order and Violence,* ed. J. D. B. Miller and R. J. Vincent (Oxford: Clarendon Press, 1990), pp. 122–24; Hedley Bull, "The State's Positive Role in World Affairs," in *The State,* ed. Stephen R. Graubard (New York: W. W. Norton, 1979), p. 115; Hedley Bull, "Society and Anarchy in *International Politics: Anarchy, Force, Imperialism,* in International Relations," ed. Robert J. Art and Robert Jervis (Boston: Little, Brown, 1973), p. 28.
5. Michael Howard, "The Military Factor in European Expansion," in *The Expansion of International Society,* ed. Hedley Bull and Adam Watson (Oxford: Clarendon Press, 1984), pp. 33–42. See also Jeremy Rifkin, *Biosphere Politics* (San Francisco: HarperCollins, 1991), Chapter 13.
6. For a detailed account of European expansion to other continents, see Adam Watson, "European International Society and Its Expansion," in *The Expansion of International Society,* pp. 13–32.
7. This description of the technological basis for European imperialism is taken from William R. Keylor, *The Twentieth-Century World: An International History,* 3rd ed. (New York: Oxford University Press, 1996); see especially pp. 27–33.
8. Ted Robert Gurr, Keith Jaggers, and Will H. Moore, "The Transformation of the Western State: The Growth of Democracy, Autocracy, and State Power Since 1800," *Comparative International Development,* Spring 1990, p. 75.
9. Ibid., p. 74.
10. Hedley Bull, *The Anarchical Society: A Study of Order in World Politics* (New York: Columbia University Press, 1977).
11. Hedley Bull, "The Emergence of a Universal International Society," in *The Expansion of International Society,* pp. 117–26.
12. Gilpin, "The Global Political System," p. 129.
13. Authored by George F. Kennan but originally signed only ["X"], "The Sources of Soviet Conduct," *Foreign Affairs,* July 1947, pp. 566–82.

14. Charles W. Kegley, Jr., and Eugene R. Wittkopf, eds., *The Future of American Foreign Policy* (New York: St. Martin's Press, 1992), pp. 253–54.
15. A useful description of these crises can be found in Gordon A. Craig and Alexander L. George, *Force and Statecraft: Diplomatic Problems of Our Time* (New York: Oxford University Press, 1990), pp. 116–33.
16. Stanley Hoffman, "The Case for Leadership," *Foreign Policy,* Winter 1990–1991, p. 22.
17. Crane Brinton, *The Anatomy of Revolution* (New York: Vintage Books, 1965).
18. John Lewis Gaddis, "Toward the Post-Cold Period," *Foreign Affairs,* Spring 1991, pp. 114–16.
19. James N. Rosenau, "The Relocation of Authority in a Shrinking World," *Comparative Politics,* April 1992, pp. 254–56.
20. These distinctions about policy arenas are taken from Marvin S. Soroos, *Beyond Sovereignty: The Challenge of Global Policy* (Columbia, SC: University of South Carolina Press, 1986), p. 20.
21. Hans J. Morgenthau, *Politics Among Nations,* 5th ed. (New York: Alfred A. Knopf, 1978), p. 4.
22. Kenneth N. Waltz, *Theory of International Politics* (Reading, MA: Addison-Wesley, 1979).
23. Robert Gilpin, *War and Peace in World Politics* (Princeton, NJ: Princeton University Press, 1981).
24. Robert O. Keohane and Joseph S. Nye, *Power and Interdependence,* 2nd ed. (Glenview, IL: Scott, Foresman, 1989), pp. 8–9, 23–24.
25. James A. Caporaso, "Introduction: The State in Comparative and International Perspective," in *The Elusive State: International and Comparative Perspectives,* ed. James A. Caporaso (Newbury Park, CA: Sage Publications, 1989), p. 10; Hedley Bull, "The State's Positive Role in World Affairs," in *The State,* ed. Stephen R. Graubard (New York: W. W. Norton, 1979), pp. 115–16.
26. Robert Axelrod and Robert O. Keohane, "Achieving Cooperation Under Anarchy: Strategies and Institutions," in *Cooperation Under Anarchy,* ed. Kenneth A. Oye (Princeton, NJ: Princeton University Press, 1986), pp. 226–27; Helen Milner, "International Theories of Cooperation Among Nations: Strengths and Weaknesses," *World Politics,* April 1992, p. 467.

CHAPTER 3

ACTORS ON THE INTERNATIONAL STAGE

The world has grown more complex and interesting as old and new actors vigorously undertake roles alongside the state on the international stage. The view of realist scholars that states dominate international relations has to give way to the recognition that multiple actors now vie for authority and influence in the world.[1] A new generation of scholars in the international relations field has gradually recognized the emergence of nonstate actors. In fact, many scholars today regard the state not as the *dominant* actor but as the *primary* actor among other influential actors.

A **political actor** is an individual or a group that seeks to achieve goals by either conflicting or cooperating with others in a policy context. Crossing national boundaries and frequently jostling with states over policy outcomes are: *transnational actors* below the state level such as ethnic groups, local governments, and individuals; international government organizations (IGOs), prominently including the United Nations; and international nongovernment organizations (INGOs) involving multinational corporations (MNCs), various churches, and even terrorists.

Some nonstate actors, such as the Roman Catholic Church, have been around a long time, while others, including most IGOs and INGOs, have existed only since the Second World War. Because the current cast of international actors is not permanent, it could grow even larger.[2] By the 1970s, many scholars recognized diverse actors and routinely included them in their descriptions and analyses of international relations.[3]

This chapter identifies and describes these actors, with an emphasis on their impact on international relations. It also examines implications of multiple actors for the evolving international society.

THE STATE

In Chapter Two, we discussed the state as central to the historical process leading to today's international system. We defined the state as a sovereign actor with a central government ruling over a population and territory as well as representing and protecting that population in the international context. We also found that the modern state wants its population to have a sense of shared identity and to give loyalty to the state.

As we study the state further and relate it to other actors, we should remember that the state intends to be a strong actor in the performance of three important political functions. The state, in full form, (1) maintains control over violence in its domain, (2) allocates resources and rewards at its discretion, and (3) stands as the major focus of identity for the large majority of the people under its authority.[4] The modern state, however, has experienced some decline, and not all entities that we commonly call countries meet the requirements of statehood in its full form. Ethnic turmoil in particular tears at the seams of some states. In addition to a concern with how well existing states meet definitional requirements and perform important political functions, we can observe much variety and change in state actors.

Diversity

Beyond sharing a definition of what constitutes a state, the nearly 200 countries are anything but cookie-cutter equivalents. Rather, the states reflect much diversity in their major characteristics. *Military power* of states ranges from the superpower status of the United States, with its long-range missiles and aircraft carriers, to small entities such as Bhutan and Nepal, which count on the protection of India. Some countries cannot protect themselves at all. Tiny, impoverished Comoros, made up of three small islands located between Mozambique in eastern Africa and the large island country of Madagascar, was invaded by a handful of mercenaries in 1995. The mercenaries took the president of Comoros prisoner and were in charge of his 500,000 citizens until French soldiers charitably came to the rescue.

Ideological differences have abated remarkably since the end of the Cold War, with the democracies emerging triumphant over the communist states of Europe. Yet China, the largest country in the world with over a billion people, remains stubbornly communist, along with Cuba, North Korea, and Vietnam. Further, nearly half the world's governments are authoritarian, being either civilian or military dictatorships or traditional monarchs. Some Islamic countries are particularly suspicious and hostile toward the Western democracies.

Other states insist on behaving as rogue states and are inimical to the norms and rules of the formative international society. The United States publicly denounces Iran, Iraq, and Libya, among others, as terrorist-sponsoring states and criticizes their human rights records. Israel is a rogue state in the eyes of most Arab states. States leave their rogue status behind only by transforming their governments or policies, as South Africa did when a mostly black leadership took the helm of a largely black country. This reform brought democracy to South Africa and ended years of near isolation diplomatically and economically.[5] Also, after decades of ostracization by the sports world, South African athletes attended the 1996 Summer Olympics in Atlanta, Georgia.

States vary enormously in *wealth,* with respect to both national wealth and the distribution of that wealth among their citizens. A major line of conflict in the world today concerns differences between the richer, industrial states, generally north of the equator, and the poorer, less industrialized countries, mostly south of the equator. In addition, the quality of life is low in many countries due to the inequitable distribution of wealth among their citizens.

Population size and growth reflect important differences too. Countries range from China, the largest country with 1.2 billion people, down to tiny states such as Tonga and Vanuatu, whose national populations number in the thousands. Population growth rate, which is usually higher in the poorer countries, pressures governments beyond their material capacities to keep up with the wants and needs of growing numbers of people. In addition, the populations of a large majority of countries are culturally heterogeneous, and

TABLE 3.1
Diversity among Selected States

	GNP per Capita (US$ 1993)	Land area (ths. of sq. km.)	Status of freedom	HDI rank	Population (est. for 2,000 in mils.)	Military expenditures (in US$ bils. 1992)
Democracies						
Australia	17,500	7,713	F	11	19.2	4,335
Canada	19,970	9,976	F	1	31.0	7,790
Germany	23,560	376	F	15	81.7	19,252
United States	24,740	9,809	F	2	275.1	242,717
Communist						
China	480	9,561	NF	111	1,284.6	22,364
Cuba	ND	115	NF	72	11.4	1,272
North Korea	ND	121	NF	83	26.0	5,087
Vietnam	170	332	NF	120	82.6	1,750
Ex-communist						
Czech Republic	2,710	17,075	PF	38	10.3	ND
Hungary	3,350	79	F	50	9.9	1,180
Poland	2,260	313	F	51	38.8	2,279
Russia	2,340	93	F	52	145.6	ND
Third World						
Egypt	660	3,288	PF	107	69.1	3,427
India	300	1,958	PF	134	1,022.0	7,550
Mexico	361	26	NF	53	102.4	951
Rwanda	210	1,001	NF	156	9.0	101
Ministates						
Comoros	530	2.2	PF	139	0.8	ND
Maldives	700	.3	NF	118	0.3	ND
Qatar	15,760	1.0	NF	56	0.6	ND
Vanuatu	1,260	12.2	F	119	0.2	ND

GNP per capita income is from *World Development Report 1995* (Washington, D.C., World Bank, 1995). Land area is in thousands of square kilometers from *World Development Report 1995*. Status of freedom is from *Comparative Survey of Freedom* (New York: Freedom House, 1993), F = freedom, PF = partly free, and NF = not free; HDI rank is the Human Development Index based on socioeconomic conditions offered as a country ranking instead of the actual index; from *Human Development Report 1995* (New York: United Nations Development Program, 1995). Population size estimated for the year 2000 is from *Human Development Report 1995*. Military expenditures reported as millions but can be read in the denomination of billions as well; from *Human Development Report 1995*. ND = no data.

the divisions along religious, language, and tribal lines often cause conflict among these ethnic groups and with their governments. The heterogeneity and conflict vary from Finland, with an apparently contented Swedish minority, to Bosnia, Lebanon, and Somalia, countries so torn with group strife that they are barely recognizable as political entities at the state level.

Even a casual look at a political map will quickly reveal that states vary tremendously in *land area*. There are the landed behemoths that include Brazil, Canada, China, and the United States. Russia, after the downsizing of the gigantic Soviet Union, remains the largest country in the world, almost double the size of any of the other large states. Australia has a unique situation because it encompasses an entire huge island continent. In contrast, the tiny states of Bahrain, Comoros, the Maldive Islands, and Qatar are among a significant number of entities possessing the trappings of statehood but lacking weighty influence. At least Bahrain and Qatar have oil wealth, however. Along with their minuscule size, their small populations and a lack of military means have led scholars to dub these states as *ministates.* As mentioned earlier, their survival can sometimes be precarious, as the people of Comoros found out in 1995.

Viability

States are not as able today as in the past to be strong, independent actors. Traditionally, a central concern of states, and a major reason for their formation, was security for the government, the people, and the boundaries of a claimed territory. The survivability of a state in the face of war was the ultimate measure of viability. However, in modern times, the militarily strongest states confront new perils. In an important article in 1957 entitled "The Rise and Demise of the Territorial State,"[6] John Herz asserted that state authority was acceptable to people because they wanted a king's protection. However, he argued, the state's protective role and its viability began to diminish as the hard-shelled impermeability of the state softened.

Modernity subjected the state to blockade, ideological influences, and air war, forces the now permeable state could not easily resist. Herz drew particular attention to a population's vulnerability to nuclear weapons. A decade later, Herz revised his views in an article entitled "The Territorial State Revisited—Reflections on the Future of the Nation-State."[7] He continued to recognize that the state was penetrable—for instance, he noted the intrusive cameras of spy satellites—but the state regained some of its viability when nuclear forces became "unavailable." Armed with sophisticated weapons systems, the Soviet Union and the United States dared not fight each other since they knew both would perish in nuclear war. As a consequence, they settled for a nuclear stand-off and a tense co-existence. Modern terrorism also tears at the viability of states in the security area. Not even Israel, with perhaps the best anti-terrorist security in the world, can stop terrorism completely.

In nonsecurity areas, states also fail to be free of outside forces. Economic interdependence is increasingly intertwining states, requiring coordinated policymaking through international organizations and interstate conferences.[8] Moreover, the sovereign authority of states is softer today because states are more prone to accepting standards formed at the international level. Their own citizens often insist on applying these international standards at home. Citizens from multiple countries even link up in transnational efforts to promote international standards such as the human rights programs of the United Nations and the environmental recommendations of the 1992 Earth Summit.

Not only are states facing new outside challenges, but internally they are less viable as well. States have become paradoxes. States are strong, with large bureaucracies holding intrusive powers in citizens' lives, including the ability to tax them heavily and to regulate their lives in many ways. Yet, during the first half of the twentieth century, states were unable to protect their citizens from the economic suffering of the Great Depression. Nor have the major industrialized democracies been able to cope with the corrosive social problems of crime, drug trafficking, family disintegration, and other signs of social decay in the latter half of the twentieth century.[9]

Some weaker states of the world, especially those in sub-Sahara Africa, are so fragile that they threaten to fall apart. The United Nations has struggled recently to restore order and safety for all citizens in Burundi, Rwanda, and Somalia in Africa and Bosnia in Europe. The fragility of some states is such an ongoing problem that Vice President Al Gore asked the Central Intelligence Agency (CIA) to explain and predict the collapse of authority in weak states. This study, known as the *State Failure Task Force* and reported in late 1995, focused on mass killings, revolutions, ethnic warfare, and violent overthrows of government as evidence of breakdowns in internal authority. This CIA study examined 600 factors in 113 case studies. The study observed that 31 variables could predict serious government failure in 70 percent of the case studies. It found success or failure by states chiefly depends on the degree of democracy, the available wealth for distribution, the infant mortality rate as an indicator of quality of life, the extent of international trade, and the numbers of unemployed youth.[10]

Therefore, the state today is less hard-shelled in its sovereignty regarding the outside world and less able to assert authority inside. Susan Strange observes the state is leaking authority above and below, with other actors supplementing the services of the state. Strange, risking some exaggeration, compares states to " . . . old trees, hollow in the middle, showing signs of weakness and vulnerability to storm, drought, or disease, yet continuing to grow leaves, new shoots, and branches."[11] In a prescient insight before the U.S. Senate Committee on Foreign Relations in 1975, futurist Alvin Toffler foresaw the state becoming an obstacle, with authority moving both down to the *subnational level* and up to the *transnational level.*[12]

Proliferation

We should be cautious, however, about regarding the state as an anachronism set on the path of a precipitous and irreversible decline. We might treat news of serious state demise as humorist Mark Twain did news of his death. When he heard such news, he wryly observed that his death was much exaggerated. So, too, any forecast that the days of the state are about over is premature. As mentioned earlier, the state holds on as the primary actor, though not the dominant one of past years.

The state's viability shows up today in the continuing proliferation of states. Many people still want states and keep creating them. The state concept, formed by the turn of the eighteenth century in Europe, eventually traveled to the rest of the world. The breakup of the European colonial systems always meant more states. Haiti became a black-ruled state in 1804 following a slave revolt against its French masters. About 20 states came out of Portuguese and Spanish empires in South America beginning in the early 1800s. Freed American slaves set up Liberia on the West African coast in 1822 and made it a republic in 1847. Japan shed its feudalistic empire to become a modern, industrial power in the latter nineteenth century, and China became a state in a republican form in 1912.

The development of European states was not yet over. Italian city-states finally merged into a state in 1861, and the German principalities became a single German state in 1871. At the end of the First World War, the collapse of the German, Austro-Hungarian, and Ottoman Turkish empires raised the number of states in Europe to 35 or so. At the end of the Second World War, over 50 states attended the San Francisco conference of 1945 to finish writing the UN Charter.

The most active stage of state proliferation occurred from the late 1940s through the 1970s as European empires in Africa and Asia crumbled. Expressing self-determination as a principle and exerting nationalistic pride, African and Asian peoples have demanded and sometimes fought for independence from their wearied colonial masters. India's independence in Asia in 1947 and Ghana's independence in Africa in 1957 set off an unstoppable wave toward independent statehood throughout most of the world. By 1980, about 165 countries shared the five inhabited continents, although Australia had a continent all to itself.

A trickle of small states continued to form in the 1980s from the remnants of dependent territories or dissolving empires. Brunei, the Marshall Islands, Micronesia, Vanuatu, and Zimbabwe found their way to independence in the 1980s. The end of the Cold War produced a spate of new countries, bringing the total number to around 200 by the mid-1990s. The fragmentation of the Soviet Union resulted in 15 new states. Turmoil in Yugoslavia in the 1990s has produced four new states so far. And Czechoslovakia, in a friendly divorce, became the Republic of Czech and the Republic of Slovakia. The Cold War's end, in a unique exception, caused the loss of one state when East Germany reunified with West Germany, creating one Germany. Most of these states poured from the cauldron of ethnic unrest once the tight lid of communist control lifted.

SUBSTATE ACTORS

The prolonged tendency for scholars to focus on the state as the dominant actor hindered their recognition of the growing importance of substate actors in addition to nonstate actors at the international level. **Substate actors** are essentially domestic actors pursuing their goals through transnational activities. Some scholars call such a merger of domestic and international political activity **intermestic politics.** Chadwick Alger calls a focus on states a "conceptual tyranny of the wall map."[13] Gradually, international relations specialists have given attention to substate actors such as political parties, interest groups, local governments, and individuals that cross permeable state boundaries. They cross these boundaries either by travel, communications, or both to accomplish goals substate actors deem worthwhile.[14] The substate actors we discuss here are ethnic minorities, cities, and individuals.

Ethnic Groups

An **ethnic group** is a set of people who share a special and enduring sense of identification based on experiences and cultural characteristics that can include a common history, regional identification, language, tribal status, indigenous status, and shared physical appearance or so-called racial traits. Frequently groups have two or more distinguishing characteristics—for instance, both a language and a religion—different from those of most of the population. Importantly, a group's identity is dependent not only on shared characteristics but also on the group's self-perception, and the perception of others in a society, that the group's members are different.[15]

Although ethnic identifications can build up and break down over time, they are lasting, and few states do not include ethnic groups, or *ethnies,* as substate actors. Perhaps 20 states with ethnic differences are free of troublesome ethnic problems, according to Ted R.

Gurr,[16] and only Iceland and the two Koreas are completely homogeneous. The remaining majority of states reflect a wide variety in the number of ethnies that share the same state territory and government and how well they get along.

Scholars once assumed that ethnic identifications would fade as the modernization process of industrialization and urbanization ground them down. By the 1970s, however, social scientists recognized the resilience and adaptability of ethnies.[17] In fact, modernization invested ethnic groups with new issues leading to group mobilization under ethnic leaders.[18] Particularly interesting, a worldwide communication network arouses an ethnic group to greater awareness and activity when they learn about ethnic kinsfolk in another country, the treatment they receive, and how they respond to this treatment. Or global communications teach techniques of advocacy, such as when African Americans, led by Martin Luther King, learned about and used the civil disobedience techniques of Mohandas K. Gandhi (1869–1948) that Gandhi developed in India.[19]

Ethnic nationalism is a strong sense of ethnic identification and advocacy for the group's interests, including statehood. This type of nationalism is *sociological* in nature and deeply rooted in strong, primordial identifications involving language, religion, or some other cultural identity. It is a pristine form of nationalism compared to the country-level nationalism that had begun in France by the early nineteenth century. Country-level nationalism is a *psychological* sense of oneness capped down over multiple ethnic differences that can rise and fall with events. Ethnic nationalism is more certain and lasting. For instance, whether ruled by the Turks, Austrians, or the recently fragmented communist state of Yugoslavia, the Serbs have burned with anger over rule by others and the loss of much of their traditional territory since at least the fourteenth century. Journalist Lance Morrow, referring to recent Serbian aggression against other ethnies in Bosnia, has said an ethnic tribe can be, at its worst, "a supermob, a fierce, virtuous assertion of the group."[20]

If a single concern bedevils efforts to build a new world order, it is the widespread occurrence of ethnic conflict. Further, the global upsurge in ethnic nationalism has yet to run its course.[21] Amid troublesome ethnic relations, we can recognize several degrees of ethnic conflict. When ethnies interact, a dominant group in a country may treat a subordinate group in a contemptuous manner and thus *dehumanize* them.[22] An ethnic group may be the victim of *discrimination* and believe their members are not receiving their fair share of roads, schools, housing, and jobs, resulting in protests and rebellious behavior.[23]

Alternatively, states may attempt *cultural nation building* by forcing minorities to assimilate into a cultural majority, creating a more homogeneous population for the state.[24] Before the fall of its communist government, Bulgaria tried to force its Turkish minority to give up their Turkish names and language. Less from coercion than from their own desire to advance, the Korean minority in Japan know they must accept Japanese names and the Japanese language if they want good jobs and housing.

Moreover, many ethnies want, and sometimes demand, a greater measure of *autonomy*, meaning a measure of self-rule separate from the central government of the state. Usually concentrated in a specific part of a state's territory, these ethnic groups want more protection from intrusions into their cultural way of life. Scots in Great Britain, Basques and Catalonians in Spain, and many indigenous peoples, such as the Sami (Lapps) of northern Scandinavia and the Amer-Indians of Brazil are groups of this kind.[25] The French speakers of the Quebec province of Canada have insisted on and received autonomy short of leaving the Canadian federal system. Many states naturally resist reduced authority over any part of their territory and adamantly object to the permanent loss of territory and people that occurs with *secession*.

Secession concerns an ethnic group's effort to withdraw from an existing state to establish a new state on territory the group occupies. Although desires for autonomy can lead to sharp conflict, secessionist efforts that dismember states' territories can mean outright warfare. The ongoing revolutions, civil wars, and international entanglements around the globe frequently have roots in ethnic problems. The Persian Gulf War gave the Kurdish and Shi'a minorities of Iraq a chance to revolt, only to face cruel defeat. The Sudan Arab–dominated government has carried on a civil war for years with the Sudanese African population in the south of the country. Eritreans founded their own country in 1993 only after a lengthy war with their former government of Ethiopia. Finally, the secessionist effort by eastern Pakistan (today's Bangladesh), involving several ethnies different from the peoples of western Pakistan, invited the successful intervention of the Indian Army in 1971. The Indian government could not resist dismembering and weakening its traditional foe.

More than 60 ethnic self-determination movements are active in the world, many causing turmoil and violence.[26] Some past and present examples easily come to mind. China suppressed Tibet in 1959 at a cost of a million lives and continues to incorporate Tibet into the body of China by placing enough Chinese in Tibet to outnumber the Tibetans. The Sikhs have fought for years for Punjab's independence from India. Two Sikh bodyguards assassinated Prime Minister Indira Gandhi in 1984, presumably to strike a blow for secession. The Kurdish minority has waged revolution for over 12 years for independence from Turkey.

A Russian minority of 100,000 people unsuccessfully attempted their independence from Moldova to become the Dniester Republic in 1992. Moldova had already broken away from the Soviet Union. Today a total of 25 million Russians live in the "Near Abroad," the ex-republics of the Soviet Union, excluding Russia, and many fear that Russia will feel an ethnic nationalist tug to come to their "rescue." Meanwhile, Russia has confronted a stubborn Chechen separatist movement that, since the eruption of violence in late 1994, has bloodied the once highly vaunted Russian army. Chechens want to create the Republic of Chechnya on Russian territory lying between the Black and Caspian seas.

It is understandable that ethnic groups would pursue these separatist movements, for they can lay claim to the democratic principle of self-determination espoused by President Woodrow Wilson and enshrined in current human rights treaties. Although President Wilson's immediate goal was to break up monarchical empires after the First World War, his Secretary of State, Robert Lansing, worried that this principle would have a resonating effect, making the world more volatile and unstable. Lansing's fears eventually became a reality. So intense is its power that ethnic nationalism calls into question the Westphalian Order of 1648 based on sovereign states with bounded territories.[27]

Ethnicity challenges this order of state actors in two ways: by offering a competing basis for identity and by threatening to make the state system, with far more than 200 states, so complex and weighty that it would become a system of complete disorder. One source counts 5,000 distinct ethnic groups in the world, and 500 of these are potential states.[28] Since most states are multinational and fear the disintegrative effects of self-determination, international law and international organizations, such as the United Nations and the Organization of African Unity, have come to take a restricted view of what self-determination can mean. According to Antonio Cassese, international law allows for only three applications of self-determination: anticolonialism, access to government by all racial groups, and opposition to foreign military occupation.[29] Many ethnic groups obviously are undeterred by this restricted view of self-determination, and they continue to insist on more autonomy if not independent statehood.

In addition to internal conflict, ethnic nationalism can mean international conflict operating in two patterns. One pattern involves the division of an ethny by a national boundary line. The other pattern occurs when rival, contentious ethnic groups control neighboring states, a situation that encourages strife and war.

The first pattern may have started with Italy when, in the nineteenth century, that state tried to annex Italian-speaking parts of Austria and Switzerland to claim their *irredenta* ("unredeemed"). Since that time, when a majority ethnic group in one country wants to annex territory from an adjoining state in which their ethnic kinsfolk live, this expression of ethnicity became **irredentism.**[30] Perhaps the best-known case of irredentism took place when Adolf Hitler, in 1938, annexed the Sudetenland of Czechoslovakia, where a German minority lived. This action was one of several aggressive acts by Nazi Germany that led to war in Europe.

Many instances of potential irredentism currently exist in the world. For example, the Balkan Mountains of southeastern Europe, always a powder keg of ethnic animosity, are more dangerous today because the Albanian minority in the Republic of Serbia resent the loss of autonomy that communist Yugoslavia once gave them. This Albanian minority might, at some point, prefer to join the adjacent state of Albania. Then there is the Armenian minority in Turkey, long dissatisfied with Turkish rule, that may want to hook up with the new Republic of Armenia formed after the breakup of the Soviet Union.

The other pattern of ethnic nationalism contributing to international conflict concerns *ethnic-states* that fight wars or live with warlike tensions. Ethnic-states have a dominant ethnic group in charge, and when two such states share a common border, conditions may be ripe for war. In such cases, ethnic nationalism merges with country-level nationalism. India, controlled by Hindus, and Pakistan, in the charge of Muslims, have fought three wars and today co-exist in a sharp-edged relationship. The Iranian-Iraqi war of the 1980s was more fierce and bloody because Iran's government had Shi'a leaders while the Sunni sect of Islam led Iraq. In an aptly titled book, *One Land, Two Peoples: The Conflict Over Palestine,* Deborah Gerner describes the historical claims that both Jews and Palestinians, an Arab people, make for the same piece of territory. Arab states have entered several wars in part to bolster the Palestinian effort to achieve a Palestinian state.[31] Many Arab people have spoken of a *Jihad,* or holy war, to drive the Israelis into the sea.

Since ethnic and state relationships entangle in complex and conflictual ways, what are the policy options for handling ethnic contention? The choices basically are *coercion* or *accommodation,* although neither guarantees to end conflict. Governments sometimes use a mixture of the two as they experimentally search for a workable policy. We can say with some assurance, however, that authoritarian states are prone to coercion while democracies increasingly pursue accommodation methods.

Frequently states coerce with *forced assimilation,* calling for an ethny to give up its cultural distinctiveness and merge with the ethnic majority. Another coercive technique is *political repression* involving imprisonment and torture to intimidate a minority into

© Tribune Media Services, Inc. All rights reserved. Reprinted with permission.

submission. *Mass deportation* can be another option. The Soviet Union, after the Second World War, forced a German population to leave eastern Prussia so Poland could have more territory on its western flank. Then there is the abhorrent practice of *genocide,* the outright destruction of a people, made infamous by Nazi Germany when the Nazis slaughtered 12 million people as "undesired" minorities, half of whom were Jews. Recently the Bosnian Serbs have practiced *ethnic cleansing* by imprisoning, killing, and raping Bosnian Muslims and Croatians to frighten and drive these minorities from lands the Serbs want.

Accommodation offers positive inducements for ethnies to get along with one another and with the governments of the states where they reside. States can extend individual and group *rights* to members of ethnic groups so they can better accept life in a country-level society. Extending *democratic participation,* through political parties and elections, empowers a group to protect their interests. Arend Lijphart recommends a package of democratic institutions for what he terms **consociational societies.** These are societies with ethnic divisions sharing the government of a country through such techniques as federalism, proportional representation in legislatures based on the size of the ethnic group, and executive leadership through a council of elites drawn from each ethnic group.[32]

Ironically, democratic techniques in countries with only two ethnies are harder to use than in more complex societies with multiple ethnic groups. Rivalry is more intense with two groups, and each side keenly fears the other when that group gains control of government. The Hutu and Tutsi tribes, existing in both Burundi and Rwanda in central Africa, have locked together on several occasions in a life-or-death struggle. When there has been a change in government, democratically or by *coup,* the losing side fears annihilation and strikes first, sometimes causing death in genocidal proportions. Hundreds of thousands of people died in these two countries in the mid-1990s. Kenya, in contrast, has multiple tribes without a single tribe constituting a majority. This partially democratic country has experienced far less ethnic violence than either Burundi or Rwanda.

Regional autonomy is a technique governments and ethnies frequently find mutually acceptable. It has pleased most Scots in Great Britain and French speakers in Canada and many other ethnic minorities in other countries. With this technique, special arrangements protect cultural practices such as language or religion and may permit a degree of self-government. Finally, some countries luckily experience *voluntary assimilation,* in which minorities adopt the culture of a majority, in part or in whole, because they choose to do so. The United States, until recently, enjoyed the reputation of being a cultural "melting pot," but today this country is oriented more toward celebrating its "cultural diversity" that preserves the identities of cultural minorities.

While ethnic violence frequently makes news headlines, many countries do successfully accommodate their ethnic divisions. Not surprisingly, the most successful are among the more established democracies such as Belgium, Canada, the Netherlands, Switzerland, and the United States. Yet ethnically based problems continue to trouble these states and others around the globe. Ethnic nationalism injects more turbulence into the progress of a new world order than any other single factor. The exact conditions and policies that would permit ethnically divided societies to stay together and dampen ethnically derived violence continue to elude scholars and leaders alike. Finally, irredentism and ethnic-state conflict fall into the purview of traditional interstate diplomacy for resolution, although the effort is not always successful.

Cities

Local governments of varied types have become transnational actors, at least for commercial reasons. Many of the 50 states within the federal system of the United States compete over foreign MNCs and send trade delegations overseas to generate business. For instance, South Carolina won a spirited context with Nebraska to attract BMW's plant to make the Z-3 sports car. However, the choice here is to emphasize cities because scholars often neglect to include them among the range of substate actors.[33]

Cities of varied sizes around the world routinely practice "citizen diplomacy," bypassing their national foreign ministries to make trade arrangements; pass resolutions on every imaginable subject, for instance, opposing nuclear bomb testing by China and France and racism in South Africa while it was under white rule; and establish "sister-city" programs to offer advice and material aid to cities in other countries.[34] In tiny Carlisle, South Carolina, with a population of under 1,000, interesting transnational connections have occurred. Mayor Janie Goree, holding office from 1987 to 1996 and the first female African American to serve as a mayor in South Carolina, attended world councils for mayors and traveled to the Bahamas, China, France, the Ivory Coast, and Japan. She used her China connections to arrange for China forestry students to study in South Carolina and to visit Carlisle.

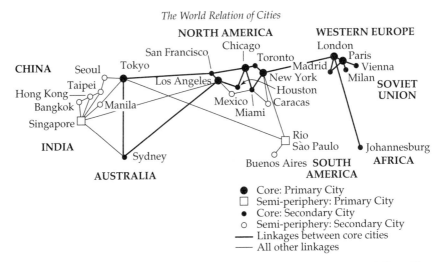

The World Relation of Cities

Source: John Friedmann, "The World City Hypothesis (Editor's Introduction)," *Development and Change* 17, no. 1 (1986), p. 74. © 1986. Reprinted by permission of Sage Publications Ltd.

Sometimes city leaders' tendency to acquire the "global bug" irritates national leaders formally in charge of foreign policy. New York City mayors often operate "foreign policies" unsuitable to Washington, D.C. As an example, Mayor David Dinkins criticized President George Bush in 1991 for rescinding economic sanctions designed to punish South Africa for its racial segregation and vowed New York City would somehow continue sanctions on its own. New York City also has required Xerox and other companies to sign a fair-employment pledge over religious discrimination in Northern Ireland before they could win New York contracts. Madison, Wisconsin, along with other cities, has passed a resolution against human rights abuses in Myabmar, Burma. In the United States alone, 7,284 municipalities, as well as 50 state legislative bodies, are prone to follow their own "foreign policies." The U.S. State Department cannot begin to keep up with their international acts, much less make them hew to its own line of policy.

Cities adjacent to one another but separated by a border can have special problems and relations. For instance, cities along the American-Canadian and American-Mexican boundaries have worked out agreements concerning roads, bridges, and water management. When Tijuana, Mexico, was dumping sewage into the ocean and fouling San Diego's beaches, the respective mayors worked out a plan to relieve the problem.

Certain major cities are the nerve centers of the world and connect countries and continents with travel and communication networks. Chadwick Alger sees a global network of cities helping to integrate the world economy.[35] To him, a few prominent cities, such as New York and London, are the "command centers" of financial and corporate decision-making. MNCs and the great banks of the world operate from these cities and radiate a web of electronic communications and air travel. Alger believes a hierarchy of cities is discernible among these "command centers." By driving communications, capital flow, and trade in goods, the most prominent cities, located in North America and western Europe, dominate lesser cities elsewhere.

Individuals

While historians have given individuals too much credit by using the "great man" theory to account for the "Age of Caesar" or the "Age of Napoleon," scholars in international relations probably have gone too far the other way by deemphasizing the impact of individual actors in favor of a traditional focus on states. We can safely regard individual actors as important because they are the only thinking, feeling, and acting entities. After all, states, international organizations, terrorist groups, MNCs, and other actors are collectives of individual people organized in special ways.

We will consider two types of individuals. The first is the individual actor that is empowered with the resources of an institution, such as a state, and may face dynamic situations that bring opportunities and dangers requiring bold steps. The second is an individual actor that becomes important as the symbol for a moral cause. The first is essentially a *public* actor, and the second is a *private* actor.

Robert Isaak observes that public leaders obviously have power if they head powerful states, but they may further enhance their impact as they operate amid world events. When leaders face crises and develop successful approaches to the problems they face, they may become great leaders.[36]

Henry Kissinger is an interesting example. He was the national security adviser and secretary of state for two presidents, Richard Nixon and Gerald Ford, between 1968 and 1976. With Nixon, he developed the *détente* policy of relaxed tensions with the Soviet Union. At about the same time, he took part in a *rapproachment* with communist China. The United States had basically turned its back on the most populated country in the world, preferring to isolate this supposedly radical state as much as possible. Henry Kissinger broke with the past on America's China policy with initiatives that, over time, eventually led to trade and diplomatic recognition. More important in the Cold War context, this bold step allowed the United States to play the "China card" as a check on Soviet power and influence.[37]

Mikhail Gorbachev, Soviet leader from 1985 to 1991, offers an interesting contrast to Kissinger's success. He received much favorable comment in the West as a leader with the vision to improve the global situation. From the Soviet view, however, he unwittingly took initiatives that led to the downfall of the Soviet Union, leaving the United States as the only superpower. Instead of meeting Isaak's criterion of successfully finding solutions in the face of a crisis, Gorbachev's efforts at limited reform quickly spun out of control, releasing powerful economic and ethnic forces that tore the Soviet Union apart. Today Gorbachev's image among Russians is quite negative.[38] His run at the Russian presidency in the election of 1996 was a complete flop.

We have seen that a public leader can make a difference, at least if that leader can work smoothly with the historical forces and world politics of the day as Henry Kissinger did. Individual private actors can be important as well. Armand Hammer, a business executive with longtime ties in the Soviet Union, persuaded Mikhail Gorbachev to renew summit conferences with President Ronald Reagan after an unusual lapse in these conferences of four years.[39] Sometimes an individual is important as a symbol of a moral cause. As a black

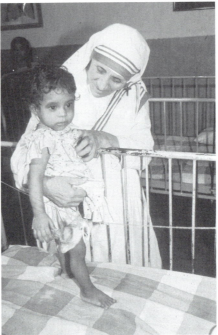

churchman, Archbishop Desmond Tutu's brave stand against *apartheid,* a harsh form of racial segregation in South Africa, helped to mobilize world opinion against discrimination at the global level. Mother Teresa has served the poor, the sick, and the abandoned of India and other countries for nearly half a century through the Missionaries of Charity that she founded. Although a tiny and humble lady with a serious heart condition, she has become a world celebrity, winning the 1979 Nobel Peace Prize. The number of good deeds Mother Teresa encourages in others is inestimable.

A private individual can be an important symbol for a cause even in death. When the Soviet Army intervened in Czechoslovakia in 1968, Jan Palach, a 20-year-old university students, set himself on fire and died to protest the Soviet intervention. For years, until the collapse of the communist regimes in eastern Europe, crowds gathered on the anniversary of his death and left bundles of flowers in the Prague square where Jan Palach made his ultimate sacrifice for Czech freedom. Unnamed individuals have made remarkable imprints on the world conscience thanks to the modern capability of televising pictures around the world. During the Tiananmen Square massacre in China in 1989, a lone, unidentified person stood in front of a column of tanks, temporarily blocking their progress. Friends finally pulled this individual aside, but this lone act may have encouraged attitudes that will resurface in the future as a defiant demand for democracy in China.

INTERNATIONAL GOVERNMENT ORGANIZATIONS

An **international organization** is an institution with membership drawn from two or more countries. Its activities transcend national boundaries as it facilitates cooperation among its

© 1997. Reprinted with permission, the *Chicago Sun-Times*.

members in the performance of one or more tasks. The international organization can be *public* or *private*. A public organization is an **international government organization (IGO)** with states as its members. The major advantage of an IGO is that it can structure communication and cooperation among member-states on a continuing basis as they deal with common needs.[40] Prominent examples of IGOs are the United Nations, the North Atlantic Treaty Organization (NATO), the International Monetary Fund (IMF), and the World Health Organization (WHO). We will cover private international organizations in the next section.

If problems and needs did not extend past the borders and jurisdictions of states, IGOs would never have come into existence. However, mail cannot move across borders any more than telegraph and telephone lines can unless states agree to accept these communications. With more people and states entering the world, accompanied by modern forms of communication, including satellite relays, the web of cooperation must grow larger and tighter. The cooperation necessary for international communication repeats itself in many task areas of states. These areas include international trade, security, the economic development of poorer countries, and the promotion of human welfare and human rights, among others.

IGOs continued to grow in prominence as an actor until some scholars once speculated that IGOs may someday encroach on states by supplanting their functions. A tapestry hanging in the *Palais des Nations* in Geneva, Switzerland, the former headquarters of the League of Nations and now the European center of operations of the United Nations, pictures the IGO as a stage in a process moving toward some form of world government.[41] More accurately, the IGO is only a supplement to the state system. Ultimate authority rests with the member-states of any IGO because they supply the money and other needed resources such as troops for UN Peacekeeping missions. Further, the states, in most instances, must implement IGO decisions. In 1990, the United Nations could declare Iraq an aggressor for invading Kuwait, but member-states had to agree with this view and raise the military forces that defeated Iraq in 1991.

Although the IGO does not operate on a par with the state as an actor, it helps to diminish the state's status from dominant to primary actor. Not only does the state partly depend on IGOs to meet its needs, but the IGO can take initiatives that shape state policy and behavior. For instance, the UN Commission on Human Rights has come to scrutinize a state policy that was once entirely within a state's domestic domain, namely the treatment of its own citizens. Scrutinizing state conduct in this area induces some states to do better regarding their citizens. At the same time, unpopular initiatives by an IGO will encourage states to be stingy with staff and money, such as when the United Nations pursues human rights protection too forcefully.[42]

Often associated with IGOs is the concept of the regime, though the two are analytically distinguishable. **Regimes** are sets of rules, norms, and decision-making procedures that actors converge around and use.[43] *Rules* are clear and usually written guides for conduct, while *norms* are general expectations concerning behavior. A regime is more an arrangement among actors than an actor itself. Frequently, regimes are *formal* and nest within the institutional framework of an IGO. Although regime rules and norms can be *informal* and lack the institutional support of an IGO, regimes tend to move toward organizational status. The rules and norms of the IMF as it hands out loans and regulates currency is a nested, formal regime. States agreeing to inspect only one unit of a new model of automobile for pollution control instead of the whole fleet can be a tacit, informal regime that does not involve a treaty or an IGO.

An important distinction concerning regimes is whether they are *hegemonic* or *cooperative* regimes. The former type is one with a dominant state imposing rules and norms, such as when the United States controlled trade terms and currency exchanges for years after the Second World War. The latter type occurs when states voluntarily agree to rules and norms, although the states still vie with one another over influence and policy outcomes. Most regimes today are basically cooperative even if the influence of states varies within these regimes. As an example, France probably has more consistent influence within the environmental regime protecting the Mediterranean Sea than any other state on the rim of this sea.

The growing interdependence of the world places a premium on cooperation; hence, the evolution of regimes.[44] While complete harmony is unexpected in regimes, the reduction of conflict is an essential part of regime operation.[45] Regimes have developed in many issue-areas, including the proliferation of nuclear weapons, international trade, sharing of fisheries, human rights, and environmental protection. We will refer to regimes often in the remainder of this textbook.

INTERNATIONAL NONGOVERNMENT ORGANIZATIONS

International nongovernment organizations (INGOs) base their membership on groups and individuals acting in a private capacity that may or may not have a political agenda. These organizations are transnational and draw membership from individuals and private associations located in several countries. Over 4,000 INGOs take part in every imaginable human activity, which may or may not concern politics. The Alliance of YMCAs, the International Chamber of Commerce, the International Political Science Association, the Muslim World League, the International Committee of the Red Cross, and the Salvation Army suggest the variety in purpose of INGOs.

INGOs have joined states and IGOs on the international stage and, in many cases, exert considerable influence. INGOs gain structure from the weakening of states; yet, paradoxically, they need strong states to carry out their agendas.[46] Amnesty International, for instance, an important human rights advocate, used its "consultative status" within the United Nations (which many INGOs have) to lobby for a treaty against torture. Only a weakened sense of sovereignty by states could permit a treaty limiting what states can do with their own citizens. Yet the treaty against torture counts on important states leading world opinion against this odious practice and pressuring states that engage in it with trade and foreign aid sanctions.

As ordinary people in various countries have become aware of sharing similar interests, modern travel and communication have facilitated the formation of transnational organizations and the holding of international meetings and conferences for the citizenry of many countries. Native Americans, as an interesting case, mobilized politically in the 1960s and learned that indigenous peoples, such as the Sami (Lapps) in Finland and Maori in New Zealand, experienced problems not unlike their own. The organizing result was the World Council of Indigenous Peoples, which protects the rights and interests of indigenous populations from their own governments.

The spread of democracy across the world has encouraged national civil societies, based on organizations of concerned citizens, that advocate proposals for new policies and reforms to their governments. Similarly, the combination of INGOs forms a loose *global civil society* that helps shape the international agenda and policy outcomes. Probably the fastest-growing INGOs, and some of the most influential, are in the environmental area. We investigate the concept of a global civil society more fully in Chapter Thirteen, which deals with environmental concerns.

Although the subject of international organizations is the focus of Chapter Twelve, several specific INGOs are prominent actors in their own right and deserve attention here. These transnational actors are multinational corporations, terrorist organizations, and churches.

MNCs

Multinational corporations (MNCs) are business organizations that extend ownership, management, production, and sales activities into several or more countries. Some

TABLE 3.2
The Good and Bad Effects of MNCs

Good effects	Bad effects
Introduce technology	Offer ill-suited technology
Encourage economic growth	Retard economic growth
Encourage interdependency	Cause dependency
Elites learn to regulate	Elites become *compradors*
Promote human rights	Harm human rights
Protect the environment	Hurt the environment
Economic actors	Political actors
Promote a cosmopolitan world	Damage the national culture

corporations, such as General Motors and Michelin, have such extensive operations that they have global reach. The MNC's head office is in a *home* state, and a cluster of subsidiary corporations carry on business in multiple *host* states.[47]

Modern communication and travel allow the various elements of an MNC to coordinate closely. Although head offices are mostly in North America, Europe, and Japan, MNCs operate from many countries around the world. Today some 35,000 MNCs with about 150,000 subsidiaries holding a total stock of foreign investment worth $1,700 billion operate in the world.[48] About 80 percent of the world's trade passes through the hands of these MNCs.

International business organizations trace back to the British East Indies Company and Hudson Bay Company of the eighteenth century, but modern MNCs began to make an impact after the Second World War. By the 1970s, many scholars and policymakers in the Third World were interpreting this impact as exploitative, with the richer countries supposedly taking advantage of the poorer ones. In the 1980s, this view began to give way to a more balanced perspective on the role of the MNC, although many observers remain skeptical of how much good MNCs do in Third World countries.

Proponents consider the MNC as a boon to economic growth and development by diffusing technology, capital, and expertise throughout the world.[49] Opponents see the MNC as a predator taking advantage of host countries. They claim MNCs mine irreplaceable natural resources, siphon capital out of the host state, bring in technology unsuited for the host's development plans, hire skilled people away from local businesses, and cause host governments to restrict human rights. Further, states deny the right to organize labor unions, keeping wages low to attract MNCs.[50] Critics even accuse the MNCs of co-opting host elites by turning them into *compradors,* allies that help exploit their own countries.

Gradually, observers have come to recognize that over time the MNC may do more good than harm.[51] Many host leaders now see the MNC as a tool of development, producing jobs and tax revenue. Competition among both modern, industrialized countries and less developed countries to attract MNCs has become intense. Proof that MNCs usually do more good than harm is the fact that host countries rarely ask an MNC to leave.[52] Nonetheless, there is the current case of India, where extreme Hindu nationalists still oppose MNCs and speak in the old-fashioned exploitative lexicon. As a result, investors move past India's potentially huge market and on to China's, where foreign investment capital dwarfs that found in India.

The reason for the overall improvement in the role of MNCs by the 1980s was a change in the approaches of the actors involved. Both MNCs and host states have encountered learning curves with favorable outcomes. The MNCs began to realize benefits from being desired, cooperative guests. Corporations have learned to bargain while keeping in mind the need for mutual advantages for themselves and their hosts. Isaiah Frank's interviews with MNC executives even uncovered sympathy for host states' economic development plans.[53] In addition, MNCs now prefer to steer clear of the designs and manipulations of their home states. MNCs want to focus on profits instead of helping to disperse foreign aid or acting as a cover for intelligence activities. They probably would prefer that home states leave them out of trade embargo policies such as the United States' effort to collapse the Cuban economy. It is difficult today to imagine any corporation allowing itself to take part in clandestine operations, as International Telephone and Telegraph (ITT) did in 1972 when it encouraged the Chilean military to overthrow an elected Marxist president.

Moreover, Third World leaders have learned much, according to political economist Joan Spero. She finds these leaders can now negotiate more effectively within MNCs for more attractive terms and know better how to regulate MNCs' operations.[54] Since corporations did not always adhere to the "codes of conduct" produced by the UN Center on Transnational Corporations, host countries developed their own supervisory resources. For example, Third World countries learned to thwart the "double accounting" techniques of MNCs by acquiring their own expert accountants to match those of the MNCs. Some corporations would keep two sets of books, one for in-house needs and the other using a lower income report to cheat on tax payments paid to the host government. In addition, some Third World countries form common bargaining fronts before MNCs so that MNCs cannot play potential host countries off against one another. The Andean Group (sometimes called the Andean Pact), based on five countries located in the Andes Mountains of South America, is an example of such a front.

The phenomenal growth of the world economy, with MNCs at the center, is one of the more spectacular international developments since the Second World War. Not only do MNCs handle most of the world's trade and investment; they draw the world together by contributing to an interdependent economy. We take up the subject of MNCs again in Chapters Eight and Nine, which focus on the international economy.

Terrorist Organizations

Terrorism is an ancient practice traceable, at least, to Jewish zealots who tried to drive the Roman army out of Palestine between A.D. 6 and A.D. 135. Sporadic episodes of terrorism have occurred down through history, focusing mostly on the governments of the terrorists' own country. The modern pattern of terrorism, beginning in the 1960s, is distinctly international in character. Although terrorist organizations may originate over local issues, they frequently discover the international advantages of traveling across multiple national jurisdictions to avoid capture and to strike at targets. Terrorist groups help one another with a transnational network of safe houses, training camps, forged passports, arms and explosives, and money.

Terrorism is an act or a threat of violence by one or more persons calculated to create an atmosphere of fear and alarm. Here we deal with privately based terrorism and save

Tailang/Hindustan Times, New Delhi. Reprinted from *World Press Review* magazine.

state-sponsored terrorism for Chapter Five. This practice is intended to make other actors, including governments, do what terrorists want.[55] Terrorists hope to break down the rational thought and willpower of leaders and citizens alike. They desire for everyone to be afraid of unattended luggage or a truck parked at a nearby curb. Terrorists may focus on particular targets as the Basque terrorists in Spain do when they assassinate generals and politicians or when Armenian terrorists kill Turkish diplomats. Other terrorists ruthlessly slay innocent, unarmed civilians at will to dramatize their cause or to punish a country. Sikh separatists blew up an Indian Boeing 747 off Ireland in 1985 because India would not grant independence to the Sikh people living in the Punjab state of India's federal arrangement, and Libyan agents bombed a Pan Am flight over Scotland in 1988, probably in retaliation for America's air strike against Libya in 1986.

Terrorist incidents rose sharply through the 1980s and then began to level off, though hundreds of terrorist incidents still occurred each year. Europe, Latin America, and the Middle East have suffered the worst of the terrorist plague. Traditionally, North America has experienced the least trouble from terrorism, but recently Americans have taken some heavy blows from terrorists. According to the *Pinkerton Risk Assessment,* in 1995 the United States joined the "top 20" states experiencing terrorist incidents.[56]

Until recently, terrorist attacks focused on American targets overseas, including the bombing of the Marine barracks in Lebanon in 1983 and the downing of the Pan Am flight over Scotland in 1988. In addition, two terrorist bombs killed American military personnel in Saudi Arabia in the mid-1990s. Now terrorism, of both foreign derivation and a home-grown kind, has come home. Radical Islamic fundamentalists bombed the World Trade Center in New York City in 1993, killing six and hurting about a thousand people. In 1995, two American individuals with a shadowy militia, antigovernment background, were accused of blowing up the Alfred P. Murrah Federal Building in Oklahoma City, killing 167 people and wounding some 400 others. Some of the casualties were children in a day care center located within the building. Then, in 1996, the explosion of TWA flight 800 near Long Island killed all 230 people on board. Although investigators now think the explosion

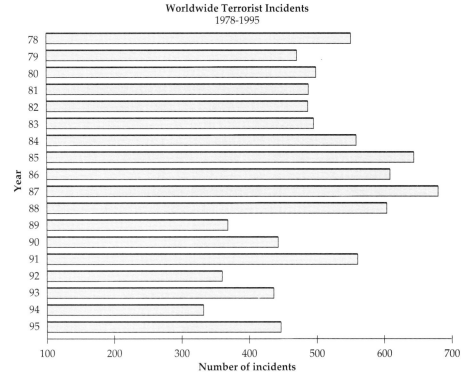

Source: *Patterns of Global Terrorism 1995* (Washington, D.C.: Department of State, 1996), p. 71.

may have been a terrible accident, this tragedy immediately raised speculation that a bomb was responsible. Finally, in 1996 a pipe bomb at the Summer Olympics in Atlanta, Georgia, killed one person and hurt several others.

The varied causes of terrorism are difficult to pin down. At one level, some terrorists may be individuals with *personality disturbances* looking for a cause, in the Eric Hoffer "true believer" sense, to give their lives meaning and purpose.[57] They may have what Richard Pearlstein, in *The Mind of the Terrorist,* calls a "narcissistic injury" leading to a profound and lasting harm to their self-images and self-esteem. Such individuals, he thinks, may turn to rage and aggression for their psychic rewards.[58] The "unabomber" may be a person of this type. He is at least a strange eccentric and a loner who, over a period of years, wanted to destroy American society by killing the creators of technology with letter and pipe bombs. Fortunately, authorities caught up with Theodore J. Kaczynski in 1996 at his shack in the wilderness of Montana.

Perhaps the most famous terrorist in history is "Carlos the Jackal." While comments here are speculative, he may be a person who sought adventure and enjoyed his escapades. Though he had only one great success, the kidnapping of 11 oil ministers from oil-rich countries in Vienna in 1975, Carlos fanned the flames of his legendary status with effective public relations. He appears to have a large ego. Carlos claims to have had 83 victims and

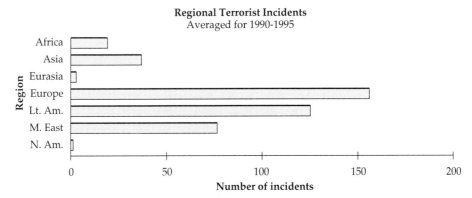

Source: *Patterns of Global Terrorism 1995* (Washington, D.C.: Department of State, 1996), p. 72.

became famous for his 1975 statement, "To get anywhere, you have to walk over the corpses." However, he probably does have legitimate Marxist beliefs and always fought for leftist causes. In the end, Carlos fell to the French in 1994 when they traded satellite photos to Sudan for his extradition. The Arab-controlled government of Sudan wanted these satellite photos to reveal the position of African insurgents in the south of the Sudan, rebels Sudan hoped to defeat. The French wanted Carlos for killing a pregnant woman with a bomb in 1982.

At another level, we should not underestimate the sense of legitimate injustice that many people living in the squalor of an oppressed society feel while venal elites live in luxury. Revolutionaries may sometimes resort to terrorism because it is the "weapon of the weak." Kidnapping, assassination, hijacking, and sabotage do not require marshaling of many resources. Many terrorist groups have a leftist or rightist *ideological view* of their situation. For instance, the Shining Path in Peru is a Marxist group that, since 1980, has killed thousands and cost Peru billions in dollars spent on security and lost through interruptions to commerce. The capture and imprisonment of their leader, Manual A. Guzman, in 1992 has slowed this group down. An example of a right-wing group is the Aryan Nation in the United States, which believes in white supremacy and has sought its own country in the American Northwest. Somehow they think this goal is achievable with murder and robbery.

Another major motive behind terrorism is the radical discontent of some *ethnic minorities*. Sikh separatists in the Punjab of India, Basque terrorists in northern Spain, the Irish Revolutionary Army (IRA) in northern Ireland, the Armenian Grey Wolves, the Tamil Liberation Front in Sri Lanka, and the Quebec Liberation Front in Canada are a few of the ethnic-based terrorists drawn from a list of many. This type of terrorist organization normally wants a substantial measure of autonomy, if not outright independence.

Radical *Islamic fundamentalism,* a special case of ethnic identity, has spawned several terrorist groups. While these groups focus mostly on socioeconomic reforms for their own countries and on a stronger role for Islam in their governments, they do terrorize Westerners on occasion. The attack on the World Trade Center in 1993 is an example. Egyptian radicals object to the ample aid America gives to a government they wish to overthrow. The two bombing attacks against Americans in Saudi Arabia in the mid-1990s happened because radical fundamentalists do not want armed "infidels" in the "holy land" of Islam. One fundamentalist leader the U.S. State Department has accused of terrorism, Osama bin Laden, has said about the time of the attacks, "Muslims burn with anger at America. For its own good, America should leave [Saudia Arabia]."[59]

Although providing high drama for worldwide news coverage for several decades, terrorists have not accomplished major goals. Nowhere has a prominent achievement resulted from terrorism. Terrorists occasionally enjoy a *tactical* success when they free a comrade from jail, hold a hostage for ransom, rob a bank, or blow up a plane. A *strategic* success—autonomy or statehood for a people or a basic change in the type of government—eludes terrorist campaigns. It would be a difficult challenge to show, event by event, how a terrorist campaign helped produce a strategic political success. Yet leaders of states sometimes feel forced to negotiate with terrorists if they have any hope of stopping campaigns of bombings, assassinations, and kidnappings.

An interesting debate could turn on whether the Quebec Liberation Front produced a measure of Quebec autonomy. Quebec cultural autonomy may have resulted more from democratic expression in popular referendums than from terrorism. Has a history of Palestinian terrorism advanced progress toward a Palestinian homeland? Or did recent terrorism by some radical Palestinian groups bring the hard-line Likud party back to power in the 1996 elections, an event that has stalled further progress toward the Palestinian homeland? Did IRA bombings over British withdrawal from northern Ireland force or stall progress toward terrorist goals? At least, the unwillingness of the IRA to disarm as a condition for further negotiations with Prime Minister John Major halted progress on the northern Ireland question.

What remedies do countries have to counter terrorism? Apparently shutting down terrorism completely is impossible as long as diehard individuals and groups are willing to make every sacrifice for their cause. In democracies especially, as open societies with many freedoms for people and with restraints on what the police can do, stopping terrorism cold is an unobtainable goal. At least democracies have one special advantage: Because democracies offer peaceful avenues for change, public opinion can backlash against terrorism, however worthy the cause may seem. As Ted Robert Gurr has put the matter, terrorist movements in democracies contain the seeds of their own destruction.[60]

Countries can and do upgrade security in areas with mass transportation, at embassies, and at special events such as the World Olympics. On occasion, countries undertake rescues and covert acts on their own. Israel is famous for its successful countermeasures. Israel's celebrated commando raid in Entebbe, Uganda, in 1976 to rescue a planeload of Israeli citizens is the subject of books and movies. Israel also has sent out teams of "hit men" to kill terrorists and launched air strikes against villages where terrorists have originated.

Countries increasingly are coordinating efforts to control terrorists as they are working together in so many other transnational problem areas. Cooperative efforts are not nearly extensive enough, but progress has occurred. For instance, after the kidnapping and murder in 1978 of Christian Democrat leader and five-time prime minister Aldo Moro of Italy by the Red Brigade, a dozen European states formed a close counterterrorist network to coordinate policy and share computerized databases on the backgrounds of terrorists.[61]

INTERNATIONAL ANTI-TERRORISM COOPERATION

Beattie and Copley News Service

A rash of terrorist attacks in the mid-1990s prompted the Group of Seven (G-7) states, as the leading trade states and democracies, plus Russia, to meet in Paris in 1996 to consider improving antiterrorist cooperation. They agreed to a 25-point plan that would help track, capture, and convict terrorists. Specifics include surveillance of bank accounts, front organizations sheltering terrorists, and terrorist communications on the Internet. The G-7 states also will ease extradition, crack down on forged travel documents, and restrict access to firearms and explosives. At this G-7 meeting, Japan announced an Asian-Pacific antiterrorist meeting in the near future.

At the same time, President Bill Clinton proposed changes in U.S. law to help constrain terrorism. He wanted authorities to have easier access to information from telephone companies and hotels, prosecute terrorists under racketeering laws that allow the seizure of their money, place "taggants" (chemical markers) in explosives to make bombs more traceable, and expand wiretapping powers. Wiretapping powers especially rankle some members of Congress, who fear imposition on the freedoms of the general public.

Perhaps the most useful step international society can take is to treat terrorism as a heinous "universal crime," calling for each state to either punish or extradite a terrorist. Historically, this principle of international law has applied to slavers and pirates. A series of treaties against terrorism have evolved, especially concerning the "skyjacking" of planes, but international cooperative efforts suffer from the political perspectives of states that color the situation. An individual who is a "terrorist" to one state may be a "freedom fighter" with a just cause to another.[62] Few states are free of this problem of political coloration. Even the U.S. government, with its solid stand against all terrorism, finds some of its Irish American citizens sympathetic to the IRA cause. These American citizens sometimes pressure Washington not to extradite IRA suspects to Great Britain. For many individuals, and probably a few governments, terrorism remains an acceptable means of force to achieve political goals.

Churches

States and churches, as international actors, frequently interact since they share the loyalty and represent the interests of many of the same people. At the transnational level, the Roman Catholic Church, Protestant churches represented by the World Council of Churches, the Islamic church, and the Jewish church are important actors.

The Roman Catholic Church has a long history of political involvement, including the appointment of the Holy Roman Emperor in the Middle Ages. The Catholic Church was always ready to regulate affairs of kings. In 1494, the pope, in the Treaty of Tordesillas, drew a line on the globe 1,100 miles west of the Cape Verde Islands. The lands discovered west of the line went to Spain, and those east of the line belonged to Portugal. This arrangement averted war between the two states. As recently as 1979, the Catholic Church mediated a dispute between Argentina and Chile over the ownership of the Beagle Islands.

Although Pope John Paul II, the current pope, was active in the liberalization of communist Europe in the 1980s, the Roman Catholic Church has increasingly turned its attention to the Third World. By the year 2000, 70 percent of Catholics will live in states of the Third World.[63] Two prominent issues have been at the center of the Church's new Third World focus. Although many social scientists regard most countries of the Third World as overpopulated, the Catholic Church has staunchly opposed birth control and abortion. In 1994, the Catholic Church allied with Muslims at the World Population Conference at Cairo, Egypt, to restrict population planning as an element of economic development strategies.

The other issue involves festering conditions of poverty and injustice found in most Third World countries. Some Catholic priests in Latin America, particularly in Brazil, have advocated a "liberation theology" supportive of revolution. Although John Paul II has tried to rein in revolutionary activism against authority by priests, the Church has not hesitated to criticize tyranny and condemn torture. In the Philippines case in 1986, John Paul II left an archbishop free to support peacefully the overthrowal of Ferdinand Marcos.[64]

In 1929, the Roman Catholic Church laid the groundwork for a more effective international role by establishing a secular state at the Vatican in Rome, an interesting and unique step for a church. The Church sends and receives ambassadors as do states in general. The pope also receives heads of state and, in turn, countries meet his visits with the grand ceremonies reserved for heads of state. Pope John Paul II regularly takes advantage of modern travel, and millions of people around the world have been able to see and hear him in person.

There are 300 Protestant denominations in the world, but they assemble into a single actor in the form of the World Council of Churches. Headquartered in Geneva, Switzerland, the World Council of Churches often takes positions on important issues, for example, calling on all churches to identify and expose governments that use torture.[65] The council also has opposed racial injustice in South Africa before that country's white citadel gave way to a black majority government. Support for revolutionary causes with humanitarian aid has been a principal business of the World Council. For instance, the council supported SWAPO, a revolutionary guerrilla group fighting for Namibia's freedom from South Africa. Their aid consisted of blankets and medicine, with the council drawing the line at weapons. Once a democratic arena becomes available for a group to pursue its objectives, the World Council suspends support for that group.

The evangelical wing of Protestant churches has grown in recent years, not only in missionary efforts for religious conversion but, similar to the Catholic Church, to promote socioeconomic reform. Oddly, revolutionaries in poor countries sometimes attack or kidnap evangelical missionaries. Charles Quarles explains this strange behavior as a fear by the revolutionaries that evangelical aid, such as food and health care, will cool the ardor of peasant populations for revolution. He claims more than half of the Americans abducted by terrorists are missionaries. Using a grant from the Evangelical Foreign Missions Association, Quarles has set up an information service known as "Project-Safe." This service can make daily risk assessments about an area for missionaries.

The Islamic religion, founded in the seventh century A.D., spread with missionary fervor from Saudi Arabia westward across North Africa and into Spain. In an easterly direction, Islam reached across the Indian subcontinent into Southeast Asia. Many of the states that formed in these regions accepted the Quran, the Islamic bible, as their secular law. A pan-Islamic movement has struggled to survive, but deep religious and cultural division fragment this effort. A bitter, centuries-old theological rivalry continues between the Sunni and Shi'a sects. Muslims also experience division because they include diverse ethnic groups such as Arabs, Kurds, Malay peoples of Southeast Asia, Persians in Iran, and Turks.

Islamic political effects are easy to find. As already mentioned, the Iranian-Iraqi War of the 1980s was particularly conflictual because these countries had Shi'a and Sunni leaderships. In addition, the Shi'as of Iran have supported terrorism in Lebanon directed at Western targets, including the truck bomb that took the lives of 241 U.S. Marines in 1983. Some acts of terrorism in the Middle East and elsewhere have been the blows of radical Islamic fundamentalists, mostly from Arab countries. These fundamentalists demand reforms by their governments and punish the West for what they perceive as intrusive support for illicit Arab governments. Finally, during the Yugoslavian breakup, concern arose that Islamic countries, Turkey in particular, might intervene to aid Bosnian Muslims hard-pressed by Serbian militias between 1992 and 1996.[66]

People of the Jewish faith lived as minorities in other peoples' countries during the centuries between the loss of Israel (Palestine) as a homeland in the first century A.D. and the establishment of Israel in 1948. Babylonian conquest first scattered Jews outside Israel about 800 B.C., an event known as the Jewish Diaspora; then Rome's crackdown on the Jews' revolt in 70 A.D. sent more Jews into exile. The *Zionist* movement, based on an INGO organized in the nineteenth century, developed to return Jews to Palestine and enjoyed much success in this effort after the Second World War. Despite the United Nations obligation to Palestinian Arabs to protect Palestine as a Trust, administered by the United Kingdom, two million Jewish refugees, having survived Nazi genocide, entered Palestine illegally. In 1948, during the first of several wars with Arab peoples, newly arrived Jewish settlers established the state of Israel after driving many Palestinians out of their homeland.

At long last, Jewish people had a state to protect Jewish people and to speak for world Jewry, although at Palestinian expense. One factor favoring Israel has been its close friendship with the United States. American recognition in 1948, along with American money and arms, have sustained Israel over the years through its several wars with Arab states, states that surround Israel on three sides. Since the oil crisis of 1973, however, the United States has moved closer to a middle position between Israel and the Arab states to serve as a peace broker. A more recent goal of the United States is to help Palestinians establish a homeland of their own. It was due to the United States' influence that Israel began negotiating directly with the Palestinians in 1992.

President Bill Clinton, in a 1996 meeting with Prime Minister Benjamin Netanyahu of the hard-line Likud Party, barely victorious in a 1996 Israeli election, made it clear that he was unhappy with Israel's new Palestinian policy. Netanyahu halted the prior policy of the Labor Party of "trading land for peace." The West Bank, an Israeli-occupied territory taken from Jordan in the Six Day War of 1967, was on its way to becoming a self-ruled homeland for Palestinians until the 1996 election brought the Likud Party to power. Prime Minister Netanyahu, by radically changing the terms of this peace process and restarting construction of Israeli settlements in the West Bank, may be sowing the seeds for more war instead of breaking the cycles of war between Israeli and Arab peoples.

In addition to Israel, the World Jewish Congress can speak out about issues affecting Jewish people, about half of whom still live as minorities in other peoples' countries. For instance, when the World Jewish Congress objected to a candidate for the German presidency in 1993 because of his tolerant views of the Nazi holocaust, Chancellor Helmut Kohl took the position that the German presidency was not the business of the World Jewish Congress. Nevertheless, the State of Israel and world Jewry try to spike any threat or animosity directed at Jewish people. Understandably, Jews have some paranoia about their survival as a people, as a culture, and as a state that Zionism had long sought to achieve. Hitler's genocide sought to take all of these away.

MULTIPLE ACTORS AND INTERNATIONAL SOCIETY

If one characteristic of modern international relations rivals the importance of tightening interdependence, especially of the economic kind, it may be the rise of multiple actors. The lasting influence of the realist model of international relations, with its state focus, slowed scholars' recognition of this important development, however. Hans Morgenthau's *Politics Among Nations,* the realists' "bible," rendered the study of international relations state-centric. For him, because power and authority channeled through the states, states were the "ultimate points of reference." Morgenthau believed that only if state leaders make rational choices about state interests, meaning power enhancement and security, does the study of international relations have a phenomenon with enough regularity to permit the development of theory. Yet Morgenthau does recognize that nothing prohibits the replacement of the state by some larger unit with different characteristics, though he fails to predict what this entity might be.[67]

Morgenthau's classic text does refer to international organizations, but his view is that international organizations exist mostly for *state convenience.* States need organizations to smooth their numerous contacts brought about by modern circumstances, such as international air travel, which resulted in the International Civil Aviation Organization. Besides offering states some convenience, international organizations merely reflect the power of states, such as when the winners of the Second World War became veto-casting members of the UN Security Council. And international courts, such as the International Court of Justice, using primitive, uncertain international law, are weak in the face of state authority and cannot define justice among states.[68]

Neorealists, led by Kenneth N. Waltz, have been intent on defending the role of the state in the face of theoretical challenges. Sometimes they give nonstate actors short shrift even more than the earlier realists did. However, growing empirical evidence forced scholars to give some attention to the role of nonstate actors, at least IGOs, as early as the 1950s and 1960s during the heyday of the realist paradigm.[69] Noteworthy is Inis Claude's *Swords Into Plowshares,* first published in 1956. This book was a careful description of the United Nations and the international organization movement, and it raised the question of whether international organizations would draw functions and authority away from states.[70] Then, in the 1970s, Raymond Vernon called attention to the growing power of the MNC in his book *Sovereignty at Bay,* which criticized the MNC for penetrating and exploiting weak states of the Third World.[71]

Regardless of growing attention to nonstate actors, Waltz's 1979 *Theory of International Politics* remains unaffected by the claim that the world has become a mixed-actor one. For instance, he makes only two brief references in his book to the United Nations, surely a nonstate actor of some weight.[72] Waltz's concentration is on the power structure among the major states in a given period and the consequences of that structure for peace. For him, nonstate actors are largely incidental and adjust to what major states do.

Robert O. Keohane and Joseph S. Nye drew attention to nonstate actors as much as any scholars did in their 1972 work *Transnational Relations and World Politics.*[73] They raised a serious question about how well realism could continue to match a changing world. Professors Keohane and Nye recognized that new actors were playing important roles in a transnational context on matters besides security and power. Their conceptual scheme on transnational actors still shapes descriptions of these actors, including those found in this chapter.

Complementing their first work on transnational matters, Keohane and Nye added *Power and Interdependence* in the mid-1970s and brought it out again as a second edition in 1989. They stressed the interdependence of the world and a growing array of new issues, unsolvable by force, that were challenging states and required the cooperation of states. In particular, Professors Keohane and Nye recognized a role for international organizations that went beyond Hans Morgenthau's "state convenience." To Keohane and Nye, the international organization became an important necessity by helping with state bargaining, arranging agendas for conferences, and serving as a catalyst for global policies. These global policies include direction and action on the environment, food shortages, trade and currency matters, ocean regulation, and many other issue-areas of concern to state and nonstate actors alike.[74]

Further, Keohane and Nye found that weak states were joining the strong in the *multilateralism* of many-sided policy negotiations. Prior to the mid-twentieth century, if not later, strong states traditionally decided and weak states acquiesced in policy decisions. Now most states, at least, have some influence in shaping the norms and rules of policy regimes.[75] Added to this complicated policy brew of strong and weak states and IGOs is the role of INGOs, involving churches, environmental groups, human rights monitors, and many other citizen-activists that lobby with moral force to make an improvable world truly improve.[76]

Shifting to the analytical construct from the first chapter, realists see a dangerous *international anarchy,* one prone to war, and call for powerful states to balance one another if peace is to prevail. States must focus on amassing power and occasionally use it in war to give realists grist for their theoretical mill. If states do arise to avert the Hobbesian twin catastrophes of civil war and international anarchy, as Bruce Porter claims in *War and the Rise of the State,*[77] can they ever be anything but an actor with a security motive? Time has proven they can be.

Despite a concentration on powerful states by realists and neorealists, slippage in the importance and change in the nature of the state seem undeniable. States now pursue goals that take them well past the simple concerns of national security and the accumulation of military power. They depend on one another for the prosperity trade brings and work together for other goals their democratically empowered citizens insist on accomplishing. Hundreds of IGOs and thousand of INGOs, as nonstate *actors,* help states set agendas and press states to cooperate, whether the goal is saving tropical forests or people from torture. Guided by common needs and growing networks of cooperation, the multiple actors of the world are pulling together into an *international society,* or at least the early stage of one.[78]

However, concerning the role of *actors,* the world falls well short of an *international community* calling for an *orientation* of close, positive interaction among multiple actors with a strong sense of common identification. Some rogue states resist the growing rules and norms of international society, and weak states collapse into turmoil. Many states face the centripetal pull of ethnic actors. Some of these ethnies want more autonomy, while others desire complete independence, or they drift into violence without clear goals. Sometimes the results are civil war, as in Bosnia in 1992–1996, or chaotic, murderous rampages, as in Rwanda in 1995. Shoring up the importance of the state and recalling the state's original security function is the role of international terrorism. Mass fear, caused by the seemingly capricious and violent acts against the innocent around the world, militates against a strong sense of world community.

In summary, positive developments currently outweigh negative ones in the mixed-actor world. Today the major states meet in trade conferences such as the G-7 and draw Russia to their meetings, encouraging their old enemy to democratize its government and privatize its economy. The cooperative patterns of the major states, along with the role of most IGOs and INGOs, are much more fundamental and important in the world than the headline-grabbing turbulence caused by ethnic conflict and the dastardly acts of terrorists. Hence, we can claim the world is an improving place at the turn of the 21st century, at least compared to the Cold War days.

CHAPTER SUMMARY

The world has grown more complex with new actors joining the states on the world stage. The new actors, especially ethnic groups, sometimes rival the states for the loyalty of people, while international organizations occasionally encroach on services once provided only by the states. Although states are no longer the dominant actors, they remain the primary actors in the world, and their numbers reflect a dramatic increase across the twentieth century. The continued demise of the state is not inevitable. Fighting terrorism partly shores up the state's traditional security function and renews the need for states. Yet, increasingly, states and their citizens are finding that states best retain usefulness when they cooperate with one another to tackle new, complex problems.

One group of actors newly recognized as important are substate actors. These actors, such as ethnic groups, cities, and individuals, arise from the domestic context of states to acquire transnational roles. Ethnic groups have conflicts that spill across borders. Cities in one country negotiate with cities in other countries. Individual leaders decide on new foreign policies, or individuals, as private citizens, can become important symbols of causes with international effects.

IGOs, with their state memberships, bring states together on the same forum and induce them to follow mutually helpful agendas. They also persuade states to look beyond traditional security concerns and work together to benefit the lives of their various citizenries, such as when they collectively fight diseases or improve human rights. The World Health Organization and the European Court of Human Rights are ready examples.

INGOs have proliferated faster than any other actor, especially since the Second World War. Citizen concerns over the environment, health, human rights, disarmament, and other issues have spawned thousands of transnational private groups that lobby for many reforms. These private organizations, in pushing for results, simultaneously approach their national governments and the multiple forums of IGOs as found in the UN System.

An international society, like any society, requires citizens. The "citizens" of today's international society are not only states, and certainly not just the most powerful states, but IGOs, INGOs, and substate actors. The majority of these actors seek ways to improve the world they share and are realizing the value of cooperation. Exceptions are the radical changes some ethnic groups and all terrorists demand. These actors, though sometimes drawing sympathy, frequently cause violence and turmoil that undermine a sense of international community.

POINTS OF VIEW

Militant nationalism is on the rise, transforming the healthy pride of nations, tribes, religious and ethnic groups into cancerous prejudice, eating away at states and leaving their people addicted to the political painkillers of violence and demagoguery.
—WORLD PRESS REVIEW, JUNE 1994, P. 28

Despite their own suffering, the Croats have plotted—with Serbia—the butchery of Bosnia. Like the Serbs, they have exposed themselves as dirty, rotten cheats—eager to inflict on Bosnia a punishment worse than that heaped on Croatia by Serbia.
—PAUL MCGEOUGH, SYDNEY MORNING HERALD

From Pakistan to Morocco, the battle for the Muslim soul is heating up. It is a context between two versions of political Islam: one pro-American, the other anti-imperialist. One is sponsored by Saudi Arabia; the other draws inspiration from Iran.
—NEW STATESMAN AND SOCIETY, LONDON

Historiography today deals with the situation and with the leader as with the egg and the chicken: They nourish each other, influence each other and together determine the course of history.
—MAARIV, JERUSALEM

You cannot hope to build a better world without improving the individuals. To that end each of us must work for his own improvement, and at the same time share a general responsibility for all humanity.
—MARIE CURIE, POLISH SCIENTIST (1867–1934)

REVIEW QUESTIONS

1. What is meant by the statement that the state is the *primary* actor instead of the *dominant* actor?
2. What are regimes? Are they actors? Explain.
3. Why do state and ethnic actors tend to conflict? What options do states have to deal with ethnic groups?
4. What activities of cities, normally seen as substate actors, demonstrate that cities can be transnational actors?
5. Under what conditions can both individual leaders and private citizens be important international actors?
6. Do you think MNCs do as much good as harm in countries of the Third World? Explain.
7. What is implied by the designation of "freedom fighters" rather than "terrorist"?
8. What are some causes of terrorism? How successful are terrorists in achieving their goals?
9. Describe the political roles of the various churches. Why can we say the Islamic faith contains important divisions?
10. Is the interaction of multiple actors mostly positive or negative in the world today? Explain.

GLOSSARY

consociational society Power sharing in ethnically divided countries using such institutional methods as federalism, proportional representation, cultural autonomy, and a council of elites as an executive drawn from the various ethnies.

ethnic group A collective of people, based on cultural identifications such as language and religion, who see themselves as a special group and are seen by others as a recognizable collective.

ethnic nationalism A strong sense of group awareness that is based on sociological identifications, such as tribe or language, and calls for an adamant assertion of the group's interests.

intermestic politics The merger of domestic and international politics.

international government organization (IGO) An international organization with a membership based on states.

international nongovernment organization (INGO) An international organization made up of private individuals or associations.

international organization A formal institution of private parties or states that transcends national boundaries and facilitates cooperation among its members.

irredentism The desire of a people of a state to annex territory from an adjoining state where their ethnic kinfolk reside.

multinational corporation (MNC) A business enterprise designed for profit in which ownership, management, production, and sales activities extend over several or more national jurisdictions

political actor An individual or a group that "plays a role" by seeking a goal in a political context.

regime A set of rules, norms, and decision-making procedures around which actor expectations converge.

secession A process in which a part of a state withdraws or attempts to withdraw to form a new state.

substate actor A political actor that usually operates below the sovereign level of a state within the domestic political arena but today often transcends national boundary lines.

terrorism Violence calculated to create an atmosphere of fear and alarm, thereby conditioning governments to accede to the demands of the agents of violence.

RECOMMENDED READINGS

Nazih N. M. Ayubi. *Political Islam: Religion and Politics in the Arab World.* New York: Routledge, 1991.

Gurutz Jauregui Bereciartu. *Decline of the Nation-State.* Reno: University of Nevada Press, 1994.

Cindy C. Combs. *Terrorism in the Twenty-First Century.* Upper Saddle River, NJ: Prentice Hall, 1997.

Deborah J. Gerner. *One Land, Two Peoples: The Conflict Over Palestine.* Boulder, CO: Westview Press, 1994.

Jean-Marie Guehenno. *The End of the Nation-State.* Minneapolis: University of Minnesota Press, 1995.

Ted Robert Gurr and Barbara Harff. *Ethnic Politics in World Politics.* Boulder, CO: Westview Press, 1994.

Eric O. Hanson. *The Catholic Church in World Politics.* Princeton, NJ: Princeton University Press, 1987.

Heidi H. Hobbs. *City Hall Goes Abroad.* Thousand Oaks, CA: Sage Publications, 1994.

Donald L. Horowitz. *Ethnic Groups in Conflict.* Berkeley, CA: University of California Press, 1985.

John Hutchinson and Anthony D. Smith, eds. *Nationalism.* Oxford: Oxford University Press, 1994.

Robert A. Isaak. *Individuals and World Politics.* North Scituate, MA: Duxbury Press, 1975.

Stephen D. Krasner. *International Regimes.* Ithaca, NY: Cornell University Press, 1983.

Daniel Patrick Moynihan. *Pandemonium: Ethnicity in International Politics.* New York: Oxford University Press, 1993.

William Pfaff. *The Wrath of Nations.* New York: Simon & Schuster, 1993.

James N. Rosenau. *Turbulence in World Politics: A Theory of Change and Continuity.* Princeton, NJ: Princeton University Press, 1990. Chapters 6 and 9.

Clare Sterling. *The Terror Network: The Secret War of International Terrorism.* New York: Holt, Rinehart and Winston, 1981.

Phillip Taylor. *Nonstate Actors in International Politics: From Transregional to Substate Organizations.* Boulder, CO: Westview Press, 1984.

Vernon Van Dyke. *Human Rights, Ethnicity, and Discrimination.* Westport, CT: Greenwood Press, 1985.

Michel Wieviorka. *The Making of Terrorism.* Chicago: University of Chicago Press, 1993.

Peter Willetts. *"The Conscience of the World": The Influence of Non-Governmental Organizations in the UN System Governmental Organisations.* Washington, D.C.: Brookings Institution, 1996.

Joanne Wright. *Terrorist Propaganda: The Red Army Faction and the Provisional IRA 1968–1986.* New York: St. Martin's Press, 1991.

ENDNOTES

1. Richard W. Mansbach, Yale H. Ferguson, and Donald E. Lampert, *The Web of World Politics: Nonstate Actors in the Global System* (Englewood Cliffs, NJ: Prentice Hall, 1976), pp. 25–29; James E. Dougherty and Robert L. Pfaltzgraff, Jr., *Contending Theories of International Relations,* 3rd ed. (New York: Harper & Row, 1990), pp. 25–26.

2. Richard W. Mansbach and John A. Vasquez, *In Search of Theory: A New Paradigm for Global Politics* (New York: Columbia University Press, 1981), pp. 7–9, 159.

3. Donald J. Puchala and Stuart I. Fagan, "International Politics in the 1970s: The Search for a Perspective," *Globalism versus Realism: International Relations' Third Debate,* ed. Ray Maghroori and Bennett Ramberg (Boulder, CO: Westview Press, 1982), pp. 40–44.

4. Amitai Etzioni, *Political Unification: A Comparative Study of Leaders and Forces* (New York: Holt, Rinehart and Winston, 1965). See also Robert Gilpin, "The Global Political System," in *Order and Violence,* ed. J. D. B. Miller and R. J. Vincent (Oxford: Clarendon Press, 1990), pp. 122–24; Hedley Bull, "The State's Positive Role in World Affairs," in *The State,* ed. Stephen R. Graubard (New York: W. W. Norton, 1979), p. 115.

5. Deon Geldenhuys, *Isolated States: A Comparative Analysis* (New York: Cambridge University Press, 1990).

6. John H. Herz, "The Rise and Demise of the Territorial State," in *The Nation-State and the Crisis of World Politics,* ed. John H. Herz (New York: David McKay, 1976), pp. 99–123.

7. John H. Herz, "The Territorial State Revisited—Reflections on the Future of the Nation-State," in *The Nation-State and the Crisis of World Politics,* pp. 226–52.

8. Vincent Cable, "The Diminished Nation-State: A Study in the Loss of Economic Power," *Daedalus: What Future for the State?* Spring 1995, pp. 23–53.

9. Geoff Eley, "War and the Twentieth-Century State," *Daedalus,* Spring 1995, p. 171; John Lukacs, *The End of the Twentieth Century and the End of the Modern Age* (New York: Ticknor and Fields, 1993), Chapter 9, especially p. 269; Ted Robert Gurr, Keith Jaggers, and Will H. Moore, "The Transformation of the Western State: The Growth of Democracy, Autocracy, and State Power Since 1800," *Studies in Comparative International Development,* Spring 1990, pp. 73–108.

10. This CIA study is not yet available to the public, though it was reported in *U.S. News and World Report,* May 6, 1996, p. 46.

11. Susan Strange, "The Defective State," *Daedalus,* Spring 1995, pp. 55–74, quote from p. 57.
12. The Stanley Foundation, "The UN System and NGOs: New Relationships for a New Era," *Report of the Twenty-Fifth United Nations Issues Conference,* February 18–20, 1994, p. 8.
13. Chadwick F. Alger, "Local Individual and Community Participation in World Society," in *The Power of Human Needs in World Society,* ed. Roger A. Coate and Jerel A. Rosati (Boulder, CO: Lynne Rienner Publishers, 1989), p. 122.
14. Similar points are made in James N. Rosenau, *Turbulence in World Politics: A Theory of Change and Continuity* (Princeton, NJ: Princeton University Press, 1990), pp. 127–28. See also Ivo D. Duchack, "Toward a Typology of New Subnational Governmental Actors in International Relations" (Working paper 87-2, University of California at Berkeley, Institute of Governmental Studies, May 1987), pp. 1–19.
15. Ted Robert Gurr and James R. Scarritt, "Minority Rights at Risk: A Global Survey," *Human Rights Quarterly,* August 1989, pp. 381, 390.
16. Ted Robert Gurr, "Ethnic Warfare and the Changing Priorities of Global Security," *Mediterranean Quarterly: A Journal of Global Issues,* Winter 1990, p. 85.
17. Cynthia Enloe, *Ethnic Conflict and Political Development* (Boston: Little, Brown, 1973), pp. 263–70.
18. Milton J. Esman, "Economic Performance and Ethnic Conflict," in *Conflict and Peacekeeping in Multiethnic Society,* ed. Joseph V. Montville (Lexington, MA: Lexington Books, 1990), p. 480.
19. Ted Robert Gurr, *Minorities at Risk: A Global View of Ethnopolitical Conflicts* (Washington, D.C.: United States Institute Press, 1993), pp. 132–35.
20. Lance Morrow, *Time,* April 12, 1993, p. 84.
21. Donald Horowitz, "Ethnic and Nationalist Conflict," in *World Security: Challenges for a New Century,* ed. Michael T. Klare and Daniel C. Thomas (New York: St. Martin's Press, 1994), pp. 175–87.
22. Herman C. Kelman, "Violence Without Moral Restraint: Reflections on the De-Humanization of Victims and Victimizers," *Journal of Social Issues* 29, no. 4 (1973), pp. 25–61; Hurst Hannum, *Autonomy, Sovereignty, and Self-Determination: The Accommodation of Conflicting Rights* (Philadelphia: University of Pennsylvania Press, 1990), p. 10.
23. Gurr, *Minorities at Risk,* pp. 122–25.
24. Hannum, *Autonomy, Sovereignty, and Self-Determination,* pp. 453–54.
25. Gurr and Scarritt, "Minority Rights at Risk," p. 385.
26. Morton H. Halperin and David J. Scheffer with Patricia L. Small, *Self-Determination in the New World Order* (Washington, D.C.: Carnegie Endowment for International Peace, 1992).
27. Charles Hauss, *Beyond Confrontation: Transforming the New World Order* (Westport, CT: Praeger, 1996), p. 70.
28. Gurr and Scarritt, "Minority Rights at Risk," p. 375.
29. Antonio Cassese, *Self-Determination of Peoples: A Legal Reappraisal* (New York: Cambridge University Press, 1995).
30. Naomi Chazan, ed., *Irredentism and International Politics* (Boulder, CO: Lynne Rienner Publishers, 1990), p. 1.
31. Deborah J. Gerner, *One Land, Two Peoples: The Conflict Over Palestine* (Boulder, CO: Westview Press, 1991).
32. Arend Lijphart, *Democracy in Plural Societies: A Comparative Exploration* (New Haven, CT: Yale University Press, 1977).
33. Exceptions are Chadwick F. Alger, "The World Relations of Cities: Closing the Gap Between Social Science Paradigms and Everyday Human Experience," *International Studies Quarterly,* December 1990. See also Heidi H. Hobbs, *City Hall Goes Abroad* (Thousand Oaks, CA: Sage Publications, 1994).
34. Michael Schuman, "Dateline Main Street: Local Foreign Policies," *Foreign Policy,* Winter 1986–1987, pp. 154–74.
35. Alger, "The World Relation of Cities," pp. 493–500, 513.
36. Robert A. Isaak, *Individuals and World Politics* (North Scituate, MA: Duxbury Press, 1975), pp. 258–60.
37. Harvey Starr, "The Kissinger Years: Studying Individuals and Foreign Policy," in *Choices in World Politics: Sovereignty and Interdependence,* ed. Bruce Russett, Harvey Starr, and Richard J. Stoll (New York: W. H. Freeman, 1989),

pp. 181–205; Walter Isaacson, *Kissinger: A Biography* (New York: Simon & Schuster, 1992).
38. Robert G. Kaiser, "Gorbachev: Triumph and Failure," *Foreign Affairs,* Spring 1991, pp. 160–74; David Halberstam, *The Next Century* (New York: William Morrow, 1991), pp. 19–29.
39. Rosenau, *Turbulence in World Politics,* pp. 120–21.
40. Marvin S. Soroos, *Beyond Sovereignty: The Challenge of Global Policy* (Columbia, SC: University of South Carolina Press, 1986), pp. 81–82.
41. Harold K. Jacobon, "The Nature of International Organizations," in *Choices in World Politics,* p. 38.
42. Howard Tolley, Jr., *The U.N. Commission on Human Rights* (Boulder, CO: Westview Press, 1987), pp. 203–5, 216–17.
43. Robert O. Keohane, *International Institutions and State Power: Essays in International Relations Theory* (Boulder, CO: Westview Press, 1989), p. 101; Stephen D. Krasner, ed., *International Regimes* (Ithaca, NY: Cornell University Press, 1983); James F. Keeley, "The Latest Wave: A Critical Review of Regime Literature," in *World Politics: Power, Interdependence & Dependence,* ed. David G. Haglund and Michael K. Hawes (Toronto: Harcourt Brace Jovanovich, 1990), p. 554.
44. Robert O. Keohane, *After Hegemony* (Princeton, NJ: Princeton University Press, 1984), p. 9.
45. Joseph S. Nye, Jr., "Political Lessons of the New Law of the Sea Regime," in *Choices in World Politics,* pp. 284–86.
46. "The UN System and NGOs," p. 3.
47. Robert Gilpin, *The Political Economy of International Relations* (Princeton, NJ: Princeton University Press, 1987), p. 232.
48. Strange, "The Defective State," p. 59.
49. Gilpin, *The Political Economy of International Relations,* p. 231.
50. Conway W. Henderson, "Multinational Corporations and Human Rights in Developing States," *World Affairs,* Summer 1979, pp. 17–30; Joan Edelman Spero, *The Politics of International Economic Relations,* 3rd ed. (New York: St. Martin's Press, 1985), Chapter 8; Gilpin, *The Political Economy of International Relations,* Chapter 6.
51. Gilpin, *The Political Economy of International Relations,* p. 248; Dougherty and Pfaltzgraff, *Contending Theories of International Relations,* p. 254.
52. David Leyton-Brown, "The Roles of Multinational Enterprise," in *World Politics: Power, Interdependence, & Dependence,* pp. 228–30; Gilpin, *The Political Economy of International Relations,* p. 252.
53. Isaiah Frank, *Foreign Enterprises in Developing Countries* (Baltimore: John Hopkins Press, 1980), pp. 144, 161.
54. Spero, *The Politics of International Economic Relations,* pp. 280–87.
55. This definition is similar to the definition used by many writers, including Brian M. Jenkins, "International Terrorism: The Other War," in *International Terrorism: Characteristics, Causes, Controls,* ed. Charles W. Kegley, Jr. (New York: St. Martin's Press, 1990), p. 30.
56. *The 1995 Pinkerton Annual Risk Assessment* (Arlington, VA: Pinkerton, 1996).
57. Eric Hoffer, *The True Believer: Thoughts on the Nature of Mass Movements* (New York: New American Library, 1951).
58. Richard M. Pearlstein, *The Mind of the Political Terrorist* (Wilmington, DE: Scholarly Resources, 1991), pp. 171–72; Jerrold M. Post, "Terrorist Psycho-logic: Terrorist Behavior as a Product of Psychological Forces," in *Origins of Terrorism: Psychologies, Ideologies, Theologies, States of Mind,* ed. Walter Reich (Cambridge, England: Cambridge University Press, 1990), pp. 25–40; Martha Crenshaw, "The Causes of Terrorism," in *International Terrorism: Characteristics, Causes, Controls,* pp. 120–23.
59. Quote from *Time,* May 6, 1996, p. 52.
60. Ted Robert Gurr, "Terrorism in Democracies: Its Social and Political Bases," in *Origins of Terrorism,* p. 102.
61. Donna M. Schlagheck, *International Terrorism: An Introduction to the Concepts and Actors* (Lexington, MA: D. C. Heath, 1988), pp. 63–66.
62. Schlagheck, *International Terrorism,* pp. 120–25.
63. Eric O. Hanson, *The Catholic Church in World Politics* (Princeton, NJ: Princeton University Press, 1987), p. 4.
64. Bryan Johnson, *The Four Days of Courage: The Untold Story of the People Who Brought Marcos*

Down (New York: The Free Press, 1987), Chapter 4.
65. Joan Dassin, ed., *Torture in Brazil* (New York: Vintage Books, 1986), Appendix II, pp. 230–34.
66. For an interesting case study of the Islamic religion at work in a political context, see Joyce N. Wiley, *The Islamic Movement of Iraqi Shi'as* (Boulder, CO: Lynne Rienner Publishers, 1992).
67. Hans Morgenthau, *Politics Among Nations,* 5th ed. (New York: Alfred A. Knopf, 1978), pp. 5, 10.
68. Ibid., pp. 281, 325–28, 444.
69. See the interesting discussion in Richard W. Mansbach and John A. Vasquez, *In Search of Theory: A New Paradigm for Global Politics* (New York: Columbia University Press, 1981), Chapter 5.
70. Inis Claude, *Swords into Plowshares,* 4th ed. (New York: Random House, 1971).
71. Raymond Vernon, *Sovereignty at Bay* (New York: Basic Books, 1971). See also Richard J. Barnet and Ronald E. Muller, *Global Reach: The Power of the Multinationals* (New York: Simon and Schuster, 1974).
72. Kenneth N. Waltz, *Theory of International Politics* (Reading, MA: Addison-Wesley, 1979), pp. 42, 164.
73. Robert O. Keohane and Joseph S. Nye, *Transnational Relations and World Politics* (Cambridge, MA: Harvard University Press, 1972).
74. Robert O. Keohane and Joseph S. Nye, *Power and Interdependence,* 2nd ed. (Boston: Scott, Foresman, 1989), pp. 35–37.
75. Ibid., pp. 36, 268–82.
76. Peter Willetts, *"The Conscience of the World": The Influence of Non-Governmental Organizations in the UN System* (Washington, D.C.: Brookings Institution, 1996).
77. Bruce D. Porter, *War and the Rise of the State* (New York: The Free Press, 1994).
78. Soroos, *Beyond Sovereignty,* pp. 75–76.

PART TWO

THE INSTRUMENTS OF INTERNATIONAL RELATIONS

CHAPTER 4

DEFINING POWER IN A NEW ERA

For many international specialists, the subject of this chapter, power, is the "life's blood" of international politics. They see states colliding in an anarchical world where might makes right and the outcome of struggle is mostly a consequence of the relative power of the combatants. Many of these scholars accept the realist paradigm, including the assumption that states are doomed to live with the threat of war. Realists, both scholars and policymakers, believe the best chance for states to achieve the all-important goal of security is through the pursuit of power. Hans Morgenthau, a leading realist, always maintained that international politics is of necessity power politics.[1]

In recent years, the nature of power and the goals sought through power have undergone significant change. A basic purpose for this chapter is to provide understanding for these changes. This understanding is important for our assessment of the current era and where it belongs on the cooperation continuum. For no other subject has the end of the Cold War been as pronounced and far reaching as it has for power. We wish to know if the post–Cold War period really is a new age leading toward an international society with an emphasis on persuasion and cooperation. We will learn that states still compete and even conflict, but most states today, continuing a trend begun in the Cold War, are more prone to use persuasion instead of force.[2] And with the Cold War over, concerned states are freer to deal collectively with threats to the peace.

This chapter will help us to understand power as a concept and the changing role of power in the post–Cold War era. First, we examine the meaning of power and identify its special dimensions. Next, we look at the measurement of power and the wide range of elements that contribute to power. Then we analyze the international power structure to see the role of power as it operates on a global scale. Next, we examine the changing faces of power to see whether power is changing in nature and in a way that promotes a desirable international society, the subject of the final section of this chapter.

THE MEANING OF POWER

Power is an elusive concept with many subtleties; yet its role is so central to international relations that an understanding of power is critical for a student of this subject. We define **power** as the capacity of one actor to persuade or coerce another, thus allowing for the control of that actor.[3] Power can be either *soft* or *hard*.

Soft power is the capacity to persuade another actor to do something through influence. The appeal of a country's ideology, culture, prestige, or success may result in that country becoming a leader to others that willingly follow.[4] The United States today, for example, as a champion of democracy and capitalism, enjoys soft power. From the post–Second World War years to the present, leaders of the United States have had influence with other democracies and have stamped their economic and political values on international institutions, for instance, the General Agreement on Tariffs and Trade and the World Bank.

Japan is the preeminent example of a country making use of soft power. Japan is unquestionably an economic and technological superpower but has a low profile politically and militarily. Japan is an economic giant but a military dwarf. Yet no major trade state can make an important trade decision without a concern for the reaction of the second largest national economy and the world's most aggressive trade competitor. Japan is the only non-Western member of the Group of Seven, made up of the world's top trade states. Japan has recently taken steps to acquire a stronger political profile by offering the world's largest national foreign aid program, sending unarmed troops to Cambodia for a UN Peacekeeping mission, apologizing for nefarious acts in the Second World War, paying billions of dollars to help with the Persian Gulf War, and showing an interest in a permanent seat on the Security Council of the United Nations. These steps also will add to Japan's influence through soft power.[5]

Hard power is a country's ability to force its will on others through military or economic clout or a combination of the two. Sometimes writers call this kind of power *compellance*, which is the ability of one actor to make another do something it would not otherwise do. For example, economic sanctions in 1990 did not force Iraq to withdraw from Kuwait, but a fierce military attack by the UN coalition forces in 1991 drove the Iraqi army home.

In general, as Joseph S. Nye, Jr., has pointed out, the use of power today has shifted from an emphasis on hard power to a focus on soft power.[6] A growing use of soft power, involving persuasion and influence, underscores the gradual evolution from an anarchical to a societal type of international relations.

Critical to the exercise of power is the compliance of the other actor.[7] If a state asks friends and allies to support a certain position in the United Nations and they do not, persuasion and influence have failed. If horrendous military coercion causes terrible destruction but does not achieve the political objective sought, the use of force has been unsuccessful. After dropping more bombs on North Vietnam in the late 1960s and early 1970s than on Germany during the Second World War, the United States failed to prevent the reunification of North Vietnam with South Vietnam under a communist government.

SPECIAL DIMENSIONS OF POWER

Power is difficult to come to grips with because it is a multidimensional subject. Power is *situational,* since the resources necessary for the exercise of power change from one context to another. Few states are likely to possess all the needed resources. In the Persian Gulf War of 1991, the United States, with its high-tech weapons, took the lead in protecting Saudi Arabia and reversing Iraq's occupation of Kuwait. Yet in 1973, following the Yom Kippur War between Israel and the Arab states, the United States was nearly as vulnerable to the pressures of the oil embargo employed by the Arab countries as the European states were. At the time, the United States imported about half of its oil and used that oil to fuel its automobiles and run much of its industry.

Also, power is always in a *state of change* because of advances in technology. In the latter part of the nineteenth century, a country's capacity for steel production became critical. By the First World War, the weapons of the period, such as steel-hulled ships, tanks, and barbwire for trench warfare, consumed huge amounts of steel. Today the single technology that serves as a proof of power capability is the ability to make computer chips critical to electronic devices used in war.

Power is important only if we understand it as a *relationship* among actors. One state exercising great power within a power vacuum would make no sense. As states interact and engage in conflicts over important interests, they make assessments of their own power as well as that of a potential opponent. As an example, in the power relationship of the Cold War in the 1960s, the Soviet Union was primarily a Eurasian land power without the ability to project power globally as the United States was able to do with B-52 bombers. In 1962, Soviet Premier Nikita Khrushchev unwisely decided to place intermediate-range missiles in Cuba, only 90 miles from the coast of the United States. From Khrushchev's point of view, placing nuclear missiles in Cuba would improve the Soviet–United States power relationship by making it more balanced than before. Unfortunately for Khrushchev, he did not anticipate that President John Kennedy would raise the stakes of this power rivalry. President Kennedy, with Cuba nearby, easily placed massive U.S. military forces in the area and insisted on the removal of the Soviet missiles from Cuba.

The distinction between *actual* and *potential* power is important. Standing military forces are perhaps the most obvious example of actual power. Another example of actual power is a strong currency based on a large gross national product (GNP). GNP is the goods and services a country can produce in a year. The GNP of a country will be extremely important as a source of influence at an economic summit and just as "actual" as military power in wartime. Potential power is capability available at a future time. Australia and Canada are rich in natural resources but have relatively small populations. As they exploit their natural wealth and combine this wealth with growing numbers of people, Australia's and Canada's economic power, and perhaps their military power, will certainly increase in the future.

Closely related to the distinction between actual and potential power is the concern over the *fungibility of power:* To what extent can leaders convert the units of one source of power into the units of another kind of power? Typically, fungible power involves converting economic power to military power or the latter to political power. Japan is an economic superpower that spends only 1 percent of its GNP on armed strength. With its large, high-tech industrial base, Japan, by spending 6 to 8 percent of its GNP on military development, could easily become a major military power. Then, with creditable military power, the Japanese could keep sea lanes open from Japan to the Persian Gulf and other areas rather than counting on the United States to perform this task for them.

Many countries deliberately try to maximize the use of their resources by carefully planning for the fungibility of power. As a specific example, the British, once they had decided to end the Argentine military occupation of the Falkland Islands in 1982, quickly rigged freighters to carry troops below decks and helicopters on the top deck. The military conversion of these freighters was possible because of special designing before the laying of the freighters' keels.

A final dimension of power is the difference between *tangible* and *intangible* power. Tangible power is a resource that is literally touchable and even countable. Steel production, assault rifles, jet planes, computers, good harbors, and much else are tangible. In contrast are concerns that are untouchable or intangible, such as wisdom, willpower, and morale. These intangibles are weighty matters in power calculations that are almost impossible to measure with reliability because they involve attitudes and values of leaders and followers. Nonetheless, intangible factors determine outcomes in contexts as varied as summit conferences and battlefields.

THE MEASUREMENT OF POWER

The central role of power in international relations draws scholars, statesmen, and soldiers alike into efforts to measure power. Observers imply power assessments of states in the names they assign, such as superpowers, great powers, middle-range powers, small powers, and even ministates. These assessments are largely impressionistic, though they may be fairly accurate. States are thought to have different interests, problems, and roles based on their positions in the power hierarchy.[8] For example, at the San Francisco Conference in 1945, held to finish the UN Charter, great powers, middle powers, and small powers wanted different institutions and functions included in the Charter.

To theorize about power, scholars need specific and reliable measures. As a result of the trend to quantify data in the social sciences, it was inevitable that scholars would measure a state's power in numerical terms and then rank states according to their power. Such an index of power represents a composite of the resources and capabilities a given scholar believes will empower states. These indexes may be useful to predict the outcomes of conflicts and wars. One of the better-known power indexes is the creation of Ray S. Cline in *World Power Trends*.[9] He tried to measure both tangible and intangible elements of power in the following manner:

$$\text{Perceived Power} = (\text{Population and Territory \{Critical Mass\}} + \text{Economic Capability} + \text{Military Capability}) \times (\text{Coherent Planning and National Strategy and Will})$$

Or, stated in symbols:

$$Pp = (C + E + M) \times (S + W)$$

Probably better known to scholars is the Correlates of War (COW) project centered at the University of Michigan for over 30 years. COW is an ongoing data collection concerning patterns of war over the last several hundred years and national capabilities based on population size, economic productivity, and military prowess.[10] The systematic study of large sets of data with computer programs moves the international relations field well beyond mere anecdotal evidence and case studies about power and war. For example, now possible in a reasonably exact form are rankings of states based on national power, measures of the distribution of power among the states forming an international system, and assessments of the implications of power arrangements for war.

The Cline and COW measures of power correspond to each other fairly closely overall, but they place some individual states at different ranks in power hierarchies. The fact that there is substantial intermeasure agreement among different measures of power, though they use various elements of power, encourages confidence that power is, in fact, measurable. Further, these measures remain fairly accurate and thus usable, though they contain "soft" elements such as willpower and morale.[11] Although power tends to be somewhat amorphous and difficult to measure, we can dispel the notion that scholars lack the methodological tools to account for power.[12]

While scholars can measure power usefully for countries taken as a whole, predicting the victor in a particular contest of wills and force is as uncertain as predicting the best football team in preseason polls. If war's outcome is unpredictable, a decision to go to war then involves great risk. The Japanese predicated their victory in war on a knockout blow at Pearl Harbor on December 7, 1941. They intended their surprise attack to give them superiority over the United States at least temporarily while they secured their goals across the Pacific region. The Japanese military command had warned the imperial government that Japan would lose the war if the war were not over within a few weeks. The Japanese, counting on a swift victory, underestimated American military resilience and support for the war despite America's bitter defeat at Pearl Harbor. Japan signed an unconditional surrender four years after attacking Pearl Harbor.

Although power resources have varied over time and with circumstances, some elements of power have been persistently important. When shifts in the emphasis on power resources take place, they are due to technological advances and to the choices leaders make as to where and how to apply power as an instrument. Most of what follows concerns the wherewithal of power from the perspective of the state level, remembering our "levels of analysis" from Chapter One.

Physical Factors

Geography favors some countries more than others in permanent ways. The United States has enjoyed two large ocean fronts that have provided a defensive barrier as well as a "fluid highway" for the U.S. navy. The British Channel, a little more than 20 miles wide at one point, saved Great Britain from invasion by Napoleon in the early nineteenth century and by Adolf Hitler in the mid-twentieth century.

The great land mass of Russia (included within the Soviet Union in the communist era) has helped that state defeat several major invasions from the West. As the invading army stretched out its supply lines and strength, the Russian and later the Soviet Army would finally turn on the invader. Only the Mongolian invasion of Russia from the East, led by Genghis Khan (1162–1227), was successful. On the downside, the former Soviet Union, now Russia, has such a cold climate that frozen ports have hampered the development of a blue-water navy with a strategic reach.

Island countries have sometimes been seafaring states with effective navies, but they frequently possess few resources and run a heavy risk of blockade in wartime. A description of Great Britain as a lump of coal with fish swimming around it is not much of an exaggeration. Germany greatly improved the submarine before the First World War with Britain's vulnerabilities as an island country in mind.

At the turn of the last century, geography was so prominent in the power bases of countries that a theoretical approach, **geopolitics,** emerged to account for geography's role in providing power advantages. One of the major geopolitical thinkers was Alfred Thayer Mahan, whose book *The Influence of Seapower on History* (1890)[13] argued that a country with the resources to support a strong navy could be a major power. Sir Halford Mackinder, taking a view supporting land power in *Democratic Ideals and Reality* (1919),[14] surmised that a state controlling the "heartland" of the Eurasian land mass could not only defend itself effectively but also advance outwardly onto other continents.

Developments in rapid communications, air travel, and missilry have undermined the relevance of geopolitics as a theory, but geography is still important in modern international politics. For instance, the traditional "choke points" of the world—the Suez and Panama canals and the Straits of Gibraltar (at the entrance to the Mediterranean Sea), the Straits of Hormuz (at the entrance to the Persian Gulf), and the Straits of Malacca (the narrow passage between Indonesia and Maylaysia)—are still critical. Those who control these choke points can easily stop or permit important movements of trade and military forces.

Another example of the current importance of geography concerns the United States, possessor of the greatest military logistical ability in the world. This country took three months placing enough equipment and personnel in the Persian Gulf to prestage for war and then had to worry about the effects of heat and sand on its high-tech weapons.

Population of a large size may impart power to a state. A country with a population sizable enough to take care of farming, industrial production, transportation, communication, and other critical activities and still field an army of millions is indeed a power worthy of respect. However, a population can be so large, as in Bangladesh, China, or India, that it weighs heavily on the country's resources and may be more of a drawback than an asset. So much the worse if the population is poor, undernourished, and uneducated. A massive-size army does not hold the advantage it once did because nowadays tactical nuclear missiles are available to several or more countries. Based on the experience of the Soviet Union, while still a superpower, and the United States today, the desired population for great power status might be 250 million to 300 million people. Such a population size can easily spare 2 to 3 million people for military service. Obviously, only a few countries have populations of such gigantic size.

European countries with much smaller populations but with a strong industrial base to supply high-tech weapons have still produced creditable, if not impressive, military forces. Small countries also may have a significant military force in terms of size personnel by following a policy called *universal military service (UMS)*. Usually in an UMS system, all young men and women (in some countries) enter military service for one to three years and then are part of a reserve force until they reach middle age. Israel also drafts young women at age 18, and, in fact, women voluntarily have served and still serve in the armed branches of many other countries. Most countries recognize that their populations are an important resource and follow policies to enhance their physical attributes and educational opportunities. As a result, their citizens can make greater contributions to the security and wealth of their countries.

The usefulness of a population as a resource diminishes when elements of that population are at odds with one another. Perhaps the most serious current concern about population is the heightened sense of ethnicity found in many countries. Cultural and racial differences among people have been divisive for decades in many Third World countries and some Western countries. Ethnic problems have recently torn at the unity of a few eastern European countries and also trouble some of the new republics formed from the Soviet Union's dissolution. Ironically, at a time in history when most states are feeling the centripetal pull of cooperative interdependence, the centrifugal force of ethnic autonomy and separatism threatens the national integrity of some states. Such states are less able to cope with international challenges when internal, divisive forces are at work.

Agriculture involves the sector of an economy most likely to receive protection through tariff walls and has stood as a hindrance to further economic integration in international trade. Not only are governments responding to the pressures of farmers who want protection, but governments often want to practice self-reliance concerning food supplies. These governments especially want to guarantee a food supply in time of war.

The United States supports a highly efficient agricultural system that not only feeds its own people and livestock but counts on earning income from the sale of food to other countries. In wartime, the United States has contributed importantly to feeding the civilian populations and armies of allies. Aware of Napoleon's adage that "an army marches on its stomach," military leaders realize that they must transport huge amounts of food over long distances to sustain a military force in the field. Some countries have become much more dependent on imported food than others as they have industrialized and grown in population and as technology has facilitated the storage and shipment of food on a global basis. Great Britain, for example, imports about half of its food daily.

Oil is critical to most states' economies and the manufacture and operation of weapons systems. Nuclear plants have only supplemented the use of oil, leaving industrialized countries dependent on imported oil despite their energy-efficient programs and searches for alternative energy resources. The Organization of Petroleum Exporting Countries (OPEC), centered around the Persian Gulf, influences, when it does not control, the bulk of the world's oil supply in price and availability. OPEC is a *cartel* because it attempts to monopolize, as much as possible, the supply and price of oil in the marketplace.

Of the industrialized countries, only today's Russia is self-sufficient in oil, and Great Britain is nearly self-sufficient since its discovery of oil in the North Sea off the coast of Scotland. The United States has imported up to 50 percent of its oil use, and Japan regularly imports over 90 percent of its energy, mostly oil. Oil dependence creates serious vulnerability with respect to national security, leading many countries to stockpile oil. The United States holds one-half billion barrels of oil in storage in the Strategic Petroleum Reserve. This oil is held in salt domes in southern Louisiana and Texas and is available in case OPEC decisions or war slow or stop the flow of oil from the Persian Gulf and other important oil-exporting areas.

Strategic minerals are imported and placed in stockpiles by many countries because these minerals are critical in some defense applications but are available in only a few places in the world. The United States, for instance, buys chromium, manganese, cobalt, vanadium, and tungsten, along with other minerals, from abroad, and $10 billion worth of these minerals is put in storage as a national defense stockpile. When the Soviet Union was intact, it was rich in strategic minerals because it possessed an adequate supply of most of the important nonfuel minerals of the world.[15] The new state of Russia, because of its huge territory, has inherited most of the Soviet Union's advantage in minerals.

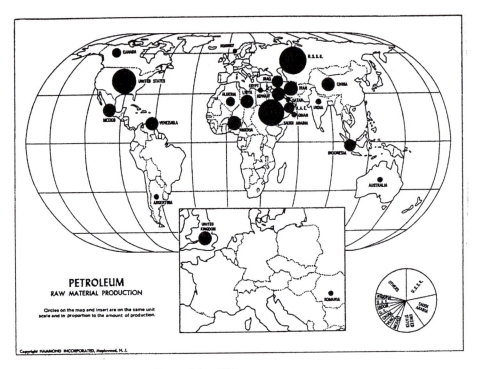

Source: *World Atlas* (Maplewood, NJ: Hammond, Inc., 1991).

Economic Factors

The *gross national product (GNP)*, already defined, is a critical factor in determining the power of a country. A country with a large economy has the industry and technology needed to produce impressively equipped armed forces. A recent theory that has attracted much scholarly attention claims that the rise of a great military power follows from economic ascendency and, conversely, the fall of a great military power results from economic decline.[16] We will return to this subject in a later section of this chapter.

The United States presently sustains the largest GNP in the world and is arguably the only true superpower now in existence if we think of both wealth and military capability together. The Soviet Union was once a distant second to the United States in GNP and probably overstrained its economy to keep up with the United States militarily. The military strength of the Soviet Union before its demise predictably waned following the near-collapse of its economy. Of course, countries vary considerably in their wealth and how much of that wealth they spend on their military capability. The figures in Table 4.1, taken from the period just prior to the end of the Cold War, make this point clear.

Industrial capability is important, especially in wars of attrition when the ability to provide military forces with resupplies of equipment and weapons for months and even years of warfare may be as important as the skill of the military forces. In the American Civil War, the

TABLE 4.1
Actual Military Expenditures and Percentage of GNP They Represent for Selected Nation-States, 1988

Nation-state	Military expenditures (in $US billions)	Percentage of GNP
Saudi Arabia	13,560	16.5
Israel	6,001	13.8
Libya	2,996	12.6
Soviet Union	299,800	11.7
United States	307,700	06.3
Chad	39 (millions)	04.3
United Kingdom	34,680	04.3
China	21,270	03.9
France	35,950	03.9
Cuba	1,326	03.8
Sweden	4,975	02.8
Spain	7,171	02.2
Canada	10,020	02.1
Finland	1,701	01.7
Japan	28,290	01.0
Mexico	1,016	00.6

Source: Military expenditures are taken from *World Military Expenditures and Arms Transfers 1989* (Washington, D.C.: U.S. Government Printing Office, 1990). The GNP for each country can also be found in this source. The percentage of the GNP the expenditure represents for each nation-state was calculated by the author.

North simply wore the South down. The North not only had a labor advantage but also a great capacity to produce weapons and other war material. In the Second World War, the United States was as critical to its allies for its industrial output as for its military forces. The massive factory system of the United States escaped the destruction of the war unscathed and was able to churn out huge supplies of war material. The British and Soviet armies made almost as much use of canned Spam and jeeps as did the U.S. Army.

Advanced technology that can support sophisticated weapons originates from the wealthy countries with the research and development capability to turn out spy satellites, laser-guided bombs, tanks with high-density armor, computer-aided radar and aiming devices, and other advanced weapons. Many sophisticated weapons have spread around the world through international trade and as gifts of military aid to client states, adding to the diffusion of power among states. The hunt for ever better technology is a constant for many states. Richard J. Samuels, in *"Rich Nation, Strong Army": National Security and the Technological Transformation of Japan,* argues that Japan raised the importance of technology to an ideological level during its modern history and for decades has focused heavily on technology to enhance its national security and become an economic superpower.[17]

Technological advantage is useful in many ways. In one celebrated case, President Ronald Reagan proposed a space-age weapons system called the Strategic Defense Initiative, or SDI (but known to many as "Star Wars"), that would cost many billions of dollars to research and billions more to deploy. This defense system would have included the development of laser-firing satellites that could destroy incoming missiles aimed at the United States. An impenetrable defense of the United States through the SDI would have left the Soviet Union completely vulnerable to U.S. offensive missiles.

Perhaps realizing that the Soviet Union did not have the money or technology to match strides with the United States, General Secretary Mikhail Gorbachev (in 1990, his title changed to president of the Soviet Union) had seriously entered into major arms and labor reduction talks with the United States by the mid-1980s. Republican partisans and supporters of President Reagan have made the claim that Soviet acquiescence to end the arms race was a result of the pressures from the SDI.

Political Factors

Leadership is important in every human endeavor, including the use of power to obtain a state's goals. Effective leadership can give a state more power than its resources alone might suggest. Many scholars, for instance, have suspected that dictatorial leaders have an advantage over democratic leaders because the former can be more efficient. Supposedly, dictators can decide rapidly without consultation and without needing to build support. Democratic leaders, however, often find that in wartime supporters coalesce around them, placing extraordinary powers in their hands.

The ideology of the leadership may affect the power of a country as well. Communism, as once practiced in the Soviet Union, may have ruined the economy in a country blessed with more natural resources than almost any other state. Japanese leadership, in contrast, using the ideologies of democracy and capitalism, has created an economic dynamo in an island country with scant resources. Without doubt, Japanese culture, involving discipline and teamwork, is an additional element of Japanese success.

Regardless of the particular ideologies of leaders, these elites must have the *political capacity* to extract and mobilize material and human resources from society and to direct these resources toward a goal.[18] Leaders unable to collect taxes or recruit soldiers cannot defend their countries much less protect interests beyond their states' boundaries.

A few leaders may enhance their power by being volatile and risk oriented. Concessions are sometimes granted to such leaders because they are so threatening. Chancellor Adolf Hitler received "bits and pieces" of Europe until it became clear that he wanted the whole continent. Would President Saddam Hussein of Iraq place any limits on his goals and means? After witnessing the brutal repression of his own people, the use of mustard gas against Iranian soldiers and Iraq's Kurdish minority, and an elaborate effort to construct a nuclear bomb, not to mention his invasion of Kuwait, we must conclude Saddam Hussein would dare any goal and use any dread weapon he could acquire. Fortunately, Desert Storm and the follow-up destruction of many of Hussein's weapons by the UN coalition forces have constrained his ambitions and military capabilities for the time being.

Alliances are a quick and direct way for a state to empower itself. An **alliance** involves two or more countries adding military forces together for mutual military support. Traditionally, alliances have existed only on paper until a war starts, and then cooperation within the alliance is usually poor. The most prominent alliances of the last half-century are the North Atlantic Treaty Organization (NATO), representing Canada, the United States, and much of western Europe, and the Warsaw Pact, based in eastern Europe and led by the former Soviet Union. These two opposing alliances were products of the Cold War. These alliances enjoy a unique status in history since they maintained regular headquarters and conducted annual maneuvers.

Fortunately, war never occurred between the two alliances during four decades of adversity. And with the implosion of the communist systems of eastern Europe and the Soviet Union, the Warsaw Pact formally disbanded in 1991. The Western allies consider NATO's record overall to be a good one and show no pending signs of terminating their alliance. From a positive point of view, NATO has helped win the Cold War without firing a shot and has contributed to the longest peace in Europe in this century. On the negative side, a possible interpretation is that NATO frightened the Soviets, leading them to create the Warsaw Pact in the first place.

In addition to NATO, the United States developed an extensive network of alliance systems during the Cold War to contain the Soviet Union and China. Except for NATO, most of these have either disbanded or declined. The Organization of American States is still viable but has served mostly to help the United States contain indigenous communist movements in the Western Hemisphere. Since NATO is today's most important alliance, given its military strength and its present and potential impact on the effort to reunite western and eastern Europe into a peaceful whole, some attention to NATO is in order.

Whether NATO now has a viable purpose is a matter of some debate among its members. NATO may be a stabilizing influence in Europe, from the Western point of view, by checking a restive and unstable Russia. At the same time, NATO is destabilizing because several states, once members of the Warsaw Pact, are seeking membership in NATO. During the third post–Cold War summit conference in 1994, the Czech Republic, Hungary, Poland, the Slovak Republic, and the Ukraine expressed a desire to join NATO.[19]

President Boris Yeltsin of Russia has condemned the efforts of some ex–Warsaw Pact states to approach NATO. Yevgeni Primakov, chief of the Foreign Intelligence Service (formerly the KGB), warned that Russia cannot "be indifferent to the fact that the world's largest military grouping plans to move close to our borders." Traditionally distrustful of the West, Russian leaders are nervous about an even stronger NATO. They see an enlarged NATO as the expansion of a Western military alliance into a sphere of influence they dominated in the recent Cold War.

The Western view of an expanded NATO is innocuous. Western leaders see an enlarged NATO as a stabilizing force to give democracy and capitalism a chance to take root in eastern Europe and even Russia. These leaders think of NATO as an important strand in a web of institutions with positive effects. The eastern European countries that wish to join NATO also seek membership, or at least a greater role in the World Bank, the IMF, and the European Union. Besides, as Westerners argue, NATO is only for defense, so why should the Russian leadership worry?[20]

At least President Bill Clinton has pursued a gradualist policy. He first proposed NATO enlargement at a NATO summit meeting in 1994. Then in the 1996 presidential election, President Clinton called for several eastern European states to join NATO. The next step was to assuage Russian fears through the 1997 NATO-Russia Permanent Joint Council that will discuss mutual security concerns. Russia already has taken part in the Partners in Peace forum, a consulting body for past Cold War antagonists. Finally, the Czech Republic,

AP Graphic (Taken from press June 23, 1993)

Hungary, and Poland will join NATO in 1999 during the fiftieth anniversary of this alliance. Victory in the Cold War may have allowed for the expansion of NATO, and could help stabilize eastern Europe, but at the expense of creating a smoldering Russian resentment that may bode ill after Russia regains its strength.

As an exception, 93-year-old George Kennan, the architect of America's original Cold War containment policy toward the Soviet Union, has sternly warned against an act that will revive great states' focus on the principles of power politics with its rival alliances and warfare. The elderly statesman has said, "I'm strongly against the idea of expanding NATO up to the Russian frontiers. That is the one thing I can think of that would really stir up a truly troublesome nationalistic military reaction in Russia."[21]

Besides the expansion of NATO, some intellectuals and political leaders also have called for NATO to assume a greater role in eastern Europe because of the outbursts of ethnic conflict. NATO, they argue, needs a new purpose to sustain its viability: "NATO must go out of area or it will go out of business."[22] For several years, NATO, operating under the mantel of the United Nations, vigorously pursued a peace settlement in war-torn

Bosnia through diplomatic means. This UN humanitarian intervention was costly in terms of lives and money but had little success. Although the Bosnian quagmire was at first divisive among NATO allies, they finally rallied in 1995 under United States plans. These plans called for NATO to intervene with a large body of troops and to enforce the peace. We will return to this subject in Chapter Twelve on international organizations.

It is difficult to forecast the fate of NATO in the years ahead. A realist would say this organization will atrophy, for it has an unclear military purpose. Standing as a counterforce to the Warsaw Pact was a formidable task, but the feeble Russian army of the Chechen operation in 1994–1995 is not a specter worthy of NATO's military clout. A transnationalist, though, might suggest the leaders in NATO can learn and adapt as an institution and, by finding new functions, remain viable and strong. The Bosnian experience may bolster NATO since an alliance without a clear danger can easily erode as alliance partners find new priorities.[23]

After reviewing these several factors of power, we must also observe some elements of power can confound the best efforts to measure power exactly, such as the *willpower* of leaders and the *morale* of a population or the armed forces. The role these intangibles can play is extremely difficult to predict, yet decision makers must somehow evaluate these elements. Willpower and morale can either compensate for military weakness or negate superior resources. In 1940, during the Second World War, Britain stood alone as Germany tried to bomb the British into submission. The British only grew in resolve, enabling them to survive the air attacks. Prime Minister Winston Churchill call the British stand "their finest hour."

In the Vietnam War, the power asymmetry clearly favored the United States as measured in the explosive ordnance of war. In spite of an unfavorable power asymmetry, the Vietnamese leaders in Hanoi intended to reunite their country and end all vestiges of imperialism. The Vietnamese people in the north gave their leaders strong patriotic support and maintained a high sense of morale. As the war wore on, in contrast, the will of the U.S. leadership faltered and the morale of the American people and armed forces sagged. The United States, unwilling to pay a higher price to win, withdrew and let Hanoi have its way. If we factor willpower and morale into the power equation of the Vietnam War, North Vietnamese power proved greater than that of a nuclear superpower.

Shorthand measures of power are tempting to use because the resources of power are so varied and ever changing. From the late nineteenth century through at least the Second World War, a primary index of power was steel production, since steel was critical to civilian and military uses. A country's reputation in war is also a shorthand measure. People naturally assume a country's military forces are as good as their last performance in war. The French, although armed with nuclear bombs, nuclear submarines, and missiles, do not have a prestigious reputation. The French military has not fought impressively since the Napoleonic era. The United States damaged its reputation in the Vietnam War but then improved this image with a dazzling display of smart bombs and Tomahawk cruise missiles in the Persian Gulf War.

The most reliable single power index, however, is the GNP of a country. Most efforts to build a composite measure of power include GNP. A strong national economy suggests economic resources for persuasion, a high level of technical capability, and the fungibility of power needed to convert economic resources into military ones. Ray Cline's list of the 10 most powerful states (Table 4.2), based on a complex formula, is very similar to the list of the top 10 states based on GNP alone, although the exact order of ranking differs.

TABLE 4.2
The 10 Most Powerful States

Ray Cline's ranking (1980)	Aggregate GNP (1985)
1. Soviet Union	1. United States
2. United States	2. Japan
*3. Brazil	3. Soviet Union
4. West Germany	4. West Germany
5. Japan	5. Italy
*6. Australia	6. France
7. China	7. United Kingdom
8. France	8. Canada
9. United Kingdom	9. China
10. Canada	10. Spain

*Cline's ranking uses "critical mass," which is based on territory, in addition to population, and this inclusion in his formula allows Australia and Brazil to enter his top 10 list.

Sources: Ray Cline, *World Power Assessment* (Boulder, CO: Westview Press, 1980). Aggregate GNP ranking is based on GNP found in *The World Factbook 1988* (Washington, D.C.: Central Intelligence Agency, 1988).

The long list of resources and conditions presented in this section affects the power of all states to some degree. If we tried to shorten this list of power resources, a *core of strength,* relevant for the present and probably for the first decades of the 21st century, would consist of a strong industrial base suffused with advanced technology and able to generate an impressive GNP experiencing a robust growth rate. This core can produce the high-tech weapons now required to fight and win. For a state with a power ambition, the core of strength is a critical necessity, while all other aspects of power are a manageable need. Food and minerals are storable, civilians for military training are usually available, and geography, while permanent, is surmountable.

Certainly countries can import high-tech weapons almost as easily as cars and television sets. Many Third World countries, unable to produce their own, do import high-tech weapons, but they acquire mostly first-generation technology. MIG-21 jet fighters and T-72 tanks cannot match F-15s and M-1 Abrams tanks, weapons of second-generation technology. In 1991, American and European planes destroyed the military and communication infrastructure of Iraq and shredded the Iraqi army in Kuwait, thus ending, for the time being, Iraq's power ambition, which was dependent on older Soviet weapons. States with military ambitions may do better in the future if an impoverished Russia sells more of its best military equipment. We will now shift from power at the state level to the distribution of power at the international level.

THE INTERNATIONAL POWER STRUCTURE

Realists, at least those of the neorealist view, and many policymakers regard the **power structure** of the world as critical to outcomes in international relations. This concept refers to the distribution of power among the major states of world. The power structure tends to change over time, with more or fewer states holding influential shares of power. Due to such happenings as economic growth or decay, victory or defeat in war, and good and bad decisions by leaders, power waxes and wanes, leading to **power transitions,** meaning changes in power significant enough to alter the statuses of states, with some rising in rank and others falling.[24] When a power transition is radical enough, one or a few newly powerful states may insist on a different order of rules for the international system. Napoleon's defeat at Waterloo in 1815, for instance, allowed a half-dozen states to coordinate the dismantling of Napoleon's empire, and later their coordination served to prevent the development of republican states in Europe.

A given power structure is best understood as a general environment for individual states as they choose options in a world of risks and opportunities. Good or bad fortune may come to a state according to how compatible its goals are with the rules and interests of the prevailing order. According to realists, the major danger in an anarchic world is war unless the successful management of power can somehow emerge from a given power structure.

Realists have developed an impressive lexicon for handling the analysis of power; however, different interpretations of historical cases of power structures and varied meanings assigned to the terms of the realist lexicon make it difficult to ascertain which scholar's view of the role of power is correct. At least we can identify the primary terms of this lexicon and outline some of the issues among realists. In addition to power structure and power transition, realists speak of a **pole** of power, referring to a major power or an alliance. The number of poles in a given power structure sharing in the distribution of power is the **polarity** of the power structure. Sometimes scholars disagree over how many important poles exist in a given period of history, but usually they consider the basic analytical options of *multipolar, bipolar,* and *unipolar* power structures.

A *multipolar* structure contains three, four, or even more poles of power, usually with power about equally divided among the major states. Concerning the multipolar structure, scholars do sometimes differ over the exact number of poles and the degree of equality in power among the poles. Many scholars would agree that classical periods of this structure appeared in Europe in the eras of 1648–1789 and 1815–1914. Supposedly the long periods of relative peace in these years resulted from the multipolar structure. Some observers also think a multipolar system is currently reemerging in the world, replacing the concentration of power divided between Soviet and United States–led alliances during the Cold War. Several considerations are leading scholars to believe a new multipolarity is shaping into place: the possible decline of the United States, the continued existence of a militarily powerful Russia, the presence of the economically strong states of Germany and Japan, the rising regional powers of such countries as Brazil, China, India, Iraq, and Israel, and even the role of OPEC as a nonstate economic actor are possible poles sharing power in an emerging multipolar structure. Just how many poles will emerge and the evenness of power among them in this multipolar system are far from clear.

Some observers have noticed variations within the multipolar structure. A *tripolar* world was thought to have developed in the early 1970s based on power divided among China, the Soviet Union, and the United States. This power division was uneven and favored the United States, since this country could play the "China card" to offset Soviet power and expansion in Asia.[25] Though both were communist states, China's antagonism toward the Soviet Union had festered since at least 1960. By the mid-1970s, some scholars and Secretary of State Henry Kissinger had begun to speak of a *quinpolar* world. Western Europe, represented through the European Union (then called the European Community), and Japan, a rising economic titan, joined the power centers of the tripolar system to form a new power structure with five poles. In the 1970s, appreciation of the European Union and Japan as poles indicated that scholars and political leaders were becoming increasingly aware of the growing importance of economic power and influence.

Another analytical option among power structures is the *bipolar* structure, with two power poles. Although earlier bipolar structures have appeared in history, the outstanding case is the Cold War relationship between the Soviet Union and the United States. Both countries led nuclear-empowered alliances set against each other. In addition to mutually held security fears, strong ideological views on each side further strengthened the respective alliances. The relationship between Moscow and Washington was tense and often reached the brink of serious conflict during crises. This power structure lasted for four decades, but what began as a *tight* bipolar structure in the 1950s, with the superpowers clearly in charge of their respective alliance systems, gradually became a *loose* bipolar structure as the allies on both sides developed wills and policy orientations of their own.

The multipolar and bipolar structures are significant only if they successfully manage power, meaning major states are able to stave off undesired wars and live within an order of acceptable rules. The multipolar system following Napoleon's era led major states to work closely together. For the Cold War era, the order of acceptable rules meant only a peaceful coexistence, not a concert of interests. The operation of the multipolar and bipolar structures, as management of power systems, depends on the clear division of power between two or more poles. Such a division deters one side from attacking the other. When this deterrence effect is in place, a **balance of power** is at work: The power of one side is a counterbalance to the power of the other side. The antidote to power is another's power. Uncertainty as to which side will win and the costs of victory for the winner discourage war.

The success or failure of balance of power arrangements in history is difficult to assess because different meanings are assigned to this concept.[26] Usually the power distribution involved is thought of as one of equilibrium, referring to both sides enjoying about equal power. Victory is especially difficult to predict if both sides realize they are equal in strength, and hence they will hesitate to choose the instrument of war to achieve a goal. The multipolar structure has a special advantage for securing a balance of power as an equilibrium. Because of several or more poles of power, a state is always available to play the role of *balancer*. The most frequently cited example is that of Britain shifting from one alliance to another to retain an equilibrium of power in European affairs. Less commonly conceptualized is a balance of power in *disequilibrium*, yet with a measure of deterrence still possible. Within a decidedly unbalanced power arrangement, Finland may have deterred the Soviet Union from attacking for several decades. Finland can expand its reserves quickly into a small, tough army that has made the Soviets hesitate to attempt seizing more Finnish soil. The stoic Finnish defense in the Winter War of 1939–1940 is not something the former Soviet Union, or Russia today, would want to experience again.

For living generations, the best-known deterrence system is that of the bipolar Cold War, a system Winston Churchill called the **balance of terror** because it was an equilibrium based on catastrophic nuclear weapons. Sophisticated weapons development on both sides led to

Thompson and Copley News Service

the long-range bombers of the 1950s and the land-based intercontinental ballistic missiles and missile-firing submarines by the 1960s and 1970s. All these weapons could operate on a strategic scale, meaning they could reach from one continent to another. These weapons systems also were hard to destroy, permitting each side to enjoy a *second-strike capacity*. If one side initiated a surprise attack, a *first-strike capacity*, enough weapons would be left over in the targeted country to destroy the attacker. This arrangement resulted in an intensely interdependent relationship of *mutually assured destruction (MAD)*. Either antagonist could drag the other into a nuclear holocaust that neither would survive. No political goal, it was believed, would be worth the attacking country's own destruction; hence, the Soviet Union and the United States became cautious about threatening each other.

Nuclear utilization theorists (NUTS) have claimed a low-level nuclear war can occur without escalating to massive destruction. The superpowers, however, always behaved as though MAD would occur if they engaged in armed conflict at any level. Caution in their dealings with each other became especially pronounced after the Cuban missile crisis of 1962, when nuclear war became a grim possibility.

The Cold War, characterized by a nuclear stand-off and sharp ideological differences, has ended during the dramatic change of the last few years. The economic demise of the Soviet Union, the ethnic unrest in that country, and the decline in confidence in the Communist Party led to a wholly different Soviet approach to the West by the latter 1980s. Before it dissolved and became 15 independent states, the Soviet Union began negotiating important disarmament agreements, withdrew its military from eastern Europe, and formally ended the Warsaw Pact. The chief dealing of today's Russia with the West has been the ignominious task of requesting loans, technical aid, and gifts of food from its old opponents. The Western countries, for their part, are busy scaling down the size of NATO forces and debating what to do with this alliance. Currently, the chief worry over nuclear weapons involves their proliferation to Third World countries and the danger of terrorists acquiring nuclear devices.

Interestingly, a recent debate has emerged among scholars contesting whether atomic weapons did, in fact, help stabilize the Cold War era and prevent war between the superpowers. Professor John Mueller has argued that even the massive conventional weapons of the Soviet Union and the United States would have prevented a war. The scale of destruction with conventional weaponry would still be unacceptable to both superpowers; besides, the historical trend among major states to avert war was already in evidence, apart from nuclear considerations.[27] Professor Robert Jervis argues for the conventional wisdom that nuclear weapons, held by both sides, did render war a completely irrational act, and a third world war, without the threat of nuclear holocaust, would be about as likely as the first two world wars.[28]

The last analytical option as a power arrangement is the *unipolar* structure, with power centered around one pole. In this structure, other states may possess important amounts of power in a hierarchical arrangement, but one dominating state, known as a **hegemon,** controls a region or the world through its preponderant military and economic prowess. The lower-ranking states in the hierarchy must accommodate themselves to the order of the hegemon. Instead of thinking in terms of equilibrium, in a unipolar context it is more sensible to think about *hegemonic stability,* when the hegemon, operating from the apex of the power hierarchy, can provide peace and stability by regulating the international system to a significant degree.[29] The **hegemony** of the dominating state remains stable until a lower-ranked state, growing in power and dissatisfaction with the order provided by the hegemon, challenges to become the new hegemon. According to Christopher Layne, potential challengers rise by experiencing economic growth rates greater than that of the hegemon and inevitably oppose the hegemon.[30] Opposition by challengers can occur through war or during peace and may fail or succeed.

The First World War, at least regarding the British-German relationship, is an excellent example of a hegemonic challenge through war. With growing German confidence in Germany's emerging industrial might and in the kaiser's high seas fleet, Germany's leaders thought their power rivaled, if not exceeded, that of the British. They were especially sure that Germany had won the naval arms race. The decisive defeat of German fleets in the Battle of Jutland and Falkland Islands during the First World War proved them wrong. Woosang Kim argues that when a rising power catches up to the hegemon, war among the great powers is most likely at this "flashpoint."[31] A peaceful and successful transfer of power from an old to a new hegemon occurred when Britain, with an economy set in decline by the Great Depression of the 1930s and an exhausting victory in the Second World War in the 1940s, gracefully stepped aside to let the United States take the lead. This transfer was easy because not only was the United States unquestionably the new global military power, but the postwar order the United States would build was, for the most part, acceptable to British leaders.

Perhaps two previous periods of unipolarity have occurred. France was a hegemon in the period 1660–1714, and Britain enjoyed such a status during the era of 1860–1914. In neither case did hegemonic status last much beyond 50 years. Unarguably, the United States enjoyed a hegemony economically and militarily for a time after the Second World War. The ascendency of the Soviet Union as a strategic nuclear power by the 1970s clearly converted the power structure to a bipolarity. Some scholars contend the bipolar world occurred much earlier than the 1970s. Recently a few observers have claimed that with the collapse of the Soviet Union, the United States again leads the world as hegemon. This hegemony, if real, is probably a "unipolar moment" that is shifting to a multipolar structure. The time when a given power structure exists is often in debate. For example, the French and British unipolarities mentioned earlier overlap the eras some scholars call the classic European periods of multipolarity.[32]

Thus far in our presentation of the international power structure, we have mostly considered the polarity of the international system. In an incisive study, Edward Mansfield takes realist scholars to task for displaying an overwhelming tendency to define the international power structure solely in terms of the number of poles. Mansfield believes that whatever the polarity of the power structure, the **concentration of power** deserves as much attention as the number of poles. Concentration is a measure not only of the number of major powers in the system but of the relative inequality among them. Mansfield surmises that realist scholars have had difficulty deciding on the best polarity for managing power because they fail to account for the effects of polarity and the concentration of power simultaneously. For Mansfield, to focus on polarity alone is too crude a measure of a power structure. He conceptualizes the concentration of power as "low," "medium," and "high" levels, and he contends that the medium level of concentration is the most likely to lead to an outbreak of war. A low concentration means major states are even in power, and victory would be costly and unpredictable. A high concentration allows the strong states to dictate, and so war is unnecessary. However, the medium level means relative inequality in the power of major states, and the costs and risks of war are acceptable to the state viewing itself as the strongest.[33]

With different meanings assigned to the terms of the power lexicon and more than one power structure assigned to the same period of history, it is hard to reach firm conclusions about how much a given structure molds the world and exactly with what effects. Consequently, the power structure that best manages power and allows for an agreeable order is almost impossible to determine. Most scholars, however, probably prefer the multipolar structure because it allows allies to join one alliance or the other, providing the best chance for equilibrium and prevention of war.[34]

If scholars and policymakers did agree on the best structure, they could not make it form into place. Power structures wax and wane due to broad-based historical forces, and policymakers can have only a limited effect as they join or quit alliances, build up weapons systems, or go to war. Indeed, some scholars outside the realist camp have cast doubts about the entire question of the international power structure affecting peace. We will return to the international system as a "level of analysis" and its connection to war in the next chapter.

To summarize up to this point, power involves persuasion and coercion to exercise control; yet it remains a somewhat elusive concept. Also, power is multidimensional and derives from many kinds of resources. It is difficult to measure power, especially because of the roles of willpower and morale, but scholars still manage to achieve fairly useful measures for power. Finally, different distributions of power mark various eras of history, none of which provides an indisputable basis for managing power.

THE CHANGING FACES OF POWER

Two fundamental changes are occurring in the world that are giving power new faces in the modern era. The changing faces of power concern the power structure and the nature of power. Any power structure appears stable at a glance, but structures are always in a state of flux. Subliminal forces are usually at work, perhaps undermining a given power structure and setting off a power transition. As we have learned, the power structure can be a multipolar, bipolar, or unipolar structure, depending on the number of great powers at a given time and their arrangement in alliances.

The collapse of the Soviet Union changed the world power structure dramatically by putting the formation of a new structure in motion. As mentioned earlier, some observers view the role of the United States in the post–Cold War era as *unipolar*. The United States clearly is the only country today that has large economic and military resources that allow it to occupy the status of superpower. Other states, however, do not occupy lesser ranks within an order clearly controlled by the United States. In fact, other states frequently follow their own policy choices. Thus, the United States does not appear to be a true hegemon able to enforce the rules of a preferred order. If a new order is forming, it is likely a collective enterprise of many states. Realizing that the present power structure is at a formative stage, we can surmise that the United States' putative "unipolar moment" has not lasted much beyond the mood of triumphalism following its decisive leadership of the UN coalition forces against Iraq in 1991.

On the matter of U.S. leadership, a fascinating debate emerged among scholars in the latter 1980s. One side of the debate thinks the decline of the United States was inevitable and well under way before the Persian Gulf War. An opposing group of scholars views the United States as a reduced power relative to other states, but not as a state in immutable decline. The declinist theorists are led by historian Paul Kennedy, who has ably expressed his views in *The Rise and Fall of the Great Powers*.[35] He argues that historically powerful states have waxed and waned, with economic decline preceding military decline. Professor Kennedy argues that economic stress worsens when a state spends too much of its wealth on military capability, especially when a country overextends itself with global commitments that he calls "imperial overstretch." Professor Kennedy regards the United States as the latest case in a long line of powerful hegemons to begin the descent in terms of power.

The declinist literature, such as Kennedy's book, cites the well-known U.S. budget and trade deficits, national debt, and money diverted to a global strategic military system as evidence of economic weakness. The declinists also point to the domestic problems of the United States, including poverty and a deteriorating infrastructure of highways and cities. This decline has resulted in domestic interest groups demanding a "peace dividend" for repairing the country. Money saved from downsizing the military system could relieve domestic problems, or so some domestic actors believe.

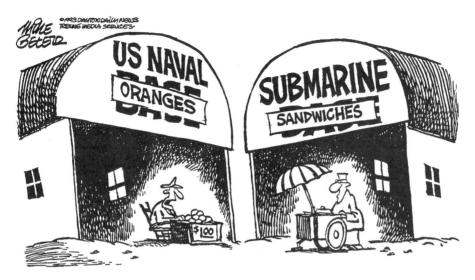

© 1993 Dayton Daily News and Tribune Media Services courtesy of Grimmy, Inc.

Perhaps the decline of the United States was inevitable when we remember that its post–Second World War economic hegemony happened only because of the economic ruin of other countries during the war. In time, the western European and Japanese economies were certain to recover from the war and have, in fact, become highly competitive in a global economy.[36] Although political scientist Joseph S. Nye, Jr., basically challenges the declinists, he does recognize that the "artificial preponderance" of the United States after the Second World War was bound to erode.[37]

If we choose to call the United States the "lone superpower," it is a diminished superpower at best. When the United States championed the cause of ending the Iraqi occupation of Kuwait, it had to call on other states to help pay for Desert Storm. This military operation was the first one in this century in which the United States took part without paying all of its own expenses. Desert Storm is a sharp contrast to the First and Second World Wars, when the United States loaned huge amounts of money and war material to allies and received only a partial repayment.

Nye, in his work *Bound to Lead,* offers a worthy counterargument to Kennedy and the declinists.[38] Nye recognizes that the United States has economic problems but sees its decline as relative, not absolute. The United States exists amid a diffusion of power involving some American decline, an increase in power by the European states and Japan, and the rise in importance of nonstate actors. Nevertheless, in Professor Nye's view, the United States can continue to be a world leader well into the 21st century simply because no other would-be hegemon is yet in a position to challenge U.S. leadership. Nye concludes that only the United States has the resource base to be a leader in a wide range of issue areas. With vision and purpose, he argues that the United States can influence and persuade others to deal cooperatively with a variety of nonmilitary problems. He believes the United States today must draw on its economic strength and leadership among the democracies as much as or more than its military clout.

Other authorities are positive about a hegemonic role for the United States well into the future. A. F. K. Organski and Marina Arbetman state forthrightly, "The world now recognizes the preeminent power position of the United States." Drawing on Henry Luce's famous prediction before the Second World War that the twentieth century would be an American century, Organski and Arbetman have asserted, "The beginning of the next millennium augurs to be a second American century."[39] For at least a few observers, U.S. dominance has roots in economic and political forces that have not nearly run their course.

The bipolar Cold War gave way to a debatable unipolar moment for the United States, but the power structure of the near future, if not of the present, is probably a multipolar one with a relatively uneven distribution of power among the states.[40] Although Edward Mansfield warns us that this structure of power can be very dangerous to international peace,[41] the saving consideration may be that the power structure today changes with the issue at hand. The same countries are not consistently strong or weak on all issues. Our discussion of the second changing face of power will make this point clear.

The second changing face of power involves the nature of power itself. Traditionally, the test of a great power was how well it handled war. Did the great power win or lose? How decisively? Military strength that could once predict international outcomes with regularity is no longer as relevant today as it once was, for several reasons.

First, allies no longer need one another for protection from a great communist superpower. Second, the use of force by major powers, even against Third World countries, has become risky. The sense of nationalism in these countries will sometimes lead them to fight tough, protracted guerrilla wars, as happened in Vietnam, and some Third World countries have acquired relatively high-tech weapons. The armed forces of these countries can shoot down jet fighters and sink modern warships. Third, and most important, the kinds of problems with which many countries must deal do not have military solutions. A would-be leader of today is not as likely to face *challengers* as much as *challenges*. These challenges, including AIDS, drug trafficking, ecological decay, and trade obstacles, among others, require a variety of resources that add up to soft power. Terrorism is one of the few current problems that may require hard power, and military solutions to that problem may be temporary without fundamental reforms.

As opposed to a reliance on military prowess, countries with advanced science and technology, a well-educated population, a prosperous economy, values admired by others (such as those associated with democracy and human rights), and a position as a major "nerve center" in the important global communications network are those that can amply empower themselves for a role of influence. Such countries not only can meet nonmilitary challenges more effectively but can lead others in doing the same. Few countries, of course, have the impressive soft power resources of the United States, which explains why the United States is "bound to lead."

Professor Nye emphasizes that with different situations and issues, power distributions vary favoring first one state as leader and then another.[42] The United States, for example, was the only state that could confront the Soviet Union in a nuclear showdown. In a Group of Seven economic summit, a meeting of the top industrial trading countries in the world, Japan and Germany may have as much influence as the United States. The United States may still have the most influence in the International Monetary Fund, a part of the World Bank system in which the United States is the largest investor. Japan, on the other hand, is the unqualified leader of the Asian Development Bank. Finally, the corporate power of MNCs may be more important than governments in generating trade and investments. These corporations control a huge portion of the world's trade goods and capital finance.

To summarize, the United States, in spite of relative decline, is the only true superpower. Because of this status, the United States is still bound to lead. Yet other countries are rising as leaders depending on the issue-area at hand, bringing the world closer to multipolarity. We also have come to appreciate that soft power now rivals hard power in importance since states require a variety of resources to meet the growing challenges of multiple human needs. These changing faces of power should help create a more peaceful and cooperative world of states in which states make collective decisions that in turn will encourage an international society.

POWER AND INTERNATIONAL SOCIETY

In this section, we will relate power to the overarching theme of the textbook, assessing progress toward cooperation within a developing international society. We begin this assessment with a brief review of the contending approaches to the subject of power. By the 1950s and onward, realists viewed power and conflict as the central concerns of international relations, with the danger of war always lurking on the horizon. States, through inexorable historical forces, inevitably clashed over their lust for power and the wealth and prestige they sought to claim with power. In recurring patterns of struggle, states tried to advance their interests by bending others to their will, that is, through the exercise of power.

In the 1960s and 1970s, neorealists shifted the focus on power away from the pursuit of power by individual states to a concern with the power structure formed by a particular distribution of power among the major states. For neorealists, different power structures will offer varying prospects for stability and peace. Both realists and neorealists at least share the view that the nature of power is essentially coercive and the ends sought are more power and the enhancement of state security. Realists and neorealists think the role of power described here is one to which history bears testimony and the future will give further credence.

By the 1970s, transnationalists, in contrast to the earlier theorists, saw power as involved in a process of considerable change. The nature of power was becoming more persuasive and less coercive, and the ends sought were increasingly the shared needs and wants of multiple actors rather than just the security of states. Today states are about as likely to base their power on a prosperous, industrialized economy and high-level technology as much as on military capability. In fact, the latter would be hard to achieve without the former two. By turning from hard power and thinking collectively, countries have not turned altruistic; they simply have different needs.

Countries now want open markets, control of pandemics, reduction of pollution, improvement in the respect of human rights, a halt to illegal drug trafficking, and other goals generally requiring nonmilitary means. These goals, beyond the power drive that realists recognize, are the results of the dual recognition that states are under pressure to make life better for their populations and that to do so, they must cooperate within a growing world structure of interdependence. Goal fulfillment in many issue-areas requires extensive cooperation.

Whether an order of cooperation is coming to prevail over one of conflict is a question of tremendous interest to many international specialists.[43] Some prominent scholars find it difficult to believe the field of international relations will ever stray far from the study of power as an instrument for conflict.[44] Definitely, we must recognize that the use of power, in a coercive sense, has not nearly disappeared. Iraq's aggression against Kuwait in 1990 and the numerous internal wars due to ethnic strife—not to mention the occasional terrorist act, as in the bombing of the World Trade Center in New York City in 1993—clearly illustrate that force remains in the world as a means to a political end.

The historical development that clearly challenges the position of the realists, however, is that the major states of the world, always their main focus, have nearly abandoned any reliance on costly military force in their dealings with one another and are usually reluctant to use force against weaker Third World states. President Bill Clinton's dispatch of troops to tiny Haiti in 1994 was cautious and tentative and, at first, done with the disapproval of the Congress and the American public. This action also occurred with a promise of multilateral participation by other states and with the approval of the United Nations. Except for halting illegal Haitian immigration to the United States, Clinton's motive was essentially benevolent, namely, the return of a democratically elected president to Haiti.

In contrast, President Clinton's punishment of Iraq with a barrage of cruise missiles in 1996 was bolder and received less support. After Iraqi troops entered the northern part of Iraq to attack an element of the Kurdish minority living there, Clinton acted without the UN Security Council's stamp of approval and won only lukewarm support from a few allies.

Moreover, with the Cold War over, the major states are now more available to assist the United Nations with conflict management. Potentially the power of these states can manage power for the good of all by stopping aggression or by dealing with other disturbances of the peace. For decades, the Cold War made cooperation by all major states difficult, if not impossible. Not only did five major states each hold veto power in the Security Council over United Nations actions, but the Soviet Union and the United States often found themselves on opposite sides during conflicts. The rapid decline of communism in Europe, marked by the tearing down of the Berlin Wall in 1989, cleared the way for the United Nations to act against Iraq in 1991. Iraq, after all, had been a client-state of the Soviet Union, receiving most of its arms from that state. Mikhail Gorbachev promised that the Soviet Union would withhold its veto and would not assist Iraq. The path was open for the United Nations to punish one of the most serious violations of international law, an act of aggression.

The lack of satisfactory results by the United Nations in Bosnia, Rwanda, and Somalia may have resulted partly from insufficient coordination in policy by the major states. At least, the chief powers of NATO finally brought some order to Bosnia in 1995. Aside from this cooperation problem, additional problems the United Nations faces are daunting. Logistical complexities, command control, and the nature of bloody ethnic quarrels are imposing obstacles to peace missions. The United Nations has failed so far to conceptualize a workable intervention, humanitarian or otherwise, to deal with an intense internal conflict in which responsible parties are unavailable to respect a cease-fire.

We can easily summarize the changes in power by thinking in terms of the analytical models from Chapter One: *international anarchy, international society,* and *international community.* An *international anarchy* is perhaps manageable to a degree if a balance of power forms or if a powerful hegemon—that is, a Leviathan in the Hobbesian sense—can control the power hierarchy consisting of ranked states. To be sure, there is no guarantee that the order provided by such an international Leviathan will be benevolent and acceptable to states ranked below the hegemon.

The nascent *international society* forming and eclipsing anarchy is a Grotian order of states able to recognize common interests and abide by many of the same rules. The deemphasis on military force by the major states, accompanied by leadership based on soft power, only bolsters such an order.

Developments in several of the eight elements used to define the models encourage confidence in a formative *international society*. The *orientation* of the major states since the end of the Cold War is toward more cooperation and less conflict. A conflict-oriented, bipolar structure has given way to a world of diversified kinds of power that is helping to form a multipolar world. Currently, the *issues* that interest states involve goals unattainable by military force, goals dealing with human needs. *Force* is giving way more and more to persuasion and influence, for which different kinds of resources are necessary.

However, contentious rivalry remains in the arena of soft power, such as potential trade wars. Further, bloody internal conflicts scattered about the world and potential wars among Third World states impede the realization of a harmonious, Kantian *international community* for the foreseeable future.

CHAPTER SUMMARY

From this chapter, we have learned much about power. Realists remind us that most power rests in the hands of states. Nevertheless, the realist world view of states, using power for their own interests within a war-prone system, now requires revision.

States, as the primary actors, appear more willing to accept constraint in their use of force than at any time in history. Certainly industrialized states have a stronger interest in developing their interdependent economies than in using force among themselves. Also, the end of the Cold War removes a major line of conflict between two ideological groups of states that lived with the threat of nuclear war from crisis to crisis. The end of the Cold War has even allowed the use of collective action against an aggressor. Desert Storm in the Persian Gulf in 1991 is the first such collective action since the Korean War over 50 years ago.

In addition to learning that efforts to measure power are complex because power can derive from many sources, we can observe that two major changes have happened concerning power in recent years. The first is the changed power structure. With the demise of the Soviet Union and the end of the Cold War, the loose, bipolar system is developing into a diffused power system called a multipolar system. The latter power system is based on a number of power centers drawing on both military and economic resources. The actual power distribution varies with the issue-context. No country, for instance, can rival the United States in military resources, but Germany and Japan are extremely important in economic summit conferences along with the United States.

The second major change in power is the shift in emphasis from hard to soft power. The capacity to persuade and lead rather than bully and force has become paramount among the most important countries in the world, the industrialized democracies. Most countries today are very reluctant to risk the costs in blood and treasure of hard power, and they have fewer goals for which force is useful.

Changes in power have moved the world farther along the cooperation continuum, from a Hobbesian anarchy toward a Grotian international society. The demise of coercive power at the international level raises hopes that an emerging international society might crystallize into clearer form, though a future Kantian community of peace and harmony is far from realizable. For today's world, the conflicts in several places in the Third World contravene any notion of a universal society free of violence and force. Power for persuasion and cooperative ventures may be in ascendency in the world today, but the use of force for political objectives can still occur.

POINTS OF VIEW

Power, like love, is easier to experience than to define or measure.
—JOSEPH NYE, JR., POLITICAL SCIENCE QUARTERLY, 1990

America may not be confronting an imperial rival anymore, but that does not mean that it can afford an empire on its own.
—MICHAEL IGNATIEFF, LONDON OBSERVER, MARCH 1993

So what does this mean, that we want to stop naked [Iraqi] aggression? Does this mean that . . . the United States will become the policeman of the world?
SENATOR TOM HARKIN, JANUARY 11, 1991

As the world's last superpower, the United States took for granted that it would rule the roost in what George Bush called the new world order. But in two days in October, with its troops gunned down in Mogadishu [Somalia] and kept out of Port-au-Prince [Haiti] by a raggedy goon squad, the Clinton administration was compelled to rethink its role.
PATRICE PIQUARD, L'EVENEMENT DU JEUDI, PARIS, DECEMBER 1993

Europe, not yet free from the heritage of the Cold War, is in danger of plunging into a cold peace.
BORIS YELTSIN, DECEMBER 1994

As NATO expands, so will security for all Europe . . . no country outside will be allowed to veto expansion.
BILL CLINTON, DECEMBER 1994

REVIEW QUESTIONS

1. Why is power an elusive concept?
2. What are some of the typical elements scholars use to measure power?
3. What do we mean by a "shorthand" measure of power, and what is the most commonly used shorthand measure today?
4. What is an international power structure? Is one type of power structure preferable to another?
5. How does balance of terror differ from a balance of power?
6. What are the two changing faces of power?
7. How do Joseph Nye's views about the future of U.S. power challenge the views of Paul Kennedy?
8. How do the concept and development of an "international society" challenge the idea of a power structure involved in realist thinking?
9. Was the United States more powerful than Vietnam during that war? Why did the United States fail to prevail over Vietnam?
10. What would be the consequences if several eastern European states joined NATO today?
11. Do you think nuclear weapons helped stabilize 45 years of Cold War? Would the Third World War have occurred without nuclear weapons?
12. Do you think the United States is enjoying a "unipolar moment"? Why or why not?

GLOSSARY

alliance An association of two or more states calling for their mutual military support in case of war.

balance of power A power division between opponents or alliances that is managed in such a way as to discourage war. The object is to deter the other side from attacking.

balance of terror Similar to a balance of power, except that the deterrence rests on the dread of a nuclear war that could easily result in the destruction of both sides.

concentration of power The relative inequality of power among the states of a given power structure.

geopolitics An approach to politics that attempts to explain the behavior and military capability of states through their physical environment.

hegemon A dominating state at the regional or international level that can set the rules for lower-ranking states.

hegemony The order established by the dominance of the top-ranked state.

polarity The distribution of power based on the number of poles.

pole A major state or alliance serving as a power center.

power The resources one actor can use to persuade or coerce another actor to do what it wishes.

power structure The distribution of power among the states on a global scale or within a particular geographical region.

power transition A major shift in power among states that allows a new power structure to form or a new hegemon to arise within a unipolar structure.

RECOMMENDED READINGS

Ray S. Cline. *World Power Trends and U.S. Foreign Policy for the 1980s.* Boulder, CO: Westview Press, 1980.

Yeichi Funabashi, ed. *Japan's International Agenda.* New York: New York University Press, 1994.

Charles W. Kegley, Jr. and Gregory Raymond. *A Multipolar Peace? Great-Power Politics in the Twenty-first Century.* New York: St. Martin's Press, 1994.

Robert O. Keohane and Joseph S. Nye. *Power and Interdependence.* 2nd ed. Glenview, IL: Scott, Foresman, 1989.

Richard L. Kugler. *Enlarging NATO: The Russian Factor.* Santa Monica, CA: RAND, 1995.

Evan Luard. *The Blunted Sword: The Erosion of Military Power in Modern World Politics.* New York: New Amsterdam Books, 1989.

Michael Mandelbaum. *The Fate of Nations.* Cambridge, England: Cambridge University Press, 1988.

Edward D. Mansfield. *Power, Trade, and War.* Princeton, NJ: Princeton University Press, 1994.

Hans Morgenthau. *Politics Among Nations.* 5th ed. New York: Alfred A. Knopf, 1978.

John M. Rothgeb, Jr. *Defining Power: Influence and Force in the Contemporary International System.* New York: St. Martin's Press, 1993.

Richard J. Samuels. *"Rich Nation, Strong Army": National Security and the Technological Transformation of Japan.* Ithaca, NY: Cornell University Press, 1994.

J. David Singer and Paul F. Diehl, eds. *Measuring the Correlates of War.* Ann Arbor, MI: University of Michigan Press, 1990.

Richard J. Stoll and Michael D. Ward, eds. *Power in World Politics.* Boulder, CO: Lynne Rienner Publishers, 1989.

Michael P. Sullivan. *Power in Contemporary International Politics.* Columbia, SC: University of South Carolina Press, 1990.

Robert W. Tucker. *Imperial Temptation: The New World Order and America's Purpose.* New York: Council on Foreign Relations, 1992.

ENDNOTES

1. Hans Morgenthau, *Politics Among Nations* (New York: Alfred A. Knopf, 1973).
2. The paragraphs above are influenced in part by John M. Rothgeb, Jr., *Defining Power: Influence and Force in the Contemporary International System* (New York: St. Martin's Press, 1993), pp. 1–14.
3. Ibid., pp. 19–22.
4. Joseph S. Nye, Jr., "Soft Power," *Foreign Policy*, Fall 1990, pp. 153–71.
5. Yoichi Funabashi, "Introduction: Japan's International Agenda for the 1990s," in *Japan's International Agenda*, ed. Yoichi Funabashi (New York: New York University Press, 1994), pp. 1–27.
6. Nye, "Soft Power."
7. Evan Luard, *The Blunted Sword: The Erosion of Military Power in Modern World Politics* (New York: New Amsterdam Books, 1989), pp. 1, 16–21.
8. Carsten Holbraad, *Middle Powers in International Politics* (New York: St. Martin's Press, 1984).
9. Ray S. Cline, *World Power Trends and U.S. Foreign Policy for the 1980s.* (Boulder, CO: Westview Press, 1980).
10. J. David Singer and Paul F. Diehl, *Measuring the Correlates of War* (Ann Arbor, MI: University of Michigan Press, 1990).
11. Michael Sullivan, *Power in Contemporary Politics* (Columbia, SC: University of South Carolina Press, 1990), pp. 16–17.
12. Ibid., pp. 134–35.

13. Alfred Thayer Mahan, *The Influence of Seapower on History 1660–1783* (Boston: Little, Brown, 1897).
14. Sir Halford Mackinder, *Democratic Ideals and Reality* (New York: Henry A. Holt, 1919).
15. Dennis Pirages, *Global Techno-politics* (Pacific Grove, CA: Brooks/Cole, 1989), pp. 121–25.
16. Paul Kennedy, *The Rise and Fall of Great Powers* (New York: Random House, 1987).
17. Richard J. Samuels, *"Rich Nation, Strong Army": National Security and the Technological Transformation of Japan* (Ithaca, NY: Cornell University Press, 1994).
18. Jacek Kugler and William Domke, "Comparing the Strength of Nations," *Comparative Political Studies,* April 1986, pp. 43–44.
19. Joseph Lepgold, "Does the United States Make Sense in NATO After the Cold War? On What Terms?" in *Post-War Policy: The International Context,* ed. William Crotty (Chicago: Nelson-Hall, 1995), p. 165.
20. Owen Harries, "The Collapse of 'the West,' " *Agenda 1994: Critical Issues in Foreign Policy* (Washington, D.C.: Council on Foreign Relations, 1994), pp. 188–200; Lepgold, "Does the United States Make Sense in NATO," pp. 165–66; Richard L. Kugler, *Enlarging NATO: The Russian Factor* (Santa Monica, CA: RAND, 1995); Gebhardt van Moltke, "NATO Moves Toward Enlargement," *NATO Review,* January 1996, pp. 3–6.
21. Quote is from *U.S. News and World Report,* March 11, 1996, p. 41.
22. Ronald D. Asmus, Richard L. Kugler, and F. Stephen Larrabee, "Building a New NATO," *Agenda 1994,* pp. 201–13; quote on p. 204.
23. The thinking here is partly influenced by Lephold, "Does the United States Make Sense in NATO," p. 170.
24. Charles W. Kegley, Jr. and Gregory Raymond, *A Multipolar Peace? Great-Power Politics in the Twenty-First Century* (New York: St. Martins Press, 1994), p. 72.
25. George Segal, *The Great Power Triangle* (New York: St. Martin's Press, 1982).
26. Inis L. Claude, *Power and International Relations* (New York: Random House, 1962).
27. John Mueller, "The Essential Irrelevance of Nuclear Weapons: Stability in the Postwar World," in *The Cold War and After: Prospects for Peace,* ed. Sean M. Lynn-Jones and Steven E. Miller (Cambridge, MA: MIT Press, 1993), pp. 45–69.
28. Robert Jervis, "The Political Effects of Nuclear Weapons: A Comment," in *The Cold War and After: Prospects for Peace,* pp. 70–80.
29. Robert Gilpin, *War and Change in World Politics* (Cambridge, England: Cambridge University Press, 1981).
30. Christopher Layne, "The Unipolar Illusion: Why New Great Powers Will Rise," in *The Cold War and After: Prospects for Peace,* p. 271. See also Charles Krauthammer, "The Unipolar Moment," *Foreign Affairs* 70, no. 1 (1991), pp. 23–33.
31. Woosang Kim, "Power Transitions and Great Power War from Westphalia to Waterloo," *World Politics,* October 1992, pp. 153–72. See also Gilpin, *War and Change in World Politics,* and Bruce Bueno de Mesquita and David Lalman, *War and Reason: Domestic and International Imperatives* (New Haven, CT: Yale University Press, 1992), Chapter 6.
32. Layne, "The Unipolar Illusion," pp. 255–66.
33. Edward D. Mansfield, *Power, Trade, and War* (Princeton, NJ: Princeton University Press, 1994).
34. Paul R. Viotti and Mark V. Kauppi, *International Relations Theory: Realism, Pluralism, Globalism,* 2nd ed. (New York: Macmillan, 1993), pp. 54–55.
35. Paul Kennedy, *The Rise and Fall of the Great Powers* (New York: Random House, 1987).
36. Michael Mandelbaum, *The Fate of Nations* (Cambridge, England: Cambridge University Press, 1988), p. 366.
37. Nye, "Soft Power," p. 153.
38. Joseph S. Nye, Jr., *Bound to Lead: The Changing Nature of American Power* (New York: Basic Books, 1990). For a more condensed version of his arguments, see Nye, "Soft Power," and Joseph S. Nye, Jr., "The Changing Nature of World Power," *Political Science Quarterly,* Summer 1990, pp. 177–92.
39. A. F. K. Organski and Marina Arbetman, "The Second American Century: The New International Order," in *Behavior, Culture, and Conflict in World Politics,* ed. William Zimmerman and Harold K. Jacobson (Ann Arbor, MI: University of Michigan Press, 1993), pp. 120–23.

40. Zalmay Khalilzad, "Losing the Moment? The United States and the World After the Cold War," in *Order and Disorder After the Cold War,* ed. Brad Roberts (Cambridge, MA: MIT Press, 1995), pp. 57–77.
41. Mansfield, *Power, Trade, and War.*
42. This discussion on soft power is taken in large part from Nye, "Soft Power."
43. The primary investigation and comparison of the two structures are by Robert O. Keohane and Joseph S. Nye, *Power and Interdependence,* 2nd ed. (Glenview, IL: Scott, Foresman, 1989).
44. Richard J. Stoll and Michael D. Ward, eds., *Power in World Politics* (Boulder, CO: Lynne Rienner Publishers, 1989).

CHAPTER 5

WAR AND LESSER CONFLICT: FORCE IN DECLINE?

War is a belligerent struggle between armed groups within a state or between states with highly incompatible goals, resulting in a sizable number of casualties. The widely used research of J. David Singer and Melvin Small distinguish the extreme conflict of war from lesser conflicts by measuring war as struggles with 1,000 battle deaths or more.[1]

Over the millennia, tribes, city-states, and empires have waged war as one type of political entity has replaced another. Since the seventeenth century, the modern state, first evolving in Europe and then spreading as a political system to the rest of the world, has been the main entity engaging in warfare. Currently, however, most wars take place inside countries, and the combatants are often rival ethnic groups, as in the recent cases of Bosnia and Rwanda.[2]

Scholars in the international relations field have probably studied war more than any other single subject, and certainly the tragedy of war deserves this attention. Wars have occurred frequently in human history and have posed a regular threat to human welfare. One estimate on warfare has claimed that over 14,500 wars have taken place between 3600 B.C. and the present, leaving only 292 years of peace, and that 3.5 billion people have perished as a result of war.[3] In almost any year of the 1980s and 1990s, war of some type has affected as many as one-fourth of the world's states.

While wars are still fought in modern times, the frequency, causes, and types of wars have changed. Even the legality of war and the conditions under which states can use force are now much different. A basic question of this chapter is whether the role of war has altered enough to allow the development of an international society with its emphasis on the use of peaceful means and a cooperative approach to problems.

In our investigation of the role of war, we will first look at traditional conceptions about this issue. Then we will review patterns, causes, and types of war to assess whether the role of war is diminishing. Next, we will look at an important question: Is there a "just" role for war that could benefit international society, or could we simply purge war from human affairs altogether? If not, can conflict choices at least operate below a warmaking level? Finally, we will attempt to ascertain whether an international society that repudiates war is forming into place.

THE TRADITIONAL ROLE OF WAR

When vital interests are at stake, the traditional instrument of choice for states in many instances has been war. Historically, warfare has occurred in a context of international anarchy, with sovereign states free to choose the course of war as their kings saw fit. However, more prudent kings, recognizing the costs of war to their treasuries, bent toward seeing war as the *ultimo ratio,* or the means of last resort. Wise kings also knew that fighting a war could have unpredictable outcomes. Modern leaders face similar choices and consequences, except that the legality of the war option has sharply declined during the twentieth century.

Thus, questions about when and how to fight wars have bedeviled leaders across the ages. Military philosophers have tried to give guidance on these questions. Few, though, take so strict a view as Emory Upton, a Union Civil War general, who emphatically stressed that war and politics are fundamentally different.[4] Upton's thinking had a lasting effect on the American military mind. Far more influential, and on both sides of the Atlantic Ocean, were the ideas of Antoine Henri Jomini (1779–1869), a Swiss-French general who served both under Napoleon and in the Russian army. Not only did he wish to turn fighting wars into a predictive science, but Jomini advocated that field commanders, relative to political leadership, have wide latitude in discretion so they could win the war.[5]

A tendency to separate politics and war especially characterized American military thinking until well after the Second World War. In the Korean War (1950–1953), President Harry Truman, exasperated with the heroic general of the Second World War, finally relieved General Douglas MacArthur of his command because the general insisted on deciding strategy and the broad course of the war. President Truman wanted the war kept limited as a United Nations enforcement action against North Korea's invasion of South Korea. Instead, General MacArthur had attempted to reunite the two Koreas only to provoke the attack of a large Chinese army, an outcome that lengthened the war and caused many more casualties.[6]

Not until after defeat in the Vietnam War (1963–1975)[7] did American military leaders rethink and revamp their views on war's place in state policy. This defeat coincided with the new, critically acclaimed translation and edition by Michael Howard and Peter Paret, in 1976, of *On War* by Carl von Clausewitz (1780–1831).[8] It is to Clausewitz whom we must turn to gain insight into the place of war in international politics, not only in the past but in modern times. For a man who rode to battle on horseback, he remains surprisingly relevant. Clausewitz offers a rational view of war as an instrument of the state. Focusing on war as a means to an end, as a careful calculation of statecraft, does not answer all our questions about war, but it is a useful starting point.

Clausewitz's *On War,* published in 1832 just after his death, connects war and politics by asserting that "war is but the continuation of politics by other means." Clausewitz developed a "trinity of war" concept to put this definition of war to work. First, political leaders decide on the goals and then control the general course of the war during its prosecution. Second, the military skillfully fights the war, choosing the specifics of strategy and tactics. Third, the populace gives material resources and passion to the war effort. Although Clausewitz did not advocate war for war's sake, he urged that ample violence be implemented "to compel our opponent to do our will."[9]

Clausewitz thought he was writing a systematic treatment of war for future Prussian officers, but scholars and political and military leaders from many countries and varied cultures have turned to *On War,* by the veteran of the Napoleonic wars, for a better understanding of the role of war. With the highly improved and accessible Howard-Paret edition, Clausewitz has informed war analysis more than he ever imagined.

Watterson. Distributed by Universal Press Syndicate. Reprinted with permission. All rights reserved.

Colonel Harry G. Summers, an infantry veteran of the Korean and Vietnam wars, uses the now classic Clausewitzian principles of war in his widely read *On Strategy: A Critical Analysis of the Vietnam War,* to assess the reasons behind the American loss in Vietnam.[10] Clausewitzian guidance also helps explain the thorough preparation and efficient waging of war in the Persian Gulf War (1990–1991) by American leadership, both military and civilian, by this time infused with the Clausewitzian approach.[11]

Even an analysis of nuclear war can occur through Clausewitz's ideas. Clausewitz might have approved President Harry Truman's decision to drop two atomic bombs on Japan to compel the Japanese to do our will by surrendering. These were small weapons compared to today's nuclear arsenals, and the United States alone possessed such weapons in 1945. In contrast, Clausewitz might well have urged leaders in the Cold War to avoid escalation and total nuclear war because, rationally, no goal of statecraft could be worth the complete destruction of one's country.

Although Clausewitz's admirers are legion,[12] eminent war historian John Keegan finds fault with Clausewitz's rational approach to war as the calculated instrument of a state. Keegan thinks Clausewitz's views are too Western in their cultural predisposition.[13] Keegan advocates instead a cultural approach: " . . . war embraces much more than politics . . . it is always an expression of culture, . . . in some societies the culture itself." To make his point, Keegan refers to Clausewitz's own description of Cossack forces during the Napoleonic invasion of Russia. These auxiliary forces burned, looted, raped, and murdered, committing hundreds of outrages that to Clausewitz appeared unnecessary for the prosecution of war. Incomprehensive to Clausewitz, these outrages were an expression not of politics but of the Cossack culture, their way of life as fighters cruel to the weak and cowardly in the face of the brave.[14]

Perhaps Keegan's critique simply tells us that no theorist is likely to cover all cases of war adequately. Clausewitz will become irrelevant only when wars end, that is, when the moral and legal proscriptions against war receive full respect. We will now look at the patterns, causes, and types of war to see if war is becoming less of a problem for humankind.

PATTERNS OF WAR

Modern social scientists would like to develop a comprehensive theory to guide research on wars, but what has resulted among today's scholars are competing and even conflicting ideas about war.[15] In the quest to understand war, many academic conferences on war are

TABLE 5.1
Notable Patterns of War

- The involvement of great powers in wars has declined sharply since the Second World War.
- Most wars are either civil wars or revolutions fought in the Third World.
- The destructiveness of wars has increased due to technological changes.
- States accused of aggression in the twentieth century have either lost or ended their wars in stalemate.
- Many scholars and leaders view nuclear wars as irrational since no goal is worth the complete destruction involved.
- One type of government (communist or democratic) is about as prone to fight wars as another.
- Democracies in the twentieth century have not fought one another.
- Confidence by scholars that wars occur in cycles (for example, every 20 years) is less firm today.

held, university institutes exist for peace research, and excellent journals (*Journal of Conflict Resolution, Journal of Peace Research,* and *Peace Research Review*) publish numerous articles about the conditions of peace and war. After years of careful study, we remain uncertain whether wars follow discernible patterns or each war is unique and idiosyncratic, making war impossible to study scientifically.

In an effort to develop a theory on war, a number of scholars have amassed impressive amounts of data, but these data have led to differing conclusions rather than integrated and coherent theory.[16] Some of the most important efforts have been Quincy Wright's *A Study of War,* originally published in 1942; Lewis F. Richardson's *Statistics of Deadly Quarrels,* published in 1960; and J. David Singer and Melvin Small's *The Wages of War, 1816–1965: A Statistical Handbook,* appearing in 1972.[17] The best-known compilation of war-related data is the *Correlates of War Project (COW)* headed by Professor J. David Singer at the University of Michigan. In spite of impressive scholarly efforts, a theory on war that will tell us why wars are fought, when they will occur, who will win, how long wars will last, and the consequences of wars has so far eluded even the best scholars. Table 5.1 lists at least some patterns of war, derived from the current literature on war.

These patterns are only current generalizations and may or may not prove lasting after further experiences with war. Perhaps the most encouraging pattern is the absence of war among the major states since 1945. This "long peace" is exceptional considering the historical behavior of great powers. The causes of war are probably multiple and exacerbate the difficulty of producing a reliable theory on war.

CAUSES OF WAR

Although a few writers may claim a single cause of war exists, such as a human instinct for aggression, most writers identify multiple causes for a given war and realize that the causes may vary from one war to another. The present state of research on the subject does not permit another conclusion. Scholars also have had to trace the causes of war in an *ex post facto* manner. After the occurrence of a given war, scholars have had to follow the historical antecedents of that war up to its flashpoint. This search for the cause or causes for war is, nonetheless, the most important consideration about war. The more we know about the causes of war, the better are the prospects for war's prevention. This situation is not unlike medical doctors who study the causes of cancer, not only out of scientific curiosity but so they might prevent or cure cancer.

We will present a brief version of the more prominent theories about the causes of war to illustrate their considerable variety. The organization follows the levels-of-analysis scheme used by Kenneth N. Waltz in his classic study *Man, the State and War*.[18] He organized the possible causes of war at the individual, state, and international levels.

Individual-Level Causes of War

Some writers theorize that the root cause of war lies in the nature of people, making them aggressive or hostile. If true, wars may be a permanent condition of humankind. Sigmund Freud (1856–1939), the pioneer of psychoanalysis, thought people have both a *life instinct* and a *death instinct*. People become aggressive, he surmised, because they convert their death wish into an act of aggression toward others, thus avoiding their own suicide. However, Freud also thought that the more civilization evolved, the more controllable the instinct for aggression would become. Freud's theory amounts to speculation, since he never adduced a body of evidence to support his ideas.[19]

Konrad Lorenz, a leading scholar in the ethology field, who studied animal behavior with emphasis on instincts, concluded aggression is instinctual among animals, but for functional purposes. In *On Aggression* (1966), Lorenz observes that aggression helps a species survive by providing food, mates, and territory. Within a species, however, aggression becomes a ritual so that attack and submission can take place with little danger to life. For example, wolf packs establish a hierarchy within the pack under the leadership of the strongest male. The other wolves roll on their backs and expose their bellies and throats to the dominant male, symbolizing their acceptance of his leadership. While some fighting may take place to identify the strongest male, killing is unnecessary.

Lorenz deduces that humans, who lacked fangs and claws for the easy killing of their own kind, developed weapons for killing long before they developed mechanisms for restraint. As a result, humans are willing to kill their own kind in acts of murder and in organized warfare.[20]

A serious criticism of Lorenz's work is that he reaches conclusions about human behavior by extrapolating from animal behavior.[21] For Lorenz to be convincing, current scholars would have to identify the genetic code that produces aggression in humans. If the genetic heritage of aggression is not demonstrable, the possibility exists that aggression and war are learned behavior for humans rather than instinctual.[22] If people do inherit aggressive behavior, or its tendency, war is not necessarily inevitable. Modern war is complex, deliberate, and planned by entire societies. The cause of war is unlikely to be as simple as the instinctive reaction of an individual or a set of individuals.

Edward O. Wilson has made some interesting observations on the role of genetics. While the field of sociobiology predates the 1975 publication of Wilson's *Sociobiology: The New Synthesis,* his work gave the field a clearer definition.[23] Briefly, this field tries to study behavior as a response to genetic evolution, an evolution that the environment also shapes. Wilson thinks a scarcity in psychological and biological needs can ultimately produce patterns of conflict and violence. Although Wilson recognizes that aggressive behavior in humans varies considerably and cooperation among people is possible, he concludes humans have a strong tendency to learn violence as a means of resolving conflict and achieving power and privilege. He thinks human brains are programmed to separate people into friend or foe.[24]

Another individual-level cause of war involves personalities. John Stoessinger, in *Why Nations Go to War*, examines seven wars as case studies and considers the role of the personalities of leaders in assessing the cause of these wars. He finds that decision makers are, after all, humans capable of irrational behavior; they are captives of emotions that psychological and physiological factors can affect. Stoessinger found many individual weaknesses contributing to war in his case studies.

For example, before the First World War, Kaiser Wilhelm had paranoid delusions about England conspiring against Germany. Adolf Hitler, in a fit of frustration, attacked the Soviet Union before defeating Britain, causing a great strategic blunder for Germany. The egos of two United States presidents lengthened an unwinnable war in Vietnam. Neither wanted to be the first president to lose a war. In 1971, Yahya Khan took Pakistan into war with India, led by Prime Minister Indira Gandi. Khan refused to make concessions, claiming he would not be "cowed by a woman."

According to Stoessinger, the personality traits of individuals may lead to misperception. When leaders decide on war, they typically expect the fighting to be brief, followed by a rewarding victory. Stoessinger surmised that leaders' misperceptions of the power of their adversaries are perhaps the quintessential cause of war.[25]

The most important question in individual-level analysis is whether aggression and war are instinctive or learned. John Stoessinger believes humans have learned war much as they once learned slavery, incest, and cannibalism. Furthermore, Professor Stoessinger is confident that humans can "unlearn" war as they have these other odious practices.[26] If war is based on instincts, humankind's future is a pessimistic one, but if humans can "unlearn" war, there is reason for hope and optimism.

Societies have existed, in fact, where violence is virtually absent. Cultural norms against violence appear to shape individuals' behavior, dampening any instincts that might call for violence and aggression. The Zuni Indians of the American Southwest and the Bushmen of southern Africa have developed such nonviolent societies.[27]

State-Level Causes of War

The people of the world today are divided into about 200 states since the disintegration of Czechoslovakia, the Soviet Union, and Yugoslavia. These states vary substantially in governmental organization, the ideologies of their leaders, and their cultures and economic conditions. These differences have led to the creation of typologies among states and to the claim that some types of states are more prone to war than others.

Some scholars have claimed that democracies are more peaceful then communist or other authoritarian states. The rationale is that in democracies, the general population controls government and most of the citizenry presumably prefers peace.[28] No one has proven with complete certainty that democracies are more peace loving, however. In a review of empirically based studies, Professors Richard Merritt and Dina Zinnes could not find consistent evidence that the option of war is necessarily a different choice for democratic and nondemocratic states.[29]

In fact, public opinion has helped push democratic governments into war, as when the American public urged President William McKinley to initiate the Spanish-American War (1898–1900), and democracies have taken part in wars in the Third World perhaps more than have communist states. Jack S. Levy also observes that democracies may fight more destructive wars because of their tendency toward moral crusading.[30]

At least we can say that democracies have not fought one another or intervened on one another's territory in this century, unlike some communist countries.[31] Is this pattern a coincidence, or is their something about democracies that inhibits these states from fighting one another? Professor Bruce Russett offers a worthwhile insight into this question. He believes the norms and procedures of democracy call for compromise in times of conflict, and so democracies avert violence among themselves.[32]

Interestingly, Professor Russett, in a study undertaken with Zeev Maoz, further investigates democracy's inhibition to engage in conflict. The two authors wish to know whether democracy's *norms* of compromise and cooperation or the *structure* of the domestic system is the more important factor in keeping the peace among democracies in conflict. Democratic structure involves the need to mobilize support and the time a democracy needs to ready itself for a clash with another country. This mobilization period gives diplomats time to work out nonviolent solutions. Maoz and Russett find that norms are a stronger explanation than structure as to why democracies are at peace with one another, although the two overlap and reinforce each other.[33]

In a separate study, Professor Russett also concludes that democracies have positive effects for economic development and provide peaceful channels for economic classes and ethnic groups to seek more just positions in society. Moreover, Professor Russett, writing before the collapse of communism in Europe, observed a shift in the world toward democracy but warned that some new democracies may be fragile and imperfect. He cautioned that the economic success of a state pursuing democratic forms may determine if democracy becomes deeply rooted and permanent in a given country.[34] Presently, Russia and eastern European countries are "living laboratories" that may confirm this observation. We return to the role of democracy in the world in Chapter Fourteen.

Another well-known assertion about the type of state is V. I. Lenin's claim in his work *Imperialism* (1918) that capitalism, in its highest stage, results in a feverish drive for more raw materials, cheap labor, and new markets. Since a number of capitalist states have the same needs at the same time, the conflict becomes intense enough to result in war as a way to eliminate trade rivals, or so though Lenin. His explanation for the First World War focused on the economic conflict among capitalist states.[35]

There have been many criticisms of Lenin's theory of imperialism, but perhaps the most telling one is that many wars appear to lack fundamental economic causes.[36] The counterclaim to Lenin, on the part of economic liberals (free trade advocates or capitalists), is that free trade and the prosperity it brings help to reinforce the peace. Capitalist states oppose war because war interrupts trade and squanders wealth.[37] We cannot easily dismiss economic motives for war, however. Imperial powers have sought empires through wars of conquest, in part for economic reasons. Whether imperial powers in the nineteenth and first half of the twentieth century gained economic advantage through empires remains a subject of debate among historians.

Certainly recent would-be empire builders have failed. In the Second World War, Germany, Italy, and Japan had economic goals in mind as well as prestige and enhancing military strength. Economic needs especially drove Japan to seek reliable supplies of oil and raw materials by seizing China, Manchuria, and the European and American holdings in the Pacific. The safe conclusion is that economic motives do play a part in some wars, but they are not the central cause of wars in the industrial age as Lenin would have us believe.

International Social Darwinism is another interesting explanation for war concerning types of societies. First, we must note that Social Darwinism is a distortion of Charles Darwin's (1809–1882) ideas about the "survival of the fittest." Darwin focused on plants and animals, and he had little to say about human evolution.[38] A few sociologists in the late nineteenth century distorted Darwin's ideas and applied them to human societies. Social Darwinism does not have much credibility with modern sociologists, who are usually more interested in cultural explanations than biological ones.[39]

International Social Darwinists believe human societies evolve and advance through competition resulting in the survival of the fittest and the elimination of the weak. They think the role of war passes the reins of power from the weak and decaying to the strong and dynamic societies. An example of Social Darwinism is one associated with the thinking of fascists and Nazis in Italy and Germany, respectively, before the Second World War. They glorified war and thought victory over other peoples would justify fascist and Nazi rule over their neighbors.[40] If states practiced international Social Darwinism widely, an especially harsh version of international anarchy would result.

Finally, we can raise the question, as feminists have: Does it make a difference that human societies have been patriarchies? A world of male-dominated national societies has, according to some feminists, produced a world of power and conflict as a result of men being in charge. National societies based on patriarchies versus matriarchies are difficult to compare, however, since few, if any, of the latter have existed. Moreover, understanding history and applying international relations theory with the benefit of feminist insights have taken place only recently.[41]

Would the involvement of more women in war-related decisions encourage moral restraint on expenditures for weaponry and reliance on war as a state instrument? Birgit Brock-Utne believes one basic cause of war is that males are more warlike than females, and traditionally males have dominated governments. She advocates that women become more involved in government to reduce the likelihood of war. Brock-Utne's only evidence for women's peace orientation is to cite polls taken in Europe and in the United States that show women are less willing to support expenditures for weapons.[42]

Kamla Bhasin, a well-known human rights advocate, believes violence, ranging from domestic violence in the home to the level of international militarization, derives from the male value of using violence to control and solve problems. For Bhasin, women become the victims of manmade violence because of the values of patriarchy.[43] Brock-Utne's and Bhasin's premise that men are more warlike and violent is at least questionable.

There is a widely held assumption that women are antiwar and antimilitarist in their values,[44] yet many examples of war involvement by women come readily to mind. Finnish women fired artillery in the Winter War of 1939–1940 with Russia, Russian women served as combat military police during the Second World War, and many of the cadre of Viet Cong regiments in the Vietnam War were women. Also, American women served with distinction in combat zones during the Persian Gulf War in 1991 and today receive training as combat fighter pilots.

The most unusual current example of women's involvement in military matters concerns the National Liberation Army (NLA) of Iran, a revolutionary group of Iranians operating from Iraqi territory. This army of 30,000 strong has 35 percent of its ranks and 70 percent of its officer corps made up of women. Their top leader is a woman as well, Maryam Rajavi. Operating since 1988, the NLA awaits the opportunity to support a general uprising against the Islamic fundamentalist regime of Iran. Rajavi explains the prominence of women volunteers in her army as the outcome of Iran's harsh repression toward women.

As leaders, women also have played important roles in war. Women monarchs, such as Catherine the Great of Russia, probably fought wars as frequently as male monarchs. Prince Albert was barely able to restrain Queen Victoria from demanding a war against the United States in 1862 after the Union navy overhauled and boarded a small British ship in the Caribbean Sea. And some democratically elected women leaders, such as Indira Gandhi of India and Margaret Thatcher of Great Britain, have made decisions to go to war and have proven to be able wartime leaders.

Cynthia Enloe regards the assertion that men are inherently violent and women are not as highly dubious. According to Enloe, not chromosomes but social processes and institutions, over generations, create and sustain gender differences. The fact that men dominate in leadership and combat roles in war is a result of the particular processes holding sway, she believes, and these processes can produce different gender patterns along national lines.[45] Ultimately, gender roles, in peace and war, may be the result only of social and cultural construction.[46] The anecdotal evidence, at least, suggests women have been effective in both prosecuting and protesting war.

A different question for feminists concerns whether women receive fair opportunities to advance in military service. This question raises the issue as to whether women can participate in combat, since such a role can be critical for career advancement. As an affirmative action cause, women in the U.S. military have entered roles bringing them ever closer to combat. During the Persian Gulf War, five American women came home in body bags and at least two were POWs. Women continue to struggle to participate in the military on the same terms as men. A lengthy legal struggle finally resulted in the admittance of women to government-sponsored military academies in South Carolina and Virginia in 1996. Women, however, can still face gross differences in treatment, as the widespread sexual harassment scandal of 1996 in the U.S. Army demonstrates.

System-Level Causes of War

The classic explanation for war rests on the sovereign right of states to go to war because they suffer the anarchy of the international system. War is a natural extension of self-help in a governmentless world. In this century, of course, the use of force became illegal except under UN Charter provisions, although some states may decide to use force anyway.

According to realists, a way exists to mute anarchy's tendency to allow, if not produce, war. These scholars are sure that the distribution of power in the world can affect the prospects for war, but they disagree about the power distribution that offers the best chance

"TWO BRAND-NEW COUNTRIES WERE FORMED TODAY AND IMMEDIATELY WENT TO WAR."

© 1997. Reprinted courtesy of Bunny Host and *Parade* magazine.

for stability and peace. Regarding the likelihood of war, the main theoretical options are a *unipolar* or power hierarchy, a *bipolar* distribution of power, and a *multipower* distribution of power. Although power configuration was a topic of the previous chapter, the focus now is more specifically on the potential of the international system to allow war. By necessity, we reiterate some points made in the last chapter, where we covered power distribution more fully.

Robert Gilpin thinks peace is more likely when a power hierarchy of states exists headed by a recognized hegemon, thus creating a *unipolar* structure. War occurs only when the growth of power by a subordinate state in the hierarchy challenges the hegemon. Competition between the hegemon and the challenger over prestige, territory, trade, and other issues creates tense and unstable conditions. If the challenger wins, a new hegemon emerges from the war. The more pronounced and unambiguous the postwar hierarchy, meaning clear dominance by the hegemon, the more likely the international system will enjoy peace and stability. This *hegemonic theory of war*, according to Gilpin, has withstood the test of time better than any other generalization in the field of international relations, and today remains an important conceptual tool. However, hegemonic theory will not, Gilpin concedes, explain all wars and will not predict exactly when wars begin.[47]

In spite of many observers' opinion that the United States is in decline as a hegemon, A. F. K. Organski and Marina Arbetman have confidence in the "massive national capabilities" of the United States that will allow it to continue maintaining the present world order. They conclude that other major states are satisfied with U.S. leadership and the dissatisfied are too impotent to force change.[48] If the *hegemonic theory of war* holds up in the future, one can only hazard guesses as to which state, in what kind of war, will become the new hegemon in the 21st century and with what rules for the international system.

Kenneth N. Waltz disagrees with Professor Gilpin's power hierarchy and concludes that a *bipolar* distribution of power, with two states or alliances balancing each other with about equal power, offers the best chance to avoid war. Professor Waltz much prefers a bipolar to a multipolar system. Peace is fragile in an anarchic system, and a bipolar arrangement will lead states to be more cautious and will make calculations about peace simpler, while a multipolar arrangement allows the miscalculation of one state to drag all the others into war.[49]

Waltz, impressed with the supposed value of bipolarity between the United States and the Soviet Union in the Cold War, would probably have trouble demonstrating the peace-preserving value of bipolarity across the breadth of history.[50] Indeed, the Soviet-American bipolarity may have been fairly unique; for instance, the mutual fear of nuclear holocaust had never characterized international relations before.

Many scholars believe the *multipolar* division of power offers the best chance to avoid war. With a number of important states available, leaders can form alliances and adjust them by attracting new members to maintain an equilibrium in power. When counter-alliances are about equal in power and unable to predict victory, both sides will be less likely to initiate war, or such is the theory.

If theorists could decide on the "best" power distribution to avoid war, no one could simply reinvent the world's power structure and form that particular distribution. Actually, history does not provide clear and conclusive evidence that any power arrangement will prevent aggression or war.

Edward Mansfield's research, an empirical study using quantified data drawn from historical cases and statistical analysis, concluded that polarity, or the number of major states in the international system, did not appear to be related to the outbreak of war. Relative inequality in the concentration of power among the states, however, does relate to the occurrence of war. Mansfield asserts that when one state thinks it holds a power advantage and the benefits will outweigh the costs of war, it may choose the course of war. Mansfield's study has reinvigorated the power distribution debate among realists, but other scholars will probably continue to question if the power distribution of the international system has anything at all to do with the catastrophe of war.[51]

A concern with various power structures at the global level may be less relevant today. The Soviet Union is no more, and the chance of war among the major states that remain is slight, if not nonexistent. Regional distributions of power, on the other hand, may be highly pertinent. Power arrangements—say, in Indian-Pakistani relations or in Iraqi-Iranian affairs—could still have a bearing on the outbreak of war.

With the large variety of possible causes of war, failure to reach consensus about a single reason for war is not surprising. Writers wishing to generalize about war's causes have had to deal with phenomena as diverse as one Greek city-state starting a war by insulting the gods of another, the Roman pursuit of glory in empire building, the concern of the Middle Ages with religion, the role of nationalism and other ideologies in the nineteenth and twentieth centuries, ethnic conflict, and the inequitable distribution of economic resources. To repeat an earlier point, the explanation of war may remain multicausal. Yet the pursuit of the causes of war remains critical, since the more we know about war, the better are prospects for preventing this bane of humankind. If we can believe that war is impermanent in the human situation, we can hope for a better and more peaceful future. Today the decline of international war among states preferring to focus on economic progress may reflect a giant step forward in the process of "unlearning" war.

TYPES OF WAR

International relations specialists interested in patterns of war always want to know about the type of war in a particular case or the type of war that characterizes a period of history. The ability to classify wars may help us answer some of the questions that arise about warfare and produce meaningful generalizations. This section describes some widely recognized types of war.

Conventional war is usually conducted by the uniformed military personnel of states that use modern weapons such as tanks, ships, artillery, warplanes, and other modern technology short of dread weapons of mass destruction, which include nuclear, chemical, and biological weapons. Conventional technology today can include the high-tech weapons that appeared in the Persian Gulf War in 1991, principally the "smart bombs" guided to their targets by a laser beam and Tomahawk cruise missiles directed to their objectives by a television camera in the missiles' noses.

Although a formal declaration of war does not necessarily precede conventional wars today, all states are accountable to the laws of war, namely the Geneva Conventions. The last declaration of war by the United States was made against Japan following that country's attack on Pearl Harbor. Conventional wars have occurred less frequently in recent decades; some examples are the Israeli-Arab wars, the Indian-Pakistani wars, the Falkland Islands War of 1982, and the Iran-Iraq War (1980–1988).

The Iran-Iraq War is a special case, since it involved **chemical warfare** as well as conventional weapons. The Iraqis used a lethal gas against Iranian troops similar to the mustard gas of the First World War. Lethal gas and germs, or **biological** warfare, are illegal to use in war, although a few states still stockpile such weapons. These, along with **nuclear weapons,** are heinous, dread weapons and are beyond the pale of conventional war.

The sole incident of nuclear war occurred when the United States dropped two atomic bombs on Japanese cities in 1945, resulting in the Japanese surrender and the end of the Second World War. The morality of that act still produces debate today. Yet, President Harry Truman had to choose between the lives of Japanese civilians and, as he thought, 225,000 American casualties that would occur in an invasion of the Japanese home islands.

Currently, the nuclear weapons of the United States and those of Russia, if used, could destroy the world in a **nuclear winter.** At this point, a nuclear winter scenario is only a theory that remains untested, and no sane person wants such a test. According to this theory, following the immediate fireball of a nuclear explosion and the widespread radioactive fallout, tremendous dust clouds will rise and block out the sun for days or weeks. Without the sun, all life will perish, leaving behind a dead planet.

The uncertainty of what will become of Soviet nuclear weapons has dampened the exultation over the end of the Cold War with the Soviet Union. The dismantling of nuclear weapons in Russia and the United States is taking place, but the much lower weapons level of the Strategic Arms Reduction Talks II has yet to reach completion. Even with all disarmament agreements fulfilled, the old Cold War antagonists will still have important nuclear arsenals. We will take up disarmament again in Chapter Ten.

Earlier, in the list of patterns of war in Table 5.1, we saw that one of the commonly held generalizations about war is that nuclear wars are irrational because no goal is worth the horrendous destruction that would result. This generalization may have held up for four decades between the United States and the Soviet Union, but there is no assurance that a nuclear war will not occur sometime in the future. As the proliferation of nuclear weapons continues, a Third World state might decide to use nuclear weapons against an opponent. Also, Israel, confronted in war by a powerful Arab alliance, might decide to use its nuclear weapons to avoid defeat.

Today **guerrilla wars** are much more common than conventional wars. The tactics of guerrilla war are ancient, but today's military experts regard them as a honed art as practiced and written by Mao Zedong (1893–1976). His war against the Nationalist government of China in the 1930s and 1940s was a textbook case of how to fight guerrilla war. General Vo Nguyen Giap (1912–), a Vietnamese disciple of Mao, successfully used similar tactics against United States forces in Vietnam. Basically, guerrilla war calls for hit-and-run tactics, ambushes, and, under Mao's teachings, a major effort to win support from the civilian population to support the guerrillas.

Another teaching of Mao advocates that guerrillas stay with hit-and-run tactics against stronger conventional forces until the guerrillas grow in strength equal to their opponent; then they can escalate to conventional tactics themselves. Guerrilla war can last for years, perhaps decades, until the conventional side tires and gives up. The tactics of guerrilla war frustrated not only American leadership in Vietnam but also the Soviets in Afghanistan and the Europeans in their colonial wars.

Counterguerrilla war or counter-insurgency tactics have developed to offset the tactics of guerrilla war, but with mixed success. The United States in Vietnam, borrowing from the military successes of the British in Malaya and Kenya, used "search-and-destroy" techniques to dislodge guerrillas and keep them on the run, "carpet bombing" by strategic bombers to destroy underground bunkers, the "hamlet" housing arrangement to separate villagers from the guerrillas, tracking dogs to find guerrillas, and many other techniques that can hurt a guerrilla enemy.

In a guerrilla war, it is willpower that often proves decisive. Frequently guerrilla wars, whether fought in deserts, jungles, or cities, bog down into a long-term slugfest of wills. These wars do not always escalate in Maolike fashion to the conventional level and then find success.

Low-intensity warfare describes a war that festers with sporadic fighting and few casualties but seemingly will not end. The lingering war between the British and the Irish Republican Army (IRA) in northern Ireland is a low-intensity war as well as an urban guerrilla war. Fighting since the mid-1970s, the IRA has terrorized northern Ireland and Great Britain, although causing comparatively few casualties. In its Christmas bombing attack in London in 1991, the IRA gave advance warning to the authorities. Apparently the IRA did not want to cause casualties so much as disrupt trade and traffic. Perhaps the message of the IRA is that while it cannot beat the British army, it can remain a thorn in the side of the British indefinitely. Sinn Fein, the political arm of the IRA, began promising negotiations with the British government about the future of northern Ireland in the mid-1990s. Negotiations faltered when the IRA refused to disarm, and some bombing was renewed. With the Labour Party coming to power in 1997, replacing Prime Minister John Major and his Conservative Party, the stymied negotiations may take on a new energy.

Civil war is another common type of war fought in the last several decades, but it has appeared in earlier centuries on occasion. A civil war is fought between two political groups within the same country. Either the two groups are fighting over which group will be the only government of the entire state or one faction wants to break away and establish a new, separate government on part of the country's territory.

In many cases, civil wars involve fighting along ethnic lines. Ethnic identities derive from cultural differences based on language, religion, tribe, and historical differences such as special territorial attachments. Culturally distinct groups often find it hard to share the same government. The fighting in Cyprus between Greeks and Turks in the 1960s, in Lebanon between Christians and Muslims from the 1970s to the present, in Rwanda between Hutu and Tutsi, and in Bosnia between Muslims and Serbs are examples of ethnic civil wars.

Civil wars also result from ideological differences such as those created by the Cold War. Both Korea and Vietnam, countries with hardly any ethnic divisions, became divided into a communist north identified with the Soviet camp and a dictatorial south identified with the United States. The wars fought in these countries in the 1950s and 1960s, respectively, were Cold War international struggles, but they were also civil wars between north and south.

Civil wars in modern times have occurred mostly in Third World countries, but with the rapid changes occurring in former communist Europe, conflicts such as that in Bosnia could occur in other countries. Finally, some of the bloodiest civil wars happened prior to the twentieth century. The Civil War in the United States (1861–1865) remains this country's most costly war. The T'ai P'ing War (1850–1864) in China may have taken 30 million lives.

Rebellion and **revolution** also have occurred frequently in the Third World, although other areas have seen these conflicts as well. A rebellion is a popular uprising usually in one part of a country, by one element of the population, and the violence involved is usually spontaneous in nature. A rebellion, however, may easily escalate into a revolution with a highly organized effort to overthrow the government and to transform society according to an ideological blueprint. When students boycott school and stone the police in South Africa or in the Gaza Strip adjacent to Israel, they are in rebellion. When organized fighters motivated by ideology, such as the Sandinistas in Nicaragua, fight for years for the chance to capture the government and then use it to restructure society, a revolution has occurred. Ethnic identities as well may fuel rebellion and revolution, as in the Chechen breakaway effort in Russia beginning in the winter of 1995.

Sometimes neatly categorizing a given war under a single type is an almost impossible task. Wars can be complex, representing several types at the same time. For instance, the Vietnam War was a guerrilla war in the south fought by the Viet Cong as a revolt against the Saigon government. This was also was a civil war, with Vietnamese elites in Hanoi and

Saigon sending uniformed troops against one another. And the Vietnam War was an international war, since the Hanoi and Saigon governments were the proxies for the superpowers locked in a global struggle during the Cold War.

Guerrilla war, civil war, low-intensity war, rebellion, and revolution are internal wars that add up to 20 to 40 conflicts going on in the world in any given year. Their frequency contrasts with today's unusual occurrence of international war. These internal conflicts have spawned a resurgence of the "warrior" type of fighter as opposed to the conventional soldier.[52] The Cossacks that puzzled Clausewitz were from a warrior society. Western countries' militaries and UN Peacekeeping forces are increasingly encountering these undisciplined, savage fighters with a "no-surrender" attitude.

Warriors hide out among civilians in the rabbit-warren slums of Mogadishu, Somali, or those in the Gaza Strip, or they may move in "shoot-and-scoot" fashion as mortar teams or snipers. They have bloodied and battered the best of troops, including U.S. Marines and French Legionnaires in Lebanon in 1983 and European troops in Bosnia after the breakup of Yugoslavia. Chechen fighters, drawing on their warrior heritage, embarrassed the once vaunted Russian army for about two years. Warriors have their own value systems that render the rules of engagement under the Geneva Conventions mostly irrelevant.

Finally, the types of wars described here are the subject for many news articles and are not unknown to the general public. Much more esoteric is the recently rediscovered just war concept.

THE JUST WAR CONCEPT

The brief Persian Gulf War in 1991 was important because a coalition of states, acting under the auspices of the United Nations, stopped Iraqi aggression in Kuwait. As in the case of Korea 50 years earlier, the United Nations implemented a version of collective security called for under the UN Charter. Collective security involves the use of force by the society of states to stop aggression. Ideally, under collective security, states are to provide help for the good of all whether or not their immediate national interests are at stake.

Moreover, this war was important because the advocates of force couched the action in **just war** terms. In his work *Just and Unjust Wars,* Michael Walzer says that a just war has a moral dualism: Its supporters must fight not only for moral *reasons* but with moral *means* as well.[53] UN collective security in Korea and the Persian Gulf represented the good of all by stopping aggression and by using a multinational force, representing international society, to do so.

Historically, the just war concept is traceable to an early Christian tradition in the fourth century A.D. The European Crusades to the Holy Land were just wars blessed by the Roman Catholic pope. Changing this situation, the Treaty of Westphalia of 1648 marked the beginning not only of sovereign states but the sovereign right to make war for practical national interests rather than moral causes. Warmakers then relegated questions about justice to the background. On occasion over the centuries, however, Catholic and Protestant clergy and political leaders have revived the just war concept to support their own causes.[54]

President George Bush's first rationale for the Persian Gulf War concerned the supply of oil to the world market and the loss of jobs that would follow an oil shortage. This practical

TABLE 5.2

Principles of a Just War

- The cause must be just—the defense of Kuwait from aggression based on a Western perception of threat.
- A lawful authority must decide to use force—the United States Congress and the United Nations Security Council authorized the use of force, but only after some U.S. forces were already on the scene.
- The use of force must be a final resort—the UN coalition applied economic sanctions first, but perhaps did not give them enough time to have a desired effect.
- The war must offer proportionality, meaning the good achieved must outweigh the damage done—the UN coalition freed Kuwait from Iraqi clutches, but with great ecological damage to the area and by killing thousands of Iraqi soldiers, not to mention "friendly fire" killing some American and British troops.
- The war must carry at least a probability of success—the superior United Nations forces won a quick victory and with lighter casualties than expected.
- The methods of the war must minimize damage to noncombatants—the accurate bombing restricted collateral damage, but probably many civilians died in Iraq as a result of the war.

rationale did not play well in the United States, and so President Bush shifted to concerns over aggression, humanitarian obligations to the Kuwaitis, and just war principles. Pentagon officials even defended battlefield practices, or means, as being in accord with just war principles.[55] However, the American effort to apply the just war dualism of moral reasons and moral means did not always consistently fit the Persian Gulf War situation, as Table 5.2 indicates.[56]

Although a just war rationale can buttress the use of collective security under the United Nations, neither the UN Charter nor contemporary written international law refers to the just war concept.[57] Also, we should bear in mind that classic just war doctrine originally allowed for *unilateral* action to enforce a *religious* morality, whereas collective security justifies *multilateral* action to enforce *secular* international law.[58] How well just war principles will fit collective security efforts of the future will be a subject of exceptional interest.

Although a just war rationale can offer moral support for taking to the battlefield, what might be better for the world would be a widely shared sense of justice that would reduce the need for fighting. Indeed, a truly well-ordered international society would protect broadly accepted values and use peaceful procedures to settle conflict to the satisfaction of the members of the society.[59] Unfortunately, differences over what entails justice can still induce the occasional state—and other actors, such as ethnic groups—to consider war as a means to redress grievances. Humankind's experience with war does not bode well for completely ridding the world of this painful and costly instrument.

TO PURGE WAR

Humankind has dreamed of purging war from their lives down through the millennia. Some exceptions are nomadic tribes with warrior cultures, fascists, and occasionally democratic publics in a mood of jingoism. Today the prospects of completely purging war from the international system may be dim, but prospects are as good as or better than at any time in history.[60] We can at least review some thought on how to purge war.

TABLE 5.3
Costs of War

First World War	$380 billion
Second World War	$3.1 trillion
Korean War	$265 billion
Vietnam War	$570 billion

Source: Congressional Research Service.

Idealists

Imaginative thinkers have offered many schemes over the centuries to eliminate war. Frequently these thinkers view war as a product of the anarchy that comes from kings, or modern governments, sending their armies to war whenever they wish. Corrective schemes typically call for centralized control over governments and military power, in other words, world government. The Quaker missionary William Penn offered his 1693 *Essay Toward the Present and Future Peace of Europe.* His plan called for the kings of Europe to form a parliament that would represent all of them, and decisions would require a three-fourths vote. Decisions by vote would preempt the use of war as a change agent.

A more recent purge scheme is the 1960 *World Peace Through World Law* of Grenville Clark and Louis B. Sohn of Harvard Law School. Their scheme called for transforming the world by converting the United Nations Charter into a constitution calling for a representative world federal government. Professors Clark and Sohn did not tell us how to persuade people to accept the uncertainties of this scheme.[61] The numerous civil wars in the world teach us that government by itself is no panacea for war. Without the underpinning of the shared value of a world culture, a world government unquestionably would be a vain effort.

Perhaps more surrealistic than idealistic is a unique and interesting approach to ending warfare. In Aristophanes' play *Lysistrata,* written in 412 B.C., the Greek women, tired of intermittent war, deny sex to their men until the fighting stops. This play is, of course, fiction, but this policy did halt warfare in the context of the play.

Intellectual Argument

In the classical state system, leaders often viewed war as an honorable and even heroic tool of foreign policy, but by the twentieth century war had become a regrettable option of last resort with declining legality. In time, intellectual arguments appeared against the utility of war, and Norman Angell's economic argument may be the best known of these. Angell first expressed his ideas on the futility of war in a pamphlet that appeared in 1909 and expanded his thinking in *The Great Illusion,* published after the First World War. He pointed out that British trade did not improve with Germany's defeat, the seizure of German East Africa did not pay one-hundredth of the cost of the war, and European countries' economies were so enmeshed with one another as a result of the industrial age that no country could benefit from war. Angell was an early student of the binding ties of interdependence. The futility of war exists, according to Angell, and yet, incredibly, people keep fighting wars because they do not recognize this futility.[62]

Clyde Wells and *The Augusta Chronicle*

Other scholars also see little gain in war or armaments. Seymour Melman claims that the predatory effects of spending money on the military erodes a state's economic growth. A wartime economy, he says, is an inflation machine that eventually causes unemployment. Further, materials made for the military rarely have civilian application; thus, military expenditures are a permanent loss to the economy.[63] For example, by 1992, the United States government had spent $7 billion trying to incinerate lethal gas stocks that it no longer wanted. Karen Rasler and William R. Thompson have found that large, global wars permanently increase government expenditures and tax revenues and play a major role in the increased centralization of power of the state.[64] At least economically, wars appear to offer only liabilities.

A balanced view of war, however, requires that we recognize that states have fought defensive wars against tyranny. In the Second World War, the Allies preserved democracy in western Europe and prevented imperialistic Japan from colonizing the Pacific region by conquest. Moreover, peoples have fought to end colonial subjugation and racism. So are all wars morally bad? Are there not at least some necessary and even just wars? Does the winning of some wars justify the loss of life on a major scale, such as when the United States lost well over 300,000 people in the combat of the Second World War? Perhaps, but the necessity of fighting a war and finding a just cause for that war depends ultimately on the point of view.

Whether a war brings an advantage to a state or whether it involves a just cause are interesting questions, but undoubtedly war always has serious consequences. In addition to lives lost and property destroyed, losing and winning wars often determine boundary lines and types of government. In the twentieth century, for example, Germany's experience

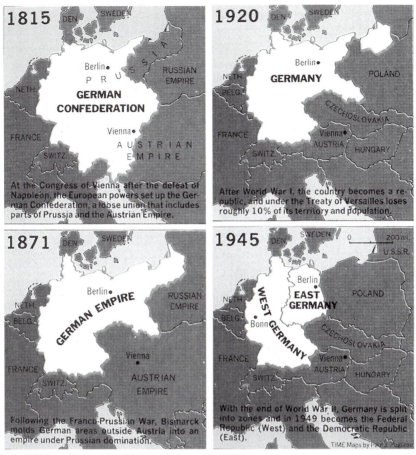

© 1989 Time, Inc. Reprinted by permission.

with war has been especially negative. Germany has lost millions of lives and much territory, and the visitors imposed democratic government on Germany's authoritarian society after each of the two world wars.

The Legal Status of War

Controlling warfare by law has been the chief issue concerning force. Before the twentieth century, the state system was permissive about states going to war. At least since the Napoleonic wars ended in 1815, a gradual but steady increase in the disapproval of war as a legitimate tool of foreign policy has taken place. Belief in the norms against war now underpins legal prohibitions, amounting to a watershed of cultural change in the evolution of international society.[65]

The acceptance of the League of Nations Covenant as international law in 1919 seriously undermined the sovereign right of states to go to war at their discretion. Articles 10 and 11 of the Covenant made any act of aggression or war the business of all states.

Articles 12, 13, and 15 required states to use peaceful settlement of issues before going to war. Moreover, states could not go to war in less than three months following the peaceful settlement effort. Under Article 16, if a state went to war without trying peaceful settlement first, it could face required economic sanctions and voluntary military sanctions by the other members. The Covenant, however, did not prevent the multiple aggressions of the 1930s or the Second World War.

The 1928 Kellogg-Briand Pact attempted to outlaw war in a categorical way except for the right of self-defense. Though a legal step beyond the League Covenant, this pact proved to be a futile and idealistic bar to war.

Today the only undisputed, legal uses of force are twofold. First, there is the right of self-defense against the armed attack of another state found in Article 51 of the UN Charter. Second, the use of collective security, under the auspices of the United Nations in Charter articles 39 and 42, is legitimate, such as when the Coalition Forces of the United Nations stopped Iraqi aggression against Kuwait in 1991. In addition to military force, the United Nations can require the use of diplomatic and economic sanctions by member-states. Without doubt, the traditional use of war as a rational cost-gain instrument of policy, in the spirit of Clausewitz, is impermissible under modern international law.

The UN Charter remains as the principal law on force as we move into the 21st century, and the Charter clearly renounces the use of force in spite of attempts by some states to argue for exceptions to the law. States, however, would be in a quandary without other remedies to solve problems besides the use of force, and alternatives to force are available. The Charter recommends the peaceful settlement of disputes by negotiation or the adjudication of disputes through the International Court of Justice as substitutes for force. Obviously, full respect for the Charter would make for a more cooperative and peaceful international society.

Realistically, the world is only at a transitional stage between the sharp conflict of war and an expanding pattern of cooperation. Sometimes states still think they need to defend their interests with force, or they simply find force expedient. Nonetheless, when states violate Charter law, they do not change it; rather, states come under scrutiny and criticism as a result of their transgression of the law. Justification for any breach of the law prohibiting force places a heavy "burden of proof" on the transgressor.

The human situation with respect to war may be improving because humankind can learn from history. Military historian John Keegan perceives a new resolution by humankind to have a less violent and disorderly world. He writes, "War, it seems to me, after a lifetime of reading about the subject, mingling with men of war, visiting the sites of war and observing its effects, may well be ceasing to commend itself to human beings as a desirable or productive, let alone rational, means of reconciling their discontents."[66] Charting the course of a human warlike past toward a potentially peaceful future is the theme of Professor Keegan's critically acclaimed *A History of Warfare*. To put the control of force in perspective, we should remember that in the domestic context of states, though central governments are present, the use of force frequently violates the law. So can we reasonably expect the international level, governmentless as it is, to do better? At least in international society, legal understanding of the use of force is clear. What is not clear is how to dissuade states from using force except in self-defense and how to stop aggression consistently through collective action. The concept of international society requires respect for a common body of law, but, as in domestic society, respect for the law is a matter of degree. Overall, we can conclude that the United Nations and charter law help constrain the use of force and reduce the degree of anarchy among states.

LESSER CONFLICTS

The traditional view of international relations is that power-oriented, ambitious states readily deploy armies on the assumption that war will bring them positive results. More realistically, many leaders have hesitated to wage war because of the huge costs in terms of blood and treasure. Searches by governments for instruments of policy less costly than war have been common in history. In Savannah, Georgia, the author once saw two Revolutionary War cannon that were part of a historical display. On the barrel of one cannon, in Latin, the phrase "The Final Answer of Kings" appears. Waging war is more often than not a last resort after attempting lesser means.

Especially in the Cold War, much conflict occurred in the "intermediacy" between peace and war. Many scholars have observed the paradox of major states having more power than ever before but less opportunity to use it. The fear of a nuclear holocaust or the frustration of fighting a guerrilla war make Carl von Clausewitz's idea of "using war to compel an opponent to do our will" a complicated matter.

Conflict below the level of war can involve many different measures, including retorsion, demonstrations of force, reprisals, military intervention, and state-sponsored terrorism. States make tactical choices about these measures according to the circumstances they face. States do not employ these measures in any particular order; in fact, a state can bypass these measures altogether, as Japan did when this country deserted negotiations to launch a surprise attach on Pearl Harbor on December 7, 1941. This "day of infamy," as President Franklin D. Roosevelt called it, immediately brought the United States into the Second World War.

Retorsion

An unfriendly but legal act by a state to protest an act by another state is **retorsion.** Retorsion does not involve armed force. The best-known instance of retorsion is the severance of diplomatic relations, an act any state has the legal right to commit at any time. The United States broke off diplomatic relations with Iran when its citizens seized the U.S. embassy in Tehran in 1979. Sometimes countries merely call their ambassadors home for "consultations," as most of Europe did when Francisco Franco, the dictator of Spain, carried out his plan to hang Basque terrorists in the mid-1970s. The European states were protesting the use of capital punishment in Spain.

Other acts of retorsion states might employ involve limiting the movements of the diplomats and citizens of foreign states, freezing the national assets of one state in the banks of another, refusing to renew trade treaties, raising tariffs, or curbing commercial fishing privileges by foreigners. An unusual act of retorsion was President Jimmy Carter's refusal to allow athletes from the United States to participate in the 1980 Summer Olympics held in Moscow. His decision was a protest against the Soviet Union's invasion of Afghanistan in 1979.

Demonstrations

A display of military force, or a **demonstration,** without firing a shot, is useful to underscore a foreign policy choice by a state. Just the availability of a standing military force at home or overseas is evidence of willpower to defend a state's interests. Placing these forces on ready-alert in a crisis can send a tacit message to another state that it is treading on vital interests.

The mere visits of ships and planes of one country to another can show interest and support. In 1946, the United States wanted a pretext for supporting Turkey against communist pressures originating from southeastern Europe. U.S. leaders chose to return the body of a Turkish ambassador who had died in Washington, D.C., aboard the *USS Missouri,* the ship on which the Japanese surrender took place in 1945. Completion of this task placed the battleship of a friendly power in Turkish waters.

In 1976, North Korean soldiers murdered two United States Army officers as they pruned a tree in the DMZ along the 38th parallel in Korea. The U.S. military placed massive forces in the area, including B-52 bombers circling overhead, and then sent infantry into the DMZ to cut the tree down. Demonstrations are discrete moves to handle an immediate and specific problem, but leaders need more basic policies to resolve serious conflict.[67]

Reprisals

A coercive measure to make a state reach a settlement or to punish another state for a past wrong is a **reprisal.** The coercion can be nonviolent, such as the seizure of property or a navel blockade, or violent, as in the case of an armed attack. Reprisals are usually thought of as illegal. A military reprisal appears to violate the UN Charter's prohibition against the use of military force. Although some leaders and legal scholars argue that reprisal may be legal according to customary international law, written law, such as the UN Charter, normally takes precedence over law based on customary practices of the past. Perhaps reprisals are best understood as the enforcements of the strong states against the weak without weighty concern for right and wrong.

A well-known act of reprisal was President Ronald Reagan's bombing attack in 1986 against Libya. It was thought, without clear evidence, that Libya had sponsored terrorist attacks against U.S. military personnel in Germany. U.S. B-111 bombers, from a base in Great Britain, and jet fighters, from aircraft carriers in the Mediterranean Sea, caused serious damage and may have killed Libyan leader Moammar Gadhafi's adopted daughter.

Two years later, in December 1988, a bomb exploded on board a Pan Am passenger plane over Lockerbie, Scotland, killing 270 people, mostly citizens of the United States. President George Bush's government indicted two Libyan intelligence officers for the bombing and would not rule out a military response. The Libyans may have blown up this flight to retaliate for the 1986 bombing of their country. The United Nations has sponsored communication, diplomatic, and economic sanctions against Libya to force it to surrender the indicted suspects, but so far to no avail.

One danger of reprisal is that it can turn into a tit-for-tat series of blows. The continuing series of reprisals and counter-reprisals between Israel and the Arab countries and Palestinians is at times hard to distinguish from continuing warfare. The current effort by the Israelis to extend a measure of autonomy to Palestinians in the occupied territories, in spite of continued violence by extremists on both sides, may help break up the cycle of reprisals. Unfortunately, the negotiations faltered when the Likud party came to power in Israel in 1996.

A rare type of reprisal, but one that deserves mention, is the *anticipatory reprisal,* a retaliation against an expected *future* wrong. A well-known case is the Israeli bombing of Iraq's Osirak nuclear reactor in 1981. The future harm is thought of as a certainty, and a preemptive blow is thus thought to be necessary.[68] The UN Charter, under Article 51, allows self-defense, but is anticipatory reprisal self-defense? The Israelis believed Iraq was preparing an atom bomb for use against their country. The Iraqis, and the French who were helping with the reactor, denied that the nuclear facility was making a bomb. The Security Council of the United Nations failed to see the bombing as self-defense and condemned the Israeli action. An anticipatory reprisal is harder to justify legally than the usual reprisal.

Intervention

"Intervention" is a vague political term rather than a legal one and reflects a panoply of definitions that range from radio interference with another country's air waves to the dropping of paratroopers on a foreign capital. Since intervention usually violates another state's sovereignty, it carries a negative connotation. As Evan Luard has observed, intervention is what other people do, not what we do ourselves.[69]

Intervention is the forceful interference in the affairs of another state. Intervention can be nonviolent, such as when foreign agents bribe a government's officials. Indirect intervention can occur through proxies, for example, when the Soviet Union used Cuban troops to fight along the Angolan-Namibian border to oppose South African racist policies and to free Namibia. Intervention can also be clandestine, such as if the CIA, or some other intelligence agency, assists foreign subversives in a *coup d'état,* the overthrow of a legal government. The interventions that raise the greatest concerns are military operations that openly cross a border.

Perhaps the most important motive behind intervention in modern times has been the desire of superpowers to guarantee the tenure of friendly governments in their spheres of influence. The former Soviet Union once dominated eastern Europe and other states along its border. The Soviet Union crushed rebellions in East Germany and Hungary in 1956 with tanks. Later the Soviet Union exercised the "Brezhnev Doctrine," a claim by the Soviet leader, Leonid I. Brezhnev, that the Soviets had a duty to protect neighboring communist governments from countercommunist forces. On this pretext, the Soviet Union intervened in Czechoslovakia in 1968 to block a democratizing movement in that state. Armored units, drawn not only from the Soviet Union but also from East Germany and Poland, carried out the intervention.

In 1979, the Soviet Union intervened in Afghanistan to prop up a communist government there, but the intervention turned into a lengthy and bloody war of frustration. Today some of the former republics of the Soviet Union worry that Russia may intervene in these republics, what the Russians call the "Near Abroad," to protect the 25 million Russians living there.

The United States has a lengthy tradition of intervention that continues into modern times, especially in Latin America. Acts of intervention by the United States had become so common by the 1930s that President Franklin D. Roosevelt felt compelled to advocate a "Good Neighbor Policy." President Roosevelt designed this policy to improve relations by promising no more interventions. Unfortunately, by the 1950s, the "threat of communist expansion" in the "backyard" of the United States led to further acts of intervention during the Cold War period.

In 1954, the United States successfully overthrew a leftist government in Guatemala through proxy forces, but failed miserably to unseat Fidel Castro's communist government with the Bay of Pigs invasion by Cuban exiles in 1961. In 1962, President John F. Kennedy intervened in Cuba by creating a unique form of naval blockade, which he called a "naval quarantine," to force the Soviet Union to withdraw its intermediate-range nuclear missiles from Cuba. The United States prevented a "communist government" from coming to power in the Dominican Republic by sending troops there in 1965. In the Dominican case, the United States chose to operate under the mantel of the Organization of American States (OAS) as a cloak of legitimacy. To symbolize this mantel, the United States asked Brazil to send troops, and by acting together, they claimed to carry out the will of the OAS. Other anticommunist interventions by the United States in Latin America involved the support of proxy forces known as "contras" in Nicaragua in the early 1980s and the United States' effort to purge a communist government in Grenada in 1983.

The last major intervention by the United States occurred in Panama in December 1989 as an action called "Operation Just Cause." Without facing a communist threat of any kind, U.S. forces defeated the Panamanian defense forces and arrested a de facto head of state, General Manuel Noriega, on Panamanian soil for crimes under U.S. drug statutes. Then, before leaving, the United States set up the government of its choice. The OAS condemned this act of bold intervention by a vote of 20 to 1, with the United States casting the lone dissenting vote.[70] The Panamanian intervention is a clear case of a great power doing as it wishes in its sphere of influence because it finds force convenient.

When the superpowers of the Soviet Union and the United States have intervened, a pattern involving several characteristics has appeared. First, a huge power asymmetry existed between the superpower and its victim, a situation offering much temptation for a quick and easy solution. Second, the superpowers often drew allies around them to shield their acts with the guise of "collective legitimacy," such as when a regional organization ostensibly approves the intervention. Third, to minimize any stigma from intervention, the superpowers preferred the "quick-in, quick-out" method of occupation so they are not on the victim's soil more than a few weeks or months. Fourth, the motive for intervention was to put a preferred government in power or to prop one up.

Numerous countries besides superpowers have followed interventionist policies, and acts of intervention amount to several hundred since the Second World War. France and Great Britain have gone to the aid of ex-colonies, and Third World countries have intervened in one another from time to time. In 1979, Tanzania intervened in Uganda to rid Africa of the pariah government of Idi Amin. In 1974, Turkey intervened in Cyprus to protect the Turkish minority there.

Finally, intervention essentially represents the "rule of the strong" instead of the "rule of law," and consequently intervention threatens the harmony of the emerging international society. In spite of a history of intervention in the world, the *duty* of nonintervention, as the corollary of the *right* to state sovereignty, remains a principle of international law

Ramirez and Copley News Service

among states. Acts of intervention face loud condemnation and strong resentment by a growing consensus of disapproval within an emerging international society.[71] The much-discussed subject of humanitarian intervention is a special case and is a topic of Chapter Twelve.

State-Sponsored Terrorism

The international society condemns terrorism of all kinds as illegal and heinous because it is beyond the pale of humanitarian standards. Yet not only do private groups seek to accomplish their goals by terrorist acts, but a few states do as well. These states are "rogue" or "outlaw" states because their behavior is so atrocious and unacceptable to international society. The State Department of the United States has identified Cuba, Iraq, Iran, Libya, North Korea, the former Soviet Union, Syria, and, as of 1993, the Sudan as states that conduct **state-sponsored terrorism.**

Sometimes a rogue state sends out its own agents as terrorists, or it may use an existing private terrorist organization. Agents of North Korea set off a bomb in Rangoon, Burma (Myanmar), in 1983 in an attempt to assassinate South Korea's top government officials while they were attending a conference. Several countries cooperated in accumulating strong evidence that two Libyan intelligence officers blew up the Pan Am flight over Scotland in 1988.

The involvement of private, or nonstate, organizations in state-sponsored terrorism is not unusual. Iranian-backed Shi'as in Lebanon were responsible for bombing the United

States embassy in Beirut and the U.S. Marine barracks in the same city in 1983. The truck bomb that killed almost 250 marines came from the Bekka Valley under Syrian control.[72] The tentacles of a state willing to foment terrorism can be far reaching. Evidence from telephone wiretaps show that Libyan leaders promised $2.5 million to a Chicago street gang to carry out bombing and assassination acts in the United States.[73]

Moreover, the targets of state terrorism are not always other states. In 1985, French agents blew up the *Rainbow Warrior* in Auckland, New Zealand, to prevent that ship from blocking a French nuclear test in French Polynesia. The *Rainbow Warrior* belonged to Greenpeace, a private, international organization involved in environmental issues.[74]

The motivation of states willing to use terrorism is difficult to fathom because this outlaw behavior usually fails to accomplish its goals. So why would some states opt for terrorism? The answer may lie in the fact that these states are usually weak, Third World countries lacking in wealth and military power that would allow them to pursue radical goals by conventional means. Acts of state-sponsored terrorism may represent the frustration of these states because they are unable to shape the world to their liking, to produce their version of justice. Nonetheless, the hundreds of people they kill creates a climate of fear for millions of others.

The Soviet Union, before its demise, offers an exception since it possessed conventional means commensurate with its goals. Perhaps the best explanation for the Soviet exception lies at the feet of Yuri Andropov, head of the KGB and later top leader of the Soviet Union in 1982 and 1983. In the late 1970s and early 1980s, Soviet terrorism was at its peak. Soviet-sponsored terrorism allegedly committed its most dastardly act with the assassination attempt on Pope John Paul II in 1981.[75]

Some scholars offer an interesting perspective on state-sponsored terrorism by relating it to the concept of *structural terrorism*. They view it as just another element in an array of violent instruments to achieve a goal in international relations.[76] The nature of force has been varied in international relations, so why not include state-sponsored terrorism? Why do we regard such terrorism as beyond the pale of acceptable conduct, making it illegal, when it too, in good Clausewitzian fashion, is the use of force to compel an opponent to comply with a particular will? The answer is that state terrorism is reprehensible and shocking to most actors of international society due to its stealth, randomness, and mayhem that often hurts and kills innocent, unarmed civilians.

Controlling state terrorism is difficult because rogue states are more than willing to conduct their violence by covert means. Unfortunately, international efforts, through trade, communications, and air travel sanctions, have not ended this odious practice. What can halt such terrorism? Perhaps progress will come primarily from the rogue states themselves.

North Korea has made diplomatic overtures to South Korea to improve relations, a promising development recently set back when North Korea reportedly built an atom bomb and executed a commando raid against South Korea in 1996. Syria has an interest in being a power broker in the Middle East and has improved its image accordingly. The Soviet Union's demise preempts future acts of terrorism by that state. Iran may have influenced the Shi'a terrorists in Lebanon to release their British and American hostages because Iran wants better relations with the West. Libya has suggested that it might send the two suspects wanted in the bombing of the Pan Am flight in 1988 to a neutral or Islamic country for trial. Most recently, in 1994, the Sudan gave up the most infamous of all terrorists, a man called Carlos, to French authorities, no doubt to better its image with Western states as well as gain French satellite pictures of Sudanese rebel positions.

Conflict is persistent because interests of various actors are not always compatible. If the elimination of this perennial phenomenon is not possible, the management of conflict becomes the optimal goal.[77] Most states prefer to handle conflict through diplomacy and other peaceful means, but when rogue states resort to state terrorism, they tear at the norms against violence and illicit behavior within the formative international society.

WAR AND INTERNATIONAL SOCIETY

Once observers looked upon war as normal and expected more warfare in the future, although war was an ugly and destructive practice. Over the centuries, a few philosophers and idealists proposed schemes to make war obsolete. Finally, across the decades of the twentieth century, war's illegality grew firmer. Yet many realists, both leaders and scholars, persisted in seeing war as an option of states. As late as the mid-twentieth century, British scholar Martin Wight would maintain that "War is the central feature of international relations, although in academic study this is sometimes forgotten."[78] About the same time, in spite of the illegality of war in the UN Charter, realist Hans Morgenthau thought the history of states reflected continuous preparation for war, fighting in wars, and recovery from war.[79] Realists did not believe the UN Charter could have much effect on the world with its natural forces of power politics operating in an anarchical world of sovereign and armed states.

However, neorealists, led by Kenneth W. Waltz, offer a significant change in the realist view of war. For neorealists, states do not lust for power; rather, they see power merely as useful for defense and providing a sense of security. States are not automatically aggressive and warlike. For Professor Waltz, peace is possible, but it exists as a fragile condition. All-important to him is the structure of power. As observed earlier, Waltz prefers a bipolar world to keep power in balance and avoid war.[80] Faith in the power structure to keep the peace has declined in recent years, however. Scholars, controlling for the power structure in empirical studies, have found that the presence of democracies, and their growth in numbers in the international system, is more important.[81]

The views of Hedley Bull represent a "conceptual bridge" across the abyss between views of realists and the improvements transnationalists perceive. For Professor Bull, war is interpretable in a more positive light, that is, as a regulator of the international system. War can help restore a balance of power and prevent dominance by a single hegemonic power, as when first Napoleon and later Hitler tried to force the European states into one empire. This useful function of war is not alien to realists, but Bull goes further. He sees war, in addition to diplomacy, international law, and the balance of power, as an international institution serving the international society of states. Moreover, Bull observes that the international society of states has agreed not only to limit the legitimate causes of war to self-defense and collective acts that oppose aggression, based on the UN Charter, but, if war breaks out, to engage in war by the "rules of war" known as the Geneva Conventions.[82]

On an even more positive note, transnationalists today observe reliance on "soft power" by states, coupled with a decline in warfare. Major states depend more on their

© Tribune Media Services, Inc. All rights reserved. Reprinted with permission.

trade advantages and have not fought wars against one another in decades. With the end of the Cold War, tensions that would induce them toward war have mostly evaporated. The major states are now busy with terms of trade and stanching war among and within Third World states. Restoring peace in Bosnia also has occupied the major states in the mid-1990s. Nowadays the option to make war appears to be excluded from the "zone of peace," the broad set of states stretching across several continents, including Australia and Japan in the Pacific Ocean, North America, and Europe. With the spread of trade priorities and democracy, war may become obsolete in more areas of the world.[83]

Referring to our analytical models will help put the role of war in a clearer perspective. Unfortunately, the world has not entirely cleared the shadow of *international anarchy*. Disruptive forces remain at work in the world. "Rogue" states still pursue dread weapons such as nuclear weapons and sponsor terrorism. Ethnic clashes, some of them once suppressed by communist control, are erupting inside several states and spilling across the borders of others. The expedient use of force by a major state, as in the "insertion" of troops by the United States into Panama in 1989, remains a possibility. Saddam Hussein of Iraq has proven, with his 1990 invasion of Kuwait, that the occasional leader may believe in the phantasm of a quick and easy victory with splendid rewards. Furthermore, states continue to rub abrasively against one another over an ancient cause of conflict, border disputes, as the Ecuador-Peru clash in early 1995 demonstrates. Yet transnationalists see an *international society* making progress, with potential for further reform that reduces reliance on naked force.

Regarding *issues,* a political evolution is leading the major states to conceptualize the problems of order and security in broadly similar terms, allowing them to cooperate to keep the peace.[84] Furthermore, states today think about the issue of security as economic and environmental concerns as well as a military matter. World leaders, in addition to scholars, are more sensitive to issues concerning socioeconomic and ethnic injustices that lead to civil war, revolution, and terrorism. These kinds of conflict might lend themselves to reform, thus further reducing warfare in the world.[85] Finally, as more states increasingly embrace the responsibility of meeting human needs, they are anxious to avoid wasting needed resources in the destruction of war.[86]

As for *force,* world-shared values more than ever support the rules and norms of the United Nations that render war illegal and call for human welfare and progress to receive due attention. United Nations rules about war have a chance to be effective not only because they are written down in the Charter but because many leaders and peoples believe in them.[87] A leading historian on war, John Keegan, has suggested that war "may well be ceasing to commend itself to human beings as a desirable or productive, let alone rational, means of reconciling their discontents."[88] War, through the evolution of the *international society,* has become less of a scourge to humankind by becoming a less viable instrument for the state.

By stages, war, as once happened with dueling and slavery, first became controversial and now may be moving toward obsolescence. The majority of states appear ready to drop war from their repertoire of instruments of policy. In the Third World, where most violent conflict occurs, many states are beginning to evince an aversion to war, as Japan once did, to concentrate on economic development.[89] War is not an inevitability but a human institution that can experience reform and even disappear.

Should peace blanket not only the prosperous, democratic states but all states in a world cohering around rules and norms for conflict management, we might then speculate about the fruition of a future *international community* similar to that envisioned by Immanuel Kant in the late eighteenth century. Only Europe approximates such a community for now, but the continued spread of democracy and the binding ties of free trade in the world may give fuller life to Kant's vision, thus setting in motion Kant's "perpetual peace."[90] Already empirical evidence from our modern period shows that Kant was right that extensive international trade and the presence of democratic governments in the world are powerful influences for peace.[91]

CHAPTER SUMMARY

War has been a serious, continual problem in the history of humankind, finally reaching a level of threat in the nuclear age that could destroy all planetary life. Warfare represents the best-known danger of international anarchy, a world system in which any sovereign state could go to war at any time for any reason.

The causes of war invite intriguing investigation, but research has found no single cause. The search for causes of war remains important, however. If we know what causes war, we have a better chance to "cure" war as a problem. Our best hope may be to "unlearn" war.

Many types of war can occur, although the most common in current times are civil war and revolution in poorer, ethnic-torn countries. Nuclear war, the most dangerous, is a type states have averted except for the two small atomic bombs dropped on Japan in 1945. Today the specter of "rogue" states acquiring and using atomic bombs and other dread weapons remains. This specter, above all else, may be the clearest element of international anarchy today.

Over time diplomacy, international law, and possibly balance of power arrangements have helped control warfare to some extent. Anarchy has begun to give way to a society of states willing to operate through the same institutions and rules despite significant potential conflict. Other actors, especially the United Nations, have entered the international society and encouraged respect for international law that prohibits war except in self-defense. New views also have developed that recognize a healthy economic interdependence in the world, an interdependence that requires cooperation among states and regards wars as interfering with international prosperity.

One of the most important patterns affecting war today is the fact that the major states are democratic and highly interested in world trade. These leading states, largely in agreement about the world they desire, are busy encouraging democracy and capitalism in other parts of the world and are possibly extending the "zone of peace" to eastern Europe, Russia, and some states in the Third World.

In general, we can conclude that the relevance of war has declined. For a nascent international society to make further progress, however, the world must abandon the war system altogether. Although purging war from the international scene is incomplete and progress in this direction is not inevitable, the potential exists for the world to move deeper into a more cooperative, less war-prone international society.

POINTS OF VIEW

(On nuclear war) *The living will envy the dead.*
—NIKITA KHRUSCHEV
PREMIER OF THE SOVIET UNION, 1957–1964

[The great questions of the day] are not decided by speeches and majority votes, but by blood and iron.
—OTTO VON BISMARK
19TH-CENTURY GERMAN PRIME MINISTER

There never was a good war or a bad peace.
—BENJAMIN FRANKLIN

There is no such thing as an inevitable war. If war comes it will be from failure of human wisdom.
—BONAR LAW
FROM A SPEECH BEFORE WORLD WAR I

I am tired and sick of war. Its glory is all moonshine. It is only those who have neither fired a shot nor heard the shrieks and groans of the wounded who cry aloud for blood, more vengeance, more desolation. War is hell.
—WILLIAM T. SHERMAN
CIVIL WAR GENERAL

Without women, we could not wage war.
—GENERAL COLIN POWELL

It is scarcely possible anywhere in the world today to raise a body of reasoned support for the opinion that war is a justifiable activity.
—JOHN KEEGAN
A *HISTORY OF WARFARE*, pp. 56–57

REVIEW QUESTIONS

1. What are Carl von Clausewitz's views on the role of war? What is John Keegan's cultural challenge to Clausewitz's views?
2. Can you explain, in Konrad Lorenz's terms, why humans are prone to kill their own kind while other animals are not?
3. What is the possibility that war is a learned rather than an instinctive practice?
4. Why do democracies refrain from fighting wars with other democracies?
5. How creditable do you think Social Darwinism is for explaining war?
6. Do you think men and women have different perspectives regarding war? Explain.

7. What kinds of power distribution do scholars relate to the outbreak of war?
8. What is the nature of guerrilla war, and what contributions did Mao Zedong make to this warfare?
9. How well does the just war concept lend itself to the United Nations' use of collective security?
10. What is the legal status of force and war today?

GLOSSARY

biological warfare The use of germs to infect the other side's troops or population to disable or kill them.

chemical warfare The use of lethal or incapacitating gas against the troops or population of the other side.

civil war A war fought inside a state over the control of the central government or because one faction wishes to secede and form a new state.

conventional war War fought by uniformed troops of different states with the standard weapons of the day, excluding dread weapons.

counterguerrilla Tactics used to block the efforts of guerrillas and to defeat them.

demonstration A show of force to indicate the seriousness a state places on a particular concern or policy.

guerrilla war "Hit-and-run" tactics by irregular troops to wear down a stronger conventional force.

intervention A vague political term, rather than a legal one, covering when one state uses dictatorial interference in the affairs of another state, especially sending its troops into the territory of that state.

just war A war fought for a moral cause and by moral means.

low-intensity warfare A festering, inconclusive war with limited casualties that is designed to wear down the willpower of a stronger opponent rather than defeat them.

nuclear weapons Atomic or hydrogen devices usable as bombs or missile warheads to attack either military targets or cities.

nuclear winter A theory of environmental disaster involving a large-scale nuclear war that, through a causal chain, would destroy all life on earth.

rebellion A popular uprising usually in one in part of a country or by one element of the population and mostly spontaneous in nature.

reprisal A coercive act to punish a state for a past wrong; if involving military force, this act has questionable legal status.

retorsion An unfriendly but legal act by one state to protest an act by another state.

revolution A war fought inside a state to overthrow the government and perhaps to reform society according to an ideological blueprint.

state-sponsored terrorism Form of terrorism in which a state sends agents or existing private groups to cause sudden acts of violence and mayhem to serve that state's political objectives.

war An armed struggle between opposing groups inside a state or between states causing a significant number of battle deaths.

RECOMMENDED READINGS

Seyom Brown. *The Causes and Prevention of War.* New York: St. Martin's Press, 1987.

Greg Cashman. *What Causes War? An Introduction to Theories of International Conflict.* New York: Lexington Books, 1993.

Bruce Bueno de Mesquita and David Lalman. *War and Reason: Domestic and International Imperatives.* New Haven, CT: Yale University Press, 1992.

Michael W. Doyle. *Ways of War and Peace: Realism, Liberalism, and Socialism.* New York: W. W. Norton, 1997.

Michael I. Handel. *Masters of War: Sun Tzu, Clausewitz and Jomini.* Portland, OR: Frank Cass, 1992.

Ruth H. Howes and Michael R. Stevenson, eds. *Women and the Use of Military Force.* Boulder, CO: Lynne Rienner Publishers, 1993.

Fred Charles Ikle. *Every War Must End.* Rev. ed. New York: Columbia University Press, 1991.

Donald Kagan. *On the Origins of War and the Preservation of Peace.* New York: Doubleday, 1995.

John Keegan. *A History of Warfare.* New York: Alfred A. Knopf, 1994.

Jack S. Levy. *War in the Modern Great Power System.* Lexington, KY: University of Kentucky Press, 1983.

Evan Luard. *War In International Society.* New Haven, CT: Yale University Press, 1986.

Terry Nardin, ed. *The Ethics of War and Peace: Religious and Secular Perspectives.* Princeton, NJ: Princeton University Press, 1996.

Robert C. North. *War, Peace, Survival: Global Politics and Conceptual Synthesis.* Boulder, CO: Westview Press, 1990.

Daniel Pick. *War Machine: The Rationalization of Slaughter in the Modern Age.* New Haven, CT: Yale University Press, 1993.

James Lee Ray. *Democracy and International Conflict: An Evaluation of the Democratic Peace Proposition.* Columbia, SC: University of South Carolina Press, 1995.

J. David Singer and Paul F. Diehl, ed. *Measuring the Correlates of War.* Ann Arbor, MI: University of Michigan Press, 1990.

Melvin Small and J. David Singer. *International War: An Anthology.* 2nd ed. Chicago: Dorsey Press, 1989.

John G. Stoessinger. *Why Nations Go to War.* 5th ed. New York: St. Martin's Press, 1990.

Kenneth N. Waltz. *Man, the State and War.* New York: Columbia University Press, 1959.

Michael Walzer. *Just and Unjust Wars.* New York: Basic Books, 1977.

David A. Welch. *Justice and the Genesis of War.* Cambridge, England: Cambridge University Press, 1993.

John A. Vasquez. *The War Puzzle.* Cambridge, England: Cambridge University Press, 1993.

ENDNOTES

1. J. David Singer and Melvin Small, *The Wages of War, 1816–1965: A Statistical Handbook* (New York: Wiley, 1972), pp. 19–22.
2. Kalevi J. Holsti, *The State, War, and the State of War* (New York: Cambridge University Press, 1996); Ken Booth, "Human Wrongs and International Relations," *International Affairs,* January 1995, p. 117.
3. Reported in Francis A. Beer, *Peace Against War* (San Francisco: W. H. Freeman, 1981), p. 20.
4. Colonel Harry G. Summers, "What Is War?" *Harper's,* May 1984, pp. 75–78.
5. Michael I. Handel, *Masters of War: Sun Tzu, Clausewitz, and Jomini* (Portland, OR: Frank Cass, 1992), pp. 155–56.
6. John Toland, *In Mortal Combat: Korea, 1950–53* (New York: William Morrow, 1991).
7. Timothy J. Lomperis, *The War Everyone Lost— and Won,* rev. ed. (Washington, D.C.: Congressional Quarterly Press, 1993).
8. Carl von Clausewitz, *On War,* trans. and ed. Michael Howard and Peter Paret (Princeton, NJ: Princeton University Press, 1976).
9. von Clausewitz, *On War;* Peter Paret, *Understanding War: Essays on Clausewitz and the History of Military Power* (Princeton, NJ: Princeton University Press, 1992).
10. Harry G. Summers, *On Strategy: A Critical Analysis of the Vietnam War* (New York: Dell, 1984).
11. Handel, *Masters of War,* pp. 12–15.
12. Handel, *Masters of War,* p. 1; Bernard Brodie, "The Continuing Relevance of *On War,*" in *On War,* p. 52.
13. John Keegan, *A History of Warfare* (New York: Alfred A. Knopf, 1994).
14. Ibid., pp. 6–9, 12.
15. Jack S. Levy, *War in the Modern Great Power System, 1495–1975* (Lexington, KY: University of Kentucky Press, 1983), p. 1.
16. David Dessler, "Beyond Correlations: Toward a Casual Theory of War," *International Studies Quarterly,* September 1991, pp. 337–55.
17. Quincy Wright, *A Study of War,* 2nd ed. (Chicago: University of Chicago Press, 1965); Lewis F. Richardson, *Statistics of Deadly Quarrels* (Chicago: Quadrangle, 1960); Singer and Small, *The Wages of War, 1816–1965.* See also Melvin Small and J. David Singer, *Resort to Arms: International and Civil Wars, 1816–1980* (Beverly Hills, CA: Sage Publications, 1982).
18. Kenneth N. Waltz, *Man, the State and War* (New York: Columbia University Press, 1959).
19. Sigmund Freud, "Why War?" in *International War: An Anthology,* 2nd ed., ed. Melvin Small and J. David Singer (Chicago: Dorsey Press, 1989), pp. 176–81; James E. Dougherty and Robert L. Pfaltzgraff, Jr., *Contending Theories of International Relations,* 3rd ed. (New York: Harper & Row, 1990), p. 227.
20. Konrad Lorenz, *On Aggression* (New York: Harcourt Brace Jovanovich, 1966); James A. Schellenberg, "The Biology of Human Aggression," in *International War: An Anthology,* pp. 162–75.
21. Dougherty and Pfaltzgraff, *Contending Theories,* p. 282.
22. Schellenberg, "The Biology of Human Aggression," pp. 170–71.

23. Edward O. Wilson, *Sociobiology: The New Synthesis* (Cambridge, MA: Harvard University Press, 1975).
24. Seyom Brown, *The Causes and Prevention of War* (New York: St. Martin's Press, 1987), pp. 9–10.
25. John G. Stoessinger, *Why Nations Go to War*, 5th ed. (New York: St. Martin's Press, 1990).
26. Ibid., pp. 205–06.
27. Brown, *The Causes and Prevention of War*, pp. 14–15.
28. R. J. Rummel, "Political Systems, Violence, and War," in *Approaches to Peace*, ed. W. Scott Thompson and Kenneth M. Jensen (Washington, D.C.: United States Institute of Peace, 1991), pp. 347–70.
29. Richard L. Merritt and Dina A. Zinnes, "Democracies and War," in *On Measuring Democracy: Its Consequences and Concomitants*, ed. Alex Inkeles (New Brunswick, NJ: Transaction Publishers, 1991), pp. 207–34.
30. Jack S. Levy, "Domestic Politics and War," in *The Origin and Prevention of Major Wars*, ed. Robert I. Rotberg and Theodore K. Rabb (Cambridge, England: Cambridge University Press, 1989), p. 85.
31. Robert J. Lieber, *No Common Power*, 2nd ed. (New York: HarperCollins, 1991), pp. 253–54.
32. Bruce Russett, "Democracy and Peace," in *Choices in World Politics: Sovereignty and Interdependence*, ed. Bruce Russett, Harvey Starr, and Richard J. Stoll (New York: W. H. Freeman, 1989), pp. 245–60.
33. Zeev Maoz and Bruce Russett, "Normative and Structural Causes of Democratic Peace, 1946–1986," *American Political Science Review*, September 1993, pp. 624–38.
34. Russett, "Democracy and Peace."
35. Dougherty and Pfaltzgraff, *Contending Theories*, pp. 229–32.
36. Ibid., pp. 234–39.
37. Levy, "Domestic Politics and War," pp. 89–90.
38. Schellenberg, "The Biology of Human Aggression," pp. 164–65.
39. Ibid., pp. 167–68.
40. Walter F. Jones, *The Logic of International Relations*, 7th ed. (New York: HarperCollins, pp. 388–90.
41. V. Spike Peterson, ed., *Gendered States: Feminist (Re)Visions of International Relations Theory* (Boulder, CO: Lynne Rienner Publishers, 1992); Rebecca Grant and Kathleen Newland, eds., *Gender and International Relations* (Bloomington, IN: Indiana University Press, 1991).
42. Birgit Brock-Utne, *Educating for Peace: A Feminist Perspective* (New York: Pergamon Press, 1985).
43. *World Press Review*, February 1992, p. 47.
44. Jean Bethke Elshtain and Sheila Tobias, eds., *Women, Militarism, and War: Essays in History, Politics, and Social Theory* (Savage, MD: Rowman & Littlefield, 1990).
45. Cynthia Enloe, *Bananas, Beaches, & Bases: Making Feminist Sense of International Politics* (Berkeley, CA: University of California Press, 1989), pp. 5–7; Cynthia Enloe, *The Morning After: Sexual Politics at the End of the Cold War* (Berkeley, CA: University of California Press, 1993).
46. Marysia Zalewski, "Well, What Is the Feminist Perspective on Bosnia?" *International Affairs*, April 1995, pp. 339–56, especially p. 350.
47. Robert Gilpin, "The Theory of Hegemonic War," in *The Origin And Prevention of War*, pp. 15–37.
48. A. F. K. Organski and Marina Arbetman, "The Second American Century: The New International Order," in *Behavior, Culture, and Conflict in World Politics*, ed. William Zimmerman and Harold K. Jacobson (Ann Arbor, MI: University of Michigan Press, 1993), pp. 99–130.
49. Kenneth W. Waltz, "The Origins of War in Neorealist Theory," in *The Origin and Prevention of War*, pp. 39–52.
50. William R. Thompson, *On Global War: Historical-Structural Approaches to World Politics* (Columbia, SC: University of South Carolina Press, 1988), pp. 196–223.
51. Edward D. Mansfield, *Power, Trade, and War* (Princeton, NJ: Princeton University Press, 1994), pp. 226–30.
52. John Keegan, "On Warfare," *U.S. News & World Report*, January 23, 1995, p. 47; Major Ralph Peters, special to *Newsday* and published in *Savannah News-Press*, August 14, 1994, section D, pp. 1, 8.
53. Michael Walzer, *Just and Unjust Wars: A Moral Argument with Historical Illustrations* (New York: Basic Books, 1977), p. 21.
54. The history of the just war concept is briefly described in Daniel S. Papp, *Contemporary*

International Relations, 2nd ed. (New York: Macmillan, 1988), p. 518; *Time*, February 11, 1991, pp. 42, 51.

55. "Confronting the New World Order: Case Studies in Ethics and Democracy," *Ethics and International Affairs*, Fall 1991, pp. 3–4.

56. These principles are taken from David J. Scheffer, "Use of Force After the Cold War: Panama, Iraq, and the New World Order," in *Right v. Might*, 2nd ed. (New York: Council on Foreign Relations Press, 1991), pp. 109–72; *Time*, February 11, 1991, pp. 42, 51.

57. Scheffer, "Use of Force After the Cold War," p. 134.

58. Ibid., p. 141.

59. David A. Welch, *Justice and the Genesis of War* (Cambridge, England: Cambridge University Press, 1993).

60. Harry B. Hollins, Averill L. Powers, and Mark Sommers, *The Conquest of War* (Boulder, CO: Westview Press, 1989); Robert Woito, *To End War* (New York: The Pilgrim Press, 1982).

61. These examples of idealists are taken from Brown, *The Causes and Prevention of War*, pp. 115–22.

62. J. D. B. Miller, *Norman Angell and the Futility of War: Peace and the Public Mind* (London: Macmillan, 1986); Norman Angell, *The Great Illusion 1933* (New York: Arno Press, 1972).

63. Seymour Melman, "Limits of Military Power: Economic and Other," in *International Political Economy*, ed. Kendall W. Stiles and Tsuneo Akaha (New York: HarperCollins, 1991), pp. 350–62.

64. Karen Rasler and William R. Thompson, "Global Wars, Public Debt and the Long Cycle," *World Politics*, July, 1983, pp. 489–516.

65. Charles W. Kegley and Gregory Raymond, *A Multipolar Peace: Great Power Politics in the Twenty-first Century* (New York: St. Martin's Press, 1994), pp. 124–26. See also Anthony Clark Arend and Robert J. Beck, *International Law and the Use of Force: Beyond the UN Charter Paradigm* (New York: Routledge, 1993).

66. Keegan, *A History of Warfare*, pp. 58–60.

67. The examples above are from Barry M. Blechman and Stephen S. Kaplan, *Force Without War: U.S. Armed Forces as a Political Instrument* (Washington, D.C.: Brookings Institution, 1978), pp. 2, 11, 517, 532.

68. Gerhard von Glahn, *Law Among Nations*, 5th ed. (New York: Macmillan, 1986), p. 566. See also Arend and Beck, *International Law and the Use of Force*, Chapter 5.

69. Evan Luard, "Collective Intervention," in *Intervention in World Politics*, ed. Hedley Bull (Oxford: Clarendon Press, 1984) , p. 157.

70. David J. Scheffer, "Use of Force After the Cold War: Panama, Iraq, and the New World Order," in *Right v. Might: International Law and the Use of Force*, 2nd ed. (New York: Council of Foreign Relations Press, 1991). pp. 109–24.

71. Hedley Bull, "Conclusion," in *Intervention in World Politics*, pp. 181–95.

72. Ray S. Cline and Yonah Alexander, *Terrorism as State-Sponsored Covert Warfare* (Fairfax, VA: Hero Books, 1986), pp. 14, 17.

73. *Time*, December 7, 1987, p. 27.

74. *Time*, August 19, 1985, p. 28.

75. Cline and Alexander, *Terrorism as State-Sponsored Covert Warfare*, pp. 11–13; Ray S. Cline and Yonah Alexander, *Terrorism: The Soviet Connection* (New York: Crane Russak, 1984), pp. 56–57.

76. Charles W. Kegley, Jr., T. Vance Sturgeon, and Eugene R. Wittkopf, "Structural Terrorism: The Systemic Source of State-Sponsored Terrorism," in *Terrible Beyond Endurance: The Foreign Policy of State Terrorism*, ed. Michael Stohl and George A. Lopez (New York: Greenwood Press, 1988), pp. 13–31.

77. "Introduction," in *Behavior, Culture, and Conflict in World Politics*, pp. 1–2.

78. Martin Wight, *International Theory: The Three Traditions* (New York: Holmes & Meier, 1992), p. 206.

79. Hans Morgenthau, *Politics Among Nations*, 5th ed. (New York: Alfred A. Knopf, 1978), p. 42.

80. Kenneth N. Waltz, "The Origins of War in Neorealist Theory," in *The Origin and Prevention of Major Wars*, pp. 40–44.

81. Bruce Bueno de Mesquita and David Lalman, "Power Relationships, Democratic Constraints, and War," in *Reconstructing Realpolitik*, ed. Frank W. Wayman and Paul F. Diehl (Ann Arbor, MI: University of Michigan Press, 1994), pp. 161–81.

82. Hedley Bull, *The Anarchical Society: A Study of Order in World Politics* (New York: Columbia University Press, 1977), Chapter 8; Ian Clark,

Waging War: A Philosophical Introduction (Oxford: Clarendon Press, 1990), pp. 23–30.
83. Hollins et al, *The Conquest of War,* pp. xiv–xv, 192; Francis Fukuyama, "The End of History," *The National Interest,* Summer 1989, pp. 3–18; Max Singer and Aaron Wildavsky, *The Real World Order: Zones of Peace/Zones of Turmoil* (Chatham, NJ: Chatham House, 1993).
84. Alastair Buchan, *Change Without War* (New York: St. Martin's Press, 1975), p. 105.
85. Graham T. Allison, "Conclusion: Windows of Opportunity," in *Windows of Opportunity: From Cold War to Peaceful Competition in U.S.–Soviet Relations,* ed. Graham T. Allison and William L. Ury (Cambridge, MA: Ballinger, 1989), pp. 312–15.
86. Clark, *Waging War,* p. 6.
87. Evan Luard, *War in International Society* (New Haven, CT: Yale University Press, 1987), pp. 21, 384, 389, 404.
88. Keegan, *A History of Warfare,* p. 59.
89. John Mueller, *Retreat from Doomsday: The Obsolescence of Major War* (New York: Basic Books, 1989), pp. 11–12, 227, 250–52.
90. Michael W. Doyle, "An International Liberal Community," in *Rethinking America's Security: Beyond Cold War to New World Order,* ed. Graham Allison and Gregory F. Treverton (New York: W. W. Norton, 1992), pp. 307–33.
91. John R. Oneal, Frances H. Oneal, Zeev Maoz, and Bruce Russett, "The Liberal Peace: Interdependence, Democracy, and International Conflict, 1950–1985," *Journal of Peace Research,* February 1996, pp. 11–28.

CHAPTER 6

PENETRATION OPERATIONS: INTELLIGENCE, COVERT ACTS, AND PROPAGANDA

Some instruments, such as diplomacy, suggest negotiation and cooperation, while penetration operations are usually instruments of conflict. Penetration operations involve actors, mostly states, that intrusively project their agents and activities into the affairs and territories of other states. These operations occur in an illegal, or at least objectionable, fashion. Actors, including those of the nonstate kind, often use these operations to gain an advantage in influence, wealth, or coercive ability. Penetration operations can take place apart from war or serve warmaking in an ancillary way. Penetration operations are threefold in type: intelligence, covert acts, and propaganda.

Such penetrations as spying, promoting *coups d'etats,* or transmitting illicit radio broadcasts into another country are clearly illegal acts of interference in the affairs of other states. The norms of international law in general, and the UN Charter in particular, prohibit these acts of penetration. The advantages of penetration may be so tempting, however, that some states will turn a blind eye to prohibited norms and laws. For some states, twentieth-century high-tech devices have provided the means, and ideological movements the motivation, to make the penetration temptation greater than ever before. Besides, states try to conduct these activities clandestinely to avoid reproach. In contrast, other states, confident about their security and without an ideological agenda for their foreign policies, may perform few or no penetration acts.

When states use penetration operations to wage conflict, they obviously hinder the evolution of international relations from an anarchy inhabited by security-conscious states to the model of a more cooperative, law-abiding society. Nevertheless, some intelligence activities, including the collection and sharing of information, can make positive contributions to an international society, as we will see later in this chapter.

This chapter's organization is as follows. First, we make clear distinctions between intelligence and counterintelligence functions and between overt and covert intelligence collection. We also evaluate the usefulness of intelligence activities and examine the techniques of intelligence. Next, we cover the role of covert acts and then review national intelligence services to illustrate some of the interesting features of intelligence organizations in selected countries. Then we look at the role of propaganda. Afterward we deal with three specialized concerns regarding penetration operations: the use of these operations by nonstate actors, the implications of secrecy for democracies, and the usefulness of penetration operations in the post–Cold War era. Finally, we assess intelligence activities in an emerging international society.

THE INTELLIGENCE PROCESS

Intelligence is the process of collecting and analyzing information for the benefit of policymakers. Traditionally, the information sought has concerned the intentions and capabilities of opponents that can threaten a country's military security. Increasingly, the desired information has come to include political, economic, and social data about other countries. Trade strategies, foreign investment opportunities, foreign aid planning, and much else may depend on massive data stored in a computer's memory. Rarely, however, does the collection of data offer a clear picture with obvious conclusions for a policymaker. Information usually comes into an intelligence agency in bits and pieces from varied sources at different times. While intelligence activities usually suggest espionage, or spying, to the mind of the public, the proper analysis of collected information may have become more important than spying itself.[1]

An intelligence agency is a veritable "think tank," and it needs to be. The information age has created an "all-source glut" of information. Millions of words pour into an agency daily from telecommunication intercepts, thousands of embassy and attaché communiqués, satellite photographs, secret agents' reports, and other sources. Someone has to distinguish the significant intelligence from all the "background noise."[2] Only after long periods of sifting and sorting can intelligence analysts produce patterns of evidence that allow them to brief policymakers with confidence. While the role of spies is historical, permanent intelligence agencies are a relatively new phenomenon. Great Britain formed the first permanent, civilian intelligence agency in 1909, followed by Germany in 1913, Russia in 1917, France in 1935, and the United States in 1947.[3]

COUNTERINTELLIGENCE

States not only collect information about other states, including military secrets, but also conduct **counterintelligence** activities. These activities include protecting one's own secrets and neutralizing any threats posed by foreign intelligence agencies. Many government offices, especially intelligence and military offices, require all confidential paperwork to be under lock and key when not in use. If this material is disposable, a standing rule may exist that agents must burn or shred papers. Some navies require that ships at sea burn classified materials and sink all trash with weights.

Paper shredders are standard equipment in many government offices. Of course, some shredders are more effective than others. The Iranians, after seizing the United States embassy in Tehran in 1979, published 54 volumes of American documents under the title *Documents from the United States Espionage Den.* Many of these documents were pages reconstituted from long, thin strips of paper, the product of the embassy shredders.[4] A few years later, when it came to light that Oliver North, a major figure in the Iran-Contra affair of the mid-1980s, had used a German-made shredder to turn pages of evidence into 10,000 flakes each, sales of that brand rose 20 percent.[5]

Intelligence agencies also carefully screen personnel recruited for their offices and other government agencies. A background check involving an applicant's elementary school teachers and friends is not unusual. Intelligence agencies also run checks on an employee's work history or test an employee's loyalty with fake offers of bribes or other temptations.

The use of drug screens and lie detector tests occurs frequently. "Sting operations" to identify and entrap foreign spies are common practices of counterintelligence as well. A clever counterintelligence technique is for a state to plant one of its own agents in a foreign intelligence agency or plant false, misleading information for an opponent to find, with the intent of confounding and disrupting the opponent's intelligence operations.

Intelligence and counterintelligence activities not only are analytically distinct functions but are conducted by specialized agencies, at least in Western countries. In the United States, for example, the Central Intelligence Agency (CIA) has responsibility for intelligence activities and usually operates outside the country, although the CIA does have a counterintelligence unit within its own ranks. The Federal Bureau of Investigation (FBI), in addition to its domestic police work, normally conducts counterintelligences activities inside U.S. borders.[6] If the arrest of a foreign spy is to take place, only the FBI has arrest powers. One of the more novel counterintelligence acts by the FBI involved placing an advertisement in a New York City Russian-language newspaper asking recent Russian immigrants to call the FBI to report any information they had on the activities of the Committee for State Security (KGB).[7]

COVERT AND OVERT INTELLIGENCE

There is an important distinction between **covert** and **overt intelligence.** Agents collect covert intelligence secretly in many ways, including the derring-do of spies made popular in movies and novels. While the focus of this chapter is on illicitly gathered information, most information reaching government policymakers comes from overt sources, openly and legally. The KGB, the most notorious of intelligence agencies, has probably obtained 75 to 90 percent of what it needs in a perfectly legal manner.[8] All sorts of information about social, economic, and, surprisingly, military matters are available in public and private publications. Much information appears in libraries, free to the public. When the British military prepared to fight the Argentine military forces in 1982, a highly unexpected development, it put together an "order of battle" on the Argentine military system through privately published works. Among these works was *Jane's Fighting Ships,* found at the Plymouth public library.[9]

THE USEFULNESS OF INTELLIGENCE

The usefulness of intelligence activities is difficult to assess because of their clandestine nature. Although in the English-speaking world intelligence is now a recognized field of academic study, the role of intelligence in history is generally a neglected field.[10] As studies improve, our ability to assess the usefulness of intelligence activities will improve with them. At this point, we at least know that many governments value intelligence activities as a way to avoid unpleasant surprises, particularly in matters of military security. Worldwide, intelligence personnel probably number well over a million people and intelligence expenditures run into the billions of dollars. These facts suggest the importance of intelligence to countries.[11]

The exact success-failure ratio of intelligence episodes is unknown, however. Failures tend to bubble to the surface, while success receives the cover of secrecy to preserve successful intelligence gambits for future use. For instance, the Japanese surprise attack on Pearl Harbor in 1941 immediately revealed failures on the part of American intelligence officers. In contrast, the British ability to decipher German communications throughout the Second World War, an ability that played a dramatic role in the Allied victory, remained secret for over 30 years.

Many states do not need intelligence activities in peacetime, at least of the covert kind, and may experience only patchy success with them in wartime. Sir Edward Creasy, in his *Fifteen Decisive Battles of the World: From Marathon to Waterloo,* published in 1851, found that intelligence was critical to the outcome of only one battle.[12] Moreover, history is replete with intelligence failures. In recent times, the CIA, as well as other intelligence sources, failed to anticipate the Shah of Iran's downfall in 1979, the collapse of communism in Europe beginning in 1989, and the Iraqi attack on Kuwait in 1990.

In all fairness to intelligence personnel, historical forces at work beneath the surface are hard to recognize, and sometimes these forces suddenly burst on the scene with revolutionary impact. It is improbable that anyone would dare claim to have seen the collapse of European communism coming and known when it would happen. Nor could any intelligence agency's personnel foresee what a quirky individual, such as Saddam Hussein, might do.

In other cases, intelligence operations may provide a treasure trove of information, but then policymakers fail to believe the data or mishandle it. Bits and pieces of information about Japanese intentions for Pearl Harbor turned up in different agencies, but in 1941 no one group of analysts had all the pieces of the puzzle.[13] The centralizing role of the CIA would come years later. Joseph Stalin had a rich information environment and was able to learn that Nazi Germany planned to attack the Soviet Union in 1941. Stalin clung to his faith in the Soviet-Nazi Nonaggression Pact of 1939 and thus found the large stock of information about a German attack unbelievable.[14]

Although the exact usefulness of intelligence is difficult to assess definitively because of its secret nature, we can be sure that some governments will always be hungry for information about the world around them and will continue to maintain intelligence agencies. Many leaders fear they must keep such agencies, especially if they see their countries' physical security in jeopardy.

THE TECHNIQUES OF INTELLIGENCE

Whether or not intelligence proves useful, the intelligence cycle—collection of information, conversion into meaningful assessments, and dissemination to appropriate policymakers who follow up with a new set of questions—must begin with acquiring information. The variety of techniques for information acquisition fall into three categories. **HUMINT** is intelligence drawn from people, such as foreign service officers, defectors, POWs, and, of course, the irreplaceable secret agent or spy. **SIGINT** is the interception of electronically based signals sent, for example, by radio, telex, teletype, and microwave broadcast antennae. **PHOINT** is the use of photography. Photography is perhaps the best known example of *imagery,* the process of producing picturelike representations of objects of interest using a variety of sensor systems.

Modern technology may have downgraded the role of the *spy,* but some information may be available only through a human agent. Satellite cameras can photograph an airfield full of fighter planes, but only a agent can pluck detailed specifications about the performance and construction of a plane from a file or a safe. Also, only a human agent can infiltrate an opponent's organization. Hence, the ancient role of the spy will probably extend far into the future.[15]

Spies can play their role in many specialized ways. An agent may be a *recruiter,* a foreign spymaster who recruits a spy ring from among the nationals of a given country. The Soviet KGB commonly placed an agent among Soviet embassy staffs, and from this protected position of diplomatic immunity, the recruiter could seek recruits inside the host country. Spies also can be *sleepers,* foreign agents who take false identities, usually including new citizenship, and then work their way up to a high-level security position. Only when the sleepers are strategically located will the *controller* back home order sleepers to commit espionage.

Daring spies have performed some striking episodes of espionage, many of them successful. The Soviet Union exploded its first atom bomb in 1949 partly through the help of Klaus Fuchs, who gave Soviet agents critical atomic secrets and later was convicted for espionage. Fuchs had worked on the "Manhattan Project," the development of the American atom bomb during the Second World War. An especially successful spy tactic involves what the British have called a *double-cross.* British counterintelligence captured most, if not all, German agents sent to their country during the Second World War and forced them to send false information back to their controllers.[16]

Not unusual are *defectors* who, through recruitment or acting voluntarily, desert their country and bring out a windfall of inside information from another government. Governments may ask defectors, when they announce their intention to switch sides or at least sell secrets, to be *defectors-in-place,* or *moles.* From such a vantage point, a mole can provide invaluable inside information for years. Defectors are interesting because they are mostly intelligence operatives from the other side rather than government bureaucrats or military personnel. Agents from different countries can have much in common and even have sympathy for one another though they represent opposing countries. When spies identify more closely with the "spy profession" than with their own countries or agencies, they find it easier to defect. Agents from opposing states sometimes know each other by name and socialize together. By the mid-1980s, as American-Soviet relations improved, CIA and KGB agents had established a friendly agreement to refrain from killing each other.[17]

There are some famous cases of intelligence operatives changing sides. Kim Philby, a mole in Britain, worked for the Soviet Union for almost three decades. He and several other British university students, from "Oxbridge" (Oxford and Cambridge universities) backgrounds, changed their allegiance to the Soviet Union because of their ideological convictions as communists. Under suspicion by British counterintelligence for several years, the British finally exposed Philby in 1963 as a Soviet mole based on the information provided by defectors from Polish and Soviet intelligence agencies.[18]

Defection can occur even between friendly countries. Jonathan Pollard, an American of Jewish heritage and a passionate Zionist, offered to spy for Israeli intelligence in 1985. For almost a year, from his position in United States naval intelligence, Pollard gave to Israeli intelligence hundreds of classified documents, including spy satellite photographs.

Kelley and Copley News Service

Pollard's capture and exposure chilled the close working relationship between U.S. and Israeli intelligence agencies.[19]

Since one of the worst disasters that can befall an intelligence agency is to have one of its own defect but stay in place as a mole, counterintelligence searches for moles can be zealous. Sometimes these searches cause almost as much harm as a mole does by destroying the careers of innocent agents and demoralizing an entire agency. In *Molehunt: The Secret Search for Traitors that Shattered the CIA,* David Wise reveals a nearly two-decades-long mole search in the 1960s and 1970s that greatly harmed the CIA, yet failed to uncover a single mole. Eventually, seven CIA moles were prosecuted between 1977 and 1985.[20]

The most infamous case of a CIA mole is that of Aldrich H. Ames, a 31-year veteran of the agency who sold information to the Soviets for several million dollars between 1985 and 1994. The help Ames gave to the Soviets probably compromised as many as 100 operations and led to the execution of 10 Soviet citizens working as CIA agents. His capture and conviction contributed to the replacement of the then current director of the CIA and to reforms of the counterintelligence procedures.[21]

A short time later, in 1996, the FBI arrested Harold J. Nicholson, a high-ranking CIA agent, who, among other transgressions, sold the identities of all new CIA agent trainees between 1995 and 1996 to Russian agents. Then a month afterward, the FBI arrested one of its own, Special Agent Earl E. Pitts, who had sold to Russian agents his key and ID badge for entering the FBI training academy. All three of these American agents began their illicit

Watterson. Distributed by Universal Press Syndicate. Reprinted with permission. All rights reserved.

activities during the Cold War and continued working for the Russians, apparently selling out their country just for the money.

Military personnel with high-level security clearances also make attractive recruitment targets for espionage activities. John Walker, as a U.S. Navy noncommissioned officer and later in retirement, spied for the KGB in the 1970s and 1980s. He also recruited a spy ring that included a friend and Walker's own children who were serving in the U.S. military. The FBI caught this spy ring, and the individuals involved went to prison for long terms.

Why do people become spies? The reasons are varied, and a combination of inducements may be at work. Blackmail, money, adventure, ego needs, patriotism, and ideological commitments are certainly among the motives for espionage. Stanislav Levchenko, a defector from the KGB, thinks Westerners are very materialistic and want so many things that they build up large debts. The KGB, he said, could find a government employee in this shape and pounce on a new recruit.[22] Another recruitment device involves sex. Israeli agents recruited a Jordanian air force lieutenant, Abdul Hafiz, in 1990 by "honeytrapping" him with an attractive Israeli agent who claimed to be an American. Hafiz turned over information on Iraqi-Jordanian aerial cooperation to the Israelis. He was soon caught and was hung in early 1991.[23]

The lives and fates of spies in general are often fearful and end in capture, followed by imprisonment or death. A death sentence is especially likely during wartime. Paradoxically, the greater the successes of spies, the greater are the prospects for their discovery and capture. A major intelligence *coup* spurs counterintelligence agents of the victimized state to make extensive efforts to catch the spy responsible. The Jonathan Pollard case is a good example.

Another technique for gathering information is to plant *bugs*, electronic listening devices, in the offices, cars, and other vehicles and places used by an opposing government's personnel. Many intelligence agencies probably do this. The telephone taps, microphones, and other means of communication intercepts used by police forces can as easily serve the purposes of intelligence agents. The placement of numerous listening devices by the Soviets in the American embassy under construction in Moscow in 1985 resulted in a decision by the United States to halt construction and abandon the uncompleted building altogether.

© 1987 Time, Inc. Reprinted by permission.

Ships and *planes* have been highly useful for collecting SIGINT, or electronic data, in both peace and war. The United States, for instance, equipped several old cargo ships with electronic sensor equipment and sent them along the coastlines of countries targeted for intelligence operations, usually communist countries. In 1967, Israeli plans attacked the *Liberty* with heavy losses to U.S. Navy personnel. The Israeli government claimed they mistakenly thought the *Liberty* was an Arab ship. This attack was in the midst of the Six Day War going on between Israel and several Arab states. North Korea seized the *Pueblo* off its coast in 1968 and held the crew prisoner for 11 months. In the same year, the *Muller* lost power and drifted toward Cuba until an American destroyer towed the *Muller* to safety. Following such unsettling experiences, the United States suspended this program.

For years, during the Cold War, the Soviets placed at least one electronically equipped trawler among their fishing fleets as they sailed near the coasts of many countries. Some countries have used submarines for similar activities. In the mid-1980s, Sweden trapped a Soviet submarine in its waters that was probably doing electronic sensing near a Swedish military base.

Planes not only can "sense" an opponent's territory and ships at sea for SIGINT but can carry out PHOINT operations as well. The United States produced the U-2 spy plane in

George Hall/Woodfin Camp & Associates

1954, and its later versions still see service. This high-altitude reconnaissance aircraft can fly at 70,000 feet and film thousands of square miles of territory in minutes. Later in development, the SR-71, nicknamed the Blackbird, can fly at 85,000 feet at over 2,000 miles an hour and film 60,000 square miles in an hour. The government retired the Blackbird from reconnaissance in 1990. Today a few Blackbirds remain in service for weather research. While the Soviet Union shot down a U-2 in 1960 and Cuba brought down another one in 1962, a Blackbird has never suffered this fate. Interestingly, U-2s, though an earlier spy plane than the Blackbird, are still in reconnaissance use; U-2s flew 800 missions in the Persian Gulf War. They have a "slant photography" capability that allows them to film terrain from an angle while flying outside the airspace of the target country.[24]

Other uses of aircraft, equipped with sophisticated sensors, include the American-made AWAC plane, which can scan ground and airspace for enemy targets across a huge area. A large plane, the AWAC is an intelligence center, with a highly trained crew, that can coordinate many planes and helicopters in the midst of major battles. Unfortunately, during the United Nations policing of northern Iraq in 1994, an American officer on an AWAC failed to alert American fighter planes that two Blackhawk helicopters were "friends," not "foes," resulting in the accidental downing of the helicopters and the deaths of all those on board.

Some countries even suspect commercial airliners of collecting PHOINT and SIGINT. In 1983, the Soviet Union shot down Korean Airlines flight 007 for straying over Soviet territory along its Pacific coastline in Asia. Possibly the Soviets thought the Korean plane was clandestinely collecting data about the Soviet Union.

A last example involves British ships and planes in the 1982 Falkland Islands war. The British so effectively collected SIGINT with ships and planes that an Argentine military analyst later speculated that the British refrained from bombing the Argentine headquarters in the Falklands because it was a prime source of intelligence for the British.[25]

The increasing capability of *spy satellites* has substantially reduced the use of spy planes. The Soviet Union and the United States launched satellites into space in the 1950s, and the United States rocketed the first spy satellite into space in 1960. Until the 1980s, the Soviet Union and the United States had a monopoly over spy satellites. Amazingly, not a single government protested the coverage of its territory by satellites operating from outer space. In contrast, when planes have flown through the airspace of other countries without

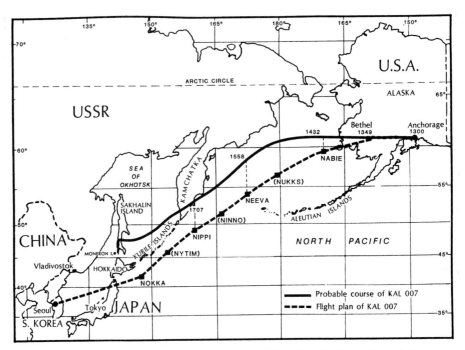

Alexander Dallin, *Black Box KAL 007 and the Superpowers,* University of California Press, Berkeley, 1985. Reprinted by permission of The Regents of the University of California.

their permission, those countries have sometimes shot them down, if they possessed the capability. Countries usually put satellites into orbit by rocket, but the United States can deploy either communication or spy satellites by releasing them from the cargo bay of a manned space shuttle.

Spy satellites can use cameras, loaded with film, to obtain high-resolution pictures of a target, or they can televise pictures back to earth stations. In addition, satellites can do *imaging* with infrared cameras when cloud cover hinders regular cameras. *Imaging radar* also can produce an image. An operator bounces radio signals off both the object of interest and its background. The timing of the radio pulses defines a picture of the object.[26]

Although the major users of spy satellites invented these devices for military purposes, during the Cold War the Soviet Union and the United States inspected each other's territory from outer space to determine if the other side was keeping arms agreements. Reassurances produced by these inspections helped stabilize the superpower relationship and prevent a nuclear holocaust.[27] Satellite inspection substituted effectively for on-site inspection that called for each side to send inspection teams to the territory of the other side. On-site inspection was never a realistic option because the Soviet Union refused to allow American inspectors on its soil.

Governments are finding more and more uses for spy satellites. Low-orbit "ferret" satellites "map" the radar systems of opponents or potential opponents,[28] a function spy ships once performed. Before the Persian Gulf War with Iraq, the United States deployed a satellite from the shuttle *Atlantis* aimed specifically at Iraq. This satellite could detect the flashes of a Scud missile launched from Iraq, providing early warning to both Israel and UN Coalition Forces in Saudi Arabia.[29] Intelligence from this satellite also helped provide target data for tank commanders and pilots in the same war.[30]

In addition to collecting information, intelligence officers must have secure communications with colleagues and allies. Since ancient times, **codes** and **ciphers** have protected sensitive communication. The relative ease of intercepting modern electronic communication has put a premium on disguised language. Codes consist of words or other symbols, such as numbers, with arbitrarily assigned meanings. Codes depend on the "sender" and "receiver" both possessing codebooks that work similarly to language translation dictionaries. In a German-English dictionary, for example, we could find a word of either language listed alphabetically and, at the same time, find its counterpart in the other language. Or we could represent all words by numbers selected arbitrarily. We could send a message such as "1140 4539." The receiver could trace numbers sequentially in a code book until the receiver found that "1140" meant "imminent" and "4539" meant "attack." Agents can transmit whole messages in the same way.

Ciphers are much more complicated. Cipher makers use complex rules of substitution for the letters of a given language. Letters are substituted from another language, numbers, or other symbols the cipher maker chooses. What letters and other symbols mean from one part of the message to another also can change. An opponent, of course, tries to discover these complex rules and *decipher* the message. Complicating matters has been the development of cipher-making machines beginning in the early twentieth century. With these machines, the range of options for structuring a cipher would run in the multiple thousands. As impenetrable as codes and ciphers can be, breaking them was the single most important source for intelligence during the twentieth century until the development of the spy satellite.[31] A rich vein of information might regularly flow to an opponent from broken codes and ciphers until the breach of security became apparent.

Through an effort begun by Polish intelligence in the 1930s and completed by British intelligence during the Second World War, a reconstruction of the German enciphering machine, known as *Enigma,* became available. British intelligence was able to intercept enciphered shortwave radio messages of the German military throughout the Second World War and shared this intelligence with U.S. intelligence officers.[32] Denying Field Marshall Erwin Rommel fuel and ammunition in North Africa, confounding German submarine "wolfpacks" in the North Atlantic, and preparing for the invasion of Normandy Beach in France were all dependent on deciphering German messages.[33]

American intelligence focused on breaking Japanese codes and ciphers and shared its findings with British intelligence, reciprocating British generosity with German codes and ciphers. The critical naval battle of Midway was a success largely because U.S. naval intelligence broke Japanese enciphered messages by learning the secrets of the *Purple,* the Japanese enciphering machine.[34] Less important but almost as satisfying to Americans was the interception of the enciphered message about the flight plan of Admiral Isoroku Yomamoto, the planner of the attack on Pearl Harbor. In April 1943, eight P-38 fighters intercepted Yomamoto's plane and its fighter escort, destroying all the Japanese planes except one fighter that escaped.[35]

The art and science of enciphering messages took a giant step forward with the development of the computer. The speed of powerful computers greatly enhances the range of options for making ciphers—and for breaking them. Today governments try to protect their communications in the computer age by frequently changing to new enciphering systems.[36] Nonetheless, governments' efforts to decipher the messages of other governments continue and can be successful.

COVERT ACTS

We have thus far described intelligence and counterintelligence functions, but several governments also have subunits among their intelligence apparati for covert acts. **Covert acts** are secret efforts to influence the behavior of leaders and to control events in other countries. A covert act can be as benign as providing a friendly government security for its leader, sharing intelligence, or offering equipment for enciphering messages.[37] More typically, covert acts involve interference in the affairs of another country, including the use of some violence, such as assassination.

Failure and embarrassment are risks when a government puts a hand into the affairs of another state, however. To be useful to the state engaging in covert acts, the act has to be circumspect, meaning small in scale and easily denied.[38] In 1990, CIA director William Webster claimed covert acts amounted to about 3 percent of his agency's expenditures and 97 percent of its problems in terms of media and congressional interest.[39] The CIA's "dirty tricks" occasionally backfire and, even if successful, may discredit American foreign policy in the eyes of many.[40] Still, the advantages that might come from a small investment of resources, as opposed to military intervention or another major option, will probably tempt some leaders to use covert acts for the indefinite future.

Loch K. Johnson thinks covert acts may have limited utility. He recommends that covert operations, if used, follow a set of guidelines that will significantly circumscribe their use. Among the guidelines he offers are: shun covert acts if diplomatic solutions are possible; avoid violating your country's laws; restrict or eliminate covert acts against other democracies; and keep all covert acts at the lowest level of intrusion possible. Overall, Professor Johnson prefers to see intelligence agencies restrict their activities to information collection and thus avoid covert acts.[41] James A. Barry, as deputy director of the CIA's Center for the Study of Intelligence, urged that the United States retain covert acts but conduct these acts with moral guidelines,[42] similar to those of Loch Johnson.

Covert acts can take many forms, limited only by the imaginations of those waging the acts. Nonetheless, some of the more common types of activities are well known. Agents use *bribery* to buy military secrets, persuade another country to purchase military equipment, influence the receipt of foreign aid, or coax foreign journalists to write positive stories about a given state.

Assassination may be a tempting choice to eliminate a troublesome government or public opinion leader. One bullet or bomb can seem a simple solution to a major problem. In the early 1960s, accusations against the CIA for hatching plots to assassinate Fidel Castro of Cuba were common.[43] These reputed attempts probably added to Castro's luster as a charismatic figure and only justified tighter security controls by his communist dictatorship. More successful were Israeli attempts in the 1960s to assassinate German scientists who were helping Egypt build rockets. In the 1970s, Israel formed the "Wrath of God" assassination squads, which went after Palestinian terrorists.[44] In 1996, the Israelis assassinated Yehia

Chapter 6 / Penetration Operations: Intelligence, Covert Acts, and Propaganda

© 1992 Jimmy Margulies, *The Record*

Ayyash, a Palestinian bombmaker, by installing a tiny bomb in his cellular phone and then simply calling his number.

Although contravening international law, *kidnapping* people allows for their punishment, interrogation for information, or use as a bargaining chip. The most famous kidnapping in history may be that of Adolf Eichmann from Argentina by Israeli agents in 1960. These agents took Eichmann to Israel, where an Israeli court tried him and sentenced him to hang as a war criminal for his role in the Nazi death camps. During the Cold War, East German agents frequently entered West Berlin and took whomever they pleased. In 1989, Israeli operatives kidnapped the militant Lebanese Shi'a leader Sheik Obeid and held him hostage. They hoped to exchange Sheik Obeid for an Israeli airman shot down over southern Lebanon.

A covert act that can bring the most immediate and thoroughgoing reward occurs when one state encourages a *coup d'état* against the government of another state. The overthrow of a foreign government may bring a major change in the policies of the other state. When American and British agents assisted a coup in Iran in 1954, they helped a monarch who was friendlier to Western oil interests replace a parliamentary government. Or the *coup d'état* may receive foreign encouragement because a particular government is highly distasteful in its form. In 1973, the CIA encouraged the overthrow of democratically elected Salvadore Allende in Chile because he was a Marxist, an act that led to his death. The drawback to *coups* is that they leave a legacy of suspicion and hatred aimed at the perpetrators.

Sometimes encouraging a *defection* produces a windfall of information. In 1966, Israeli agents bribed an Iraqi pilot to fly his MIG-21 to Turkey and then on to Israel.[45] Israeli intelligence not only could debrief the pilot but had access to their opponent's main fighter plane for hands-on examination.

A covert act to destroy or harm equipment or vehicles or to sidetrack or delay the plans of others is *sabotage.* Countries commonly use sabotage in wartime, but episodes of sabotage occur in peacetime as well. In the early 1960s, the CIA persuaded a German manufacturer to ship off-centered ball bearings to communist Cuba, and the CIA sabotaged British-made buses intended for Cuba while they were still on the docks awaiting shipment.[46]

Blackmail is a common covert act to force people to become spies against their own countries. For instance, in 1962, the KGB honeytrapped Jeremy Wolfenden, a British reporter for the *Daily Telegraph,* in a homosexual affair and forced him to work for them. Later Wolfenden reported the blackmail to British intelligence, and they pressured him to become their double agent and spy on the KGB. Under the strain, Wolfenden's health declined, and he died at age 31 when he apparently fainted and struck his head in his own bathroom.[47]

The last example of covert acts presented here is *disinformation.* This activity is communication to confuse, deceive, and undermine the policymakers, military leaders, and even the public opinion of another country. Ladislav Bittman, a defector from the Czechoslovakian Disinformation Department, has revealed that the KGB frequently injected forged documents, fake press releases, spurious letters, and other communications into world media channels. Foreign presses, thoroughly deceived about the source of their information, have attacked KGB foes and defended its friends. Bittman points out that open, free societies of the West were easy to penetrate with disinformation.[48]

One of the most interesting cases of disinformation concerns the Strategic Defense Initiative (SDI), also known as the "Star Wars" defense program. To make this high-tech defense program credible, the American military, in a 1984 experiment, allegedly attached a homing beacon to a missile to make it easy to shoot down. This fake credibility not only pressured the Soviets to spend billions they could not afford on a similar program but helped the American military secure more billions of dollars from Congress for the SDI. Officials in charge of the SDI program have denied that they rigged the missile test.

When President Bill Clinton appointed John Deutch as CIA director in 1995, Deutch discovered that the CIA had passed some disinformation to Presidents Bush and Clinton in the guise of reliable intelligence. This disinformation was *feed,* information used by Soviet agents as a lure so the CIA would accept them as double agents. By 1991, the CIA knew this intelligence on Russian aircraft and missile capabilities was tainted.

To conclude, covert acts are acts to disrupt and confuse an opponent, and sometimes involve violence, as in the case of assassination. Covert operations can easily backfire on the sponsoring state, causing that state much embarrassment. Some intelligence specialists question the overall usefulness of covert acts, especially by democracies.

NATIONAL INTELLIGENCE AGENCIES

Every state has some sort of agency, perhaps with an innocuous-sounding name such as the "Ministry of Information," that collects and disseminates information in a perfectly overt way. The collection function may involve nothing more than routinely gathering information from the media and other governments, and the dissemination function may generate only a favorable public relations image. The more a country must focus on its security, however, the more likely that country will set up agencies to perform clandestine penetrations. A look at several of these agencies will provide insights as to how they organize and function.

The United States

The United States has an intelligence history traceable to George Washington's administration, but historically the American emphasis on intelligence has been a weak one except in time of war. The Organization for Strategic Services (OSS), formed during the Second World War, gave America a complete intelligence dimension for its war effort. Only after postwar tensions with the Soviet Union developed did a permanent civilian intelligence organization, the CIA, begin operations in 1947. The intelligence operations of the United States amount to an *intelligence community* because, in addition to the CIA, the community includes the Defense Department's Intelligence Agency, the intelligence component of the State Department, the National Security Agency (NSA), the counterintelligence component of the FBI, and the intelligence units of each of the branches of military service. The CIA director is the titular head of the intelligence community, but questions often arise over how smoothly this community works together.

Most of the staff of this community work in offices and analyze data until they form "pictures" of a situation, leading to reports for policymakers. All parts of the community collect information, but it falls to the CIA to conduct covert acts. The FBI, as mentioned earlier, tries to block spying by others within the United States. The NSA, with its sophisticated computers, has the interesting task of making and breaking codes and ciphers. One last specialized component of the intelligence community deserving mention is the National Reconnaissance Office. This office, located in the Pentagon, manages the critical spy satellite program.

The intelligence community is large and may have, at its peak size, used 7 to 8 percent of the defense budget, or nearly $30 billion. The budget axe that has reduced America's military spending to provide a "peace dividend" in the post–Cold War era has threatened the intelligence community as well. Pointing out that the old Soviet Union, though now disassembled, leaves behind four republics that may still have some nuclear weapons and the economic and ethnic unrest of that crumbled empire, intelligence heads and their congressional allies have fought to hold onto the intelligence community's significant share of the defense budget. The focus of America's intelligence organizations over the decades has been the communist threat within the Cold War context, but in recent years, terrorist organizations and radical Third World governments, such as Iraq and Libya, have increasingly demanded attention.[49]

Despite the threats in the post–Cold War era, the CIA has come under attack from Congress as the dangers of the Cold War have faded. Director William Casey's clandestine efforts to assist the "Contras," guerrilla soldiers fighting the Marxist regime in Nicaragua during Ronald Reagan's tenure, angered both the Congress and public opinion.[50] James Woolsey, the first CIA director under President Bill Clinton, further antagonized Congress by refusing to fire those responsible for allowing the Aldrich Ames spy escapade to drag on for years without detecting Ames as a mole for the Soviets. Senator Patrick Moynihan proposed to do away with the CIA, as if it were no longer necessary. Adding to CIA woes was a class action suit in the 1990s by as many as 100 CIA female employees over sex discrimination.

In the aftermath of a deflated CIA image, President Bill Clinton set up a commission to study the CIA and its future. He also replaced Director Woolsey in 1995 with John Deutch, a Defense Department administrator with a solid reputation; Deutch promised reforms and better relations with Congress. CIA Director Deutch proved to be a temporary appointment, however, as President Clinton, once elected for a second term in 1996, sought to appoint Anthony Lake, his national security adviser, as the new CIA director. Lake's appointment, never an assured one because of congressional opposition, failed in early 1997 with his withdrawal from the nomination process. The next CIA director will be the sixth in five years, a turnover rate that has made continuity in policy and in responsibility difficult. The new director is George Terent, for a time the acting director. This nominee received a warm reception by the Senate and was confirmed in the summer of 1997.

The Soviet Union (Russia)

The largest and most aggressive example of intelligence agencies in the world is the KGB when the Soviet Union was intact. The Soviet Union may have engaged in state-sponsored terrorism, particularly in the 1970s and early 1980s, when Yuri Andropov directed the KGB, and in 1984–1985, when he became the top political leader of the Soviet Union. Although the KGB applied most of its resources internally to maintain the Soviet Union as a police state, it had sufficient resources left to put agents in every country of the world. The KGB focused most of its external attention on the defeat of the United States during the globally based Cold War. Andropov's leadership in the 1970s guided the KGB toward a reputation for efficiency and competence as Andropov recruited from among the elite of Soviet youth. The image of KGB thugs in bad suits gave way to one of bright, well-dressed university graduates serving an elite institution.

Soviet military intelligence, the Main Intelligence Administration (GRU), augmented the KGB's espionage. Eastern bloc countries, especially Czechoslovakia and Poland, also produced intelligence agencies that worked as subsidiaries of the KGB. These states and those new states that have emerged from the Soviet Union will form new "KGBs," probably to protect themselves from Russian tentacles.[51]

The demise of the Cold War and the failure of communism in the Soviet Union brought what may prove to be significant changes to the KGB. First, by 1991, the KGB began serving a much reduced country, territorially and militarily speaking, as Russia and other republics of the old Soviet Union divided into separate states. Second, the new democratic government of Russia, under President Boris Yeltsin, split the internal and external functions of the KGB to control that organization more effectively.[52] The two new agencies became the Foreign Intelligence Service of Russia and the Ministry of Security, which focused on the domestic context. President Yeltsin took this step to defuse the anger of a public long suffering the weight of a secret police, especially following the KGB's complicity in the attempted military overthrow of the new Russian republic in 1991.[53]

Now the intelligence services of Russia are free from the ideological straitjacket of fighting the Cold War and focusing on the danger of a United States nuclear attack. They

Zehentmayr/Kurier, Vienna. Reprinted from *World Press Review Magazine*.

can turn to the multiple threats of nuclear and chemical weapons proliferation to radical states, terrorism, gangsterism with international reach, drug trafficking, and the volatile Muslim states along the southern border of Russia. And, as before the end of the Cold War, Russian spies will likely continue to pursue Western technological know-how to help Russia boost its new privatized economy within a global marketplace. Finally, Russian authorities have claimed that they recalled one-third of their KGB spies operating in other countries. However, Robert Gates, CIA director in 1992, countered by saying Russia was spying more than ever by replacing KGB spies with GRU spies.[54]

People's Republic of China

Much less is known about the intelligence services of China than those of the defunct Soviet Union. The United States and other Western states have focused mostly on the Soviet bloc because of its military power during the Cold War days. We can be sure, at least, that China conducts intelligence activities aggressively against industrial states. The United States has publicly identified China as the most intrusive country concerning the surreptitious acquisition of U.S. technology.[55] Chinese intelligence successes are due more to the numerous attempts made than to the skill of its intelligence efforts. China's intelligence operatives also enjoy a measure of achievement because they seek mid-level technology that exists below U.S. counterintelligence priorities.[56]

Chinese intelligence services have a couple of other interesting characteristics. First, China's agents sometimes steal intelligence themselves instead of recruiting the nationals of a target country to do it for them, and they often use commercial and academic covers rather than the safer cover of a diplomat with immunity. Second, China has a poor record of keeping its own secrets under wraps, for some of China's most sensitive matters are rumored on public streets. If Western states are uninformed about China, it is because their intelligence analysts may have trouble telling fact from fiction amid the flow of rumors and because they do not try hard to gather information on China. However, there can be little doubt that China's intelligence services will improve and will come of age as their espionage efforts reflect China's growth as a military and economic power.[57]

Great Britain

British intelligence has a distinguished reputation based on a centuries-old history. Perhaps British intelligence reached its apogee in the Second World War. In addition to breaking German ciphers, produced by Enigma, and managing a "double-cross" by using captured German agents to plant disinformation in German decision-making circles, Britain controlled a double agent code-named Garbo. In 1944, Garbo deliberately sent information to German intelligence claiming that the Allies would invade France at Normandy, but stressed that the attack on the beach of Normandy would be a diversion. This ruse kept German tank divisions located at other places along the French coast. Garbo so impressed Adolf Hitler with his accuracy about the landing at Normandy, though it proved to be the primary landing by the Allies, that he awarded Garbo the Iron Cross second class, one of Germany's highest military awards.

In the First and Second World Wars, British intelligence had been the senior partner in the relationship with America's intelligence service because of British experience and expertise. After the Second World War, with Britain's economic decline combined with the great expense of operating banks of computers and developing SIGINT capabilities, America's wealth and new concern with the Soviet Union shifted leadership in intelligence matters to agencies of the United States.

Today Britain has the Secret Intelligence Service (SIS) for clandestine collection of information outside Britain and for covert operations, although covert acts receive less emphasis since the 1950s. The Security Service, frequently called MI-5, its old military designation, has domestic responsibility for counterintelligence and surveillance. MI-5 also deals with terrorism and sabotage. The Scotland Yard Special Branch contributes by performing arrests in counterespionage operations. Finally, the Government Communications Headquarters (GCHQ) assists with ciphers and codes and helps with SIGINT intelligence.

The modern focus of British intelligence has been on the Cold War struggle. Counterintelligence, however, has had to give substantial attention to the Irish Republican Army, terrorists based in northern Ireland, as well as the communist spies. Furthermore, British intelligence will undoubtedly have to share with American intelligence many of the same post–Cold War concerns such as the instability of eastern Europe and Russia, the future of the Persian Gulf, and the spread of dread weapons to radical states.[58]

Israel

Probably no other country has given the priority to intelligence that Israel has. For over four decades, almost surrounded by hostile Arab states and beleaguered by a variety of terrorist organizations, Israel has channeled an unusual amount of money and personnel into intelligence activities to buttress its military security. Israel's intelligence apparatus has operated as though Israel were in a perpetual state of war. Israel's impressive success with its armed forces and intelligence operatives conjures up the image of a long, dangerous arm controlled by a cunning mind. For instance, Israeli intelligence aided in the preemptive, defensive strike on Egypt's air force in 1967 and the stunning commando raid at Entebbe, Uganda, in 1976. At Entebbe, Israeli commandos rescued a planeload of Israeli citizens and brought them safely to Israel. On balance, Israeli intelligence also has had some striking failures; for example, Israel failed to anticipate and properly prepare for Egypt's successful military breach of Israeli defenses at the Suez Canal in 1973.

The focus of Israeli intelligence, understandably, has been on the intentions and capabilities of Arab states. Israel also once gave some attention to Soviet bloc countries. Israel's deserved reputation for effectiveness rests mainly on HUMINT rather than either SIGINT or computer applications for enciphering and deciphering. Moreover, Israel's intelligence has probably performed better at the level of tactical military information than that of strategic political assessments. If there is one serious omission in the Israeli intelligence system, it is the absence of satellite intelligence of its own. On the other hand, if one capability stands out, covert acts have to be the signal achievement of the Israelis. The long list of covert acts, such as kidnappings, assassinations, commando raids, the interception of terrorists, the incitement of disturbances within Arab states, and the aggravation of divisions among those states, has been the Israeli forte.

Israel has the Mossad for foreign intelligence gathering, and the Mossad has a subunit, the Special Operations Division, for covert acts. The General Security Service (Shin Beth) deals with counterintelligence at home and internal security, whether the problem is Palestinian terrorists or Israeli right-wingers. A group called Aman handles military intelligence. The Bureau of Scientific Liaison, also known as Lakam, specialized in scientific information and controlled the spy Jonathan Pollard. The bureau disbanded in the wake of the Pollard affair.

More recently, in 1997, news has leaked that the FBI is searching for an even better-placed spy, code-named "Mega," who may be passing U.S. diplomatic intelligence to the Israeli government. The FBI also has complained that Israeli agents routinely take part in economic espionage for technical secrets, and, in 1996, the CIA reported to the Senate Intelligence Committee that Israel was one of six countries with a government orchestrated clandestine effort to collect U.S. economic secrets.

Before these incidents, the intelligence services of Israel and the United States traditionally worked closely together. For instance, Israel has shared information about captured Soviet weapons taken from Arab armies and information collected from immigrants recently arrived from the Soviet Union. The United States, in turn, has shared selected satellite photographs with Israel.[59]

The vaunted reputation of Israeli intelligence suffered a blow in the fall of 1995 when Shin Beth failed to protect Prime Minister Yitzhak Rabin from an assassin's bullets. Shin Beth agents mistook Yigal Amir for a VIP driver and allowed him near the prime minister. Amir is a right-wing religious extremist violently opposed to the Palestinian peace process that Prime Minister Rabin was leading.

Countries do not just spy on their enemies and share intelligence with their friends. Sometimes countries clandestinely collect information from friends. Israel's use of Jonathan Pollard to gain access to satellite photographs belonging to the United States is a prominent example. Other examples are France's spying on the Green movement in Germany, the United States' efforts to find out if Britain and other allies are selling American technology to the Soviet bloc, and British spying on trade partners to discover their trade strategies.[60] What is fairly exceptional is to expose an ally's spies, as France did in 1995 when the French government ordered five CIA employees to leave France. The French government claimed they were stealing audiovisual and telecommunication secrets.

To summarize this section of the chapter, we have seen that national intelligence agencies are highly specialized groups of people that serve their governments by providing them with extensive amounts of information used to formulate policy. Most employees of an intelligence agency actually work in offices and sift and weigh information as it flows into the agency. Occasionally these agencies spy on allies as well as opponents. We turn now to another type of penetration that deserves separate attention: propaganda.

PROPAGANDA

Long before the academic field of psychology developed, actors in pursuit of goals recognized that the values and attitudes of other people might affect their prospects for success. Individuals, churches, business organizations, terrorists, and undoubtedly the governments of states have wanted other actors to take a friendly and positive attitude toward their own purposes and activities. In modern times, almost every kind of institution at every level performs some kind of public relations effort to project the most favorable image possible.

States in particular have made sophisticated efforts to penetrate other societies with their messages. These efforts fall under the rubric of **propaganda.** In the international context, *propaganda* refers to a process of using information and symbols to change the attitude and thus the behavior of a target population in another country. Usage has rendered the term pejorative in its connotation. To refer to a message as propaganda is to suggest somehow that the message involves falsehood and fabrication. Sophisticated efforts at propaganda frequently include a deliberate mixture of fact and fiction to make a message more palatable. Ultimately, in politics what is true, what is false, and what is merely slanted or distorted is a matter of perspective.[61]

The Intensity of Propaganda

A useful "color code" has emerged to characterize the degree of deceptiveness in a message. *White* propaganda is information disseminated that an actor thinks is true and is at least an honest point of view. The information is from a known source. Most public relations programs by various actors are no worse than white propaganda. *Grey* propaganda involves selective reporting, if not some actual falsehood, and it is combative in tone. The sources of the message normally announce their identities with the message. In a hostile relationship, such as war, a message designed to confuse, weaken, demoralize, and divide an opponent is *black* propaganda. Frequently this type of communication purports to operate from a country other than the actual source, an operation called a "false flag."[62] Radio broadcasts from the Soviet Union once claimed to be from a station inside China speaking on behalf of Chinese military dissidents who resented the low priority the Chinese military received in economic planning.[63]

Subversive propaganda amounts to **psychological warfare** and carries the purpose of undermining an opponent. Radio messages, leaflets dropped from planes, and other means encourage the enemy's soldiers to surrender or an abused minority to revolt. Or the message, freighted with discouragement, may intend to break the willpower of the leadership. One reason so much film of pinpoint-accurate bombing appeared on CNN during the Persian Gulf War was to dishearten the Iraqi leaders. In wartime, there are usually few misgivings about identifying the actual source of the propaganda message.

"That's Goebbels; he's in advertising."
Lowry/The Spectator/London

Lowry/The Spectator. London. Reprinted from *World Press Review* magazine.

Propaganda's History

Propaganda is traceable to ancient times, but its real impact began in the First World War. During that war, mass media amounted to high-speed presses that could turn out daily newspapers for largely literate populations in Europe and the United States. In addition, special government propaganda organizations tried to influence public opinion, for example, by printing colorful posters rallying support for their side and condemning the motives and methods of their enemies.

Critical in the First World War were the questions of whether the United States would enter the war and on which side. America had millions of citizens of German and Irish descent who were unsympathetic to Great Britain, one of the major participants in the war. Yet, after the British navy cut the German Atlantic cable, the British gained a near-monopoly over war news reaching America's major newspapers and hence the American public. For example, both sides executed women as spies, but the British successfully portrayed Germans to Americans as barbaric "Huns" for doing so.[64] American public opinion gradually shifted to favor the British, partly as an outcome of British propaganda.

Radio and film became common forms of entertainment in the interwar years, and Nazi Germany took full advantage of the spoken word and the dramatic effect of moving pictures. German propaganda had considerable impact domestically, especially after 1933 when the Nazis eliminated all competition among ideas within their totalitarian state. Directed toward a highly cultured German population was a base, emotional appeal designed to stimulate an extreme sense of nationalism and the vilification of a "scapegoat" ethnic group, the Jewish minority of Germany. This base form of propaganda largely succeeded with the German people in spite of Germany's high level of cultural achievement. The fact that the minister of propaganda, Joseph Goebbels, was one of Adolf Hitler's top lieutenants in the Nazi Party testifies to the importance of propaganda to the Nazis.[65]

Goebbels' propaganda was less effective outside Germany. The release of film of the resplendent German Army, with its goose-stepping troops and the war machines of its *blitzkriegs* as Hitler moved on Europe, had at best a mixed result. Movie newsreels of the successful Nazi *juggernaut* may have discouraged some people but prompted others to rally in defense of their homelands.

The history of propaganda during the Cold War involves a range of media, including newspapers, magazines, radio, and especially television. A worldwide communication grid, linked by satellites, became available before the end of the Cold War. Democratic and communist countries could use this multimedia network to attract the world's population to their respective ways of thinking. Nevertheless, news of the economic success of the West and the economic failure of the communists had more influence on the Cold War outcome than any propaganda concocted by either side. Experiencing hard realities can frequently transcend any flow of words or pictures designed to "reinvent" reality. A brief review of the propaganda efforts by the protagonists of the Cold War will help make the role of propaganda clear.

United States Propaganda

The two titans of the Cold War built up substantial propaganda instruments over nearly half a century. The United States has broadcast to the world through the Voice of America radio station since 1943. Broadcasting in many languages, Voice of America mixes a range of news stories and entertainment with information about life in the United States and supportive arguments for American foreign policy. In 1993, President Jean-Bertrand Aristide of Haiti, ousted by a military coup in 1991, used Voice of America to speak to Haitians. He urged his people to resist migrating to America illegally and to stay home until he returned, bringing with him democratic reforms. President Aristide did return to Haiti in 1994, thanks to the intervention of American military forces.

Radio Free Europe and Radio Liberty began radio broadcasts in the 1950s to send radio messages to eastern Europe and the Soviet Union, respectively. For years, the CIA secretly supported these stations, but today the United States Board for International Broadcasting operates them openly. Their programs offered news of the outside world to a people given access only to the media of a totalitarian state. Although communist governments have collapsed in eastern Europe, supporters of these radio stations want them to continue to operate and to encourage the struggling democratic movements in these ex-communist states.[66]

In 1985, Radio Marti began to broadcast the American viewpoint to Cuba, and TV Marti started operations in 1990. TV Marti telecasts only late at night and, at that, Cuban authorities heavily jam these last-night telecasts. Congress conducted a study in 1992 concerning broadcasts behind the bamboo curtain by a proposed Radio Asia to the communist countries of China and Southeast Asia.[67]

Some other countries have represented the Western point of view through radio as well. *Deutsche Welle* of Germany and the British Broadcasting Corporation (BBC) of Great Britain are good examples. For several generations, millions of people around the world have listened to BBC radio and still regard it as the most reliable and relatively objective source available. Although BBC has established World Service Television, the privately owned CNN global television network has probably shouldered BBC aside as the preeminent "picture" news source for the world. By the 1980s, at least 80 countries were broadcasting a variety of radio programs internationally in as many as 30 languages.[68]

The United States Information Agency (USIA), known as the United States Information Service overseas, added a new dimension to America's propaganda efforts. Often located near U.S. embassies and loosely associated with the State Department, USIA centers contain libraries with books on America, exhibit rooms, TV and movie theaters, and press and information offices. The USIA can arrange programs as varied as student and scholarly exchanges with other countries, speaker tours, and visits by astronauts. Through its Worldnet satellite service, USIA can set up interviews with major figures in Washington while foreign journalists ask their questions from a USIA center. The job of the USIA is to create favorable public opinion of America in other countries. Most American propaganda has been white propaganda that has at times been shaded into grey propaganda.

Soviet Propaganda

Radio Moscow, always a powerful station in transmitting wattage, sent its messages around the world in many languages. Soviet newspapers, such as *Pravda* and *Izvestiya*, were usually available in the large cities of the world and in the appropriate language. The Soviet propaganda was closer to the grey type, with messages selected and slanted to imply that America and its CIA were responsible for many of the unfortunate happenings around the world. Radio Moscow, as well as Soviet television news for domestic consumption, aired mostly negative stories that dealt with American poverty, crime, and the mistreatment of minorities.[69] For years, Leonard Peltier, a Lakota (Sioux Indian) convicted for slaying two FBI agents in 1975, was a favorite topic of Soviet propaganda. Many Americans also believe Peltier received a wrongful conviction.[70]

Of course, Radio Moscow aired only positive stories about the Soviet Union. This writer remembers a Radio Moscow broadcast extolling the freedom of religion in the Soviet Union. Later, while visiting Leningrad (now once again called St. Petersburg), this writer went to several churches to find them converted to museums and locked up during the hours posted as open.

Today some of the same propagandists operate from a downsized Russia, and in a more open society at that. Russian news services are able to be more critical about their own authorities and give much attention to the physical environment, human rights, organized crime, and human services inside their country. However, President Boris Yeltsin's restrictions on the opposition press since 1993, following the suppression of recalcitrant communist in the Russian Parliament, represent a more limited role for the Russian press than is usually the case in a true democracy. In the future, Russian foreign propaganda may pay more attention to Slavic issues in Europe to Russia's west, the Islamic revolutionary movement to the south, and developments in China to the southwest.

With the Cold War at an end, propaganda efforts at the regional level will probably be more noticeable. For instance, both sides in the Bosnian war used a relatively harsh grey propaganda in the fight over territory before NATO established peace in 1995. Muslims and Serbs attempted to outdo each other in leveling charges of atrocities. Stories of horrible prison camps, mass rapes, and constant sniper fire aimed at unarmed civilians were common. The Serbians lost the propaganda war probably because they deserved to; they had more weapons and so gave greater vent to their ethnic hatred. Most of the suspects wanted for trial by the International War Tribunal, sponsored by the United Nations, are Bosnian Serbs.

Propaganda's Usefulness

The usefulness of propaganda to the propagandist is difficult to assess. At first glance, the use of mass media, the increase in literacy, and the greater involvement of people in their governments around the world suggest propaganda is potentially effective. Yet the target population may not pay attention, their government may jam the airwaves, and messages may amount to hard, ideological diatribe that is unintelligible to most listeners, if not boring. To be effective, propaganda has to be simple, be credible, and follow a constant theme over time. Propaganda is often made more believable by mixing it with well-known facts. If the target population is a modern, industrial country, relatively sophisticated, and living in an open society with a "marketplace" of free ideas, propaganda will have less chance to be effective than if the target population has the opposite characteristics.

"Action speaks louder than words" is an old saying that is germane to the question of propaganda's usefulness. Winning gold medals at the Olympics, shipments of free food to a famine-ridden area, and spectacular accomplishments in space may cast a more favorable image for a country than all the concocted words imaginable. The Soviet's two *Sputniks*, which orbited in outer space in 1957, had a momentous impact around the world, including the reorientation of America's public education priorities toward math and science. A similar impression on world opinion occurred in 1969 when the United States decisively captured the lead in the "space race" by landing astronauts on the moon. A major rationale for the U.S. space program has always been its propaganda value.[71]

Both superpowers' expenditures in the Cold War peaked at $300 billion on defense, $30 billion on intelligence, and several hundred million dollars on propaganda. These expenditures suggest the relative importance states attribute to these instruments. Propaganda is, then, a relatively low priority as an instrument. Yet countries involved in intense, protracted struggles are likely to use any instrument that has some usefulness, including propaganda. In the nonshooting environment of the Cold War, with its emphasis on ideological choices between democracy and communism, antagonists felt especially compelled to champion the worth of their receptive systems. Obviously, countries that choose to use propaganda believe they can win friends and discourage enemies.

To conclude, propaganda strives to shape the opinions of people and their governments and therefore their choices and behavior. Propaganda can be soft and subtle, producing general images, or vociferous and intense, such as when subversive efforts are made against rival governments. Propaganda's value is not as certain as that of impressive acts, such as placing a human on the moon; thus, propaganda does not receive nearly the funding and personnel other instruments of government do. Nevertheless, almost all actors are public relations conscious, especially with a global communications grid in place. We can expect states and other actors to treat propaganda as useful in some degree for the indefinite future.

PENETRATION OPERATIONS AND NONSTATE ACTORS

States are not the only actors to use operations that interfere with other actors, including clandestine techniques. MNCs have sought to collect all sorts of information about investment opportunities, governments' policy on nationalization of foreign industry, and other information related to the hospitality a MNC can expect to find in a potential host country. Sometimes a MNC has gleaned information by means of bribery. MNCs have even used covert acts. For example, International Telephone and Telegraph (ITT) contributed money to help bring down the democratically elected Marxist government in Chile in 1973.

In another case, from about 1990 to 1992, British Airways resorted to subterfuge against a much smaller airline, Virgin Atlantic. Among its "bag of dirty tricks" was one technique code-named "Mission Atlantic." This technique called for British Airways workers to meet Virgin Atlantic passengers and lead them straight to the British Airways gate, claiming that Virgin Atlantic had scheduling problems. These workers deliberately gave the impression that they worked for Virgin Atlantic. A British court leveled considerable damages and court costs against British Airways. MNCs also have advertised, or propagated, their contributions to various countries concerning the investment of capital and skills.

Terrorists commonly gather intelligence about their targets and use counterintelligence techniques to thwart police efforts to catch them. Covert acts are at the heart of all that terrorists do. Bombings, assassinations, and kidnappings are carried out with stealth, but later terrorists may seek to gain publicity for their acts. Typically, after a bombing incident, several terrorist groups will call radio and television stations claiming credit for the bombing. Terrorists have used propaganda to justify their violence and demand that their group receive justice or some other desired goal. They wish to establish a climate of opinion that will pressure governments to give them what they want.

The Roman Catholic Church collects intelligence on many subjects, including countries' human rights practices, which it supports, and countries' birth control policies, which it mostly opposes. The Church approves only of the "natural rhythm" method of limiting the number of births as opposed to artificial means. Covert acts are not unknown within the Roman Catholic Church's domain. Remember from Chapter Three the role of the "Marxist priests" in Brazil, acting against the directive of the Church hierarchy, and the partly surreptitious role of the Church in the fall of the Marcos regime in the Philippines. And certainly the Roman Catholic Church propagates its values, that is, what it considers to be the gospel, or religious truth.

Another example involves an ethnic group. In the winter of 1992–1993, Israel deported almost 400 members of the Hamas, an Islamic fundamentalist group of Palestinians. They wound up in a "no-man's land" in south Lebanon from which they were unable to return to Israel and could not proceed into Lebanon. The plight of this ethnic group had resounding political effects, as the United Nations and the world media gave the Hamas considerable attention. These deportees became a "live stage of propaganda" appearing as the innocent victims of Israeli repression. The Hamas, living in a crude camp in wintertime, were able, for a time, to damage the Israeli-American friendship and jeopardize the United States–backed peace talks between Palestinians and the Israeli government.

In sum, nonstate actors collect information for their policy decisions, propagandize, and, at least in the case of terrorists, use violent, covert acts. These roles by nonstate actors are another example of the growing importance of the mixed-actor world.

SECRECY AND DEMOCRACY

Democracies that use spies, covert acts, and at least grey propaganda face an inherent dilemma. To protect national security, many states, including a number of democracies, have undertaken a variety of clandestine activities, treating them as justified means to protect their countries. Realists have argued that providing national security to citizens is a high moral obligation of all leaders. However, the deep secrecy involved in protecting national security through penetration operations is usually incompatible with the open nature of democracy. Secrecy can lead to secret power and thereby can corrode democracy. Secrecy allows governments to avoid accountability for some of their actions to the people they serve, a fundamental requirement of democracy. As intelligence agencies expand, democracy may contract.[72] The enduring irony of clandestine activities is their potential to destroy as well as to guard democracy.[73]

The most immediate problem is the temptation for those with secret power to act against the society they are to serve and protect. Examples are easy to provide. The FBI once illegally broke into a psychiatrist's office to gather information about the individual who copied the classified *Pentagon Papers,* documents that exposed the decision making behind the Vietnam War. Also during this war, the CIA spied on war protesters in the American domestic context, where the CIA cannot legally act. Shin Beth in Israel has mistreated prisoners to extract information and may have murdered some terrorists on Israeli soil. Britain's MI-5, or Security Service, has surveiled labor unions and antiwar campaigners. Canadian operatives have surveiled and infiltrated labor unions and teacher organizations.[74]

Outside their own territories, questions also arise about the proper conduct of intelligence agencies representing democracies. As mentioned earlier, one argument is that secret intelligence collection is allowable for a democracy, but not the use of covert acts. British intelligence may have suspended covert acts altogether in the 1950s, and today the United States, under law, must limit and review covert acts carefully. Israel, in contrast, actively engages in assassinations and kidnappings to exact revenge and to defend itself.

A dilemma arises because if intelligence operations of any kind are justifiable, some degree of secrecy is inevitable. A United States case clearly illustrates this point. Philip Agee, an ex-CIA employee, published a book that included the name of every CIA agent he could remember. However, Agee denies ever mentioning in print the name of Richard Welch, CIA station chief in Athens, before his murder in 1975. Because Barbara Bush, a former first lady in her book *A Memoir,* alleges that he did, Agee slapped her with a $4 million libel suit in 1995. Should the freedom of press allow a writer to identify secret agents? Whether or not Agee is responsible for Welch's death, the CIA asked for and got a law making it illegal to print the names of CIA agents, thus limiting the freedom of the press. Must a government always choose between effective clandestine activities and viable democracy?

The proper balance between secret, efficient intelligence operations and the requirements of democracy is difficult to establish. An option for democracies is to limit the activities of intelligence agencies by law and establish oversight arrangements so these agencies are held accountable. The United States has gone further than other democracies in this regard. Not only does the United States require administrative review for covert acts, including a role by the president, but congressional oversight committees now exist in the Senate and House to review the entire intelligence community.[75] Yet, from 1947 to 1974, the executive branch dominated intelligence policy, with senior members of the Armed Services and Appropriation Committees, charged with oversight responsibilities, merely deferring to the president. In the aftermath of the Watergate scandal and the loss of the Vietnam War, Congress created oversight committees in 1975, though the tendency to defer to the president persisted. Congress, however, has gradually emerged as a partner to the executive branch in intelligence policy.[76]

David D. Gries, director of the CIA's Center for the Study of Intelligence, has claimed the CIA is a more open organization and is more responsive to the democratic society it serves than in times past.[77] In spite of Director Gries's confidence in congressional oversight, however, we can justifiably raise the question of whether the oversight function is thorough enough. Although Congress had forbade aid other than humanitarian help to the Contras in Nicaragua, the CIA managed to ship arms and other assistance to the Contras in the early 1980s. The secret nature of the CIA, as an instrument of policy, may remain a temptation for presidents to circumvent Congress.[78]

In Britain, a number of Whitehall, or administrative, committees are supposed to oversee British intelligence, but exposing intelligence of any kind in the British Parliament has been anathema to British leaders for years.[79] In 1989, Britain did admit the existence of MI-5 and, in a public brochure, described its activities that today mainly focus on the terrorist Irish Republican Army (IRA). The identity of the chief of MI-5, Stella Rimington, became available in 1993. Scandals over Shin Beth's use of torture have led to greater administrative review in Israel, but the balance remains heavily tilted toward secrecy in that country.[80]

Because of the secret nature of intelligence agencies, it is unknown whether oversight committees in democracies regularly receive notification of penetration operations. Probably it is safe to say that democracies are too protective and tolerant of intelligence agencies. Little, if any, accountability ties intelligence operatives to their political masters and these, in turn, to the voting public. Democracies place much faith in intelligence personnel that they will remember they represent democratic governments and behave accordingly. The occasional misdeed that comes to light shows that democracies sometimes misplace this trust.

PENETRATION OPERATIONS IN THE POST–COLD WAR ERA

Intelligence communities on both sides of the Cold War targeted and penetrated each other's countries. When facing the prospect of nuclear war, Moscow and Washington focused most of their spies on each other. In the post–Cold War era, however, the foci of these intelligence agencies began to shift to new concerns. In 1991, President George Bush issued National Security Review no. 29 directing intelligence agencies to review and make an assessment of intelligence priorities. Then, in 1993, CIA director James Woolsey and the Russian Foreign Intelligence Service (the successor to the KGB abroad) director, Yevgeni Primakov, began meeting to discuss how their intelligence agencies could cooperate over new concerns: the spread of weapons of mass destruction, terrorism, and drug trafficking. On the shift from the focus on the Cold War and nuclear destruction to a mixture of new concerns, Director Woolsey said, "We have slain a large dragon, but we live now in a jungle filled with a bewildering variety of poisonous snakes."[81]

Security remains among intelligence priorities, though its nature has changed markedly. Soviet nuclear arms are now in four separate national arsenals as a result of the breakup of the Soviet Union. Also, several states in the Third World, some with strong animosity toward Western countries, are striving to acquire nuclear, chemical, and biological weapons capabilities. Information on these capabilities and what leaders plan do with them will remain vital. Today, the CIA has the important mission of tracking the spread of nuclear and chemical weapons. CIA satellite cameras and sensors have discovered proof that a facility in Libya was making chemical weapons, that Iraqi agents tried to move nuclear equipment to avoid detection by UN inspectors, and that North Korea may have enough plutonium for at least one nuclear weapon.

Terrorists occupy the attention of counterintelligence agencies, and these agencies may remain focused on terrorists for an indefinite time. For example, MI-5 gives most attention to the IRA, as mentioned earlier. The FBI, in its counterintelligence mode, successfully apprehended a radical Islamic group subsequent to its bombing of the World Trade Center in New York City in 1993 and prevented them from bombing a tunnel for automobile traffic in the same city. Terrorists, backed by rogue states such as Iraq and Libya, may especially require the watchful eye of intelligence agencies. Terrorists with international connections, including the availability of safe houses, false passports, and the support and training of rogue states, may be more difficult to intercept and capture than domestic terrorists such as the bombers of the federal building in Oklahoma City in 1995. In that year, CIA director John Deutch announced a new priority on terrorism and shifted resources within the CIA to its counterterrorism organization.

Desperation over failed efforts by the United States to counter drug trafficking has led to the enlistment of the CIA as well as the armed services to block the transborder movement of illicit drugs. As recently as five years ago, CIA officials refused to dirty their hands by joining the war against drugs, but more recently the CIA has infiltrated drug cartels and reportedly helped organize the 1989 ambush of a Colombian drug cartel leader.

The newest use of intelligence is the collection of ecological information through satellites. Measuring snowpacks and estimating future flooding, mapping the rate of deforestation, photographing the movements of oil slicks, fighting forest fires, assessing hurricane damage, and making weather forecasts are some recent uses of satellite reconnaissance. In 1984, Albert Gore, Jr., as a legislator, asked for and received help from satellite-produced intelligence to find hazardous waste dumps in western Tennessee. In 1992, the CIA indicated it would give scientists 30 years of satellite photographs to help them study global warming.[82] CIA satellite intelligence also has helped friendly states locate valuable oil and gas reserves.

Another ecologically useful device from the "cloak-and-dagger world" is the Sound Surveillance System, designed to track Soviet submarines globally with 1,000 microphones linked together with 30,000 miles of cable. Today the system can track whales, spy on illegal fishing, and monitor volcanoes and earthquakes at sea. Unfortunately for ecological uses, this undersea surveillance system is experiencing huge budget and personnel cuts with the post–Cold War downsizing of America's security apparatus.

The hottest current topic in intelligence policy is industrial espionage. Global trade competition intensified as the Cold War issues subsided. The economic position of states regarding international trade and technological know-how has risen to challenge the attention that leaders and scholars previously gave to military power. Collecting data on countries' trade strengths and strategies could be useful for economic summits when the leading trade states meet. Moreover, counterintelligence has a role in protecting a country's economic secrets from foreign industrial espionage.

Yesterday's political and military allies are more clearly seen as today's economic competitors. Increasingly, international conflict is including competition for economic and commercial success as well as competition over military power. Suspicions and accusations over industrial spying abound as some governments and companies seek a shortcut to a more competitive position by stealing technological, scientific, and commercial secrets from other countries and industries. Industrial theft characterizes not only Third World and former communist states, which are far behind in technology, but also the most modern and active trading states. The United States, for instance, worries about industrial espionage directed at its companies from France, Germany, Israel, Japan, South Korea, and even Canada.

Peter Schweizer, author of *Friendly Spies: How America's Allies Are Using Economic Espionage to Steal Our Secrets,* thinks spying among friends and allies will only intensify because billions of dollars in trade advantages are at stake.[83] To Schweizer, economic clout rather than military strength is the new currency of national power. Consequently, he believes spying for commercial resons will grow while military espionage will recede. Although the United States has exercised some commercial espionage, an FBI report shows that 57 countries have attempted covertly to obtain advanced technology from the United States, with France being the most aggressive of these states. If the highly skilled intelligence agencies of Cold War days turn to commercial espionage as a deep pattern, they risk causing major disruption to international trade. Countries will not jeopardize their proprietary rights by selling or displaying their best technology to trade competitors that steal.[84]

The prospect of many U.S. companies displaying their technological wares at the 1993 Paris Air Show with the danger of theft of their ideas prompted a systematic study by the U.S. intelligence community of the problem of foreign spying on American companies. The FBI and the CIA have made public commitments to a counterintelligence policy of blocking foreign industrial espionage.

Less clear is whether the CIA will conduct retaliatory espionage to gather technological secrets for U.S. business. Stansfield Turner, director of the CIA from 1979 to 1981 but commenting recently, appears to have little compunction about recommending the theft of economic intelligence from foreign sources. He reasons that economic viability is part of our national security and, after all, other countries steal from us.[85] In 1993, CIA director James Woolsey offered a plan before Congress for economic spying by the CIA. Considerable opposition exists to this plan, but Director Woolsey doubtlessly was trying to avoid the budget cuts of post–Cold War downsizing and was searching for a way to impress Congress with the potential usefulness of the CIA. Some of America's friends are already convinced the CIA has chosen the course of economic espionage. The French government asked several CIA agents to leave France in 1995, and the German government made one

CIA agent depart its soil in 1997. These governments accused the agents of snooping out their technological secrets.

The most fundamental challenge to intelligence efforts is the unexpected. Trends in science, technology, economics, and politics can bring revolutionary change at any time. The leading edge does not always go to the actor with the most raw power; rather, it can go to the actor with the best vision, the best grasp of key trends.[86] Collecting information on nonmilitary subjects, with proper analysis, could hold a payoff for perceptive actors.

In sum, intelligence collection can serve in positive ways to improve conditions in the world in addition to promoting security. Establishing new intelligence priorities and the amount of national resources to give them is an ongoing process.

INTELLIGENCE ACTIVITIES AND INTERNATIONAL SOCIETY

In their debate over the fundamental nature of international relations, realists and transnationalists generally give little attention to the so-called black art of penetration operations. Nonetheless, espionage and other convert deeds are an inherent part of the conflictual and anarchical world as seen by realists. Spies, counterintelligence efforts, and covert acts directly relate to a state's national security, the ultimate concern of realists. At least, realist Hans Morgenthau recognizes the entanglement of espionage and diplomacy since spies often operate under the cover of service as diplomats.[87] Traditionally, intelligence activities fit neatly into the analytical model of *international anarchy.*

Only recently have observers viewed intelligence activities in positive terms. The end of the Cold War has meant intelligence activities can turn away from much of the skullduggery of the past. Even before the end of the Cold War, leaders of the Soviet Union and the United States were using satellites to verify arms control agreements. After Mikhail Gorbachev came to power in the Soviet Union in 1985, and the great sea change that ended the Cold War began, both sides agreed that the more they knew about each other, the safer they were.

Gathering and sharing information, whether of an overt or a covert kind, may facilitate cooperation needed to deal with problems experienced in common. Such matters as preparation for a trade summit, prevention of dread weapons falling into the hands of terrorists or radical states, protecting the world's environment, and halting transnationally organized crime and illegal drugs require the cooperation of many states, and that will happen only if there is a common appreciation of these problems. For instance, conferences involving states and nongovernment actors are more likely to reach agreement over rules and norms for guiding policy when conference participants share a common stock of information. As in the case of uneven wealth and military power, some countries with advantages in information gathering, such as satellite imagery or skilled intelligence agencies, may have more information and thus more influence when states pool information for common action.

In a positive way, intelligence can make a contribution to the growth of a cooperative *international society* based on actors coping with global problems. However, the *orientation* of the world is still toward a mixture of cooperation and conflict. Among old allies and old enemies of Cold War days, the industrial espionage of today tends to fray the bonds of an emerging international society. Finally, the continued use of covert acts against terrorists and secret intelligence gathering about radical countries, such as Iraq, remind us that significant fissures remain in the world among some actors. This conflict leaves the world well short of the *consensus,* including a common identity among all humankind, needed for an *international community.*

CHAPTER SUMMARY

Spying, covert acts, and propaganda violate international law and the norms of international society. These operations routinely intrude on national sovereignty. Yet, in various forms, penetration operations have taken place for centuries and continue to be in use for one simple reason: These operations empower the user. Traditionally states, acting from a central concern with power in an anarchical environment, have turned to penetration operations to protect their national security. These operations help deflect intended harm by others and can help a state achieve its ambitions. Sometimes states have even spied on allies and friends to ensure loyalty and learn about their secret weapons. Much about penetration activities supports the views of realists on the role of power in an insecure world. As states deal with arms races, prepare for war, and fight wars, the more they know about an opponent, the better their chances of surviving.

Penetration operations, as we have learned from this chapter, include intelligence (the gathering and interpretation of information) and counterintelligence (steps to block spying on one's own country). Most of the information on which states act is probably collected overtly, or openly and legally. Sometimes, however, critical pieces of information may be available only by covert, or secret and illegal, means.

The most controversial penetration efforts concern covert acts, usually viewed as a "bag of dirty tricks" that occasionally rely on acts of violence. Some intelligence analysts think kidnapping, assassination, and other covert acts may do more harm than good for the country perpetrating them. The more states worry about security, the greater the prospects that they will develop agencies to conduct intelligence, counterintelligence, and covert acts.

Propaganda probably has limited usefulness, since it is not easy to change the minds of other government leaders and their populations. Then, too, with the Cold War over, a pressing need for both sides to extol the virtues of their ideologies is no longer present. Nonetheless, the modern means of communication in the world encourage propaganda's use.

This chapter dealt with three specialized concerns involving penetration operations. First, non-state actors use penetration operations in limited ways. The Roman Catholic Church, for example, may use only overt intelligence collection inside countries to support human rights. Terrorists regularly focus on violent covert acts.

Second, democracies struggle morally with the use of penetration operations. Secrecy, a lack of accountability, and covert acts against other states are bothersome for states with democratic scruples.

Third, perhaps the most interesting special dimension of penetration is the use of intelligence agencies in the post–Cold War period. The opportunity now exists to use intelligence activities in positive ways to make improvements in the world instead of enhancing conflict. Such penetration operations, once emblematic of the harder, more conflictual aspects of the world, may be in decline. Shared intelligence may help states deal with common problems in the areas of global trade, ecology, and terrorism and may encourage the evolving international society. The use of intelligence agencies for stealing trade secrets is one post–Cold War penetration act, however, that perpetuates unhealthy competition, creating some friction for the evolving international society.

POINTS OF VIEW

[Regarding the list of cold war mysteries about covert activities that might be in the now open files of ex-communist states] One word of caution to historians before they celebrate: of some of the darkest deeds there may be no record at all.

—DAVID WISE,
MOLEHUNT

[On the possible reorientation of the CIA from international to industrial espionage] I am willing to die for my country but not for "widget" motors.

—UNNAMED CIA AGENT'S COMMENT AS
REPORTED BY FORMER CIA DIRECTOR
ROBERT GATES IN AN INTERVIEW

If a company needs the CIA to tell them what's going on in their area of business, then they're already in Chapter 11 [bankruptcy].

—AMERICAN CORPORATE EXECUTIVE

. . . the photoreconnaissance satellite is one of the most important military technological developments of this century, along with radar and the atomic bomb. Without it, the history of this century would be very different. Indeed, without it history might have ceased.

—JEFFREY T. RICHELSON,
AMERICA'S SECRET EYES IN SPACE

I should have been more careful.

—ALRICH H. AMES,
CONVICTED SPY

One of the great benefits of the end of the Cold War is the opportunity it presents to reexamine secrecy and to end a great deal of it.

—PAT M. HOLT,
SECRET INTELLIGENCE

REVIEW QUESTIONS

1. What is meant by the statement "Penetration operations are associated with an anarchical, conflictual world"?
2. What is the difference between covert and overt intelligence? Which do you think is more important?
3. What are some of the specialized roles spies can carry out? Why do people become spies?
4. What happens to individuals when they are said to be "honeytrapped"?
5. Name as many techniques for collecting intelligence as you can.
6. What is the importance of codes and ciphers to intelligence, and what is the distinction between the two?
7. What do states try to accomplish through covert acts, and what are some examples of these acts?
8. Why does a dilemma occur over secret operations and democratic principles? To what extent do democracies maintain "oversight" of intelligence activities?
9. Now that the Cold War is over, can you think of useful applications for intelligence activities?
10. How do intelligence activities relate to an evolving international society?

GLOSSARY

ciphers Complex rules of substitution for the letters of a language into other symbols, with the meaning of a symbol changing from one part of the message to another.

codes Words or other symbols, such as numbers, that are assigned meanings understandable only by someone with a list of those meanings, that is, a codebook.

counterintelligence The process of protecting one's own secrets and intelligence organization and deflecting the efforts of foreign spy organizations.

covert acts Secret acts, sometimes violent, taken in a foreign country to influence political outcomes; usually small in scale and feasibly deniable.

covert intelligence Information gathered secretly and illegally in foreign countries.

HUMINT Intelligence collected from human sources.

intelligence The process of collecting and analyzing information for policymakers, especially concerning the intentions and capabilities of opponents.

overt intelligence Information gathered openly and legally in foreign countries.

PHOINT The use of photographs and other forms of imagery, taken by cameras placed in planes or satellites, to collect information about a target country.

propaganda The dissemination of information, often tainted by falsehood, to affect the attitudes and behavior of a target population.

psychological warfare Subversive propaganda designed to demoralize and weaken the will of a target population and its government.

SIGINT Intelligence collected from intercepts of electronically based communications.

RECOMMENDED READINGS

Christopher Andrew, ed. *Codebreaking and Signals Intelligence.* London: Frank Cass, 1986.

Christopher Andrew. *For the President's Eyes Only.* New York: HarperPerennial, 1996.

Christopher Andrew and David Dilks, eds. *The Missing Dimension: Governments and Intelligence Communities in the Twentieth Century.* Urbana, IL: University of Illinois Press, 1984.

Martin Ebon. *KGB: Death and Rebirth.* Westport, CT: Praeger Publishers, 1994.

Nicholas Eftimiades. *Chinese Intelligence Operations.* Annapolis, MD: Naval Institute Press, 1994.

Michael Herman. *Intelligence Power in Peace and War.* New York: Cambridge University Press, 1996.

Pat M. Holt. *Secret Intelligence and Public Policy: A Dilemma of Democracy.* Washington, D.C.: Congressional Quarterly Press, 1995.

Loch K. Johnson. *Secret Agencies: U.S. Intelligence in a Hostile World.* New Haven, CT: Yale University Press, 1996.

Garth S. Jowett and Victoria O'Donnell. *Propaganda and Persuasion.* Newbury Park, CA: Sage Publications, 1986.

Samuel M. Katz. *Soldier Spies: Israeli Military Intelligence.* Novato, CA: Presidio Press, 1992.

Phillip Knightley. *The Second Oldest Profession: Spies and Spying in the Twentieth Century.* New York: W. W. Norton, 1987.

Mark Perry. *Eclipse: The Last Days of the CIA.* New York: William Morrow, 1992.

W. Michael Reisman and James E. Baker. *Regulating Covert Action.* New Haven, CT: Yale University Press, 1992.

Jeffrey T. Richelson. *A Century of Spies: Intelligence in the Twentieth Century.* New York: Oxford University Press, 1995.

Jeffrey T. Richelson. *America's Secret Eyes in Space: The U.S. Keyhole Spy Satellite Program.* New York: Harper Business, 1990.

Jeffrey T. Richelson. *Foreign Intelligence Organizations.* Cambridge, MA: Ballinger, 1988.

Jeffrey T. Richelson. *The U.S. Intelligence Community.* 3rd ed. Boulder, CO: Westview Press, 1995.

Abram N. Shulsky. *Silent Warfare: Understanding the World of Intelligence.* Washington, D.C.: Brassey's (US), Inc., 1991.

Frank J. Smist, Jr. *Congress Oversees the United States Intelligence Community, 1947–1994.* 2nd ed. Knoxville, TN: University of Tennessee Press, 1990.

Russell Jack Smith. *The Unknown CIA: My Three Decades with the Agency.* Washington, D.C.: Pergamon-Brassey's, 1989.

David Wise. *Molehunt: The Secret Search for Traitors That Shattered the CIA.* New York: Random House, 1992.

ENDNOTES

1. Herbert E. Meyer, *Real-World Intelligence: Organized Information for Executives* (New York: Weidenfeld and Nicolson, 1987), p. 8.
2. At least this situation has been reported about the CIA. See Christopher Andrew, *Her Majesty's Secret Service: The Making of the British Intelligence Community* (New York: Viking, 1985), p. 498.
3. Phillip Knightley, *The Second Oldest Profession: Spies and Spying in the Twentieth Century* (New York: W. W. Norton, 1987), pp. 3–4.
4. Edward Jay Epstein, "Secrets from the CIA Archive in Tehran," *Orbis,* Spring 1987, pp. 33–41.
5. *Time,* February 29, 1988, p. 93.
6. Stephen J. Cimbala, ed., *Intelligence and Intelligence Policy in a Democratic Society* (Dobbs Ferry, N.Y.: Transnational Publications, 1987), p. 6.
7. *Time,* October 23, 1989, p. 43.

8. Knightley, *The Second Oldest Profession*, p. 383.
9. Jeffrey T. Richelson, *Foreign Intelligence Organizations* (Cambridge, MA: Ballinger, 1988), p. 54.
10. Christopher Andrew and David Dilks, eds., *The Missing Dimension: Governments and the Intelligence Communities in the Twentieth Century* (Urbana, IL: University of Illinois Press, 1984), p. 2; Abram N. Shulsky, *Silent Warfare: Understanding the World of Intelligence* (Washington, D.C.: Brassey's (US), Inc., 1991), p. xv.
11. Knightley, *The Second Oldest Profession*, p. 5; Ian Black and Benny Morris, *Israel's Secret Wars: A History of Israel's Intelligence Services* (New York: Grove Weidenfeld, 1992), pp. xi–xii.
12. This observation is made in Knightley, *The Second Oldest Profession*, p. 389.
13. Russell Jack Smith, *The Unknown CIA: My Three Decades with the Agency* (Washington, D.C.: Pergamon-Brassey's, 1989), p. 4.
14. Cimbala, *Intelligence*, pp. 233–34.
15. On the usefulness of human agents, see David L. Boren, "The Intelligence Community: How Crucial?" *Foreign Affairs*, Summer 1992, p. 55.
16. Richelson, *Foreign Intelligence Organizations*, p. 13.
17. Knightley, *The Second Oldest Profession*, p. 385.
18. Andrew, *Her Majesty's Secret Service*, p. 493.
19. Black and Morris, *Israel's Secret Wars*, p. xv.
20. David Wise, *Molehunt: The Secret Search for Traitors that Shattered the CIA* (New York: Random House, 1992), pp. 292–95.
21. An account of Ames's treachery can be found in Peter Mass, *Killer Spy* (New York: Warner Books, 1995).
22. Stanislav Levchenko, *On the Wrong Side: My Life in the KGB* (Washington, D.C.: Pergamon-Brassey's, 1988), pp. 242–43.
23. Black and Morris, *Israel's Secret Wars*, pp. 522–23.
24. This information on spy ships and planes is taken from Jeffrey T. Richelson, *The U.S. Intelligence Community* (Cambridge, MA: Ballinger, 1985), pp. 116–17, 128.
25. Richelson, *Foreign Intelligence Organizations*, p. 54.
26. Most of this information on spy satellites is taken from Jeffrey T. Richelson, *America's Secret Eyes in Space: The U.S. Keyhole Spy Satellite Program* (New York: Harper Business, 1990). A good description of imagery is found in Richelson, *The U.S. Intelligence Community*, Chapter 7.
27. Richelson, *America's Secret Eyes in Space*, p. vi.
28. Richelson, *The U.S. Intelligence Community*, p. 122.
29. Black and Morris, *Israel's Secret Wars*, p. 515.
30. Ernest R. May, "Intelligence: Backing into the Future," *Foreign Affairs*, Summer 1992, p. 64.
31. At least this is the opinion of Andrew and Dilks, *The Missing Dimension*, p. 8.
32. Andrew, *Her Majesty's Secret Service*, pp. 448–51.
33. See Andrew and Dilks, *The Missing Dimension*, p. 1.
34. James R. Chiles, "To Break the Unbreakable Code," *Smithsonian*, June 1987, p. 141.
35. Associated Press, October 30, 1988.
36. Knightley, *The Second Oldest Profession*, pp. 374–75.
37. Shulsky, *Silent Warfare*, p. 78.
38. Smith, *The Unknown CIA*, p. 220.
39. George A. Carver, Jr., "Intelligence in the Age of Glasnost," *Foreign Affairs*, Summer 1990, p. 162.
40. Andrew and Dilks, *The Missing Dimension*, p. 6.
41. Loch K. Johnson, "On Drawing a Bright Red Line for Covert Operations," *American Journal of International Law*, April 1992, pp. 284–309.
42. James A. Barry, "Covert Action Can be Just," *Orbis*, Summer 1993, pp. 375–90.
43. Richelson, *The U.S. Intelligence Community*, p. 229.
44. Richelson, *Foreign Intelligence Organizations*, pp. 207–9.
45. Ibid., p. 201.
46. Richelson, *The U.S. Intelligence Community*, p. 230.
47. Knightley, *The Second Oldest Profession*, p. 386.
48. Ladislav Bittman, *The KGB and Soviet Disinformation: An Insider's View* (Washington, D.C.: Pergamon-Brassey's, 1985), pp. 2, 13, 217–19.
49. A useful overview of America's intelligence community can be found in Richelson, *The U.S. Intelligence Community*; Smith, *The Unknown CIA*; Boren, "The Intelligence Community"; and Loch K. Johnson, "Smart Intelligence," *Foreign Policy*, Winter 1992–1993, pp. 53–69.

50. Mark Perry, *Eclipse: The Last Days of the CIA* (New York: William Morrow, 1992).
51. Martin Ebon, *KGB: Death and Rebirth* (Westport, CT: Praeger Publishers, 1994).
52. A great deal can be learned about Soviet intelligence activities by reading Levchenko, *On the Wrong Side;* Bittman, *The KGB and Soviet Disinformation;* and Jeffrey T. Richelson, *Sword and Shield: The Soviet Intelligence and Security Apparatus* (Cambridge, MA: Ballinger, 1986).
53. Ebon, *KGB,* p. xii.
54. Associated Press, May 29, 1992.
55. Nicholas Eftimiades, *Chinese Intelligence Operations* (Annapolis, MD: Naval Institute Press, 1994), pp. 5–6.
56. Ibid., pp. 113–14.
57. Ibid., pp. 114–16.
58. British intelligence and its history is interestingly described in Andrew, *Her Majesty's Secret Service.*
59. Black and Morris, *Israel's Secret Wars;* Richelson, *Foreign Intelligence Organizations,* Chapter 7.
60. Knightley, *The Second Oldest Profession,* p. 382.
61. This understanding of propaganda has been influenced in part by Garth S. Jowett and Victoria O'Donnell, *Propaganda and Persuasion* (Newbury Park, CA: Sage Publications, 1986), pp. 15–16.
62. These three types of propaganda are summarized in W. Michael Reisman and James E. Baker, *Regulating Covert Action* (New Haven, CT: Yale University Press, 1992), p. 125.
63. Richelson, *Sword and Shield,* pp. 153–54.
64. Jowett and O'Donnell, *Propaganda and Persuasion,* pp. 118, 123–26, 131.
65. This description is based in part on Jowett and O'Donnell, *Propaganda and Persuasion,* pp. 138–39.
66. Kevin J. McNamara, "Reaching Captive Minds with Radio," *Orbis,* Winter 1992, pp. 23–26, 29–31.
67. Ibid., pp. 38–40.
68. Stephen Kramer, "Global Communications and National Power," *World Politics,* April 1991, p. 345.
69. *Iowa Alumni Review,* Nov–Dec 1985).
70. See the engaging argument against Peltier's conviction by Peter Matthiessen, *In The Spirit of Crazy Horse* (New York: Viking, 1991).
71. See Vernon Van Dyke, *Pride and Power: The Rationale of the Space Program* (Urbana, IL: The University of Illinois Press, 1964), Chapters 8, 9.
72. Richelson, *Foreign Intelligence Organizations,* p. 311; Knightley, *The Second Oldest Profession,* p. 392.
73. Johnson, "Smart Intelligence," p. 69.
74. Some of these examples are taken from Richelson, *Foreign Intelligence Organizations,* pp. 309–10.
75. Reisman and Baker, *Regulating Covert Action,* pp. 120–21.
76. Frank J. Smist, Jr., *Congress Oversees the United States Intelligence Community,* 2nd ed. (Knoxville, TN: University of Tennessee Press, 1990), pp. 19–24, 279–80.
77. David G. Gries, "Opening Up Secret Intelligence," *Orbis,* Summer 1993, pp. 365–72.
78. Pat M. Holt, *Secret Intelligence and Public Policy: A Dilemma of Democracy* (Washington, D.C.: Congressional Quarterly Press, 1995), pp. 239–43.
79. Knightley, *The Second Oldest Profession,* p. 370; Andrew and Dilks, *The Missing Dimension,* p. 14.
80. Black and Morris, *Israel's Secret Wars,* pp. xii–xiii.
81. Quoted in *Newsweek,* April 12, 1993, p. 30.
82. For general discussions of the role of intelligence in a new era, see Carver, "Intelligence in the Age of Glasnost"; Johnson, "Smart Intelligence"; May, "Intelligence: Backing into the Future"; and Boren, "The Intelligence Community." Some of the examples used in this section are from *Time,* July 5, 1993, pp. 27–33; *Newsweek,* April 12, 1993, pp. 30–32; and *Time,* February 22, 1993, p. 60.
83. Peter Schweizer, *Friendly Spies: How America's Allies Are Using Economic Espionage to Steal Our Secrets* (New York: Atlantic Monthly Press, 1993).
84. Peter Schweizer, "The Growth of Economic Espionage: America Is Target Number One," *Foreign Affairs,* January–February 1996, pp. 9–14.
85. Stansfield Turner, "Intelligence for a New World Order," *Foreign Affairs,* Fall 1991, pp. 150–66.
86. Meyer, *Real-World Intelligence,* p. 6.
87. Hans J. Morgenthau, *Politics Among Nations: The Struggle for Power and Peace,* 5th ed. (New York: Alfred A. Knopf, 1978), p. 534.

CHAPTER 7

THE ROLE OF DIPLOMACY: A TRADITIONAL TOOL IN CHANGING TIMES

Diplomacy is the process of conducting communication among states through officially recognized representatives. The communication is almost continuous among states as their representatives, or diplomats, protect state interests and reduce conflict. Diplomacy is a major dimension of a state's foreign policy, with foreign ministers (the secretary of state in the case of the United States) and their diplomats living abroad carrying out state business. In recent years, however, scholars are becoming increasingly aware of diplomacy practiced by nonstate actors, including international organizations, human rights groups, and multinational corporations, among others. Nonstate actors may not have accredited diplomatic representatives, but nonetheless they negotiate and bargain with states and with one another.

Although most diplomacy is still *bilateral,* between two states, *multilateral diplomacy,* which involves various numbers of states and nonstate actors, has been on the rise since the nineteenth century. At such multilateral conferences as the UN Conference on Population and Development held at Cairo, Egypt, in 1994 and the UN World Conference on Women at Beijing, China, in 1995, country representatives try to move toward agenda-setting programs for international society while nonstate actors attempt to influence the rules and norms of any agreements made.

The value of diplomacy is that its communication and negotiation offer a cost-effective way to head off problems such as wars and trade conflicts. Were there total conflict or complete cooperation, diplomacy would be either ineffective or unnecessary. When states perceive their conflict as one of impasse and desert diplomatic methods for force, the price in lives and money can be high. Moreover, diplomacy's value goes beyond the settlement of specific conflicts because diplomacy contributes to the development of international society. Diplomacy helps actors understand one another and provides a channel for sharing values and developing agreement on policy matters.[1]

We begin this chapter with a brief history of diplomacy, followed by a look at the functions of diplomats and the central importance of negotiation and bargaining to diplomacy. Next, we examine the legal setting of diplomacy, then the style of diplomacy and its operating conditions. We discuss diplomacy by nonstate actors and the importance of multilateral, or conference, diplomacy. Finally, we gauge the contribution diplomacy is making to an emerging international society.

A BRIEF HISTORY OF DIPLOMACY[2]

Diplomacy probably made its appearance in prehistoric times when cave dwellers discovered it was useful to hear the message of an emissary instead of killing him. Better-known diplomatic practices are those of the ancient Greeks and Romans. By the fifth century B.C., emissaries traveled regularly within the Greek city-state system. These emissaries were "orator" types of diplomats who made appealing speeches as they pleaded the cause of one city to another city. Frequently the "orator" diplomat was a resident of the city receiving the appeal. For example, Sparta might pay an Athenian to represent Sparta's interests to Athens.

The Romans exchanged diplomats with the tribes and empires existing on the periphery of the Roman Empire. The Romans were better known for placing their relations with foreigners under law than for practicing the art of negotiations. The Roman *jus gentium* (law of nations) is a legal development scholars regard as an early contribution to international law. Evidence also exists that other ancient peoples, such as the Chinese, Indians, and Persians, found a need for diplomacy.

The form of diplomacy we are familiar with today emerged from the Italian city-state system. In Italy, the method of using a trained, professional representative developed in the thirteenth and fourteenth centuries and replaced reliance on an "orator" diplomat. By the fifteenth century, the important Italian concept of a permanent mission, or **embassy,** appeared because of an increase in diplomatic business. Other European capitals soon followed this Italian precedent. An additional boost to professional diplomacy in Europe was a recognition of the need for a shared definition of diplomacy and for the regulation of diplomacy at the Congress of Vienna in 1815. The Congress of Aix-la-Chapelle that soon followed established diplomacy as a distinct branch of public service in each country of Europe.

Europe's global explorations and search for trade in the seventeenth and eighteenth centuries created a need for diplomatic envoys to far-flung kingdoms and empires on other continents. Diplomacy of an intercontinental kind did not flourish at first, however, because European exploration and early trade ties led to the colonial subjugation of most of the peoples living on other continents. Thus, relations between European capitals and other continents became mostly hierarchical and administrative in nature rather than diplomatic.

With the breakup of colonial empires, first in the Americas in the eighteenth and nineteenth centuries and then in Africa and Asia after the Second World War, the number of states rapidly expanded to about 160 by the 1960s. With additional colonial breakups and the downfall of European communism accompanied by ethnic separatism, the number of states has risen to about 200. The parallel increase in capitals has greatly enlarged diplomatic intercourse that now enjoys a global setting. The rise in the number of states will require the appointment of many new diplomats and the creation of new embassies.

FUNCTIONS OF DIPLOMACY

Most countries operate far-flung diplomatic systems of embassies and diplomatic corps because diplomacy has several useful functions. These functions focus on the diplomatic corps headed by an **ambassador.**

Representing State Interests

Ambassadors act as the spokespersons for their governments and serve as channels of communication between the countries that send them and the host states. Ambassadors must, above all, be "interpreters" who can help host governments understand the sending countries' points of view. Similarly, ambassadors also must sensitize their own governments to the conditions and points of view of the host governments. As the conduit of this channel of communication, the first concern of ambassadors is always their own governments' interests. Some governments transfer their ambassadors periodically to prevent them from becoming too sympathetic with another government's point of view.

The interests ambassadors can pursue for their own countries are manifold. The interest may be as ordinary as arranging for airline flights between two countries, setting lower tariffs for trade, or arranging a treaty of extradition. At mid-level, an ambassador may lodge a protest over the action of another government, such as a border violation or the maltreatment of foreign nationals while on the soil of another country. More critically, the interest may cause a deterioration in relations unless countries correct the problem. For instance, in 1995 President Bill Clinton threatened to sharply increase tariffs on Japanese luxury cars, such as the Lexus and the Infiniti, if Japan did not initiate reforms to open up its car dealerships to American-made cars. Had compromise failed, a trade war between the two largest national economies in the world would have been a real possibility.

More spectacular than specific actions are *diplomatic campaigns* to explain a country's policy as a way to win the understanding and cooperation of other countries. In 1979, Egypt tried in vain to persuade African and Arab countries to view its recognition of Israel as a wise and necessary step. Great Britain was more successful in restraining other governments from supporting Argentina in the Falkland Islands War of 1982, painting Argentina as an aggressor and a violator of one of international society's most hallowed rules. To build an international consensus opposing Iraq's invasion of Kuwait, President George Bush employed his secretaries of state and defense in a 1990 diplomatic campaign that made overtures to many states. Highly successful, U.S. diplomacy produced a powerful coalition against Iraq, a coalition that first used economic sanctions and then military means to punish Iraq for invading Kuwait.

Two special methods of representing countries' interests have evolved above the ambassadorial level in the post–Second World War period. One of these is **summit diplomacy,** a meeting in person by heads of state to expedite agreement and avoid misunderstanding. Although examples of summit diplomacy go back to the age of absolute monarchs, summitry is usually identified with the strained, confrontational politics of the Cold War between the United States and the Soviet Union. The promise and outcome of these summit meetings often served as the barometer of the American-Soviet relationship, a relationship always overshadowed by the threat of nuclear war. The Geneva Summit of 1955, the first held after the Second World War and the first called a *summit,* raised hopes for a "thaw" in the Cold War.

Later the downing of an American spy plane over Soviet territory dispelled any chance for the 1960 summit, a never-realized meeting between President Dwight Eisenhower and General Secretary Nikita Khrushchev. During his first term (1980–1984), President Ronald Reagan failed to have a summit meeting with a Soviet leader, and this failure symbolized a

Reprinted by permission of John Trever, *Albuquerque Journal*

deterioration in the American-Soviet relationship. In President Reagan's second term (1984–1988), as relations over armaments and eastern Europe greatly improved, several meetings between Reagan and Gorbachev took place. President George Bush continued these productive meetings in his presidency until the Soviet Union dissolved as a state. President Bill Clinton has attended mostly economic summits but met with President Boris Yeltsin of Russia several times. This instance of summit diplomacy took place to bolster President Yeltsin's status in the eyes of the Russian people. President Clinton risked fastening American policy to a man who might easily fall from power, but support for President Yeltsin was the best hope of stabilizing a peaceful, democratic Russia.

The rise in importance of several countries as economic powers has moved summitry into the trade context as well as the security context. In particular, the economic interdependence of the major industrial powers of the world periodically has drawn many leaders together to attend economic summits. The representatives of top industrial countries have met for years, in variously sized groups. The Group of Ten met in the mid-1960s to consider loans to the International Monetary Fund to help that organization stabilize a currency crisis. The Group of Five met in 1985 to stabilize world currency exchanges and money supplies. The best-known example of economic summitry today is the Group of Seven, the leading industrialized democracies, which has met every year since 1975. The Group of Seven summits have largely determined the rules and norms of international trade. Agreements among the Group of Seven usually set the agenda of the General Agreement on Tariffs and Trade and, undoubtedly, now influence decisions of the new World Trade Organization. These various "groups" include the most influential economic states of the day.

The advantage of summitry, above the ambassadorial level, is that it can generate broad areas of agreement or break diplomatic deadlocks that have lingered at lower levels of diplomacy. The great danger of summitry is that it can raise high expectations for success on the part of the public and make failure more noticeable. Summit diplomacy has a better chance to succeed when lower diplomatic levels arrange an agenda for the meeting and produce some broad areas of agreement before the summit begins.

An interesting variant of summit diplomacy is *proximity discussions.* The idea is to place disputing parties near each other—for example, on separate floors of the same hotel—when they refuse to meet in person. Then a third party, a team of mediators, can easily move back and forth between the parties in dispute. Some diplomats also call this variant the "Rhodes formula," drawn from the case of Israeli and Arab negotiations on the island of Rhodes to end their first war in 1948.

Shuttle diplomacy is another means of representing a country's interests above the ambassadorial level. This form of diplomacy involves negotiation that takes place through the travels of a high-ranking official serving as a mediator between the capitols of disputing states. A well-known case of shuttle diplomacy concerns Secretary of State Henry Kissinger. In the 1970s, Secretary Kissinger traveled back and forth between Tel Aviv (Israel) and Arab capitals to try to find a basis for peace between Israel and its Arab neighbors. While a clear legacy of peace may not have resulted from Kissinger's efforts, another secretary of state tried shuttle diplomacy and definitely failed. Secretary Alexander Haig flew back and forth from Buenos Aires (Argentina) to London, an exhausting 8,000-mile, one-way trip, in a failed effort to prevent the Falkland Islands War of 1982.

Perhaps shuttle diplomacy has the advantage of using high-level officials who can lend their prestige and that of their states to the mediation effort, but there is a downside to shuttle diplomacy. A major criticism of Henry Kissinger has been that his personal style of diplomacy made foreign ministries unwilling to deal with anyone other than the secretary. Shuttle diplomacy concentrates authority near the top of government and undermines the role of ambassadors. The few well-known cases of shuttle diplomacy do not recommend this form of diplomacy. Perhaps ambassadors and their staffs, who have the time and skill to devote to a problem, should handle stubborn issues that persist for a long time.

Symbolic Representation

Normally, the exchange of ambassadors between two countries accomplishes their formal recognition of each other. Before an ambassador's appointment to a country, the approval, or **agrément,** of the future host state must occur. Upon arrival at a diplomat's new post, the ambassador presents a set of credentials to the head of state in a formal ceremony.[3]

The United States–Chinese experience in the 1970s bears out the symbolic importance derived from the presence of an accredited ambassador. President Richard Nixon began the normalization process with China in 1972 by appointing a "liaison officer" to Beijing, and the People's Republic of China reciprocated by sending a similar emissary to Washington. The 1970s offered a trial relationship that culminated in an exchange of ambassadors between the two states in 1979. Only then did the long-delayed recognition occur. The United States refused to recognize China in 1949 when a communist government came to power. The United States preferred to recognize Nationalist China (Taiwan) in the hope that the Nationalists would somehow regain control of mainland China. Finally exchanging ambassadors with Beijing meant the United States was diplomatically forsaking Nationalist China and accepting the reality of a huge mainland China awakening to its economic and military potential.

The half-measure of appointing a liaison officer appears to be a useful pattern for the United States, at least concerning communist states with long-standing hostilities toward this country. President Bill Clinton's administration opened a liaison office with Vietnam in early 1995 as a precursor to full recognition, and later that year upgraded this facility to embassy status. In early 1997, Pete Peterson, who spent over six years as a POW of the Vietnamese, took up the first U.S. ambassadorial post in Hanoi, Vietnam. Also in 1995, President Clinton sent a team to North Korea to find a site for a liaison office in Pyongyang, the North Korean capital.

The continuous presence of an ambassador is not necessary for recognition, however. Governments frequently call their ambassadors home for consultation, and the case of Mongolia shows that ambassadors can be absent from their posts most of the time. When the United States recognized Mongolia in 1987, the United States planned for its ambassador to visit Ulan Bator periodically rather than take up residence. Of 100 states that have recognized Mongolia, only 17 keep ambassadors in residence in Ulan Bator.[4] Obviously Mongolia is not a major center of international diplomacy.

Not only can the diplomat's presence be important but the diplomat's conduct also can be a significant living symbol. The ambassador becomes the personification of his or her own country. The diplomat's skill, professionalism, charm, and understanding of the host country's customs may have as much impact as the official communications the diplomat transacts. The thoughtful diplomat can promote a positive image by dutifully attending numerous state functions of the host, making many speeches to private groups, and taking part in civic activities such as charities.

A particularly interesting way in which a diplomat can be useful symbolically involves personal characteristics, although the intended effect does not always happen. In 1987, President Ronald Reagan appointed Edward Perkins, an African American and a distinguished career diplomat, as U.S. Ambassador to South Africa. South Africa was then a country well known to practice a strict form of legal racism known as *apartheid*. From a human rights point of view, President Reagan undoubtedly wanted the Afrikaner government to understand that blacks could serve competently in leadership roles. Incredibly, many South African whites regarded Perkins's appointment as a symbolic snub, and South African blacks saw the appointment as insulting tokenism. Ambassador Perkins completed his tour with distinction, however, and later became Director General of the Foreign Service and Director of Personnel for the Department of State.[5]

Moreover, the failure of two states to recognize each other through an exchange of ambassadors or a decision to sever existing diplomatic ties does not mean communications will fail to take place.[6] The United States, for example, has not had an ambassador in Havana, Cuba, since Fidel Castro took power through revolution in 1959 and later declared himself a communist. And, acting reciprocally, Cuba has not sent an ambassador to Washington. Without mutual recognition, the two countries have still needed to discuss Cuba's nationalization of American property, the U.S. naval base at Guantanamo, the return of skyjacked planes, and the mass effort by many Cubans to migrate illegally to the United

States in 1995. Facilitating such discussion, the Swiss and Czechoslovakian embassies in Havana exchanged communications for the United States and Cuba for many years.

In another case, the United States continues to communicate with Taiwan, although America ended recognition of Taiwan at China's insistence. China regards Taiwan as a Chinese province in revolt and, therefore, as unqualified for recognition as a state. The United States maintains a trade mission in Taiwan that serves as a de facto diplomatic link to the leaders of Taiwan. Although communications can take place in some manner, mutual recognition and the exchange of ambassadors certainly are preferable to nonrecognition if resolving differences is to have a maximum chance of success. Mutual recognition by two countries with a long-term hostile relationship is the clearest evidence that both want improved relations.

Obtaining Information

Every state that is wisely led pays attention to what is happening in its environment, such as the military activities of neighbors or major global economic trends that could affect its domestic economy. If a state's government is going to react intelligently to new challenges or take advantage of an opportunity, it must have information to formulate and conduct an appropriate policy. States' capabilities for obtaining information vary considerably, but they can include, as we learned in Chapter Six, satellite pictures, spies' activities, information from globally based news services, and reports from other governments. Much of the information that leaders of states trust flows back to them from around the world via the diplomatic corps of the various states.

The value of a diplomat's information lies in a carefully studied assessment of a given situation from the point of view of the diplomat's home state. The depth of study and expertise behind diplomatic reports are what makes them useful. Diplomats monitor situations on a long-term basis so they can anticipate developments and give timely warning to their countries.[7] Unfortunately, after the Iranian Revolution in 1979, President Jimmy Carter disregarded reports from American diplomats that the visit of the deposed Shah of Iran to the United States would have serious consequences. In angry retaliation for the Shah's visit, Iranians seized the American embassy in Tehran, setting off a painful hostage crisis for America that lasted 444 days.

Leaders especially want to know about potential revolutions, civil war, and *coups d'état* in other states. These special events can bring about sudden, dramatic shifts in policy. The true character and intentions of a new government on a range of issues are critical to a state considering recognition of the new government. Modern technology allows states to have on hand capability for the rapid processing and interpretation of incoming information from embassies; in fact, the United States has one of the most sophisticated communication networks available. The State Department's Communications Center is a clearinghouse for thousands of diplomatic cables that come in or go out daily to embassies. U.S. specialists encrypt or encode cables and rank them by a priority designation according to their importance. The center sends many cables on to other government agencies and to the president if they are critical. The center operates 24 hours a day, 365 days a year. Operations are increasingly sophisticated, using communication satellites and underwater fiber optic cables that can carry State Department messages around the world in an instant. Reliance on electronic distribution techniques and computer monitors is gradually replacing the need for paper copy.[8]

Most reports are periodic and routine, but they can still be useful. For instance, the United States has published its *Country Reports on Human Rights* annually for many years; these reports derive from information supplied by all U.S. embassies. These reports not only describe the human rights conditions of almost every country in the world but, according to congressional law, also provide a basis for distributing American foreign aid.

Attachés send much of the information that routinely flows back to the home state. An **attaché** works in an embassy under the control of an ambassador but represents a government department other than the foreign ministry. Military, cultural, agricultural, immigration, and tourism attachés are typical of the specialized information seekers that countries send out to their embassies. The types of attachés depend on the interests of the sending state.[9] A military attaché, for example, might make recommendations concerning weapons acquisitions for an ally. An agricultural attaché may make crop reports about the host country that will guide food aid or agricultural sales on the part of the sending country. Also, intelligence-gathering organizations, such as the U.S. Central Intelligence Agency (CIA), may place personnel in undercover roles inside embassies.

Not only do embassies obtain information for the home capitals, but information flows from the home capitals to the embassies as well. An important element of a country's diplomatic corps is the **diplomatic courier.** Couriers travel thousands of miles each year carrying sensitive documents and transporting cargo to embassies and consulates around the world, all done without fear of interference with the courier or what the courier carries.

Promoting and Protecting the Interests of Nationals

The diplomatic corps of a given state will try to serve the interests of fellow nationals in two ways: promoting the general interests of nationals abroad and protecting individual citizens while they are in other countries.[10] Diplomats are frequently busy carrying on activities such as seeking preferential tariffs, arranging flights for their countries' aircraft, and negotiating trade contracts that will benefit companies from the home states. An interesting example of this activity is the effort to promote American football in Great Britain. National Football League teams play in the "American Bowl" annually each summer at London's Wembley Stadium. The U.S. ambassador and his staff organized this event with more on their minds than the camaraderie of sports fans. This annual game has generated enough enthusiasm for American football that British football players spend over $600 million on American-made football equipment.[11]

Diplomats also aid individual nationals in foreign countries when the latter suffer harm to their persons, lives, and property and when they break the local laws. In one case known to the author, an American couple, while touring Italy, had their car broken into and lost all their property. This couple was able to return to the United States only by borrowing money and arranging temporary passports through American diplomats.

One of the sadder duties for a diplomat is to assist fellow citizens under arrest. Diplomats cannot, of course, demand the release of their nationals, for they are under the jurisdiction and control of the host government's laws. However, the diplomat can help with mail and money sent from home, arrange for a local attorney, and insist on humane treatment. Many arrests are related to illicit drug offenses. Sometimes Americans incorrectly assume drug laws in other countries are much more liberal than at home, when often they are far stricter. In some countries, trafficking in drugs can lead to a life sentence or even the death penalty.

In theory, ambassadors and their embassies are responsible for their nationals, but ambassadors usually concentrate on intergovernmental problems. In practice, a consular network is more likely to take care of the specific concerns of nationals. This network is based on consular posts or **consulates** headed by a **consul** in important cities that serve as seaports and trade and tourist centers. A sending country may have several consuls in the same country. The consular staff can exist in a separate hierarchy from the diplomatic staff, but most countries today, including the United States, combine the diplomatic and consular staffs. American foreign service officers (FSOs) can serve interchangeably in either consular or diplomatic missions.[12]

A consul's work deals mostly with trade interests, helping stranded or incarcerated nationals, and handling passports. A consul serves a national "colony" of fellow citizens as a "family lawyer." A concentration of a particular nationality in a foreign city on a long-term basis can easily keep a consul busy serving as a witness and notary, handling weddings, births, and deaths.[13] Rapid, modern travel also puts millions of foreign nationals in other countries for short-term visits. The transnational sojourns of tourists, students, athletes, journalists, and others guarantee busy lives for consuls and their staffs.

Policymaking by Diplomats

Traditionally, the diplomat is the official channel of communications between the sending and host states. At a minimum, the diplomat can pass on information and receive instructions, but the diplomat also can play a role in policymaking. In past centuries, when diplomats received a letter or two a year from their kings, they were important policymakers. In the absence of regular instructions, diplomats had to make many policy decisions alone.

Although modern communications and travel have made possible more policy directives from the home capital, diplomats on the scene are still important because of their personal impressions about leaders and policy trends in host capitals. Diplomats at least set the stage for decisions with a backlog of advice and reports.[14] The individual diplomat's experience and wisdom may lead to significant influence in the home capital in some cases. One context in which ambassadors are still policymakers is at the multilateral level. Some conferences are so irregular about their meetings and so esoteric in their subject matter that a government may have to defer to its diplomats by giving them much leeway in decision making.

Despite the fact that the United Nations is more structured than conferences, ambassadors active in policymaking roles continue to operate within this world body. For instance, American ambassadors to the United Nations sometimes have presidential cabinet rank and can bypass their Department of State overseers to visit the president directly. Some American ambassadors to the United Nations have been tough, persistent advocates of particular policies.[15] Madeline Albright, President Bill Clinton's ambassador to the United Nations, enjoyed such a reputation. In his second term, President Clinton moved Albright to the Secretary of State job, which made her perhaps the highest-ranking woman official in U.S. history.

In summary, diplomats are useful in several ways. Their presence in a host's capital signifies that the sending country legally recognizes the government of the host state, and ambassadors can present the interests and concerns of their states to their hosts. Diplomats also are able to help fellow nationals abroad who are in trouble and to obtain a great deal of information about the host states. In an age of modern communication, ambassadors are still important in the policymaking hierarchy because of impressions they derive from personal interaction with their hosts' leaders.

NEGOTIATION AND BARGAINING

Although diplomacy involves formal communications among states and concerns several functions, the most important stage of the diplomatic process is *negotiation*. This stage is a communication specifically to resolve conflict and avoid the use of force. Negotiation normally takes place in face-to-face meetings. The means of negotiations is *bargaining* based on two sides making offers and counteroffers until both sides reach agreement. Bargaining requires a give-and-take spirit of compromise, since each side is prone to push for maximum gains and to make the fewest concessions necessary.

The assumption behind bargaining is that both sides desire a negotiated end to a problem or conflict. If one side thinks it can achieve an all-out success by nondiplomatic means, a negotiated settlement is unlikely. Both sides must need a settlement they cannot achieve alone before serious negotiation can take place. In 1968 in Paris, the United States and North Vietnam began lengthy talks to end the Vietnam War as neither side could bring the war to a conclusion by force of arms.

After protracted and painful conflict, the most embattled and deadlocked opponents may decide they would rather negotiate than fight. Since 1993, Prime Minister John Major of Great Britain has communicated with Gerry Adams of the Sinn Fein, a political party stand-in for the terrorist organization known as the Irish Republican Army. Over 20 years of low-intensity warfare probably wore down both sides. Further progress faltered when Prime Minister Major insisted that the IRA disarm, which the IRA has refused to do. The victory of the Labour Party and its assumption of governmental powers in early 1997 may bring new energy to the negotiations.

Since 1993 until his death by assassination in 1995, Prime Minister Yitzhak Rabin of Israel pinned his hopes for peace on Israel's old nemesis, Yasser Arafat of the PLO, as Israel tried to trade a homeland to the Palestinians for peace. The PLO appeared to Israelis to be an attractive negotiating partner in contrast to the terrorist Hammas of the Palestinians. Radicals in Israel and among the Palestinians have done their best to derail the peace negotiation process. Moreover, the 1996 election brought the hard-line Likud Party to power in Israel, resulting in a more aggressive policy to build Israeli settlements in the West Bank. It is here where an independent Palestinian homeland is to take shape. Though hardened rivals, Prime Minister Benjamin Netanyahu and Yasser Arafat at least were able to shake hands and, at the end of 1996, worked on an agreement to turn the last West Bank city, Hebron, over to Palestinian control. Their negotiations have stalled, however, over the issue of the Israelis continuing to build Israeli settlements in the West Bank area during 1997.

The negotiating process often begins with *preliminary talks* to make sure negotiations are potentially useful, set the meeting place, decide who will attend, and agree on the level

AP Photo/Adel Hana

of negotiations. Once negotiations start, both parties frequently make a formal *opening statement* establishing their position and offering a rationale for that position. Then the two parties must somehow compromise their respective positions into a settlement. The result of a negotiation is not necessarily a "win-lose" situation hammered into place by the stronger side but may be a "win-win" outcome with both sides benefiting. Trade arrangements are frequently of the latter type, although one side may do relatively better than the other under the agreement. States only occasionally have equal bargaining strength on entering negotiations but strive to be successful anyway because it is in the mutual interest.

Yet negotiations do not always occur in good faith and may have no other purpose than to stall for time, provide an opportunity for propaganda, or gather intelligence from the other side. In his widely read book *How Nations Negotiate,* Fred Charles Iklé recommends rules for facilitating successful negotiations, beginning with both parties engaging in the negotiation process in good faith. Iklé also calls for avoiding disputes over status, following the agenda agreed on, honoring agreements, staying flexible, and reciprocating favors.[16]

Another especially useful practice is to invite *intermediaries* to assist the disputing parties to reach agreement. An impartial intermediary can serve as a conduit when disputants' communications collapse, suggest a site for face-to-face talks, offer terms potentially agreeable to both sides, and provide a face-saving means for backing away from fighting. An intermediary can be a state, such as when Algeria intervened between Iran and the United States over the 1979–1980 hostage crisis, or a nonstate actor, such as the Quakers' role in the Nigerian Civil War of 1968, or even an individual. Journalist John Scali carried messages between the Soviet Union and the United States during the Cuban missile crisis of 1962. The effect of the intermediary may not be all-determining, but the intermediary could tip the balance from a contentious to a cooperative approach.[17] Chapter Twelve on international organization identifies the formal roles the United Nations asks member-states to play as intermediaries.

Of course, no matter how much good faith diplomats display, how many rules diplomats obey, and how useful intermediaries are, insistence on terms by one side that violate the vital interests of the other side will lead to failed negotiations. The use of force is all that may shake another state loose from a position it regards as critical to its interests. However, if a state initiates force to achieve its goals, it will pay an unpredictable price in blood and treasure, as will the victim of its attack.

Finally, Linda P. Brady makes an interesting distinction between the *art* and *science* of negotiation. As art, negotiation is thought to be a fairly unique phenomenon that experienced diplomats cannot teach to beginners. Supposedly diplomats are born, not made through education. Practicing diplomats are inclined to think of negotiation as an art and are sensitive to personalities, cultural differences, and national styles that affect bargaining. In contrast, negotiation as a science recognizes a rational process of bargaining, with similarities from case to case that permit understanding in theoretical terms. Some scholars have tried to duplicate the negotiating process in laboratory simulations to conduct experiments.[18] Whether art or science, negotiation and diplomacy operate under rules that constitute a well-established area of international law.

THE LEGAL SETTING OF DIPLOMACY

Diplomatic **immunity** is a fundamental rule of international law that allows a diplomat to engage in international diplomacy without fear or interference. Governments would be reluctant to send ambassadors to other states if someone might harm them or take them hostage. Immunity is broad enough to protect the diplomat from normal law enforcement and civil suits. After centuries of customary and legal development, widely accepted diplomatic practices were set down in the *Vienna Convention on Diplomatic Relations* of 1961.[19] A diplomatic staff also enjoys the same immunity the ambassador does, and this immunity extends to the attachés and the spouses and families of the diplomats.[20] Diplomatic immunity is an early and clear example of states preferring to find ways to cooperate rather than accepting greater conflict.

If war breaks out, diplomatic immunity continues until diplomats have departed from the host country. In 1941, Japanese diplomats were in Washington, D.C., at the time of the attack on Pearl Harbor. Nevertheless, the American government allowed Japanese diplomats to pack and leave the United States in good order.[21] Immunity even extends to a deceased diplomat. In 1916, someone shot dead the first secretary of the French embassy in a London hotel. A local coroner started to hold an inquest when the French ambassador objected. The British government had to concede that even a diplomatic corpse had immunity.[22]

If the host government wants to get rid of an individual with diplomatic immunity, it must declare that person **persona non grata** and ask for his or her recall by the sending government. An unacceptable diplomat has to return to the sending state, and the host state does not have to give an explanation. The principal reasons a host state might declare a diplomat *persona non grata* are personal misconduct, espionage, and retaliation by a state that has had one of its diplomats found unacceptable.[23] In 1994, President Bill Clinton's administration expelled the senior Russian intelligence officer, Aleksander Lysenko of the Russian embassy, the first such expulsion since 1986. The Clinton administration was upset over the espionage of a CIA employee, Aldrich Ames, who continued spying for Russia after the end of the Cold War.

The forced recall of a diplomat following a charge of espionage was common during the Cold War. In many cases, the charge of espionage against diplomats was understandable because many countries placed spies among their diplomatic corps. On several occasions, the United States caught Soviet diplomats recruiting Americans for acts of espionage and asked for the recall of those diplomats. Sometimes the Soviet Union retaliated by sending American diplomats packing, some of whom were, in fact, practicing espionage. This problem has diminished somewhat with the breakup of the Soviet Union, the country with the largest number of foreign spies. In 1991, at the beginning of the post–Cold War era, the FBI reassigned 300 agents from counterintelligence duties to domestic crime on the assumption there would be fewer spies to detect and to arrest.

The image of diplomats portrayed in novels and movies suggests that diplomats casually abuse their extensive immunity and do so with impunity. In fact, most do not. Professional diplomats follow an ethical code that requires them to obey local laws.[24] Diplomats can hardly convey their governments' views to the host governments and convince the host governments to accept those views, even partially, if the diplomats become an embarrassing spectacle. As one observer has put it, "The best guarantee of the diplomat's immunity is the correctness of his own good conduct."[25] When episodes occur such as the diplomat Gueorgui Makharadge from the Republic of Georgia (formerly part of the Soviet Union), who, in January 1997, while intoxicated near "embassy row" in Washington, D.C., crashed his car and killed a teenage girl, the relationship between the two countries suffers, as does the reputation of diplomats in general. Upon a request by the U.S. government, the Republic of Georgia, after some deliberation, finally lifted the immunity of this diplomat, allowing officials in Washington to bring criminal charges.

Host governments certainly expect good conduct and are not always tolerant about speeding, traffic accidents, parking in front of fire hydrants, and other violations of law. Diplomatic immunity covers parking tickets, and some diplomats do take advantage by accumulating thousands of such tickets in a short period of time (see Table 7.1). The Soviet Union's collapse left behind a Cold War legacy of $4 million worth of unpaid tickets in Washington, D.C. These problems have continued into the post–Cold War era. Members of delegations to the United Nations received 68,637 tickets in 1994, amounting to over $3 million in unpaid fines. Moreover, some of the same diplomats take advantage of diplomatic immunity by refusing to pay their rent and ignoring payment notices.

Officials have even restrained diplomats when they have become violent, although such cases are rare. In 1935, Maryland police officers stopped the Iranian ambassador for speeding and, when he became violent, handcuffed him. Although the United States expressed regrets, the U.S. government intimated that the privilege of diplomatic immunity imposes on the diplomat the obligation to obey the laws of the host country.[26]

TABLE 7.1
The American Experience with Diplomats' Parking Tickets

Number of tickets			
New York (consulates and UN missions)		**Washington (embassies)**	
Russia	8,138	Russia	73,797
Nigeria	2,556	Nigeria	2,295
Israel	2,363	Egypt	1,465
Indonesia	1,582	South Korea	1,265
Egypt	1,421	Zimbabwe	1,223
Brazil	1,260	India	1,070
South Korea	1,239	Bulgaria	992
Ukraine	956	Oman	831
Venezuela	919	Argentina	818

Source. *Time,* November 8, 1993, p. 25. New York figures are from January to June 1993; Washington figures are from June 1990 to June 1993.

Most countries house their diplomatic missions in a building commonly called an *embassy.* The grounds around an embassy can be elaborate, containing a swimming pool, parking garage, and other structures that add up to the **premises.** Frequently embassies of many countries cluster together in the capital of the host country and often stretch along one street, referred to as "embassy row." Massachusetts Avenue in Washington, D.C. is such an embassy row.

Historically, the embassy of the sending state might have enjoyed the privilege of **extraterritoriality.** This status meant that embassy personnel could follow their own country's laws inside the embassy, though those laws might be incompatible with the laws of the host state. This historical view is not accurate today, if it ever was. An embassy is inviolable only in the sense that the diplomats and their diplomatic business are not to suffer interference and that local authorities will not enter the embassy without permission.

An activity sanctioned by the sending state in one of its embassies will not necessarily hold up as legitimate in the eyes of the host state. The *Radwan v. Radwan* case of 1972, held in a British court, serves as a good illustration. An Egyptian man divorced a British woman in an Egyptian consulate in Great Britain. The divorce was based on Egyptian and Muslim law. Following the woman's objection to the divorce, the British court ruled that an embassy (or consulate) was not the "soil" of the sending state but the host state. The British court found a Muslim divorce in an Egyptian consulate located in Britain to be invalid.[27] This British case illustrates that modern practice disavows extraterritoriality. Thus, nondiplomatic acts, civil or criminal, that occur in an embassy fall under the jurisdiction of the host state.

Host states have a legal obligation to protect embassies and consulates; however, this protection does not always hold up in practice. On rare occasion, mobs storm embassies and sometimes burn them. The Chinese "Cultural Revolution" of the late 1960s led to the ransacking of several embassies in Beijing. During 1980, a Pakistani mob burned the American embassy in Islamabad and killed a Marine guard. Perhaps the most egregious

A U.S. Marine guard holding a shotgun keeps watch over the entrance to the U.S. Embassy from behind a column shortly after an attack on the diplomatic compound in Moscow.

attack on an embassy in history is the 1979 seizure of the United States embassy in Tehran, Iran. Many months of pained waiting and negotiation followed the seizure of the embassy before the return of the embassy staff took place. Over this flagrant violation of international law, namely the Vienna Convention on Diplomatic Relations of 1961, the United States broke off diplomatic relations with Iran and has yet to restore them. In another dramatic violation, in late 1996, rebels known as the Tupac Amaru Revolutionary Movement stormed into the Japanese ambassador's residence in Peru during a party and took about 500 hostages.

Embassy security is never a certainty. In the fall of 1995, a rocket grenade was fired into the U.S. embassy located in Moscow. Fortunately, it struck an equipment room and no one was harmed. Russian police believe the attack took place to protest the NATO bombing of Serbian positions in Bosnia a short time before. The Russians are ethnic kinsmen to the Serbs and historically have taken a protective attitude toward other Slavic peoples in Europe.

The covert placement of listening devices, or "bugs," by the Soviets in what was to be the new American embassy in Moscow also was a clear violation of an embassy's immunity. Work stopped on the unfinished embassy in 1985 when the discovery of the "bug infestation" occurred. The United States would not let the Soviets move into their new embassy in Washington without first resolving this violation. In 1992, under President George Bush's direction, the solution was to build a new American embassy on a new lot at an estimated cost of $220 million. The Soviet Union agreed to pay a compensation of $45 million, and in return the Soviets could move into their new embassy in Washington, D.C.

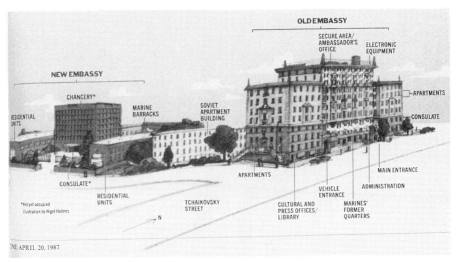

© 1987 Time, Inc. Reprinted by permission.

For a time, the U.S. embassy staff remained in the "old" embassy, and the "new" embassy remains unfinished since 1985. President Bush began a "newer" embassy in Moscow after the Cold War ended. The United States used American labor and prefab construction in the United States as much as possible to avoid having the "newer" embassy "bugged." During this dispute, the Soviet Union similarly accused the United States of "bugging" its embassy and embassy cars in Washington, D.C.

Immunity also covers the home of the ambassador. When one Lebanese partisan group burned the U.S. ambassador's home in Lebanon in 1983, American leadership decided to punish the partisans responsible by firing on them with the 16-inch guns of the battleship USS *New Jersey*.[28]

Asylum in an embassy is interesting and sometimes leads to controversial matters. **Asylum** is the protection from arrest or extradition given to a local political refugee by an embassy. The International Court of Justice has said that states generally do not recognize a right of asylum associated with embassies, but embassies can grant asylum for humanitarian reasons when a political refugee is threatened by mob violence.[29]

Although embassies would naturally prefer to avoid clashes with the host government over asylum cases, the American Foreign Service regulations allow asylum if the refugee is in mortal danger from a mob.[30] However, when the People's Republic of China suppressed the student protesters in Tiananmen Square in 1989, the top dissident and his wife fled to the United States embassy. The United States refused to put him out of the embassy, though it was the Chinese government in pursuit, not a mob. A better-known case of asylum in U.S. experience is that of Cardinal Josef Mindszenty. He fled from the Hungarian communists in 1956, after serving eight years in prison, and sought asylum in the U.S. embassy in Budapest. Cardinal Mindszenty stayed at the embassy for 15 years before the Hungarian government signed an agreement allowing him to leave the country.[31]

In a recent example of asylum seeking, Hwang Jang Yop, a top-ranking official of the North Korean government, defected to South Korea in early 1997 by fleeing to a South

Korean consulate in Beijing and then asking for asylum. The already high tensions between the two Koreas reached an even higher state for a few days, but then calmed as North Korea refocused attention on its famine conditions and the food aid South Korea is providing.

In most of the world, embassies rarely grant asylum, but Latin American states are much more receptive to the practice of asylum. Since their use of asylum is significantly different from general practice, Latin American countries are, in effect, practicing "regional" international law. The *Caracas Convention Diplomatic Asylum* of 1954 allows these states to grant asylum and determine whether an offense is criminal or political.[32] Because of this convention, asylum cases occur with some frequency in this region.

When Manuel Noriega fled to the Vatican embassy of the Roman Catholic Church following the United States' intervention in Panama in 1989, he only complied with established practice in Latin America. Yet, after a few days, he surrendered to American soldiers who had surrounded the embassy. While the matter is unclear, Vatican authorities probably decided not to grant asylum to Noriega. They may have reckoned his status was criminal and not political in nature, since he was wanted in the United States on drug-smuggling charges. We return to the subject of regional international law in Chapter Eleven.

Consuls and consulates do not have quite the same immunities and inviolability diplomats and embassies do, even though the International Law Commission of the United Nations has recommended the same protection. Instead of granting the same protection, states chose to create the *Vienna Convention on Consular Relations* of 1963 in addition to the *Vienna Convention on Diplomatic Relations* of 1961. In general, the consuls have less protection from civil and criminal prosecution than diplomats, and host authorities can enter consulates in matters of public safety such as fire. However, the protection of consulate records, the freedom of communication, and the freedom of movement for consuls is about the same as for diplomats. In recent years, the privileges and immunities for consuls and diplomats have drawn closer together through custom and bilateral treaties. Many countries, including the United States, have integrated their diplomatic and consular staffs into one.

Another special guideline for diplomatic conduct exists. **Protocol** is the proper conduct and procedures involved in diplomacy. Protocol has grown out of need and is a matter of custom more than formal international law. Over the centuries, diplomats have arranged elaborate rules of conduct to avoid problems before they occur rather than to set an impressive social style. In the seventeenth and eighteenth centuries, diplomats wasted much time and occasionally dueled over matters of prestige and status. Each diplomat wanted a seat at the head of a table, or one closest to a host, or to be put first in line in a procession. The diplomats' positions symbolically reflected their countries' power and importance.

An example will help make the need for protocol clear. In 1661, both French and Spanish delegations went to a London dock to greet the new Swedish ambassador, as was the custom then. The French contingent tried to squeeze behind the Swedish ambassador's carriage in the place of honor. The Spanish delegation, which was better prepared, brought a party of armed men who hamstrung the Frenchmen's horses and wounded their coachman. Through this mean deed, the Spanish achieved the place of honor. Matters of prestige, status, and honor remain important to states and their diplomats, but, thanks to well-established protocol, incidents of this kind are unlikely to occur today.

Much of the havoc in diplomacy ended with the Congress of Vienna of 1815 after it adopted a principle of seniority based on the dates of accreditation of the ambassadors in a given capital. From that time on, seniority would control position on formal occasions. Matters of dispute among ambassadors in the same capital fall to a "dean of the diplomatic corps" who arbitrates for the others. The dean of diplomats is the most senior of the diplomatic corps.[33]

Host governments usually appoint a chief of protocol to ensure that proper procedures, including deference to seniority, always receive respect. Shirley Temple Black, a famous child movie star of the 1930s, after serving as United States ambassador to Ghana, was appointed chief of protocol in Washington, D.C., by President Gerald Ford. Although the general public may find diplomatic protocol too ceremonial and ostentatious, proper protocol diffuses conflict over symbols so issues of substance can receive due attention.

The most important point to remember about the legal setting of diplomacy is that the rules governing diplomacy, first based on custom and then codified in law in the early 1960s, exist to protect diplomats with immunity and to facilitate their work through protocol. Because of immunity and protocol, diplomats have a better chance to represent the interests of their states and, at the same time, to preserve peace.

DIPLOMATIC STYLES

All states practice diplomacy, but in varied ways because their diplomacies reflect particular national styles. *Diplomatic style* is the characteristic way states and other actors approach and handle their foreign policies.[34] National cultures can hold different prescriptions for the behavior of people, including worldly diplomats. A "national way" of performing diplomacy is controversial, however, since some observers believe national diplomatic styles are nothing more than unreliable stereotypes. Yet Harold Nicolson, probably the best-known diplomat of the twentieth century, firmly believed that European diplomatic styles reflect national differences.[35] If national cultures affect diplomatic style, diplomats are likely to bring different sets of assumptions to the bargaining table, thus producing "cultural static" along their lines of communication.

A degree of cultural consensus in diplomacy may have existed in the era Ambassador Nicolson called "Old Diplomacy" before the First World War (1914–1918). He points out that before this war, in every European capital, a professional diplomatic service existed as an almost identical model of other capitals. These European diplomats had similar education, experience, and aims, the chief one being to keep the peace. These diplomats established a sense of identity among themselves above their respective national styles.[36] This identity could have only European roots at the time, and consensus over this identity had to decline once dozens of non-European countries joined the existing international society. Clearly, the "international diplomatic culture" is weaker today than before the First World War.[37]

In a study of many countries, Raymond Cohen, in *Negotiating Across Cultures*, concludes that cultural differences run deep and obstruct the resolution of conflicts. Significant cultural differences, he thinks, can worsen the conflict over issues and lead to failure in negotiation. Misperceptions, misunderstandings, and even offended sensitivities can flow from meetings among negotiators representing variety in cultural heritages. The cultures of the world—including, in part, Anglo-Saxon countries, Islamic countries of the Middle East, the Hindu national society of India, the ancient Buddhist-influenced countries of China and Japan, and the many Hispanic national societies of Latin America—display a remarkable variety of customs, manners, and forms of social organization developed by the human race.

Cohen sees a particularly serious problem between Westerners and non-Westerners. As an example of cultural disharmony in negotiations, he contrasts the American style of diplomacy with the non-Western style based on some mutual misperception. Non-Westerners think the American style overly emphasizes frankness, impatience, insensitivity, a resort to new initiatives, and a tendency to view issues as crises. Americans think the non-Western style focuses too much on a concern with social form, history, preference for principles over specifics, intransigence to bargaining, and a willingness to end meetings without agreement. Mutual misperception can exacerbate any problem of substance. Cohen concludes that if cross-cultural ignorance hurts negotiation, cross-cultural knowledge and appreciation should facilitate negotiation.[38]

Perhaps a better-known case of "cultural static" was the collision between Soviet and American styles of diplomacy during the Cold War. The Soviets traditionally were suspicious and accusatory in negotiation. The Soviet Union's diplomats used threats and bluffs and often demanded the whole loaf instead of compromising for half a loaf.[39] The United States style, like that of most Western countries, calls for skill in negotiation and compromise as well as major powers working cooperatively within international organizations in which multilateral diplomacy takes place.[40]

Different diplomatic styles can be a problem, but even worse is the misperception that other countries share one's own conception of the art of diplomacy. American leaders had to free themselves from the idea that Joseph Stalin (1879–1953), Soviet leader for many years, including the Second World War and postwar years, would negotiate with the same style they used.[41]

OPERATING CONDITIONS OF DIPLOMACY

The temptation may arise to think diplomats will succeed or fail according to their skills. While skills are important, several operating conditions enhance or limit the diplomatic instrument of a state.

Expense

The rapid rise in the number of states since the 1960s has required expanded diplomatic operations for many states and involves a serious financial burden for most of them. Since the demise of the Soviet Union, the United States probably has the largest diplomatic establishment in the world. The United States has over 140 embassies abroad, maintains more than 100 consulates in other countries, and hosts more than 130 embassies in Washington, D.C. In addition, the United States has about 75 diplomatic missions that regularly attend international organizations such as NATO and the United Nations. The diplomatic establishments of most states are usually much smaller. Cost-cutting pressures led the United States to close 18 consulates and two embassies in Africa in 1993 and 1994. Other installations and 2,000 staffers have felt the budget axe too. President Bill Clinton's administration is asking for a $1 billion foreign affairs budget increase in 1997, bringing the total budget to a mere $19.3 billion.

When governments fail to establish an embassy—or to close one, as Gambia did its Washington embassy in 1985—the reason is often the financial costs involved. Even the United States, as the wealthiest country in the world, does not have an embassy in every country. In 1988, when the United States decided to open a diplomatic post in Ulan Bator, the capital of landlocked Mongolia, the State Department decided to save money by posting the U.S. ambassador to Mongolia in Washington. Only a small staff of State Department employees live in a rented apartment in Ulan Bator, with the American ambassador making occasional visits.[42] States without the financial resources for a large network of diplomatic posts often compensate by communicating with other governments through their respective diplomatic missions to the United Nations in New York City or by sending the same ambassador to several states adjacent to one another.

War

When leaders suspend negotiations to make war, the role of the diplomat is severely limited. The use of military force implies that the goals of the warring states are irreconcilable. Diplomacy can be effective only when room for negotiation exists and compromise is possible. Japan decided on a surprise attack against Pearl Harbor in 1941 when that country's leaders concluded the United States would and could stop Japan's expansion in Asia and the Pacific. More recently, Argentina grew weary of protracted negotiations for the return of the Falkland Islands and seized those islands by force in 1982. In 1990, President Saddam Hussein of Iraq deserted diplomacy in a dispute over the ownership of oil wells along Iraq's border with Kuwait. He simply grabbed Kuwait for a time with the Iraqi Army.

Although the concern here is with war's interference with diplomacy, a diplomat may unwittingly contribute to war. U.S. Ambassador April Glaspie met sharp criticism for telling President Saddam Hussein that the United States did not have much to say about Arab border problems. Critics have thought this remark gave a "green light" to Saddam for his invasion of Kuwait. Ambassador Glaspie has defended her role and claimed reporters took her comments out of context. Unfairly to Ambassador Glaspie, Iraqi leaders, as Muslims, may have failed to take her as seriously as they would have a male ambassador.[43]

States, once engaged in a war, may find it very difficult to return to negotiations while the war continues. Concessions are difficult to make to an enemy, and each side hopes to score a great success on the battlefield that will improve its prospects at the bargaining table. Wars usually stop when one or both sides have taken as much punishment as they are willing to bear. After much suffering in the lengthy Vietnam War, the United States desired negotiations when the American public grew restive over casualty rates and the plight of the American POWs. Vietnam, for its part, had suffered massive American bombing strikes. Sometimes countries have only the option to surrender, as Germany and Japan did at the end of the Second World War. Their military defeat was complete, and little remained to negotiate as these two countries accepted unconditional surrenders.

Power

While diplomacy is ongoing, military strength may be useful to support diplomacy. The common view that diplomats and soldiers are in separate businesses is a mistaken one. The two professions should support the same foreign policy, and in a coordinated way.

Diplomats from weak countries may not receive attention, and military power unguided by diplomatic advice may prove to be a blind, reckless force. For example, American diplomacy needed power to back America's objection to Japan's imperialism in Manchuria in the 1930s, and the military rulers in Japan needed diplomatic advice before they began a war they could not win. Frederick the Great, King of Prussia (1740–1786), once remarked, "Diplomacy without an army is like music without instruments." From the other perspective, Karl von Clausewitz, a Prussian general and military philosopher of the early nineteenth century, has said, "War is the continuation of diplomacy by other means."[44]

Skilled diplomats, then, are more likely to achieve success if considerable military might backs their goals. A plausible interpretation of recent U.S. foreign policy is that this country, flushed with victory over Iraq in the Persian Gulf War, attempted an emboldened diplomacy confident that a combat-proven military could reinforce its objectives in any context. The use of this force, however, has proven more complicated than anticipated. President George Bush sent 25,000 U.S. troops to Somali in 1992, but in 1993, after a number of casualties, President Bill Clinton promised to withdraw American troops by March 1994, and did so. American forces, along with troops from other countries operating under the United Nations aegis, were unable to establish a lasting solution to the clan warfare in Somalia.

In the case of the Bosnian imbroglio, the United States and several European states accurately calculated that UN peacekeepers were inadequate to restore peace in Bosnia and turned to their own organization, NATO. Large units of well-trained troops with fighter planes and tanks preserved the peace brokered by the United States in 1995. In a final analysis, the wisdom and feasibility of using force to support diplomacy must, by necessity, involve decisions made on a case-by-case basis.

Alexander George has an interesting view about coordinating power and diplomacy as instruments of policy in his book *Forceful Persuasion: Coercive Diplomacy as an Alternative to War.* He defines **coercive diplomacy** as a defensive strategy that attempts to persuade an opponent to halt an aggressive action. In addition to diplomatic ploys, the threat of force, or the actual use of limited force, can serve to restore peace. The idea is to use some coercion now to avoid the use of greater force later, even though a purely diplomatic solution is preferable. The abstract theory of coercive diplomacy assumes rationality on the part of an aggressor, that is, an ability to receive relevant information and make proper judgments. Unfortunately, miscalculations about power and misperceptions of intentions can easily disrupt a strategy that otherwise would successfully confront an aggressive state.[45]

The strategy to stop Japan from further aggressions and force Japan's withdrawal from China in 1941 depended on the American threat to cut off U.S. oil shipments to Japan. Ironically, in this case, Japan's need for American oil was so great that the threat boomeranged: Japan decided to fight the Western countries holding colonies in the Pacific Ocean and win a quick victory before Japan ran out of oil. Early in the war, Japan counted on seizing the Dutch East Indies (now Indonesia), where it could secure a regular supply of oil.[46]

In contrast, the most successful case of coercive diplomacy in modern history involves the Cuban missile crisis of 1962. President John F. Kennedy, in communications to General Secretary Nikita Khrushchev, leader of the Soviet Union, properly mixed diplomatic overtures with a demonstration of force and produced a successful outcome. The "naval quarantine," or naval blockade, and the threat of an air attack against Cuba got Khrushchev's attention. Then the exchanges of letters and messages between Kennedy and Khrushchev convinced the latter of Kennedy's resolve to have the missiles out of Cuba and, at the same time, offered concessions to Khrushchev as a face-saving device. As a result, a nuclear holocaust between the Soviet Union and the United States over the crisis was averted.[47]

Coercive diplomacy has to operate in a very flexible way and takes much skill to implement. Just how much persuasion and how much coercion to use, and when or in what order, are difficult matters to ascertain. After all, coercive diplomacy is a form of crisis management with developments occurring swiftly and unexpectedly, and usually portending great danger.[48]

Finally, we should not confuse coercive diplomacy with *gunboat diplomacy*. The latter is an offensive tactic rather than a defensive gambit to head off an aggressive act. The term arose in the age of imperialism, at the turn of the last century, when a naval vessel or river gunboat was the state-of-the-art means for forcing a strong state's policy on a weak state. European states' activities in Africa and Asia and those of the United States in Latin America have produced many examples of gunboat diplomacy. This offensive tactic is not unknown in modern times. In 1995, China placed flags on unoccupied atolls in the Spratley Islands, between China and the Philippines, and enforced this territorial claim with destroyers. At stake are rich oil deposits that several Asian countries claim.

Terrorism

Terrorists have probably existed as long as governments have, but they have been especially active since the 1960s. Terrorists use violent acts to dramatize their grievances and wear down the will of governments that resist them. Terrorists have sometimes focused on diplomats because the latter's traditional, peaceful role has made them vulnerable. One terrorist group called the Grey Wolves, a group of Turkish Armenians who want autonomy from Turkey, has specialized in assassinating Turkish diplomats and their families. Bombings and other terrorist-related matters frequently disrupt embassy activities. In the summer of 1987, the French, wanting to question a terrorist suspect hiding in the Iranian embassy, surrounded the embassy with 200 police officers. In retaliation, the Iranians cordoned off the French embassy in Tehran and threatened to arrest French suspects.[49]

The reaction of many countries to terrorism is to turn their embassies into fortresses with steel doors, surveillance cameras, barbed wire, and search procedures. Secretary of State George Shultz, serving under President Reagan, asked Congress for $4.5 billion to protect American diplomats and embassies. The State Department's memorial plaque testifies to the dangers of diplomacy by listing over 160 diplomats who have lost their lives on duty.

Most early deaths of diplomats were from sickness and disease. Thomas Nast, the famous political cartoonist who gave us our modern conception of Santa Claus, died in 1902 in Guayaquil, Ecuador. He succumbed to yellow fever shortly after arriving at his station to serve as an American consul. In Bosnia in 1995, three American representatives who were involved in the effort to bring peace to Bosnia died when their armored car tumbled 400 yards off a mountain road near Sarejavo and caught fire. Since the Second World War, however, most deaths have resulted from acts of terrorists. Murder during the 1980s accounts for one-fourth of the names on the memorial plaque.

Although states have refused to admit that terrorism has reduced the diplomatic role, diplomacy is more difficult to carry out because of terrorist activities.[50] As recently as 1995, two men attacked an American diplomatic van in Karachi, Pakistan, and killed two

Chapter 7 / The Role of Diplomacy: A Traditional Tool in Changing Times   223

Photo by American Foreign Service Association

and wounded one of the occupants. Suspected in the attack are Muslim terrorists angry at America for extraditing a suspect from Pakistan, an individual who may have masterminded the bombing of the World Trade Center in New York City in 1993. To date, terrorists have seized or interfered with embassies of 40 countries, and diplomats from nearly 50 countries have been the victims of kidnappings.[51] The leftist rebels who seized the Japanese ambassador's residence in Peru in late 1996 and took hundreds hostage objected to the press calling them terrorists.

In an unfortunate development for the viability of diplomacy, some countries have used their diplomatic pouches to carry bombs and other weapons from one country to another so their agents could carry out acts of state-sponsored terrorism. This practice is clearly illegal, as is searching these pouches by host countries. In light of numerous terrorist acts, some states want to change the provision in the Vienna Convention on Diplomatic Relations dealing with diplomatic pouches. They propose that instead of having complete inviolability, a diplomatic pouch be subject to inspection by a country's customs officers. Some states already use detection equipment to screen these pouches for guns and explosives. A few years ago, groans from diplomatic bags led to the discovery of two kidnapped and drugged individuals in a Rome airport.[52]

Technology

The role of summit diplomacy and shuttle diplomacy, dependent today on the jet airplane, can downgrade the role of ambassadors, as can electronic communication. Diplomats sometimes receive the derisive description as "clerks at the end of a telephone line." The implication is that they are merely the messengers of their governments rather than important advisers and policymakers.

Hans Morgenthau has observed that diplomacy arose as an important political function due largely to a lack of speedy communication. Consequently, diplomacy would naturally decline with the onset of modern communication technologies such as the telephone, telegraph, cable, and communication satellite. Professor Morgenthau suggests that the decline of diplomacy, due to the telephone as well as the telegraph, became noticeable after the First World War.[53]

Following the Cuban missile crisis in 1962, Washington and Moscow set up a teletype system that delivered printed copy from one capital to the other almost instantaneously. Leaders' willingness to use telephones has carried communication a step further. In the Persian Gulf crisis of 1991, President George Bush and President Mikhail Gorbachev (the latter's title became "president" in 1990) conducted an unprecedented 75-minute telephone conversation, including the time needed for translation. Other telephone links between the two leaders occurred as well. President Bill Clinton also has talked to several leaders by telephone. A telephone conversation is the next best thing to a meeting in person. Unfortunately for diplomats, telephones largely bypass their roles.

Diplomats, including the top-ranked ambassador, operate within a hierarchy of authority that stretches from the embassy back to the sending country's capital. Modern communication doubtlessly tightens the authority and control over a diplomat. Nevertheless, a perceptive representative in a foreign capital can always be useful for his or her advice and information. An ambassador's understanding of another leader's intentions and another state's capabilities could prove critical. Charles W. Thayer, an experienced American diplomat, has said, "An intimate knowledge of the psychological processes of your diplomatic adversary is invaluable, especially if he is more powerful than you."[54] Person-to-person contact is highly useful to achieve such perceptions.

Extent of Agreement

If states share common interests and have few disagreements, the diplomat's task will be relatively easy. The United States and Canada have the longest demilitarized border in the world, and they resolve their minor problems in a spirit of friendship. In contrast, China and the Soviet Union (now much of China's northern border is with Russia) shared a hostile border at which each had placed about a million troops. In 1969, their border dispute led to an exchange of shots along the Usurri River. An American ambassador to Canada dealing with acid rain or a new trade treaty has a simple task in contrast to the experience of a Chinese or Soviet ambassador sent to the other's capitol in the recent past. Today China and Russia warily struggle for a better relationship. Understandably, countries send some of their most skilled ambassadors to unfriendly but powerful countries.

Secret versus Open Diplomacy

After the First World War, the change from secret to open diplomacy diminished the influence of skilled diplomats. One of the causes of the First World War may have been a series of military obligations that the participants of the war had made in secret. Once two combatants began fighting, their respective allies, responding to secret treaties, entered into a widening circle of war. President Woodrow Wilson's famous Fourteen Points aimed at structuring a better world included a recommendation that the diplomatic process, as well as the agreements of states, receive public scrutiny. The League Covenant, following President Wilson's recommendation, required that countries publish and register every treaty with the League of Nations.[55]

The problem with open diplomacy is that diplomats cannot be effective in a "fishbowl" environment. Public negotiating will lead to posturing for public effect, with diplomats either making empty gestures or taking rigid positions. The more democratic the country, the more pressure the diplomat will feel to practice open diplomacy. Diplomacy calls for concessions and compromise, and these are difficult to achieve with media and anxious publics watching. Modern diplomacy faces a serious dilemma: To be effective, diplomacy must be secretive, but to meet the requirements of democracy, it must be open. A way to "jump between the horns" of the dilemma exists, and democratic countries usually take this outlet. States can conduct negotiations secretly, or at least temporarily behind closed doors. When completed, the public can learn the terms of the agreement.

Henry Kissinger's negotiations in Paris with the North Vietnamese started as a secret process in 1968, but later the American public knew the talks were taking place. Still, the terms under discussion were kept secret. Only with the signing of the Paris Peace Accords of 1973 did the public learn the terms ending the war in Vietnam. At the first stage, diplomats maintain secrecy so a success can occur. At the second stage, publication of the agreement meets the requirements of democracy. Such an arrangement may be the surest way to deal with the conflicting needs of diplomacy and democracy.

Diplomatic Skill

Whatever the obstacles a diplomat faces, considerable skill will enhance successful diplomacy. Although the skills and high integrity of "Old Diplomacy" before the First World War may have passed into history, quality performance in diplomacy still occurs. European countries are widely thought of as maintaining the traditionally high standards of diplomacy, but in fact quality performances by individual diplomats around the world are not uncommon. However, some countries have received a variety of criticisms regarding their diplomatic corps.

Third World countries, except perhaps for the states of Latin America, have not yet had time to build strong traditions of diplomacy. While excellent individual diplomats have come from African, Asian, and Middle Eastern countries, many others are political appointees. These are the relatives of the rulers, political opponents, or troublemakers appointed as diplomats to get them out of the country. Nonprofessional diplomats often seek the pleasures of their station rather than work. A retired Foreign Service Officer (FSO) once told the author that the most dreaded duty for an American FSO was to be a host-diplomat in New York City, the headquarters of the United Nations. Foreign diplomats frequently besiege this unfortunate FSO with requests for women, liquor, and drugs. Examples of less than professional diplomacy are easy to find, especially among the missions sent to the United Nations. In 1986, Iran's ambassador to the United Nations, Said Rajaie-Khorassani, tried on a $100 raincoat in a New York department store. He ripped off the price tag and headed for the exit. When he got caught, he told the police he was merely looking for a three-way mirror to see if the coat would fit.

The United States is the subject of much criticism for its numerous political appointments to its diplomatic corps. Typically, one-third of the ambassadors of the United States receive appointments through presidential patronage. It is incredible that the world's greatest economic and military power uses so many unskilled diplomats, a situation that portends problems for international diplomacy. These appointees lack knowledge as to how embassies function, they do not know the language and culture of their host country, and they produce a low morale among FSOs because they deny these professionals a deserved ambassadorship.

President George Bush outdid other presidents in making some particularly ignominious appointments. Joy Silverman, ambassador to Barbados, held no college degree, nor did she have an impressive job record, but in 1987–1988, she donated more than $180,000 to Republican candidates. Peter Secchia, a former National Republican Party committeeman, became ambassador to Italy. Before arriving in Rome, he endeared himself to his future hosts by joking that the new Italian navy boasts glass-bottom boats so Italian sailors can see the old Italian navy. Another candidate the American Academy of Diplomacy rated unqualified was Joseph Gildenhorn, ambassador to Switzerland. He and his family donated $230,000 to Republican coffers.[56]

Soon after President Bill Clinton assumed office, a group circulated a petition in London requesting that the new president retain Raymond Seitz as the U.S. ambassador to Great Britain. Ambassador Seitz was the first professional FSO to occupy the British post, usually the preserve of political appointees. The British believed Seitz, who was informed about and sensitive to European complexities, would be capable of maintaining the special American-British relationship under a new Democratic administration. Although once promising to move beyond politics in appointing ambassadors, President Clinton appointed 40 percent of his emissaries from the ranks of financial contributors to the Democratic Party.

Not all political appointments are poor choices, however. A successful political appointee of President Bush was Shirley Temple Black, ambassador to Czechoslovakia. As noted earlier, this former child movie star already had served President Gerald Ford in two diplomatic capacities. President Bill Clinton appointed Pamela Harriman (1920–1997) the U.S. ambassador to France in 1994. She was a much-married, British-born lady who helped raise funds for the Democratic Party. Well-informed and fluent in French, Ambassador Harriman served the United States well and died while on station in her post as ambassador to France.

Most ambassadors (about two-thirds) are FSOs, well trained, and skilled, but it was only in 1924 that a professional diplomatic corps resulted from the Rogers Act.[57] In addition to studying foreign languages, the diplomatic corps go through the Foreign Service Institute staffed by a faculty drawn from the most experienced diplomats. Only after a long and distinguished career do the most successful FSOs become ambassadors.

As a related matter, we must maintain skilled diplomacy while representing the diversity of America in the diplomatic corps. In 1971, John Campbell's *Foreign Affairs Fudge Factory* observed that the State Department was a far cry from being a microcosm of the American people, especially concerning minorities and women. Minorities, Campbell surmised, saw the State Department as an "Establishment" with little relevance to their domestic concerns. Women fared better, but more often than not were shunted into consular and administrative duties instead of the more prestigious embassy duty.[58] Incidentally, President Harry Truman appointed the first woman ambassador, Helen Anderson, in 1949.

More African Americans and women have become FSOs in the last 20 years because of major efforts by the State Department to recruit people from these categories. By 1990, African Americans accounted for at least 6 percent of the FSOs, and women represented 24 percent. Unfortunately, morale among the corps of FSOs, already damaged by political appointees taking ambassadorships, may have sagged further because of affirmative action policies.[59] However, in the first year of the Clinton presidency, only 11 women, 6 African Americans, and 1 Hispanic held ambassadorships. Efforts to represent America's diversity continue.

At least, recruitment below the ambassadorial rank and other appointive posts has been generous to women. A middle-level State Department official told this author that with the trend across America of so many college graduates going into business and business graduate schools, many qualified males no longer applied to become FSOs. The solution, as he saw it, was to focus recruitment on the files of women, who continued to send in qualified applications and were easy to hire under affirmative action guidelines.

Currently, the State Department continues to make extensive efforts to recruit minorities and women. Minority numbers, however, remain low among FSOs, especially black males. The 1996 entry pay level of $30,000 to $40,000 per year for FSOs hampers recruitment efforts since corporations, able to pay three times as much, go after the same pool of qualified black males. Efforts to attract women have been far more successful, with women now accounting for over one-fourth of the FSO workforce.

NONSTATE ACTORS AND DIPLOMACY

Discussion about diplomacy traditionally has concerned the activities of states, but nonstate actors conduct diplomacy too. An interesting concept, **track-two diplomacy,** has emerged in recent years to refer to the phenomenon of unofficial, informal interaction among members of adversarial groups or citizens from different states. *Track-one diplomacy,* of course, is formal diplomacy in the hands of diplomats and their states. Unofficial, private diplomacy of the track-two kind strives to exchange information, prepare public opinion for compromise, and develop strategies for conflict resolution. Such "citizen diplomacy" takes place because other actors view governments as entangled in the issues and processes, unable to make progress, and so private actors bypass governments to allow "the people" to do the job.

This transnational phenomenon involves international nongovernment organizations (INGOs), for instance, farm organizations, churches, environmental groups, human rights advocates, and multinational corporations such as Exxon or Mitsubishi. Some of these INGOs favor workshops in which private adversarial groups can come up with solutions to conflicts that have eluded governments. Third parties usually mediate these workshops to guarantee fairness and to offer understanding for the two parties locked in conflict. Track-two diplomacy, for example, may have had some moderating effect on the conflicts between Catholics and Protestants in northern Ireland and between Israelis and Palestinians.[60]

Then there is the case of one individual performing a track-two diplomatic act. In 1977, news anchor Walter Cronkite of CBS interviewed President Sadat of Egypt and Prime

Minister Begin of Israel. He interviewed them separately by a satellite hookup and then spliced the two interviews together for broadcast. A dramatic presentation of the two adversaries expressing a desire for better relations may have facilitated their meeting in person. The mutual diplomatic recognition of their countries soon followed, with Egypt becoming the first Arab country to recognize Israel. The two leaders might have gotten together anyway, but at the time, Cronkite was a catalyst.

Sometimes, track-one and track-two diplomacies blend together, as in the example of Israel, as a state, negotiating with the PLO, an INGO, since 1993. The Israeli-Palestinian declaration of principles, agreed to in 1993, provides for a significant measure of Palestinian self-administration in the Israeli-occupied territories of the Gaza Strip and in the West Bank. Israelis hope they can trade land for peace; Palestinians hope they are moving toward self-rule and their own state after spending two generations as refugees. The two sides previously had refused to meet face to face but were able to come together after decades of exhausting, bitter conflict and violence. We should note that some actors have treated the PLO as a "state-to-be" for years; for instance, the United Nations has long given "observer status" to the PLO. As noted elsewhere, a change in Israeli leadership and violence by extremists on both sides threaten the peace process.

The case of diplomacy by the Roman Catholic Church also is an interesting one, and Chapter Three, dealing with actors, briefly describes the Church's diplomacy. At least as early as the Treaty of Tordesillas 1494 between Spain and Portugal, the pope and his emissaries have been active as diplomats and mediators. In fact, the Roman Catholic Church is one of at least two nonstate actors possessing the right of diplomatic representation normally reserved for a sovereign state. The Vatican, or papal state in Rome, exists as a minuscule spot of land but has diplomatic relations with over a hundred states. The Vatican also has recognized the PLO since 1994, though another nonstate actor. The other nonstate actor, completely without territory, is the Knights of Malta, a Rome-based organization that devotes care to the sick and wounded. The Knights have diplomatic relations with over 40 states.[61]

If a single nonstate actor stands out in the diplomatic arena, unarguably it is the multinational corporation (MNC). Once castigated by leftist thinkers as agents of exploitation, MNCs now receive appreciation by some Third World leaders as allies in economic development. MNCs can offer a country capital funds, expertise, technology, and an outlet into world markets. Rulers everywhere are under pressure to better economic conditions for their populations, and MNCs can aid governments in this priority task. This situation draws the MNC to the center of the world stage as a significant actor that can negotiate and bargain with states. Political economist Susan Strange has observed that political scientists once focused on the power differences between "strong" and "weak" states but now would do better to distinguish between the "shrewd" and the "sleepy" states as to which ones make good deals with MNCs.[62]

In some instances, "corporate diplomacy" with states receives the assistance of other INGOs acting as intermediaries. This assistance is especially important among the Pacific region countries. Intergovernmental arrangements in the Pacific region are less equipped to integrate states into tight, cooperative trade arrangements than those in Europe and North America. Filling in the void are several INGOs that bring government representatives, economic scholars, and business leaders into contact with one another. The Pacific Economic Cooperation Council, formed in 1980, is perhaps the most interesting because it is a *tripartite,* placing all three groups together on one forum. This INGO permits a risk aversion strategy in an informal environment where corporate and government leaders can consider new policy ideas, possibly spiced with the suggestions of scholars.[63]

INGOs are increasingly approaching states in diplomatic arenas of varying kinds. In a mixed-actor world, the increase in the number of private actors and their participation in international relations only broadens the base of the international society. Reaction to the rise in importance on the part of nonstate actors should stay in perspective, however. The state is still the primary actor on the world stage. Private citizens and INGOs can establish informal diplomatic communication and propose solutions, but principally it is the state that has the authority to negotiate and to make binding decisions. INGOs are probably more influential in the "low politics" areas, such as human rights and the environment than in the "high politics" areas of security, such as disarmament issues.

MULTILATERAL DIPLOMACY

Most diplomacy has been and remains bilateral, but since the nineteenth century, countries have been using conference diplomacy, or multilateral diplomacy. As indicated in the introduction to this chapter, this form of diplomacy involves a meeting of several or more states to deal with one or more shared problems. Conferences involving many countries have become common since the Second World War. An increasingly interdependent world has made countries realize that not only well-known international subjects such as disarmament, jurisdiction of the seas, trade, human rights, and the environment but also more technical, esoteric subjects such as atomic waste disposal, seabed resources, radio wavelengths, and the pollution of the oceans cannot receive proper attention by countries acting unilaterally. More than ever before, states understand that the problems they face are transnational in nature, and these problems must receive multiple-state attention and cooperation.

Multilateral diplomacy is inherent to global organizations such as the United Nations and to regional organizations such as the Arab League, the Organization of African Unity, and the Organization of American States that meet regularly in annual sessions. Multilateral diplomacy also occurs on ad hoc occasions or for conferences that take place periodically. Often INGOs attend these conferences with states. About 6,000 state representatives attended the Beijing World Conference on Women in 1995, while at the same time 24,000 women gathered at the Non-Governmental Organizations Forum. The Earth Summit of 1992 is another good example of hundreds of private organizations attending a conference, in this case to help shape environmental norms and goals proposed for agreement by states.

Sometimes these conferences lead to treaties that are available for ratification by the participating states. The Law of the Sea Conference of 1982 offered a treaty containing 320 articles covering most concerns about the seas. A total of 159 states signed the treaty in 1982, and in 1994 the required number of 60 states ratified the Law of the Sea Treaty, bringing it on line for implementation. The United States, however, had failed to sign the treaty for some time. During the presidency of Ronald Reagan in the 1980s, America remained steadfast on its capitalist principles and objected to the "seabed regime" provision in the treaty. President Bill Clinton, in his first term, did sign the Law of the Sea Treaty. The seabed regime, or organization, established in Kingston, Jamaica, was to distribute the resources of the seabed as the "common heritage" of all peoples instead of allowing the capitalist states, with superior technology, to harvest commodities such as manganese nodules for themselves.

Multilateral diplomacy, as in the case of the Conferences on the Sea, brings up the interesting question of whether or not a majority of signatory states can pull a minority of non-signatory states their way and eventually expect them to accept the rules of the treaty. Such a development becomes a *quasi*-legislative step and threatens the traditional sovereignty of states. A successful quasi-legislative step is especially impressive if it draws a reluctant major power into compliance. The United States, early on, complied with some of the articles of the treaty, such as a 12-mile territorial jurisdiction at sea that replaced the several-hundred-year old three-mile jurisdiction. One or a few countries out of sorts with rules the majority embraces may find themselves constantly involved in unwanted squabbling and conflict.

In conclusion, multilateral diplomacy allows all concerned parties to meet together, thus facilitating problem solving and agreement. As a long-term effect, sharing experiences and problems and seeking joint solutions are helping to form a sense of an international society among states and INGOs.

DIPLOMACY AND INTERNATIONAL SOCIETY

Following a discussion of multilateral diplomacy is a good place to evaluate the overall effect of diplomacy on the formation of an international society. An understanding of realists and transnationalists' views on diplomacy will help with this evaluation. How different are the views of these theorists, and has the role of diplomacy transformed sufficiently to allow us to conclude that realists and transnationalists hold two completely different views?

Scholars identify realists, led by Hans Morgenthau, with the role of power and the danger of war within an international anarchy. Yet this identification should not suggest that realists prefer these conditions or that they reject the notion that conditions can improve. Morgenthau, for instance, gives significant attention to the preservation of peace through diplomacy. While he recognizes that the interests of states can clash and that one state may receive a benefit only if another state suffers a disadvantage, Professor Morgenthau also is aware that diplomacy can serve the common interests of states.

In his *Politics Among Nations,* Morgenthau proposed that diplomacy could lend itself to the common good in areas as diverse as overpopulation, the control of nuclear weapons, and the misuse of the environment. However, Morgenthau further observed that diplomatic institutions and procedures generally fail to serve the common interest adequately.[64] For realists, diplomacy can moderate the anarchy of the world only in degree; hence, prudent states will stay well armed and rely on the skillful management of the balance of power among adversaries.

While prominent neorealist Kenneth N. Waltz's *Theory of International Politics* is mute on the subject of diplomacy, it is reasonable to conclude that the role of diplomacy is implicitly important in his thinking.[65] Waltz's emphasis on a nuclear-enforced peace between two superpowers would have to depend heavily on the useful communications of diplomacy. If two antagonists are to come to a mutual understanding, reinforced by the stabilizing effect of arms control agreements, success is unimaginable without skilled diplomacy. In fact, regular summit-level diplomacy, though often tense, allowed the two superpowers to share the same world without directly firing a shot at each other for nearly a half century. Diplomacy helped restrain the superpowers from turning the Cold War into a hot war.

As in some other areas, the writings of Hedley Bull are an important conceptual bridge between the realists and transnationalists on the subject of diplomacy. Bull thinks the quality of diplomacy declined after the First World War, but diplomacy still survived the turbulence of the twentieth century, including the Cold War. Diplomacy offered a bond for a growing number of states with diverse cultures, allowing them to find their common interests. Professor Bull writes, " . . . the diplomatic profession itself is a custodian of the idea of international society, with a stake in preserving and strengthening it."[66] While Morgenthau understood that diplomacy could help several states establish and keep the peace, Bull realized further that diplomacy could help pull together a large number of diverse states into a society.

Transnationalists acknowledge a useful role for diplomacy regarding an international society. Scholars of this approach give three aspects of diplomacy special attention. One, nonstate actors take part regularly in diplomacy. Two, multiple issues, many technical in nature, draw states together to make life easier and more convenient for all concerned. Three, states emphasize multilateral forums to forge cooperation toward common goals. In fact, Robert O. Keohane and Joseph S. Nye's *Power and Interdependence* ends with a salute to rising multilateralism because of its production of international rules and norms and of strengthened cooperation in the world.[67] Both realists and transnationalists see diplomacy as a positive instrument. For realists, however, diplomacy may or may not mitigate conflicts among states that can lead to war, while for transnationalists, diplomacy, with its three new aspects, is helping to shape a formative international society.

Diplomacy, as a traditional tool in changing times, is helping to move the world from the model of *international anarchy* to the model of *international society*. Perhaps more effectively than any other subject of this textbook, diplomacy draws together and affects all of the eight elements used to form the models instrumental to our analysis. Today's diplomacy generally supports respect for the *authority* behind international law and international organizations and is the chief instrument for providing many more rules and norms to guide conduct in international society. Nonstate *actors* now join in diplomacy, often facilitating cooperation among the more primary state actors.

The *orientation* of diplomacy is clearly toward cooperation and the avoidance of conflict, especially the use of *force*. The *interaction* of the world is now one of interdependence created through the sharing of multiple *issues* that requires regularly engaging the *problem-solving level* of multilateralism. Multilateralism is simply diplomacy in which many actors meet in the same place, either in ad hoc conferences or in the more structured international organizations. Today there is a *consensus* on the diplomatic process and, to a lesser degree, on issues for which diplomacy is appropriate. Most actors today much prefer diplomacy over force, though they still have meaningful differences over issues.

Conditions supporting the international anarchy model of the realists definitely have faded; yet overstressing the positive effects of the diplomatic process can lead to exaggeration. Diplomacy is currently shaping an international society, but has not completed this task. In addition, the shared world culture, essential for an *international community*, is nowhere in sight. Differences in national cultures, national interests, and diplomatic styles can still occur and create turbulence in diplomatic relations.

If an international community were in place, the role of diplomacy probably would decline. The basic purpose of diplomacy is to open lines of communication among disparate societies that are within physical range of one another and face potential conflict. A true community reflects integration through shared values and interests, as well as a common sense of identity, and has a web of regularly used internal lines of communication.

CHAPTER SUMMARY

In this chapter, we learned that the ancient practice of diplomacy developed through custom as the history of the state system evolved; more recently, in the early 1960s, the diplomatic process came under treaty law. Diplomacy provides communication among international actors and offers opportunities to negotiate differences arising from clashes in interests. Diplomats usually prefer peace and wish to avoid the use of force. In spite of important cooperative patterns, however, force remains an option today in the minds of a few leaders. Diplomacy is not so effective that it can entirely abrogate anarchy and stop all warfare.

As diplomats strive for national goals, including peace, many conditions affect their prospects for success. These conditions range from the specific acts of terrorists to the amount of power backing the diplomats' efforts. Although telecommunications and the jet plane have reduced the operational independence of the ambassador, no technology can replace an ambassador's perceptive assessment of foreign leaders' characters and intentions.

A growing reliance on multilateral diplomacy characterizes modern diplomacy. Multilateral diplomacy has helped to mix the elements of a formative international society: a large array of transnational issues in an interdependent world, a growing number of states and important nonstate actors, and a greater reliance on rules and norms to guide conduct. The regular use of multilateral diplomacy indicates that the singular pursuit of national interests in a state-centric anarchy is no longer affordable for the world.

Sharing policy choices by multiple actors is clearly becoming a pattern and is basic to the incipient international society. Undoubtedly, diplomacy has drawn many states and nonstate actors together to pursue the same goals—for instance, the improvement of human rights and protection of the world's environment—and has helped spread respect for international law around the world. A true test for diplomacy is the subject of the next chapter: competition and conflict over structuring the world's trade and sharing the world's wealth.

POINTS OF VIEW

When a diplomat says yes he means perhaps; when he says perhaps he means no; when he says no he is no diplomat.

—ANONYMOUS

These then are the qualities of my ideal diplomatist. Truth, accuracy, calm, patience, good temper, modesty and loyalty. They are also the qualities of an ideal diplomacy. "But," the reader may object, "you have forgotten intelligence, knowledge, discernment, prudence, hospitality, charm, industry, courage and even tact." I have not forgotten them. I have taken them for granted.

—HAROLD NICOLSON
DIPLOMACY

The views of foreign governments are no longer fashioned by the advice of their ambassadors. They are formed by what the politicians themselves see on CNN.

—ADRIAN HAMILTON
OBSERVER, LONDON

It is difficult to sit by and watch Bosnia die. And all reasonable diplomatic means should be used to get the combatants to stop; at some point, they may exhaust themselves sufficiently to make a negotiated solution possible.

—Joe Klein
Essayist in *Newsweek*, 1993

I see no diminution in the need for a really good diplomatic apparatus. But our whole diplomatic apparatus is vastly overbureaucratized today. Diplomacy is basically the responsibility of the president and the secretary of state, and they've allowed far too much of it to slip into other semi-independent hands. Washington needs a housecleaning.

—George Kennan
92-year-old dean of diplomats
March 1996

REVIEW QUESTIONS

1. What is the basic role of diplomacy in interstate relations, and what is a good test for successful diplomacy?
2. Name and describe the specific functions that diplomats carry out for the sending state.
3. How broad is the coverage of immunity for diplomats, and why do they enjoy this privilege under international law?
4. How reliable is a given country's reputation for a certain diplomatic style?
5. Does a diplomatic subculture exist to an appreciable degree, or are national cultures still a problem for diplomacy?
6. What are some of the operating conditions that can determine diplomatic success or failure?
7. How should power and diplomacy work together in coercive diplomacy?
8. How does track-two diplomacy bring nonstate actors into international relations?
9. Why are political appointees to ambassadorships harmful to U.S. diplomacy?
10. Why can we say that multilateral diplomacy contributes to the development of an international society?

GLOSSARY

agrément The formal acceptance of a diplomat by the future host state before the nomination of the diplomat is made public.

ambassador The highest rank for an accredited agent of a state who represents the state in international relations.

asylum The protection from arrest or extradition given to a local political refugee by an embassy (though not a general practice).

attaché A specialized agent attached to an embassy whose job is to report to and represent the home state in a particular area of policy.

coercive diplomacy A defensive strategy designed to retard aggression with a combination of diplomacy and force.

consul An agent of a state, usually without the complete immunity of a diplomat, who represents commercial interests and protects fellow nationals in the major cities of other states.

consulate The offices of the consul, which enjoy limited immunity concerning communications and records.

diplomacy The process of conducting communications among states through official representatives to represent state interest and minimize conflict.

diplomatic courier A special messenger with immunity who carries information or cargo from the home state to the state's embassies or from embassy to embassy.

embassy The location of a diplomatic mission in a host country; enjoys substantial immunity for diplomatic purposes.

extraterritoriality The exercise of one state's sovereign authority outside its boundaries (but today it is an anachronism regarding the operation of embassies).

immunity Protection of a diplomat from civil and criminal charges and from detention or personal harm.

persona non grata The principle that a person can be found unacceptable by a host government and can be expelled.

premises The grounds and buildings associated with an embassy, which are inviolable.

protocol The formal rules and courtesies of procedure that diplomats enjoy so that problems of prestige and status will be less likely to interfere with substantive issues.

shuttle diplomacy An effort at mediation that requires travel back and forth between the capitols of the disputing parties.

summit diplomacy Negotiations conducted personally by heads of state.

track-two diplomacy Unofficial, informal interaction among members of adversarial groups that is outside of government channels and is designed to find solutions to conflict.

RECOMMENDED READINGS

Linda P. Brady. *The Politics of Negotiation: America's Dealings with Allies, Adversaries, and Friends.* Chapel Hill, NC: University of North Carolina Press, 1991.

Raymond Cohen. *Negotiating Across Cultures: Communication Obstacles in International Diplomacy.* Washington, D.C.: United States Institute of Peace, 1991.

David Cortwright. *Peace Works: The Citizen's Role in Ending the Cold War.* Boulder, CO: Westview Press, 1993.

Gordon A. Craig and Alexander L. George. *Force and Statecraft: Diplomatic Problems of our Times.* New York: Oxford University Press, 1983.

R. G. Feltham. *Diplomatic Handbook.* 3rd ed. New York: Longman, 1980.

Roger Fisher, Andrea Kupfer Schneider, Elizabeth Borgwardt, and Brian Ganson. *Coping with International Conflict: A Systematic Approach to Influence in International Negotiation.* Upper Saddle River, NJ: Prentice Hall, 1997.

Chas. W. Freeman, Jr. *Arts of Power: Statecraft and Diplomacy.* Herndon, VA: USIP Press, 1997.

Alexander L. George. *Forceful Persuasion: Coercive Diplomacy as an Alternative to War.* Washington, D.C.: United States Institute of Peace Press, 1991.

Martin F. Herz, ed. *The Modern Ambassador: The Challenge and the Search.* Washington, D.C.: Georgetown University Press, 1983.

Fred Charles Iklé. *How Nations Negotiate.* New York: Harper & Row, 1964.

Victor A. Kremenyuk, ed. *International Negotiation: Analysis, Approaches, Issues.* San Francisco: Jossey-Bass, 1991.

Robert Hopkins Miller. *Inside an Embassy: The Political Role of Diplomats Abroad.* Washington, D.C.: Congressional Quarterly, 1992.

Harold Nicolson. *Diplomacy.* New York: Oxford University Press, 1964.

Elmer Plischke, ed. *Modern Diplomacy: The Art and the Artisans.* Washington, D.C.: American Enterprise Institute for Public Policy Research, 1979.

B. Sen. *A Diplomat's Handbook of International Law and Practice.* 3rd ed. Boston: Martinus Nijhoff, 1988.

Andrew L. Steigman. *The Foreign Service of the United States: First Line of Defense.* Boulder, CO: Westview Press, 1985.

Charles W. Thayer. *Diplomat.* New York: Harper & Brothers, 1959.

ENDNOTES

1. Adam Watson, "Diplomacy," in *Dilemmas of World Politics: International Issues in a Changing World*, ed. John Baylis and N. J. Rengger (Oxford: Clarendon Press, 1992), p. 160.
2. This historical coverage of diplomacy is largely dependent on Harold Nicolson, *Diplomacy*, 3rd ed. (New York: Oxford University Press, 1964), pp. 1–14; B. Sen, *A Diplomat's Handbook of International Law and Practice*, 3rd ed. (Boston: Martinus Nijhoff, 1988), pp. 3–7.
3. R. G. Feltham, *Diplomatic Handbook*, 3rd ed. (New York: Longman, 1980), pp. 1–7.
4. *Update,* September–October 1988, p. 1 (a bimonthly publication of the U.S. Department of State).
5. *Update,* January–February 1990, p. 2.
6. William R. Slomanson, *Fundamental Perspectives on International Law* (St. Paul, MN: West Publishing Co. 1990), p. 197.
7. Sen, *Diplomat's Handbook,* p. 66.
8. *Update,* May–June 1990, p. 4.
9. Feltham, *Diplomatic Handbook,* pp. 18–19.
10. These two methods of serving nationals are identified in Sen, *Diplomat's Handbook,* p. 73.

11. *Update,* March–April 1989, p. 2.
12. Charles W. Thayer, *Diplomat* (New York: Harper & Brothers, 1959), p. 130.
13. Ibid., pp. 130–38.
14. Sen, *Diplomat's Handbook,* pp. 57–58.
15. Seymour Maxwell Finger, *American Ambassadors at the UN* (New York: United Nations Institute for Training and Research, 1990).
16. Fred Charles Iklé, *How Nations Negotiate* (New York: Oxford University Press, 1964).
17. Thomas Princen, *Intermediaries in International Conflict* (Princeton, NJ: Princeton University Press, 1992).
18. Linda P. Brady, *The Politics of Negotiation: America's Dealings with Allies, Adversaries, and Friends* (Chapel Hill, NC: University of North Carolina Press, 1991), pp. 12–19.
19. Slomanson, *Fundamental Perspectives,* pp. 204–5.
20. Sen, *Diplomat's Handbook,* pp. 185–87.
21. Ibid., p. 107.
22. Thayer, *Diplomat,* p. 202.
23. Feltham, *Diplomatic Handbook,* pp. 1–7; Thayer, *Diplomat,* pp. 215, 218.
24. Thayer, *Diplomat,* p. 214.
25. Sen, *Diplomat's Handbook,* p. 109.
26. Michael H. Cordozo, "Diplomatic Immunities, Protocol, and the Public," in *World Politics,* 2nd ed., ed. Arend Lijphart (Boston: Allyn & Bacon, 1971), p. 151; Thayer, *Diplomat,* p. 216; Sen, *Diplomat's Handbook,* p. 109.
27. Slomanson, *Fundamental Perspectives,* pp. 212–14.
28. Sen, *Diplomat's Handbook,* p. 111.
29. Slomanson, *Fundamental Perspectives,* pp. 215–17.
30. Thayer, *Diplomat,* p. 207.
31. Suzanne Riveles, "Diplomatic Asylum as a Human Right: The Case of the Durban Six," *Human Rights Quarterly,* February 1989, p. 157.
32. Slomanson, *Fundamental Perspectives,* pp. 216–19.
33. Thayer, *Diplomat,* pp. 225–27.
34. R. P. Barston, *Modern Diplomacy* (New York: Longman, 1988).
35. Harold Nicolson, *Diplomacy* (New York: Oxford University Press, 1964), Chapter 6.
36. Harold Nicolson, "The Old Diplomacy," in *Crisis and Continuity in World Politics,* ed. George A. Lanyi and Wilson C. McWilliams (New York: Random House, 1966), pp. 413–16. See also Nicolson, *Diplomacy,* Chapter 3.
37. Paul R. Kimmel, "Cultural Perspectives on International Negotiations," *Journal of Social Issues* 50 (1994), pp. 179–96.
38. Raymond Cohen, *Negotiating Across Cultures: Communication Obstacles in International Diplomacy* (Washington, D.C.: United States Institute of Peace, 1991).
39. Iklé, *How Nations Negotiate,* pp. 234–35.
40. Ibid., pp. 238–53.
41. Thayer, *Diplomat,* p. 84.
42. *Update,* September–October 1988.
43. Kimmel, "Cultural Perspectives on International Relations," p. 191.
44. The point about a joint military-diplomatic policy and these two quotes appear in Michael Roskin and Nicholas Berry, *IR: An Introduction to International Relations,* 2nd ed. (Englewood Cliffs, NJ: Prentice Hall, 1990), pp. 324–27.
45. Alexander L. George, *Forceful Persuasion: Coercive Diplomacy as an Alternative to War* (Washington, D.C.: United States Institute of Peace Press, 1991), pp. ix–xii, 4–5.
46. Ibid., pp. 19–23.
47. Ibid., pp. 31–37.
48. Ibid., pp. 73, 82.
49. *Time,* July 27, 1987, p. 46.
50. *Update* (September–October 1989), p. 3; *Parade Magazine,* March 30, 1986, p. 16.
51. Andrew L. Steigman, *The Foreign Service of the United States: First Line of Defense* (Boulder, CO: Westview Press, 1985), p. 220.
52. Harris O. Schoenberg, "When Terrorism Travels by Diplomatic Pouch," *Christian Science Monitor,* December 4, 1986, p. 29.
53. Hans J. Morgenthau, *Politics Among Nations,* 6th ed. (rev. by Kenneth W. Thompson) (New York: Alfred A. Knopf, 1985), pp. 569–70.
54. Thayer, *Diplomat,* p. 88.
55. Frederick H. Hartmann, *The Relations of Nations,* 6th ed. (New York: Macmillan, 1983), p. 104.
56. *Time,* July 31, 1989, p. 17.
57. Thayer, *Diplomat,* p. 265.
58. John Franklin Campbell, *The Foreign Affairs Fudge Factory* (New York: Basic Books, 1971), pp. 246–48.
59. John Owens, "The U.S. Foreign Services: An Institution in Crisis," *Mediterranean Quarterly,* Summer 1991, pp. 27–50.

60. Joseph V. Montville, "Transnationalism and the Role of Track-two Diplomacy," in *Approaches to Peace: An Intellectual Map,* ed. W. Scott Thompson and Kenneth M. Jensen (Washington, D.C.: United States Institute of Peace, 1988), pp. 255–69.
61. Sen, *Diplomat's Handbook,* pp. 20–21. See also H. J. A. Sire, *The Knights of Malta* (New Haven, CT: Yale University Press, 1994).
62. Susan Strange, "States, Firms and Diplomacy," *International Affairs,* January 1992, pp. 1–15.
63. Lawrence T. Woods, *Asia-Pacific Diplomacy: Non-Governmental Organizations and International Relations* (Vancouver: UBC Press, 1993).
64. Hans J. Morgenthau, *Politics Among Nations,* 5th ed. (New York: Alfred A. Knopf, 1978), pp. 529–30, 541.
65. Kenneth N. Waltz, *Theory of International Politics* (Reading, MA: Addison-Wesley, 1979).
66. Hedley Bull, *The Anarchical Society: A Study of Order in World Politics* (New York: Columbia University Press, 1977), pp. 177–78, 183.
67. Robert O. Keohane and Joseph S. Nye, *Power and Interdependence,* 2nd ed. (Glenview, IL: Scott, Foresman, 1989), pp. 268–82.

CHAPTER 8

THE INTERNATIONAL POLITICAL ECONOMY: INSTRUMENTS OF COMPETITION AND CONFLICT

Since the 1970s, the **international political economy (IPE)** has been a growing specialty within the field of international relations. Traditionally, economics and political science are separate departments in universities, but in the real world, scholars find it difficult to disentangle economic and political variables since they overlap and intermix in complex ways.[1] The *economy* is the system of producing, distributing, and using wealth, while *politics* involves the set of institutions and rules that govern social and economic interactions. Each molds the other.[2] For instance, trade competition drew the United States to recognize Vietnam in 1994 before Japan gobbled up all the prize markets in that country. And with better relations, the United States can use Vietnam, an ancient enemy of China, as a hedge against the expansion of Chinese military power and economic influence in Southeast Asia. Consequently, we define IPE as the study of economic and political interactions in the world arena, with causal relations recurring between the two phenomena.[3]

The end of the bipolar nuclear stand-off of the Cold War has brought greater attention to economic questions. With the decline of the United States as **economic hegemon** and the concurrent rise of rival trade states, will antagonisms over the basic rules of competition lead to a trade war among Western states?[4] Or will these states bargain successfully over the rules and norms that govern trade to preserve global and regional prosperity? How disruptive will the entrance of the ex-communist states of Europe into the global free trade economy be as they focus their needs and hopes on the prosperous West with beggar-thy-neighbor growth strategies? Can the Third World find a way to close the huge economic gap between countries and the prosperous, industrialized West? Trade competition among Western states, drastic adjustment to capitalism and democracy within the now fragmented Soviet empire, and the underdevelopment of the Third World are unsettling tensions in today's world.

This textbook has two chapters on the IPE. In this chapter, we emphasize the competitive and conflictual side of the IPE. In Chapter Nine, we focus on the institutions and efforts within the IPE context that are bringing economic cooperation and mutual benefit to the global and regional levels. Recognizing that both conflictual and cooperative economic tendencies are present in the world, enough evidence may be available to allow us to speculate about which tendency will prevail as we enter the 21st century.

We begin this chapter with a discussion of three contending perspectives on the rules and norms governing the international economy. Next, we assess whether trade competition will induce the major trade states into a trade war. Then we inquire about the prospects of the ex-communist states of Europe to successfully convert to free market economies and democracy. We then examine whether the developed states and Third World states will find a way to bridge the huge divide between them. Next, we explore the range of economic instruments that actors find useful for accomplishing political goals. Finally, we look at the obstruction that economic competition and conflict can bring to the formative international society.

CONTENDING PERSPECTIVES ON THE INTERNATIONAL ECONOMY

Over time, several perspectives have developed on the political-economic arrangement of world order. We will see that the liberal, or free trade, perspective has taken primacy over mercantilism and Marxism, though elements of all three are visible somewhere in the global economy. History first favored **mercantilism** (also known as *economic nationalism*) as it evolved along with the state system starting in the seventeenth century. **Liberalism** advanced an intellectual challenge to mercantilism in the latter part of the eighteenth century and began to win the upper hand as a free market system of rules and norms during the late nineteenth century. Well after the setback to free trade brought about by the Great Depression in the 1930s, liberalism appeared triumphant when the ex-communist states of Europe chose market economies and democracy in the early 1990s. Liberalism, in turn, faced challenges by the mid-nineteenth century when socialists, especially Karl Marx (1818–1883), impugned the morality of liberalism. Practical challenges to a free market economy occurred when Russia in 1917 and other states after the Second World War followed schemes of **Marxism** known as communism.

Mercantilism

As we learned in Chapter Two, mercantilism, in its classic form, called for the state to build up its economy to pay for military power and enhance state security. Mercantilists desire to advance their own states' industries and avoid economic dependence on others as much as possible. Dependence can lead to vulnerability, creating an opportunity for one state to dominate another. For mercantilists, economic relations are conflictual as states seek relative gains at the expense of other states rather than mutual gains based on cooperation with them.

Mercantilism's influence continues today and will persist as long as the state remains the primary actor and is willing to subordinate economic activities to its interests. For example, critics from among its trade rivals accuse Japan of practicing *neomercantilism*. While classic mercantilism sought military power and security, today's neomercantilism seeks a prosperous national economy for its own sake. In this new form of mercantilism, Japan creates a trade surplus by deliberately exporting more than it imports and has little concern about leaving trade partners with a trade deficit. Through *managed trade,* the Japanese government produces a trade surplus by setting export goals and limiting imports. Limiting imports is basic to **protectionism,** an economic policy designed to reserve home markets for a state's own producers and sellers. Protectionism clearly conflicts with liberal free trade among countries; yet some protectionism still lingers even after negotiations finalized the Uruguay Round of the General Agreement on Tariffs and Trade (GATT) in 1994.

Liberalism

Scottish economist Adam Smith (1723–1790) argued for the benefits of a free market economy that depended on capitalism and recommended practicing free trade at the domestic and international levels. **Capitalism** is the private ownership of the means of production, distribution, and exchange of wealth. Liberals, if purists, want free trade completely unfettered by governments. Smith believed an economy should receive only the guidance of the "unseen hand," the market forces of supply and demand. In his classic *Wealth of Nations,* published in 1776, he observed that mercantilism may serve the state, but it is economically inefficient. Smith envisioned national and international economies that would be spontaneous. Humankind naturally trades what it produces for something useful it does not have. According to Smith, goods should move both internally and across borders based on supply and demand, not the dictates of states. Cheaper, better goods would be available through the competition of the marketplace, allowing a rising prosperity for all people.

Encouraging international prosperity, as Adam Smith conceived it, would be a *division of labor* that occurs when countries make different products and exchange them for mutual benefit. Later, English economist David Ricardo (1772–1823), in his *Principles of Political Economy and Taxation* of 1817, refined Smith's thinking by contributing the idea of *comparative advantage,* meaning a relative advantage. Ricardo assumed each country could make one thing better and cheaper than any other country. Ricardo recognized that several countries could make the same product competently, but for international trade, each state should specialize in its best product. If Portugal could produce both wine and wool but produce wine with less cost, Portugal should concentrate on wine and leave wool production to another country. All states would then enjoy a savings with the resulting efficiency. Finally, liberals emphasize that expanding webs of trade interdependence sustain peace since states do not want the prosperity from trade interrupted by war.

Enthused with capitalism's efficiency and productivity, liberals have been less prone to deal with the maldistribution of wealth within national societies and among states that has accompanied all economic systems to date. The glaring economic inequities of the world are behind much of the economic conflict in both domestic and international relations. For instance, because of sharp class differences, some governments have interfered in their national economies to arrange more egalitarian societies. Further, when poorer states demand from richer states a redistribution of the world's wealth, they are seeking a more egalitarian international society.

Echoing the title of Adam Smith's classic *Wealth of Nations,* Douglas Dowd's modern *Waste of Nations* blames capitalism for inequities because, as he sees it, capitalism is exploitative and wasteful of labor, investment monies, and natural resources. However, recognizing the productive power of capitalism, Dowd wants not to jettison this economic system but reform it to serve humanity.[5] James Q. Wilson would agree about the productive power of capitalism but would disagree with Dowd and others who deal with capitalism as if it were bereft of morality. He finds that all economic systems have reflected greed and maldistribution, but at least capitalism helps democracy to flourish and encourages a more peaceful, cosmopolitan world. Moreover, when harnessed with democracy, the inequities and environmental damage from capitalism are reformable.[6]

Many leaders of states, though sometimes holding reservations similar to Dowd's, are increasingly choosing the prescription of liberalism for their domestic economies over the other two options. For these leaders, capitalism offers the best chance to raise their countries' level of wealth. Today liberalism guides not only the policies of many national decision makers but the policies of international trade regimes. In practice, national economies, as well as the global economy, are variants of liberal ideas that have not achieved the full-blown model of completely free economies based entirely on market forces.

Marxism

Karl Marx, as a nineteenth-century socialist, focused on the class conflict within the national economies of industrial Europe, where he expected the downtrodden working classes to revolt and overturn a capitalist system controlled by the factory owners and their government protectors. To explain why the Marxist revolutions never happened, Vladimir Lenin (1870–1924), a disciple of Marx, changed emphasis from the national to the international level. In his theory, published as *Imperialism* in 1918, Lenin argued capitalist states avoided a showdown with their working classes by shifting exploitation away from their workers to colonies in Africa and Asia. Unfortunately for the capitalist states, according to Lenin, additional economic expansion was impossible because of limited natural resources and markets. Consequently, fierce competition within a constricted world economy drove the capitalist states toward the First World War. For Lenin, a world dominated by capitalist states is a war system, an international structure prone to war. To the disappointment of Marxists, class revolutions and the demise of the capitalist states never occurred, and modern communist theorists have struggled to explain why ever since.[7]

A modern extension of Marxism is the **dependency theory,** usually attributed to Argentine economist Raul Prebisch. Widely accepted in the 1970s as an explanation for the enormous wealth gap between the "North," the rich, industrial states generally above the equator, and the "South," the poor Third World states in Africa, Asia, and Latin America mostly below the equator. According to this theory, the industrial states are the "core" of the world economy, while the poor states exist in the "periphery," the outer region of decision making and profit sharing. In a pernicious division of labor, the core draws on cheap raw materials and labor in the periphery and sells expensive finished products back to the periphery. The dependency theorists accused the North of practicing *neocolonialism,* the economic exploitation of ex-colonies through the co-option of the South's leaders and by unfair trade. The South's situation is hopeless if the division of labor between North and South operates unchanged, because without major reforms, the South can never hope to catch up in economic development.[8]

Modern socialist scholar Immanuel Wallerstein believes hardship for the South worsens whenever capitalist economies of the North are in the downturn of a recession. Wallerstein surmises that the world capitalist economy expands and contracts in Kondratieff cycles spanning 40 to 60 years.[9] N. D. Kondratieff, a Russian economist, offered his empirical observations about the capitalist economy in the 1920s, but could not offer a theoretical explanation of the expansion-contraction cycle before the Soviet government sent him to

TABLE 8.1
A Comparison of the Economies of the Two Koreas, 1993

	North Korea	South Korea
Per capita GDP	$904	$7,466
Economic growth rate	–4.3%	5.6%
Debt as a percentage of GDP	50.3%	13.4%
Military spending as a percentage of GDP	27.4%	3.6%
Textile production	1.9 million tons	60.4 million tons

GDP = gross domestic product.
Source: Data are from the research of Pat Carr using information from Runzheimer International; data reported in press October 21, 1994.

Siberia.[10] Wallerstein concluded that the present Kondratieff cycle began in the 1960s, and so it will be about the year 2000 before an upturn in economic growth can begin and bring some relief to economic hardship. For Professor Wallerstein, lasting relief requires transition from a capitalist to an international socialist system, a process that will take 100 to 150 years.[11]

Dependency theory lost some credibility in the 1980s when several states of the South became *newly industrialized countries (NICs)*. For instance, the "Asian Tigers" of Hong Kong, Taiwan, Singapore, South Korea, and now China experienced impressive double-digit economic growth rates with capitalist methods, thus overcoming the alleged dependency relationship. To the delight of capitalists, countries divided by the Cold War—Germany, Korea, and Vietnam—had struggling communist halves and prosperous capitalist halves. The contrast in the standard of living between the communist and capitalist halves was sharp, and widespread knowledge of this contrast helped bring down communist governments in Europe after 1989. The indicators in Table 8.1 for the economic standing of the two Koreas in 1993 illustrate the benefits of a capitalist development strategy.

Liberalism has triumphed over mercantilism and survived the challenge of Marxism. It has been the provider of rules and norms for the world's economic order since the Second World War. Today, however, the liberal trade order experiences three significant stresses. First, the major trade states—members of the European Union (EU), Japan, and the United States—have at times veered toward adversarial competition. Second, eastern and western Europe exist at two distinct economic levels. Third, a seemingly ineradicable economic gulf separates the North and the South. We turn now to the efforts of the major trade states to preserve the liberal trade order.

MAJOR TRADE STATES: LIBERAL ORDER OR ADVERSARIAL COMPETITION?

Before the Second World War ended, the United States leadership pushed hard to set up a liberal trade order. In 1944, the United States led in the creation of a World Bank to make loans and the International Monetary Fund (IMF) to regulate the value of national currencies. A short time later, the United States was the primary force behind the General Agreement on Tariff and Trade (GATT) that, through a series of summits, would grind down **tariffs** (a fee charged on imports), **quotas** (a numerical limit on imports), and **nontariff barriers (NTBs)** (an indirect means of restricting imports). The outcome of this liberal order would be a trade system that Adam Smith would approve; that is, rising levels of free trade that would contribute to the prosperity of all countries participating. We will elaborate on the institutions behind the liberal order in Chapter Nine.

The United States, with its large industrial system emerging unscathed by the war and its strong dollar serving as the standard for currency exchange in world trade, quickly moved out front as an economic hegemon, a hegemony that lasted until the 1970s. As a dominant and self-confident economic power, the United States did everything possible, through generous trade terms and by providing military security, to bolster the western European and Japanese economies in the epic struggle against world communism. The U.S. economic hegemony was not to last, however. Its decline was due to a combination of reasons that included chiefly a weakened U.S. dollar, a growing dependence on foreign oil, a swelling consumer appetite for foreign goods, and poor saving habits by Americans that denied capital for investment and expansion.

At the same time, the European and Japanese economies rebounded from the war's damage, and these countries became significant competitors to the United States in world markets by the 1970s. A constricted world economy in the 1980s, as a result of recessionary tendencies, intensified this situation. With the end of the Cold War and a reduced need for American protection, these allies boldly asserted themselves as trade competitors in search of a bigger share of tightening global trade. As competition for markets grew more adversarial, including the threat of a trade war involving such mutually destructive techniques as high tariffs and low quotas, how could a liberal trade order survive without a hegemon to insist on appropriate trade rules?[12] Robert Keohane's *After Hegemony* challenges the neorealist claim that a hegemon is a necessity and argues that a cooperative trade regime can manage trade effectively if the major trade states stay focused on their economic interdependence and mutual interests.[13]

Indeed, it appears that a long-term, nonhegemonic era is unfolding, but will the major trade states continue to converge around a free trade order at the turn of the 21st century, or will they back into a trade war? Cooperation among the states of the EU, Japan, and the United States is critical because together they account for more than half of global trade and their MNCs handle 80 percent of the world's **foreign direct investment,** the movement of capital across borders to develop a profit-making enterprise.[14]

On a broad scale, it is defensible to regard the major trade states as approximate coequals, a point the data in Table 8.2 support. At least these countries are unable to push one another around over trade terms. Each major trade actor has its strengths and weaknesses. For example, the EU integrates 15 national economies into one bargaining force that has ably represented Europe in a series of GATT rounds that has negotiated the terms of world trade over the years. For several years, however, the EU has experienced slower growth rates and higher unemployment rates than either Japan or the United States.

Japan emerged from the ruins of the Second World War to become a world-class economic dynamo. Operating from an island country of limited resources, Japan has built an economy almost two-thirds the size of that of the United States. Although Japan does not have a safe nest within a regional organization such as the EU or the North American Free Trade Agreement (NAFTA), it has established strong trade ties with many Asian states, mainly through bilateral relations with states that are experiencing some of the fastest economic growth in the world.[15] Unfortunately for Japan, its "economic bubble" partially deflated due to an overheated banking and real estate market in the late 1980s and early

TABLE 8.2
Comparative Data on the Economic Power of Major Trade Actors

	Hourly labor costs	% of World GNP	% Unemployment	Unrestricted consumers (millions)
United States	$17.10	26%	6.7% (NAFTA)	380
Japan	$21.42	15%	2.5%	127
EU	$19.47	32%	10.9%	370

	Exports as % of imports	GNP PC	PPP$	% GDP on education	Growth rate of GNP	GNP (trillions)
United States	76%	$23,830	$23,760	3.7%	3.1%	6,081
Japan	147%	$28,690	$20,520	5.5%	4.3%	3,565
EU	97%	$20,043	$17,792	4.8%	2.0%	7,379

Sources: Hourly labor costs are from U.S. Bureau of Labor Statistics, reported by Pat Carr in press September 1995. Percentage of world GNP calculated by the author. Percentage of unemployment is for 1993. Unrestricted consumers calculated by the author, exports as a percentage of imports, GNP per capita, and purchasing power parity are for 1992. Percentage of gross domestic product spent on education, growth rate of annual gross national product, and gross national product are taken from *Human Development Report 1995* (New York: Oxford University Press, 1995).

1990s, marked by business bankruptcy and unemployment rates unusual for Japan. Only in the mid-1990s did Japan's economy regain its footing based on stable growth. Finally, Japan receives 90 percent of its energy from abroad, mostly oil from the volatile Persian Gulf.

The United States, though now roughly on the same plane with other major trade states, is the *primus inter pares,* or first among equals. The United States retains the largest national economy, with over 260 million free-spending consumers, a market every country wants to enter. Its currency is still a *safe-haven* currency, meaning governments and financiers are glad to hold American dollars, and its cutting-edge technology is the envy of most of the world. The United States also can claim the largest export-import trade in the world. Moreover, after painful downsizing and reorganization, American MNCs have become more flexible and effective by using information-oriented technologies and benefiting from the deregulation occurring since the Ronald Reagan presidency. Presently, the U.S. enjoys a steady economic growth rate, low inflation, and a record low in unemployment.

Largely because of American corporate strength, the United States now ranks as the number one most competitive national economy, defined as a capacity to generate wealth for a country. Japan fell from third place to fourth place in 1995 after having headed the rankings from 1986 to 1993. States of the EU and the Group of Seven, or G-7 (the top industrialized democracies), also frequent the top rankings as Table 8.3 shows.

The downside to American success is that many white-collar workers have received pink slips and the pay of American blue-collar workers is less than that of workers in some of the other major trade states. More important, the United States suffers a huge national debt of about $5 trillion; a yearly unbalanced government debt of billions that feeds the national debt; a trade deficit that amounted to $160 billion by the mid-1990s; and a consumer debt, based mostly on credit cards, of several hundred billion dollars. These matters are the economic clay feet of the country that is number one in competition.

TABLE 8.3
A Ranking of the Most Competitive States

*1.	United States	11.	Taiwan
2.	Singapore	*12.	Canada
3.	Hong Kong	†13.	Austria
*4.	Japan	14.	Australia
5.	Switzerland	†15.	Sweden
*†6.	Germany	†16.	Finland
†7.	Netherlands	*†17.	France
8.	New Zealand	*†18.	Great Britain
†9.	Denmark	†19.	Belgium
10.	Norway	†	Luxembourg
		20.	Chile

* G-7 membership.
† EU membership.
Source: Data are derived from a 1995 report of the World Economic Forum as reported in *U.S. News & World Report,* September 18, 1995, p. 24. The author added the G-7 and EU membership designations.

Clearly, diffusion of authority for managing international trade is the order of the day, since one major trade actor cannot dominate the others. Without a hegemon available to set the rules and without the unifying common cause of the Soviet threat, along with the recessionary trends begun in the 1980s, fractious trade relations among the major trade states intensified as each sought to carve the largest slice possible from the limited international trade available. The economic growth rate of the world dropped from about 5 percent in the late 1980s to 1 or 2 percent in the early 1990s.

Instead of completing the Uruguay Round of GATT in the 1990s and raising free trade to a new level, major trade states might have given free rein to economic nationalism, or neomercantilism. This kind of trade would likely have two dimensions: stealthlike protectionism in the form of NTBs to block imports and aggressive, export-led growth strategies. Sometimes a major trade state even tries to capture a market by **dumping** goods into a foreign market at a sale price below production costs as a way to drive away competitors.

Instead of giving neomercantilism its head, however, states actually expanded world trade through **reciprocity** that called for them to reduce trade barriers on a mutual basis under fair trade rules. Reciprocity is essential to the liberal model of the IPE. If, however, states cheat by restricting their markets to trade partners in devious ways or insist on expanding their own national economic growth by exporting much more than they buy, rancor in trade relationships is likely to occur. Threats of punitive retaliation have risen among the leaders of the major trade states with some regularity in the 1990s. If an escalating spiral of trade punishments did develop, a full-blown trade war might erupt, possibly taking the world into a depression.[16]

The adversarial nature of relations is easy to illustrate. When export-led strategies by all major trade states operated amid the slow-growth world economy of the 1980s and early 1990s, trade negotiations turned antagonistic. The EU became more restrictive toward foreign MNCs and outside trade at the same time it liberalized trade among its

© 1992 *The Florida Times-Union*

membership. The Manstricht Treaty of 1992, in particular, forced American and Japanese MNCs to quickly locate behind EU borders before a deadline fell. Although the EU's traditional hostility to Japanese trade and MNC investment is more pronounced than toward American economic flows, President George Bush, in 1992, threatened trade retaliation through tariffs on some French products if the French did not buy more agricultural products from the United States, the perennial issue in the American-EU relationship.

The antagonism between Japan and the United States has been especially intense because Japan has an export dependence on the United States and the latter has a debt dependence on Japan. Many Americans believe the billions of dollars of annual surplus favoring Japan (once $60 billion and down to under $48 billion in 1996) occur only because the Japanese keep out American goods in illicit ways. Japanese leaders and public, for their part, think the surplus is a proper reward for producing high-quality, competitively priced products that Americans choose to buy.[17] Japanese trade surpluses may remain irksome for some time. The Japanese trade surplus with all partners for 1996 dropped to $83 billion but threatens in 1997 to rise as high as an estimated $120 billion because Japanese leaders continue to solve economic difficulties at home through export trade. Occasionally, the trade debate has taken a vitriolic turn in tone. American businesspeople have resorted to "Japan bashing," comparing Japan's trade aggression to Japanese military aggression during the Second World War. Some Japanese leaders have responded by referring to America as a country of lazy, mixed-race people.

On a more serious level, respected parliamentarian and writer Shintaro Ishihara, in a book titled *The Japan That Can Say No,* urged Japan's obsequious leaders to stop trying to please American leaders who are responsible for their own trading inadequacies.[18] In a later book, *The Voice of Asia,* written with Prime Minister Mahathir Mohamad of Malaysia, Ishihara claims Asia will replace the West as the center of the world economy.[19]

Fortunately, patient and intense negotiations on both sides have prevailed and held the Japanese–United States relationship together. Convinced that Japan has practiced *corporatist* policy, meaning Japanese government and industrial leaders have worked closely together to ensure a favorable trade above and beyond normal market forces, American negotiators have insisted that Japan buy American finished products such as aircraft and cars as well as raw materials that include wood products and some foodstuffs. To back up its negotiators, the U.S. Congress passed the "super 301" provision of the Omnibus and Competitiveness Act of 1988 allowing the executive branch to fight unfair trade with retaliatory punishments.[20]

Carla Hill, trade representative for President George Bush, called "super 301" her "crowbar" to open the markets of Japan.[21] Selling cars to Japan has been a special goal and a sensitive issue, since the Japanese have always claimed their cars are better, perhaps a legitimate claim considering that Americans buy them by the thousands. In fact, American cars have risen sharply in quality because of the competition from Japanese imports. Improvements in American cars helped Mickey Cantor, trade representative for President Bill Clinton, finally hammer out an agreement permitting American automobile corporations to operate their own dealerships in Japan. In addition, in 1997, several American car companies shipped right-hand-drive cars to Japan, removing another legitimate complaint against American cars.

With calm heads on all sides prevailing, an adversarial relationship is giving way to renewed trade vigor as we move into the 21st century. The leaders of the major trade states know the Great Depression of the 1930s worsened when trade partners intensified protectionism to save their respective home markets for themselves. Any form and degree of trade war would only hurt all states today as in the Great Depression. For instance, as mentioned earlier, Japan cannot do without our consumer market, and the United States must borrow back our spent consumer dollars from Japan to operate our government in the face of a chronic annual deficit. No finer example of intense economic interdependence is available.[22]

In addition to states renewing relations bilaterally, revived global trade patterns are receiving a boost from the completion of the GATT Uruguay Round in 1994 that reduced trade restrictions to historical lows and provided the World Trade Organization (WTO) with a process for trade dispute settlement. In fact, the recent global slump may be over. Easing trade relations today is a world GNP growth rate that rose from 1 percent in 1991 to 4 percent in 1997, a rate of growth that may continue into the early 21st century. Further, inflation rates and unemployment rates are improving for most leading industrialized states.[23] World trade exploded from $7 trillion in 1990 to nearly $11 trillion by 1996.

Undoubtedly, Paul Krugman is correct to warn against an obsession with competition that treats an entire country as a single corporation doing battle with other states, as depicted in Lester Thurow's 1992 book *Head to Head: The Coming Economic Battle Among Japan, Europe, and America.*[24] Krugman correctly points out that international trade is not a zero-sum game of winners and losers; rather, when countries prosper, they prosper together by providing one another with markets.²⁵ The metaphor about a rising tide floating all boats is an apt one here.

ECONOMIC HEALING IN THE POST–COLD WAR ERA

Until recently, a major source of tension in the world was the nuclear stand-off between the United States–led western European countries and the Soviet Union–led eastern European countries. Behind this stand-off were their vast ideological differences, which included opposing perspectives about the organization of the IPE. The West embraced the liberal perspective of free trade, and the communists implemented a form of centralized control and government ownership. The communist states, under the leadership of the Soviet Union's Joseph Stalin (1879–1953), intended their economy to operate independently from the Western free trade system. Stalin even rejected about $7 billion slotted from the U.S. Marshall Plan of 1947 to help eastern Europe recover from the destruction of the Second World War.

The communist states also turned their backs on the IMF, World Bank, and GATT for years. To maintain communist **autarky,** or independence, from the world economy, with its "evil, exploitative capitalist ways," Joseph Stalin forged together an economic bloc of the Soviet Union and eastern European states. Known as the Council for Mutual Economic Assistance (CMEA, but sometimes called COMECON), this bloc had the goal of rivaling and even surpassing capitalist economies in the West. Working through the centralized planning of a **command economy,** the expected economic growth failed to materialize. CMEA implemented a set of complex five-year plans that actually stifled initiative and production throughout the region. Goods often moved only by bartering among the communist countries, and benefits, as Western critics gleefully pointed out, favored the Soviet Union, as it seemed to enjoy neocolonial advantages over eastern Europe.

So disappointed were the peoples of eastern Europe with the economic results that revolts occurred in Hungary and Poland in 1956, and economic motives partly caused the revolt in Czechoslovakia in 1968. Communist leaders' frustration with their system's poor economic performance led to a loss of willpower, the first inkling of which appeared during the second Polish revolt of 1981–1982. The Polish Solidarity movement experienced some repression but not the onslaught of the Soviet Army, as had previous eastern European revolts.

To the chagrin of the Soviet Union, eastern European countries responded favorably to the overtures of trade and loans from the West, beginning with *Ostpolitik,* or "eastern policy," of West Germany in the latter 1960s. Willy Brandt, as foreign minister and then chancellor of West Germany, offered trade and loans against the wishes of the United States. Then, in the 1970s, Secretary of State Henry Kissinger tried to link trade to Soviet good behavior regarding its military and political policies. By the 1980s, the drift toward westward economic involvement by more Soviet bloc countries proved unstoppable as their governments sought loans and membership in the World Bank, IMF, and GATT to boost their hard-pressed economies. Between 1989 and 1991, the economic failure of communist governments and loss of self-confidence by their leaders led the European communists to surrender power. Only in Romania did a popular revolt have to topple the communist government by force.

When Boris Yeltsin ascended to power in Russia in 1991, he chose a fast-track strategy to transform Russia into a democratic and capitalist state. To receive Western loans and foreign aid, President Yeltsin tried to play by Western rules, including privatizing state-owned enterprises and converting military industries to civilian industries. To encourage Yeltsin's reforms, Western leaders wisely offered an aid package of $24 billion to Russia in 1992, mostly in loans reluctantly approved by the IMF. At a G-7 meeting in 1993, Western leaders announced a $44 billion package for Russia from the IMF, World Bank, and other sources. The IMF and World Bank accepted Russia as a member in 1992, and Russia also received observer status in GATT, now the World Trade Organization. In subsequent G-7 summits, President Boris Yeltsin of Russia attended as a special guest and continues to lobby for Western economic support. This summit is critical to Russia because the G-7 states have much to say about not only their direct loans but what the IMF and World Bank decide to do.

Already, Russia's inability to collect taxes and pay miners, soldiers, and pensioners and to control rising gangsterism almost cost this country a $336 million installment of a $10 billion loan by the IMF in late 1996. Out of a concern that the Russian government had not done enough to prevent the crash of its finance institutions, in early 1997, the World Bank refused to loan $1 billion to Russia to revamp its banking system.[26] Yet, in the summer of 1997, the World Bank announced that it would loan $10 to $12 billion more to Russia for a broad range of projects, provided the Russian government stayed on the road of capitalist reform.

Additional help to Russia and eastern Europe from the United States and western Europe has come through offering the ex-communist states most favored nation status, the best terms available for a trade partner. These same states also created the European Bank for Reconstruction and Development aimed at helping eastern Europe.[27] Moreover, these Western countries have freed up badly needed technology for Russia and eastern Europe during the improved security atmosphere of the post-Cold War period.

The rapid changes involved in the capitalist changeover have proved painful for the ex-communist states, especially the Russian people. High inflation and unemployment rates, vicious organized crime rings, declining production, ethnic disturbances, and threatened tax revolts by republics within Russia have been the price that country has paid for attempting to follow the Western model.[28]

During this painful transformation, a popular joke made the rounds in Russia: "What has one year of capitalism achieved that 75 years of communism could not?" The answer: "To make communism look good."[29] The once authoritarian states of Russia and eastern Europe, which only recently had stable central planning, may now be too weak to produce a reliable market system any time soon.[30]

Because of hardscrabble economic lives in Russia and eastern Europe, leaders are having difficulty building and sustaining democratic institutions. If economic failure pushes the governments of these countries in a radical direction, military insecurity for Western countries will recur as well. Western countries can ill afford a slack effort at promoting the economies of the old Soviet bloc. These ex-communist states may need economic help for a generation or more before capitalist and democratic societies can take hold.

Despite all the West is doing, however, its response to this region may be lukewarm given the region's importance. The EU states in particular, after years of bemoaning the artificial presence of the Iron Curtain dividing Europe, have not readily welcomed eastern

© Tribune Media Services, Inc. All rights reserved. Reprinted with permission.

Europe into the EU. Certainly, the ex-communist states want nothing more than to merge with the fast traffic of the EU economy. So far, the EU has agreed only to a vague European Confederation and extended EU associate membership in 1991 to the Czech Republic, Hungary, and Poland.[31] The large economic disparity between the two halves of Europe would make any form of economic integration difficult and expensive for the western half. For the foreseeable future, the two halves, economically speaking, will constitute a two-speed Europe. The economic healing of a whole Europe has only begun.

THE NORTH-SOUTH RELATION: A DIMINISHING CONFLICT?

East-West tensions have greatly eased with the passing of European communist governments and their alliance for fighting war, the Warsaw Pact. Although the eastern European countries and Russia are undergoing turbulence while transforming to democracy and capitalism, their industrial bases and skilled populations offer them a good chance to acquire a higher level of prosperity. In contrast, the conflict between the industrialized North above the equator and the underdeveloped South below the equator portends a disturbing permanence.

The intensity of the conflict may have slackened somewhat, however. The North has lost much interest in the conflict because the Cold War competition that brought aid to the states of the South is over, and the North's desire to remedy the South's underdevelopment has flagged through "compassion fatigue." The North has grown weary of helping for decades without much improvement in the South. The South, for its part, contains great

© Tribune Services, Inc. All rights reserved. Reprinted with permission.

diversity, involving over 100 African, Asian, and Latin American countries. Some states, such as Haiti, are miserably poor and aid dependent, while others, such as South Korea, are experiencing rapid economic growth in industry, improving their standard of living, and even moving into democratic practices. The common front the South could once present to the North, beleaguering them to redistribute the earth's wealth, has broken apart. More and more states of the South are deserting socialist experiments of various hues to join the global trend of practicing capitalism and free trade.

If the North and South now experience less conflict, the economic gap between them, paradoxically, has probably widened. The old adage that "the rich get richer and the poor become poorer" seems to apply. Can a global economic house, so divided, stand? Since the world has moved past the tensions of the Cold War, the biggest problem for an international society may be the North-South economic disparity. A review of, first, the conditions of the South and then the economic flows that link the North and South will help to elaborate this disparity.

We can describe several typical conditions of the South, although they vary in degree. These conditions involve inequality, class systems, low level of industrialization, infrastructure weakness, overpopulation, the traditional role of women, and a history of turmoil.

Inequality

The South's overall inequality with the North is striking when we compare incomes of the G-7 in Table 8.4 with incomes of selected countries from the South. The G-7 are among the "high-income" countries, with the states of the South showing varied but much lower income levels. However, some states of the South have a chance to move upward in

TABLE 8.4
Inequality among and within Selected Countries

	GNP (U.S. $ billions)	GNP per capita (U.S. $ thousands)	(PPP $)	Percentage of national income held by top 20%	PQLI
High income					
United States	6,081 (trillion)	23,830	23,760	41.9	98
Japan	3,565	28,690	20,520	37.5	101
Germany	1,877	23,360	21,120	40.3	98
Great Britain	1,046	18,110	17,160	44.3	98
France	1,296	22,630	19,510	41.9	99
Italy	1,187	18,090	18,090	41.0	98
Canada	600	21,070	20,520	40.2	99
Upper middle income					
Brazil	432.2	2,810	5,240	67.5	79
Venezuela	59.7	2,920	8,520	49.5	87
Middle income					
Philippines	50.1	790	2,850	47.8	83
Columbia	45.1	1,350	5,480	55.8	86
Peru	30.3	1,350	3,300	51.4	78
Ivory Coast	8.7	680	1,710	44.1	56
Jamaica	3.3	1,390	3,200	48.4	96
Low income					
India	274.2	310	1,230	41.3	60
Indonesia	128.3	680	2,950	42.3	74
Pakistan	54.3	420	2,890	39.7	54
Bangladesh	24.8	220	1,230	38.6	47
Sri Lanka	9.9	560	2,850	39.3	90
Ghana	7.3	460	2,110	44.1	61

Sources: GNP, GNP per capita, and PPP are from *Human Development Report 1995* (New York: Oxford University Press, 1995). Income categories and percentage of wealth held by the upper 20 percent of the population are from *World Development Report 1995* (New York: Oxford University Press, 1995).

income. The NICs of Brazil, India, and Mexico, as well as the "Asian Tigers" (so-called because of their robust economic growth rate) of Singapore, South Korea, and Taiwan, are such states. Although China has 1.2 billion people, its annual economic growth rates in recent years have been high enough to raise the annual per capita income of its masses from an estimated $300 to $600 per year. A few states have pitifully low incomes, and their prospects for improvement are not good. Some scholars call these impoverished countries "basket cases"—for instance, Chad and Niger located on the southern belt of the Sahara Desert—that may be aid dependent indefinitely.

While scholars commonly work with income data, such as GNP per capita, such data are not always a reliable indicator of exactly how well off or poor a country may actually be. Even when we anchor comparisons in the same currency, such as U.S. dollars, purchasing power can vary from country to country, as the *purchasing power parity* data in Table 8.4 show. A Big Mac may cost $1.25 in a poor Asian country and $6.00 in a European country. Then, too, GNP per capita is a mathematical average based on the money that, theoretically, is available for each citizen. A GNP per capita of $20,000 does not mean that each citizen of that country has $20,000 to spend. The actual distribution of wealth among a country's population can take many variations.

Inequality *within* states parallels the inequality *among* states. Although all countries have uneven distributions of wealth, the states of the North usually have large middle classes and a fairer distribution of wealth than states of the South. From Table 8.4, we can see that among the "high-income" countries of the North, the upper 20 percent of the population controls about 40 percent of the national income, while the same upper quintile in the South usually owns 40 to over 60 percent of the national wealth. This maldistribution of income has led some scholars to call states of the South "pyramid states," with a class of elites at the apex enjoying great wealth and the masses huddling at the base in poverty. As such, middle classes are much smaller in the South.

Because not all scholars trust the reliability of income data, whether comparing countries or investigating the general welfare of the people within a country, many scholars have turned to the *physical quality of life index* (PQLI). The PQLI, as given in Table 8.4, is a composite measure of literacy, life span, and infant mortality rates.[32] The higher the PQLI, the higher the standard of living in a country, meaning the wealth of the country is reaching the people and benefiting their lives. When a country does especially poorly or particularly well for its income level, we call that country an "outlier" case. The Ivory Coast, as a "middle income" country, has a PQLI score of 56, well below the other countries in its income group. Sri Lanka has a PQLI score of 90, which is high for a "low income" country. Leaders and scholars who are interested in developmental strategies will want to know what the Ivory Coast is doing wrong and what Sri Lanka is doing right. Finally, Japan has done so well in its PQLI indicators that its score is slightly above the expected range, which tops at 100. Not surprisingly, Japan leads the world in centenarians, with 7,000 people at age 100 years or more, 80 percent of whom are women.

Class Systems

Closely associated with the distribution of wealth in societies are class systems that all countries have in some form. The class systems of the South tend to be more rigid because of the maldistribution of wealth between the "apex" and the "base" of society. Often class lines overlap with ethnic and racial differences, creating *ethnoclasses.* Unfortunately, elites may feel little obligation to improve the lives of people outside their class or ethnic group and may even look on the mass population with disdain. Some of these leaders are *predatory elites,* meaning they exploit their societies for their families and supporters without regard for the common good of the general population. Offering some promise, the worldwide trend toward democracy is removing some of these unresponsive, authoritarian leaders. It will be interesting to see if the removal of the military elites from Haiti and the restoration to power of democratically-elected president Jean-Bertrand Aristide, followed by an elected successor, can somehow improve the lot of desperately impoverished Haiti.

Reprinted with permission of John Trever, *Albuquerque Journal*

Industrialization

The NICs of the South have found ways to industrialize at least some sectors of their economies, although their industrial base may rest on older first-generation technology. Industry, nevertheless, means a chance to move toward export-led economic growth with the ability to sell finished products at higher prices than raw materials bring. Countries in the South also wish to diversify their economies through industrialization and to avoid dependence on a *primary product*. Producing a single commodity as the main export can hold a country's economy hostage to the vagaries of the global marketplace. If the price of that commodity suddenly drops, the price loss will ripple across the national economy with harsh effects. Zambian copper, for instance, accounted for over 90 percent of Zambian exports in the 1970s. When copper prices fell suddenly in 1974, the impact was hard felt through all sectors of the Zambian economy.[33] The reason many states of the South now compete for MNCs rather than turn them away is to draw on the technology and capital of the MNCs to boost the industrialization process of an underdeveloped country.

Infrastructure

Most countries below the equator have a weak infrastructure of transportation and communication. Roads can be impassable in bad weather, dock equipment inadequate or nonexistent, and airport runways too short and without proper safety equipment. Executives of foreign MNCs feel frustration when they cannot fax, telephone, and telegraph messages from any point in the world to any other point. A country without modern telecommunication outlets, including satellite links, is behind the speed of the international business game. A MNC investigating a new site for locating a subsidiary will give careful attention to a country's infrastructure capabilities.

Overpopulation

More than 4.5 billion people live in the South, while 1.5 billion live in the North with most of the wealth. The population growth in the world, 100 million new people a year, occurs mainly in the South. Increasing numbers of people need housing, jobs, schools, and hospitals, needs that absorb any extra capital. Consequently, population pressures hold back the development of national economies in the South. When a population grows faster than the economy, a serious shortfall develops between people's needs and wants and what is available. Unable to keep up, governments in the South and the United Nations become frustrated over insufficient progress.

In spite of rising world population numbers, living conditions in Asia and Latin America have improved a little, but they are in decline in Africa, where population growth rates are the highest in the world. If resources in the world are finite and a limits-to-growth situation exists, as many scholars believe, the population explosion of up to 12 billion people by the middle of the 21st century will doom millions more people to harsh lives. An even wider pattern of malnutrition and starvation will occur than presently exists.

Traditional Role of Women

Closely related to overpopulation is the traditional role of women as mothers to large families and as farm laborers. Women who receive a good education and can enter all sectors of the economy have fewer children, and they contribute more to the growth of the economy. In contrast, a woman in Kenya who picks coffee beans with several small children straggling behind, another on her back, and yet another in her womb, would benefit the Kenyan economy more had she married later, received a good education, and taught agricultural science in high school or college. Her own life might be more gratifying as well.

The Report of the South Commission, *The Challenge of the South,* has stressed the point that a gender-sensitive approach to development is a basic condition for sustained economic and social progress.[34] The International Population Conference in 1994, the International Women's Conference in 1995, and various development forums of the United Nations have echoed this message time and again. As Catherine Scott points out in *Gender and Development,* women have all too often received attention only within the context of "household economics," the business of raising children and tending garden plots.[35] Today women are increasingly at the center of grass-roots efforts to develop economies and to improve lives.[36]

History of Turmoil

The national societies of the South are often the victims of internal wars. Most wars in the last half of the twentieth century have been civil wars or revolutions in the countries of the South. The eastern horn of Africa has suffered warfare perhaps more than any other region, with wars continuing for years concurrently in Ethiopia, Somalia, and the Sudan.

Kal/*The Economist*/London

Warfare disrupts food supplies, destroys homes and hospitals, and causes human misery through disease and death. Turmoil does occur outside the South, to which the Bosnian crisis bears grim testimony, but the North usually escapes violent interruptions of its national economies.

This list of conditions in the South is not all-inclusive, as other conditions that harm development no doubt exist, but it at least suggests the long odds faced if three-fourths of the human population living in the South are to live as well as the one-fourth in the North.

We now turn to the economic flows serving as linkages between the North and the South to better understand the conflict between these two hemispheres. These linkages are trade, foreign aid, loans, and investment.

Trade

Most of the South's income through foreign exchange depends on trade rather than foreign aid, loans, or even investment. The North, applying the liberal model of trade, expects reciprocity arrangements under GATT rules. The South, in turn, wants to derogate from the norm of reciprocity by charging more tariffs to protect its new industries and paying fewer tariffs to enter the markets of the North. The South hopes the flow of money from such an unbalanced arrangement would gradually increase its wealth. The *UN Conference on Trade and Development (UNCTAD),* once called the "poor man's lobby," managed to persuade some countries of the North in the 1970s and 1980s to accept such an arrangement, called the *Generalized System of Preferences.* Usually, however, the reciprocity norm stands.[37]

A standard complaint of the North against the South, especially against the fast-growing NICs, concerns *intellectual property rights (IPRs),* which deal with patents, copyrights, trademarks, and trade secrets. The North may lose as much as $60 billion a year in IPR thefts. Countries with the most attractive investment opportunities are frequently the violators of IPRs. Some of the better-known offenders are Brazil, Mexico, Singapore, South Korea, Taiwan, and Thailand. The fast-growth countries naturally attract investments, but they are often the ones that take the shortcut of stealing intellectual rights from others to help propel this growth. Pharmaceuticals have been an especially hot issue in the IPR area. Some NICs, such as Brazil, risk trade retaliation from the United States when they duplicate patented medicine. Brazilian officials reason that for cheap, effective medicine for their people, the trade retaliation they suffer is worth it.

For the United States, China is probably the worst offender, pirating CDs, computer software, designer jeans, and much else. In 1996, under U.S. pressure, Chinese officials destroyed 48,000 tapes that were copies of U.S.-owned property. The United States also has filed complaints with the WTO because of IPR violations by India, Pakistan, Portugal, and Turkey, and keeps other possible violators on a "priority watch list."

Efforts to protect IPRs go back to the *Paris Convention* of 1883 and reach forward to the recently completed Uruguay Round of GATT ending in 1994. This last round of GATT, as well as the World Intellectual Property Organization (WIPO), a specialized agency of the United Nations, encourages states to pass legislation to protect IPRs, a step compatible with the norms of the North.[38]

Foreign Aid

Gifts of money to the South have never accounted for much of Southern income, and future aid will probably decline. Because of the end of Cold War competition between the superpowers, global recession, the South's reputation for corruption, and a growing awareness that aid has not brought fundamental improvement in the South's conditions, "donor fatigue" has become apparent. For instance, the United States has cut some of its development aid monies by as much as half and, among the top industrialized states, gives the smallest percentage of its GNP as foreign aid.

Bilateral aid, government-to-government aid, is often on a short-term basis that hampers long-term planning and frequently has political strings attached. U.S. foreign aid recently dropped from $16 billion a year to $13 billion, and for 1996, foreign aid may have been as little as $11 billion. Japan now exceeds the United States as the world's largest aid donor. Japan promised $8 billion at the Earth Summit in 1992 just for environmental projects.

Multilateral aid has been available from the United Nations, the World Bank system, the Asian Development Bank, and other international government organizations (IGOs). Since the 1960s, the United Nations has treated each decade as the "Decade of Development," focusing up to 90 percent of its budget and personnel on developmental projects for the South. Over the years, the United Nations has asked member-states to contribute 0.7 percent of their GNPs for aid projects, but only a few Scandinavian countries have exceeded 0.5 percent of their GNPs. By 1993, the average aid level of member-states had fallen to 0.29 percent of GNP.[39] The needs of eastern Europe and Russia are further siphoning off already limited aid money, a matter of consequence to the South.

Not only does much aid become "spillage," lost to corruption, but large portions of aid go to "white elephant" projects favored by elites that do little good for their populations. The

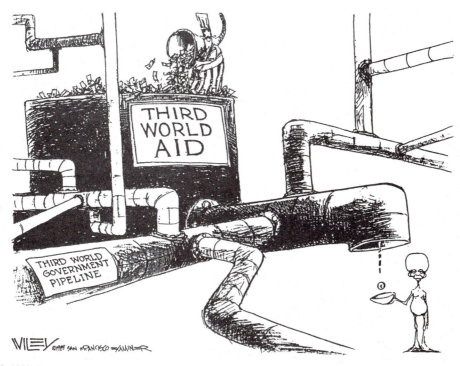

© 1989 *San Francisco Examiner.* Reprinted with permission.

most effective foreign aid may be *microloans,* an outlay of $50 to $300 by a private humanitarian organization as start-up money for a small entrepreneur. These "people-to-people" aid flows frequently do more to improve the lives of people than "government-to-government" aid that goes above the heads of the people into corruption or grandiose projects.

In February 1997, a summit of 100 countries involving 2,000 delegates, including First Lady Hillary Clinton and Treasury Secretary Robert Rubin, studied ways to raise over $20 billion to use for microloans to help the 2.5 billion people living in abject poverty. Dozens of nongovernment organizations arranged the summit partly to draw governments into the microloan development venture.

Global Debt

Huge debts connect the North and South in a particularly sensitive form of interdependence. Since the early 1980s, the world's financiers have worried that the global "debt bomb" would finally explode. They fear that a major debtor country owing billions of dollars will default on its loans. This default might trigger a chain reaction through a pyramid structure of interconnected banks causing a financial collapse on a global scale. The South's debts total over $1.3 trillion, a sum that is impossible for them to repay. The interest to service the loans of the South amounts to over 30 percent of the total GNPs of the Southern states. To handle this "debt bomb," the North and South maintain the fiction that the South will pay the debt. To repudiate a debt means a state would negate any chance for future loans and investments. The general strategy for dealing with the South's debt involves forgiving part of the debt, rescheduling the time allotted for repayment, and lowering the interest rate.[40]

The "debt bomb" originated when the Organization of Petroleum Exporting Countries (OPEC) invested its billions of dollars in profits from oil sales in the 1970s in Western banks. These banks, in turn, put the money to work in the form of loans for the South's economic development. The South expected to develop rapidly and to join in the world's export trade, which would provide them with profits for servicing the loans. Recessionary trends in the 1980s spoiled chances for repayment, and the global debt crisis began. Susan George, author of *The Debt Boomerang,* has observed far-reaching harms from the debt problems of the South. Not only do debt payments eat into export earnings and restrict economic growth in the South, but debt payments cause additional problems. The cutting of rain forests results when countries sell timber to pay debts, and illegal immigration from the South to the North takes place because people are desperate for work.[41]

Investment

Although more foreign direct investment, or long-term capital commitment, moves from one country of the North to another, an increasing number of MNCs from Europe, Japan, and the United States are seeking opportunities in the South.[42] The NICs are providing investment money through their own MNCs as well. MNCs build industries, develop transportation and communication systems, and create networks of commodity and merchandise flows. Chapter Three discussed the pros and cons of the MNCs in the developing context of the South. We learned from that discussion that scholars and leaders now view the MNC less as a predator and more as a desirable force for economic development.[43] Political economist Susan Strange believes activities of MNCs will outmatch the effort of governments through the GATT regime to stimulate world trade.[44] Abusive effects of MNCs, intentional or not, may still occur on occasion, but the investments by MNCs mostly lead toward positive interdependence.

Response of the South: Strategies for Development

Operating from within limiting conditions and recognizing the impact of the North-South links on their economies, leaders from the South have reacted to the North's dominance of the world economic order with several development strategies for economic growth. These strategies reflect aspects of the political-economic perspectives described early in this chapter: mercantilism (or economic nationalism), liberalism, and Marxism. States of the South have followed these strategies in haphazard ways, leaving one for another and sometimes mixing them.

Economic nationalism, especially popular in Latin America in the 1970s, followed an *import substitution* program calling for the domestic manufacture of many needed products and the restriction of foreign goods through high tariffs. Young industries could then get a toehold and grow. Economic nationalism also called for the seizure of foreign MNCs' subsidiaries, sometimes without payment. States choosing this path often became corporatist in nature, meaning their governments tried to run their economies. They usually dampened the spontaneity of the economies with inefficient bureaucracy and complex planning.

The *modernization strategy* in the South accepted most of the rules and norms of the liberal model that presently guides the global economy. Some leaders believed that by embracing capitalism at home and participating more fully in international free trade, they could rapidly improve their economies. Some of these leaders even accepted the liberal premise that they should democratize, because capitalism and democracy reinforce each other. Usually their governments were "guided democracies," or dictatorships with the trappings of democratic forms. The Asian Tigers of Singapore, South Korea, and Taiwan are countries that used a form of the modernization strategy but did eventually move toward real democracy. Finally, an element of economic nationalism appears in their modernization strategies when the Asian Tigers seek export-led growth and a trade surplus, following the close-by model of Japan.

China is an oddity because it remains a communist country but employs market techniques in "special economic zones." The largest country in the world eagerly seeks international trade, especially foreign trade that is producing a trade surplus favoring China. Unlike the Asian Tigers, China studiously avoids democratic reforms and violates human rights at will, including the use of prison labor to make trade goods.

The *dependency theory,* an extension of the Marxist perspective, was popular in the South for years, but it is more a moral demand for reform than an economic plan. As noted earlier in this chapter, the South blamed its economic weakness on "class" exploitation by the North. The North presumably seized wealth from the South with GATT rules and through MNCs, causing a world of rich and poor states delineated by the equator. Latin American countries have trumpeted the dependency argument the most as a rationale for their version of economic nationalism based on import substitution. The dependency theory began to give way to the modernization strategy as more Southern states achieved notable success with it.

Whatever their development strategy, leaders of the South looked for avenues of approach and institutions to lobby and pressure the North for systemic reform of the global economic structure. After all, the North had the G-7, GATT, and the bulk of the world's wealth. Even the IMF and the World Bank have played roles as tools of the North rather than serving the general good. The IMF, for example, has shifted from its original role of overseeing currency exchanges to policing debts, thus ensuring that borrowers in the South and eastern Europe meet strict conditions to obtain balance of payment financing. The World Bank, set up to make easy-to-repay loans for economic development, along with the IMF, became net takers of funds from the South in the 1980s instead of net givers, a result of the South paying off its huge debts.[45]

The avenues of approach and institutions for the South were the United Nations and various conferences, where the weight of their numbers, in a multilateral context, might produce some accomplishments. True, the United Nations did commit most of its budget and staff to helping the South, but these efforts were never enough since the North would not turn over more than a miserly amount of its GNPs for aid. The formation of UNCTAD in 1964 by Southern states, known at the time as the *Group of 77 (G-77)* amounted to conference diplomacy but could do little more than make moral arguments calling for the North to shift wealth southward. UNCTAD continues to meet every four years and today has a membership of approximately 120 states.

In the Law of the Sea Conferences, held between 1958 and 1982, the South used its influence to achieve one small success. A seabed mining regime was to regulate the extraction of minerals from the ocean floor. The regime would make sure all states, rich and poor, shared in the bounty, though only a few rich states had the necessary technology to mine minerals from the ocean floor. The seabed would be the "common heritage" of all states, and the technology-enabled states were to surrender their capitalist claim that the minerals they mined belonged to them. Now that the Law of the Sea Treaty has enough ratifications to begin implementation, it will be interesting to see how fully the technology-enabled states share minerals and profits.

The major success of the South occurred for a small subset of Southern states, the dozen countries of OPEC. As an organized effort to control the market price of oil, the OPEC **cartel** demanded princely sums for its oil in the 1970s. Prices rose from a few dollars a barrel to over $30 a barrel by 1980. Instead of giving this money away to fellow Southern states, OPEC members looked for investment opportunities through Western banks, a financial step that greatly contributed to the debt crisis, as mentioned earlier. OPEC's role as an economic actor declined in the 1980s because the industrial states of the North became more energy efficient and found sources of energy besides oil. In addition, non-OPEC oil producers, such as Mexico, Norway, and Russia, placed more oil on the international market.

The set of reforms the South desired became known in the mid-1970s as the **new international economic order (NIEO).** The NIEO called for shifting wealth to the South through more foreign aid, new loans and forgiveness of old loans, preferential tariff treatment instead of reciprocity, more control over the MNCs through international codes of conduct, and a voice more commensurate with the South's numbers in the GATT, the IMF, and the World Bank. The NIEO was a direct challenge to the liberal economic order that the major trade states have promoted, first under the hegemony of the United States and then through the cooperative regime of approximate co-equals. The South was asking the North for nothing less than a revolution in the IPE, a surrender of the North's political power over the world economy. The North, however, held on to its control of the IPE until it was able to witness more and more states of the South joining the global trend of practicing capitalist economies and democracy.

Has the North-South conflict diminished? The fiery rhetoric may be over, but the original cause of the conflict remains, namely, the gross inequality between two hemispheres of the world. Such inequality, with its invitation to conflict, is a persistent and pernicious obstacle to a formative international society. An upturn in world economic growth, such as that predicted by the Kondratieff cycle, is occurring as we approach the 21st century, and this world economic growth has the potential to help narrow the gap between North and South.

ECONOMIC INSTRUMENTS: POSITIVE AND NEGATIVE TOOLS

In this section, we shift away from the political struggle over producing and sharing the world's wealth to the use of economic instruments to achieve noneconomic goals as states compete and conflict in an effort to control outcomes. Economic tools can be *positive*, such as using foreign aid to win goodwill, trade restrictions to protect the environment, and rewards for promoting human rights; or economic tools can be *negative*, such as when states manage trade to enhance their security, wage economic warfare to bring down another government, or fight a war partly relying on economic means.

Economic tools hold a central place in the foreign policy repertoire of most states. Economic instruments often impose costs on both the states employing them and the target-states, since both lose trade. Sanctions may not always achieve their goal, but they do signal resolve and exert pressure for policy change.[46] At least economic sanctions are an effort to manage conflict by other than military means. Often economic instruments make a statement about the preferred norms of international society. These instruments punish aggressors by denying them trade or instruct dictators to respect human rights if they want more foreign aid.

Positive Tools

Foreign aid is usually outlays of gifts or generous loans to help the economic development of the South, although foreign aid probably produces less than 5 percent of the developmental capital the South needs. Gifts of food and medicine in natural disasters or during wartime for civilians are frequently the most appreciated aid. Perhaps the rich countries genuinely want to help others, but they also want to make a good public relations impression.

Some countries use trade policies to protect the environment. Nowadays more governments and publics are sensitive to environmental problems and make some economic sacrifices to save the environment. For instance, many countries refuse to import ivory to protect elephants from poaching, even if ivory importers and ivory carvers suffer economically. Also, private groups of citizens have refused to buy fish from countries that hunt whales or kill sea turtles and dolphins in mile-wide dragnets.[47]

Two major problems stand in the way of furthering environmental protection through the management of trade. One is that countries sometimes use environmental protection as an NTB to keep out goods of foreign competitors. Real motives are hard to expose in cases of this kind, but at least when Denmark would not import beer and soft drinks in cans, preferring recyclable bottles, the European Court of the EU ruled that Denmark's concern for environmental benefits outweighed the constraint on trade and ruled in Denmark's favor.[48] The other problem is that states without environmental laws can produce goods more cheaply than states with environmental laws, thus creating an unfair trade advantage for the former. GATT has not done enough to harmonize environmental rules among states to preserve fair trade, while the EU has made some progress for its 15 states.[49]

In another positive step, some countries hope to promote human rights practices by either offering or withdrawing aid and trade. Since 1976, the United States has claimed to link its foreign aid to the human rights records of aid recipients, although matching the amount of aid given with human rights improvement has been difficult to demonstrate.[50]

The best-known recent case of connecting trade and human rights involves China. The United States has threatened to withhold **most favored nation (MFN)** status if China does not end repression and stop using prison labor to produce products for international trade. China signed an agreement with the United States in 1992 promising it would not export prison-made goods to the United States.[51] However, Guangdong Province, the Chinese industrial base for export trade, has 135 prison camps on the border near Hong Kong and Asia Watch, a respected human rights group, has accused China of lying about the exportation of prison-made goods.[52] In spite of China's poor human rights record, President Bill Clinton's administration has annually renewed the MFN status for China.

Raeside/*Times-Colonist*/Victoria, British Columbia

In 1994, the late Commerce Secretary Ronald Brown and Chinese Minister of Foreign Trade Wu Yi signed an agreement setting the stage for long-term trade and investment opportunities, effectively marking the separation of human rights and trade by the Clinton administration. In 1996, the United States experienced a trade deficit to China that almost reached the $40 billion mark in trade surplus favoring China. Some trade experts predict China's trade surplus with the United States will exceed Japan's in a year or two. Because of China's huge population and rapid economic growth rate, the trade and investment opportunities for the United States tend to overpower its concern for human rights. China's economic size, which will expand even more in the 21st century, gives China considerable "soft power" in international circles. China probably did lose the Olympics for the year 2000 to Australia because of its human rights record, however.

Other actors in addition to states can bring economic pressures to bear on the cause of human rights. The United Nations orchestrated sanctions, an **embargo** forbidding the sale of goods and a **boycott** stopping purchases, against both Rhodesia (later Zimbabwe) and South Africa. The objective of the United Nations was to persuade the white minorities in charge to accept democracy by allowing the black majorities to form governments. Private groups and MNCs joined the pressure on South Africa with **divestment.** MNCs sold their subsidiaries and private groups sold their stocks to South Africans. Both sets of white minorities eventually gave way to black majority rule, due partly to economic pressures.

During the Cold War, only the two efforts against racist governments were possible, but after 1990, the United Nations has been able to coordinate a half-dozen multilateral economic pressures to bring about some type of improvement.[53] In the best-known case, the United Nations has maintained a tight boycott on Iraqi oil before and since the Persian Gulf war of 1991, hoping to persuade Saddam Hussein to give up his dreams of producing weapons of mass destruction and carrying out aggression in the Persian Gulf region. In

Chinese Minister of Foreign Trade Wu Yi, right, toasts the late U.S. Secretary of Commerce Ron Brown after signing an agreement aimed at expanding trade and economic cooperation in 14 areas between the two countries.

1996, the United Nations allowed Iraq to sell $2 billion worth of oil to pay for food and medicine for the Iraqi people.

Sanctions to bring positive change in accord with international norms are not always successful, but they have a better chance to the extent that the following conditions are in operation. First, the sanctions must make the elites of a country feel the pinch, such as when their international travel and communication are under restriction. Second, economic sanctions need time, usually three years or more, to be effective. Third, the cost of the sanctions should amount to at least 2 percent of the target-state's GNP. Fourth, the full cooperation of the major trade partners of the target-state is necessary. Fifth, the cost to the sanctioning states must be bearable. Finally, political opposition within the target-state to lift the sanctions is an advantage.[54]

Negative Tools

Frequently states are willing to sacrifice trade benefits to wage power struggles against opponents in peacetime and enemies during war. The best-known case is the United States–led Coordinating Committee (CoCom), which conducted a strategic embargo against the Warsaw Pact during the Cold War, costing the West billions of dollars in sales. CoCom, which included NATO countries (except for Iceland), Australia, and Japan, regularly reviewed technology allowable for sale to the Soviet Union and other communist countries. CoCom began operations in 1949 in a small annex of the United States embassy in Paris, and its annual budget never exceeded half a million dollars. It probably dealt a hard blow to Warsaw Pact weapons sophistication, since the latter countries tended to lag behind Western countries in technology. With the military drawdown by many states in the latter 1980s, even before the collapse of the Soviet state, CoCom began turning its attention to the spread of weapons technology to radical Third World states, especially Iran, Iraq, and Libya.[55]

In addition to CoCom, the United States has promoted the development of specific weapons regimes to prevent the proliferation of missiles, weapons of mass destruction, and some conventional weapons to Third World countries. Chapter Ten deals at length with weapons regimes.

During President Ronald Reagan's first term (1980–1984), the United States led CoCom into an era of **economic warfare** in an attempt to weaken the military and political system of the Soviet Union by undermining the entire Soviet national economy through a broad set of trade restrictions.[56] The United States also practiced economic warfare against Cuba. The intention has been to make life so miserable for Cubans that they would overthrow Fidel Castro. An embargo-boycott set of sanctions, organized through the Organization of American States (OAS), began soon after Castro announced he was a communist in 1961.

More recently, economic warfare led to the Cuban Democracy Act of 1992. This law forbade even foreign subsidiaries of American MNCs from trading with Cuba. Later, in 1996, the Helms-Burton Act allowed Americans to sue foreign companies that used American property seized after Fidel Castro came to power. European MNCs are involved, and they are protesting to the WTO, claiming the Helms-Burton Act violates international trade law. Many Americans would prefer the opposite strategy to topple Castro's regime: They would like to carry the benefits of capitalism to impoverished Cuba, and through such icons of American consumerism as McDonald's and Toys-R-Us, marginalize Castro's importance. Tightening the economic noose around Cuba has not brought Castro down, however, for he remains popular with the Cuban people in spite of their economic distress. Sanctions have created a "rally-around-the-flag" response, making many Cubans determinedly loyal to Castro. The clearest outcome of United States sanctions is that the poverty of Cuba has propelled waves of illegal Cuban immigrants to Florida.

Economic means also can be a useful ancillary to warfare, though their role is rarely decisive. Obviously states at war normally will not trade with an enemy. They can, however, **blacklist** businesses of neutrals that trade with their enemies. The country producing such a list of businesses will exclude them from its own trade. Arab states have for decades considered themselves at war with Israel whether or not there was shooting. In 1994, with an improving political climate, Saudi Arabia and five smaller Persian Gulf states ended their blacklisting of businesses that trade with Israel. Also, states at war have used **preemptive purchases,** not to get war supplies for themselves but to deny the supplies to an enemy. By paying inflated prices, the United States bought materials from neutral Sweden during the Second World War that otherwise would have wound up in German hands. **Confiscation** of an enemy national's property also can occur in wartime under international law, and that property, such as a ship, can serve the confiscating state during the war.

Better known are **blockades,** the prevention of cargo carriers, planes, ships, or trucks from reaching an enemy country with goods that could help it in a war effort. While the laws of war govern blockades, their role in war is almost always controversial. A *pacific blockade* permits cargo carriers of neutral countries to enter the territory of either warring state as long as they do not transport "contraband," or war materials. Defining contraband

© 1990 Clyde Wells, *The Augusta Chronicle*

is always controversial. Countries may prefer to apply a *belligerent blockade,* forbidding all shipments to an enemy. To be legal, such a blockade must be completely enforceable as opposed to a "paper blockade" with sporadic enforcement.

ECONOMIC INSTRUMENTS AND INTERNATIONAL SOCIETY

In addition to instances of states using economic instruments for competition and conflict, a more basic pattern of cooperative trade interdependence is taking place that is drawing the world into a societal relationship. A brief investigation of realist, neorealist, and transnationalist views will help put this question in perspective.

Realist Hans Morgenthau, writing years earlier, would not agree that trade is helping to push the world into a societal arrangement. Although well aware of the centuries-old intellectual tradition that claims the binding ties of commerce will rid the world of anarchy and war, Morgenthau believes world trade is more often a source of conflict among states. As for technology and industry, realist Morgenthau views these as resources of national power and tools for fighting war when necessary.[57] Professor Morgenthau has a kinship with neomercantilists or economic nationalists.

Kenneth N. Waltz, offering his major neorealist writing in 1979, attempted to "unpack" the notion of a positive interdependence benefiting the world by revealing it to be a myth. He realized the world had a degree of interdependence in its economic structure, but he regarded this interdependence as negative in nature. It meant mutual vulnerability among states that allows states to hurt one another economically. Making matters worse,

TABLE 8.5
A Comparison of Economic Flows at the Global Level Converted to Trillions of Dollars, 1982–1992

	Investment	Exports	Imports	WGDP
1982	0.4395	1.7160	1.7920	11.13
1983	0.4454	1.6660	1.7360	11.39
1984	0.4610	1.7840	1.8630	11.89
1985	0.5598	1.8080	1.8780	12.33
1986	0.6902	1.9900	2.0530	14.32
1987	0.8839	2.3480	2.4190	16.17
1988	1.0113	2.6860	2.7560	18.16
1989	1.2496	2.8209	2.9750	19.07
1990	1.4959	3.4250	3.4300	21.02
1991	1.6504	3.5310	3.5500	21.85
1992	1.6934	3.7530	3.7770	23.21

Sources: Foreign direct investment data are from Table V; Direct Investment Position Abroad of OECD Countries (N = 24), *International Direct Investment Statistics Yearbook* (Paris: Organization for Economic Co-operation and Development, 1994). Export and import trade data are from *International Financial Statistics Yearbook* (Washington, D.C.: International Monetary Fund, 1990–1995). World GDPs provided by reference librarian Nancy Lambert of USC-S via a telephone contact with Robert Lyman of the International Economics Department of the World Bank, Washington, D.C.

the vulnerability is uneven, putting greater economic power in the hands of some states. Thus, Waltz chides transnationalists both for claiming that interdependence is growing tighter and for concluding that interdependence is positive.

Professor Waltz points out that trade interdependence operated at a high level just before the First World War, with great powers deriving 30 to 50 percent of their GNPs from international trade versus 8 to 15 percent in the 1970s. And if trade interdependence is positive, as transnationalists and liberals claim, then why, Waltz asks, did Germany fight Russia (its best trade partner), Britain (its second-best trade partner), and France (its third-best trade partner) in the First World War? Waltz took comfort in the fact that the bipolar world of 1979 did not reflect significant economic interdependence between the Soviet Union and the United States during the nuclear-armed Cold War.[58]

In recent years, transnationalists can easily point to dramatic growth in world trade and the world's total domestic product that international trade helps produce. World trade and world GDP more than doubled in a decade, as Table 8.5 shows. Further, although Professor Waltz focused on trade, the more dramatic growth is the tripling of the international flow of foreign direct investment, as shown in Table 8.5, based on the 24 industrialized countries of the Organization for Economic Cooperation and Development (OECD). The major states of today, unlike the Soviet-American relationship in the Cold War, have positive connections in trade and investments that bring mutual benefits. Their leaders now put more time and energy into economic summits and the GATT rounds than into the workings of military alliances. Transnationalists can argue that recent history disputes Waltz given the clear importance and positive nature of economic interdependence.

We can treat more seriously neorealists who acknowledge the central importance of the world economy in international relations but observe that transnationalists take an uncritical view of the extent of cooperation stemming from trade ties. Neorealist Joseph Grieco carefully studied the Tokyo Round of GATT in the 1980s and concluded that multilateral efforts to cooperate over trade did not always succeed. During the Tokyo negotiations, he found that members of the EU would shy from an agreement, even though it might produce mutual benefits, if an outside trade partner would receive greater benefits than the EU states. In the Tokyo Round, the EU refused to accept an agricultural subsidy arrangement because the United States might gain a larger share of trade benefit than the EU's members.[59]

In another study of a different trade agreement, two researchers from the Fraser Institute of Vancouver, Canada, concluded the opposite: that Canada accepted the NAFTA agreement knowing that Mexico and the United States would receive greater economic benefits.[60] How far apart can benefits be for trade partners before their cooperation breaks down? This question does not yet have a clear, empirical answer.

Another noted neorealist, Stephen D. Krasner, argued some years ago that to develop according to rules and norms, the structure of international trade needed an economic hegemon.[61] Since Krasner's original publication on this subject in 1976, the hegemony of the United States has passed into history, but cooperative regimes still take place among trade partners.[62] Leaders of states can learn through their states' historical experiences, and their experiences may suggest the value of cooperation even in the absence of a trade hegemon.[63] Without a doubt, recent generations of leaders have learned from the Great Depression of the 1930s and the disastrous effects of resorting to protectionism. Despite the absence of an economic hegemon, states, wanting more trade and prosperity through cooperation, have managed deeper integration in the EU, the formation of NAFTA, and completion of the Uruguay Round of GATT, including in this round the creation of the WTO with more regulatory power in world trade than the GATT possessed.

Neorealists sometimes exaggerate the position of the transnationalists, thus setting up an easier target to attack. True, transnationalists, such as Robert Keohane and Joseph Nye, have faith in the liberal assumption that the rising economic flows of trade and investment can have mutual benefits for states. They also would agree that one benefit of economic interdependence is to retard war, since states do not want valuable trade interrupted. However, these scholars do not claim that interdependence will dismiss conflict, including war, from the scene. Further, they realize interdependence can be uneven, with some states more dependent and vulnerable than others. They understand too that interdependence can lead to sharp competition over the relative shares of benefits. Keohane and Nye's view of interdependence, a complex type with several dimensions of state relations leading to webs of cooperation, is an idealization. The real world, as they see it presently, lies between the realist view of power conflict and the more cooperative one of complex interdependence.[64]

Is the basic trend today more conflict or cooperation in international trade? Edward Mansfield's work on the concentration of power, referred to in Chapters Four and Five on power and war, respectively, offers help with this question. Recall that Mansfield focuses not only on the number of major actors present, as in a tripolar or multipolar system, but also on how evenly the actors possess power. Based on empirical evidence, Mansfield concluded that the highest and lowest concentrations of power in the international structure bring the highest levels of trade, while a medium concentration of power produces the lowest level of trade.[65]

International trade grew rapidly after the Second World War under the tutelage of American hegemony, a time of high concentration in power when a hegemon's rules could facilitate a rising pattern of trade. After American hegemony diminished, trade did not become stagnant; rather, a slow-growth world economy emerged as the pattern in the 1980s and early

1990s, a period we might call a medium concentration of power based on approximate co-equals. The co-equal major trade states have at least averted trade wars and have created or extended the development of several trade regimes. With more trade states becoming important and sharing power behind trade terms and agreements, as in the cases of China, Indonesia, and Malaysia—and, perhaps one day, the ex-communist states, of Europe—a structure of low concentration in power may be taking shape. If so, then, based on Mansfield's theoretical work, we can expect a higher level of trade in the future as multiple trade actors produce more goods and must accommodate one another to keep the growing volume of goods moving across many national borders. The present growth in the world GNP from 1 percent in 1991 to about 4 percent today is compatible with this observation.

Overall, the role of international trade helps move the world past the model of *international anarchy* with its emphasis on military security and preparations for war among power-focused state actors. Yet today's evolving *international society* is not a certainty. Several elements used to form our analytical models are pertinent here. Considering the *orientation* element, some conflict does occur over trade along with the stronger pattern of cooperation. Although *interaction* through economic interdependence usually creates binding ties, interdependence can sometimes mean uneven dependence and vulnerability.

For major states, regarding the element of *issues,* global trade has pushed aside national security as the chief concern. However, most observers would probably agree that a measure of conflict over producing and sharing the world's wealth is healthier than focusing on superpower alliances and arms production for mass destruction. Then, too, despite some states' efforts to leverage trade terms into place with threats of tariff retaliation, the *problem-solving level* of multilateral conferences and trade regimes is firmly in place. These conferences, however, have been and may remain arenas where trade states seek relatively higher gains than others receive.

The model of *international community* applies only to western Europe. There an *orientation* of competition, in the liberal spirit, means cheaper prices and better-quality goods through healthy competition and the removal of all border barriers to trade in the spirit of Adam Smith. For western Europe, *interaction* is mostly wholesome interdependence that overshadows the occasional fuss among the EU membership. Regarding *issues,* in contrast to the North-South void at the global level, the EU has redistributive programs to help all members overcome inequalities and attain high economic standards. Finally, the *problem-solving level* in western Europe is the most advanced in the world, based on a significant degree of political integration among 15 sovereign states. We can expect more positive societal and community developments in the future, for varied cultures and governments can perform the same complex task with a surprising degree of common purpose: They can do business together.[66]

CHAPTER SUMMARY

Producing and distributing wealth are regular human concerns. At least three different perpectives have existed about wealth and the role of political authority concerning the production and distribution functions. The international political economy, according to mercantilists, is one in which the state manages the economy for its own interests. Liberals believe the state should stay out of the economy and leave it to market forces. Marxists claim the international political economy historically has been a system of class exploitation among both social classes inside countries and states at the global level. For them, the focus should be on a fair distribution of wealth. The perspective of liberalism has the strongest hold on the world today, especially because of American hegemony after the Second World War.

The prosperous trade arrangement under American hegemony began to experience considerable turbulence by the 1970s, starting the world on the road to a cooperative trade regime replacing hegemonic stability. Then, in the early 1990s, major trade actors, no longer forced into unity by the Cold War and worried over the slowdown in the world economy, threatened their cooperative trade regime by quarreling over shares of the world market. Each one followed an export-led growth strategy though markets were already tight. A tension exists today between centripetal forces pulling states toward cooperation within the WTO and centrifugal forces pushing states into tense competition that threatens a trade war. So far, the major trade states have stanched a trade war with last-effort compromises.

World trade never really included Russia and eastern Europe in a major way while these countries practiced economic autarky as communists, nor did it raise significantly the level of economic prosperity of the South. In addition to resolving trade differences among major trade actors, further tasks center on integrating the ex-communist states and the large number of diverse states of the South into a prosperous world economy.

Most economic competition is healthy because it means better goods at lower prices, but occasionally states depart from fair trade to employ imaginative devices such as NTBs, or they brazenly steal IPRs to gain an unfair advantage. Sometimes states implement economic tools for noneconomic purposes. Positive goals may be to help people with foreign aid, protect the environment, or promote human rights. Negative goals can serve to undermine another state's military capacity, wage economic warfare to bring down another government, or weaken an enemy economically during wartime.

Although sharp trade competition and the specter of a trade war have been present in recent years, the positive, integrating forces of the world economy are holding their own. A positive force such as diplomacy can help facilitate the emergence of the international society, but prosperity through trade can give international society a strong motive to exist. In spite of Europe's two-speed economy and the North-South gulf, the states of the world increasingly are sharing the same sense of economic order based on liberal trade premises. A period of significant world economic growth as we enter the 21st century would reinforce faith in the liberal trade order.

POINTS OF VIEW

... history is not made by politics. It is made by economics, by demographics and, above all, by science and technology.

—CHARLES KRAUTHAMMER
TIME, MAY 1990

Interdependence is not simply a word created by idealistic world-order reformers, but a very real condition of life bonding the fate of the rich to the fate of the poor.

—SEYOM BROWN
INTERNATIONAL RELATIONS IN A CHANGING GLOBAL SYSTEM, 1992

This two-way street of transatlantic investment is indicative of a larger trend: foreign direct investment—not just international trade—is increasingly propelling the globalization of the world economy.

—JURGEN W. MOLLEMANN
ECONOMIC MINISTER OF GERMANY

The truth about Japan sometimes hurts especially for Americans who are used to being number one but who are being told that by the year 2000 their economy will be number two.

—PETER MCGILL
OBSERVER, LONDON

The process of trade liberalization in Japan, it seemed, was like peeling an onion, where the core of the onion was not quickly reached as layers were removed.

—PIETRO S. NIVOLA
REGULATING UNFAIR TRADE, 1993

So long as the free market economy is not more severely controlled and submitted to our new set of moral values, it will be as cruel and unjust as the law of the jungle we have rejected.

—Captain Jacques Cousteau
Calypso Log, 1992

The Russian economy will never recover unless the country's industry is restructured to respond to market needs and to produce goods that consumers at home and abroad want to buy when they want to buy them.

—Michael Heseltine
President of Britain's Board of Trade

REVIEW QUESTIONS

1. What are the economic strengths and weaknesses of the major trade actors? What is meant by the United States as *primus inter pares*?
2. Why is Europe a two-track economy since the fall of communism?
3. What typical conditions of the South are holding back its economic development?
4. Why is the status of women critical to economic development?
5. What is dependency theory, and why has its legitimacy declined?
6. What is the role of competition according to a supporter of free trade?
7. Why was OPEC a mixed blessing for the South?
8. What are NTBs, and why do states use them?
9. What role did CoCom perform as an act of economic warfare against the Soviet Union?
10. What are some of the economic tools available in war?

GLOSSARY

autarky Economic self-sufficiency by a state or group of coordinated states.

blacklist A list of businesses with which a country will not trade because they trade with the enemy.

blockade Preventing cargo from reaching an enemy's territory in wartime on land, at sea, and by air.

boycott A refusal to buy one or more commodities or products from a specific country or countries.

capitalism An economic system based on private ownership and controlled by market forces of supply and demand with minimal government interference.

cartel A device used by a group of major suppliers to control the availability and hence the price of a product or commodity.

command economy A centrally controlled economy involving extensive planning and management by the government; usually associated with communist countries.

confiscation Seizure of an enemy state's property or that of its citizens during war.

dependency theory The hypothetical claim that rich, industrialized states above the equator exploit poorer states below the equator in economic relations.

divestment The withdrawal of investment money from a foreign country; usually associated with a political goal.

dumping The sale of a product by one country to another in large quantities at prices below the normal market value to capture a share of that country's market.

economic hegemon A dominating power, regionally or globally, that can determine the rules of trade.

economic warfare The use of trade restrictions to cripple an opponent's economy and possibly bring down the government of the opponent.

embargo A refusal to sale and ship a material or product that another country wishes to buy.

foreign direct investment The movement of capital across borders on a long-term basis to develop a profit-making enterprise.

international political economy (IPE) The study of the interaction of international political and economic forces, with each able to have effects on the other.

liberalism A perspective on the international economic order calling for competitive free trade for the mutual benefit of states, including the avoidance of war to maintain the trade system.

Marxism A socialist view claiming capitalism means the exploitation of one group by another and calling for a fair redistribution of wealth.

mercantilism An economic order that focuses on states running their economies to promote the military power and security of the state; in its modern form, neomercantilism focuses on a state's economic enrichment at the expense of other states.

most favored nation (MFN) Trade terms given to a trading partner that are guaranteed to be as good as the terms allowed any other trading partner.

new international economic order (NIEO) A broad set of reforms the South expected of the North that are basically designed to redistribute the wealth of the world in the South's favor.

nontariff barriers (NTBs) Devices to serve protectionist policy as an alternative to relying on the obvious use of tariffs or quotas.

preemptive purchases The purchase of materials useful for a war effort from neutrals to prevent their sale to an enemy.

protectionism A trade policy that discourages the purchase of foreign goods and encourages the purchase of domestically produced goods.

quota A numerical limit on certain imports.

reciprocity The granting of corresponding privileges by trade partners.

tariff A duty or fee charged by a state for importing a good from another country.

RECOMMENDED READINGS

Vinod K. Aggarwal. *Debt Games: Strategic Interaction in International Debt Rescheduling.* New York: Cambridge University Press, 1996.

David A. Baldwin. *Economic Statecraft.* Princeton, NJ: Princeton University Press, 1985.

The Challenge to the South. The Report of the South Commission. New York: Oxford University Press, 1990.

John A. C. Conybeare. *Trade Wars: The Theory and Practice of International Commercial Rivalry.* New York: Columbia University Press, 1987.

David Cortright and George A. Lopez, eds. *Economic Sanctions: Panacea or Peacebuilding in a Post–Cold War World?* Boulder, CO: Westview Press, 1995.

Susan George. *The Debt Boomerang: How Third World Debt Harms Us All.* London: Pluto Press, 1992.

Robert Gilpin. *The Political Economy of International Relations.* Princeton, NJ: Princeton University Press, 1987.

Joanne Gowa. *Allies, Adversaries, and International Trade.* Princeton, NJ: Princeton University Press, 1994.

Joseph M. Grieco. *Cooperation Among Nations: Europe, America, and Non-Tariff Barriers to Trade.* Ithaca, NY: Cornell University Press, 1990.

Robert A. Isaak. *Managing World Economic Change: International Political Economy.* 2nd ed. Englewood Cliffs, NJ: Prentice Hall, 1995.

Ethan Barnaby Kapstein. *The Political Economy of National Security.* New York: McGraw-Hill, 1992.

Edward J. Lincoln. *Japan's New Global Role.* Washington, D.C.: The Brookings Institution, 1993.

Edward D. Mansfield. *Power, Trade, and War.* Princeton, NJ: Princeton University Press, 1994.

Lisa L. Martin. *Coercive Cooperation: Explaining Multilateral Economic Sanctions.* Princeton, NJ: Princeton University, 1992.

Michael Mastanduno. *Economic Containment: CoCom and the Politics of East-West Trade.* Ithaca, NY: Cornell University Press, 1992.

Lee E. Preston and Duane Windsor. *The Rules of the Game in the Global Economy: Policy Regimes for International Business.* Boston: Kluwer Academic Publishers, 1992.

Carolyn Rhodes. *Reciprocity, U.S. Trade Policy, and the GATT Regime.* Ithaca, NJ: Cornell University Press, 1993.

Herman M. Schwartz. *States versus Markets: History, Geography, and the Development of the International Political Economy.* New York: St. Martin's Press, 1994.

Catherine V. Scott. *Gender and Development: Rethinking Modernization and Dependency Theory.* Boulder, CO: Lynne Rienner Publishers, 1995.

Thomas Richard Shannon. *An Introduction to the World-System Perspective.* Boulder, CO: Westview Press, 1989.

Lester C. Thurow. *The Future of Capitalism.* New York: William Morrow, 1996.

ENDNOTES

1. Edward D. Mansfield, *Power, Trade, and War* (Princeton, NJ: Princeton University Press, 1994), p. 28.
2. Jeffry A. Frieden and David A. Lake, eds., *International Political Economy: Perspectives on Global Power and Wealth,* 3rd ed. (New York: St. Martin's Press, 1995), p. 1.

3. Ibid.; Robert Gilpin, *The Political Economy of International Relations* (Princeton, NJ: Princeton University Press, 1987).
4. Yong S. Lee, "U.S. Trade Policy in the Post–Cold War Era: A Search for New Directions," in *Post–Cold War Policy: The International Context*, ed. William Crotty (Chicago: Nelson-Hall, 1995), p. 67.
5. Douglas Dowd, *The Waste of Nations: Dysfunction in the World Economy* (Boulder, CO: Westview Press, 1989).
6. James Q. Wilson, "Capitalism and Morality," *The Public Interest*, Fall 1995, pp. 42–60.
7. The descriptions of the three perspectives draw on Gilpin, *The Political Economy of International Relations*, Chapter 2.
8. Robert S. Walters and David H. Blake, *The Politics of Global Economic Relations*, 4th ed. (Englewood Cliffs, NJ: Prentice Hall, 1992), pp. 45–55.
9. Immanuel Wallerstein, *The Politics of the World Economy* (Cambridge, England: Cambridge University Press, 1984); Immanuel Wallerstein, *The Modern World-System* (New York: Academic Press, 1974); Christopher Chase-Dunn, *Global Formulation: Structures for the World Economy* (Cambridge, MA: Basil Blackwell, 1991).
10. William R. Thompson, *On Global War: Historical-Structural Approaches to World Politics* (Columbia, SC: University of South Carolina Press, 1988), pp. 167–71.
11. Wallerstein, *The Politics of the World Economy*, p. 9.
12. Stephen D. Krasner, "State Power and the Structure of International Trade," in *International Political Economy*, pp. 19–36.
13. Robert O. Keohane, *After Hegemony: Cooperation and Discord in the World Political Economy* (Princeton, NJ: Princeton University Press, 1984).
14. Herman M. Schwartz, *States versus Markets: History, Geography, and the Development of the International Political Economy* (New York: St. Martin's Press, 1994), p. 329.
15. Edward J. Lincoln, *Japan's New Global Role* (Washington, D.C.: The Brookings Institution, 1993), p. 9.
16. Carolyn Rhodes, *Reciprocity, U.S. Trade Policy, and the GATT Regime* (Ithaca, NY: Cornell University Press, 1993), p. xi.
17. Kazuo Inamori, "U.S.–Japan Relations from the Viewpoint of Japanese Multinational Corporations," in Glenn Hastedt, ed., *One World, Many Voices: Global Perspectives on Political Issues* (Englewood Cliffs, NJ, 1994), pp. 225–32.
18. Shintaro Ishihara, *The Japan That Can Say No: Why Japan Will Be First Among Equals* (New York: Simon & Schuster, 1991).
19. Shintaro Ishihara and Mahathir Mohamad, *The Voice of Asia: Two Leaders Discuss the Coming Century* (Kodansha International, Ltd., 1996).
20. Lee, "U.S. Trade Policy in the Post–Cold War Era," pp. 77–80.
21. Benjamin J. Cohen, "A Brief History of International Monetary Relations," in *International Political Economy*, p. 522.
22. Lee E. Preston and Duane Windsor, *The Rules of the Game in the Global Economy: Policy Regimes for International Business* (Boston: Kluwer Academic Publishers, 1992), p. 5.
23. *The Economist*, January 4–10, 1997, pp. 67–68.
24. Lester Thurow, *Head to Head: The Coming Economic Battle Among Japan, Europe, and America* (New York: William Morrow, 1992).
25. Paul Krugman, "Competitiveness: A Dangerous Obsession," *Foreign Affairs*, March–April 1994, pp. 28–44.
26. *World Press Review*, January 1997, p. 9.
27. Richard T. Cupitt, "Coping with Uncertainty: U.S. Trade and Financial Policies Toward Central and Eastern Europe in a Post–Cold War World," in *Post–Cold War Policy*, pp. 95–112.
28. Thomas E. Weisskopf, "Russia in Transition: Perils of the Fast Track to Capitalism," in *International Political Economy*, pp. 476–80; Deborah Anne Palmieri, "Russia's Foreign Economic Relations with the West," in *Russia and the NIS in the World Economy: East-West Investment, Financing, and Trade*, ed. Deborah Anne Palmieri (Westport, CT: Praeger Publishers, 1994), pp. 1–18.
29. Weisskopf, "Russia in Transition," p. 488.
30. Beverly Crawford, *Economic Vulnerability in International Relations: The Case of East-West Trade, Investment, and Finance* (New York: Columbia University Press, 1993), p. 224.
31. Desmond Dinan, *An Ever Closer Union?* (Boulder, CO: Lynne Rienner Publishers, 1994), pp. 477–80.

32. The PQLI is taken from *U.S. Foreign Policy and Developing Countries* (Washington, D.C.: Overseas Development Council, 1991), Table 15.
33. Walters and Blake, *The Politics of Global Economic Relations,* p. 49.
34. *The Challenge of the South.* The Report of the South Commission (New York: Oxford University Press, 1990), pp. 128–31.
35. Catherine Scott, *Gender and Development: Rethinking Modernization and Dependency Theory* (Boulder, CO: Lynne Rienner Publishers, 1995).
36. Gay Young, Vidytamali Samarasinghe, and Ken Kusterer, eds., *Women at the Center: Development Issues and Practices for the 1990s* (West Hartford, CT: Kumarian Press, 1993). See also Thomas F. Carroll, *Intermediary NGOs: The Supporting Link in Grassroots Development* (West Hartford, CT: Kumarian Press, 1992).
37. Walters and Blake, *The Politics of Global Economic Relations,* pp. 48–49.
38. *Intellectual Property Rights and Foreign Direct Investment* (New York: United Nations, 1993).
39. *Our Global Neighborhood: The Report of the Commission of Global Governance* (New York: Oxford University Press, 1995), p. 191.
40. Vincent Ferraro and Melissa Rosser, "Global Debt and Third World Development," *World Security: Challenges for a New Century,* 2nd ed., ed. Michael T. Klare and Daniel C. Thomas (New York: St. Martin's Press, 1994), pp. 332–55.
41. Susan George, *The Debt Boomerang: How Third World Debt Harms Us All* (London: Pluto Press, 1992).
42. Gilpin, *The Political Economy of International Relations,* p. 232.
43. Walters and Blake, *The Politics of Global Economic Relations,* p. 151.
44. Susan Strange, "Protectionism and World Politics," *International Organization,* Spring 1985, pp. 233–60.
45. *Our Global Neighborhood,* pp. 181, 185; Ivan L. Head, "Haves and Have-Nots: Upheaval Between North and South," in *At Issue: Politics in the World Arena,* 6th ed., ed. Steven L. Spiegel (New York: St. Martin's Press, 1991), pp. 261–62; Ferraro and Rosser, "Global Debt and Third World Development," p. 343.
46. Lisa L. Martin, *Coercive Cooperation: Explaining Multilateral Economic Sanctions* (Princeton, NJ: Princeton University Press, 1992), p. 3.
47. Alison Butler, "Environmental Protection and Free Trade: Are They Mutually Exclusive?" in *International Political Economy,* pp. 493–505; Daniel C. Esty, *Greening the GATT: Trade, Environment, and the Future* (Washington, D.C.: Institute for International Economics, 1994), pp. 10–27; Hilary F. French, *Costly Tradeoffs: Reconciling Trade and the Environment* (Worldwatch Paper 113) (Washington, D.C.: Worldwatch Institute, 1993), p. 9.
48. French, *Costly Tradeoffs,* p. 43.
49. Ibid.; Esty, *Greening the GATT,* pp. 2–7.
50. Stephen Poe, "Human Rights and U.S. Foreign Aid: A Review of Quantitative Studies and Suggestions for Future Research," *Human Rights Quarterly,* November 1990, pp. 499–512.
51. Andrew J. Nathan, "Influencing Human Rights in China," in *Beyond MFN: Trade with China and American Interests,* ed. James R. Lilley and Wendell L. Willkie II (Washington, D.C.: The AEI Press, 1994), pp. 77–90.
52. *World Press Review,* July 1994, pp. 13–14.
53. George A. Lopez and David Cortright, "Economic Sanctions in Contemporary Global Relations," in *Economic Sanctions: Panacea or Peacemaking in a Post–Cold War World?* ed. David Cortright and George A. Lopez (Boulder, CO: Westview Press, 1995), pp. 4–6.
54. Cortwright and Lopez, *Economic Sanctions,* p. 9; Ivan Eland, "Economic Sanctions as Tools of Foreign Policy," in *Economic Sanctions,* p. 34.
55. Michael Mastanduno, *Economic Containment: CoCom and the Politics of East-West Trade* (Ithaca, NY: Cornell University Press, 1992).
56. Ibid., pp. 234–42.
57. Hans Morgenthau, *Politics Among Nations: The Struggle for Power and Peace,* 5th ed. (New York: Alfred A. Knopf, 1978), pp. 123–28.
58. Kenneth N. Waltz, *Theory of International Politics* (Reading, MA: Addison-Wesley, 1979), pp. 140–45, 151–59.
59. Joseph M. Grieco, *Cooperation Among Nations: Europe, America, and Non-Tariff Barriers to Trade* (Ithaca, NY: Cornell University Press, 1990).

60. Steven Globerman and Michael Walker, eds., *Assessing NAFTA: A Trinational Analysis* (Vancouver, BC: The Fraser Institute, 1993), p. xxvii.
61. Krasner, "State Power and the Structure of International Trade," in *International Political Economy,* pp. 57–64.
62. Keohane, *After Hegemony.*
63. Robert Axelrod, *The Evolution of Cooperation* (New York: Basic Books, 1984).
64. Robert O. Keohane and Joseph S. Nye, *Power and Interdependence,* 2nd ed. (Boston: Scott, Foresman, 1989), pp. 8–11, 40–41, 222, 247–54.
65. Mansfield, *Power, Trade, and War,* p. 23.
66. Robert Heilbroner, *21st Century Capitalism* (New York: W. W. Norton, 1993), p. 20.

CHAPTER 9

THE INTERNATIONAL POLITICAL ECONOMY: THE INSTITUTIONS OF COOPERATION AND INTEGRATION

Before the Second World War, the world's economy consisted of about 50 loosely connected, protectionist-oriented national economies and the colonies of European countries. After the war, over several decades, a much larger number of national economies emerged within a network of growing interdependence. This network led to countries counting on economic flows from outside their borders for part of their national economic growth and prosperity. The primary flows have been rising rates of international trade goods and foreign capital investment. As interdependence has tightened its hold on national economies, the governments of sovereign countries have had to find ways to provide *governance* for the increasingly complex global economy that they share.

Governance has come about through economic policy regimes that have converged mostly around the liberal rules and norms of free trade and capitalism. There are global regimes such as the General Agreement on Tariffs and Trade (GATT), which recently became the World Trade Organization (WTO), and regional regimes such as the European Union (EU), the North American Free Trade Agreement (NAFTA), and the Association of Southeast Asian Nations (ASEAN). There also are functional regimes for specialized tasks, including the International Monetary Fund (IMF), the International Telecommunications Union (ITU), and the International Finance Corporation (IFC). State involvement in policy regimes varies from low levels of *cooperation* to significant levels of *integration*.

Although cooperative and integrative processes are robust in the global economy, dissonance is still present. Important trade states continue to practice some degree of economic nationalism while still enjoying the rise in the liberalized trade environment that GATT has produced. Also, ex-communist states in Europe and rising newly industrialized countries (NICs) from the South are scrambling to participate in the benefits of the liberalizing economic order but have trouble adjusting to its rules and norms. Nonetheless, the completion of the Uruguay Round of GATT, the continued rise in trade and investment, the formation of NAFTA, and further progress in the integrative process of the EU mark a tilt in the world's economic forces favoring cooperation over conflict.

We begin this chapter with an account of the world economic system that emerged after the Second World War. This liberal order, produced under American hegemony, has survived

America's decline as a global hegemon and, through major adjustments, has continued to promote cooperation and economic growth. Then we question whether regional strategies for cooperation and integration are undermining or enhancing the global economy. Next, we assess the extent of regional cooperation in Europe, North America, and Asia. Finally, we consider the argument that burgeoning economic cooperation is contributing to an international society.

POSTWAR ECONOMIC COOPERATION

Near the end of the Second World War, two factors, soon followed by a third, provided the impetus for postwar economic cooperation. First, the recent memory of the rapid decline in world trade due to the disastrous Great Depression and the protectionism it brought led Allied planners to pursue an open world economy of free trade. Second, the war's devastation in industrial countries other than the United States compelled economic cooperation if postwar recovery was to proceed speedily. Third, not long after the close of the Second World War, the Cold War divided the former Allies that had defeated Germany. Western leaders realized that Europe and Japan's economic development was necessary to resist the appeals of communism and to pay for military strength needed to deter an increasingly hostile Soviet Union.

At the war's end, the United States was not only a superpower with an atomic bomb but an economic dynamo able and willing to serve as the world's hegemon. For about 25 years, America's hegemony stimulated world economic growth through its trade, loans, and foreign aid. America brought order to the world's monetary system by stabilizing currency exchanges, and American multinational corporations (MNCs) provided investment capital for development. Above all, hegemony permitted the United States to insist that other countries gradually replace protectionist policies with a free trade system. Similar to Adam Smith's thinking, based on his 1776 *Wealth of Nations,* the intent was to remove all trade barriers possible, thus allowing a greater volume of shared trade and commonly enjoyed prosperity. However, unlike Adam Smith's idea of regulating the international economy by the "unseen hand" of market forces alone, the United States pushed for the governance of international trade through international institutions.

The Bretton Woods System

The story of postwar economic cooperation and governance begins with the Bretton Woods meeting of the Allies in 1944, just months before the war's end. The product of the Bretton Woods meeting was a set of hegemonic regimes embedded in formal institutions, largely created and led by the United States. The *World Bank,* formally known as the International Bank for Reconstruction and Development (IBRD), first helped war-torn Europe to recover through loans and then later shifted loans to the Third World. The IBRD has traditionally focused loans on middle-income countries at market interest rates with up to 20 years to repay. Now over 50 years old with about 180 member-states, the World Bank has contributed significantly to world economic output and the rapid rise in global trade. World Bank loans peaked at nearly $24 billion in 1993 and have since declined to about $20 billion a year. The World Bank is the world's largest single lender and occupies the epicenter of the international financial system. Thus, its loans are more important than their dollar amounts might suggest. These loans are "seals of approval" that enable countries to attract much larger amounts of loan money from private banks. World Bank loans usually pay for about 25 percent of the projects this bank supports, with other banks and national revenues covering the rest.

The Bretton Woods system expanded the World Bank with the creation of the *International Finance Corporation (IFC)* in 1956, the *International Development Association (IDA)* in 1960, and the *Multilateral Investment Guarantee Agency (MIGA)* in 1988. With the IBRD, these affiliates comprise the *World Bank Group.* The IFC provides loan capital for private development, funneling small amounts of money as "pump primers" to attract other private capital. The IFC's capital loans were only $330 million in 1993. The IFC forms part of the world's investment regime, with its rules and norms suspended between Third World countries that want MNCs' investments regulated and the industrialized countries that desire more open opportunities for investment and greater protection from the expropriation steps of host governments.[1] The IDA specializes in "soft loans" to the poorest countries with less than $805 dollars per capita income. Of World Bank money, the IDA loaned about $7 billion in 1993 without interest and with a payback period of up to 40 years. The MIGA's role is to encourage private investment by insuring these investments against political risks such as war, civil strife, and government expropriation of foreign property. MIGA has had at least modest success at encouraging foreign investment.

Elements of the World Bank Group are independent agencies within the UN System, each with its own budget and decision-making criteria and process. A board of governors makes basic decisions using a weighted voting system based on the amount of investment of each member-state. The management teams of the different elements of the World Bank Group overlap, and some policymakers simply change hats when making different kinds of loans. The United States has provided about 20 percent of the World Bank's capital and has a corresponding voting power. Although American hegemony has given way to an economic structure of approximate co-equals, it is safe to say the World Bank remains under the primary influence of Western, industrialized countries that support a capitalist, liberal order. The location of the World Bank Group in Washington, D.C., reflects American hegemony at the time of the bank's formation.

The World Bank has experienced plenty of criticism. Perhaps the most fundamental criticism is that the World Bank has remained too fixed on its original purpose of developing the infrastructures of countries. World Bank policy intended that large-scale, government-backed projects involving roads, telecommunication systems, and the development of industry would have systemwide impact on national economies. By focusing too much on national economic growth indicators, according to critics, the World Bank has paid too little attention to environmental harms, the role of women in development, and the basic needs of people. The World Bank may have lacked sensitivity to these problems because the bulk of its employees work in Washington, D.C., with few operating in the field.

Responding to criticisms, the World Bank has participated in the *Global Environment Facility* set up in 1991 and created a *Vice-Presidency for Sustainable Environmental Development* in 1993. These steps resulted in the screening of loans according to their environmental impact. The World Bank also created the *Women in Development Program* in 1987 and aimed more loans toward the advancement of women. Further, to meet human needs in education, population control, health, and nutrition, the World Bank devised the

Program of Targeted Interventions, which spent $3 billion of World Bank money on human needs in 1992.[2]

If the World Bank Group is the first pillar of the Bretton Woods system, the *International Monetary Fund (IMF)* is the second. In its early years, the task of the IMF was simple: stabilize the rate of exchange among the world's currencies to encourage international trade. Countries accepting foreign currencies as payment for goods obviously need to know what the currencies are actually worth. Otherwise, states with weak economies can and will inflate their currencies to buy more goods than they can afford. Another, related problem is that without a global standard for currencies, countries might drift into *currency blocs* because they have confidence in only one currency. Ex-French colonies might trade in francs with France and other ex-French colonies. Perhaps the British Commonwealth would trade primarily among its member-states using the British pound. Further, Europe might trade in German marks, and North and South American countries might trade among themselves through the American dollar. True global trade patterns would collapse.

The original task of the IMF was fairly easy as long as the IMF could peg the world's currencies to the American dollar, the currency of the postwar's economic hegemon. The Federal Reserve of the United States valued the American dollar's worth in gold, with $35.00 equaling one ounce of gold. All went well while the United States owned $25 billion in gold, almost 75 percent of the world's known gold.[3] Unfortunately, the voracious appetite of American consumers for foreign goods created a trade deficit accompanied by a glut of dollars accumulating in foreign central banks. These banks chose to exchange their dollars for gold, an exchange promised on the face of American currency. American gold dwindled to an amount worth $10 billion by 1970.[4]

Many economists mark the demise of the Bretton Woods system, and with it American hegemony, by President Richard Nixon's decision in 1971 to sever the link between the dollar and gold. This decision permitted the dollar to drop to a realistic level of worth based on the country's sales and services. As a result, currency exchanges among trade partners became more erratic, and the use of currencies of uncertain worth inhibited growth in international trade. The IMF turned to a "float system," valuing a given country's currency against a "basket of currencies" of the major trade states. Currency exchange rates now stay in flux with the currency speculation of private traders, making matters worse.

As discussed in Chapter Eight, because of the "debt bomb" of the 1980s, the IMF had to take on a new role as "lender of last resort." Heavily in debt, many Third World countries could borrow only from the IMF, giving this body tremendous bargaining power. Other loans and investments would not be forthcoming without the IMF "seal of approval."[5] Managed by Western bankers, the IMF insisted on a strict guideline of austerity, regardless of impoverishing effects that might result, before it would finance a country's balance of payment deficit in international trade. The World Bank also has responded to world indebtedness by shifting some of its money to "adjustment lending" to ease balance of payment problems.[6] To assist with loans, the IMF created its own reserve fund in 1969, called *Special Drawing Rights (SDRs),* which exists merely on accounting records. The central bank of one country can borrow and pay these SDRs to the central bank of another country because the IMF guarantees their worth.

The IMF is an independent agency of the UN System, with about 180 member-states taking part. The IMF has a board of governors that meets annually to devise general policy and an executive board that handles day-to-day business. Countries share a weighted voting system on the two boards depending on their investments in the IMF. Similar to the World Bank, Western states control the IMF and its policies, and the IMF too is in Washington, D.C. Coordination between the World Bank and the IMF occurs through the World Bank/IMF Development Committee drawn from the two respective boards of governors.

Overall, most writers in the IPE field give the Bretton Woods system high marks for promoting stable international cooperation and economic growth along the lines of the liberal trade model. More recent revisionist thinking, however, claims the power of the Bretton Woods system's influence is an exaggeration.[7] Only more careful historical analysis will lead to firm conclusions, but it is safe to say the Bretton Woods system contributed significantly, even if the degree of contribution is in doubt by some.

The General Agreement on Tariffs and Trade (GATT)

We learned in Chapter Eight that the GATT helped increase the world's trade levels by removing trade barriers through eight rounds of negotiations stretching across five decades, ending with the highly volatile Uruguay Round of 1986–1994 (Table 9.1). Originally, GATT was not the intended organization to construct a liberal free trade order for the world. The GATT would be only a temporary means for negotiating tariff reductions while ratification of the International Trade Organization (ITO) took place. Following easy agreement over the Bretton Woods system in 1944, the United States had proposed the creation of the ITO in 1945. However, the negotiations over the ITO did not begin until 1947 in Havana, Cuba, permitting time for postwar cooperation to erode and other conditions to change. For example, the Republican Party captured Congress in 1946 and refused to support a trade regulatory body that might reduce the sovereign trade choices of states. And Great Britain, agreeable to tariff reductions in general, wanted to keep its Imperial Preference System favoring trade units within its empire.

As a proposed treaty, the ITO did not receive enough ratifications, including the ratification of the United States. The collapse of plans for the ITO led President Harry Truman to accept GATT by executive agreement, thus bypassing the need for Senate approval. The GATT process officially got under way on the first day of 1948 and carried on its work for nearly half a century.

GATT operated around several specific norms. All member-states would trade under the most favored nation (MFN) principle, with all trade partners treated equally. Also, trade would be *transparent,* meaning the exclusion of hidden barriers to trade. GATT permitted only tariffs and quotas that were to fade over time. Further, each new trade rule would apply to all member-states through reciprocity. Finally, states had to accept dispute settlement when disagreement over trade rules occurred. By converging around these norms, GATT contributed to a growth of billions of dollars in world trade. GATT accomplished this feat by forging even freer trade agreements across eight rounds of protracted negotiations. The GATT process began with 21 states at the Geneva Round in 1947 and ended with over 100 states taking part in the Uruguay Round from 1986 to 1994. Counting associate members, approximately 120 states agreed to the terms of the Uruguay Round. This last round took as long as it did, and sometimes nearly collapsed, because of the large number of diverse participants and a range of controversial issues. This last round of GATT went

TABLE 9.1
GATT Rounds

Round	Year	Number of GATT members	Tariff cuts
Geneva	1947	21	20+%
Annency (France)	1949	22	21.1
Torquay (Britain)	1950–1951	33	0
Geneva	1955–1956	34	2–3
Dillon Round	1960–1961	43	1
Kennedy Round	1964–1967	75	20
Tokyo Round	1973–1979	86	35
Uruguay Round	1986–1994	102	38

Note: The number or states attending rounds and the tariff reductions by percentages vary among sources.
Source: Ingomar Hauchler and Paul M. Kennedy, ed., *Global Trade: The World Almanac of Development and Peace* (New York: Continuum Publishing Company, 1994), p. 243.

beyond trade in merchandise goods, unlike previous rounds, and tackled the divisive matters of agricultural subsidies, intellectual property rights, textiles, and trade in services such as insurance and banking.

Because GATT was to be temporary, it had a skeletal structure. It did, at least, have a headquarters in Geneva, Switzerland, with a small, permanent staff. In addition to a political oversight body that met once a year, GATT had a council of representatives consisting of delegates from member-states that met several times a year. The council reviewed trade disputes after a panel of experts investigated and made a report. A key accomplishment of the Uruguay Round was to add more body to the skeleton of GATT by creating the World Trade Organization (WTO). Beginning in 1995, the WTO absorbed GATT's role as a regime for merchandise trade and will operate separate policy regimes for services, as opposed to trade in goods, and for intellectual property protection. The WTO has a stronger dispute settlement capability than GATT and can resolve disputes more quickly. A WTO council manages daily operations and appoints investigative panels for trade disputes when the need arises. Although basic questions will require a consensus in the WTO, a two-thirds vote in the WTO council can speed up a panel's recommendation to level penalties against a country for trade rule violations.[8]

The WTO remains essentially a **preferential trade system** because the 120 or so states involved only reduce tariffs and other barriers to an agreed-on level. However, these states do give one another their best trade terms under the MFN principle. Completely free trade, without any tariffs or other barriers, is the long-term goal of the WTO, based as it is on liberal economic norms. The WTO will hold regular meetings, as it did in Singapore in late 1996 to continue deciding the pace and depth of further liberalized world trade. The WTO will encounter stiff resistance before achieving a completely free trade world by 2010, if such a goal is possible among diverse and numerous states operating at different economic levels. Renato Ruggiero, director-general of the WTO, and some other leaders have spoken vaguely of such a goal. Another problem encumbering free world trade is that China and Russia are not yet members of the WTO, though they may be in a year or two.[9]

Minilateral Economic Cooperation

While GATT has provided a *multilateral* forum for the majority of the world's states to reach agreement on global trade, the *Organization for Economic Cooperation and Development (OECD)* and the *Group of Seven (G-7)* offer *minilateral* forums in which the 25 leading industrialized states of the OECD (South Korea received an invitation and joined in 1996) and the seven major trade states of the G-7 work out problems arising from high levels of interdependent trade. In these smaller forums, rich, Western states have often reached a measure of consensus before tackling the same policy issues in GATT rounds. The OECD (Australia, Canada, Japan, New Zealand, Turkey, the United States, and much of western Europe) began in 1961, emerging from an earlier organization that had planned European postwar recovery.

The OECD promotes economic growth through freer trade and coordinates member-states' foreign aid to the Third World. The OECD researches and offers respected reports on matters such as industrial output, consumer demand, price stability, inflation controls, and unemployment levels. The OECD has a Paris headquarters with a secretariat led by a secretary-general. A council of representatives meets annually allowing member-states to challenge the trade policies of others and defend their own.

The G-7, introduced in Chapter Eight, started its annual summitry in 1975 in time to help construct a cooperative trade regime among major trade states as America's hegemonic descent began. The 1971 collapse of the American dollar as the world's currency standard and the first oil crisis of 1973 made clear the need for coordination among the major trade states. Meeting annually since 1975, these minilateral summit meetings have been successful overall by promoting free trade and periodically revitalizing the GATT process. That success waned in recent years, however, as relations became more adversarial in an intensely competitive world economy experiencing slow growth in the 1980s and the early 1990s.[10] For instance, the 1994 summit in Naples, Italy, hardly accomplished anything worthwhile. Cooperative patterns held, nevertheless, and a rise in world trade in the latter 1990s eased G-7 relations. The G-7 is an informal arrangement, but the staffs of foreign and economic ministers do plan the agenda and position papers before national leaders meet. After the Denver summit of 1997, the G-7 became known as the G-8 with Russia's deepening participation.

Although the OECD and G-7 help guide a cooperative regime of major trade states, on occasion bitter quarrels portending trade wars have tested the limits of the regime's resilience. For instance, a major dispute in 1992 between the United States and the EU over agricultural subsidies threatened to collapse the Uruguay Round. The states involved were barely able to step back from the brink of a trade war. The United States wanted agricultural subsidies in Europe reduced so American farm products would be more competitive in the European market. The EU has a long-standing Community Agricultural Policy (CAP) that includes farm subsidies the EU regarded as off limits for cuts. This fracas became so intense that it harmed progress in other economic sectors of GATT, and twice, in Montreal in 1988 and Brussels in 1990, frustrated negotiators suspended talks.

The farm subsidy issue reached the flash point over French subsidies for oilseeds in 1992. The United States announced a punitive 200 percent tariff on $300 million worth of EU products, mostly French white wine. United States and European negotiators were finally able to devise a compromise that resuscitated the stalled Uruguay Round. The EU

© Tribune Media Services, Inc. All rights reserved. Reprinted with permission.

reformed the CAP by lowering the amount of support for Europeans farmers, and the United States agreed not to carry the issue before a GATT panel for investigation.[11]

How can a few farmers drive their governments to the point of a trade war and the probable collapse of the GATT process? In the United States, the agricultural sector amounts to 2 percent of this country's GNP, farmers number 3 percent of the American workforce, and agricultural products comprise 9 percent of America's foreign trade. In Europe, the agricultural sector is under 4 percent of the EU's total GNP, farmers make up 7½ percent of the workforce, and farm products account for 12 percent of foreign trade. Yet the rancor over agricultural trade between Washington and Brussels has accounted for almost half the charges of "unfair trade" under GATT rules.

The answer to the question about farmers' influence involves a paradox: The small number of farmers, on both sides of the Atlantic Ocean, allows them to be extremely well organized and to have powerful effects through lobbyists in their respective capitals. This paradox concerning the influence of farmers holds true for all the Western industrialized states.[12] Keeping in mind that farm subsidies were a new and volatile issue for the GATT process, we can say the agricultural compromise helped save the Uruguay Round from collapse. This compromise between the United States and the EU testifies to the viability of the cooperative regime as it operated through the OECD and G-7 networks. Ultimately, cooperation prevailed over conflict.

GLOBALISM VERSUS REGIONALISM

The question now is whether global patterns in trade will hold and even grow when regional alternatives for economic cooperation are available. The belief that policy management at the global level is the most useful is called **globalism.** To the supporters of globalism, most human problems occur around the globe in some form. For this reason, concerted world action is necessary to handle matters such as pollution, human rights violations, and economic problems. **Regionalism** is the belief that regional management provides the most efficient way to serve states' interests. Regionalism offers the advantages of a smaller number of states that must agree, closer geographical proximity for meetings and the shipment of goods, and perhaps a shared culture that will facilitate agreement. Although scholars have argued over the respective merits of globalism and regionalism, the two are not necessarily incompatible cooperative ventures whether the functional area is human rights promotion, military security and peacekeeping activities, or economic cooperation.

When the Uruguay Round occasionally stalled, fearful concern turned to promising regional developments in the anticipation that intraregional trade would become the prominent international pattern. Miles Kahler has called this regional forecast a "factoid," a "created fact" repeated frequently and widely believed. Kahler, however, does not anticipate that national leaders will step back from global multilateralism to focus on regional arrangements.[13] No major trade state today has committed itself solely to a regional strategy, not even in Europe, where intraregional trade is strongest.[14] In 1988, the EC (later the EU) issued a declaration called the "International Role of the European Community" that claimed further economic integration in Europe would not only contribute to economic growth in that region but stimulate global growth as well.[15]

The successful completion of the Uruguay Round, following immediately behind advances in the EU and NAFTA, suggest regional developments are compatible with global ones and may even boost them. The reason for this compatibility is that the forces propelling regionalism are liberal, not protectionist. In practice, regional arrangements not only stimulate national economic growth for member-states but prepare those countries to face growing competition outside their region. Although the EU has the highest level of intraregional trade, it has always shown great interest in GATT rules and norms for global trade, and it remains a pioneering experiment for further global liberalization by developing the most elaborate set of institutions for cooperation. In addition, NAFTA is proving to be a trade arrangement contributing to global trade, not one diverting previously global trade into an intraregional pattern within North America. As NAFTA MNCs become more efficient through regional trade, they can look outward for more trade opportunities.

Presently interregional trade has a share of international trade equal to that of intraregional trade. This pattern should hold because major trade states from different regions remain dependent on one another.[16] The mutual dependence and mutual vulnerability of Japan and the United States epitomize this situation. As mentioned in the last chapter, Japan counts on sales to American consumers, and the United States needs Japanese loans to operate its government. Trade in this bilateral relationship involves $150 billion a year, and Japanese investors hold more than $100 billion in U.S. Treasury bonds.[17] By region, more than half of the Western Hemisphere's exports and two-thirds of Asia's exports move outside their respective regions. For instance, Mercosur (a common market for Argentina, Brazil, Paraguay, and Uruguay formed in 1991) has the EU as its major trade partner.[18] In contrast, Europe's extraregional exports are only one-third of its trade. Nonetheless, the United States, Japan, and the countries of western Europe all count on their extraregional trade to sustain their national economies.[19] For instance, U.S. exports amounted to 12 percent of its national economy in 1996, up from 7 percent a decade ago. Last year's exports were $607 billion, and U.S. corporate affiliates overseas produced and sold $2 trillion in goods.

Several important forces that support the global pattern of trade are at work. First, a global framework for the governance of international trade is in place and continues to evolve. In addition to the Bretton Woods system and the WTO, agencies within the UN System, such as the International Telecommunications Union, the International Civil Aviation Organization, and the International Maritime Organization, help regulate and facilitate global communications and global shipping networks. Second, although the United States' hegemon status has declined, its free trade norms now infuse global governance, and the world is more receptive to Western economic and democratic values than ever before.[20] Third, the fact that the major trade states are on different continents while other important, rising trade states—the NICs such as Brazil, China, and Mexico—are scattered about the globe buttresses the global pattern. Fourth, nearly 200 states have a wide range of needs and wants that only a global base of resources can satisfy since natural resources exist unevenly on the planet. If we recall David Ricardo's principle of comparative advantage from Chapter Eight, we can reason that a global set of trading states will be more cost efficient in products than a regional set. Finally, MNCs, as important economic actors controlling ever-larger volumes of trade and capital investments, have global reach as part of their strategies for efficiency's sake. Consequently, they compel a global marketplace to form and encourage multilateral trade liberalization to span the globe.[21]

We have learned that postwar cooperation, beginning with the Bretton Woods system, has expanded into a global liberal order moving ever deeper into free trade practices. As a result, just between 1990 and 1996, world trade grew from $7 trillion to $11 trillion. Ex-communist states and many states of the South are anxious to join the mainstream liberal order. Further, the global pattern of cooperation is holding even though several important regional developments co-exist with the WTO. The regional developments are mostly compatible with and actually boost world economic growth. Unmatched European economic integration, the North American Free Trade Agreement, and Asian consultation over economic matters are the most important regional developments today.

EUROPEAN ECONOMIC INTEGRATION

Facing the Second World War's devastation and an increasingly hostile Soviet Union, western Europe followed a special strategy. Learning from the cooperation of dispersing funds from the Marshall Plan of 1947, and with the strong encouragement of the United States, European leaders worked together to rebuild the western European economy. Since the postwar era, European national economies have merged into a deepening **economic integration.** This merger of national economies came about through a series of progressive steps that represent the highest level of integration in the contemporary state system. The

European accomplishment is a spectacular one when we recall that Europe provided the world with the legal concept of sovereign state independence and the emotion-laden identity of nationalism.

Steps of Economic Integration

The first step toward European economic integration was the formation of the *European Coal and Steel Community (ECSC)* in 1951, followed by the *European Economic Community (EEC,* sometimes called the "Common Market") in 1958, and the *European Atomic Energy Community (EURATOM)* in 1958. The ECSC was a **free trade area** that dropped tariff barriers among its member-states. The EEC was both a free trade area and a **customs union,** meaning that besides free trade, the member-states practiced a common tariff policy toward nonmember states. Then the member-states of these three organizations merged into the *European Community (EC)* in 1967. The six countries in the merger were Belgium, France, Germany (then West Germany), Italy, Luxembourg, and the Netherlands. Although the EEC occasionally had enjoyed the sobriquet of "common market," the EC was much closer to **common market** status by practicing not only free trade in merchandise goods but also free transborder movement of labor and capital. In addition, the EC developed a permanent political structure for coordinating joint economic policy.

The expansion of the EC to 12 states, doubling its size, was itself a major step. Joining the EC in 1973 were Denmark, Great Britain, and Ireland. Greece entered the EC in 1981, and Portugal and Spain joined in 1986. In 1978 and 1979, the EC agreed to move toward a *European Monetary System (EMS)* to regulate its currency exchanges and proposed the *European Currency Unit (ECU)* (also called the "Euro") as a future single currency for all member-states. In time, steps took place as well to move the participating European states into an **economic union.** Besides a common currency, the new European Union (EU) is to have a central bank, a common fiscal policy, open borders with the end of customs inspections, and harmonization of tax and social policies. These major developments arose from the *Single Europe Act* of 1986 and the *Treaty of Maastricht* of 1991.

When Jacques Delors, a French Socialist and former French finance minister, became president of the EC Commission at the end of 1984, he reinvigorated the EC integration process by persuading member-states to accept the Single Europe Act (SEA).[22] Proposed in 1985, agreed to in 1986, and ratified in 1987, the SEA called for a "borderless Europe" by the end of 1992, allowing goods, persons, capital investment, and services to move across member-states' borders without hindrance, including the elimination of customs inspections.[23] As intended, the SEA boosted the EC economy with a rise in employment, investment, and GNP growth rates.[24] The SEA allowed Europe to offer stronger global competition to Japan and the United States.[25] To make decision making more efficient, the SEA changed the unit-veto system of the European Council to a qualified majority rule, a change needed as the EC increased from 6 to 12 members.[26] The SEA was not an act of idealism, unity for unity's sake, but a matter of converging national interests around an intensified liberal order to bring greater prosperity to the member-states.[27]

Building from the momentum of the SEA, the EC member-states negotiated the Treaty of Maastricht (also known as the Treaty of European Union) in December 1991 calling for extensive integration in several areas. Ratifications by the 12 member-states were to be complete by the end of 1992. Primarily, Maastricht terms called for a central European bank and the use of the ECU as a common currency by 1997, if possible, but no later than 1999. Probably banks will regularly use the ECU in that year and ECU notes will be available to the EU publics in 2002. The bank and currency changes would occur in 1997 only if seven countries properly strengthened their economies along the following criteria: a low inflation rate, similar interest rates for loans, a reduced government budget deficit, an accumulated national debt below 60 percent of a country's GDP, and a stable national currency. If seven member-states failed to meet these criteria, then in 1999, those that were ready would join the central bank, and the citizens of the qualified states would use the ECU currency.[28] Denmark and Great Britain reduced the potential of the unionization process by opting out of using the single currency and resisting participation in a central bank.

The banking and currency steps would change the EMS into an *Economic and Monetary Union (EMU)*. The EMS began in 1979 as a **monetary union,** or a system for regulating currency exchanges. The ECU was a reserve currency after 1979 with bank transfers, letters of credit, traveler's checks, and other economic flows denominated in ECUs. By at least 1999, some citizens of the participating countries may have ECU money in their pockets. The ECU is to be a composite currency, based on member-state currencies, that could range from the inflation-prone Italian lira to the sound German mark, appreciated in many quarters as a "safe haven" currency. A common currency eliminates transaction costs and questions about the convertibility of one country's currency into another's. Understandably, a single currency for a region will facilitate and increase trade.[29] Yet a single currency also calls on Europeans to cross not only a monetary line but an important psychological one by giving up the prominent national symbol of a national currency. With this unionization process under way by 1992, many writers began to call the EC the European Union (EU).

Another term of the Treaty of Maastricht was to accept and implement the *Social Charter* of 1989. Great Britain refused to be a party to the Social Charter at Maastricht, producing a major setback in the European integrative process. Previously, all member-states of the EU had accepted new terms together and took no backward step from the integrative process. The Social Charter dealt with socioeconomic rights of workers, including such issues as safety and health standards, the protection of children, and equal treatment of men and women.[30] Great Britain's government, long controlled by the Conservative Party, had spent years beating back labor's privileged position in the British economy and its demands for more socioeconomic protection. The political costs might have been high at home if the Conservative Party had accepted a policy agenda similar to that of its nemesis, the Labour Party. Choosing not to harmonize with Europe's liberal labor policy, the consequence for British workers may be less freedom to move about Europe in search of work.[31] The Labour Party's victory in 1997 probably will not change matters much since its ideological stance is less socialist today and more moderate.

The Treaty of Maastricht also provides for EU citizenship in addition to national citizenship. A citizen of France or Germany, for instance, is a citizen of the EU as well. Citizens of the EU member-states can travel freely among EU countries, vote in any country if in residence, work in any country, petition the European Parliament, and use the diplomatic service of any EU country if needed. Whether psychological feelings of "Europeanness," similar to national identities, will wax into place and reinforce EU citizenship is an unknown.[32]

EU Defense and Foreign Policy

Further, Maastricht terms provide for common defense and foreign policies, although these policy areas lack the definition associated with economic unionization. The EU adopted the *Western European Union (WEU*—Belgium, France, Germany, Great Britain, Greece, Italy, Luxembourg, the Netherlands, Portugal, and Spain), a defense arrangement that dates back to the 1948 Brussels Pact and today includes most of the EU membership. This WEU development has caused some uneasiness on the part of the United States, the traditional leader of NATO. The EU, however, claims the WEU will strengthen Europe's role in NATO rather than supplant NATO. WEU forces may grow as large as 50,000 troops by building around a French-German brigade of 4,000 soldiers, organized in 1988 outside the NATO framework. The "Eurocorps," as planned, will locate in Strasbourg, France, and will be on call for NATO services in an emergency.[33]

The EU's chief achievement and greatest source of unity in foreign policy has been the protection of its interests in GATT rounds. Another economic interest concerns European neighbors. In its EC days, the EU maintained a healthy trade relationship with the *European Free Trade Area (EFTA),* which in 1991 included Austria, Finland, Iceland, Liechtenstein, Norway, Sweden, and Switzerland. In 1991 and 1992, as the EC was moving toward economic union status, it tightened trade relations with the EFTA by forming the *European Economic Area.* However, some members of the EFTA, witnessing the unionization of the EC and fearing economic marginalization, applied for membership in the new EU. EFTA countries, after all, contained only 10 percent of the population of the EU countries, and their total GDP was less than that of Germany.[34] Austria, Finland, Norway, and Sweden applied for membership and held popular referendums on joining the EU in 1994. These countries became members in the EU in 1995, except for Norway. Through popular voting, Norway has said no twice to the EU. Norway has oil wealth and well-managed fisheries that it does not care to share with others. Evidently, Norwegians, correctly or incorrectly, calculated they had a better economic future outside the EU framework.

Another policy area of note is the EU's concern over eastern Europe. In addition to loans, aid, and trade, some eastern European countries want membership in the EU. The republics of Czech, Hungary, and Poland have adopted SEA-type legislation to harmonize their national economies with the EU in the hope of entering in 1999. The EU officials have remained noncommittal.[35] In addition to problems of privatizing a communist economy, parts of eastern Europe have experienced the turmoil of ethnic strife, particularly Bosnia. In 1993 and 1994, the EU, along with the United Nations, sent mediators, who struggled patiently but vainly to end the fighting. In 1995, NATO became the international organization taking center stage in Bosnia and, through negotiations and the placement of a large NATO military force, ended ethnic warfare there.

The Prospect of Political Integration

An interesting question is whether the EU, if it completes the economic integration process, can evolve further through a **political integration** process, with the 15 member-states becoming a single political entity, eliminating separate sovereign statuses. Some theorists have thought that economic and even political integration would occur through **spillover** effects: cooperation in one functional area leading to cooperation in another area, gradually drawing states into a new entity. For instance, free trade in coal and steel led to a "common market" in merchandise goods that, in turn, produced EC political institutions to coordinate an increasingly complex economic arrangement.

Today the EU clearly reflects "pooled sovereignty" of separate states willing to forge policy together for the common interest, but the EU does not amount to a general surrender of sovereign authority to a higher level. The EU is **supranational,** meaning EU institutions suggest the decisions member-states frequently accept. In some cases, especially concerning the decisions of the European Court of Justice, member-states must accept authoritative decisions. The essence of traditional state sovereignty remains intact, however.

The conflict over the EU's political potential is a long-standing one between the *supranationalists* and the *intergovernmentalists.* Speaking for the supranationalists, in 1950, French Foreign Minister Robert Schuman called for European unification in a historical document now known as the *Schuman Plan.* Better known is Jean Monnet, a leader with a 40-year career in the public service of France and European organizations. Decades ago, he promoted the idea of an ultimate unification into a federal arrangement, a "United States of Europe." The most recent advocate of deeper integration has been Jacques Delors, president of the EU Commission from 1985–1995, who pressed for the SEA and the Treaty of Maastricht. Following Delors's zeal, the selection of Jacques Santer, a former Luxembourg prime minister, probably is a more conservative choice. The EU bureaucracy also is a repository of pan-European values, always wanting to harmonize more aspects of European life.

The best-known intergovernmentalists are President Charles de Gaulle of France in the 1960s and Prime Minister Margaret Thatcher of Great Britain in the 1980s. Intergovernmentalists, in keeping with a realist tradition, see EU cooperation basically as a bargaining process among sovereign states. Both de Gaulle and Thatcher decried the notion of a "European superstate" and insisted that Europe remain a "Europe of sovereign states." More recently, Prime Minister John Major of Great Britain makes sure the intergovernmentalist view remains influential in the EU. Great Britain has regularly been a lukewarm participant in the EU, for example, choosing not to participate in the EMU and the Social Charter. Jacques Chirac, the conservative and nationalistic president of France, may prove to be an intergovernmentalist on EU issues as well.[36] Left to Germany is the leadership role for federalist ambitions that may someday create a "United States of Europe."

A review of EU institutions will reflect the tension between supranationalism and intergovernmentalism. Supranationally oriented institutions are the Commission, the European Parliament, and the Court of Justice. The Council of Ministers and the European Council represent the intergovernmental point of view.

The *Commission* consists of representatives appointed by the member-states. However, these commissioners are not the representatives of their governments; rather, together they are the embodiment of the European unity idea, and they take an oath of allegiance to the EU. Commissioners are free from any political interference by their home governments. The Commission symbolizes supranationalism more than any other European institution. Located in Brussels, Belgium, the Commission takes the initiative to recommend policy to the Council of Ministers and often sets the agenda for government decision making. A president guides the Commission in its work and supervises over 13,000 civil servants who help administer EU policy and rules. Under President Jacques Delors, the Commission was vigorous in setting the pace for the EU, but, as mentioned, President Jacques Santer may prove less bold about integrative proposals.

The EU *European Parliament,* located in Strasbourg, France, is the first and only experiment in transnational democracy. The Parliament dates from 1952 as part of the ECSC. Although the Parliament cannot pass laws, as parliaments normally do, it can review the EU budget and sometimes block executive proposals. The European Parliament has the power to dismiss the Commission with a two-thirds vote, though this act has never taken place. The Parliament's public profile and importance increased after 1979 when the citizens of the member-states elected delegates directly. When there were 12 member-states, the Parliament had 518 delegates, but with three new EU members, it will probably have at least 550 delegates. The Parliament has requested that its size not exceed 599 delegates irrespective of the future number of EU member-states. Although the number of parliamentarians each country has is approximately commensurate with the country's population size, these delegates do not sit as national blocs. Parliamentarians usually sit in political groups reflecting the ideological spectrum current in Europe. Although national positions can occur, Parliament is basically supranational in its views.

The EU's *Court of Justice* also is in Strasbourg. The Court formed in 1952 as an element of the ECSC and has remained an important factor in European integration. The Court has 13 judges appointed to 6-year terms by the member-states. The Court adjudicates disputes and, using the EC/EU treaties as the "highest law," can overrule conflicting laws of member-states. The Court of Justice acts as final arbiter of the EU system and has gone further than any other EU institution in limiting national autonomy. The caseload of the Court exploded from 50 cases a year in the 1960s to 300–400 cases a year by the 1980s. Norms that Court decisions reflect are free trade, democratic conduct, human rights, and high environmental standards. The Court of Justice has been a staunch adversary of the intergovernmental viewpoint over the years.

As an intergovernmental body, crucial decisions still belong to the *Council of Ministers.* Cabinets of the member-states send ministers that form the Council. These ministers are the spokespersons of the current governments of the member-states. The particular ministers sent from the national cabinets depend on the subject at hand, but most Council meetings involve agricultural, finance, and foreign ministers. The 15 member-states enjoy voting power according to their size. Since the SEA, the Council now approves policy decisions by majority vote except for a unanimity requirement regarding new members and broad, new policy choices. Three states can block a decision, but collective decision making tends to pull ministers together, with ministers sometimes voting in ways they normally would not choose because of group influences.

It is at the high executive level of the Council that some members want more majority decision making and less protection for national sovereignty as exercised through the use of vetoes. British leaders especially resist any further watering down of their veto power. The exact procedures of the EU are regularly under review, such as in the "Intergovernmental Conference" held in Turin, Italy, beginning in 1996 and lasting into 1997.

In 1975, the *European Council* formed outside the EC/EU process and is a meeting of heads of government (the prime ministers and presidents) of EU member-states. Only with the SEA of 1986 did the European Council become a legal part of the EC and now continues its role in the EU. The European Council, through summit diplomacy, tries to

TABLE 9.2
Intraregional National Characteristics of EU Countries

Country	GNP (1992 US$)	GNP per capita (1992 US$)	Population (2000 est.)	PQLI
Germany	1877 (trillion)	23,360 (thousand)	81.7 (million)	98
France	1296	22,630	59.0	99
Italy	1187	20,790	57.3	98
Britain	1046	18,110	59.0	98
Spain	561 (billion)	14,230	39.8	98
Netherlands	316	20,850	15.9	100
Sweden	238	27,500	9.0	100
Belgium	214	21,360	10.2	98
Austria	178	22,790	8.1	97
Denmark	136	26,310	5.2	98
Finland	114	22,690	5.2	99
Greece	76	7,390	10.6	97
Portugal	74	7,510	9.8	91
Ireland	45	12,850	3.5	97
Luxembourg	14	35,000	0.4	98

Sources: GNP is from Table 38, GNP per capita is from Table 28, and population size estimates for the year 2000 are from Table 33 of the *Human Development Report 1995* (New York: Oxford University Press, 1995). The physical quality of life index is from *Foreign Policy and Developing Countries* (Washington, D.C.: Overseas Development Council, 1991).

reach agreements on broad issues and policy directions. The European Council is critical to the EU process and can block or promote supranationalism with its intergovernmental, sovereign powers. Ultimately, the future of the EU is in its hands.[37]

Against a historical backdrop of war-prone European states that jealously guarded their sovereignty, the deep integration of an economic union with supranational institutions is a monumental accomplishment. It is as though western Europeans, in a short time, decided to catapult themselves from the Hobbesian world of anarchy and war into the Kantian community of "perpetual peace" held together by commerce. After the Second World War, these Europeans barely doffed their collective hat to a Grotian society of appreciable cooperation before loading themselves into the catapult.

Western Europe has accomplished a common market, moving into economic union status, of 15 states with about 370 million people enjoying an economy of more than $7 trillion. The EU has helped provide one of the highest standards of living in the world. A major reason European integration has been possible is that wealth among most of the member-states of the EU is fairly even. The GNP per capita income and physical quality of life index (PQLI), introduced in Chapter Eight, are in the same broad range for most of the EU membership, as Table 9.2 shows. Although population size and GNP differences are large, one set of states within the EU does not tend to exploit another set. In fact, the EU leadership worries about raising the economies of the "Poor Four"—Greece, Ireland, Portugal, and Spain—to avoid a "two-speed EU" and to promote economic justice. If it happens, the entrance of several eastern European countries into the EU will almost certainly intensify EU disparities for a time.

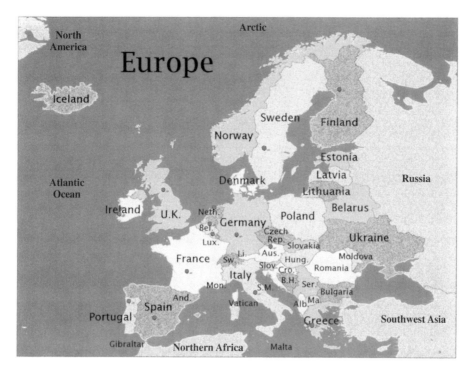

Members of the EU

A problem that dampens enthusiasm over movement to an EU central bank and a single currency is the "Eurosclerosis" of a slowed economy, a problem shared throughout Europe. The European economy has not picked up from the recent world recession as well as that of the United States, with inflation and unemployment behaving negatively and sometimes reaching double-digit figures. Further integration, however, may be the remedy that will open up European economic arteries and push economic growth in the region.

Another problem that causes concern is the key role Germany plays in the EU. This role will loom larger as the reunified, ex-communist, former East German *lander* catch up to the economic speed of the former West German *lander* and add to the overall economic "critical mass" of Germany. The German central bank and German currency will have an even greater impact on EU affairs. If Germany's EU partners perceive too much power and too many advantages flowing to Germany, this perception could have some disturbing effects on the unity of the EU.

Sometimes a special episode erupts and causes much divisiveness within the EU membership, as in the case of mad cow disease (a fatal brain infection called BSE). Mad cow disease killed more than 10 people in Britain in 1996, and the rest of Europe refused to import British beef, thus threatening an annual income for Britain of $780 million. In retaliation, Britain began vetoing decisions within the EU framework until it leveraged a compromise into place. Britain tightened its inspections for the disease and destroyed 150,000 potentially contaminated cattle in the hope that exports of British beef would resume.

Despite its monumental accomplishment, the process of European integration obviously has not always been a smooth one, and future disappointments are possible. While the SEA came through with considerable government and public support in the mid-1980s, the ratification of the Treaty of Maastricht ran into strong resistance during 1992. Although Ireland's referendum adequately approved the Treaty of Maastricht, Denmark had to vote twice in a public referendum before winning approval, and France's public barely accepted Maastricht's terms. It may have been fortunate for the European integration process that the other EU member-states did not use public referendums in their ratification processes. The European public has not been as supportive of integration as have European leaders in general.

The Maastricht treaty did emerge ratified but tarnished as economic unionization struggled to move forward. The largest setback may prove to be Denmark's and Great Britain's decisions to avoid the single currency and the EU's coordination of national central banks. A true economic union can evolve only if all member-states use the same currency and coordinate their central banking systems. The combination of a recessionary European economy in the early 1990s and the Maastricht terms, reaching into key areas of sovereignty such as displacing national currency, have combined to raise profound doubts about the legitimacy of further integration.[38] Completing all stages of the EMU for all member-states will be difficult. Even the stronger economies may not be ready for a central bank and a single currency by 1999. These qualifications regarding the smoothness of the integration process do not, however, diminish the historically important accomplishment of an integrated and prosperous western Europe. This accomplishment deserves the admiration of other regions and offers a worthwhile model for a global-level international community in the future.

THE EMERGENCE OF NAFTA

Early European success with economic cooperation has encouraged some 25 regional economic organizations of some type. These are mostly free trade areas and do not aspire to the deep integration of the EU. Some are hobbling along and fading, while others are vibrant and growing. One does not read nearly as much about the Central American Common Market (1961—five member-states) and the Andean Pact (1969—five member-states) as about the EU or NAFTA, but these organizations and others are continuing to improve the national economies of their member-states. Still other organizations are new but promise economic rewards to states in return for opening their trade to others, for example, the Black Sea Economic Cooperation (1992—11 member-states, including ex-communist countries) and the Group of Three (1995—Colombia, Mexico, and Venezuela).

The most important regional organization to form since the beginning of the European integration process is the North American Free Trade Agreement (NAFTA). Its importance derives from the participation of the world's leading trade state, the United States, anchoring a trilateral arrangement with Canada and Mexico. The United States, motivated by highly competitive global trade, is trying to improve its economic efficiency to compete more effectively on the global level.

American, Canadian, and Mexican leaders negotiated NAFTA in 1992, ratified it in 1993, and set this free trade arrangement in motion in 1994. This arrangement has a total population and GNP about as large as the EU, but does not nearly match the EU's depth of integration. NAFTA creates a free trade area with 380 million people sharing a $6.9 trillion combined GNP.

NAFTA calls for the elimination of most tariffs and NTBs over a period of 10 years. Some free trade agreements cover only merchandise trade, but with NAFTA service industries, such as banking, advertising, and insurance, also are to become transborder opportunities. Further, foreign investment flows can more easily cross borders with less hindrance, including investments in the Mexican oil industry previously operated as an exclusive government corporation.

NAFTA does not go nearly as far as the EU in practicing economic norms of the liberal model. It is not even a customs union arrangement for coordinating tariffs against those outside NAFTA. Nor does NAFTA have a plethora of institutions to give it a supranational life. There is only a commission of arbitration to handle trade disputes, a commission inherited from the American-Canadian free trade agreement of 1989. Also, the three trade partners do not have plans to move toward an economic and monetary union or to operate according to a common social and economic charter.

Although the EU has economic differences among its member-states, the differences within NAFTA are much greater. The per capita income difference between Canada and the United States on the one hand and Mexico on the other is sharp, as Table 9.3 shows. The PQLI score for Mexico is notably lower too. Moreover, NAFTA does not have sharing

TABLE 9.3
Intraregional National Characteristics of NAFTA Countries

Country	GNP (1992 US$)	GNP per capita (1992 US$)	Population (2000 est.)	PQLI
United States	6081 (trillion)	23,830 (thousand)	275.1	98
Canada	600 (billion)	21,070	31.0	99
Mexico	310 (billion)	3,510	102.4	87

Sources: GNP is from Tables 20 and 38, per capita income is from Tables 12 and 28, and population size is from Tables 16 and 33 of the *Human Development Report 1995* (New York: Oxford University Press, 1995). The PQLI is from *Foreign Policy and Developing Countries* (Washington, D.C.: Overseas Development Council, 1991).

arrangements to raise Mexico's economic level as the EU does for its "Poor Four." At least Mexico has the advantage of being the country of the South with the best access to the behemoth, consumer-oriented economy of the United States. Another difference is the contrast between the "critical mass" of the United States in terms of population and GNP size (see Table 9.3) and the population sizes and GNPs of Canada and Mexico.

If the United States is no longer a global hegemon it is a towering regional hegemon in the Western Hemisphere. The danger here is that when disparate states integrate their economies, a good chance exists that uneven benefits will flow from the cooperative arrangement. As neorealists warn, uneven benefits can cause dissatisfaction with the arrangement and undermine cooperation. NAFTA's future may depend on all three parties perceiving enough major benefits, though possibly uneven, to make the free trade arrangement worthwhile.

The NAFTA venture should last because it builds on the platform of a long-standing trade pattern. Canada and Mexico conduct over 80 percent of their foreign trade with the United States. The United States, in turn, carries on about 20 percent of its foreign trade with Canada and nearly 10 percent with Mexico. Canadian-Mexican trade is tiny by comparison but may grow because of NAFTA. Particularly interesting is the point that over a span of years, Canada has been America's most important trade partner. Inundated with news about Japanese imports to the United States and the adversarial relationship between these two countries, most Americans fail to realize Canada's historic economic importance to their country. Finally, if NAFTA expands trilateral trade, Canada, Mexico, and the United States, with more efficient national economies and MNCs, will compete more vigorously on the global level.

Formalizing historic trade ties through NAFTA has involved some difficulty, however. International economic arrangements, such as marriages, are good ideas that do not come together and operate without some problems. Canadians worried, as they did before NAFTA, that closer economic relations with the United States would hurt the Canadian national identity. These closer relations could result in the American economy and culture absorbing the economy and culture of Canada. For instance, only about 3 to 5 percent of the movies shown in Canada are of Canadian origin, with the bulk of the remainder coming from the United States.[39] Also, Canadian leaders have feared more Canadian industries will move southward to the United States or Mexico seeking cheaper labor pools.

Mexican reservations about joining NAFTA were probably fewer than those in Canada or the United States. A critical problem did arise in Mexico in the first year of NAFTA's

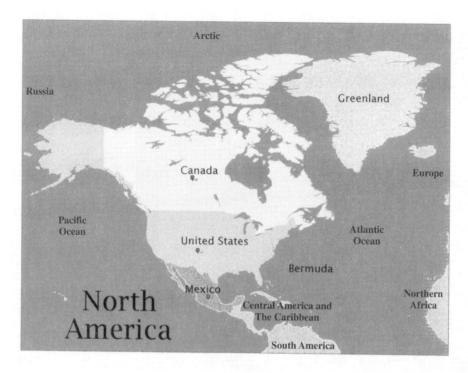

NAFTA Members

operation and caused concern well beyond NAFTA. President Ernesto Zedillo Ponce de Leon was not in office for even a month in December 1994 when a run on the Mexican peso began, dropping the peso's worth by more than one-third. Mexico's balance of payments in foreign trade suffered a $28 billion deficit during 1994, and the Mexican government did not have the reserves to pay for the goods. Nor could the Mexican government buy up its own currency in foreign countries to prevent the peso's decline. Further, foreign investors began to withdraw their funds, and currency speculators rapidly exchanged pesos for other currencies. Consequently, the Mexican government could not sustain the peso, which was pegged to the American dollar, and delinked the two currencies.

Not only did Mexicans find themselves poorer almost overnight and unable to continue their rising purchases from the United States, but Mexico's NAFTA partners, the World Bank, and the IMF worried that Mexico's default on payments would lead to national bankruptcy. In 1995, President Bill Clinton and leaders of the World Bank and the IMF arranged an emergency loan package of nearly $50 billion, with the U.S. share of this amount growing to about $20 billion. In the same year, President Zedillo made a repayment of $700 million on this emergency loan to symbolize Mexican responsibility and stability, and, in 1996, Mexico made advance payments on the loan to further bolster confidence in the Mexican economy. Nevertheless, it will probably be several years before Mexico can return to the vitality in foreign trade that it enjoyed in the early months of 1994.

Much social unrest continues to plague Mexico, a country traditionally prone to rebellion by an impoverished peasantry in need of basic reforms. Today there are three active

© 1992 Jimmy Margulies, *The Record*

guerrilla forces in the rural north and south of Mexico, though violent contact with the Mexican Army is light. Corruption at high governmental levels, in part fueled by drug trafficking, also exists, as does a reluctance to move to full-blown democracy, especially on the part of the PRI, Mexico's historically dominant political party. Problems such as these, as well as the peso crisis, discourage foreign investors that could help expand the Mexican economy. Yet Mexican finance minister Guillermo Ortiz told a press conference in late 1996 that Mexico could expect a 4 percent economic growth rate, 800,000 new jobs, and $8 billion in foreign direct investment in 1997.[40]

For the United States, NAFTA was a sharp issue in the presidential campaign of 1992. Republican president George Bush was a free trader by principle and a strong advocate for NAFTA, as was Democratic presidential candidate Bill Clinton. Ross Perot, an independent candidate for the presidency, played heavily on fears that thousands of American jobs would move to Mexico. Organized labor fought against NAFTA for the same reason. Labor leaders, moreover, feared working conditions and pay might decline to meet new Mexican competition. In addition, many environmental groups raised the concern that NAFTA would encourage more factories to set up in the *Maquiladoras* belt below the Rio Grande River in Mexico, where authorities have been lax about enforcing Mexican environmental laws. Environmentalists have claimed that for American goods to compete, American industries would demand weaker environmental laws. Environmental laws presumably drive up production costs, resulting in higher prices for consumers that leave a company less competitive.

President Bush argued that under NAFTA arrangements, the rise in exports to Mexico would create as many new jobs within the United States as old jobs lost to Mexico. The jobs lost would be the simpler "screwdriver" assembly jobs, and the jobs won would be better-paying high-tech and service industry employment. It was fallacious for Ross Perot and organized labor to argue, in "zero-sum" terms, that jobs won in Mexico were jobs lost in the United States. Until the devaluation of the peso, the rise in export-import trade between Mexico and the United States stimulated job growth in both countries. Nonetheless, ultra-conservative Pat Buchanan, who held strong protectionist views on trade, continued to harp on the issue of lost jobs due to NAFTA in the 1996 presidential race.

Ratification of NAFTA occurred in 1993 after Bill Clinton had won the presidency. President George Bush had assumed NAFTA was on a "fast track" to congressional acceptance without changes. However, to please labor and environmentalists, and their congressional supporters, President Clinton had to move quickly to save NAFTA by arranging "side agreements" with America's trade partners that guaranteed labor and environmental standards.[41]

NAFTA's early boost to trade and jobs in 1994 prompted the *Summit of the Americas* to meet and propose a free trade association for North and South America. This association might take the name "American Free Trade Association" or the "Free Trade Association of the Americas." The Summit of the Americas took place at the end of 1994 in Miami, Florida, with 34 countries in attendance. Already Mexico has new ties in the Group of Three with two South American countries, Colombia and Venezuela. As South America, once the hotbed for dependency theorists and economic nationalists advocating import substitution, continues to democratize and to open its economies to market forces, the chances that a Free Trade Association of the Americas will take place increase. If this free trade association occurs in 10 to 20 years, it will involve nearly a billion people and possibly a $15 trillion economy. A meeting of trade ministers from the Western Hemisphere, including U.S. trade representative Mickey Kantor, met in 1996 in Colombia, still expressing hope for a free trade association to include all or most of the American states of the Western Hemisphere.

In addition, in early 1997, President Bill Clinton invited President Eduardo Frei of Chile to visit and try to sell Congress on the idea of Chile joining a reconstructed NAFTA. President Clinton has expressed the ambitious aim of creating a Western Hemispheric free trade zone by the year 2005. Although critics stress further job losses on top of those that have already gone to Mexico, America has experienced a net gain of 8 million jobs since 1991 as this country has become more efficient.

PROSPECTS FOR REGIONALISM IN THE ASIAN-PACIFIC AREA

Because of the residual effects of colonialism, Cold War distractions, and a huge geographical expanse, the Asian-Pacific area has a low degree of interaction.[42] Although a recent focus on regionalism in the Asian-Pacific area is discernible, this area has the least organization for economic cooperation of the three regions under study in this chapter. Yet several motives exist for stronger economic cooperation than is now observable. As Pacific traders, Canada and the United States want to make sure they will continue their trade roles in the Asia-Pacific area. Japan flirts with the idea of forming an organization around itself to match its actual hegemonic status. Moreover, some Asian countries wish to see freer trade increase already robust growth rates. Finally, Japan and the "Asian Tigers," with their export-growth strategies aimed largely at North America and Europe, fear that

Courtesy of *Free China Journal*

economic integration in North America and particularly in Europe will squeeze them out of critical markets. An Asian organization raising trade levels would provide compensatory trade for losses that might occur elsewhere.

Not surprisingly, a call from Australia in 1989 for a meeting of Pacific Rim countries found a responsive audience. The *Asia Pacific Economic Cooperation* forum (APEC) held its first summit in Seattle, Washington, in 1993. APEC is primarily a consultative forum with a small secretariat in Singapore. Its membership includes 18 countries (see Table 9.4). At a second summit in Bogor, Indonesia, in 1994, the APEC group called for its member-states to embrace both free trade and unrestricted transborder investments at some future time.[43] Yearly summits continue, with President Bill Clinton advocating at the 1996 summit in Singapore that tariffs on computers and other technology end in the year 2000, a position the APEC forum endorsed in principle.

While any further steps toward organization are uncertain, the consultative forum of APEC receives reinforcement from interested international nongovernmental organizations (INGOs). Since 1968, the *Pacific Trade and Development Conference* draws together government and university economists for discussions. Businesspeople and MNCs frequently consult together through the *Pacific Basin Economic Council* since 1967. Finally, the *Pacific Economic Cooperation Council,* from 1980 onward, allows academics, businesspeople, and government representatives to intermingle and exchange views.[44] These organizations were mentioned in Chapter Seven on diplomacy.

A core of six countries within APEC, the *Association of Southeast Asian Nations (ASEAN),* listed in Table 9.4, offers the only true intergovernmental organization for economic cooperation in the Asian-Pacific area. ASEAN formed as a political and

TABLE 9.4
Intraregional National Characteristics of APEC Countries

Country	GNP (1992 US$)	GNP per capita (1992 US$)	Population (2000 est.)	PQLI
United States	6,081 (trillion)	23,830 (thousand)	275.1 (million)	98
Japan	3,565	28,690	126.5	101
Canada	600 (billion)	21,070	31.0	99
China	568	480	1,284.6	84
South Korea	315	7,220	47.1	92
Mexico	310	3,510	102.4	87
Australia	308	17,730	19.2	99
Taiwan	209	10,000	21.3	95
Hong Kong	91	15,710	6.0	92
New Zealand	44	12,660	3.8	98
Chile	38	2,780	15.3	92
Papua NG	4	990	4.0	61
ASEAN states				
Indonesia	128	680	212.7	74
Thailand	105	1,840	61.9	87
Malaysia	53	2,830	22.3	86
Philippines	50	790	74.6	83
Singapore	47	16,970	3.0	93
Brunei	3.5 GDP	8,800 GDP per capita	0.3	79

Sources: Data for this table are from the same sources as Table 9.3. Data for Brunei are missing, and Taiwan is not in the tables of *Human Development Report 1995*. Economic data for Brunei (GDP) and Taiwan (GNP) are from *The World Almanac* (Mahwah, NJ: World Almanac Books, 1994).

economic consultative group in 1967, but, in 1992, decided to embark on a free trade arrangement that would gradually reduce tariffs over a 15-year period.[45] The approach of ASEAN to a free market status is tentative at best. Following a preferential trading arrangement in the 1980s, the ASEAN heads of government announced in 1992 the "Singapore Declaration." They called for an "open international economic regime" to make ASEAN countries more competitive at the global level.

The ASEAN Free Trade Agreement (AFTA), as planned, will have tariffs no higher than five percent of a good's worth by 2008. Non-Tariff Barriers (NTBs) are another issue that AFTA will discuss at a later, unspecified date. Not only is AFTA moving slowly on its free trade schedule, but it allows each member-state an "exclusion list" of goods that are outside the free trade system. If AFTA succeeds, it will be a free trade area of 330 million people with a combined GDP of $300 billion.[46] Finally, ASEAN recently accepted Myanmar (previously called Burma) into its fold as an observer and potential member. This happened in spite of the military government's repression of the Burmese democracy movement led by 1991 Nobel Peace Prize winner Aung San Suu Kyi.

One other Asian Pacific development is worthy of mention. In 1990, Malaysian prime minister Mahathir Mohamad proposed that an *East Asian Economic Group* organize around ASEAN under Japan's leadership. The Malaysian prime minister thought this organization

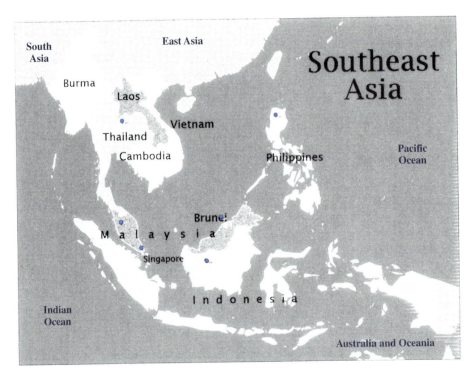

ASEAN Members

would loosen Asian dependence on exports to the United States. Japanese leaders have toyed with such a leadership role in recent years. They have referred to the analogy of Asian countries moving together as geese do in a V formation, with Japan as the lead goose. While Japanese leaders may speak of broad Asian-Pacific cooperation on diplomatic forums, at home these same leaders focus their attention on ASEAN countries and other nearby NICs.[47]

Economic cooperation through a free trade organization is an uncertainty in the Asia-Pacific area, except for tepid efforts by AFTA. The large number of states alone would make an organization difficult, but then too the economies and governments in the Asia-Pacific area are highly dissimilar. Besides the different economic levels of development and trade strategies, these countries include communist China (the largest Islamic country in the world), Indonesia, and several Western democracies such as Canada and the United States.[48]

A specific issue that looms over the Asian-Pacific group of states concerns human rights. Many Asian countries respond with vexation over Western views on prison, child labor, and other human rights issues. So far, their leaders have successfully gambled that their trade opportunities will keep Western economic flows coming while they continue to control their domestic economies and national populations as they see fit.[49]

Further, the more vibrant national economies in the area depend on neomercantilistic trade strategies with governments managing trade. These governments focus on shifting trade deficits to partners. Their trade philosophies leave them unprepared to let trade move freely across borders based entirely on market forces.

Finally, many Asian states already are enjoying robust trade and growth, with two-thirds of their trade being extraregional.[50] An intraregional shift in trade probably seems unnecessary and would be a departure from a trade pattern that has brought several Asian states considerable wealth. The Asian-Pacific area will have to handle its intraregional trade through consultative forums and the global WTO arrangement for the near future.

ECONOMIC COOPERATION AND INTERNATIONAL SOCIETY

The corresponding section of Chapter Eight on international society dealt with instruments of economic competition and conflict and the resulting stress placed on economic cooperation. Here we focus on the instruments of economic cooperation that are institutions states create to expand regional and global economies. In this era of economic cooperative ventures, transnationalists enjoy their heyday. The major states of today are trade states that are anxious to maintain and extend economic cooperation, not the military high achievers of realists. Because of major states' emphasis on trade, growing cooperation for mutual economic benefit is a pervasive feature of international society. Posing security threats is the ugly business of radical Third World states and terrorists.[51]

Transnationalists also observe that states have developed cooperative patterns through a learning process. Joseph S. Nye refers to "sociological liberalism," a process through which states learn new attitudes and a new definition of their interests.[52] The payoff of mutual benefits, such as economic rewards, draws states into this learning process.[53] Moreover, this learned cooperation occurs in a world of self-interested states without the authority of a world government.[54] The guiding force that allows economic cooperation to continue, according to transnationalists, is the governance of trade regimes. States are willing to cohere around rules and norms to receive the benefits of trade, benefits that derive from the free trade rules of economic liberalism. Regimes, including the WTO, EU, and NAFTA, allow states to feel secure about the future because these regimes institutionalize and enforce agreed-upon trade rules for the common good.

Modern cooperative patterns clearly outdate the views of realists, such as Hans Morgenthau, prevailing from the 1940s to the 1960s. Realists viewed economic policies merely as a tool to bolster political and military power.[55] Neorealists arrived on the academic scene in the 1970s and 1980s, in time to mount a charge against the increasingly recognized role of regimes. Stephen Krasner, for instance, views regimes, including those involved in trade arrangements, not as facilitators of cooperation among states but merely as institutions one step removed from sovereign states. For this reason, Krasner is doubtful that the supposed authority of regimes can shape state behavior in cooperative directions. For neorealists, regimes are epiphenomena that merely reflect the power distribution among states. They claim that regimes are unable to do much to mitigate the divisive aspects of power-seeking states operating amid anarchy.[56]

Joseph Grieco's study of the Tokyo Round of GATT, referred to in the corresponding section of Chapter Eight, found the GATT regime lacking because the European states resented the extra advantage for the United States that led to conflict. As a neorealist, Grieco concluded transnationalists underestimate the conflict problem of relative gains in trade.[57] With the advantage of hindsight, the author can say that Grieco saw a glass half empty when he could have seen one half full. This Tokyo Round finally ended with 35 percent tariff reductions in spite of United States–European quarreling. Then an even more successful Uruguay Round, though with its own attendant problems, took place some years later. Had either the Tokyo or Uruguay Rounds collapsed, Grieco's concern over relative gains would make a more lasting impression. Instead, the advantages of cooperation won out over the threat of relative-gains conflict.

Precious little about the trade relations of most states supports the model of *international anarchy,* despite some friction that occurs in negotiations. Actually, much about economic cooperation supports the model of *international society,* with an international system of states recognizing their growing interdependence. Rather than resisting the pulling force of interdependence, states respond positively to this global force and expand their economies through it. The epitome of international economic cooperation is the regional efforts of the EU.

The EU's *authority* is an extensive use of rules and norms through a highly developed IGO, but it does not amount to a central government. As a result, the states of the EU, as sovereign *actors,* are less important today than in the Europe of the 1930s and 1940s. The *orientation* of modern European states is to submerge their statehoods deeply into cooperative patterns for the greater good of all, although this process is not problem free.

Force is not a useful option among EU states as these states, through EU institutions, promote an *interaction* of economic and some political integration. The *issue* of redistributing wealth from richer to less fortunate states is able to exist in the EU, in contrast to the failed redistribution of wealth between North and South on the global level. Supranational *problem solving,* based on pooled sovereignties, goes well beyond the multilateral efforts in other regions and at the global level. The *consensus* within the EU over democracy, capitalism, and human rights is solid.

Furthermore, the successful economic cooperation of the EU, more than any other subject in this textbook, foreshadows the *international community* the world might hope to achieve. While no known inexorable force is pulling the world toward the EU model of international community, the EU does offer a living example of possibilities. The community notion falls short for the EU only because the 320 million people living in these countries probably invest their identities largely with France, Germany, or Great Britain instead of the EU. Their approach to the EU may be primarily pragmatic rather than emotional. A completed community has a strong, emotive sense of common identity.

CHAPTER SUMMARY

This chapter has focused on the institutions of economic cooperation and integration as the instruments of states. Leaving protectionism behind, the United States, as the undisputed global hegemon in the post–Second World War era, launched the beginning of a free trade regime in the form of the Bretton Woods system and, shortly afterward, the GATT. The Bretton Woods institution of the World Bank started organizational life as an aid to postwar recovery but then, with European recovery, shifted emphasis to the development of the Third World. The other major Bretton Woods institution, the IMF, began as a regulator of the world's currencies concerning their convertibility.

With balance of trade problems and threatened defaults of payments by many Third World countries, the IMF became a "lender of last resort" for the poor of the world economy.

GATT, intended as a temporary arrangement, lasted almost half a century until it became the WTO in 1995. Through a series of negotiation rounds, GATT reduced tariffs and NTBs, thus moving the world toward a liberal trade order. The WTO has operated similarly as a free trade regime but has had more institutional flesh than the GATT skeleton. Once, when the GATT process almost completely broke down during the Uruguay Round, the minilateral regimes of the OECD and the G-7 helped fashion a saving compromise.

One of the more troublesome developments for global economic cooperation, to some observers, has been the emergence of regional organizations that might divert trade away from a global pattern. More probably, the regional arrangements of the EU, NAFTA, and APEC forum are having the effect of increasing trade at the regional and global levels simultaneously. It appears that regional developments are strengthening the three regional economies, making it possible for the states involved to stay with global competition. The upshot is that the several regions remain as important markets for one another.

The EU is a well-integrated organization of 15 western European states. These states are moving far beyond free trade to form an economic union. EU policymaking is supranational, meaning it involves "pooling sovereignties." The EU countries are able to reach agreement among themselves and then act as a unit during negotiations in the GATT rounds. NAFTA is still new and involves the three North American states in a free trade arrangement that includes service industries but mainly trade goods. In the Asia-Pacific area, the 18 member-states are disparate in kind and follow such different policies that the conversion of the APEC forum, a consulting body, into a free trade regime is highly problematic. The subset states of ASEAN have done better about free trade, although the six member-states are moving sluggishly to reduce their tariffs within their free trade arrangement.

This textbook has followed a theme emphasizing the prospects for cooperation in international relations. Among the many dimensions of this subject, the international economy may represent the most impressive area of cooperation. Transnationalists have pointed to the emerging liberal economic order as proof that the world is knitting together through economic interdependence, an interdependence encouraging states to learn cooperative patterns for mutual benefits. While neorealists can correctly point out that uneven benefits may lead to some conflict, recent cooperative ventures, such as the completion of the Uruguay Round, appear to override and surpass the conflict that does occur.

POINTS OF VIEW

A clutch of data suggest that the U.S. recovery is finally beginning to take off. And the economy that is emerging from recent structural upheavals is looking like a potential world beater.
—MICHAEL PROWSE
FINANCIAL TIMES, LONDON

Though the wealth class makes up no more than 5 percent of China's 1.3 billion population, it still represents some 65 million consumers—a market larger than Thailand or Malaysia. Foreign films have begun targeting this group, known as baofa-hu, or "households exploding with wealth."
—OTTO MANN
DIE PRESSE, VIENNA

From the viewpoint of Mexican President Carlos Salinas de Gortari, what defines the economic relationship between the United States and Mexico is not asymmetry but complementarity.
—JORGE G. CASTANEDA AND CARLOS HEREDIA
NEXOS, MEXICO CITY

Portugal's economy has behaved like one of Asia's tigers' economies since the country was admitted to the European Community (EC) in 1986.
—PETER M. JOHANSEN
KLASSEKAMPEN, OSLO

In its growing obsession to lend progressively larger amounts of money, the [World] Bank lost sight of the reason it was created.
—HILARY FRENCH
THE STATE OF THE WORLD 1994

REVIEW QUESTIONS

1. What are the institutions of the World Bank Group, and what do they do?
2. Why did the GATT become permanent, at least for five decades, and around what norms did it operate?
3. How did minilateral negotiations help save the Uruguay Round of GATT?
4. What forces are sustaining global patterns of trade as regional developments occur?
5. Why can we say that the European integration process has been a monumental accomplishment?
6. Does "pooling sovereignty" in the EU represent a reduction in state sovereignty? Explain.
7. What evidence can you offer to contrast the degree of economic integration between the EU and NAFTA?
8. Why would we expect the disparities among the three states of NAFTA to be a problem for their economic integration in a free trade union?
9. Considering the APEC forum and ASEAN, how far has the Asian-Pacific area gone into economic integration, and what are the prospects for further integration in this region?
10. Do transnationalists or neorealists make the stronger argument concerning economic cooperation? Why?

GLOSSARY

common market An arrangement among states to conduct free trade in merchandise goods and allow the free transborder movement of labor and capital.

customs union An agreement among states that provides for free trade among the participating states and a common tariff policy for those outside the agreement.

economic integration A general process involving the merger of two or more national economies to some degree.

economic union An arrangement between two or more states that involves common internal and external policies on trade and strives to harmonize capital, labor, tax, and monetary policies.

free trade area Two or more states that remove all trade barriers among themselves but engage in separate trade policies with states outside the arrangement.

globalism A belief that policy management operating from the global level is the most useful approach toward policy issues.

monetary union An agreement on currency exchange rates, or possibly an agreement to share the same currency, between two or more states.

political integration The joining of two or more governmental entities under a central decision-making structure. The joining process is thought of as reducing or eliminating separate sovereign status.

preferential trade system The reduction of tariffs among a group of states that falls short of completely free trade.

regionalism A belief that regional management of policy issues is the most efficient way to handle such issues.

spillover The theoretical process of cooperation in one functional area leading to cooperation in another area on the part of nation-states.

supranationalism The pooling of state sovereignties on a regular basis to provide centralized decision making for a group of states in agreed-upon policy areas.

RECOMMENDED READINGS

Michael Calingaert. *European Integration Revisited: Progress, Prospects, and U.S. Interests.* Boulder, CO: Westview Press, 1996.

Peter Coffey. *The Future of Europe.* Brookfield, VT: Edward Elgar, 1995.

Desmond Dinan. *Ever Closer Union? An Introduction to the European Community* (Boulder, CO: Lynne Rienner Publishers, 1994)

Steven Globerman and Michael Walker, ed. *Assessing NAFTA: A Trinational Analysis.* Vancouver, BC: The Fraser Institute, 1993.

Dean M. Hanink. *The International Global Economy: A Geographical Perspective.* New York: John Wiley & Sons, 1994.

Martin Holland. *European Community Integration.* New York: St. Martin's Press, 1992.

Gary Clyde Hufbauer and Jeffrey J. Schott. *NAFTA: An Assessment.* Rev. ed. Washington, D.C.: Institute for International Economics, 1993.

Robert O. Keohane and Stanley Hoffmann. *The New European Community.* Boulder, CO: Westview Press, 1991.

David P. Lewis. *The Road to Europe: History, Institutions and Prospects of European Integration, 1945–1993.* New York: Peter Lang, 1993.

Bruce E. Moon. *Dilemmas of International Trade.* Boulder, CO: Westview Press, 1996.

Kenichi Ohmae. *The End of the Nation-State: The Rise of Regional Economies.* New York: The Free Press, 1995.

Sidney Weintraub. *NAFTA: What Comes Next?* Westport, CT: Praeger Publishers, 1994.

David M. Wood and Birol A. Yesilada. *The Emerging European Union.* White Plains, NY: Longman, 1996.

Lawrence T. Woods. *Asia-Pacific Diplomacy: Nongovernmental Organizations and International Relations.* Vancouver, BC: UBC Press, 1993.

ENDNOTES

1. Lee F. Preston and Duane Windsor, *The Rules of the Game in the Global Economy: Policy Regimes for International Business* (Boston: Kluwer Academic Publishers, 1992), p. 239.
2. Hilary French, "Rebuilding the World Bank," in *State of the World 1994* (New York: W. W. Norton, 1994), pp. 156–76.
3. John Charles Pool and Stephen C. Stamos, Jr., *International Economic Policy: Beyond the Trade and Debt Crisis* (Lexington, MA: Lexington Books, 1989), pp. 3–4.
4. Ibid., pp. 104–8.
5. Miles Kahler, "Bargaining with the IMF: Two-Level Strategies and Developing Countries," in *Double-Edged Diplomacy: International Bargaining and Domestic Politics,* ed. Peter B. Evans, Harold K. Jacobson, and Robert D. Putnam (Berkeley, CA: University of California Press, 1993), pp. 363–66; *Our Global Neighborhood: The Report of the Commission on Global Governance* (New York: Oxford University Press, 1995), p. 181.
6. French, "Rebuilding the World Bank," p. 158.
7. Francis J. Gavin, "The Legends of Bretton Woods," *Orbis,* Spring 1996, pp. 183–98.
8. Carolyn Rhodes, *Reciprocity, U.S. Trade Policy, and the GATT* (Ithaca, NY: Cornell University Press, 1993); Daniel C. Esty, *Greening the GATT: Trade, Environment, and the Future* (Washington, D.C.: Institute for International Economics, 1994), pp. 243–48.
9. Charles R. Carlisle, "Is the World Ready for Free Trade?" *Foreign Affairs,* November–December 1996, pp. 113–26.
10. G. John Ikenberry, "Salvaging the G-7," *Foreign Affairs,* Spring 1993, pp. 132–39.
11. Desmond Dinan, *Ever Closer Union? An Introduction to the European Community* (Boulder, CO: Lynne Rienner Publishers, 1994), pp. 438–45.
12. Robert L. Paarlberg, "Agricultural Policy," in *U.S. Foreign Policy: The Search for a New Role,* ed. Robert J. Art and Seyom Brown (New York: Macmillan, 1993), pp. 192–212.
13. Miles Kahler, "A World of Blocs: Facts and Factoids," *World Policy Journal,* Spring 1995, p. 19.
14. Ibid., p. 25.
15. Dinan, *Ever Closer Union?* p. 438.
16. *Our Global Neighborhood,* p. 171.
17. Bruce E. Moon, *Dilemmas of International Trade* (Boulder, CO: Westview Press, 1996), p. 94.
18. Moises Naim, "Latin America: The Morning After," *Foreign Affairs,* July–August 1995, p. 58.
19. Robert Z. Lawrence, "Emerging Regional Arrangements: Building Blocs or Stumbling Blocs," in *International Political Economy: Perspectives on Global Power and Wealth,* 3rd ed., ed. Jeffrey A. Frieden and David A. Lake (New York: St. Martin's Press, 1995), pp. 411–12; Gary Clyde Hufbauer and Jeffrey J. Schott, *NAFTA: An Assessment,* rev. ed. (Washington, D.C.: Institute for International Economics, 1993), pp. 111–17.
20. Henry Nau, *The Myth of America's Decline: Leading the World Economy into the 1990s* (New York: Oxford University Press, 1990), pp. 326–33, 370.
21. Jeffrey E. Garten, "Is American Abandoning Multilateral Trade?" *Foreign Affairs,* November–December 1995, p. 51.
22. Roland Vaubel, "A Public Choice View of the Delors Report," in the *Political Economy of International Organization,* ed. Roland Vaubel and Thomas D. Willett (Boulder, CO: Westview Press, 1991), pp. 306–7.
23. Martin Holland, *European Community Integration* (New York: St. Martin's Press, 1992), p. 68;

Carolyn Hotchkiss, *International Law for Business* (New York: McGraw-Hill, 1994), p. 102.
24. Spyros G. Makridakis and Michelle Bainbridge, "Evolution of the Single Market," in *Single Market Europe: Opportunities and Challenges for Business,* ed. Spyros G. Makridakis and Associates (San Francisco: Jossey-Bass, 1991), pp. 3–26; Spyros G. Makridakis, "Future Challenges for Single Market Europe: Feedback from Business and Government Leaders," in *Single Market Europe,* p. 358.
25. Derek W. Urwin, *The Community of Europe: A History of European Integration Since 1945* (New York: Longman Group, 1991), p. 231.
26. Robert O. Keohane and Stanley Hoffmann, "Institutional Change in Europe in the 1980s," in *The European Union: Readings on the Theory and Practice of European Integration,* ed. Brent F. Nelsen and Alexander C-G. Stubb (Boulder, CO: Lynne Rienner Publishers, 1994), pp. 250–51.
27. Keohane and Hoffmann, "Institutional Change in Europe in the 1980s," p. 253.
28. Wayne Sandholtz, "Choosing Union: Monetary Politics and Maastricht," in *The European Union,* p. 288.
29. Tanya M. Atwood, "Monetary Union in the European Community," in *The Road to Europe: History, Institutions and Prospects of European Integration 1945–1993,* ed. David P. Lewis (New York: Peter Lang, 1993), pp. 358–66.
30. Dinan, *Ever Closer Union?* pp. 398–400.
31. Holland, *European Community Integration,* pp. 154–55.
32. George Ross, "After Maastricht: Hard Choices for Europe," *World Policy Journal,* Summer 1992, p. 507; Makridakis and Bainbridge, "Evolution of the Single Market," pp. 5–6; Elizabeth Meehan, "Citizenship and the European Community," *The Political Quarterly,* April–June 1993, pp. 172–86; John Pinder, *European Community: The Building of a Union* (New York: Oxford University Press), p. 227.
33. *Political Handbook of the World* (Binghamton, NY: CSA Publications, 1995), pp. 1160–61; David Garnham, "European Defense Cooperation: The 1990s and Beyond," in *The 1992 Project and the Future of Integration in Europe,* ed. Dale L. Smith and James Lee Ray (Armonk, NY: M. E. Sharpe, 1993), p. 211; Frederic S. Pearson, "European Security Policy and the Single European Act," in *The 1992 Project.*
34. Dinan, *Ever Closer Union?* p. 447.
35. Ibid., *Ever Closer Union?* pp. 478–79.
36. Holland, *European Community Integration.*
37. The description of the EU institutions is generally taken from Urwin, *The Community of Europe;* Pinder, *European Community;* Holland, *European Community Integration,* Chapter 4; and Francis Jacobs and Richard Corbett with Michael Shackleton, *The European Parliament* (Boulder, CO: Westview Press, 1990).
38. Jeffrey J. Anderson, "The State of the (European) Union," *World Politics* (April 1995), vol. 47, no. 3, pp. 450–451.
39. Moon, *Dilemmas of International Trade,* pp. 140–41.
40. David Barkin, Irene Ortiz, and Fred Rosen, "Globalization and Resistance: The Remaking of Mexico," *NACLA: Report on the Americas,* January–February 1997, p. 24.
41. Good accounts of NAFTA appear in Steven Globerman and Michael Walker, eds., *Assessing NAFTA: A Trinational Analysis* (Vancouver, BC: The Fraser Institute, 1993); Gary Clyde Hufbauer and Jeffrey J. Schott, *NAFTA: An Assessment,* rev. ed. (Washington, D.C.: Institute for International Economics, 1993).
42. Edward J. Lincoln, *Japan's New Global Role* (Washington, D.C.: The Brookings Institute, 1993), p. 161.
43. Kahler, "A World of Blocs," p. 24.
44. Lawrence T. Woods, *Asia-Pacific Diplomacy: Nongovernmental Organizations and International Relations* (Vancouver, BC: UBC Press, 1993).
45. Preston and Windsor, *The Rules of the Game in the Global Economy,* pp. 136–37; Dinan, *Ever Closer Union?* pp. 454–55.
46. Narongchai Akrasanee, "The ASEAN Free Trade Agreement," in *Foreign Direct Investment: OECD Countries and Dynamic Economics of Asia and Latin America* (Paris: OECD, 1995), pp. 137–45.
47. Lincoln, *Japan's New Global Role,* p. 170.
48. C. Fred Bergsten, "APEC and World Trade," *Foreign Affairs,* May–June 1994, pp. 20–26.
49. Stephen A. Douglas and Sara U. Douglas, "Economic Implications of the U.S.–ASEAN Discourse on Human Rights," *Pacific Affairs,* Spring 1996, pp. 71–87.

50. Lawrence, "Emerging Regional Arrangements," pp. 411–12.
51. The essence of this point is borrowed from Seyom Brown, *International Relations in a Changing Global System: Toward a Theory of the World Polity* (Boulder, CO: Westview Press, 1992), p. 30.
52. Joseph S. Nye, Jr., "Neorealism and Neoliberalism," *World Politics,* January 1988, p. 246.
53. Kenneth A. Oye, "Explaining Cooperation Under Anarchy: Hypotheses and Strategies," in *Cooperation Under Anarchy,* ed. Kenneth A. Oye (Princeton, NJ: Princeton University Press, 1986), p. 19.
54. Robert Axelrod, *The Evolution of Cooperation* (New York: Basic Books, 1984), p. 20.
55. Hans J. Morgenthau, *Politics Among Nations: The Struggle for Power and Peace,* 5th ed. (New York: Alfred A. Knopf, 1978), pp. 34–35.
56. Stephen D. Krasner, *Structural Conflict: The Third World Against Global Liberalism* (Berkeley, CA: University of California Press, 1985), p. 28; Linda Cornett and James A. Caporaso, " 'And Still It Moves!' State Interests and Social Forces in the European Community," in *Governance Without Government: Order and Change in World Politics,* ed. James N. Rosenau and Ernst-Otto Czempiel (New York: Cambridge University Press, 1992), p. 233.
57. Joseph M. Grieco, *Cooperation Among Nations: Europe, America, and Non-Tariff Barriers to Trade* (Ithaca, NY: Cornell University Press, 1990).

PART THREE

THE STRUGGLE FOR WORLD ORDER

CHAPTER 10

ARMS LIMITATIONS: PASSAGE INTO THE POST–COLD WAR ERA

Humankind evolved as an intelligent animal, but without the powerful claws and fangs of many animal species. To compensate, humans fashioned tools for hunting and for fighting. As a force multiplier, humans also formed bands for these activities. Over time, arms became more sophisticated and lethal, culminating in nuclear warheads attached to long-range missiles. Eventually, the bands of warriors became permanent armies ready to defend their states and to pursue the political goals of kings. For centuries, the power and status of a state depended ultimately on its arms and armies. The hostile world that resulted forced states to live in fear of one another, and thus agreements to limit weapons proved rare.[1] Until the end of the Cold War, governments were reluctant to slash weapon budgets and downsize armies to save money for human needs.[2]

The decline and then collapse of communism in Europe produced an epochal change in the relations of the states of the opposing alliances of NATO and the Warsaw Pact. The nuclear and missile arms races in the 1970s, when the Soviet Union was at the height of its power, had permitted only a few agreements between the superpowers. Because of the severe economic problems of the Soviet Union in the 1980s, the opportunity arose for arms reductions. Arms negotiations are always difficult, but the act of demobilizing arms has been nearly impossible unless one side accepted a lower position in the power hierarchy of states.[3]

A further encouragement to arms reductions came in 1991, when the behemoth Soviet Union collapsed into multiple states, leaving a new Russia holding on to most of the Soviet nuclear forces. This Russia, though still possessing a major nuclear capability, gladly accepted unprecedented arms reductions. Russia desperately needed to concentrate on its ramshackle economy and ethnic struggles. The reduction in nuclear arms by the superpowers signaled a wholly new political relationship between these old enemies.

The most pressing current arms problems are in Asia and the Middle East, where some governments strive to acquire not only sophisticated conventional weapons but missiles with atomic, biological, and chemical (ABC) warheads. A major cooperative effort by states today is to promote weapon regimes that can stanch the flow of weapons into regional conflicts, thus slowing the escalation of arms races.

In this chapter, we identify the objectives of arms limitations and the obstacles that make these limitations difficult to achieve. Then we distinguish among several types of arms limitations. Next, we will see that in spite of significant breakthroughs in arms reductions, the proliferation of weapons in the world is still a formidable problem. Weapon regimes are the subject of the next section; these regimes represent the status of the rules and norms states use to regulate arms. Then we discuss the role nonstate actors play in arms limitations. Finally, we focus on a question interesting to realists and transnationalists: Can an anarchy of war and arms races transform into an international society that involves arms limitation?

THE OBJECTIVES OF ARMS LIMITATIONS

There are two principal objectives of arms limitations. One is peace; the other is cutting costs associated with arms races and wars.

Achieving Peace

As we approach the end of the twentieth century, almost everyone wants peace. The massive destruction of two world wars, followed by decades of living under the shadow of nuclear holocaust, has sensitized a generation to the value of peace. Since 1945, the loss of 40 million lives through 250 wars and conflicts in the Third World also has been sobering.[4] A downturn in world military expenditures and a world effort to control weapon flows mark a generation of humankind desirous of peace and prosperity. For this generation, the destruction wrought by wars and the waste of economic resources on arms are major setbacks to human progress. However, ambitious rogue states, such as Iraq, and vicious ethnic strife in several countries continue to trouble the formative international society.

Can arms limitations contribute to peace? While some scholars assume arms races produce tensions that in turn, contribute to war the evidence on the relationship between arms and war is complex. Robert Wesson thinks arms agreements not only slow arms races but reduce the prospects for war.[5] For instance, the Nuclear Test Ban Treaty of 1963 and the Nuclear Non-Proliferation Treaty of 1968 may have set the stage for the détente of the 1970s, a period of relaxed tensions between the Soviet Union and the United States. From their case studies, Michael Brzoska and Frederic S. Pearson reach the converse but compatible conclusion that major arms acquisitions usually precede wars.[6]

Other scholars assume arms races are dangerous but focus on specific aspects of the arms race: Have the weapons of a challenging state surpassed those of the current hegemonic state? Do the chances of war decline the longer an arms race lasts? Are rising quantities of weapons more dangerous than a change in the types of weapons? These and other questions about arms races remain unanswered to the satisfaction of many scholars.[7] Colin S. Gray even questions whether there is a phenomenon known as an arms race. As a matter of definition, he asks how we are to distinguish the abnormal occurrence of an arms race from the normal self-defense of countries that arm themselves under the conditions of anarchy.[8]

Some scholars view weapons merely as the symptoms of hostility that result from more fundamental issues.[9] For these scholars, peace depends on resolving the underlying issues. Hans Morgenthau has observed, "Men do not fight because they have arms. They have arms because they deem it necessary to fight."[10] Nevertheless, conventional wisdom holds that arms agreements at least ease tensions and slow steps toward war, and leaders frequently speak and behave accordingly.

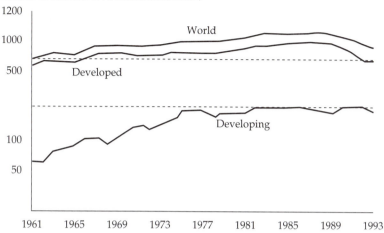

World Military Expenditures, 1961–1993

Source: *World Military Expenditures and Arms Transfers* (Washington, D.C.: U.S. Arms Control and Disarmament Agency, 1995), p. 1.

Costs to Bear

Global military spending since the Second World War amounts to $30 to $35 trillion.[11] It is flabbergasting to think of the cumulative negative effects of such expenditures on the world's population and its needs. These vast sums could have alleviated global human suffering by providing all the schools, hospitals, medicines, and homes that humankind has needed over the past five decades. According to the *World Military Expenditures and Arms Transfers (WMEAT)* report of the U.S. Arms Control and Disarmament Agency, world military expenditures rose steadily until 1987, when they peaked at over $1 trillion, then dropped to $868 billion in 1993. The decline in military expenditures between 1987 and 1993 includes a savings of over $1 trillion, a reduction in military personnel around the world from 28.7 million people in 1988 to 24.8 million in 1992, and a sharp decline in world arms imports and exports.

Most of these savings resulted from the decline in *developed* countries' spending. The developed countries spent much greater sums on arms and then reduced their spending more sharply than the *developing* countries.[12] The developed countries, according to the U.S. Arms Control and Disarmament Agency's definition, are 28 industrialized countries with high GNP per capita incomes and a favorable quality of life. The developing countries are the remaining 143 countries in the Arms Control and Disarmament Agency's report that have a lower level of industrialization, less income, and a poorer quality of life.[13] The developing countries essentially are the Third World. Considering the historic political transformation of the world at the end of the Cold War, the peoples of the world might have expected much larger savings. However, world military spending may be stuck at over $800 billion and may not decline in the foreseeable future.[14] Presently military expenditures for the planet about equal the yearly incomes of half the world's population.[15]

Most military spending occurs in peacetime, but when wars do break out, costs quickly accelerate, diverting even more monies from human needs. For example, during the rapid buildup in the Vietnam War between 1964 and 1966, the United States spent over 8 percent of its GNP on the military. The height of war expenditure occurred in 1968 when the United States invested $23 billion in the lost cause of the Vietnam War. This figure might be four times higher in today's dollars. President Lyndon Johnson, in trying to cover costs of the war as well as the domestic priorities of his "Great Society" program, used deficit spending and began the United States' long-lasting national debt.[16] In another case, military preparations and fighting in Desert Shield and Desert Storm cost the coalition forces $80 billion in an unusually brief war.[17]

Legacies of wars are often costly and slow to disappear. Wars can cause a massive exodus of refugees. The UN High Commissioner for Refugees had expenses of $1.1 billion in 1993, and, in the next year, had to handle 23 million refugees at the international level and 26 million internally displaced persons.[18] Sometimes refugees languish in camps for years. Several generations of Palestinians have lived in refugee settlements in Arab countries since the 1948 Arab-Israeli War. Many Palestinians have never seen Palestine (Israel).

The environmental impact of war and war preparation is an unfortunate legacy as well. Kuwait has spent a huge portion of its oil wealth to clean up after Desert Storm, including recapping many oil wells that Iraqi invaders blew up. An enormous task awaits the U.S. Department of Energy (DOE) as it decides how to clean up nuclear weapons plants that are no longer of any use. Finally, destroying old stocks of chemical weapons in Russia and the United States is a dangerous, expensive, and so far incomplete task. Apparently both sides in the Cold War created sumptuous ABC weapon materials without any forethought as to their disposal at a future time.

A particularly heinous legacy is the presence of old land mines and the setting of new mine fields. When he was UN secretary-general, Boutros Boutros-Ghali wrote that 100 million land mines lay buried in 62 countries, and millions more are currently appearing in wars and conflicts. Land mines are indiscriminate maimers and killers of civilians years after a war is over. Secretary-General Boutros-Ghali observed that around the world, "the legless, blinded, ravaged bodies of the living are an increasingly common sight." The medical costs are prohibitive for Third World countries. Additional costs come from clearing mine fields. Iraqi troops laid 7 million mines in Kuwait during the Persian Gulf War, and the Kuwaiti government spent millions of dollars a year to remove these mines.[19] After completing land mine clearance, Kuwait had spent a total of $1 billion, and 80 deminers brought in to clear the mines died in the process.

Another legacy concerns the demobilization of military forces after a war or a peacetime drawdown of the armed services. Governments must reintegrate military personnel into the civilian workforce, convert military industries to civilian products, and close military bases. U.S. base closings in the post–Cold War era is costing $15 billion between 1990 and 1999, with $4 billion of this amount going to environmental cleanup at the bases. Russian costs, due to conversion, are in the billions of dollars as well and surpass Russian financial capabilities. Russian conversion is moving slowly because of expenditures of only $500 million a year.[20] Nonetheless, over the long term, these changes will mean savings for the countries willing to cut their military programs.

A final legacy of cost concerns the diversion of government expenditures from human services to military spending that can hurt the growth of a national economy. In a study on 103 countries, Alex Mintz and Randolph T. Stevenson found that in only 10 percent of the cases did military expenditures contribute to economic growth. Overall, nonmilitary spending by governments is far more important to help national economies to expand.[21]

With the downsizing of military forces in the post–Cold War era, can we expect a large amount of savings, known as a "peace dividend," that can improve schools and the environment, reduce health costs, and meet other human needs? Unfortunately, the peace dividend so far is mostly an illusion. First, the cuts are less than 20 percent of what countries were spending on their militaries in 1987. Second, governments are using the savings to reduce budget deficits and lower taxes.[22]

OBSTACLES TO ARMS LIMITATIONS

The potent motives of peace and saving money encourage arms limitations, but serious obstacles stand in the way of their success. The main obstacle to arms limitations is the fear countries have about their security. Another obstacle involves the technical problems that undermine sincere efforts to control weapons.

Fear in a Still Dangerous World

The post–Cold War era is a mix of promise and peril, perhaps with emphasis on promise. The end of the Cold War, with its spiraling nuclear arms race, was a triumphant moment not only for the West but for the world. The threat of a strategic nuclear war, already diminished in a fairly stable bipolar world, declined even further. At the regional level, however, serious hostilities remain. North Korea and South Korea share the most hostile border in the world. As recently as 1994, both sides put their military forces on alert status during the controversy over North Korea's effort to make an atomic bomb. India and Pakistan have fought three wars and are barely holding back from fighting a fourth. Each is probably capable of attacking the other with small atomic bombs. Israel's troubles with its Arab neighbors have been so continuous that wars and conflicts tend to shade into one another. However, improved relations with a few Arab states and the Palestinians offer the promise of peace. Finally, the bitter ethnic fighting in the Balkan Mountains continues as Croatians, Muslims, and Serbs, of former Yugoslavia, try to carve out separate states.

These and other hostilities have generated fear, leading some countries to follow the dictum of a Roman general from centuries ago, "If you want peace, prepare for war." Almost certainly other countries will follow the same advice, leading to an arms race and tense relations. War is almost a certainty if a country is building up arms not for its defense but as a strategy for taking what is unobtainable except by force. The designs of Adolf Hitler on his neighbors' territories and, more recently, the plans of Saddam Hussein for Kuwait are such cases. Fortunate are the European countries that live in a *security-community*. Within this set of countries, an attack on one another is inconceivable. These states are democratic and integrated into a regional economy; they have no goals concerning one another that require military force. Enviable as well is the American-Canadian relationship. These two countries share the longest unarmed border in the world. While security requirements of states vary, almost all countries remain armed because the world continues to offer much uncertainty. Few countries will risk their safety by doing away with their military forces, as Costa Rica has.

Technical Problems

Even if states can move past their fears and political ambitions toward arms limitation, they still face several technical obstacles. The most common technical obstacles are power ratios, the distinction between offensive and defensive weapons, the identification of strategic versus theater weapons, and verification problems.

Power ratios require an evaluation of the force represented by weapons, both the weapons states can keep and the weapons states agree to demobilize. Since states can have military forces and weapons configured in different ways, measuring one country's weapons compared to another's can be complex. For instance, how does the American M-1 tank measure up against the Russian T-72? A problem of quality versus quantity arises. An American M-1 tank, equipped with TOW missiles or laser-sighted cannon, can shoot its weapons accurately while cruising at considerable speed. Other factors to consider are the cruising range of the tank, ease of maintenance, and the training of the crew. So how many Russian T-72s will equal one American M-1?

Weapon negotiations may be one of the few times when adversaries compliment each other. They exaggerate the worth of an opponent's weapon in power ratio assessments to limit the number of that weapon. Perhaps the best-known treaty using a ratio is the *Washington Naval Agreement* of 1922. This treaty involved the capital surface ships of five states that promised to arrive at the following ratio over a 20-year period: Great Britain (5), the United States (5), Japan (3), France (1.67), and Italy (1.67).

In weapon negotiations, states also disagree about the orientation of weapons: whether they are **offensive weapons** or **defensive weapons.** Basically, military forces use an offensive weapon when on the attack and a defensive one to repel an opponent's attack. In practice, the distinction between the two orientations tends to blur. In ancient Greece, Sparta objected to Athenians building a wall around their city. Spartans worried that Athens, as a naval power, could attack Sparta at will since the Athenian wall would stop the Spartan infantry. The role of the bayonet by European infantry is another interesting example. The bayonet began in seventeenth-century France as a defensive weapon. Attached to a musket, a bayonet freed a soldier from having to carry both a musket and a pike, a spearlike weapon for fending off offensive charges at close quarters. In the early eighteenth century, after a Russian army attacked and routed an encamped, larger Swedish army with a bayonet charge in the midst of a snow storm, other armies followed the Russian example of using the bayonet on the offensive.

The most important modern case of determining the offensive or defensive status of a weapon occurred over the *Strategic Defense Initiative (SDI),* first proposed by President Ronald Reagan in 1983. Planned as an elaborate, high-tech defense system, SDI was to intercept and thoroughly destroy incoming missiles, thus placing an aerial shield over the United States. The expensive technology involved remains incomplete, but the specter of the SDI's potential frightened Soviet leaders. As the Spartans feared Athens, Soviet leaders feared the United States could fire its missiles against Soviet targets with impunity. The Soviets viewed SDI as part of a broad offensive strategy, while President Reagan considered SDI to be purely defensive. This proposed weapon system was highly destabilizing to American-Soviet relations and could have set off an arms race with unprecedented costs. President Reagan and his supporters claimed, to the contrary, that the SDI program helped draw the Soviets into serious talks on arms reductions.

Another technical obstacle concerns the difference between a strategic weapon and a theater weapon. A **strategic weapon** can travel intercontinentally with a highly destructive payload. Long-range bombers and *intercontinental ballistic missiles (ICBMs)*, which can travel thousands of miles, are the primary strategic weapons in modern times. These strategic projections of power usually carry nuclear bombs or warheads. In contrast, a **theater weapon** has a range of approximately a thousand miles, limiting it to an attack range within a given continent or region. These weapons too are usually bombers or missiles, but with a shorter range.

Arguments easily develop over the category appropriate for a particular weapon. The United States insisted for years that the Soviet "backfire" bomber was a strategic weapon because, with refueling in the air, it could reach the United States and return to the Soviet Union. The Soviet Union, for its part, wanted cruise missiles, basically a theater weapon that can carry a nuclear warhead and is counted as a strategic weapon. The U.S. Air Force can attach several cruise missiles to each American long-range bomber. The bombers can then carry these highly accurate missiles close to an enemy's territory and launch them toward separate enemy targets.

Verification through inspection has always been the technical problem of paramount importance. States invest their security not only in their own arms but in the knowledge that the other side is not cheating on arms agreements. The outer limits of what states might hope to achieve in arms limitations rest largely on verification possibilities. Verification techniques include aerial surveillance, spy satellites, on-site inspections, and monitoring devices.

In 1955, President Dwight Eisenhower called for an "open skies" arrangement that would allow the United States and the Soviet Union to fly over each other's territory to inspect military facilities. Following mutually satisfactory reconnaissance, disarmament negotiations could begin. The Soviets, highly resistant to any form of inspection, refused the "open skies" arrangement by claiming they wanted disarmament to come first. However, another proposal for aerial surveillance has succeeded. The Open Skies Agreement of 1992 allowed 27 countries, ex–Cold War adversaries, to fly over one another's territory. The purpose is for these states to assure one another that no state is mobilizing to attack another.

Spy satellites were important in the 1970s to encourage arms control agreements between the Soviet Union and the United States concerning limits on ICBMs. Satellites do not violate the air space of a country as planes do, yet sophisticated camera technology can film missiles above ground and missile silos. Spy satellites gave assurances to both sides that each was respecting the agreed-on ICBM limits.

On-site inspections between the superpowers were almost impossible because of the traditional Russian suspicion of foreigners on their soil. For instance, the Soviets turned down the *Baruch Plan* of 1946 proposed by the United States. This plan, offered before the Soviet Union had its atomic bomb in 1949, intended to eliminate nuclear weapons from the planet. The plan also called for an Atomic Energy Commission to make sure nuclear facilities were only creating energy for peaceful purposes. Later, in 1968, the nuclear *Non-Proliferation Treaty (NPT)* sought to limit nuclear weapons to the five states already in possession of these weapons. Included in the NPT was the International Atomic Energy Agency (IAEA), which would inspect the facilities of the states without nuclear weapons. Since the Soviet Union was one of the accepted nuclear weapon states, the IAEA did not pose a problem for the Soviet Union.

© 1991 by Herblock, *The Washington Post*

The IAEA, however, has been in the thick of the struggle to prevent Iraq from returning to an atomic bomb program and to dissuade North Korea from making an atomic weapon. Maintaining access to the facilities of both countries has been difficult for the IAEA. In 1997, the IAEA, pushed hard by the United States, adopted new, tougher rules for inspecting peaceful nuclear programs to make sure countries such as Iraq and North Korea do not stray into nuclear weapons development.

With the arrival of Mikhail Gorbachev in 1985 as the Soviet top leader, what had been impossible suddenly became possible. An intermediate-range missile agreement in 1987 led to the withdrawal of these missiles from central Europe by the United States and the Soviet Union. Each side would observe the other, on its own territory, destroy the rocket launchers for the intermediate-range missiles. Then, in 1991, just before the Soviet Union collapsed, a major agreement on the reduction of ICBMs and nuclear warheads took place between the Cold War rivals that allowed "short-notice" inspections of each other's ICBM missile sites.

Monitoring devices also have appeared in arms agreements. In 1974, the Soviet Union and the United States agreed to reduce the size of underground nuclear explosions below the level allowed by the 1963 treaty on underground tests. Part of the 1974 agreement required both sides to exchange seismic data that measured the nuclear explosions. In time, each side allowed the other's scientists, armed with sensory equipment, to visit its test site for monitoring purposes. More recently, in the early 1990s, the IAEA placed cameras at nuclear facilities in Iraq and North Korea. IAEA camera-monitors face some limits, however. Before the Persian Gulf War, Iraq hid weapon facilities in underground bunkers that may be unknown to the IAEA, and North Korea for a time simply refused to allow the IAEA to see two of its nuclear facilities, much less place cameras in them.

Through several treaties, the inspection process has become elaborate enough that the U.S. Defense Department has set up an On-Site Inspection Agency. The United States also is one of the few states to go beyond the ubiquitous defense department almost all countries have to form the U.S. Arms Control and Disarmament Agency.[23]

In conclusion, the basic obstacle to arms pacts is the fear states have of one another. Arms limitations, if successfully negotiated, can build trust and thus provide an opportunity for more arms agreements. However, a pattern of arms agreements over time is not an inexorable process, for negotiations can stall for years or collapse, or states may violate the agreements already standing. Finally, many technical problems can stand in the way of arms negotiations. The greatest such obstacle is verification. Only when states inspect one another's territory can they operate with confidence that others are keeping arms agreements. In spite of an improving world in the area of arms limitations, states remain fearful actors and will not leave their security to blind trust. Arms agreements require guarantees.

TYPES OF ARMS LIMITATIONS

States can reach three basic types of arms limitations agreements, and all three have played a role in winding down the Cold War. **Arms control** refers to limitations, or caps, on weapon levels. **Disarmament** calls for either the complete or partial elimination of weapons. **Disengagement** is the withdrawal of two potentially hostile military forces from positions of direct contact to reduce the potential for friction. Disengagement can involve weapons, military personnel, or both.

Although analytical distinctions can separate the three basic types of arms limitations, in practice they often overlap. The *Intermediate Nuclear Forces Treaty (INF)* of 1987, for example, involved destroying intermediate-range missiles with nuclear warheads as a disarmament action, but the elimination of these American and Soviet missiles from proximity in Europe also reduced tensions as a step of disengagement.

In addition, states may choose to limit or reduce their armaments on a *unilateral* basis or by controlling *arms transfers*. Unilateral steps take place when one country removes or reduces its forces in an area in the hope that the other side will reciprocate. Countries acting alone or in concert with other countries can halt or limit the international transfer of one or more types of weapons as gifts or sales.

We will see that arms control agreements became the centerpiece of Cold War cooperation. From the 1950s through the 1980s, the United States and the Soviet Union held incompatible views of what the world order should be, but imposing their respective views on each other and the world could have meant a nuclear Armageddon. Instead of war, the superpowers came to focus on war avoidance, and arms control helped reduce tensions and costs in a nuclear stand-off that appeared insoluble. Then Soviet reforms under Mikhail Gorbachev's leadership, followed by the dissolution of the Soviet empire, suddenly ushered in disarmament successes that had previously been unimaginable.

Withdrawing weapons and personnel, as acts of disengagement, accompanied disarmament successes.

Arms Control

On August 6, 1945, a B-29 bomber, the *Enola Gay,* named after the pilot's mother, dropped a small atomic bomb on Hiroshima. The nuclear age began, and nothing has ever been the same since. Most historical periods rest on the impact of ideas and heroes, but the nuclear age centers on a weapon. After the Soviet Union exploded its first atomic weapon in 1949 and, by the 1970s, had ascended to a power level rivaling that of the United States, the two superpowers were in deadlock. Each had a *triad system* of bombers, submarines, and ICBMs. The dual triads produced a *mutually assured destruction (MAD)* arrangement in the event that war broke out. If one side attacked, even with complete surprise, the other could counterattack, leaving both sides to perish beneath nuclear mushroom clouds. Neither side dared use its nuclear arsenal offensively to advance its interests. In time, both nuclear titans recognized that having the capacity to destroy each other five or ten times over had become pointless.

Nevertheless, the chances for halting an inconclusive and endless arms race were slight. In the midst of the Cold War, Hans Morgenthau noted that arms agreements on conventional weapons had failed altogether, and while arms control successes were precarious, disarmament appeared impossible.[24] Even before the nuclear age, disarmament had enjoyed little success under the League of Nations auspices, and, by 1960, the United Nations had shifted emphasis from disarmament proposals to arms control pacts. Several arms control agreements were possible during the Cold War because they brought mutual advantage to the two ideological foes. Arms control steps could only slow the nuclear arms race.[25] At least arms control agreements eased tensions and costs for a few years at a time, and each successful agreement improved diplomatic relations and encouraged future agreements.[26]

An early arms control agreement was the *Limited Test Ban Treaty* of 1963. Although numerous states have accepted this treaty, the original signatories in 1963 were Great Britain, the Soviet Union, and the United States. Many Third World states, using the United Nations as a forum, pressured the three nuclear powers to halt bomb tests. These tests shifted from atom to hydrogen bombs and became increasingly "dirtier" with radioactivity. Between 1945 and 1963, the nuclear powers exploded over 400 nuclear devices. An environmental concern added to the desire to reduce tension. The ban restricted nuclear tests from the atmosphere, outer space, and the oceans. Only underground tests were allowable. For years more, however, China and France used above-ground tests before changing to underground tests.

The *Threshold Nuclear Test Ban Treaty* of 1974 supplanted the Limited Test Ban Treaty of 1963. The 1974 test ban treaty is a bilateral one between the United States and the Soviet Union. This treaty reduced the size of bomb tests to 150 kilotons or smaller. Numerous appeals by governments and environmental groups have called for a *comprehensive test ban treaty (CTBT)* agreement. Early in President Bill Clinton's administration, research to produce "mini-nukes," small, low-yield warheads, continued from the previous administration. More recently, however, President Clinton has become a strong supporter of a

CTBT, and he signed such a treaty in 1996. Other major states, including China and France, finally moved in this direction. France probably conducted the last tests, detonating eight nuclear devices in 1995 and 1996 near Tahiti in the South Pacific.

The Cuban Missile Crisis of 1962, which almost resulted in a nuclear war, led to the *"hotline" agreement* of 1963, another Soviet-American bilateral arrangement. For future crises, the nuclear rivals agreed to have direct communications by a cable connection between Washington and Moscow. In the early 1970s, the two countries upgraded their hotline with a communications satellite link.

Another important act of cooperation between the superpowers was the promotion of the *Nuclear Non-Proliferation Treaty (NPT)* of 1968, a multilateral treaty with 168 signatories. A nonproliferation treaty was a recognition by the superpowers that the national security of each country was bound up with the "common security" of all countries. The treaty prohibits signatories from giving or receiving nuclear weapons, or the means to make them, as transfers among states. Some states did not ratify the NPT, and others have cheated on its terms. India, Israel, Pakistan, and South Africa probably have an atom bomb, or its facsimile. These states may be "threshold" nuclear powers, meaning they have the parts of an atomic weapon and can quickly assemble one. Undoubtedly, other states in the Third World wish to build an atomic weapon. Many scholars and leaders agree that the more states that have nuclear weapons, the greater is the chance for a nuclear war, if only because of statistical probability. The NPT has slowed nuclear proliferation, but it needs stronger regulatory powers.

As the two superpowers finally came to realize that further nuclear escalation was pointless, the *Strategic Arms Limitation Talks* agreements of 1972 and 1979 (*SALT I* and *SALT II*) became possible. These agreements took place during the détente period of relaxed tensions between the Soviet Union and the United States during the 1970s. With SALT I, the superpowers agreed to place a ceiling on land- and sea-launched ICBMs for a period of five years.

The superpowers negotiated an *Anti-Ballistic Missile (ABM)* agreement in Helsinki to accompany the SALT I treaty. The ABM limited the United States and the Soviet Union to two defensive missile sites. The ABM agreement reflects a mutual interest as well as considerable practicality by the superpowers. Not only would ABM sites for every American and Soviet city and military facility cost billions of dollars, but an attacking country could always saturate the defensive missile sites of the defending country with a larger number of ICBMs. As a result, the Soviet Union chose to install only one ABM site at Moscow, and the United States also built one site, now inoperable, to protect a cluster of ICBM silos in North Dakota.

With SALT II, the superpowers intended to limit the *multiple independently targetal re-entry vehicles (MIRVs)*. MIRVs could use a single rocket to gain outer space and from there fire multiple nuclear warheads from the rocket at separate targets on an opponent's territory. The Soviet and American negotiators also agreed in principle to limit the number of bombers carrying cruise missiles. The SALT II agreement was to apply in 1977 when SALT I came to an end. However, the opinion of many U.S. senators that SALT II would strategically disadvantage the United States delayed the ratification of the treaty. When the Soviet Union intervened in Afghanistan in 1979, President Jimmy Carter withdrew SALT II from further consideration by the Senate. Unrestrained by SALT II, the Soviet Union developed an even more potent MIRV system on the SS-18 ICBM, an ICBM several stories high that carried 14 separate warheads.

Another type of arms control agreement is a *preclusion treaty*. Under this type of treaty, countries ban weapons before they build or deploy them. The *Environmental Modification Convention* of 1977 bans the development of hostile techniques for altering weather or climate patterns, ocean currents, the ozone layer, or ecological balance for military purposes. The *Antarctic Treaty* of 1959 bans any military uses of Antarctica, especially of a nuclear kind. The *Outer Space Treaty* of 1967 forbids nuclear weapons from orbiting earth or stationing these weapons in outer space. The advantage of a preclusion agreement is that it occurs prior to countries making financial investments in weapons and before they count on those weapons for their security. The preclusion treaty, as a vehicle of arms control, is easier to negotiate than other arms treaties. The NPT is a preclusion treaty in the sense that it requires nonnuclear states to forgo nuclear weapons.

Disarmament

In 1990, the world had a stockpile of nuclear warheads, with the Soviet Union and the United States owning 97 percent of these weapons.[27] The total explosive power of these nuclear weapons was 18,000 megatons. The total explosive power of conventional weapons in the Second World War, Korean War, and Vietnam War was 11 megatons, and yet these conventional weapons took 44 million lives.[28] Nuclear warhead production in the Soviet Union and the United States appeared as if it could go on indefinitely.

Regrettably, the first term of Ronald Reagan (1980–1984) reintensified Cold War hostility. President Reagan viewed disarmament talks as a forum for Soviet propaganda and busied himself with doubling the U.S. defense budget.[29] A succession of sick, elderly Soviet leaders mirrored President Reagan's animosity. He went through his first term without a summit meeting with the top Soviet leaders until after Mikhail Gorbachev's ascendancy to power in 1985. His rise to power led to "new thinking" within the Kremlin, providing the opportunity for serious arms negotiations.[30] Gorbachev called for a 50 percent reduction in nuclear weapons and a nuclear-free world by the year 2000.[31] Instead of fomenting the usual communist propaganda about complete disarmament, he proved sincere about specific disarmament steps because he regarded growth in nuclear weapons as unnecessary and expensive.[32] Soviet domestic problems, chiefly a failing economy and ethnic dissatisfaction, had narrowed Gorbachev's options. The Soviet Union desperately needed rest and repair from the debilitating arms race.

The first summit of the two leaders at Reykjavik, Iceland, in 1986 marked a shift in arms negotiation from arms control to disarmament. Both leaders expressed a strong interest in strategic nuclear disarmament involving ICBMs, but Reagan's insistence on having the SDI program temporarily hamstrung progress. At least the two leaders could agree to disarm in the area of theater nuclear weapons, and the Intermediate Nuclear Forces Treaty of 1987 was the result.[33] The INF called for the destruction of nearly 3,000 intermediate-range vehicles, both planned and operational missiles, in Europe and on the Soviet-Chinese border. The INF is of striking importance for two reasons. First, the INF was the first ratified arms agreement between the superpowers in about 15 years. Second, negotiators eliminated an entire class of weapons.[34] Both sides removed the warheads, and one side watched while the other either blow-torched or blew up the rocket vehicles. Accompanying the onsite inspection arrangement was a Special Verification Commission that would deal with any inspection problems that arose.

The terms of the INF treaty removed more Soviet than American intermediate-range missiles in Europe and represented the American negotiating position held since 1981. The INF was emblematic of a power asymmetry favoring the United States. More important, the INF disarmament step was the most significant event in the wind-down of the Cold War until the tearing down of the Berlin Wall in 1989.[35]

The rapid transformation in the atmosphere of the Cold War from 1989 to 1991 ushered in an even more dramatic disarmament step than the INF. After long years of fruitless negotiation over strategic arms, the superpowers were ready to demobilize some of their most potent weapons, their ICBMs. The *Strategic Arms Reduction Talks Treaty (START I)* of 1991 called for a significant reduction of nuclear warheads carried mostly by ICBMs, missiles that could travel 8,000 or 9,000 miles in minutes. By the 1970s, the ICBMs surpassed bombers as the key weapon sustaining the military order of the Cold War based on MAD.[36]

With START I, the world military order began a retreat from a massive to a minimum deterrent. In 1992, the superpowers had about 10,000 warheads each, with a strategic delivery capability based on the triad of land- and sea-launched ICBMs and long-range bombers. By 1999, under START I, the United States was to have about 8,500 warheads, and the Soviet Union (now Russia and three other former Soviet republics, or "FSRs") would have approximately 6,500 warheads. The nuclear rivals also would accept a limit of 1,600 ICBMs carrying no more than 6,000 warheads. Each side could place its remaining warheads on cruise missiles carried by bombers. Of the ICBMs, no more than 880 could be *sea-launched intercontinental ballistic missiles (SLICBMs)* fired from submarines. SLICBMs are the nuclear weapons most difficult to knock out with a first-strike blow and thus are the most prized strategic weapon today. Finally, the Soviets agreed to reduce by one-half their much-feared stock of SS-18s MIRVed missiles, leaving them with 154 SS-18s.[37]

As in the case of the INF treaty, the two sides must destroy the rocket vehicles agreed on. Also, similar to the INF treaty, they could store warheads within the allowable limit if they so chose. The inspections under START I are more stringent than the INF and include "short-notice" visits to each other's territory.[38] The terms of START I left the United States in a relatively stronger position. Not only was the United States allowed more warheads, but its bombers and submarines are of better quality. Some observers have claimed the United States deserves nuclear superiority, confirmed with START I, because it clearly won the Cold War.[39] Traditionally, the peace terms after a war reflect the success or failure of the participants. In 1991, the United States' military technology and values, involving democracy and capitalism, were in ascendancy while the Soviet state was beginning to unravel.

Mikhail Gorbachev's political fortunes faded with those of the Soviet Union in 1991. His political demise left President Boris Yeltsin of Russia to sign a follow-on treaty, known as *START II*. The terms of START II brought even more drastic cuts in strategic nuclear forces and added to America's nuclear edge. By the year 2003, the United States is to have 3,500 nuclear warheads compared to 3,027 for Russia. Compatible with lowering the number of nuclear warheads, both sides agreed to discontinue their MIRV systems, leaving

TABLE 10.1
Disarmament in Nuclear Warheads

	1992 levels	START I (1999)	START II (2003)
Russia/FSRs ICBMs	6,115	3,153	531
United States ICBMs	2,370	1,400	500
Russia/FSRs SLBMs	2,696	1,744	1,744
United States SLBMs	3,840	3,456	1,728
Russia/FSRs bomber weapons	1,426	1,552	752
United States bomber weapons	3,776	3,700	1,272
Total Russia/FSRs	10,237	6,449	3,027
Total United States	9,986	8,556	3,500

Source: Data are from the Arms Control Association as reported in *Newsweek,* June 29, 1992, p. 26.

ICBMs that can carry only one warhead per missile. Consequently, Russia had to give up its remaining SS-18s. In the last years of the Cold War, if the Soviet Union had ever hoped to catch the United States by surprise with a "bolt from the blue," it would have been with its MIRVed SS-18s. Despite slightly fewer SLICBMs for American submarines compared to Russia, the present qualitative differences in nuclear sea power and bombers work to the United States' advantage. Finally, President Bill Clinton and President Boris Yeltsin agreed in 1994 to speed up weapon cuts and reach START II limits before 2003.

The U.S. Senate ratified START II in early 1996, but more than a year later, in 1997, the same treaty languished in the Russian Parliament. Russian leaders, upset over the eastward expansion of NATO, have been reluctant to ratify. This reluctance probably will fail to leverage a halt to NATO's expansion, and the Russians will then likely ratify START II. Their ICBMs are aging, and they cannot afford to maintain them properly or to replace them. Failing to ratify will leave Russia with increasingly unreliable missiles while the United States can afford to move on to a new generation of ICBMs. The missile system of Russia, before START II reaches fruition, presently consists of 1,300 strategic missiles with 6,000 warheads, and these missiles are kept on hair-trigger alert. Unfortunately, not only are Russian conventional forces disheveled, but the Strategic Nuclear Forces are largely unpaid, unfed, and demoralized. Safeguards that prevent accidental or unauthorized launches are fraying.

The historically significant accomplishments of START I and START II are without complete assurance of success, however. For a time, three FSRs (Belarus with 54 warheads, Kazakhstan with 1,360 warheads, and the Ukraine with 1,408 warheads) hesitated to surrender their nuclear weapons to Russia for disposal, but finally did so.[40] Now the Russian

Parliament, reflecting a pricked sense of nationalism over the eastern expansion of NATO, makes START II an uncertainty. Finally, assuming START II reaches its goals at least by 2003, the danger of a nuclear war between Russia and the United States will not evaporate. Both countries still have enough nuclear weaponry to obliterate each other.[41] Hence, Russian success with a capitalist economy and democracy remains critical to world peace.

Are other nuclear weapon states that admit to having a nuclear weapon planning any disarmament? China, France, and Great Britain are unwilling to join Russia and the United States in cutting nuclear weapons. In their view, their nuclear arsenals are so minuscule that they will not disarm to any degree, at least not until Russia and the United States make much deeper cuts in their own nuclear arsenals. China has 450 nuclear weapons, France 524, and Great Britain 200.[42] Then there are the undeclared nuclear states of India, Israel, and Pakistan. Their exact number of nuclear weapons are unknown. As mentioned earlier, their nuclear capability may be at the "threshold" stage, with stored parts, nuclear fuel, and trigger devices ready for assembly. Countries under suspicion for currently working on an atomic bomb are Algeria, Iran, Iraq, Libya, North Korea, and Syria. These states are unlikely to give up their nuclear programs. In contrast, Argentina, Brazil, South Africa, South Korea, and Taiwan have ceased nuclear weapons development, or so they claim.

Finally, disarmament steps have also taken place in the area of biological weapons and chemical warfare. *The Geneva Protocol* of 1925 banned the use of biological weapons, but not the making and stockpiling of these weapons. The *Biological Weapons Convention* of 1972 prohibits the production and stockpiling of bacteriological and toxic weapons, known as "germ warfare." The *Hague Conferences* at the turn of the last century prohibited the use of chemical weapons, sometimes called "gas warfare." In spite of this prohibition, European armies used lethal gas in the First World War. This use led to the Geneva Protocol, which also bans lethal gas and which states respected through the Second World War and for years afterward. However, Iraq released gas against Iranian troops in the 1980s and dropped bombs, armed with gas, on its Kurdish minority. Iraq's use of gas led to the *Chemical Weapons Convention (CWC)* of 1993, which disallows the production and storage of chemical weapons and requires states to dispose of any existing stocks by the year 2005.

Disengagement and Confidence Building

The process of removing troops and weapons of different states from proximity to one another, sometimes accompanied with confidence and security-building measures (CSBMs), also has helped stabilize peace among states. A famous disengagement pact, and the most successful to date, is the *Rush-Bagot Agreement* of 1817. The British and American governments agreed to withdraw their troops and warships from the Great Lakes region, and the Canadian government has continued to respect this agreement. Today the American-Canadian border is the longest unarmed border in the world.

An excellent example of a modern CSBM comes from the *Conference on Security and Cooperation* of 1975 in Europe. Among other agreements, European countries on both sides of the Iron Curtain decided to give warning before either NATO or the Warsaw Pact would practice maneuvers. Thus, neither side would mistake maneuvers for the launching of a surprise attack. Furthermore, the *Stockholm Talks* of 1986 allowed observers from each alliance to watch the others' maneuvers.[43] A recent example is the agreement by

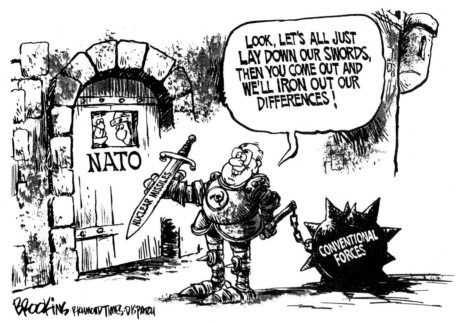

© 1987 Gary Brookins, *Richmond Times-Dispatch*

President Bill Clinton and President Boris Yeltsin in 1994 to re-aim American and Russian ICBMs at isolated areas of the oceans instead of military bases and cities. Should the accidental firing of a missile take place, minimal damage would result. Evidently pleased with a consulting role with an expanded NATO, President Yeltsin also promised in 1997 to re-target missiles aimed at Europe toward the Atlantic Ocean. These steps are mostly symbolic since the Russians can re-aim their missiles in minutes by computer.

As with disarmament, disengagement among the NATO and Warsaw Pact states was not possible until Mikhail Gorbachev came to power in the Soviet Union in 1985. At first, American leaders thought Gorbachev would insist on the same position previous Soviet leaders had taken, to urge nuclear disarmament in Europe without reductions in conventional forces. A large numerical advantage in tanks, planes, and troops by the Warsaw Pact over NATO meant the United States ultimately had to rely on nuclear weapons to deter a Soviet-led attack. Disposing of nuclear weapons alone in Europe would only magnify the Warsaw Pact advantage.

In a surprising move, however, Mikhail Gorbachev made offers of arms and troop reductions in Europe to begin as early as 1988, and this offer led to the *Conventional Forces in Europe Treaty (CFE)* of 1990. The CFE greatly reduced the number of tanks, combat helicopters, and artillery of the Warsaw Pact, leaving the two sides about equal in conventional weapons. Since the Warsaw Pact had a three-to-one advantage in several important weapons, the CFE improved NATO's position on conventional weapons. The CFE called for elaborate on-site inspections to guarantee the terms of the agreement. Although the dissolution of the Soviet Union jeopardized the CFE, the FSRs involved promised in 1992 to abide by the CFE terms. Russia got to keep about half of the conventional weapons in central Europe once controlled by the Soviet Union.

Following close behind the CFE, the *Troop Levels in Europe Agreement* of 1992 limited American and Russian troops to 195,000 each in central Europe. President Bill Clinton also promised to further reduce American participation in NATO to 100,000 troops. During the Cold War, America's contribution to NATO reached 300,000 troops. Finally, in our earlier discussion of verification, we covered the *Open Skies Agreement* of 1992, another confidence-building measure intended to show that an attack is not in preparation.

Unilateral Actions

Occasionally a country, on its own initiative and without consulting other states, will simply reduce its arms to save money or because it evaluates its security needs differently. In other cases, states unilaterally make a strength reduction in the hope that other states will understand the tacit message that they should reciprocate. The hope is that reciprocal actions will go back and forth in a pattern called GRIT, or graduated and reciprocated initiatives in tension reduction.[44] Before 1963, the United States and the Soviet Union halted nuclear tests on occasion, with one signaling the other that a respite from testing would be welcome. The United States put locking devices on its ICBMs to prevent their accidental launch, hoping the Soviet Union would do the same. Further, President George Bush, on his own, withdrew **tactical weapons,** short-range nuclear missiles (95 to 310 miles) from Europe in 1991. Then Russia responded by agreeing to pull all of its tactical weapons back on Russian soil by the summer of 1992. Cooperation is possible among states without formal negotiations, even in the sensitive area of national security.

Arms Transfers

An opportunity to restrict weapons exists in the areas of selling weapons and giving them away as foreign aid. Countries can limit arms transfers unilaterally or cooperatively with other states. Arms exports were a major policy tool during the Cold War to acquire and control client-states, but today the motive of arms sales is to earn income from abroad. The tight, competitive world economy of the late 1980s and early 1990s helped sustain a pattern of arms sales, since many countries were anxious to earn foreign income. In spite of a drop in the world market for arms, arms-exporting countries still scramble to make whatever sales they can instead of halting the flow of weapons as a boon to humankind.[45]

A PROLIFERATION OF ARMS

Nuclear Weapons

With the end of the Cold War, we can observe some impressive disarmament steps, such as the START treaties. As part of the START treaties, former Soviet republics have transferred missiles to Russia for disposal. Moreover, the United States also carried out "Project Sapphire" in 1994 to remove 600 kilograms of enriched uranium from the former Soviet republic of Kazakstan. This amount of uranium fuel would allow for building 20 nuclear bombs. Another ongoing program is the Nunn-Lugar Project (named after two U.S. senators) for dismantling old Soviet nuclear submarines near Vladivostok on the Russian Pacific coast.[46]

Mike Thompson and Copley News Service

Yet several states may still wish to join the "nuclear club." What has happened is a shift from *vertical proliferation,* with the original nuclear club of five ascending to ever greater heights of nuclear power, to *horizontal proliferation,* involving an increase in the number of states acquiring an atomic bomb or at least trying to build one.[47] The generating power behind nuclear proliferation is strong. The Soviet Union responded with fear over the United States' nuclear capability, China to that of the Soviet Union, India to the Chinese nuclear bomb, and Pakistan to the nuclear threat of India. Prime Minister Zulfikar Bhutto of Pakistan, upon learning that India had exploded an atomic device, said his people would "eat grass if necessary to finance their own bomb."[48] Israel and South Africa developed nuclear weapons because they felt beleaguered by multiple nonnuclear states on their borders that held strong animosities toward them.[49]

Michael Mandelbaum offers an interesting trilogy of states that may help account for possible nuclear proliferation in the future. First, the United States *allies* of Germany and Japan, long accustomed to the protection of the American nuclear umbrella in the Cold War, might develop new fears if they see the multipolar world as unstable and unpredictable. Can they count on the United States to back them up in the face of new threats in the post–Cold War era?

Second, the *orphans* are states without an alliance to a strong nuclear state. These states include Israel, Pakistan, the Ukraine, and possibly India and Taiwan. These states probably

Chapter 10 / Arms Limitations: Passage Into the Post–Cold War Era

© 1994 Jimmy Margulies, *The Record*

have a nuclear capability, but will they pursue additional nuclear power? Dangers for these states are at the regional level and are unrelated to the passing of the Cold War. These states hope the United States, through diplomacy, will help defuse the issues with their neighbors. At least the Ukraine helped stanch horizontal proliferation by signing a tripartite accord with Russia and the United States in 1994. The Ukraine not only is to move its nuclear weapons to Russia for disposal but has also promised to sign the NPT.

Third, the *rogues* are several Third World states that have shown a keen interest in an atom bomb, apparently to increase their power and prestige. These states include Algeria, Iran, Libya, Syria, and especially Iraq and North Korea.[50] The West, for business profits, helped Iraq assemble a massive, high-tech military system before the Persian Gulf War in 1991. This help proved to be an abysmal error by the West. Luckily, Iraq still needed three to six months before having an atomic bomb when the attack of the coalition forces began on Baghdad.[51]

The example of Iraq, with its attack on Kuwait in 1990, suggests what might happen if a reckless and ambitious leader should acquire a nuclear weapon. If Iraq had possessed a nuclear warhead that would fit on its Scud missiles, would the coalition forces have dared rescue Kuwait at the cost of seeing Tel Aviv in Israel and Riyadh in Saudi Arabia evaporate in a nuclear fireball? For a rogue state, the value of a nuclear bomb might be to discourage interference by other states as the rogue state attacks a neighbor with conventional weapons.

By 1993, North Korea had become the nuclear problem-child for the world after Desert Storm quashed Iraq's military strength. North Korea had signed the NPT in 1985 but decided to construct an atomic bomb anyway. No one outside North Korea knows with certainty whether this country really has a bomb, but this poor state, with some of its population facing famine and starvation, probably has enough plutonium on hand for one to three bombs. After generous inducements by President Bill Clinton, including possible trade and diplomatic relations with the United States, North Korea still failed to cooperate satisfactorily with the IAEA. One reason for President Clinton's patience with China's trade and human rights violations is that China may be able to exert a positive influence with North Korea's leaders concerning their nuclear weapons program. China may be the only country with regular and dependable communications with Pyongyang, the North Korean capital.

An inducement for North Korea to steer away from a nuclear weapons program is the promise of two light-water reactors for peaceful energy use. A consortium of the European Union, Japan, South Korea, and the United States, known as the Korean Peninsula Energy Development Organization (KEDO), is building these nuclear reactors to replace the aging Soviet-type reactors that create weapons-grade waste materials. As planned, the first reactor will be ready for operation in 2003.

In case North Korea does make and use an atomic weapon, President Clinton, bearing in mind the United States' bilateral defense treaties with both Japan and South Korea, has said, "we would quickly and overwhelmingly retaliate. . . . It would mean the end of their country [North Korea] as they know it."[52]

Possible enablers to the spread of nuclear weapons are the unemployed or low-paid scientists in Russia and eastern Europe whose weapons know-how is no longer in demand at home. The knowledge of a Russian nuclear physicist could help convert a country such as Iraq or North Korea into a nuclear power in a brief period. To the credit of Russian authorities, they have tried to stop Russian scientists from moving to rogue states for lucrative pay. The International Science and Technology Center (ISTC) in Moscow, set up in 1993, is spending more than $60 million, given by the European Union, Japan, and the United States, to employ 5,000 scientists on nonmilitary projects.

Largely because of the ISTC, the expected exodus of Russian scientists has not happened. However, some enterprising scientists have sold their expertise by electronic mail, a communications network the IAEA and other monitoring bodies will have trouble controlling. One enterprising Russian physicist, for $3,000 pay, worked out a missile guidance problem for Iran via E-mail. Recruitment of scientists and their responses can easily take place over the Internet by enciphered messages, if necessary, to avoid censoring.

Chemical and Biological Weapons

Proliferation in the areas of chemical and biological weapons is a concern second only to the spread of nuclear weapons. Concerning knowledge and necessary materials, these weapons are more available and cheap to produce. Gas and biological weapons are the "poor man's A-bomb" whenever a Third World country desires a weapon with mass destruction capabilities. Gas weapons are probably the first choice of the two. Although neither is easy to control as battlefield weapons, gas is easier to manage. Despite international conventions to rid the world of the dangers of chemical weapons, 15 to 20 countries, mostly Third World states, may have a gas warfare capability or one in development.[53] Any country that is willing to convert a pesticide factory and has a few easy-to-obtain chemicals can make lethal gas for warfare.[54]

Germ warfare may have less military application than gas warfare, but anthrax and cholera are storable in military containers and are directable to a target.[55] At least some countries have tried to create a germ warfare capability. Japan had a large research facility in Manchuria where Japanese scientists experimented on POWs during the Second World War. Evidence of possible anthrax development appeared in Iraq following the Persian Gulf War. In 1979, Russian scientists accidentally released anthrax spores from a germ warfare facility

Palma/Expresso/Lisbon

in Sverdlovsk, killing a thousand of their own civilians.[56] An occasional scientist, departing Russia permanently, has claimed that Russia carries on chemical and biological warfare capacities despite President Boris Yeltsin's best efforts to shut them down.

Missile Proliferation

The acquisition or development of missiles by radical Third World states compounds the proliferation of ABC weapons to these countries. For example, North Korea has the No-Don I missile, with a range of 650 miles, and India has the Agni, with a range of 1,500 miles, that it has fired into space and has controlled its reentry into the atmosphere. Wanting hard currency, Russia has been willing to sell rocket engines, and China has sold its Silkworm missile, with a range of several hundred miles, to a few Third World states and has probably sold the M-11, with a range of 180 miles, to Pakistan. Once these states fashion ABC weapons into warheads for missiles, their capacity to project mass destruction multiplies. Algeria, Egypt, Iraq, Iran, North Korea, Pakistan, and South Africa are in the *intraregional ballistic missile (IRBM)* club, although they may not yet have suitable ABC warheads. Twenty states may have IRBM capability by the turn of the 21st century.[57] Only Russia and the United States are in the business of destroying missile vehicles.

Intermediate-range missiles, combined with submarines that can fire them, will give some Third World countries intercontinental range. Over 40 countries collectively have more than

Lambert Der, *The Greenville News*

600 submarines. For instance, North Korea has 35 submarines.[58] The most modern nuclear submarines are not necessary to fire missiles. Submarines based on the older technology of diesel/electric propulsion are adequate to carry and fire intermediate-range missiles.[59]

It is the fear of facing missile attack by rogue states that has renewed interest in an antiballistic missile (ABM) defense system on the part of some major states. Russia and the United States, however, are in a quandary over this matter because they signed a treaty together in 1972 binding themselves to one ABM defensive missile site each. If they are to develop antimissile missiles, beyond the ability of the Patriot missile batteries that had a mixed record shooting down Iraqi Scuds in the Persian Gulf War, Russia and the United States will have to develop a rationale to sidestep the 1972 ABM treaty. One rationale they can consider is to claim the 1972 treaty concerns only defensive missiles for shooting down ICBMs traveling strategically from one continent to another. This rationale would leave Russia and the United States free to develop new ABM systems for operating in a tactical or regional context.[60]

Terrorists

The proliferation of ABC weapons to terrorists may be as threatening as radical Third World states acquiring these weapons, if only because of their proclivity to use them. Many terrorists are fanatical, and they are willing to pay any price to serve their cause, including their own lives and the blood of the innocent. Terrorists have maimed and killed people at will in many countries for a variety of causes. A Japanese religious cult's release of gas in Tokyo's subway

The Globe and Mail, Toronto

system in 1995 is a frightening preview of what may happen in the future when terrorists acquire or make more lethal ABC devices. The use of chemical and biological agents is not beyond terrorists' capabilities, and their acquisition of an atomic device is not impossible.

Most countries are highly vulnerable to terrorist attacks against civilian populations. In 1997, as a beginning at protecting its people, the United States commenced the *Domestic Preparedness Program (DPP)* in Denver that will eventually protect 120 cities from terrorist use of ABC weapons of mass destruction. In the largest civil defense program since the Cold War, the DPP starts small by placing in Denver a detection system for sniffing out deadly airborne microbes. Under a 1996 congressional law, the U.S. Department of Defense is backing this program.

Atomic weapons in the hands of terrorists are the most feared. Only two resources are necessary to make an atomic bomb: knowledge and materials. Knowledge about atom bombs is now widespread. The primary but thin barrier to terrorist acquisition of a workable atomic bomb is government control of plutonium and uranium. All that is needed for the simplest atomic device is 100 pounds of enriched uranium or 20 pounds of plutonium. While these materials are under tight security wraps in the United States, several efforts to smuggle them out of Russia have occurred, and one effort may have succeeded. Disarray in Russia and poor pay have created opportunities for government employees and Russian organized crime syndicates to move these materials into black market channels as a profitable business venture.

Conventional Weapons

While the proliferation of ABC weapons and missiles captures the most attention concerning weapon transfers, a flourishing international market in conventional weapons

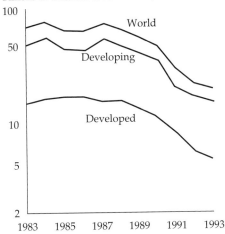

WORLD ARMS IMPORTS 1983-1993

Billions of constant 1993 dollars *(ratio scale*)*

Source: *World Military Expenditures and Arms Transfers 1993–1994* (Washington, D.C.: U.S. Arms Control and Disarmament Agency, 1995).

also has significant negative effects. Tanks, artillery, gunship helicopters, planes, rifles, and hand grenades moving into troubled regions raise international tensions to higher levels and provide the means for internal strife and political repression. The good news is that weapon imports in most areas of the world have declined in recent years. Figure 10.2 shows the slope of the decline in world arms imports, the bulk of which are conventional weapons.

The figures involve a world decline from about $76 billion in arms imports in 1984 down to about $22 billion in 1993. The breakdown for the developed countries (28 countries with high-tech industry and high living standards) is a decline from a $16 billion peak in weapon imports in 1986 to $5 billion in 1993. The developing countries (the 143 remaining countries in the WMEAT 1993–1994 report) reflect a similar drop in imports, from $61 billion in their peak year of 1984 to $17 billion in 1993.[61]

The explanation for the decline in weapon imports is threefold. First, the end of the Cold War stopped the competition between the United States and the Soviet Union to recruit and control client-states through attractive arms deals and gifts. Second, more countries nowadays are democracies, a type of government that is prone to negotiate differences with other governments instead of fighting. This observation is especially true when democracies are dealing with one another. Third, a constrained world economy means less money available for arms, and, in a democratizing world, active publics are demanding "peace dividends."

Although the decline in weapon imports is a clear pattern, weapon flows are still significant in size. Cumulative arms imports for the world totaled over $76 billion for the period 1991–1993. Table 10.2 shows a breakdown of imports by region. Assuming western Europe is a stable area, except for the possible dangers of a revanchist Russia and the Bosnian

TABLE 10.2
Regional Arms Imports, 1991–1993

Region	Expenditures (U.S. $bil.)	Percentage of world total
Middle East	$31,690	41%
Western Europe	12,940	17
East Asia	10,635	14
North America	5,840	8
South Asia	4,515	6
Africa	2,015	3
South America	1,400	2
Eastern Europe	1,300	2
All others	6,215	8
World	76,550	100

Source: *World Military Expenditures and Arms Transfers 1993–1994* (Washington, D.C.: U.S. Arms Control and Disarmament Agency, 1995), p. 10.

imbroglio, the Middle East and East Asia are the current regions most prone to arms races. The Middle East has experienced many wars, and even in times of peace, this region absorbs a major share of weapon imports. Iraq alone was the world's fourth leading arms importer from 1986 to 1990. Iraq received over $10 billion in arms purchases as this country finished its war with Iran and readied for the invasion of Kuwait.[62]

War has spared East Asia in recent years, but several countries are building up arms, including China, Japan, and Taiwan. These countries focus on arms modernization rather than raising troop levels. With a healthy economic growth rate, East Asia can pay for the high-tech weapons that are modernizing its military forces. For example, China recently purchased from Russia two new destroyers equipped with Sunburn missiles that can attack ships in the U.S. 7th Fleet, a large number of SU-27 fighters armed with Archer air-to-air missiles that pilots guide to target with a helmet-mounted sight, and four Kilo-class submarines. China is following the well-worn historical path of many states by converting new wealth into military strength and, in doing so, has made its neighbors nervous.

Accompanying the world decline in arms imports is the drop in the arms sales of the United States. Despite vigorous efforts to sell arms abroad to offset America's trade debt, arms sales for the United States plunged from $36 billion in 1993 to $14.5 billion in 1994.[63] Although international weapon sales have declined markedly since the end of the Cold War, the United States has gained a larger proportionate share of the market that does exist. Table 10.3 shows that the United States' percentage share of the arms market rose each year, while Russian arms exports declined. Other countries' percentage shares of the arms market remained stable. The largest single route of arms sales in the world market is from U.S. weapon plants to the armed forces of NATO allies.[64] Undoubtedly, America's paramount role in arms sales comes from a need to earn foreign income, but the U.S. government and some scholars make the dubious claim that America's arms sales help stabilize regional conflicts.[65]

The United States also transfers a lot of weapons as "giveaways" to friends and allies or sells them cheaply as surplus weapons. The United States has transferred over $7 billion

TABLE 10.3
Shares of World Arms Exports, 1989–1993

Year	United States	Soviet Union/ Russia	Britain, France, Germany	Other Europe	China	Others
1989	27%	39%	17%	17%	5%	5%
1990	30	34	25	5	3	3
1991	36	22	29	5	5	3
1992	42	10	29	9	4	6
1993	47	12	28	6	4	3

Source: *World Military Expenditures and Arms Transfers 1993–1994* (Washington, D.C.: U.S. Arms Control and Disarmament Agency, 1995), p. 15.

worth of surplus weapons since 1990. These include older tanks, jet fighters, and ships. As many as 60 countries receive these weapons free or at far below their cost. Israel has received most of these weapons.[66]

Light Weapons

Just as the proliferation of ABC weapons overshadows conventional weapons as a concern, high-tech tanks and jet fighter planes shoulder aside the importance of light weapons such as mortars and assault rifles. Yet it is these weapons, along with machine guns, mines, and grenades, that destabilize many societies and fuel the violent conflict found in internal wars, including those of Bosnia and Rwanda. Heavily armed militias can even challenge UN Peacekeepers and U.S. troops, as they did in Somalia. Because of a much lower price range, an expansion in small arms has taken place, bucking the trend of declining sales in the major conventional arms such as jet fighters and modern battle tanks. In addition, sales of small arms are difficult to monitor because the *UN Register for Conventional Weapons* does not cover small arms.[67]

Many countries are happy to focus on the market niche of small arms. In some cases, drug cartels, with their money and smuggling routes, act as middlemen in small-arms sales. A drug cartel has supplied the Peruvian guerrilla group Shining Path with American-made M-60 machine guns and 81mm mortars. The drug cartel bought these weapons from a licensed exporter instead of a black market source, because it could acquire better-quality weapons at lower prices.[68]

Finally, a special worry in weapons proliferation is the sale of land mines, a subject discussed earlier. While some countries refuse to sell mines, others, particularly Italy, sell cheap, hard-to-detect, plastic-encased mines that are a bane to human life and limb. There are 100 million mines in the ground today and another 100 million in stockpiles, and millions more are coming off assembly lines, although UN secretary-general Boutros Boutros-Ghali and the International Committee of the Red Cross advocated a complete ban on the export of all land mines.[69] Recently the United States announced it would cease the export of land mines and would use land mines only to defend South Korea and to stop aggression in the Persian Gulf area. Finally, a 1996 United Nations conference on land mines called for any mines laid after 2005 to have detectable metal parts and to deteriorate over time to an unworkable state.

In addition to land mines, another weapon, in development by five states, including the United States, belongs under the coverage of the *UN Inhumane Weapons Convention* of 1980. The weapon is a laser device designed to blind enemy soldiers from miles away. All weapons of war seem inhumane, but some are especially deplorable.

THE STATUS OF WEAPONS REGIMES

At least five recognizable weapons regimes have come into existence to check the proliferation of weapons in the world. Three of these deal with the ABC weapons, while the others focus on export controls for missile technology, trade between Western and communist countries, and trade in conventional weapons. Recall that regimes are rules and norms supported by a group of states, either through a hegemon's leadership or through a cooperative venture. Weapons regimes are basically cooperative in type and offer opportunities for states to accumulate lessons that can shape more effective weapons control institutions for the future.[70]

The Nuclear Weapons Regime

The nuclear regime centers on the NPT and the inspection role of the IAEA. Five nuclear powers are members (China, Great Britain, France, Russia and the United States), along with 163 nonnuclear members, although several of these latter states are almost certainly "threshold" states able to assemble an atomic bomb. The holdouts—China, France, and South Africa—joined the NPT in 1991. Signatories of the NPT agree not to give or receive the technology and fissionable materials needed to make a nuclear weapon. The nuclear regime is the most developed weapons regime, yet several members have tried to make an atom bomb in direct contravention of IAEA rules. For instance, the NPT has loopholes that permit states to accumulate legally all they need for a bomb short of assembling a weapon with a trigger device. Nuclear powers met as the London Group in 1974, and later as the Nuclear Suppliers Group, to control exports that might aid a nonnuclear state in building a nuclear weapon.[71]

The fundamental problem of the nuclear regime is its glaring hypocrisy as a two-tier regime. A few powerful states allow themselves nuclear bombs while attempting to deny them to others. The nuclear powers are saying to nonnuclear states, "Do as I say, not as I do."[72] The Chemical Weapons Convention, in contrast, has the moral advantage of calling for a universal agreement with all states subscribing to the same rules.[73] To its disadvantage, the NPT has no clear means of enforcing its rules. The only direct enforcement against a rogue state so far has been the highly controversial preemptive air strike by the Israeli Air Force against Iraq's nuclear facility at Osiraq in 1981. The legitimacy of a unilateral act of enforcement strains credibility, however. In contrast, the United Nations effort to demobilize Iraq's ABC facilities following the Persian Gulf War does carry the imprimatur of widely accepted legitimacy.[74]

An interesting extension of the nuclear regime is the effort to halt all nuclear testing and to sign a *comprehensive test ban treaty (CTBT)*. A moratorium against testing stood from 1992 to 1995 until the French government resumed a schedule of eight nuclear tests that were to last into 1996. States supporting the CTBT have called for the CTBT moratorium to become permanent and universal in 1996. France resumed tests because it wanted to make a more compact weapon and to test this weapon against computer models. France has claimed computer models will replace actual nuclear explosions in the future. With the end of French testing, China became the prime state needing to make a firm commitment to the nuclear test ban regime.

After many years of discussing a complete test ban for nuclear weapons in the Geneva Conference on Disarmament and failing consensus, the issue moved to the General Assembly of the United Nations, where the CTBT received an approving vote of 158 to 3 in September 1996. The five declared nuclear powers (China, France, Great Britain, Russia, and the United States) voted for the CTBT, with President Bill Clinton being the first leader to sign this treaty. These five states are responsible for the 2,045 nuclear explosions that have occurred since 1945, except for the one platform-type explosion by India in 1974. Bhutan, India, and Libya voted against the treaty. Interestingly, India, in 1954, was the first country to call for a complete ban on nuclear explosions. Today India wants all countries to disarm all nuclear weapons instead of leaving an unequal world with a small "nuclear club" and all other states devoid of nuclear weaponry. The CTBT is now open for ratification, and it calls for zero yield, which means no explosion of any size, and for a complete test ban treaty organization (CTBTO) that can inspect testing and radiation on land, at sea, and in the atmosphere.[75]

The Biological Weapons Regime

The *Biological Weapons Convention* (BWC) of 1972 is the center of the biological weapons regime, with over 130 states subscribing to it. No certain inspection of verification takes place, but a state can call on the UN Security Council to investigate a state suspected of work in this area. The BWC of 1972 forbids the production or use of germ warfare, while the earlier *Geneva Protocol* of 1925 prohibited only the use of germ warfare. A set of Western states known as the *Australia Group* has sought since 1990 to control exports of equipment and material that might contribute to the development of a germ warfare capability by a state.

As yet no major use of germ warfare has taken place, but the biological weapons regime needs strengthening by using short-notice inspections.[76] Enough suspicions and activities take place to warrant these inspections. Iraq, based on evidence found following the Persian Gulf War, had a biological weapons program. In 1995, President Bill Clinton's administration accused China of conducting biological warfare experiments. Finally, President Boris Yeltsin of Russia may have failed to end biological and chemical tests in his country.

The Chemical Weapons Regime

Unlike biological weapons, chemical weapons have appeared on the battlefield, causing 1.8 million casualties in the First World War and thousands more in the Iranian-Iraqi War in the 1980s. Yet 25 states had signed the Hague Declaration of 1899 pledging to refrain from "asphyxiating or deleterious gases."[77] The Geneva Protocol of 1925, in addition to prohibiting germ warfare, tried to outlaw the use of lethal gas in war. In 1985, the Australia Group took on the added responsibility of monitoring equipment and material that might contribute to the development of a gas warfare capability.

Corbis-Bettmann

A stronger contribution to the chemical weapons regime is the *Chemical Weapons Convention (CWC)* of 1993, which has 164 signatories and 75 ratifications as of April 1996. The CWC not only prohibits gas warfare but also requires states ratifying the treaty to destroy all stocks of gas by 2005. After a tough fight between President Bill Clinton and some opposing senators, the U.S. Senate ratified the CWC in April 1996. The original ratifying states will exercise authority over any future rule changes concerning chemical weapons.

The United States and Russia have by far the largest gas stocks, and Russia is a special problem because it cannot afford the almost $4 billion the destruction of its stocks would cost.[78] Overall, as many as 25 countries may have achieved a gas warfare capability by the 1980s.[79] Libya, in its usual rogue state capacity, is an extreme problem. Libya has been busy for several years building a nerve gas factory in a cavern deep inside a mountain where spy satellites and air attacks cannot reach. Given Libya's record of state-sponsored terrorism and support for privately based terrorists, the potential harm it could do is inestimable. Fortunately, Iraq's gas-making ability received a severe setback in the aftermath of the Persian Gulf War. Iraq has had to dismantle gas-making facilities under United Nations supervision. The CWC established the *Organization for the Prohibition of Chemical Weapons (OPCW)* with authority to conduct short-notice inspections and to ensure that signatories respect all rules. The OPCW began operations in 1995 but with a smaller staff and budget than the original plan called for: 365 employees instead of 1,000 and a 1995 budget of $60 million instead of $150 million.[80]

The Missile Technology Control Regime

The missile regime began only in 1987 because, for a time, states regarded missiles as conventional weapons. However, concern arose over a widening circle of states trying to develop ABC warheads for their missiles. Thus, export controls became necessary to restrict the sale of missiles and missile technology. About 25 countries take part in the export controls. Specifically, the missile regime calls for exporting states to halt the transfer of missiles that could carry a payload of 500 kilograms at a range of 300 kilometers. The thinking at the time was that Third World countries could not make a nuclear warhead smaller than 500 kilograms. The Persian Gulf War heightened fears that missiles could also carry a lighter gas or germ-type warhead, and so the missile regime tightened standards to include any missile with a range over 300 kilometers, regardless of warhead size or type. Each supplier unilaterally implements the rules of the missile regime and shares information about a violation with other states in the regime. Before the end of the Cold War, the states of the Soviet bloc and China, though not original supporters, agreed to apply the regime rules.

A major issue between China and the United States, in addition to human rights questions and trade terms, was China's sale of missile technology to Pakistan until China recently stopped those sales. The United States retaliated against a 1993 sale that violated the missile regime by refusing to allow $1 billion of trade in high-technology goods between 1993 and 1995. The U.S. Congress has made mandatory trade punishments for violating the missile regime.

The Conventional Weapons Regime

A *United Nations Register for Conventional Weapons,* after 25 years of discussion, finally opened in 1992. The goal behind this UN register is transparency for arms sales. If weapons sales are out in the open, those selling weapons may become more prudent concerning what and to whom they sell. The role of the Register is not effective enough, however, since participation is voluntary and the 70 or more countries taking part are able to report just what they choose. The UN Register is still a significant accomplishment if we bear in mind that the participating actors are sovereign and have a long history of selling arms to influence other states as well as to make money.

In his term of office from 1976 to 1980, President Jimmy Carter attempted to cap American arms sales. However, weapon sales and gifts were too useful to cement relations with client-states, and so conventional weapon sales remained robust until after the Cold War.[81] Only when member-states of the United Nations became dramatically aware, through Iraq's example, of the damage that unrestrained weapon sales can cause did they move to create the UN Register.

Other types of regimes could emerge as well. Japan and the United States have cooperated over the sale of supercomputers to keep them out of the hands of warlike states. Small, high-speed computers are useful for building high-tech weapons such as missile-aiming devices. Also, an emerging regime may be taking shape in scientifically advanced countries calling for these states to restrain their weapon scientists from taking employment in a Third World state.[82] Finally, if the Iranian-Iraqi War is not to be a grim harbinger of the Third World's future, weapons control regimes will have to do a better job.

THE ROLE OF NONSTATE ACTORS

Arms limitations activities do not belong to states alone. International government organizations (IGOs) and international nongovernment organizations (INGOs), as well as domestic actors, exert strong voices against military expenditures and the dangers of weapons accumulation.

Arms limitations are traceable to the *Hague Conference* of 1899, which sought to outlaw poisonous gases, and to the League of Nations as an IGO, dating from 1919, that called for general disarmament. The League also promoted the *Geneva Arms Traffic Convention* of 1925, which failed to receive enough signatures and did not enter into force. At least the League was able to level economic sanctions against Italy and Japan for aggressions in the 1930s, sanctions that failed to stop those aggressions but did hurt the aggressors economically.[83]

The United Nations came to see complete disarmament as idealistic by the 1960s and turned its energies to controlling the weapons that did exist. The United Nations set up organizational machinery for dealing with arms questions, including the Disarmament Commission and the UN Institute for Disarmament Research. This IGO also publishes the *Disarmament Yearbook,* a record of arms activities. The United Nations has served as a forum urging the nuclear powers to arrive at the Nuclear Test Ban Treaty of 1963, encouraged the NPT's acceptance, and sponsored the Outer Space Treaty of 1967 and the UN Convention Against Inhumane Weapons of 1980. Finally, the United Nations has not only lent its imprimatur to the coalition forces for stopping Iraq's invasion of Kuwait but has insisted on the destruction of Iraq's ABC weapons facilities as the price for ending the economic embargo against Iraq.

Paralleling state and IGO efforts are the activities of domestic actors to halt expenditures on weapons and to promote peace and focus more money on human welfare.[84] Should the world continue to democratize, more domestic actors will be able to demand of governments a justification for military expenditures. In the United States, for instance, over 30 organizations that lobby against arms operate in Washington, D.C. The Council for a Liveable World is the oldest of these organizations. Women in Western countries have been in the forefront of the disarmament movement, including the U.S. organizations of Peace Links and Women's Action for Nuclear Disarmament. Disarmament groups in Washington coordinate under a loose association called the Monday Lobby Group.

Citizen activity can lead to ad hoc cooperation across borders. During the 1980s, the National Resources Defense Council in the United States and the Academy of Sciences in the Soviet Union arranged for seismic devices to monitor the size of underground nuclear explosions. These seismic devices guaranteed that the explosions would not exceed the size agreed to by treaty. Some citizen transborder activities form into permanent organizations, or INGOs. The International Physicians for the Prevention of Nuclear War, made up of American and Soviet doctors, won the Nobel Peace Prize in 1985.[85]

In 1989, an INGO formed in Monterey, California, to track the spread of nuclear materials missile technology. Formed on the campus of the Monterey Institute of International Studies, the Center for Non-Proliferation Studies can use as many as 60 different language speakers to monitor journals, newspapers, business reports, and all other open sources to keep track of sales and thefts. Stored in computer banks, the center shares its data with governments and weapons regimes attempting to stop the flow of dangerous weapons.[86]

A widely respected organization is the Stockholm International Peace Research Institute (SIPRI). The SIPRI is a quasi-INGO, reflecting both a domestic and an international

Agence France-Presse

status. While the SIPRI receives important funding from the Swedish parliament, it also takes money from private donors from any country. The SIPRI's personnel come mostly from Sweden, but they include members from many countries. The SIPRI dedicates its activities to world peace and delivers its most important service through its highly respected *Yearbook of World Disarmament.* The *Yearbook* reports arms information from a majority of the countries of the world.[87]

An INGO that takes a more energetic approach than most organizations is Greenpeace. This INGO is an environmental group that objects to nuclear testing because of environmental damage. Greenpeace has tried to disrupt the series of eight French underground tests 650 miles from Tahiti in the South Pacific Ocean. As Greenpeace sailed *Rainbow II* into French territorial waters in French Polynesia in 1995, French marines tear-gassed and arrested the crew. This act occurred on the eve of the 10-year anniversary of the sinking of *Rainbow I* in a New Zealand harbor in 1985. French agents planted a bomb on *Rainbow I* that took one person's life. During the series of eight nuclear bomb tests, both spontaneous and organized demonstrations besieged French embassies and consulates around the world.

The 1995 Nobel Committee unabashedly sent a message to the world, and particularly to the French government, by awarding its peace prize jointly to Joseph Rotblat and the Pugwash Conferences on Science and World Affairs located in Pugwash, Nova Scotia. Rotblat is a founder of the Pugwash Conferences, which has been meeting since 1957, dedicating its resources to eliminating nuclear weapons from the world. In 1944 Rotblat left the "Manhattan Project", which was designing an atom bomb for the use of the United States during the Second World War. In 1955, he joined with Bertrand Russell and Albert Einstein to sign a manifesto calling for a nuclear-free world.

ARMS LIMITATIONS AND INTERNATIONAL SOCIETY

The presence of arms in the world mirrors the insecurity and fear characteristic of states in an uncertain world. States on edge, always ready to defend or to attack, will not interact in a way favorable to an international society. If the realist's view of the world as a dangerous anarchy of endless power struggles were entirely correct, states could do no better than arm themselves to deter the strong and prey on the weak. For a realist, the only hope for peace occurs when states form a balance of power arrangement to establish mutual deterrence from attack. Realists recognize, however, that equality in armed strength may provide only a brief rest from a pattern of war. Even if a balance of power works for peace, new developments in arms on one side, tension from an arms race, or the formation of a new alliance can easily upset a balance of power system, encouraging conflict and war.

Thus, realists tend to make bleak assessments about arms agreements contributing to a better world. A stable system of states, much less an international society of states building a web of norms and rules, cannot last long if the perverse logic of realism is correct: Under anarchy, as states pursue their own security, they endanger the security of other states.[88] As a result, a continuous scramble for arms and allies permeates a system of hostile states. Even if states prefer to disarm, their best strategy in a self-help, anarchic world leads to armaments instead of disarmament. When it is "every state for itself," states cannot envision a common interest in arms limits.[89] Leading realist Hans Morgenthau further deprecates the chances for arms agreements by pointing out that there is a more fundamental problem than simply the possession or riddance of arms: It is states' lust for power that produces the fear and insecurity in the state system in the first place.[90] For Morgenthau, the power struggle among states is inexorable and timeless, making arms agreements difficult if not impossible.

For neorealists, led by Kenneth N. Waltz, the prospects for arms limitations are less gloomy. Neorealists still see a dangerous world, especially because of nuclear weapons, but the Soviet Union and the United States were able to reach a stable understanding based on a bipolarized world with a MAD arrangement.[91] Neither side could afford militarily to impose its view of a global order on the world because a nuclear war would destroy all the countries in the communist and democratic camps, if not the world. The superpowers, with their shared interest of survival at hand, fine-tuned their nuclear stand-off with arms agreements of the arms control type. According to neorealists, the Cold War adversaries came to behave similarly in a reciprocal, cooperative way, thus preventing nuclear war.[92]

Transnationalists, in contrast to realists and neorealists, are more optimistic about progress toward peace. They recognize a capacity by leaders of states to adopt new perceptions about national interests and arms. According to Joseph S. Nye, Jr., states are coming to understand that the national interest of security for each state depends on the "common security" of all states.[93] Arms agreements are not superfluous, as realists think, or merely a stabilizing device for a bipolar stand-off, as neorealists believe, but a tool to help former Cold War enemies transform the world into a new and better international order.[94] Since the end of the Cold War, with its vast ideological gulf, major states no longer have the clash of differences requiring huge arsenals of mass destruction and therefore can begin the historically unusual step of at least partial disarmament. Further, new norms, aided by the spread of democracy, call on governments to reduce their armed forces so that more economic resources can flow to meet people's needs.

Further understanding of the role of arms limitations in international relations can come from reference to the three models guiding the analysis of this textbook. The possession and use of arms stem naturally from an *international anarchy,* in which central *authority* is absent and actors must meet their own security needs. Although world developments have progressed beyond the simple conflict orientation of realists, a few rogue states still live on the periphery of the developing *international society* and are willing to operate outside the rules and norms of this society. They choose the older values of anarchy involving the pursuit of power through armaments and the achievement of goals by force as the normal conduct of states.

However, the nascent international society has largely supplanted anarchy in the world, with most states, certainly the major states, making choices to fulfill mutual interests. States are increasingly realizing that national security, as an *issue,* is indivisible from the common security of all. Force must give way to persuasion and is usable in only two instances. One is in self-defense. The other is "collective security," meaning states can pool their force capabilities to stop an act of aggression. These two exceptions derive from the UN Charter and are firm rules of international society. Force is not absent from the international scene, but it is in decline, and now states can distinguish legitimate from illegitimate uses of their arms.

Finally, an *international community,* in which states have no conceivable objective that calls for force by arms, exists only in western Europe. These states have arms because they once feared aggression by the Soviet Union, not threats within their ranks. For this reason, the future of NATO has been in doubt ever since the Soviet Union collapsed. In late 1995, NATO found a new function, however: policing peace in Bosnia, where the light arms of a small number of UN Peacekeepers, as well as the nature of their mission, proved inadequate. Bosnia is the one part of Europe that clearly has been in a state of anarchy with all the misery, brutality, and death that philosopher Thomas Hobbes might conjure. Now uncertainties about Russia's future propel an expansion eastward.

CHAPTER SUMMARY

Unless a country intends to use arms to gain a goal that is otherwise unachievable, they are usually interested in some form of arms limitation. Arms limitations on the part of states can signal a desire for peace, avoid an arms race, and save large sums of money. However, the chances for arms limitations sometimes collide with states' ancient fears about the intent of others. Down to what level can a state disarm without inviting imposition or invasion? Moreover, several technical problems are hindering arms limitations, arrangements for verification usually being the major obstacle. Verification procedures are a standard element of arms agreements today.

Three basic types of arms limitations are available to countries. Arms control places a ceiling on the existing system of weapons. Disarmament calls for partial or complete reduction of armaments and had been extremely difficult to achieve until the Cold War began to wane. Disengagement is the withdrawal of forces from proximity to one another to ease tensions. Unilateral steps for tacit reciprocation by the other side and controlling arms transfers are additional techniques of arms limitations.

The total volume of arms and arms expenditures in the world are in decline since the Cold War ended. Yet specific weapon transfers to rogue states, including some materials for ABC weapons and the construction of missiles, are worrisome for the large majority of states preferring peace. Several weapons regimes have formed to control the transfer of weapons. Although the regimes slow proliferation, none are complete successes.

Domestic actors, IGOs, and INGOs work hard to push governments toward disarmament. Some use a moral appeal; others, such as Greenpeace, use the tactics of civil disobedience. Anti-arms groups of all hues receive support from public opinion that increasingly calls for shifting money away from weapons to human services. The evolving democratization process in the world, in turn, bolsters this public opinion.

The recent disarmament steps between Russia and the United States make it clear that the major states are willing to live in peace and share a similar world order, including democracy and capitalism. The Cold War arms race, with bigger missiles and "dirtier" nuclear explosions, has passed into history. A greater consensus about the rules and norms of the world order and the peaceful interaction of the major states serves to reinforce the evolving international society. Today the major worries for this society are tensions and arms races in Asia and the Middle East and the danger of terrorists getting their hands on ABC devices.

POINTS OF VIEW

Since 1945 all our arts—our literature, our music, our religion, our moral philosophy—have paled beside our creative science of death.

—E. L. DOCTOROW
CALYPSO LOG
JUNE 1992

... from the dawn of consciousness until August 6, 1945, man had to live with the prospects of his death as an individual; since that day when the first bomb outshone the sun over Hiroshima, mankind as a whole has had to live with the prospect of its extinction as a species.

—ARTHUR KOESTLER,
QUOTED IN RIFKIN'S *BIOSPHERE POLITICS*

Every gun that is made, every warship launched, every rocket fired signifies, in a final sense, a theft from those who hunger and are not fed, those who are cold and are not clothed. This world in arms is not spending money alone. It is spending the sweat of its laborers, the genius of its scientists, the hopes of its children.

—DWIGHT D. EISENHOWER
PRESIDENT AND GENERAL OF THE U.S. ARMY
CALYPSO LOG, JUNE 1992

When the Army marches abroad, the Treasury will be emptied at home.

—SUN TSU
THE ART OF WAR, 500 B.C.

If you want peace, prepare for war.

—ATTRIBUTED TO A ROMAN GENERAL

If you really want peace, you have to prepare for peace.

—DR. RODRIGO CARAZO
PRESIDENT OF COSTA RICA, 1978–1982

Iraq is hellbent on redeveloping and restoring its chemical, nuclear and biological weapons capabilities.

—REPRESENTATIVE TOM LANTOS
HOUSE FOREIGN AFFAIRS COMMITTEE, *NEWSWEEK*,
JULY 12, 1993

REVIEW QUESTIONS

1. What are the basic objectives of most states concerning arms limitations?
2. What obstacles to successful arms limitation agreements can you identify?
3. Why has verification been a particularly obdurate problem for arms limitations?
4. What are the types of arms limitations? How does the end of the Cold War bear on disarmament?
5. What were the different fates of SALT I and SALT II?
6. What impact did Mikhail Gorbachev have on arms limitations?
7. What problem did three FSRs pose for the START agreements?

8. Why are rogue states interested in ABC weapons?
9. Why are weapons still proliferating in the world even with the Cold War over?
10. What is the SIPRI, and what does it do?
11. How successful have weapons regimes been?
12. What are the views on arms limitations on the parts of realists, neorealists, and transnationalists?

GLOSSARY

arms control An arms limitation agreement that places a ceiling on the number or type of weapons in either the present or the future.

defensive weapons Instruments used to deter an opponent from attacking or to ward off the attack if it occurs.

disarmament An arms limitation agreement that calls for the partial or complete reduction of a type of weapon or all weapons.

disengagement The mutual withdrawal by two parties in conflict, or potentially in conflict, from a point of proximity to reduce the likelihood of fighting.

offensive weapons Instruments used by one side to attack an opponent.

power ratios The military power of one state's weapons relative to the weapons of another state as a measurement for facilitating arms limitations.

strategic weapon A long-range instrument, such as a missile or a bomber, capable of traveling intercontinentally and normally carrying a nuclear warhead or bomb.

tactical weapon Short-range missiles with a 95-to-310-mile range that can carry a nuclear warhead or an artillery-fired shell and has a range of approximately 20 miles.

theater weapon A medium-range vehicle, such as a missile or a plane, with a range of about 500 to 1,200 miles, that is usable at the regional level.

verification A means of inspection to assure each side in an arms agreement that the other side is keeping the agreement.

RECOMMENDED READINGS

Michael Brzoska and Frederic S. Pearson. *Arms and Warfare: Escalation, De-escalation, and Negotiation.* Columbia, SC: University of South Carolina Press, 1994.

Stephen J. Cimbala. *U.S. Nuclear Strategy in the New World Order: Backward Glances, Forward Looks.* New York: Paragon House, 1993.

Paul Cornish. *Controlling the Arms Trade: The West versus the Rest.* London: Bowerdean Publishing, 1996.

Hugh D. Crone. *Banning Chemical Weapons: The Scientific Background.* Cambridge, England: Cambridge University Press, 1992.

"Arms Control: Thirty Years On." *Daedalus,* Winter 1991.

Jeffrey M. Elliot and Robert Reginald. *The Arms Control, Disarmament, and Military Security Dictionary.* Santa Barbara, CA: ABC–CLIO, 1989.

Randall Forsberg, William Driscoll, Gregory Webb, and Jonathan Dean. *Nonproliferation Primer: Preventing the Spread of Nuclear, Chemical, and Biological Weapons.* Cambridge, MA: MIT Press, 1995.

Gary T. Gardner. *Nuclear Nonproliferation: A Primer.* Boulder, CO: Lynne Rienner Publishers, 1994.

Colin S. Gray. *Weapons Don't Make War.* Lawrence, KS: University of Kansas Press, 1993.

Evan Luard. *The Blunted Sword: The Erosion of Military Power in Modern World Politics.* New York: New Amsterdam, 1988.

Michael J. Mazarr. *North Korea and the Bomb: A Case Study in Nonproliferation.* New York: St. Martin's Press, 1995.

Edward Reiss. *The Strategic Defense Initiative.* New York: Cambridge University Press, 1992.

Mitchell Reiss and Robert S. Litwak, eds. *Nuclear Proliferation After the Cold War.* Washington, D.C.: Woodrow Wilson Center Press, 1994.

Paul Rogers and Malcolm Dando. *A Violent Peace, Global Security After the Cold War.* Washington, D.C.: Brassey's (UK), 1992.

Richard Smoke. *National Security and the Nuclear Dilemma: An Introduction to the American Experience in the Cold War.* 3rd ed. New York: McGraw-Hill, 1993.

Leonard S. Spector and Virginia Foran. *Preventing Weapons Proliferation: Should the Regimes Be Combined?* Muscatine, IA: The Stanley Foundation, 1992.

Sheldon Ungar. *The Rise and Fall of Nuclearism.* University Park, PA: Pennsylvania State University Press, 1992.

Burns H. Weston, ed. *Alternative Security: Living Without Nuclear Deterrence.* Boulder, CO: Westview Press, 1990.

ENDNOTES

1. Stanley M. Burstein, "Arms Control in Antiquity," *Encyclopedia of Arms Control and Disarmament,* ed. Richard Dean Burns (New York: Charles Scribner's Sons, 1993), p. 16.
2. Michael G. Renner, "Swords into Consumer Goods," *Worldwatch,* July–August 1989, p. 18.
3. Arthur A. Stein, *Why Nations Cooperate* (Ithaca, NY: Cornell University Press, 1990), p. 187.
4. Nicole Ball, "Demilitarizing the Third World," in *World Security: Challenges for a New Century,* 2nd ed., ed. Michael T. Klare and Daniel C. Thomas (New York: St. Martin's Press, 1994), p. 216.
5. Robert Wesson, *International Relations in Transition* (Englewood Cliffs, NJ: Prentice Hall, 1990), p. 63.
6. Michael Brzoska and Frederic S. Pearson, *Arms and Warfare: Escalation, De-escalation, and Negotiation* (Columbia, SC: University of South Carolina Press, 1994), p. 238.
7. Greg Cashman, *What Causes War?* (New York: Lexington Books, 1993), pp. 172–84.
8. Colin S. Gray, "Arms Races and Other Pathetic Fallacies: A Case for Deconstruction," *Review of International Studies,* July 1996, p. 329.
9. Joseph S. Nye, Jr., "Arms Control and International Politics," *Daedalus,* Winter 1991, p. 47.
10. Hans J. Morgenthau, *Politics Among Nations: The Struggle for Power and Peace,* 5th ed. (New York: Alfred A. Knopf, 1967), p. 410.
11. Michael Renner, *Budgeting for Disarmament: The Costs of War and Peace,* Paper 122 (Washington, D.C.: Worldwatch Institute, 1994), p. 10.
12. *World Military Expenditures and Arms Transfers 1993–1994* (Washington, D.C.: U.S. Arms Control and Disarmament Agency, 1995), p. 1.
13. Ibid., p. 165.
14. Renner, *Budgeting for Disarmament,* p. 5.
15. *Courier,* Winter 1995, p. 11.
16. Ethan Barnaby Kapstein, *The Political Economy of National Security: A Global Perspective* (New York: McGraw-Hill, 1992), pp. 66–86.
17. Ibid., p. 66.
18. Renner, *Budgeting for Disarmament,* pp. 12, 13.
19. Boutros Bourtros-Ghali, "The Land Mine Crisis: A Humanitarian Disaster," *Foreign Affairs,* September–October 1994, pp. 8–13.
20. Renner, *Budgeting for Disarmament,* pp. 34–35.
21. Alex Mintz and Randolph T. Stevenson, "Defense Expenditures, Economic Growth, and the 'Peace Dividend,'" *Journal of Conflict Resolution,* June 1995, pp. 283–305.
22. Renner, *Budgeting for Disarmament,* pp. 5–6.
23. Ibid., p. 14.
24. Morgenthau, *Politics Among Nations,* pp. 415–16.
25. Stein, *Why Nations Cooperate,* pp. 131–32.
26. William J. Dixon and Dale L. Smith, "Arms Control and the Evolution of the Superpower Relations," *Social Science Quarterly,* December 1992, pp. 876–89.
27. Carl Kayser, Robert S. McNamara, and George W. Rathjens, "Nuclear Weapons After the Cold War," *Foreign Affairs,* Fall 1991, p. 96.
28. Ruth Leger Sivard, *World Military and Social Expenditures 1989,* 13th ed. (Washington, D.C.: World Priorities, 1989), p. 14.
29. Sheldon Ungar, *The Rise and Fall of Nuclearism* (University Park, PA: Pennsylvania State University Press, 1992), p. 1.
30. Richard Smoke, *National Security and the Nuclear Dilemma,* 3rd ed. (New York: McGraw-Hill, 1993), pp. 264, 267.
31. James E. Dougherty and Robert L. Pfaltzgraff, Jr., *Contending Theories of International Relations* (New York: Harper & Row, 1990), p. 416.
32. Smoke, *National Security,* p. 281.
33. Harry B. Hollins, Averill L. Powers, and Mark Sommer, *The Conquest of War: Alternative Strategies for Global Security* (Boulder, CO: Westview Press, 1989), p. 52.
34. Nye, "Arms Control and International Politics," p. 51; Allan S. Krass, "Death and Transfiguration: Nuclear Arms Control in the 1980s and 1990s," in *World Security: Trends and Challenges at Century's End,* pp. 78–79; Linda P. Brady, *The Politics of Negotiation* (Chapel Hill, NC: University of North Carolina Press, 1991), pp. 120–47.
35. Smoke, *National Security,* pp. 268–71.
36. Hollins, Powers, and Sommer, *The Conquest of War,* p. 79.
37. Smoke, *National Security,* pp. 303–5.
38. Ibid., p. 306.

39. Paul Rogers and Malcolm Dando, *A Violent Peace: Global Security After the Cold War* (Washington, D.C.: Brassey's (UK), 1992), p. 2.
40. William Walker, "Nuclear Weapons and the Former Soviet Republics," *International Affairs*, April 1992, p. 258.
41. Dixon and Smith, "Arms Control and the Evolution of the Superpower Relations," p. 888.
42. Robert S. Norris, *Nuclear Weapons Databook, Volume Five* (Boulder, CO: Westview Press, 1994).
43. Smoke, *National Security*, pp. 272–73.
44. Cashman, *What Causes War?*, pp. 186–87.
45. William D. Hartung, "Breaking the Arms-Sales Addiction," *World Policy Journal,* Winter 1990–1991; *Calypso Log*, June 1992; William D. Hartung, "Curbing the Arms Trade," *World Policy Journal,* Spring 1992, pp. 219–47.
46. Richard Wolkomir and Joyce Wolkomir, "Where Staving Off Armageddon is All in a Day's Work," *Smithsonian* February 1997, pp. 126–27.
47. This distinction is taken from Marvin S. Soroos, *Beyond Security: The Challenge of Global Policy* (Columbia, SC: University of South Carolina Press, 1986), p. 165.
48. Jeremy Rifkin, *Biosphere Politics* (New York: HarperCollins, 1991), p. 143.
49. Michael McGuire, "Is There a Future for Nuclear Weapons?," *International Affairs,* April 1994, p. 220.
50. Michael Mandelbaum, "Lessons of the Next Nuclear War," *Foreign Affairs,* March–April 1995, pp. 22–37.
51. Kenneth R. Timmerman, *The Death Lobby: How the West Armed Iraq* (Boston: Houghton Mifflin, 1991), pp. ix–xi.
52. Tom Minehart, AP article, July 13, 1993.
53. Rogers and Dando, *A Violent Peace,* pp. 55–56.
54. William Wilson, "Chemical and Biological Warfare," *In Depth,* Spring 1993, p. 115.
55. Rogers and Dando, *A Violent Peace,* p. 59.
56. Wilson, "Chemical and Biological Warfare," p. 112.
57. Seth Cropsey, "The Only Credible Deterrent," *Foreign Affairs,* March–April 1994, p. 17.
58. U.S. Navy Department data appearing in Knight-Ridder newspapers, January 1995.
59. Cropsey, "The Only Credible Deterrent," p. 17.
60. Marc Dean Millot, "Facing the Emerging Reality of Regional Nuclear Adversaries," in *Order and Disorder After The Cold War,* ed. Brad Roberts (Cambridge, MA: MIT Press, 1995), pp. 177–207; Michael Krepon, "Are Missile Defenses MAD?", *Foreign Affairs,* January–February 1995, pp. 19–24.
61. *World Military Expenditures,* p. 9.
62. Brzoska and Pearson, *Arms and Warfare,* p. 222.
63. William D. Hartung, "Nixon's Children: Bill Clinton and the Permanent Arms Bazaar," *World Policy Review,* Summer 1995, p. 25.
64. Frederic S. Pearson, *The Global Spread of Arms: Political Economy of International Society* (Boulder, CO: Westview Press, 1994), p. 16.
65. Ethan A. Epstein, "America's Arms-Trade Monopoly," *Foreign Affairs,* May–June 1994, p. 18; Hartung, "Nixon's Children," pp. 26–31.
66. Lora Lumpe, "Costly Giveaways," *The Bulletin of the Atomic Scientists,* September–October 1997, pp. 30–38.
67. Stephen D. Goose and Frank Smyth, "Arming Genocide in Rwanda," *Foreign Affairs,* September–October, 1994, pp. 86–96.
68. Pearson, *The Global Spread of Arms,* p. 61.
69. *World Press Review,* September 1994, p. 48.
70. Nye, "Arms Control and International Politics," pp. 155–57.
71. Mandelbaum, "Lessons of the Next Nuclear War," pp. 31–32.
72. Barry M. Blechman and Cathleen S. Fisher, "Phase Out the Bomb," *Foreign Policy,* Winter 1994–1995, pp. 79–82.
73. McGuire, "Is There a Future for Nuclear Weapons?", p. 225.
74. Mandlebaum, "Lessons of the Next Nuclear War," pp. 32–35.
75. Rebecca Johnson, "The In-Comprehensive Test Ban," *The Bulletin of the Atomic Scientists,* November–December 1996, pp. 30–37; Jaap Ramaker, "Towards a Nuclear Test Ban Treaty," *NATO Review,* November 1996, pp. 26–30.
76. Bleachman and Fisher, "Phase Out the Bomb," p. 93.
77. Wilson, "Chemical and Biological Weapons," pp. 101–2.
78. J. P. Perry Robinson, "Implementing the Chemical Weapons Convention," *International Affairs,* January 1996, pp. 73–89; Sergui Batsanov,

"Preparing for the Entry into Force of the Chemical Weapons Convention," *NATO Review,* September 1996, pp. 16–20.
79. Wilson, "Chemical and Biological Weapons," pp. 107–8.
80. Renner, "Budgeting for Disarmament," p. 31.
81. Pearson, *The Global Spread of Arms,* pp. 71–72.
82. Spector and Foran, *Preventing Weapons Proliferation,* p. 6.
83. Pearson, *The Global Spread of Arms,* pp. 76–77.
84. Ernest R. May, "National Security in American History," in *Rethinking America's Security: Beyond Cold War to New World Order,* ed. Graham Allison and Gregory F. Treverton (New York: W. W. Norton, 1992), p. 114; Renner, "Swords into Consumer Goods," p. 18.
85. Mary Lord, "Nongovernment Organizations in Arms Control and Disarmament," in *Encyclopedia of Arms Control and Disarmament,* pp. 5–10.
86. Wolkomir and Wolkomir, "Armageddon," pp. 115–28.
87. *Calypso Log,* pp. 10–11.
88. Robert Axelrod, *The Evolution of Cooperation* (New York: Basic Books, 1984), p. 4.
89. Stein, *Why Nations Cooperate,* pp. 24, 40, 124, 187.
90. Morgenthau, *Politics Among Nations,* pp. 402–5.
91. Kenneth N. Waltz, *Theory of International Politics* (Reading, MA: Addison-Wesley, 1979), pp. 174–75.
92. Ernst-Otto Czempiel, "Governance and Democratization," in *Governance Without Government: Order and Change in World Politics,* ed. James N. Rosenau and Ernst-Otto Czempiel (New York: Cambridge University Press, 1992), pp. 253–55; Richard A. Falk, "Theory, Realism, and World Security," in *World Security: Trends and Challenges at Century's End,* ed. Michael T. Klare and Daniel C. Thomas (New York: St. Martin's Press, 1991), pp. 11–13, 16–17; R. D. McKinlay and R. Little, *Global Problems and World Order* (Madison, WI: University of Wisconsin Press, 1986), p. 255.
93. Nye, "Arms Control and International Politics," p. 152.
94. Emanuel Adler, "Arms Control, Disarmament, National Security: A Thirty Year Retrospective and a New Set of Anticipations," *Daedalus,* Winter 1991, pp. 17–18.

CHAPTER 11

INTERNATIONAL LAW AS THE FRAMEWORK FOR INTERNATIONAL SOCIETY

Upon telling a colleague in a different field that I was preparing a course in international law, he laughed and claimed my subject was an oxymoron. He said the terms *international* and *law* contradict each other. He thought that wherever international conditions prevailed, law would have little meaning. Some observers deny that international law is law since it does not have a central government for enforcement.[1] In contrast to the domestic situation of states with their *vertical,* or hierarchical, authority arrangement, international society is a *horizontal* structure with authority divided among sovereign states.[2] Other observers hold the idealistic belief that international law can solve most of humankind's problems. The truth, as so often is the case, lies somewhere in the middle.

International law is the rules and norms that states, and other actors as subjects of law, feel an obligation to obey in their mutual relations and commonly do obey. Rules are formal, often written expectations for behavior. Norms are less formal, customary expectations that members of a society tend to obey. All societies develop rules and norms for conducting relationships. In societies made up of cave dwellers, tribal people, citizens of a city-state, or the population of a modern state, these rules and norms instruct members of a given society about their behavior. People want the security and predictability that accompany a shared understaing of how they are to deal with one another; that is, people want a body of law to provide a social order. The nature of orders can vary considerably, however. Laws can be the draconian rules of the strong for controlling and exploiting the weak, or laws can provide for a democratic and just order.

Humankind has become a global society and needs a framework of law to guide behavior so people around the world, politically organized into states, can get along with one another. Despite the absence of a world government, a clear understanding about expected behavior operates in international society and in such a way as to control conflict. The main reason laws work in any society is that subjects willingly obey them without facing coercive sanctions.[3] International law may be weak and imperfect compared to many domestic legal structures, but its several hundred years of development and usefulness are incontestable.

States and other actors usually obey laws because it is in their mutual interest to do so. In the modern complex, interdependent world, actors cannot merely co-exist. To handle common interests satisfactorily, cooperation is more necessary than ever. The body of evolving international law is a response to a broadening array of new activities binding states together in cooperative patterns. If the **codification** of the rules of the high seas arose as a need in the seventeenth century, rules about sharing broadcast wavelengths and

351

geostationary positions for satellites in the field of telecommunications are now a necessity in the latter part of the twentieth century. Most states cooperate to place widely understood rules and norms in treaties on a variety of subjects, thus codifying them.

Our first step in this chapter is to explore the sources of international law. For beginning students of international relations, aware that a world government does not exist, their first question concerns these sources. Next, we identify the actors subject to international law. We will see that international law's jurisdiction has relevance not only for states but for other actors as well. Also, we will describe the broadening scope of international law that reflects a growing array of issues. Then a comparison between the uses of domestic and international law will demonstrate international law's appreciable effectiveness. An evaluation of the operation of international law in a multicultural world follows. Finally, we will assess the role of international law in establishing an international society.

THE SOURCES OF INTERNATIONAL LAW

The first question of beginning students of international law concerns its sources. Historically, we can trace the roots of international law back to Western Christendom, Roman law, divine law, canon law, and natural law.[4] Precedents and principles flowing from these multiple sources became a confluence in Europe by the time of the classic European state system. This system dates from the *Treaty of Westphalia* of 1648, which established state sovereignty. Some scholars date international law in Europe as early as the writings of Hugo Grotius (1583–1645), known as the "father of international law." His *Freedom of the Seas* of 1609 and *The Law of War and Peace* of 1625 became classic sources for later scholars and jurists.

International law continued to evolve in Europe for several centuries and, from its Eurocentric channel, flowed to the rest of the world through European trade and colonization. The extent to which other states around the world have accepted the European state system, including international law, is remarkable. Third World states in particular have used international law, along with diplomacy and international organizations, to redress their grievances against Western states, the main proponents of international law.[5]

Different philosophies have arisen concerning the origin and foundation of international law. **Natural law** originated in ancient Greek and Roman thinking. Europeans adopted this philosophy believing that right principles of a divine origin were available if reasoned out and followed. These principles supposedly were inherent in nature, and legal scholars thought they could deduce specific laws from them as guides for the conduct of states. In the seventeenth century, most scholars accepted natural law philosophy as the foundation of international law. After 1776, Americans would even assert that their rights were natural birth rights as opposed to the rights of English subjects, protected by an English king.

Positivism came to challenge natural law as the primary source of international law in the seventeenth and eighteenth centuries. This legal philosophy holds that the practice of states defines international law, that is, what states agree to accept in the form of customs and treaties. Positivism blended well with the rise of the modern state with its emphasis on sovereignty. Independent states would accept only those agreements and treaties they chose to embrace. Hugo Grotius, writing in the early seventeenth century, represents a bridge between the natural law and positivist philosophies. He thought the two philosophies were compatible and states were bound to obey both. However, the higher claims of a moral and ethical nature that derived from natural law gradually lost currency among states and legal philosophers, allowing positivism to dominate by the nineteenth century.

Positivism is practical and realistic, emphasizing "what is" instead of "what ought to be" based on moral principles. This philosophy held the potential for the powerful states to force their views of rules and norms into the body of international law, that is, to make this law the "rule of the strong." After the Congress of Vienna of 1815, a concert of powerful European states, embracing many shared views, became the core of the state system and the driving force behind positivist international law.

Moral principles of justice are not entirely absent from international law, however. Since the First World War, states have been willing to write moral-based strictures into treaties, as in the case of limits and prohibitions against war in the League Covenant and the UN Charter. In another case, the modern human rights movement, beginning after the Second World War, has a natural law heritage and began its expression as the "Universal Declaration of Human Rights." Finally, whatever the content of the treaties, moral or otherwise, states still can agree to accept or reject treaties, thus confirming the prevailing positivist philosophy.[6] We can now turn our attention to more specific sources of international law.

The Statute of the International Court of Justice identifies four specific sources of international law: treaties, customs, general principles, and judicial decisions. These sources are listed here in the order of their importance. Only in the case of treaties do sovereign states clearly give their consent to accept specific rules.[7]

Treaties

A **treaty** is a written international agreement concluded by states, and sometimes international organizations, that commits the signatories to future terms of interaction. The *Vienna Convention on the Law of Treaties* of 1969 governs the legal process of making and using treaties among states. Treaties have been in evidence throughout history, and their role as the primary source of international law has become increasingly pronounced.

Treaties cover every imaginable kind of subject in international relations. States normally register them with the United Nations, and today over 30,000 treaties are in the registry of this world body. Treaties can be bilateral, binding on two states, or multilateral, applying to three or more states. Any state, or a set of states acting in a conference, can sponsor treaties. Alternatively, an international organization, such as the United Nations, can recommend a treaty. The United Nations charter is a multilateral treaty supported by the largest number of state signatories of any treaty.

Customary Law

Customary behaviors in the international context can become legal obligations if they receive respect and compliance over time. **Customary law** is recognized but unwritten law. Article 38 of the Statue of the International Court of Justice states, "international custom is evidence of a general practice accepted as law, . . . " Obligations by states are at stake, and sanctions and retaliation are available when states violate customary law. How to determine when customary law is firm, however, is unclear. How many states have to respect a practice, how often, and how long to produce a customary law?

A common pattern of development in international law concerns the conversion of customary law into treaty law. After centuries of diplomatic customary law, the ratification of the *Vienna Convention on Diplomatic Relations* of 1961 produced a global-level treaty. Customary law has included rules governing such diverse areas as jurisdiction over territory, freedom of the high seas, the privileges and immunities of states, and the rights of aliens.

An old and still troublesome area of customary international law concerns territorial sovereignty. For example, in 1990, agents in the employ of the United States kidnapped a Mexican doctor accused of torturing to death an American drug agent working in Mexico. The agents turned the doctor over to American authorities at the border for trial. President George Bush ordered this kidnapping, and the U.S. Supreme Court ruled the federal government could try the doctor even though the kidnappers had seized him on foreign soil. In 1992, the release of the doctor for lack of evidence by a federal district judge only partially calmed the anger of Mexican leaders.[8] Private bondsmen also have brought wanted individuals back to the United States from Canada for trial in state-level courts. Under customary international law, these acts violated Mexican and Canadian territories. Sometimes states elect to have an extradition treaty that prohibits such acts of snatching individuals from their home country for trial in another country.

The most famous case in history of territorial violation as a way to bring a person to trial concerns Adolf Eichmann. Eichmann had been a German SS officer at a Nazi death camp that helped carry out the Nazi policy of genocide against the Jews of Europe. Israeli agents kidnapped Eichmann in Argentina and took him to Israel. The Israeli government then tried and hung Eichmann for war crimes in 1961. Such acts are clear violations of customary law concerning territorial sovereignty, but sometimes the practice occurs when legal extradition procedures are not available or these efforts fail.

In a newly declassified presidential directive, the policy of the United States appears to be that of snatching suspected terrorists from foreign soil if extradition does not provide a remedy. President Bill Clinton signed the Presidential Decision Directive, or PDD-39, in 1995. A provision of PDD-39 that came to light in early 1997 allows for the forceful return of terrorist suspects from foreign soil. Because the seizure of the Mexican doctor in 1990 sparked such an uproar in Mexico, the United States and Mexico signed a 1994 agreement prohibiting "grab-and-snatch" operations. Consequently, Mexico is exempt from the PDD-39 policy.

General Principles of Law

Guidelines used widely by states as a source of law are the **principles of law.** These principles often arise from **municipal systems,** that is, domestic or national internal systems. (References to municipal law in the international law context should not lead to confusion with the governing of cities.) Principles that have derived from court cases are good faith, morality, equity, and fair hearings, among other matters. The "good faith" principle, for instance, symbolizes the essence of international law to many legal theorists. Natural law also can be a source of general principles.

Some diplomats and international lawyers, however, are reluctant to accept general principles as a truly usable source of international law. For some legal experts, general principles appear to repudiate the positivist philosophy, relying only on formal treaties and general customs as valid law.

Judicial Decisions

Decisions by judges in domestic courts, international courts, or ad hoc tribunals of arbitration may create precedents that will guide future decisions. Strictly speaking, **judicial decisions** under international law are binding only for the parties involved in a particular case. Precedents are not as firm in international law as, say, judge-made law in the American and British tradition that respects *stare decisis* (to stand by a decision or precedent). Nonetheless, international adjudication creates a record of norms that can influence later cases of international law. Judges naturally take heed of decisions by their peers domestically and internationally.

National courts are playing an increasingly important role in international law by filling in the gap between the national and international levels of jurisprudence. International law requires that the international legal obligations of a state apply on the domestic scene of countries when they are pertinent. National judges have contributed to the harmonization of the two levels of jurisprudence, especially in the areas of human rights, labor laws, environmental laws, and banking laws when foreign banks are of concern.[9] Some legal scholars call the application and integration of international law on the national, or municipal, level the *incorporation of international law*.

Ancillary to court decisions are the opinions of legal scholars known as **publicists**. These scholars provide an extra source of law when other sources fail to give clear guidance. Publicists, such as Hugo Grotius, were especially useful when little of international law was codified. Even in modern times, the research and ideas of scholars can help break a path in new areas needing legal guidance. Scholars have suggested rules for guiding states in areas such as marine pollution, deep seabed mining, and outer space. Diplomats, as well as judges, also quote learned writers on matters concerning international law.[10]

To sum up, international law does not have the strong statutory frame that the federal laws of America or the common law and parliamentary law of Great Britain do. International law generally is less clear and affirmed than many domestic systems. Yet treaties and customary law are continuously binding international society together as states and other actors interact within increasing degrees of interdependence. States voluntarily undertake international legal obligations and customarily obey the rules and norms involved because they find them useful to facilitate cooperation. The other sources of international law supplement the more basic sources of treaties and customs.

THE SUBJECTS OF INTERNATIONAL LAW

Traditionally, states have been the only *subjects* of international law with rights and duties. Today states are still the primary subjects, but not the only ones. Some nonstate actors, once *objects* of international law without rights and duties, are transforming into subjects. If an object of the law, an actor can receive only the effects of international law. In the twentieth century, international organizations with states as members (IGOs), international nongovernment organizations (INGOs), individuals, and some other groups do have some degree of **international legal personality,** meaning they are subjects of international law with rights and duties.[11] Identifying and defining the subjects of international law is an ongoing process.

States

The state, as the primary actor and subject of international law, enjoys a unique position in international relations as an actor with a territorial base. States frequently have wide latitude in decision making as sovereignties—that is, as legal entities without a higher authority over them—and many states have great resources of economic and military power. We gave the state considerable attention in Chapter Two on history and in Chapter Three on actors.

In international law, the *Montevideo Convention on Rights and Duties of States* of 1933 gives the state a legal definition.[12] States, of course, have extraordinary differences in territorial size, population size, and economic and military power; yet, under international law, as sovereigns, they are not only independent of authority above them but are legal equals. States, however, commonly reduce their sovereign independence to some degree by committing to the obligations of specific treaties. A state that offers *most favorable nation* status to another state in a trade treaty, for example, loses its option of discriminatory tariffs.

International Government Organizations (IGOs)

IGOs, as we recall, are public organizations that states form to help them cooperate in an interdependent world. Prominent examples are the United Nations, the Organization of American States, and the European Union. IGOs have the rights and duties that states assign to them in the treaties of their creation. A tension is usually present because the state-creators are not anxious for IGOs to develop any more independence than they already have. Yet in practice, because states divide over policy choices, a partial vacuum is created in which the staffs of IGOs have a good deal of independence. In fact, IGOs can send and receive ambassadors, make treaties, and develop policy directions of their own that shape the behavior of states.[13] The fact that the president and the top civil servants of the European Union lead member-states in choices about trade policies is a well-known case.

Approximately 15 independent agencies or IGOs, as part of the UN system, are actually affiliates of the United Nations through treaty arrangements. Perhaps the best known of these agencies are the International Monetary Fund and the World Health Organization. In a 1949 advisory opinion, the International Court of Justice ruled that the United Nations had a legal personality, but its rights and duties were specific and less than those of a state.

International Nongovernment Organizations (INGOs)

INGOs are private international organizations that promote cooperation on a transnational basis and behave similarly to interest groups and lobbyists as they approach the governments of states and attend meetings of IGOs. Although technically not subjects of international law, 300 or so INGOs, such as the human rights organization Amnesty International, have consultative status with the Economic and Social Council of the United Nations. The International Committee of the Red Cross, however, does enjoy a legal personality when it works in the area of humanitarian law, including the inspection of POW camps.

Multinational Corporations (MNCs)

MNCs are a special case of INGO. They originate under the domestic or municipal law of one state, but their business transactions take place in several states. This particular type of INGO acquires the nationality of the state that licenses its creation. While MNCs are not subjects of international law in a clear, full way, they operate under the regulations of the several states where they do business. MNCs also enter into arbitration with states. The impact of the MNCs is so great, especially on Third World states, that weaker states have felt the need for protection from these nonstate actors. In the 1970s, the United Nations offered a code of conduct for the operation of MNCs, and in 1974, the United Nations formed the Center on Transnational Corporations to report on MNC activities.[14]

MNCs are part of the emerging *private international law* that involves the intersection of several state jurisdictions trying to regulate the same business activity. Once the principle of territoriality sufficed, meaning the courts and laws of the state whose territory was the primary location of the business would resolve any problems. With the rapid growth of international business, the activities of MNCs stretching across several countries, and business contracts tying governments and MNCs together in complex relationships, identifying one territory and one national method to settle a dispute to the satisfaction of all parties became impossible.

Since no universal law governing transnational business disputes exists, jurisdictions of states frequently clash with the MNCs caught in the middle. In a spirit of reciprocity, states have been willing to use one another's laws and court decisions in their own national courts to handle contract disagreements, management-labor conflicts, product liabilities, environmental obligations, and other commercial complexities. Moreover, states can and do use private arbitration, such as through the International Chamber of Commerce. Gradually, some agreement about how to handle international business is falling into place.

The wiser states, looking ahead, will try to work out problems not only over choice in law but over forums for settlement and remedies before trade patterns intensify. States can put agreements dealing with such business problems into treaties. When states negotiate these treaties, private international law concerning business begins to merge with *public international law* that normally governs the way states treat one another. We will return to the subject of private international law when we discuss international law in a multicultural world.

Individuals

Tentative advances under international law treat individuals as subjects with rights and duties.[15] Traditionally, individuals have been objects of law and, consequently, treated only as citizens of a state that could give its citizens benefits and impose burdens. In modern times, when prosecution against pirates, slavers, perpetrators of genocide, and war criminals occurs, the accused individuals stand trial as subjects of law. Such crimes fall under the *universality principle,* meaning they are so repugnant to civilization that they are crimes against all states and humankind. Any state can prosecute those so accused or extradite them at will.

The Nuremburg and Tokyo War Crimes trials following the Second World War marked a substantial change concerning individuals as subjects. These trials discounted the rationale "I was only obeying orders," which meant individuals were merely an extension of the state and not acting in their own capacity. From the precedent of these trials, individuals now have the duty under the laws of war to distinguish between a lawful and an unlawful order based on the laws of war.[16]

In the 1990s, Bosnia, rent with ethnic strife and bloodshed, has run amok with war crimes that have included murdering unarmed civilians, beating and starving prisoners in detention camps, and the systematic rape of Bosnian Muslim women, all calculated to assist in "ethnic cleansing." Bosnian Serbs have waged a war to drive the Muslims from their towns and territory. Croats have fought too, and all three groups probably have individuals guilty of war crimes. It is the Serbians who apparently have committed the most widespread and egregious acts, perhaps because they have been the strongest ethnic group in Bosnia in military terms.

In 1993, the UN Security Council voted unanimously to set up a War Crimes Tribunal at the Hague in the Netherlands to deal with the Bosnian atrocities. The War Crimes Tribunal can issue international warrants, and, if individuals elude custody, they will at least be pariahs, unable to leave the safety of their locales for fear of arrest. Restrictions are that trials cannot be *in abstentia* should authorities fail to make an arrest, and the tribunal cannot give a defendant the death penalty. Finally, a new and important development of the authority of the tribunal is that the use of rape as a weapon of war is now triable as a war crime.

A moral issue arises when those accused are brought to trial for war crimes. Can they get a fair trial? Are war criminal trials little more than a "victor's peace"? The trials of captured German and Japanese military personnel and civilian officials by American, British, and Soviet judges have never satisfied everyone that they produced justice and did not exact vengeance. The tribunal will have a more objective basis for providing justice than was the case at Nuremburg. The 11 judges who constitute the tribunal come from a variety of countries and receive their authority from the United Nations, not a set of states victorious in war.

Problems can arise even when a state tries one of its own citizens for war crimes, a fairly unusual occurrence. In the case of Lieutenant William Calley, whose platoon killed over 300 unarmed civilians at the village of My Lai in 1968 during the Vietnam War, some critics, instead of praising the United States for being willing to punish one of its own, concluded that Calley's punishment was too light. A United States military court held Calley responsible for at least 22 of the murders and gave him a life sentence. President Richard Nixon allowed Calley to live under house arrest during the appeals process and later pardoned him. No one disagrees with the principle of punishing war criminals, but different perceptions about justice are likely to color the process.

Thus far, in the case of Bosnia, the War Crimes Tribunal has charged about 60 people with war crimes, most of them Bosnian Serbs and a few Bosnian Croats and Bosnian Muslims. Especially important, in 1995, the War Crimes Tribunal issued warrants for the

Corrigan/Canada/Cartoonists & Writers Syndicate

two top Bosnian Serb leaders, President Radovan Karadzic and General Ratko Mladic, charging them with genocide against the Bosnian Muslims. Karadzic, feeling safe in his stronghold in Pale, Bosnia, derides the prospect that he will ever face the War Crimes Tribunal. Under pressure from NATO leaders and neighboring Republic of Serbia, these two men have stepped down from official positions but remain at large inside the Serbian portion of Bosnia. They dare not venture far for fear of arrest.

Most of the Bosnian war participants charged with war crimes are not in custody, since they are not prisoners of war as were thousands of Germans and Japanese at the end of the Second World War. Amnesty International, the human rights organization, has advocated that the strong NATO forces seize those wanted for war crimes in the Serb sector of Bosnia; however, NATO leaders were reluctant to do so out of a concern for disrupting the Dayton Peace Accords that finally ended the war in Bosnia. The tribunal's president, Justice Antonio Cassese, warned in late 1996 that if the major states of NATO do not make arrests in the next 10 months, the tribunal may as well pack up and go home. In the summer of 1997, NATO forces began a more aggressive campaign to arrest war criminals.

So far in 1997, while other individuals are on trial for war crimes, only Dusan Tadic, a Bosnian Serb, has received a conviction. Once a guard at a harsh camp holding Muslim prisoners, Tadic was found guilty of brutalizing some of these prisoners. He was acquitted of more serious crimes including murder.

The bloodletting in Rwanda that began in the summer of 1994 led to the UN Security Council creating a second tribunal in late 1994, the International Tribunal for Rwanda. When the majority Hutus finally came to power in this African state in 1994, this act triggered a massive and vengeful attack by Hutu soldiers and citizens against the minority Tutsi. The Hutu have long regarded the Tutsi as their oppressors. The slaughter of men, women, and children quickly reached genocidal proportions, with as many as a half-million people dying in a three-month period.

When the Tutsi fought their way back to control of the country, they wisely did not wreak revenge but called on the United Nations to create the Tribunal for Rwanda. The tribunal, based on its authorization, does not have to connect genocide to warring conflict, as in the Bosnian case, but can punish for the murderous rampaging that amounted to the crime of genocide.[17] One aspect of the authorization for an international tribunal that disappointed the new Tutsi government of Rwanda was that the tribunal could not give the death penalty. Ironically, after asking for the tribunal, the Rwandan government voted against it at the United Nations over the death penalty issue. The International Tribunal for Rwanda began its first trial in early 1997, while thousands of suspects languished in Rwanda jails awaiting indictment and trial. The tribunal, unfortunately, begins its trial session within a climate of criticism. UN Inspector-General Karl Paschke had just completed an investigation of the tribunal, finding some truth to the allegations of misconduct and ineptness. Because of slow progress, Rwanda began its own trials in July 1997.

In addition to war crimes, the modern human rights movement, beginning after the Second World War, has encouraged the treatment of individuals as subjects of international law. The discovery of Adolf Hitler's genocide attempts against the Jews of Europe at the end of the Second World War set off a long and broad human rights treaty-making process. This process continues today and encourages the treatment of individuals as subjects of international law. Several dozen global and regional human rights treaties are now in effect or await ratification. Under a few of these treaties, individuals with grievances over their rights can appeal for help above their governments' heads, a remarkable development in a world of sovereign states.

Under the *Covenant of Civil and Political Rights* of 1976, an individual can petition a Human Rights Committee for help if the government in question has signed the optional protocol of the covenant. Much more notable is the right of people living in a European country, if the country is a signatory to the *European Convention on Human Rights* of 1955, to appeal their cases before the European Court of Human Rights. As an example, in 1985, several immigrant women in Great Britain brought a case claiming sex discrimination. They could not, under British law, bring their husbands to Britain, but immigrant men could bring their spouses to Britain. The European Court of Human Rights ruled in favor of the women.[18]

In another British case, in 1990, a male Englishman who underwent a sex-change operation brought a case to the European Court of Human Rights. His grievance was that the British government would not change his birth certificate to say that "he" was now a "she." Under the law of Great Britain, a male could not marry a male, and so this law blocked a legal marriage for this individual. The European Court turned down this appeal.[19]

Other Actors

If insurgents, or rebels, control a significant amount of their country's territory and operate a government on this territory, they can receive treatment as a subject by other states. The assumption behind this treatment is that such insurgents are at the threshold of creating a new, breakaway country, or they may win and control the entire country, operating under a new government. Since there are so many secessionist movements, the trend increasingly is to withhold recognition for insurgents. The Chechen fighters, in revolt against Russia in early 1995, enjoyed some sympathy in the media, but governments, including that of President Bill Clinton, studiously avoided saying or doing anything that might suggest Chechnya should become an independent country. The application of international law today leans in favor of the original, legal government in its effort to block a breakaway effort by rebels.[20]

Liberation movements, seeking an end to foreign rule, also have received occasional treatment as subjects. The legitimacy of these movements derives from the hallowed principle of self-determination, especially when a case of colonialism or foreign occupation is at stake. A liberation movement may become a state, as the National Liberation Front did in Algeria in 1962. The Palestine Liberation Organization, formed in 1969, hopes to lead a Palestinian state someday and has for years enjoyed "observer status" in the United Nations.[21] A degree of limited autonomy for Palestinians resulted from negotiations with Israel in the early 1990s, a status that now appears to be jeopardized since the Likud Party came to power in Israel in 1996.

This survey of the subjects of international law clearly demonstrates that the world is indeed a *mixed-actor world*. States, international organizations, and individuals have established legal personalities. INGOs and MNCs and liberation movements fall into a quasi-subject status, but their development as legal personalities is probably on the rise. Insurgents have enjoyed subject status, but their legal personality is in decline. Without serious qualification, the state has the broadest set of rights and duties, while the other actors, as subjects, have more limitations in this respect. Clearly, the mixed-actor world bases relationships on legal standing, in addition to political and economic ties, as the various actors intermingle in complex ways.

THE SCOPE OF INTERNATIONAL LAW

The scope of international law covers almost every kind of activity of a transborder character. These activities have grown over time, propelled by such concerns as a global human rights movement, patterns of rising international trade, and changing technology. The examples presented here are illustrative, as we do not attempt to give complete coverage of international law's scope, a task that would require volumes.

As we have discussed, international law identifies the actors, or subjects, that have legal status and provides for their rights and duties. The *Montevideo Convention on Rights and Duties of States* of 1933 is a good example of this law. States have such rights as equality under law and self-defense. They are required to refrain from the use or force or from intervening in other states, to fulfill the obligations of treaties, and to respect human rights, among other duties. The *Convention on Privileges and Immunities of the United Nations* of 1946 spells out the status of the United Nations as a subject of law.

An area of law among states that has often received much attention in movies and novels is **extradition,** the formal procedure of returning a fugitive from the state of residence to the state where the criminal act occurred. Traditionally, the procedure operated under customary law, but since the early twentieth century, extradition has operated

© 1991 by permission of Johnny Hart and Creators Syndicate, Inc.

increasingly under bilateral treaties. The *Treaty on Extradition Between the United States and Japan* of 1978 is a fairly typical example. States normally use extradition for a list of crimes that both states recognize. If a state views an act as a "political offense" and not a crime, the state may not extradite. States often disagree as to whether an agent of violence is involved in a political act or is a common criminal. Terrorists are sometimes difficult to extradite for this reason.

War has been an ever-present danger for states and their peoples; thus, *laws of war* to "civilize" war have arisen. Numerous laws dealing with the opening and ending of hostilities, fighting on land and sea, the kinds of weapons allowed, and other concerns became accepted rules of war at the *Hague Conventions* of 1899 and 1907. Two of the most fundamental laws of war are that aggressive war is unlawful and that self-defense in cases of aggression is lawful. The *Kellogg-Briand Pact* of 1928 and the *United Nations Charter* of 1945 established these written rules. The *Geneva Conventions* of 1949 say a lot about how to fight wars and with what weapons, and lay down rules about the treatment of enemy civilians and POWs during war.

The treatment of civilians and POWs in wartime is often inhumane in spite of laws to the contrary. Whether in guerrilla war or strategic bombardment, civilians are caught in the midst of war, and their casualties may be greater than those of the combatants. The recent experience of the United States with POW issues, a legacy of the Vietnam War, has been a long and painful one. The North Vietnamese claimed captured American flyers were war criminals, not POWs, because the war was undeclared and the United States was an aggressor. American pilots held in North Vietnam experienced terrible treatment, including torture, over a period of years. American infantrymen, captured in action in South Vietnam and held in jungle camps, fared little better, and as many as one-third died.

The *Protocols to the Geneva Conventions* of 1977 made it clear that prisoners from any conflict, whatever its nature, should receive humane treatment as POWs.[22] The important question remaining today from the Vietnam War is whether over 1,200 missing-in-action (MIA) Americans could have become POWs and whether Vietnam has accounted for all of its American prisoners. An increasing number of MIAs are now listed as deceased because of Vietnam's cooperation in finding the remains of those Americans killed in action (KIA). Some American veterans of the Vietnam War have returned to Vietnam in recent years to help the Vietnamese locate the remains of an incredible 300,000 MIAs from the Vietnamese side of the war.

Another concern of war is the prospect of limiting the destruction of war or even preventing war through arms limitations. The reduction of weapons means fewer casualties if war occurs, and weapons reductions may reduce the war-provoking tensions associated with arms races. These agreements, particularly those between the Soviet Union (these same agreements now apply to Russia) and the United States, are the subject of Chapter Ten.

A body of law important to states in wartime concerns the *laws of neutrality.* When can neutrals face blockades to their trade, what constitutes contraband if trade is possible, and what is the required legal treatment of a neutral's civilians caught in a war zone are the kinds of questions covered under the laws of neutrality.

Normal times among states fall under the *laws of peace,* which deal with territoriality, nationality, diplomacy, and trade, among other subjects. One of the oldest areas of international law is the law of the sea, which goes back, at least in written form, to the work of Hugo Grotius. A new version, the *Law of the Sea* of 1982, received the necessary 60 signatories to put the treaty into effect in 1995, including the ratification of the United States. Before the completion of the ratification process, many states already were applying this new version of the law of the sea.

Among other rules, the seaward jurisdictions of states from their *baselines* have standing under the Law of the Sea. The baseline is the point where the sea meets a coast. From their baselines, states have complete territorial jurisdiction 12 miles out to sea. For an additional 12 miles, there is a *contiguous zone* that allows limited sovereignty to deal with problems such as smuggling. Then there is a 200-mile *exclusive economic zone* along each country's coast along which a country enjoys a monopoly over natural resources.

Technology can bring up new concerns over jurisdiction as first the invention of the airplane and then the development of powerful rockets demonstrate. Air space as a jurisdiction began as codified law with the *Chicago Convention on International and Civil Aviation* of 1944. The atmosphere above land boundaries belongs to a given state, and many states are sensitive to any intrusion. Radar scans this space carefully, and jet fighters and ground-to-air missiles stand ready to confront an intruder. In what was surely an overreaction in the post–Cold War period, Belorussia shot down a balloon, killing two men who were harmlessly taking part in a transborder balloon race.

The *Outer Space Treaty* of 1967 applies to activities in the space beyond the atmosphere and covers heavenly bodies such as the moon and other planets. States basically can explore these "space territories" but cannot arm them with weapons of mass destruction or declare heavenly bodies their national territory.

Laws of nationality are important in an age characterized by strong migration patterns and many people living abroad. Countries have categorically different rules about nationality. States in the Western Hemisphere usually follow the *jus soli* principle, or law of the soil. Under this principle, any person born on a territory can claim to be a citizen regardless of the nationality of the parents. Most European states, in contrast, use the principle of *jus sanguinis,* law of blood. A child's nationality is the same as that of the parents, regardless of the place of birth. Some states even tolerate dual citizenship, allowing a person to be a citizen of two states.

States at peace carry on normal diplomatic relations, the subject of Chapter Seven. In addition to the *Vienna Convention on Diplomatic Relations* of 1961 and the *Vienna*

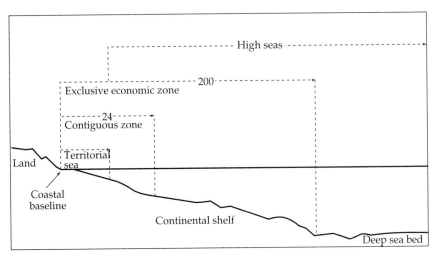

Sea Zones

Convention on Consular Relations of 1963, there is the *International Convention Against the Taking of Hostages* of 1979, which followed from the shocking act of seizing the American embassy by an Iranian mob in 1979. Under this treaty, diplomats and private citizens receive protection from hostage status. States where the hostage taking occurs are responsible for the safety of diplomats and citizens from other countries.

An area of law that has probably produced the largest number of treaties is trade. Bilateral and multilateral treaties abound. The *Free Trade Agreement* of 1989 between Canada and the United States expanded into the *North American Free Trade Agreement (NAFTA)* of 1993. With this latter agreement, Mexico joined the trade bloc.

A regional treaty with long-term success is the *Treaty of Rome* of 1957, which created the European Economic Community. This trade arrangement later grew into the broader European Union (EU). The integration of the EU has deepened with the acceptance of the *Maastricht Treaty,* signed in December 1991 by the then 12 members of the EU. This treaty ended all border restrictions on trade at the beginning of 1992 for the 12 states, now expanded to 15.

Finally, the *General Agreement on Tariffs and Trade (GATT)* of 1947 attempts to pull the world together under the free trade philosophy. The top trading states have led in upgrading this treaty every few years, always extending free trade further through the reduction of tariffs and other trade barriers. The World Trade Organization (WTO), which would offer more extensive free trade management than GATT, has now replaced GATT. Extensive and natural trade ties become formal arrangements through treaties to provide a measure of stability and predictability in trade. Cooperation in trade is the subject of Chapter Nine.

An impressive area of growth in international law in modern times is the body of law dealing with human rights. Under the shield of their sovereignty, states have claimed they can treat their citizens as they wish. This notion of sovereignty stems from the *Peace of Westphalia* of 1648. Yet, after the Second World War, a spate of human rights declarations and treaties, global and regional, have steadily appeared as international law. These usually require the governments of states to treat their citizens in a way that favors the well-being of the citizen.

A fairly complete list of rights is found in the *Universal Declaration of Human Rights* of 1948. These human rights principles reappeared as two treaties, the *Covenant on Civil and Political Rights* of 1976, mentioned earlier, and the *Covenant on Economic, Social and Cultural Rights* of 1976.

More specialized areas of human rights law are the treaties sponsored since the 1920s by the International Labor Organization that protect laborers and their unions. Then there is the *UN Convention on Genocide* of 1948, which "ethnic cleansing" in Bosnia has probably violated during the 1990s.

A special problem for children has been custody disputes of a transborder nature, resulting in the *Hague Convention on the Civil Aspects of International Child Abduction* of 1988. The broader *Convention on the Rights of the Child* is now open for ratification. Finally, the rights of indigenous peoples, such as Native Americans (Indians) of Canada and the United States, Maori of New Zealand, and Sami (Lapps) of Scandinavia, have come into prominence. These rights are found in a draft of the proposed "Universal Declaration on the Rights of Indigenous Peoples," offered by a UN Working Group.

Several regional human rights arrangements also echo the Universal Declaration of Human Rights. These include the *African Charter on Human and Peoples' Rights* of 1986, the *American Convention on Human Rights* of 1978, and the *European Convention on Human Rights* of 1955, among others. A full-length discussion of human rights appears in Chapter Twelve.

Treaties in the areas of terrorism, the environment, intellectual property and copyright laws, health, communication technology, and many other areas demonstrate that international law is an evolving body of law. This evolution is the product of an interdependent world that needs the organizing framework international law can provide. This law guides cooperation in areas of mutual concern and pulls states, as well as other actors, into a shared international society.

THE EFFECTIVENESS OF INTERNATIONAL LAW

The effectiveness of international law is its capacity to produce desired results, that is, to develop and apply rules. A useful way to assess this effectiveness is to compare international law's situation to that of the municipal or national level. Every society experiences three governmental functions in some form: rulemaking, rule adjudication, and rule enforcement. A chief may perform all three functions for a tribe, or a complex, modern government may have highly specialized branches for each function, as in the United States. Since the world is without a central government, international law is almost certain to be less effective than the laws of governments in strong, well-ordered states. Yet international law reflects the three governmental tasks in some degree and manner.

The Legislative Task

When a legislative body in a democratic state passes a law, a majority of representatives in the legislature has legitimated a rule that everyone in society must obey. In contrast, sovereign states are not bound by any rule they do not accept. The League of Nations recognized this principle through a unanimity rule under which one state in the League Assembly could veto a resolution. A **resolution** is simply a decision or recommendation of the League or the United Nations and does not carry the force of a world law.

The General Assembly of the United Nations, unlike the League, can pass resolutions by majority rule. Though not lawful, resolutions have helped set a climate of moral opinion that, in the long run, shapes world opinion and the policies of states. Over the years, resolutions against the racist policies of South Africa and Israel's handling of Palestinian matters have hampered these states in their freedom of action.

Moreover, the several declarations of the General Assembly against racism and colonialism have set the stage for some human rights treaties and the downfall of colonial empires. **Declarations** are clear statements of policy that take on the importance of an international norm. Declarations by the General Assembly may amount to a stage in the treaty-making process.

For instance, the General Assembly's *Declaration on Torture* of 1975 became the *Convention on Torture* in 1984. The conversion of a declaration into law occurs when states ratify the declaration's content as a convention or treaty. When norms are set down in a treaty, they are, of course, considered codified, a step comparable to putting norms into statute law in a municipal, or national, system. The legal effect is the equivalent of a genuine piece of international legislation. The fact that states have to ratify before they are bound by this law is what sets international law apart from majority rule in the lawmaking process of democratic states.[23]

Sometimes multilateral conferences have produced policy proposals and treaties. The *Stockholm Conference on the Human Environment* of 1972 encouraged states to support environmental policies, and the *UN Conferences on the Law of the Sea* between 1959 and 1982 led to a treaty that has recently received the 60 signatories needed for the treaty to take effect.

The UN General Assembly has specialized committees, similar to a legislative body, and one of these, the Sixth (legal) Committee, has dealt with a wide range of legal problems. The Sixth Committee has drafted at least one treaty opened for ratification by states, the *Convention on Genocide* of 1948. In addition, the Commission on Human Rights, acting under the aegis of its parent body, the Economic and Social Council of the United Nations, has encouraged the development of several human rights treaties.

Finally, there is the International Law Commission, established by the General Assembly in 1949. This body reviews legal norms and sometimes recommends them for codification into a treaty. This commission conducted groundwork for the Law of the Sea Treaty, the Vienna Conventions on Diplomatic and Consular Relations, and the Convention on the Law of Treaties. It has also helped define the important concept of aggression and has offered a set of rules as a model to guide states in their use of arbitration.

Article Thirteen of the UN Charter requires that the United Nations take responsibility for developing international law, and the United Nations carries out this task in ways that substitute for an international legislative body. In sum, the United Nations has recommended law, but only the acceptance by sovereign states can turn norms into law.[24]

The Judicial Task

Normally, within the national context, a court's decisions are firm and are enforceable by executive authorities. Court decisions are enforceable because national courts have **compulsory jurisdiction** over domestic subjects of the law. People, corporations, and officials must come to court if subpoenaed as witnesses or charged with a crime. International judicial efforts are significant but do not nearly match the role of national courts in power and effect.

In the nineteenth century, the use of **arbitration,** an ancient Greek practice, achieved popularity among states. This technique for dispute settlement involves a third, neutral party that can make a binding decision of a judicial type. The Hague Conventions of 1899 and 1907 created the Permanent Court of Arbitration. This "court" was really neither permanent nor a court but a list of 120 jurists who were on call as arbitrators.[25] The First World War interrupted the potential of this judicial effort.

In modern times, arbitration at the international level has dealt mostly with problems between business groups and host states. The *New York Convention on the Recognition and Enforcement of Foreign Arbitral Awards* of 1958, ratified by over 80 states, provides for an international arbitral panel that can rule on claims. Domestic courts of the signatory states enforce the decisions of the panel. For instance, three claims were made against Libya in the 1970s when that state nationalized foreign private oil companies operating on its soil. In each of the three cases, the arbitrators found for the plaintiffs, the oil companies. Libya had to pay out millions of dollars or face the loss of its property in other countries as punishment. The International Chamber of Commerce receives many requests for arbitration services. In some years, this arbitral service handles over 300 cases.

The World Bank has created the International Center for the Settlement of Investment Disputes to deal with disputes between foreign investors and host countries. This center can use both conciliation (political negotiation) and arbitration (binding judicial settlement). The center has had only 26 cases since 1971, however. Also, the *United States and Canada Trade Agreement* of 1989 called for binding arbitration through a joint commission set up for this purpose. Already 15 requests for arbitration have occurred under this trade agreement. These cases have concerned mostly government interpretations of trade laws.[26]

In at least one nonbusiness area, arbitration may play a role. The Law of the Sea Treaty will offer the services of an International Tribunal with arbitral services.[27]

Adjudication, or the process of making judicially binding decisions, can include not only arbitration but also courts with regular sessions and full-time judges and staffs. Establishing a permanent international court reflects great hopes as to what is achievable among sovereign states that occupy a world without a world government.

The first significant effort to build a world court to resolve disputes peacefully was the Permanent Court of International Justice, created in 1921 by the League of Nations. This court handed down 32 decisions and 27 advisory opinions. *Advisory opinions* are authoritative statements of legal opinion. The League institutions, and later those of the United Nations system, would request such an opinion of the world court and usually abide by it. An advisory opinion, in the Anglo-Saxon tradition of Britain and the United States, falls within the purview of an attorney-general and is never given by a judicial body. In these two countries, an actual case with litigants must take place before a court hands down a decision.

Given the anarchical nature of the world, the Permanent Court of Justice usually receives good marks by scholars for accomplishment, though most of its cases involved "low politics" with a minimal level of conflict. The aggressions of the 1930s and the outbreak of the Second World War, which ended the League's life, halted the Permanent Court's activities as well. After the Second World War, the states, with renewed confidence, created another court to replace the Permanent Court. The International Court of Justice, one of the six original institutions of the United Nations, parallels closely the formal role of the Permanent Court in the world. The International Court is available to adjudicate disputes for states if states choose to make use of the Court's services.

The Statute of the International Court also allowed for an "optional clause," under which a state would accept the Court's jurisdiction automatically if another state brought a claim against it. Over 50 states accepted the optional clause, but sometimes with significant reservations. The United States was one of those 50 states. However, the United States withdrew from all commitments to compulsory jurisdiction in 1986. The International Court's decision in 1984 that it had jurisdiction in the suit brought by Nicaragua over the United States mining Nicaragua's harbors greatly upset President Ronald Reagan's administration. The withdrawal of the United States, along with ten other states, from compulsory jurisdiction has undermined the legitimacy and effectiveness of the International Court.[28]

Such states are willing to support a world court only if it decides in their favor. The mark of a true international society would call for states to accept disappointing decisions much as citizens must do when national courts rule against them. If we were to apply the Anglo-American concept of *rule of law* to President Reagan's decision to ignore the Court's judgment, we would conclude that the supremacy of the law failed while the discretionary power of a strong, sovereign state succeeded. The anarchical potential of the state system can sometimes make a glaring appearance by subverting international law.

In spite of the many disputes in the world, the International Court does not have a full docket of cases. Moreover, similar to the Permanent Court, the cases are usually "low-politics" issues and do not represent the important disputes of the times. For example, the United States and Canada had a case before the International Court that dragged on from 1981 to 1984. At stake was a fisheries dispute in the Gulf of Maine. The central issue called for the Court to decide the maritime boundary between the two states. Overall, the International Court has handled about 60 cases and given over 20 advisory opinions to institutions of the United Nations system.[29]

In addition to the reluctance of states to bring major disputes to the International Court, some cases before the Court have hurt its reputation. The Court failed to rule on the Southwest African cases in the 1960s and harmed the International Court's image, perhaps irreparably, in the eyes of the Third World. States from this bloc wanted the Court to take southwest Africa (now Namibia) away from the racist Republic of South Africa and place it in the UN trusteeship system. The International Court feared hurting its prestige if it decided against a South Africa that would ignore its decision. The upshot was that South

Africa remained in charge of the old League Mandate of South-West Africa and was able to continue its racist policy of apartheid in this territory for some years.[30]

The inability of the Court to enforce decisions it has made against recalcitrant states has done damage to its reputation as well. The 1949 ruling against Albania for damaging British ships with mines, the ruling against Iran for seizing the American embassy in Tehran in 1979, and the ruling against the United States for mining Nicaraguan harbors are examples of rulings that accused states have ignored.[31]

In general, the International Court of Justice has not been a busy court, nor has it handled truly important cases in the affairs of states. Some authorities even think the Permanent Court achieved a more impressive record. The Permanent Court may have had an easier path because, as a "world court," the world it served was mostly the European society of states while much of the remaining world existed in colonial empires. In contrast, the International Court has faced major dissension from one element of the world after another. First, the communists saw this court as a Western tool. Then the Third World lost confidence in the International Court after the Southwest Africa cases. Finally, the United States, though a Western state, became disillusioned over the International Court during President Ronald Reagan's administration.[32] The International Court's most important accomplishment to date may be the fact that it has existed for four decades and no one is talking about getting rid of it.[33]

Several regional courts have come into being on the assumption that there would be enough cohesion within a region, based on shared interests and cultures, to allow a court to be effective. Such courts exist in Europe. The European Court of Justice began in Luxembourg in 1952 as part of the economic integration leading to the European Union and has made effective decisions on hundreds of cases on trade relationships. We have already referred to the European Court of Human Rights in the context of individuals as subjects of international law. This court began in Strasbourg, France, in 1959 and is an impressive court because human rights complainants can appeal over the heads of their governments. In a world where the state is still the primary actor, an appeal by an individual beyond a state's sovereign control is a momentous development. This court has been busy and currently hears about 30 new cases a year.

In Latin America, the Andean Court of Justice began operation in 1983 in Quito, Ecuador, to hear cases concerning trade among five Andean Mountain states under a trade association known as the Andean Pact. The Inter-American Court of Human Rights was established in 1979 in San José, Costa Rica. This court can hear only cases brought by states and has heard but a few cases. For example, in 1988, Honduras agreed to appear before the court regarding the political murder of thousands of its citizens from the 1950s onward. Then there is the Central American Court of Justice, established in 1965, which makes rulings on trade among the states of this subregion. The judges are the highest judicial official of each country, since the design of this court did not call for a full-time judicial body. The Central American Court has been the least active of the regional courts.[34]

The most frequent use of international law in courts is, paradoxically, in national courts. Any national court system can hear appropriate cases based on international law. Both citizens and governments bring cases when more than one state's citizens, territory, ships, airplanes, and other extensions of states are involved in a dispute. The owners of ships that have collided at sea, for example, can seek an answer as to blame and damages in the nearest national court if they so choose, though neither ship flies the flag of this nearest national jurisdiction. National judges can also draw on treaties and other sources of international law and incorporate them in their domestic context. If a country is a signatory of the Covenant on Civil and Political Rights, that country's judges might decide to define a citizen's freedom through the Covenant, thus overriding a national executive decree or legislative act.

The Executive Task

At the international level, a world attorney-general does not exist to guarantee compliance with international laws. Nevertheless, as in most domestic contexts, subjects willingly obey international laws most of the time. When states carry on normal business by living in peace, conducting diplomacy, exchanging goods and currency, facilitating tourist travel, and making agreements of all types, they are continuously involved in acts of obedience to international law.[35]

The executive side of the United Nations faces serious limitations regarding international law's effectiveness. The Secretary-General of the United Nations is the chief executive officer of this organization, but is mostly a symbolic spokesperson for humankind. This office is without coercive powers. Instead, secretary-generals have practiced "quiet diplomacy," persuasive discussions to move a state to stop fighting or to halt odious human rights practices. Their success is hard to gauge, but unquestionably secretary-generals experience failures as well as successes.

Around the Secretary-General is a large staff of experts who help shape and clarify international law. One such individual has been B. G. Ramcharan, Special Assistant to the Assistant Secretary-General for Human Rights. Ramcharan has published several important books in the human rights field, including *The Right to Life in International Law,* which has shaped the meaning of law in this area.[36]

In addition, world opinion, as reflected by the United Nations, can offer a sanction of sorts. To regularly and grievously violate international law is to take on the status of a pariah, resulting in a harder international life for such a state. Prospects for trade, foreign aid, tourism, a capacity for influence, and other matters of value diminish with pariah status.

Below the international level, states frequently serve in their own executive capacity to encourage respect for law. In customary law, the fundamental principle of *pacta sunt servanda,* that agreements are to be observed, has a long record of respect and is now codified in the *Law of Treaties* of 1969. Because of *pacta sunt servanda,* states cannot choose the laws they will obey, and years of digression from obedience to one or more laws does not alter their duty to obey.

Noncoercive means are available to states to bring about compliance with international law. Perhaps obedience occurs, more than for any other reason, because of *reciprocity.* The potential offender is also the potential victim. If one state performs a negative act, such as violating the immunity of another state's diplomats, or declares a diplomat *persona non grata,* the victimized state may retaliate.[37] By the same token, a positive act, such as returning hijacked planes, can produce similar behavior by another state. If states expect international law to receive respect when it favors their interests, their governments must respect international law when it benefits other states. Werner Levi has maintained that state practice shows reciprocity to be the largest contributor to the binding force of law and may be the best way to achieve profitable, cooperative, and friendly relations.[38]

States can shift from noncoercive to coercive means, if they choose to, in the **self-help** centuries-old tradition of customary law. This tradition emerged because international law is *primitive law,* meaning a central government for enforcement is absent.[39] Self-help enforcement can amount to simple acts of *retorsion,* acts that are legal though unfriendly, such as breaking off diplomatic relations. Or self-help can involve a naval blockade or military intervention to protect property and citizens on another state's territory.

However, during the twentieth century, unilateral, coercive force has declined in legitimacy. Most of the world, for instance, did not approve of the attack on Libya by American planes in 1986 or the United States' military intervention in Panama in 1989. These acts of unilateral force are retrograde from the point of view of progress under international law; they make this law seem more primitive than it is and remind us of an order based on "might makes right."

In the twentieth century, states have had means available beyond the self-help tradition. The development of the League of Nations, and later the United Nations, established a basis for economic and military sanctions that states could exercise as a society instead of acting unilaterally. Not only does the UN Charter require peaceful settlement of disputes, but force is legal only for self-defense. Unfortunately, for an emergent international society, the United Nations' role in collective enforcement is a mixed record at best.

On occasion, states may calculate that self-help will be worth the potential international disapproval and proceed on their own, including the use of force. Or states may recruit a few other states to join them for appearance's sake and pretend their act is collective and legitimate. For instance, when President Ronald Reagan sent military forces into Grenada in 1983, a federation of tiny Caribbean states supposedly gave a legitimating imprimatur to this action. It is unclear if other Caribbean states feared the expansion of communism from Grenada, but definitely President Reagan objected to the presence of a communist government on Grenada and one friendly to Cuba.

Finally, foreign ministers and diplomats of states, as executive officers, probably interpret and use international law more than any other group, including national judges. International law in this executive context is the foundation of many negotiations among states.

To conclude the analysis for this section of the chapter, states operate in a relatively primitive legal environment in which it is difficult to force a subject's compliance. Nevertheless, the legitimacy of international law has wide acceptance around the world, and states normally do choose to obey the law. The acceptability of international law derives from the simple fact that compliance frequently serves the various interests of individual states and the common good of all states. We can think of international law operating through three classic governmental functions—the legislative, judicial, and executive—performed in some manner. Compliance with laws, backed as it is by punitive sanctions, is probably greater in well-ordered states; yet compliance with international law is impressive given the condition of authority in a *horizontal* international society. As a structured order, international law is truly the framework of international society.

INTERNATIONAL LAW IN A MULTICULTURAL WORLD

Presumably, complying with law and perceiving law as just are more likely to happen if law derives from a culture all subjects share. Definitely, the world does not enjoy these positive effects, but given the world's multicultural nature, can there be at least one legal order to cement the deep fissures of multiculturalism? Adda Bozeman observes a significant incongruency between a culturally diverse world on the one hand and an international law drawn from the context of "Euro-American jurisprudence" on the other. Professor Bozeman believes the fissures of cultural diversity among the legal cultures of Africa and Asia, the communist world, and the Western world will not permit the world to evolve as one legal system. Bozeman concludes that the dominance of a Western political order is passing into history and that the rest of the world will not abide by Western standards of international law.[40]

Werner Levi, in contrast to Bozeman, thinks it is erroneous to say that for international law to exist, there must be substantial agreement among national legal cultures. Professor Levi has a strong opinion that cultural differences among national societies do not undermine international law. For him, it is the interaction of states that provides the fertile soil for the growth of international law. Moreover, Levi believes, "The weakness of international law stems less from different outlooks and much more from similar but clashing interests antagonistically pursued."[41] Thus, Professor Levi believes it is national interests that endanger a world under one law and not manifold cultures, although cultural differences are hardly supportive of a worldwide legal system. Actually, clashing interests and cultures have a formative function and are helping to develop common rules and norms that mitigate diversity.

Although international society does not tightly cohere around a firm core of norms, progress toward a web of bilateral and multilateral relationships, guided by a normative system supporting international law, is well under way. The measure of this progress is the avoidance of disputes because of the agreement over the law.[42] Agreement is partial and imperfect, but the international society, for instance, condemned Iran's seizure of the U.S. embassy in Iran in 1979, Soviet aggression against Afghanistan in the same year, and Iraqi aggression against Kuwait in 1990. States and other actors hammer out agreements and plans of action at environmental, human rights, and trade summit conferences. Numerous countries send thousands of peacekeepers to the far-flung corners of the world, where they have no interests, all in the name of peace. Further, United Nations human rights bodies continue to define and shape the norms of universal human rights, leveling criticisms of violations that cut across all the major cultures of the world.[43]

Nonetheless, a single and clear body of world law is not yet a fact of international life. Especially noticeable are the international law observances that differ along bloc and cultural-regional lines. Given a world of diversity, preference for some differences in norms and rules is not surprising, especially when we recognize that within domestic societies, legal practices can be disparate as well. The United States, for example, has some states in its federal system that use capital punishment while others do not, and Great Britain devolves authority to Scotland to allow different educational and juvenile laws.

Hedley Bull and Adam Watson find the extent to which Third World states have embraced elements of a Eurocentric system remarkable. In fact, these states use international law and diplomacy to redress their grievances against Western states.[44] Third World states have readily accepted many Western institutions as a means of interaction with the rest of the world; however, they want to use some of these institutions, such as diplomacy, to achieve a larger share of the world's wealth. Along with their integration into the world system, especially regarding trade, Third World states want to place new principles in treaties. For instance, these states want to alter the reciprocity principle to allow them more favorable trade terms than the better-off countries receive. The argument of the Third World is that such arrangements are a better means than foreign aid for their economies to catch up with the richer industrialized states.

What has allowed the norms of international law to operate throughout much of the Third World despite a special outlook, an almost ideological view, especially concerning world trade? Since colonial times, non-Western elites have attended Western universities and, in other ways, paid attention to the Western mode of conduct. They realize the existing international system is well established, and so most Third World leaders choose to work through this system to gain the advantages of trade, a sense of security through the recognition of their sovereignty, and an outlet to the world by sending diplomats to global conferences and to the United Nations. Although commitment to these norms in the Third World is a matter of degree and layered on top of other cultural values, these shared norms manage to facilitate a world order of law.[45] As a result, coordination among states is smoother because interstate relations receive guidance from Western legal values.[46]

The demise of European communist states as a block will probably aid the promotion of a world legal system. These former communist states seem eager to embrace the rules and norms of their past Western opponents as long as doing so brings peace and prosperity. The Soviet Union had led its allies and friends in the struggle to block Western influence and the growth of a world capitalist system. Yet, while they survived, Soviet-bloc communist states did not object completely to Western-derived international law. True, communist theorists saw the law of capitalist states as the rule of the strong designed to exploit others, but the same law also gave communist states the protection of sovereignty in the face of capitalist encirclement, intervention, and domestic interference. As the Soviet bloc of states came to accept "peaceful co-existence" with the West, they began to view international law as a contractual arrangement between two different worlds, capitalist and communist.[47] International law helped to structure and stabilize the bipolar Cold War.

Although the obstacle to world law posed by European communism is largely gone, other examples of different international legal practices by blocs of states remain. For instance, the Universal Declaration of Human Rights became two covenants for ratification purposes, one for Western states that emphasized civil and political rights and the other for socialist and communist countries that appreciated social and economic rights. Some states ratified both covenants. Also, we referred earlier to the nationality principles based on *jus soli* in the Western Hemisphere and *jus sanguinis* in Europe.

As for cultural regions, they have their own values and practices that set them apart from the international system at large concerning international law. Among cultural regions, Latin America may be the most distinct region. The "Calvo Doctrine," found in many Latin American countries, claims that a state is not responsible for harms done against aliens on its soil during an insurrection, while most states accept such a responsibility.

Also, it is in Latin America, as discussed in Chapter Seven on diplomacy, that embassies can grant political asylum under the *Inter-American Convention for the Granting of Asylum* of 1928, although states in the rest of the world refrain from doing so. Cultural influences as hindrances to a single body of law are perhaps best understood by looking at a specialized area of law and following it through the prisms of varied cultures.

It is in the underdeveloped but emerging area of *private international law* that cultural diversity especially confounds the notion of world law. This point is crucial, since the world is experiencing the integrating effects of economic interdependence, and thus finding agreeable ways to deal with transnational business disputes is a shared concern. A ubiquitous set of rules for business transactions is only at an early stage of development. Legal cultures around the world contain different histories, attitudes, and principles. *Common law* countries cover contracts, torts (damages), and remedies, not only through laws of legislative bodies but through precedents drawn from specific cases and disputes. Common law also derives from long-standing custom. Australia, Canada, Great Britain, New Zealand, and the United States are states with common law traditions.

European, Latin American, and some African and Asian states have *civil law* legal traditions. Civil law depends on extensively coded rules and regulations that attempt, well ahead of any anticipated problems, to cover every aspect of regulated life, including business activities. Civil law has a long tradition, going back to at least the Roman Empire. Germany, as a civil law state, has great importance because of its central role in the European Union and as the leading state inducing Russia and eastern Europe to join the capitalistic world trade system. German views can easily imprint on formative international business law, especially Germany's benevolent and protective treatment of labor.

Latin America is, in part, an extension of the European civil law tradition, and, at the same time, its identification with the Third World encourages many Latin American countries to share in the dependency theory that they are victims of capitalist exploitation by the richer states. To protect themselves from coercion and intimidation from powerful states, many Latin American countries abide by the "Calvo Clause" (do not confuse with the "Calvo Doctrine"), which requires foreign businesses to use a Latin American national court and to refrain from appealing for diplomatic help from their home states.

Japan, even more than Germany in international business, has achieved the widely recognized status of an economic superpower. Japan's civil law, including the regulation of commerce, originated from German codes of the late nineteenth century. Japan uses this law when Asian values of harmony and consensus fail to satisfy Westerners. Japanese businesspeople want openness and flexibility in trade arrangements with other countries, while Westerners want specifics. Westerners who want exact terms of trade, such as lists of trade goods the Japanese promise to buy and a known time of purchase, have a tough negotiating task ahead of them.

Socialist law (or communist law) is a legal tradition that began with the Russian Revolution of 1917. Marxist, anticapitalist values spread to China, Cuba, eastern Europe, North Korea, Vietnam, and a few countries in Africa. The socialist law tradition called for highly centralized economies, usually planned in five-year time segments. State ownership of almost all property left little tolerance for private property. International trade developed among the communist states, but trade with Western states, as Cold War opponents, was limited. The inability of communist countries to convert their monies into the currencies of other countries and the necessity of bartering in goods, among other hindrances, prevented the integration of a true world economy. The collapse of communism in Europe, a change of attitude about international trade and some use of capitalist techniques in China and Vietnam, and forces for change in Cuba and North Korea are helping to create a more fully integrated world economy unimaginable during the Cold War.

Of the states from the socialist law tradition, China is rapidly proving to be the most important. China is experiencing billions of dollars of import-export trade with Western states and is an important investment target for Western MNCs. As Hong Kong, a major financial and industrial center, reverts from British colonial status to Chinese ownership in 1997, China's economic role in the world will be even more prominent. China probably will influence the world economy as an economic superpower before the middle of the 21st century.

Today, however, China is an oddity to the world. Never completely losing ancient Confucian values calling for honorable negotiations and the avoidance of litigation, China, which currently has a centralized economy, is busy converting socialist law into civil law more conducive to a healthy business climate. In spite of this promising step, negotiating terms of trade between China and Western countries remains prickly for both sides. Strife arises easily, as in the case of President Bill Clinton's threat of trade sanctions in 1995. China had allowed the violation of American intellectual property rights concerning computer software and movie videos.

The *Islamic law* tradition is important because it applies in a large number of countries, including most of the countries of North Africa, the Middle East, Central Asia, and Indonesia and Malaysia in Southeast Asia. Some of these countries contain large amounts of oil critical to the Western economy. Islamic law is God's law revealed in the Quran, the Islamic bible, and Islamic law is often one and the same as secular law in Islamic states. The content of Islamic law poses some difficulties for international trade, such as treating interest on loans as usury and making interest rates illegal. Contracts, on the other hand, are similar enough as a concept between the West and Islamic states to allow a huge amount of trade. Saudi Arabia, the chief exporter and holder of oil in the world, has used oil revenues to produce an impressive domestic economic and technological development without its Islamic status posing a serious drawback.[48]

About business and law, we can conclude that multiple billions of dollars in trade and investment are occurring in an interdependent world economy in spite of the significantly different legal cultures found among the trading partners. Yet many misunderstandings can occur over contracts, investment terms, the settlement of and remedies for disputes, and other problems because of the need to communicate through cultural filters. As states come to share similar versions of *private international law,* they can reduce misunderstandings and facilitate higher levels of trade that all of them profess to want. States sometimes place shared understandings of private international law in treaties, thus converting such law into the *public international law* of states. These understandings are increasingly coming to reflect a Western flavor.

In the current era, we rightfully pay attention to the multicultural nature of the world, and many scholars are sensitive to different cultures, arguing they have equal worth. Despite these fair-minded academic views, Western conquest of the past and, more recently, Western capitalism and democracy appear to be the driving forces behind the transcendence of Western norms of law over those of other cultures such as Buddhism, Hinduism, and Islam.

The extent of acceptance of different parts of the body of international law varies substantially, at least in part because of cultural differences. Three levels of compliance operate in the context of international law. First, we can speak of legal norms being so fundamental that compliance is thought of as *universal* whether or not a particular state has consented to the norm. An example would be the principle of *pacta sunt servanda,* that all states must obey agreements.

Second, a *general* international law derives from a multilateral treaty with many signatories. Most of the world accepts this kind of law and, at some time in the future, this law has a chance to become universal. The Law of the Sea, including a 12-mile seaward territoriality, is such a law.

Third, there is the *particular* international law that binds only two states or a limited group of states. The St. Lawrence Seaway arrangement involves Canada and the United States, and the Maastricht Treaty now draws 15 European states into deeper trade ties. Some international laws are germane only for a specific cultural region, such as when the Organization of African Unity or the Arab League deals with common problems through treaty arrangements. Sometimes such cultural regions accept human rights treaties and declarations designed especially for their respective regions, taking care that these agreements will not contravene their cultural values.

INTERNATIONAL LAW AND INTERNATIONAL SOCIETY

Now we will focus more directly on the role international law is playing in an emerging international society. As we have mentioned, international law, along with diplomacy, has served as a vital institution for pulling together a society of states. International law continues today to be an important formative force behind international society. International law's scope continues to expand, and states and other actors increasingly respect and apply the rules of international society.

Assessing the importance of the role of international law reminds one of the proverbial glass filled to mid-level with water. To the pessimist the glass is half empty, and to the optimist it is half full. The reality of international law allows us to see considerable failure and success. International law is inadequate when states are in serious conflict, and leaders regard force as a viable option. Richard Falk, a principal contributor to the scholarly "world order movement" and a scholar usually positive about international law's prospects, once called the outlook for these rules and norms bleak after reviewing a number of serious violations of law prohibiting the use of coercive power.[49]

Yet Thomas M. Franck observes that international law can affect state behavior even in time of war, presumably the epitome of anarchy. Professor Franck cites the example of Argentina's aggression against the Falkland Islands in 1982. Argentina had diplomatically disputed Britain's possession of these islands for decades. Normally, many Third World countries would have been sympathetic to Argentina, but aggression is a gross violation of international law. Argentina's aggression largely isolated that state diplomatically.[50] Argentina was unable to acquire more Exocet missiles from Latin American neighbors that

Argentine pilots had used successfully against several British warships. Argentina lost the war decisively, mostly because of superior British forces but also due to its lack of diplomatic and material support from other countries.

Undoubtedly, international law gives much guidance to states.[51] Burns H. Weston views international law as a positive and formative tool. He thinks international law can and will create a more secure world among states by controlling weapons through arms agreements and will promote social justice, foster economic well-being, and improve the global ecology for the benefit of humankind.[52] The sanguine view that Professor Weston expresses about international law's future is encouraging, but does the actual role of international law deserve such optimism when put to close scrutiny?

We can assess international law's role in the evolution of international society through a review of the theoretical positions of realists, neorealists, and transnationalists. Realists give more credence to international law's importance than the later neorealists, who largely ignore the subject. For transnationalists, international law is a cornerstone of the burgeoning international society.

Realist paragon Hans Morgenthau recognizes that many states, in their normal business, regularly follow international law, but he views this law as weak, primitive, and decentralized concerning enforcement. Morgenthau finds that international law cannot effectively regulate the pursuit of power by states, a failure shown in the histories of the League of Nations and the United Nations.[53]

Charles W. Kegley, Jr., and Gregory Raymond would almost surely disagree with Professor Morgenthau. They recognize that powerful states could flout international law, but they usually do not. The leaders of great powers have nearly always seen themselves as constrained by principles, norms, and rules. As the destruction of war has increased in history, especially after the massive toll of the First World War, great powers tried to establish ever-firmer rules to prevent struggles from boiling over into war.

More exactly, Professors Kegley and Raymond believe a given period in history can be a *permissive normative order* or a *restrictive normative order* concerning the leeway states enjoy over the use of force. These different orders contain rules that affect when it is appropriate to wage war and how to fight a war. After the huge costs in blood and treasure of the Second World War, the great powers mostly adhered to alliance treaty commitments and the clear law of the UN Charter against war, thus producing a restrictive normative order or the "long peace" of the Cold War era. Recognizing that realists focus on alliance systems and distributions of power, Professors Kegley and Raymond have reviewed historical cases of these matters and discovered that realists fail to give norms and rules their due in explaining outcomes of war and peace and political outcomes in general.[54]

In an interesting study comparing the power of norms to shape outcomes versus national interests that realists espouse, Gary Goertz and Paul F. Diehl found norms more important. Worldwide norms calling for decolonization outweighed states' economic interests and need for military security bound up with their colonies. As a result, colonial empires, designed to last indefinitely, collapsed within a few short decades.[55]

In addition, Louis Henkin regards Morgenthau's realist view of international law as too narrow. Morgenthau thought he observed an "iron law" of power politics that treats legal obligations and national interests as separate matters. For this reason, Professor Morgenthau could not see important national interests fulfilled through the law of states; rather, for

Morgenthau, the focus was on power interests that could easily conflict with states' legal obligations. Professor Henkin believes that international law is a major force in international relations shaping state behavior, although he recognizes that other forces outweigh law on occasion.[56]

Similarly, Professor Henkin believes realist George F. Kennan, the chief architect of American containment policy in the Cold War, depreciated the role of law in his classic study *American Diplomacy 1900–1950*. Kennan tended to dichotomize diplomacy and law as though they had little to do with each other.[57] Because realists emphasize the use of force and war, they unduly marginalize the role of international law.[58]

Kenneth N. Waltz, the spearhead of neorealists, fails to recognize a meaningful role for international law. For Waltz, norms of any kind lack independent causal force. The power structure of the world and the number of states sharing in this structure are all-determining for Professor Waltz. In the index of his classic study *Theory of International Politics,* there is no reference to the subject of international law.[59] Certainly we can assume Waltz is aware of the history of law in international relations, but for him the role of international law does not explain what is important to scholars in the field of international relations.

A useful way to understand the position of transnationalists concerning international law is through the writing of legal scholar Anne-Marie Burley. Professor Burley points out that international specialists failed to pay enough attention to international law until the 1970s, when some of them began to focus on the regulatory effects of regimes, a subject we discussed in Chapter Three on actors. She observes that transnationalists, such as Robert O. Keohane, have rediscovered international law through a the study of rulemaking regimes as institutions promoting the national interests of multiple states.

Regimes can regulate trade, the environment, human rights, or any subject affecting the common interests of several or more states. Regimes vary considerably regarding the formalization of their rules, however. Such institutions, whether informal regimes based on norms or treaty-based organizations with clear rules, promote the common interest and raise multilateral cooperation to a higher level than would be the case without regimes. Professor Burley points out that international lawyers have long known that law is more than a constraint system because law encourages the good behavior of cooperation. Professor Burley concludes that "regimists," with their interest in the convergence of state behavior around rules and norms, have simply used international law by another name.[60]

Putting the transnationalist view succinctly, the state system, decentralized in authority and inhabited by autonomous states as well as other actors, is in transition to a network of interdependent states regulated by rules or laws. International rulemaking, in contexts ranging from bilateral negotiation to multilateral conferences, is a social process giving definition to an international society.[61] International law stems from basic political, economic, and cultural determinants that are pulling international society together. International law is not itself the main pulling force but follows the path taken by the determinants of society and serves as an organizing framework. As R. J. Vincent has put the matter, international law "is a cart, not a horse."[62]

We can restate the role of international law through the three analytical models used in this text and the appropriate elements from Table 1.1 of Chapter One. The realist view of the world is giving way to the transnationalist view as theory catches up to changes in the real world. Realism cannot account for an ongoing transformation from *international anarchy* to an *international society* because realists are tied to the notion that states will not trade their autonomy for other interests through cooperative ventures.[63] Nor do realists believe international law can do much to control the use of force. For realists, failure in this endeavor seems to cast doubt about the effectiveness and legitimacy of all international law.[64] The actual record of the evolving international society is a mixed one. A sense of "triumphalism" after the UN Coalition stopped Iraqi aggression in 1991 seemed to undercut the realist assertion about controlling force, but more recently, the United Nations has had great difficulty quelling internal disputes.

However, overall, a shift from the order of international anarchy to a more cooperative order is taking place. The spread of law into more areas of concern and the growing appreciation of law as an institution promoting the common good clearly allows an international society to integrate more fully than ever before. International law has been beneficial since at least the seventeenth century and has become even more salient during the twentieth century. The strongest potential for international law may be in the post–Cold War era, when a greater consensus about rules and norms is possible. To be sure, international law is helping humankind by providing a framework for cooperation in diverse areas such as peace, human rights, diplomacy, trade, and environmental protection.

Several elements used in our analytical models are relevant here. First, international law exudes *authority* because it represents rules that more and more actors are willing to respect. Second, international law represents a *problem-solving level* at the regional and global levels of multilateral cooperation. Laws evolving at both levels hold agreements about how states are to conduct their relations. States and other actors find they can routinize behavior around common standards and avoid unnecessary problems in the future when states agree to rules such as those in the Law of the Sea Treaty. Finally, states can apply similar policies to given *issues*—for instance, to human rights practices—when they agree to these policies through treaties.

A Hobbesian struggle of all against all, the model of international anarchy, is transforming into a Grotian order of rules that reduces conflict to form an international society. This change from one order to another has taken centuries but is now intensifying, pushed favorably by the end of the Cold War. This order may not be as good, normatively speaking, as the Kantian perpetual peace we wish for in an international community with a closely identifying, global citizenry. Still, an international society, focused on the achievement of peace even in the face of stubborn squabbles within this society, is no small accomplishment.

CHAPTER SUMMARY

Every human society establishes security and predictability through rules. International law is the formal rule framework for a nascent international society. Most states find the law useful to promote and guide cooperation over a wide range of interests.

International law derives from several sources in the absence of a world government. Treaties and customary law are the principal sources. The subjects of international law now include several actors other than the state. International organizations and individuals, in addition to states, are the subjects of international law. These actors, however, enjoy varying degrees of legal personality. The scope of international law affects most human activity that is transnational in nature, and this scope is broadening as actors find new issues requiring negotiation and agreement.

The effectiveness of international law, however, does not match the way a strong state can apply law in its territory and to its citizens. Nevertheless, international society performs the three tasks of government—rulemaking, rule adjudication, and rule execution—in some manner and degree. The more states are in agreement, the better is the performance of these three tasks. For the future, international law will increase in importance, not to the extent that it serves as the "rules of the strong" as a constraint system but to the extent that it can help shape a consensus around the vision of a stable, predictable, and just world order.

Once realists thought of international law as incidental to the core of international relations, the pursuit of power by states. By the 1970s, transnationalists, in contrast, began to give attention to regimes, or international law by another name. Regimes, with their norms and rules, encourage cooperative behavior by states.

The role of international law clearly moves the world away from anarchy and toward a more cooperative international society. International law, perhaps more than any other subject, helps establish the framework of a cooperative Grotian order over a Hobbesian order of anarchy.

POINTS OF VIEW

. . . law is a major force in international affairs; nations rely on it, invoke it, observe and are influenced by it in every aspect of their foreign relations.
—Professor Louis Henkin

When Kansas and Colorado have a quarrel over the water in the Arkansas River, they don't call out the National Guard in each state and go to war over it. They bring suit in the Supreme Court of the United States and abide by the decision. There isn't a reason in the world why we cannot do that internationally.
—President Harry Truman
April 1945

In short, Third World governments do not want to replace the society of sovereign states but rather to improve their own positions within that society.
—Professors Hedley Bull and
Adam Watson

What makes the situation in the former Yugoslavia particularly repugnant is evidence that rape has apparently become a strategy of the war; a terror weapon aimed specifically at women.
—Editorial in *Say It Now,*
April–May 1993, p. 2

The credibility of international humanitarian law demands a war crimes tribunal to hold accountable those responsible for gross violations in the former Yugoslavia.
—Theodor Meron
Professor of International Law
in *Foreign Affairs,* Summer 1993

REVIEW QUESTIONS

1. What are the sources of international law, and how do they rank in importance?
2. What is the difference between natural law and the positivism tradition in international law?
3. What do scholars mean when they speak of the incorporation of international law?
4. What are the subjects of international law in addition to states?
5. Identify the international courts that exist today, and describe their importance to international law.
6. What has been the role of the UN in developing international law?
7. Does the multicultural world obstruct international law? Explain.

8. Why is Latin America a special region in terms of international law?
9. What areas fall within the scope of international law?
10. How does private international law become public international law?
11. Why does scholar Anne-Marie Burley think regimes are another way of talking about international law?
12. What role does international law play in forming an international society?

GLOSSARY

adjudication The process by which a regular court makes a judicially binding decision.

arbitration The process in which a third, neutral party makes a binding decision in an *ad hoc* or temporary judicial procedure.

codification The process of converting understood rules and norms into written law, primarily as a treaty.

compulsory jurisdiction An arena of power of a court that allows it to compel an actor to come to court and accept the court's ruling.

customary law Recognized but unwritten law that receives respect and compliance over time.

declaration A clear statement of policy that may be interpreted as an international norm and sometimes leads to a treaty.

extradition The formal procedure for returning a fugitive from one state to another; usually governed by treaty.

international law The rules and norms that states, and other actors as legal personalities, are bound to obey in their mutual relations and commonly do obey.

international legal personality A subject of international law that has rights and duties.

judicial decisions Rulings of national and international court judges that can set precedents in international law.

municipal systems Domestic or national internal legal systems; not to be confused with city governments.

natural law Fundamental principles bound up in the universe that allow additional rules to be discovered and deducted to build a body of the appropriate laws for human society.

positivism A practical and realistic philosophy that believes true laws are the rules actors agree to be bound by and actually obey.

principles of law Broad guidelines for actors to follow that can be drawn from natural law or municipal sources and are considered sources of international law.

publicists Legal scholars who offer legal opinions in published law journals as a solution to a legal problem.

resolution A decision or recommendation of an international body such as the General Assembly of the United Nations.

self-help A customary law practice that has allowed a state to enforce international law on its own volition.

treaty A written agreement concluded by states, and sometimes by international organizations, that commits the signatories to future terms of interaction.

RECOMMENDED READINGS

Carol C. Adelman, ed. *International Regulation: New Rules in a Changing World Order.* San Francisco: Institute for Contemporary Studies, 1988.

S. James Anaya. *Indigenous Peoples in International Law.* New York: Oxford University Press, 1996.

Anthony Clark Arend and Robert J. Beck. *International Law and the Use of Force: Beyond the UN Charter Paradigm.* New York: Routledge, 1993.

Geoffrey Best. *War and Law Since 1945.* New York: Oxford University Press, 1994.

Adda B. Bozeman. *The Future of Law in a Multicultural World.* Princeton, NJ: Princeton University Press, 1971.

Hedley Bull. *The Anarchical Society: A Study of Order in World Politics.* New York: Columbia University Press, 1977, Chapter 6.

Antonio Cassese. *International Law in a Divided World.* Oxford: Clarendon Press, 1986.

Lung-chu Chen. *An Introduction to Contemporary International Law: A Policy Oriented Perspective.* New Haven, CT: Yale University Press, 1989.

Anthony D'Amato. *International Law: Process and Prospect.* Dobbs Ferry, NY: Transnational Publishers, 1994.

Lori F. Damrosch, ed. *The International Court of Justice at a Crossroads.* Dobbs Ferry, NY: Transnational Publishers, 1989.

Richard Falk. *Revitalizing International Law.* Ames, IA: Iowa State University Press, 1989.

Wolfgang Friedmann. *The Changing Structure of International Law.* New York: Columbia University Press, 1964, Chapter 18.

Rosalyn Higgins. *Problems and Process: International Law and How We Use It.* Oxford: Clarendon Press, 1994.

Carolyn Hotchkiss. *International Law for Business.* New York: McGraw-Hill, 1994.

Werner Levi. *Contemporary International Law.* 2nd ed. Boulder, CO: Westview Press, 1991.

Vaughan Lowe and Malgosia Fitzmaurice. *Fifty Years of the International Court of Justice.* New York: Cambridge University Press, 1996.

Vaughan Lowe and Colin Warbrick, eds. *The United Nations and the Principles of International Law.* New York: Routledge, 1994.

Terry Nardin. *Law, Morality, and the Relations of States.* Princeton, NJ: Princeton University Press, 1983.

J. G. Merrills. *The Development of International Law by the European Court of Human Rights.* Manchester: Manchester University Press, 1988.

Daniel P. Moynihan. *On the Law of Nations.* Cambridge, MA: Harvard University Press, 1990.

Burns H. Weston. *International Law and World Order: Basic Documents.* 5 vols. Irvington, NY: Transnational Publishers, 1996.

ENDNOTES

1. Hedley Bull, *The Anarchical Society* (New York: Columbia University Press, 1977), p. 129.
2. Werner Levi, *Contemporary International Law,* 2nd ed. (Boulder, CO: Westview Press, 1991), pp. 145–46.
3. A. LeRoy Bennett, *International Organizations: Principles and Issues,* 6th ed. (Englewood Cliffs, NJ: Prentice Hall, 1991), p. 182.
4. Bull, *The Anarchical Society,* p. 142.
5. Hedley Bull and Adam Watson, "Conclusion," in *The Expansion of International Society,* ed. Hedley Bull and Adam Watson (Oxford: Clarendon Press, 1984), p. 435.
6. A useful description of legal philosophies is found in Levi, *Contemporary International Law,* pp. 17–18; Gerhard von Glahn, *Law Among Nations,* 6th ed. (New York: Macmillan, 1992), pp. 29–30, 33–34.
7. Bull, *The Anarchical Society,* p. 147.
8. Monroe Leigh, "Editorial Comment: Is the President Above Customary International Law?" *American Journal of International Law,* October 1992, pp. 757–63.
9. John H. Barton and Barry E. Carter, "The Uneven, But Growing, Role of International Law," in *Rethinking America's Security,* ed. Graham Allison and Gregory F. Treverton (New York: W. W. Norton, 1992), pp. 289–90.
10. These four sources are taken from Robert L. Bledsoe and Boleslaw A. Boczek, *The International Law Dictionary* (Santa Barbara, CA: ABC-CLIO, 1987); William R. Slomanson, *Fundamental Perspectives on International Law* (New York: West, 1990), pp. 8–22; von Glahn, *Law Among Nations,* pp. 12–24.
11. Bull, *The Anarchical Society,* p. 129
12. Lung-chu Chen, *An Introduction to Contemporary Law* (New Haven, CT: Yale University Press, 1989), pp. 25–49; Antonio Cassese, *International Law in a Divided World* (Oxford: Clarendon Press, 1986), pp. 77–85.
13. Chen, *An Introduction to Contemporary Law,* pp. 50–62; Cassese, *International Law in a Divided World,* pp. 85–90.
14. Chen, *An Introduction to Contemporary Law,* pp. 63–75; Cassese, *International Law in a Divided World,* p. 103.
15. Bull, *The Anarchical Society,* p. 152.
16. Chen, *An Introduction to Contemporary Law,* pp. 76–81; Cassese, *International Law in a Divided World,* pp. 99–103.
17. Payam Akhavan, "The International Criminal Tribunal for Rwanda: The Politics and Pragmatics of Punishment," *American Journal of International Law,* July 1996, pp. 501–10, especially p. 503.
18. *Time,* June 10, 1985, p. 55.
19. *Parade* magazine, November 25, 1990, p. 18.
20. Cassese, *International Law in a Divided World,* pp. 81–85.
21. Taken in part from Bledsoe and Boczek, *The International Law Dictionary.*
22. Slomanson, *Fundamental Perspectives on International Law,* p. 363.

23. Hans J. Morgenthau, *Politics Among Nations: The Struggle for Power and Peace*, 5th ed. (New York: Alfred A. Knopf, 1978), p. 285.
24. A good description of the UN's contribution to international law can be found in Bennett, *International Organizations,* Chapter 8. An early and detailed analysis is in Rosalyn Higgins, *The Development of International Law Through the Political Organs of the United Nations* (New York: Oxford University Press, 1963).
25. Morgenthau, *Politics Among Nations*, p. 294.
26. This description of modern business arbitration is taken from Barton and Carter, "The Uneven, But Growing, Role of International Law," pp. 285–87.
27. Ibid., p. 288.
28. Mark W. Janis, *An Introduction to International Law* (Boston: Little, Brown, 1993), p. 128.
29. A useful description of the ICJ is found in Bennett, *International Organizations,* pp. 186–203.
30. Ibid., pp. 197–98.
31. Barton and Carter, "The Uneven, But Growing, Role of International Law," pp. 283–84.
32. Georges Abi-Saab, "The International Court as a World Court," in *Fifty Years of the International Court of Justice,* ed. Vaughan Lowe and Malgosia Fitzmaurice (New York: Cambridge University Press, 1996), pp. 3–7.
33. For a general assessment of the ICJ, see Lori F. Damrosch, ed., *The International Court of Justice at a Crossroads* (Dobbs Ferry, NY: Transnational Publishers, 1987).
34. A good description of regional courts can be found in Slomanson, *Fundamental Perspectives on International Law,* pp. 297–304.
35. Bull, *The Anarchical Society,* p. 137.
36. B. G. Ramcharan, ed., *The Right to Life in International Law* (Boston: Martinus Nijhoff, 1985).
37. Roger Fisher, "Bring Law to Bear on Governments," in *The Conquest of War,* ed. Harry B. Hollins, Averill L. Powers, and Mark Sommer (Boulder, CO: Westview Press, 1989), p. 144; Barton and Carter, "The Uneven, But Growing, Role of International Law," p. 281.
38. Levi, *Contemporary International Law,* p. 20.
39. Bull, *The Anarchical Society,* pp. 131–39; Morgenthau, *Politics Among Nations,* pp. 297–300.
40. Adda Bozeman, "The International Order in a Multicultural World," in *The Expansion of International Society,* pp. 387–406; Adda B. Bozeman, *The Future of Law in a Multicultural World* (Princeton, NJ: Princeton University Press, 1971).
41. Werner Levi, *Law and Politics in the International Society* (Beverly Hills, CA: Sage Publications, 1976), pp. 135–50. The quote is from p. 146.
42. Rosalyn Higgins, *Problems and Process: International Law and How We Use It* (Oxford: Clarendon Press, 1994), p. 1.
43. Lincoln P. Bloomfield, "The Premature Burial of Global Law and Order: Looking Beyond the Three Cases from Hell," in *Order and Disorder After the Cold War,* ed. Brad Roberts (Cambridge, MA: MIT Press, 1995), pp. 163–64.
44. Bull and Watson, "Conclusion," pp. 433–34.
45. Ibid., p. 435.
46. Mark W. Zacker, "The Decaying Pillars of the Westphalian Temple: Implications for International Order and Governance," in *Governance Without Government: Order and Change in World Politics,* ed. James N. Rosenau and Ernst-Otto Czempiel (New York: Cambridge University Press, 1992), pp. 97–98.
47. Excellent descriptions of different views of international law are found in Cassese, *International Law in a Divided World,* pp. 106–25; Walter S. Jones, *The Logic of International Relations,* 7th ed. (New York: HarperCollins, 1991), pp. 530–40.
48. Carolyn Hotchkiss, *International Law for Business* (New York: McGraw-Hill, 1994), Chapters 3 and 4.
49. Richard Falk, *Revitalizing International Law* (Ames, IA: Iowa State University Press, 1989), pp. 60–61.
50. Thomas M. Franck, "The Strategic Role of Legal Principles," in *Choices in World Politics: Sovereignty and Interdependence,* ed. Bruce Russett, Harvey Starr, and Richard Stoll (New York: W. H. Freeman, 1989), pp. 295–304.
51. Robert Wesson, *International Relations in Transition* (Englewood Cliffs, NJ: Prentice Hall, 1990), p. 292.
52. Burns H. Weston, "Law and Alternative Security: Toward a Just World Peace," in *Alternative Security: Living Without Nuclear Deterrence,* ed. Burns H. Weston (Boulder, CO: Westview Press, 1990), pp. 78–106.

53. Morgenthau, *Politics Among Nations*, pp. 281, 297–99.
54. Charles W. Kegley, Jr. and Gregory Raymond, *A Multipolar Peace: Great-Power Politics in the Twentieth Century* (New York: St. Martin's Press, 1994), Chapter 6.
55. Gary Goertz and Paul F. Diehl, "International Norms and Power Politics," in *Reconstructing Realpolitik,* ed. Frank Wayman and Paul F. Diehl (Ann Arbor, MI: University of Michigan Press, 1994), pp. 101–60.
56. Louis Henkin, *How Nations Behave: Law and Foreign Policy,* 2nd ed. (New York: Columbia University Press, 1979), pp. 329–31.
57. Ibid., pp. 322–24, 329.
58. Anne-Marie Slaughter Burley, "International Law and International Relations Theory: A Dual Agenda," *American Journal of International Law,* April 1993, p. 217.
59. Kenneth N. Waltz, *Theory of International Politics* (Reading, MA: Addison-Wesley, 1979).
60. Burley, "International Law and International Relations Theory," pp. 205–39.
61. Zacker, "The Decaying Pillars of the Westphalian Temple," p. 98; Franck, "The Strategic Role of Legal Principles," p. 304.
62. R. J. Vincent, "Order in International Politics," in *Order and Violence: Hedley Bull and International Relations,* ed. J. D. B. Miller and R. J. Vincent (Oxford: Clarendon Press, 1990), pp. 55–56.
63. Zacker, "The Decaying Pillars of the Westphalian Temple," p. 98.
64. Henkin, *How Nations Behave,* p. 319.

CHAPTER 12

INTERNATIONAL ORGANIZATIONS FOR SECURITY AND PROGRESS

In Chapter Three on actors, we defined international organizations as institutions that transcend national boundaries and facilitate cooperation among the members of the organization. As institutions, international organizations provide a process for handling recurring concerns in security, economic, and social problem areas. Scheduled meetings allow states to negotiate, form rules, and agree on policy in the international arena, where governments, operating separately, cannot exercise control. The global web of rules and policies coming from international organizations thus provides a measure of *governance* at the international level, where no central government exists.

The United Nations and its specialized agencies, known as the *UN System,* provide the best available instrument for coping with global-level problems. Only the United Nations can offer a collective vision of what the world can be, according to the recent UN Secretary-General, Boutros Boutros-Ghali.[1] The central importance of the United Nations in the world derives from its nearly universal membership among states and its comprehensive mandate that allows the United Nations to tackle most issues.

Although cooperation and conflict intertwine in every human enterprise, most international organizations tilt decisively toward promoting cooperation over conflict. The founders of organizations usually design them to have positive effects for some or all states and their peoples. Clear exceptions would be a trade cartel that seeks to monopolize a commodity or a military alliance that forms to wage war more effectively. Ultimately, international organizations must constrain conflict so cooperation can bring about an improved world. When international organizations are successful, the world is less volatile and violent than if conflict were free to play out its force, causing a more anarchical order. At the international level, international organizations represent the high-water mark of humankind's venture in promoting cooperation over conflict.

In this chapter, we first distinguish the types of organizations that exist, then look at a brief history of the development of international organizations. Next, we assess the progress made in the promotion of peace, economic and social progress, and cooperation in technical areas such as telecommunication. Then we evaluate the vitality of the United Nations in terms of its costs and efficiency. Finally, we analyze the contribution international organizations have made to the formation of an international society that transcends the anarchy of conflict-prone states.

FIGURE 12.1 Classification of International Organizations

	GLOBAL		REGIONAL	
	Unifunctional	Multifunctional	Unifunctional	Multifunctional
IGO	WHO	UN	NATO	OAS
INGO	AI	ICRC	ALU	PLO

WHO = World Health Organization; UN = United Nations; AI = Amnesty International; ICRC = International Committee of the Red Cross; NATO = North Atlantic Treaty Organization; OAS = Organization of American States; PLO = Palestinian Liberation Organization; ALU = Arab Lawyers Union.

TYPES OF INTERNATIONAL ORGANIZATIONS

We can learn much about any organization by asking and answering three questions. These questions can lead to the classification scheme of Figure 12.1. First, is the organization a public or private one? A *public* organization has a membership of states and is an international government organization (IGO). Most scholars estimate the number of IGOs at 300 or more, and these include the United Nations, the European Union (EU), the North Atlantic Treaty Organization (NATO), and many other important organizations that can influence and shape the behavior of states. A *private* organization has a membership of individuals or groups and is an international nongovernment organization (INGO). INGOs number from 3,000 to over 4,000. INGOs can include organizations that originate for reasons other than politics, such as the Association of International Libraries or the International Confederation of Mid-Wives. Additional organizations, such as the International Criminal Police Organization (Interpol), the International Commission of Jurists working on behalf of human rights, and the environmental group Sea Shepherd, may lobby or work regularly with governments and IGOs.

Second, is the organization *multifunctional* or *unifunctional*? Obviously, the United Nations is multifunctional because it works in several distinct areas, principally peacekeeping, social and economic progress, and technical services. We also can regard the International Committee for the Red Cross (ICRC) as multifunctional. This organization began working with the wounded in wartime, then extended its services to helping POWs, and eventually aided refugees fleeing both war and natural disasters. In contrast, Amnesty International (AI) works only in the area of human rights and focuses on persons imprisoned because of their political and religious opinions. As the name implies, the World Health Organization (WHO) deals with health questions such as AIDS and is one of the better-known organs of the UN System.

Third, what is the venue of the organization? Does it operate at the *global* or *regional* level? Frequently the name provides the answer. The WHO and the Baptist World Alliance are clearly global, while the Organization of American States (OAS) and the Arab Lawyers

Union (ALU) are regional. Sometimes a name—for instance, the Salvation Army—suggests little about venue, and so one has to investigate. In other cases, categorization brings out some peculiarities. Most scholars regard the British Commonwealth as a regional organization because the membership draws from ex-colonies of Britain; yet the member-states exist on several continents. We might naturally assume that NATO would have members only with Atlantic Ocean coastlines, but Greece and Turkey, on the Mediterranean Sea, are member-states. Germany also is a member-state, but is located on the Baltic Sea. At least regional status implies a special subset of actors, usually with a geographical connection. Regardless of some oddities, most organizations are easily identifiable as either global or regional.

Global organizations rest on the belief that many problems are worldwide in scope and will respond only to a global effort. Environmental problems, human rights, trade, and even peace seem to be less and less divisible into geographical parts. War, for example, can spread from a region to become a world war, such as when problems in the Balkans in 1914 escalated into the First World War. Moreover, an effort to place sanctions against an aggressor will do little good unless all states take part. In modern times, any aggressor can easily obtain needed resources outside its region.

However, the world is too heterogeneous to allow for the global handling of all problems. Regional organizations form from the assumption that groups of people or states, sharing similar geography, culture, and concerns, can more effectively solve many of their local problems. The Organization of American States (OAS) deals with the security, economic, and human rights concerns of most of the states in the Western Hemisphere. The Organization of African Unity (OAU) brings over 50 African states together to focus on matters ranging from border issues to a common strategy for the forum of the United Nations. The Arab League frets over conflict with Israel, Palestinian refugees, and keeping the peace among Arab states. Nonetheless, global and regional organizations need not be incompatible. In fact, the UN Charter encourages robust performance by regional organizations as long as they complement the activities and principles of the United Nations.

A BRIEF HISTORY OF INTERNATIONAL ORGANIZATIONS

Some form of organization among sovereign entities is traceable to the Greek city-states of more than two millennia ago or, more recently, to the Hanseatic League of German towns in the eleventh century. However, the real history of the modern international organization begins in the nineteenth century. The institutional precedents of the nineteenth century, along with the accumulating effects of other historical forces, have helped create and sustain international organizations. The most important organizations have been the League of Nations and the United Nations because they sought to achieve a universal membership of all states and to carry out a broad mandate of services for the world.

Nineteenth-Century Precedents

The earliest modern international organizations were the *river commissions* of Europe, mainly the Central Rhine Commission of 1804 and the Danube River Commission appearing in 1856. These commissions still function in some form and promote cooperation among the states sharing these rivers. A canal and a system of locks now join these two rivers, a dream since the time of Charlemagne in the ninth century. Today commercial and pleasure boats can traverse a river system that reaches from the Baltic Sea in Scandinavia to the Black Sea, which borders the northern coast of Turkey.

Another important precedent was the growth of *conference diplomacy* among leading European powers. These major states (Austria, France, Great Britain, Prussia, and Russia) met often beginning with the Congress of Vienna in 1815. The purpose of these conferences was to deal with issues such as the status of France after Napoleon's exile and the placement of colonial boundary lines in Africa. Without the attention of conference diplomacy, these issues might have led to friction and war. Conference diplomacy also established the precedent of great-power responsibility for keeping the peace, a precedent that carried into the Council of the League of Nations and the Security Council of the United Nations.

The nineteenth century's series of conferences ended with the Hague Conferences of 1899 and 1907. Twenty-six European states attended the 1899 Hague Conference, which created the Court of Arbitration, among other developments. An idea that would later bear fruit as the League of Nations, the 1907 Hague Conference gave the first clear hint of a world body that would extend beyond Europe. In addition to European states, many Latin American states attended. The 1907 Hague Conference proposed a permanent body that would locate at The Hague, Netherlands. The First World War both interrupted this plan and, at the same time, proved the need for a world body to preserve peace.

Another important institutional precedent of the modern international organization was the birth of the *international public union* for cooperation in technical areas. The two most important unions were the International Telegraph Union of 1865 and the Universal Postal Union of 1874. These unions demonstrated that states have transborder interests beyond any one state's territorial jurisdiction. Today's world, keenly aware of its interdependence, had its first clear preview of international interdependence, and the need for international governance, in the form of the public unions.[2]

Forces Contributing to International Organizations

In addition to institutional precedents, several historical forces helped to create and today continue to support international organizations. One such force is the spread of *democracy*. Western states and their leaders have long assumed that democratic states, with their bent toward negotiation and compromise through parliaments and other assemblies, could easily form and use IGOs. The major supporting states first of the League and then of the United Nations have been Western democracies. The recent collapse of European communism and the growing number of democratic states in the world are a positive development, encouraging states to cooperate through international organizations.

The fact that the *number of states* is expanding raises the usefulness of IGOs. About 20 states were prominent at the time of the first Hague Conference, approximately 50 states negotiated and ratified the UN Charter, and today at least 185 states are members of the United Nations. With a total of around 200 states existing in the world, and with more probably to form, the chances for clashes and friction over a host of issues are greater than ever. The presence of more states places a premium on the services of international organizations to promote cooperation and solve problems. Added to the increasing number of states are *thousands of INGOs* contributing to a burgeoning civil society at the global level. These INGOs are eager to lobby international organizations and participate in world conferences. Supporting these INGOs is an avid world cry for a voice in the international policymaking that is shaping lives around the globe.

Population growth in the world now totals about 6 billion, and that number is due to double by the middle of the 21st century. The needs and wants of these people are growing at an astounding rate too. Frequently international organizations are having to step into the vacuum left by weak or failed states to deliver multiple services. Humanitarian aid regularly involves the activities of IGOs and INGOs as they furnish distressed people with such basics as physical security, shelter, food, and health care.

Then there are the *technological changes* that began with transborder telegraph and mail services in the nineteenth century and now include sharing communication satellites and telecommunication frequencies for radio and television. Modern travel by jet aircraft allows millions of people to be constantly on the move as migrants, refugees, businesspeople, tourists, and exchange students. The rising interaction of the world's peoples enables influenza and the deadly pandemic of AIDS to spread quickly. To cope with the growing problems stemming from technological developments, specialized international organizations bring some order to the void where 200 states, acting apart, cannot be effective. The International Telecommunications Union (ITU), the International Civil Aviation Organization (ICAO), and WHO contribute irreplaceable services to states and their peoples.

Finally, most of today's states find *military force* less useful. The issues their leaders consider important, trade matters in particular, do not lend themselves to settlement by force. Consequently, states are more open to relying on negotiation that international organizations and conferences facilitate.

Although we touch on these historical forces elsewhere in this textbook, we should recognize that the culmination of these forces has provided the world, despite some disappointments and setbacks, with sufficient reason to keep building and relying on international organizations. This process appears healthy. According to Mark Zacker, by 1909, 37 IGOs and 176 INGOs existed; in 1951, 123 IGOs and 832 INGOs were on the international scene; and, by the 1980s, 337 IGOs and 4,649 INGOs had formed.[3] Doubtlessly, a more complex, interdependent world of the 21st century will require even more international organization activity for the coordination of multiple human enterprises.

The League of Nations

The League of Nations (1919–1939) formed immediately after the First World War, following the harsh lesson of 20 million war dead. Leaders probably regretted that the 1907 Hague Conference's grand ambition of building a world organization went unfulfilled before the First World War. Such a world organization might have blocked the drift toward war. Led by President Woodrow Wilson, now known as the "father of the League of Nations," the founders attempted to build a world system based on a just peace shared by democratic states. President Wilson wanted the League to replace the traditional practice of dividing the spoils of war among the victors before forming a new balance of power.

The League became the first multifunctional organization with permanent institutional arrangements. The membership consisted of most of the states of the day, although the

United States failed to join. The League still represented much diversity. Its membership included European states, South American states, Haiti in the Caribbean, Ethiopia and Liberia in Africa, and Japan in Asia.

The League was important chiefly because it called for the use of coercion to halt the bane of anarchy, aggression, and war. According to the League Covenant, states were to wait three months to allow for the peaceful settlement of disputes before resorting to force. If the League determined that an act of aggression had taken place, it could require the member-states to apply economic and diplomatic sanctions against the aggressor. The League also could ask states to volunteer their help for military sanctions, but could not demand such help. A stronger version of coercion by the United Nations would be used, a subject we will discuss further in this chapter.

Unfortunately, the League faltered in the 1930s as several revisionist states pursued their radical goals by acts of aggression. The League, however, did make a full-faith effort to halt Italy's 1934 invasion of Ethiopia through the use of economic sanctions in 1935–1936. The League almost bankrupted Italy, but this attempt at collective security finally failed, one central reason being that the United States, which was not a member, felt free to supply Italy with war material. Further aggressions of the 1930s damaged the League's reputation, leading to serious questions about the feasibility of collective security. At least the League did establish the principle that states were not free to use force as they pleased. Following the creation of the League, the society of states had a duty, responded to or not, to halt aggression and to protect the weak from the strong.

Although it closed its doors in 1939, the League of Nations left a legacy that guided the founders of the United Nations. This new world body largely followed the pattern of the League, but the founders of the United Nations sought to improve and strengthen the new organization based on League experiences. In fact, some scholars have called the United Nations a resurrected League.

The United Nations

Despite misgivings, the world had not given up completely on the pursuit of peace through the international regulation of power. The United Nations' founders proceeded to strengthen collective security by authorizing the Security Council to require military sanctions by member-states as well as economic sanctions. In addition, the founders knew the aftermath of the Second World War would hold many socioeconomic problems requiring a coordinated international effort. A world organization could help with the expected flood of refugees, starving and orphaned children, numerous health problems, and a world economy in disarray, to name only some postwar troubles.

The immediate problem for Allied leaders was to create a postwar public opinion mood supportive of a "new League." Sometimes it is a useful marketing technique to give an old business or product a new name, to dress it up a bit for consumer consumption. The founders gave the new world body the title "United Nations," a popular name appearing early in the Second World War to designate the Allies. Not surprisingly, the structure of the United Nations paralleled that of the League, but the United Nations would be more elaborate and specialized. Table 12.1 illustrates the skeletal similarity between the League of Nations and the United Nations. For each major element of the League, a United Nations

TABLE 12.1
Organizational Similarities of the World Bodies

League of Nations (1919–1939)	United Nations (1945–)
Secretariat	Secretariat
Council	Security Council
Assembly	General Assembly
Social and Economic Committee	ECOSOC Council
Mandate System	Trusteeship Council
Permanent Court (1922)	International Court

counterpart came into being. Both organizations had a **secretariat,** an international bureaucracy headed by a secretary-general, the chief executive officer. Secretary-General Sir Eric Drummond of the League never aspired to the political leadership role of some of the later UN secretary-generals. He behaved as the League's top civil servant, patient and neutral regarding the power politics of his day. In contrast, UN secretary-generals, caught in the throes of the Cold War and the North-South economic divide, have been more active as leaders, causing controversy over the secretary-general's role and the selection of individuals to fill this role.

Each organization also had a council that became responsible for keeping the peace. This responsibility drew on the tradition of the great powers keeping the peace in the nineteenth century, but, regrettably, great-power rivalries obstructed both councils. Anticipating such conflict, the framers of the UN Charter made five powerful states (China, France, Great Britain, the Soviet Union, and the United States) permanent members of the UN Security Council and gave them veto power over most of the United Nations' proposed actions. The United Nations had to avoid an enforcement action against one of these powerful states and, presumably, one of the permanent members would veto such an unwise act. Only after the Cold War, with the Soviet Union's veto passing to a more compliant Russia, has the new, but tentative, cooperation in the Security Council been possible.

Whereas the Assembly of the League used a unanimity rule for voting on resolutions, the UN General Assembly could act on resolutions and declarations by majority voting. This advantage became important by the 1960s, when the increase in the number and variety of states appeared in the General Assembly. States voting as legal equals, regardless of population size, wealth, or military power, allowed the Third World to become the controlling bloc of states in the General Assembly by the 1970s.

The Economic and Social Council of the United Nations has a less clear precedent from League days. The League was setting up a committee to coordinate social and economic programs when the Second World War ended its institutional life. Drawing on this limited experience, the Economic and Social Council became one of the six original institutions of the UN System, and this body has authorized a host of programs, including the advancement of women, protection of children, promotion of environmental improvements, and preparation for disaster relief, to name but a few.

The League had a Mandates Commission to guarantee the ultimate independence of the colonies of the defeated powers of the First World War, Germany and Turkey. Trusted members of the League were responsible for the supervision of the ex-colonies until they became independent. This arrangement was significant because it prevented the victors from claiming the colonies as the spoils of war, the usual fate of territories and peoples under the traditional norms of power politics. In time, Iraq, Lebanon, and Syria received independence under the Mandate System, while the other colonies passed to the supervision of the UN Trusteeship Council in 1946. All of the UN Trust territories eventually became independent except a few Pacific Islands held as a "trust" of the United States for its security reasons. An exceptional case was Southwest Africa, a Mandate of South Africa, which remained controversial for years. South Africa imposed its policy of strict racial segregation on this territory and refused to relinquish Southwest Africa to the UN Trust System. The United Nations designated this territory as Namibia in 1966 and, after years of warfare, Namibia became independent in 1990.

The League established the first "world court," designing it to be permanent with regular sessions held every year. The League member-states approved the Permanent Court of International Justice (PCIJ) in 1921, and the PCIJ began its first session in 1922. This court handled 29 contentious cases and delivered 27 advisory opinions. Although not an original organ of the League, scholars have given the PCIJ high marks for its performance. Perhaps the PCIJ's most important decision was its advisory opinion in the 1923 *Nationality Decrees Issued in Tunis and Morocco*. In this advisory opinion, the PCIJ decided that "domestic jurisdiction" of a state was a relative concept, not an absolute one. This legal ruling meant the sovereignty states so jealously guard is a matter of degree. The Statute of the PCIJ, the treaty creating the jurisdiction of the world court, passed to the International Court of Justice (ICJ). While beginning as one of the six original organs of the United Nations, the ICJ never quite achieved the status and importance of its predecessor.

The skeletal frameworks of the two world bodies are similar, but the United Nations has extended far beyond the six original institutions. The UN System has evolved to meet the rising demands of a world populated by 200 states and over 6 billion people. Joining the six original institutions of the United Nations are the highly specialized agencies that answer to the General Assembly and the Economic and Social Council. Figure 12.2 shows the elaborate structure of the UN System today.

A final difference is that the United Nations located its primary home in New York City instead of Geneva, Switzerland, where the League had its headquarters. This change followed naturally from the early U.S. support for the new world body. The United States, as the world's new hegemon, intended for the United Nations to play an important role in its postwar plans. After all, New York City was America's "capitol" of communications, travel, and finance in 1945. The United Nations does use the Geneva facilities for some of its agencies and Secretariat staff.

Why did the League of Nations struggle mostly in vain and finally collapse in 1939 while the United Nations seems to have a perennial life? At least three standard reasons are given to account for League failure. First, the League suffered from being part of a victor's peace. The *Treaty of Versailles* of 1919 not only ended the First World War but also authorized the creation of the League. In effect, this treaty held Germany responsible for the First World War and required Germany to pay large war reparations to France. Understandably, Germany never truly committed itself to the League any more than it sincerely accepted the Weimar Republic, a government formed following Germany's defeat. Second,

FIGURE 12.2 The United Nations System

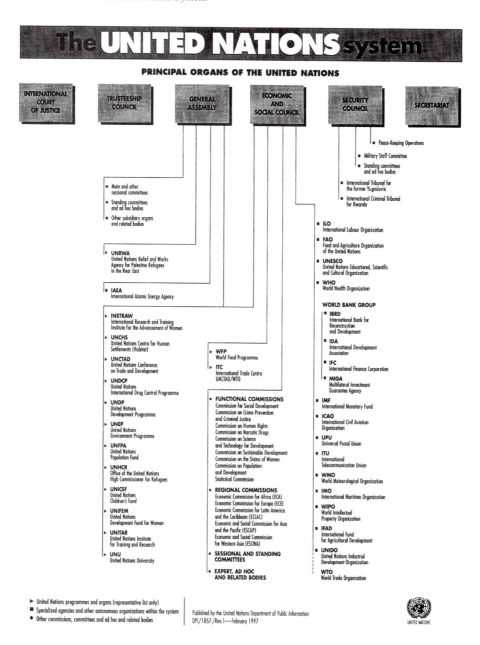

the League did not have the United States as a member. Had the United States joined the League and participated in the 1936 embargo against Italy, Italian aggression against Ethiopia might have come to a halt. Finally, the League Covenant did not allow the Council to require military sanctions to carry out collective security.

At least, these reasons are the usual causes scholars offer to explain the demise of the League. It is equally correct to observe that the League was a wonderful idea for breathing more life into a fledgling international society, but the League was an idea ahead of its time.

The United Nations is proving more enduring than the League for several reasons. First, the large growth in numbers and types of states makes the United Nations an attractive forum for pursuing needs and wants, especially for Third World states that can take advantage of their voting strength as they confront the powerful oligarchy of Western states. Second, the United Nations came into the world as an international organization completely separate from the treaties that ended the Second World War, and the United States threw its impressive resources and prestige behind the world body during its early development. Finally, the creation of the United Nations derived from the destructive lesson of two world wars. If a world body had any chance at all to prevent or stop a war in progress, it deserved the chance to do so. This belief nurtured the United Nations through the decades of the Cold War and continues to do the same today as the world body struggles to preserve peace.

THE PURSUIT OF PEACE

Most goals of the United Nations support peace. The United Nations calls on states to settle disputes peacefully according to international law. Economic development reduces tension between the "haves" and "have-nots" of the world. Respect for human rights encourages ethnic groups to interact with less conflict. Further, arms limitations may reduce prospects for war. Finally, certain Charter provisions and innovations aim specifically to preserve or restore peace. Designed for this purpose are the peaceful settlement of disputes, peacekeeping operations, and collective security, the subjects of this section.

Peaceful Settlement

The Charter offers the means to resolve disputes other than by the use of force. The specific options under **peaceful settlement** appear in Article 33 of the Charter. These means are the *political procedures* of negotiation, which include good offices, inquiry, mediation, and conciliation. *Negotiation,* already dealt with in Chapter Seven, usually refers to bilateral bargaining. **Good offices** involve a third state offering neutral communication between the disputing parties. An **inquiry** is a search by a neutral third party for the facts in a dispute. In **mediation,** a third party offers suggestions about the terms of settlement in a dispute. When the third party is a commission, involving several states or a body from an international organization, the mediating effort is an act of **conciliation.** The terms, as a proposal for settlement, are more explicit and formal than with mediation. As political techniques, these procedures are often helpful, but the parties in a dispute do not have to accept any proposed terms.

Peaceful settlement also includes *judicial procedures,* which, unlike political procedures, are binding. The disputing parties must accept the terms of a decision. Judicial decisions can come from arbitration or the decisions of a court, subjects discussed in the previous chapter on international law. States have strongly preferred political settlement over judicial decisions because states have more control over the outcome. Neither the political nor the judicial techniques provided in the Charter represent entirely new innovations, since these techniques are traceable, in some form, to antiquity.

States often refer disputes to the Security Council. The Security Council can suggest any of the peaceful settlement procedures available or refer a dispute to a regional organization such as the OAS or OAU. Finally, the Secretary-General sometimes personally handles a dispute or appoints a mediator.

In more than a half-century, the United Nations has effectively handled over 200 disputes, with most of these disputes reaching a settlement. Some disputes, however, appear interminable; for example, the feud over Israel occupying Arab territories has festered for decades. An arguable point is that the involvement of the United Nations only perpetuates a conflict when the traditional clash of arms might offer a final resolution, though the outcome may be unjust to one side. Most scholars, while recognizing that the role of the United Nations does not always resolve disputes, believe the United Nations dampens conflicts and saves thousands of lives.

Peacekeeping

When negotiations between disputants fail and war breaks out, the UN Charter calls for the Security Council to marshal a military force to punish the aggressor. However, in many disputes an aggressor is not readily identifiable, nor is a large, punitive force easy to put together. When collective security has been unusable, the United Nations has turned to the bold innovation of **peacekeeping.** In over 40 disputes, the United Nations has placed either lightly armed troops or unarmed observers between opposing forces after the shooting has ceased. The peacekeeping troops have come mostly from medium-size to small countries and behave neutrally toward the combatants. One exception today is Russia, which contributes one of the largest contingents of troops to UN Peacekeeping. As a small body of troops, with easily recognizable blue headgear and white vehicles, the peacekeepers operate as a moral presence, restraining combatants from renewing fighting until a peaceful settlement procedure can take hold.[4]

Closely associated with peacekeeping are the concepts of cease-fire and preventive diplomacy. Based on a precedent set in League days, the United Nations "orders" a *cease-fire* between warring parties before entering the dispute with lightly armed peacekeepers. Cease-fires are not always secure, as in the recent cases of Bosnia and Somalia, when renewed fighting caught peacekeepers between heavily armed combatants.

Preventive diplomacy calls for the United Nations to enter a dispute early and, through diplomacy, prevent the outbreak of fighting or stop the fighting from escalating. Preventive diplomacy was notably useful in the Cold War, when two superpowers, bristling with nuclear weapons, were prone to take opposing sides in any small, "brush fire" conflict. After preventive diplomacy restrained the superpowers, the United Nations would take over the conflict by inserting peacekeepers and engaging the peaceful settlement process. Applying preventive diplomacy to internal conflicts has proven more difficult. Gaining sufficient early warning to deal effectively with explosive outbreaks of ethnic violence in internal conflicts, before they result in massive casualties and flows of refugees, is an elusive goal for preventive diplomacy.

Peacekeeping has been an evolving concept as the United Nations has responded to the challenges of an ever-changing world. Early in the history of the United Nations, peacekeeping efforts involved small numbers of unarmed observers placed on tense

AP Photo/Peter Northall

A UN soldier carries a child evacuated in Bosnia.

borders. Observer teams remain important today; for example, UN observers have been sustaining the cease-fire between India and Pakistan over the disputed territory of Kashmir. In recent years, the most important United Nations observation team has been the 350 unarmed personnel sent to the Iranian-Iraqi border in 1988. UN observers guaranteed a cease-fire after the longest and bloodiest interstate war since the Second World War.

Peacekeeping reached its full-blown form as a concept with the 1956 UN Emergency Force (UNEF). The neutral philosophy, the means of financing, and the size and selection of troops owe much to Secretary-General Dag Hammarskjold. After British and French troops seized the Suez Canal following Egypt's nationalization of this critical, humanmade link between the Mediterranean Sea and the Red Sea, a world crisis ensued. Fortunately, both the Soviet Union and the United States wanted the British and French forces withdrawn. Secretary-General Hammarskjold negotiated the removal of these forces and sent in 6,000 peacekeepers drawn from 10 countries. The UNEF kept the Suez Canal safe from intervention and began the process of reopening the canal to ship traffic. The UN Peacekeepers stayed on Egyptian soil until the Egyptian government asked them to leave in 1967, precipitating the third war between the Arab states and Israel.

UN Peacekeeping continues to play an international role, for instance, supervising the Soviet withdrawal from Afghanistan and monitoring the Iranian-Iraqi cease-fire in the late 1980s. The nature of conflict in the world, however, has shifted from international to mostly internal conflict. Of the 30 or more conflicts going on in the world at any given time, most involve fractious ethnic groups. The United Nations, showing less trepidation over sovereignty questions than in its early years, has been willing to tackle some of these internal conflicts. Refugees spilling outside Rwanda into other African countries, arms shipments to Bosnia, or outside powers threatening intervention easily allow the United Nations to call a primarily internal conflict a "threat to international peace."

In addition to restoring peace in internal conflicts in the 1990s, the United Nations has stepped up its peacekeeping missions to perform acts of national political transition. After disarming combatants and clearing land mines, the United Nations has supervised elections in Cambodia, El Salvador, Haiti, Mozambique, and Namibia. The United Nations has

Danziger/*The Christian Science Monitor*

helped ease these strife-torn countries with a history of authoritarian rule, toward democracy. Except for some obstruction by a military government in Haiti, which has suffered from political repression on a massive scale, these war-weary countries have been receptive to a new and peaceful way to handle their political affairs.

The United Nations was less fortunate with the internal conflicts in Bosnia and Somalia, troublesome cases that went beyond the capabilities of peacekeeping. In these two cases, the warring factions had not spent their energies; yet the United Nations, heady with optimism after quashing Iraqi aggression, plunged into these maelstroms of violence to do good deeds. In the "nobody-in-charge" environments of Bosnia and Somalia, neither governments nor factions would respect a cease-fire. A multiplicity of "authorities," three ethnic groups in Bosnia and a complex set of clans in Somalia, followed erratic policies that produced anarchy.

In spite of these anarchical conditions, Secretary-General Boutros Boutros-Ghali decided that humanitarian priorities were so great in Bosnia and Somalia that the United Nations had to act. Instead of the traditional peacekeeping mission, the United Nations role took the form of *humanitarian intervention.* United Nations workers attempted to convoy food and medical supplies to the starving and dying in the middle of sporadic fighting.

In Somalia, beginning in 1992, clan groups regularly attacked and seized United Nations convoy supplies. In frustration, Secretary-General Boutros Boutros-Ghali embraced a mission of *peace enforcement.* "Operation Restore Hope," as Americans knew the mission, finally reached a total force of 38,000 troops from 21 countries. Although much improvement resulted from this new protection of supply lines for humanitarian relief, a general state of peace and order failed to develop. From the outset, the Secretary-General wanted the United States, with its 20,000 Marines in Somalia in 1992, to disarm the clan factions and impose a cease-fire. U.S. leaders and other governments, however, wanted a limited mission.[5] At least acts of military retaliation against the clans that attacked convoys took place, and U.S. elite troops tried to capture the primary warlord, Mohamed Farrah Aidid. The United Nations had issued an arrest warrant for Aidid and offered a $25,000 reward for his capture.

AP Photo/Peter Harris/*The Washington Times*

British and U.S. soldiers cross the Sava River in Bosnia as part of NATO operation.

For the United States, cooperation with the United Nations proved embittering. "Command and control" problems took place when U.S. Army Rangers found themselves surrounded during the attempted capture of Aidid. The United Nations commanders took hours to send armored vehicles to relieve the rangers, a delay resulting in heavy casualties among the U.S. forces. A total of 100 peacekeepers died in Somali, of which 42 were American troops. In March 1995, unable or unwilling to take on the heavily armed militias, the United Nations mission backed out of Somalia under the protection of U.S. Marines.

The Bosnian case, which also started in 1992, posed problems similar to the Somalian experience. Again the United Nations tried to convoy food and medicine to desperate people. The convoys trucked mostly to enclaves of Muslims, while the other two ethnic groups, Bosnian Serbs and Croatians, interfered. The United Nations placed over 30,000 peacekeepers from 36 countries in Bosnia. Scattered about, these troops occupied hilltops as observation posts and protected Sarajevo and five other "safe areas" for the benefit of besieged Muslims. Amid bitter ethnic fighting, involving war atrocities unequaled in Europe since the Nazi terror 50 years before, the United Nations made little headway in protecting human rights or restoring peace, as one cease-fire after another collapsed.

Finally, a particularly deadly Serb shelling of a Sarajevo marketplace in the summer of 1995, which killed 43 civilians, brought the United Nations to the point of complete frustration. UN decision makers called on NATO jets to retaliate with punishing bombing strikes on Serb positions. Then Serbs not only shelled United Nations "safe areas" but took 370 UN Peacekeepers prisoner. The Serbs chained some peacekeepers to potential targets that NATO jets might attack. The time had come for the United Nations to entrust, or "subcontract," its mission to the more powerful organization of NATO, a development that resulted in an active role by the United States.

Following United States–led negotiations at Wright Air Force Base in Dayton, Ohio, NATO took over the Bosnian mission from the United Nations in December 1995. In a place far removed from the conflict, the Dayton negotiations brought together leaders of the three ethnic groups in Bosnia, and the United States pressured these leaders to accept a division of Bosnian territory and a cease-fire. With a heavily armed 60,000 Implementation Force (I-For), NATO set out to enforce the new cease-fire and carry out the distribution of

The West's quick check list to determine whether to get involved in another country's affairs....

	YES	NO
DO THEY HAVE OIL?	☐	☐
ARE U.S. BUSINESS INTERESTS THREATENED?	☐	☐
ARE WE DOWN IN THE POLLS?	☐	☐
CAN WE USE OUR NIFTY NEW WEAPONS?	☐	☐
IS CNN COVERING IT?	☐	☐

Raeside/*Times-Colonist*/Victoria, British Columbia

Bosnian territory among the ethnic groups. This force was to downsize, according to plan, in the spring of 1997, leaving a Sustainment Force (S-For) of 30,000 troops that would include 8,000 Americans. While I-For separated the warring ethnic factions, S-For had the responsibility of rebuilding Bosnia as a united country—a much tougher task.

The Bosnian case represents a decisive shift from humanitarian intervention to peace enforcement, but the Somalian experience, which also began as a humanitarian mission, faltered when the clear need for peace enforcement arose. Why did the United Nations go the extra distance for Bosnia? Are Africans less valued than Europeans? Was the United Nations dismayed over the African situation, known as the "basket case" of the world, because of its economic regression and internal conflicts? Was it more helpful to deal with only three ethnic groups instead of multiple clans? Or was the critical difference simply that Bosnia is logistically feasible with NATO close at hand? Further, could NATO countries see their national interests at stake in the Bosnian case since fighting could spread to the rest of Europe while Somalia posed no threat to European countries? These questions may haunt the United Nations for some time to come.

As UN Peacekeeping missions have entered more internal conflicts, United Nations mediators are encountering vicious warfare stemming from ethnic animosities, such as when Muslims and Serbs loosened pent-up hatreds in Bosnia, or Hutu and Tutsi attack each other's women and children without mercy in Rwanda. Military historian John Keegan has called these conflicts "primitive wars," conflicts fed by long-standing rancor and passion that do not yield to reason and mediation.[6] Unless the United Nations is ready to step up to peace enforcement under its own blue flag, it will have to continue subcontracting enforcement actions to member-states when internal conflicts exceed UN Peacekeeping capabilities.[7] Such entrustment has happened already in the cases where French troops provided a safe area in Rwanda for fleeing Hutu in 1995, the United States intervened in Haiti in 1994 to clear the way for UN Peacekeepers, the United States provided the same service in Somalia in 1992, and NATO assumed control of the peacekeeping mission in Bosnia in 1995.

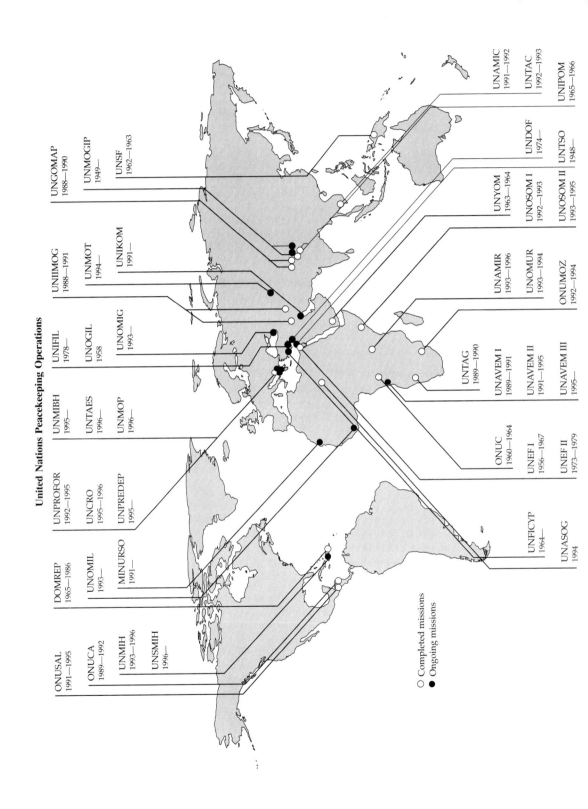

1. UNTSO
United Nations Truce Supervision Organization
June 1948–

2. UNMOGIP
United Nations Military Observer Group in India and Pakistan
January 1949–

3. UNEF I
First United Nations Emergency Force
November 1956–June 1967

4. UNOGIL
United Nations Observation Group in Lebanon
June 1958–December 1958

5. ONUC
United Nations Operation in the Congo
July 1960–June 1964

6. UNSF
United Nations Security Force in West New Guinea (West Irian)
October 1962–April 1963

7. UNYOM
United Nations Yemen Observation Mission
July 1963–September 1964

8. UNFICYP
United Nations Peacekeeping Force in Cyprus
March 1964–

9. DOMREP
Mission of the Representative of the Secretary-General in the Dominican Republic
May 1965–October 1966

10. UNIPOM
United Nations India–Pakistan Observation Mission
September 1965–March 1966

11. UNEF II
Second United Nations Emergency Force October 1973–July 1979

12. UNDOF
United Nations Disengagement Force Observer Force
June 1974–

13. UNIFIL
United Nations Interim Force in Lebanon
March 1978–

14. UNGOMAP
United Nations Good Offices Mission in Afghanistan and Pakistan
May 1988–March 1990

15. UNIIMOG
United Nations Iran–Iraq Military Observer Group
August 1988–February 1991

16. UNAVEM I
United Nations Angola Verification Mission I
January 1989–June 1991

17. UNTAG
United Nations Transition Assistance Group
April 1989–March 1990

18. ONUCA
United Nations Observer Group in Central America
November 1989–January 1992

19. UNIKOM
United Nations Iraq–Kuwait Observation Mission
April 1991–

20. UNAVEM II
United Nations Angola Verification Mission II
June 1991–February 1995

21. ONUSAL
United Nations Observer Mission in El Salvador
July 1991–April 1995

22. MINURSO
United Nations Mission for the Referendum in Western Sahara
April 1991–

23. UNAMIC
United Nations Advance Mission in Cambodia
October 1991–March 1992

24. UNPROFOR
United Nations Protection Force
March 1992–December 1995

25. UNTAC
United Nations Transitional Authority in Cambodia
March 1992–September 1993

26. UNOSOM I
United Nations Operation in Somalia I
April 1992–March 1993

27. ONUMOZ
United Nations Operation in Mozambique
December 1992–December 1994

28. UNOSOM II
United Nations Operation in Somalia II
March 1993–March 1995

29. UNOMUR
United Nations Observer Mission Uganda–Rwanda
June 1993–September 1994

30. UNOMIG
United Nations Observer Mission in Georgia
August 1993–

31. UNOMIL
United Nations Observer Mission in Liberia
September 1993–

32. UNMIH
United Nations Mission in Haiti
September 1993–June 1996

33. UNAMIR
United Nations Assistance Mission for Rwanda
October 1993–March 1996

34. UNASOG
United Nations Aouzou Strip Observer Group
May 1994–June 1994

35. UNMOT
United Nations Mission of Observers in Tajikistan
December 1994–

36. UNAVEM III
United Nations Angola Verification Mission III
February 1995–

37. UNCRO
United Nations Confidence Restoration Operation in Croatia
March 1995–January 1996

38. UNPREDEP
United Nations Preventive Deployment Force
March 1995–

39. UNMIBH
United Nations Mission in Bosnia and Herzegovina
December 1995–

40. UNTAES
United Nations Transitional Administration for Eastern Slavonia, Baranja, and Western Sirmium
January 1996–

41. UNMOP
United Nations Mission of Observers in Prevlaka
January 1996–

42. UNSMIH
United Nations Support Mission in Haiti
July 1996–

43. MINUGUA
United Nations Verification Mission in Guatemala
January 1997–

Note: The last peacekeeping mission to form (MINUGHA) is so recent that it does not appear on the map in this figure.

Before the post–Cold War era, only UN Peacekeeping in the Congo (now Zaire), from 1960 to 1964, presaged the role of peace enforcement. Secretary-General Dag Hammarskjold intended for the Congo operation to follow the pattern molded in the 1956 Suez operation. However, conditions in the Congo became so chaotic, with only an excuse for a central government, that the UN Peacekeeping mission quickly began to experience "mission creep." To restore order, UN Peacekeepers had to go beyond monitoring duties by disarming Congo Army mutineers and defeating the secessionist movement in the Katanga province. UN Peacekeepers captured and expelled hundreds of mercenaries. A total of 93,000 troops from 34 countries served in the Congo over a four-year period, at a cost of over $400 million (probably more than $2 billion in today's currency). A great deal of rancor and disappointment occurred among the United Nations member-states, however, because the Congo mission went well beyond the Suez model.[8]

In addition to the problems associated with internal conflict, the United Nations is experiencing *case overload*. The United Nations has never pretended that it could handle all of the more than 100 wars and conflicts that have taken place during its history.[9] During the Cold War, the 279 vetoes cast in the Security Council partly saved the United Nations from case overload, but since 1990, with the end of the Cold War, demands for UN help have surged.[10] In 1988, the year UN Peacekeepers won the Nobel Peace Prize, the United Nations handled 14 conflicts involving 8,600 peacekeepers at a cost of $400 million.[11] In the early 1990s, the costs and numbers of troops shot up by tenfold. By 1994, costs had risen to $3.6 billion a year to support 80,000 peacekeepers in the field. Fortunately, costs are more under control today, with under 26,000 UN Peacekeepers located at 16 sites. Without clear criteria for entering conflicts, the United Nations must somehow choose among the 30 or more conflicts that are present in the world at any given time.

Collective Security

Although some scholars attempt to trace **collective security** to earlier eras, this means of managing power is really a twentieth-century concept. Collective security is bold conceptually and has had only two applications in United Nations history, the Korean War (1950–1953) and the Persian Gulf War (1990–1991). Under collective security, the United Nations intended to control power through a societal concept of indivisible peace: The peace of one state would be the peace of all states. Collective security logically corresponds to a "neighborhood watch" program in which all neighbors watch one another's houses for common protection against break-ins.

The United Nations hoped states would desire peace sufficiently to apply economic and military sanctions jointly against a transgressor of the peace. For the framers of the UN Charter, the feasibility of collective security rested on the assumption that a UN military force would constitute a preponderance of power, either deterring a potential aggressor or punishing an actual aggressor with defeat. As a concept, collective security is attractive because it goes beyond the balance of power system that forces states to defend themselves, alone or through an alliance.

As already mentioned, the UN Charter strengthened collective security beyond League capabilities. Chapter VIII authorized the Security Council to use military sanctions as well as economic sanctions under Article 42, to call on member-states to provide the necessary military forces under Article 43, and to organize a Military Staff Committee under Articles 46 and 47 for "command and control" purposes of the UN military force.

Two problems inherent in the state system, however, undermine collective security. The first problem is the strong sense of national interests and national security that characterizes states. A focus on immediate state concerns restrains states from fully embracing a sense of indivisible global security supportive of collective security. With the end of the Cold War, agreement over security questions is easier, but a world with Western states, a communist China, a nationalistic Russia, and fundamentalist Muslim states may confound a consensus over whose security is in jeopardy and how to deal with it. The second problem concerns assembling enough power to constitute a preponderant advantage over an aggressor. Checking an atomic power through collective security certainly would be fraught with great danger. States armed with a considerable amount of conventional weapons also can be difficult to control.

The first application of collective security, in the Korean War, was not in strict accord with the Charter. When communist North Korea invaded South Korea in 1950, the United Nations, led by the United States, responded with the "Uniting for Peace Resolution" of 1950. This resolution allows the General Assembly to deal with threats to the peace if the Security Council is in deadlock and unable to do so. The Soviet Union, irked over the refusal of the United Nations to accept the new state of communist China as a member, decided to boycott the Security Council. During its brief absence, the Soviet Union could not veto the Uniting for Peace Resolution. The United Nations also departed from the Charter by not using the Military Staff Committee that was called for; rather, the world body set up a unified UN command under the direction of U.S. Army General Douglas MacArthur. This unified command was euphemistic because General MacArthur actually answered to President Harry Truman, not to the Security Council.

Although 16 states voluntarily contributed to United Nations forces in Korea, the United States and South Korea provided the bulk of the combatants that repelled the North Korean invasion of South Korea and then fought a large Chinese Army to a standstill. The chief motive for collective security in Korea was not stopping aggression for its own sake but halting communist aggression as a United States Cold War objective. Further, while communist China was a new country, it was able to send a quarter of a million troops across the Yalu River into Korea with devastating effect on United Nations forces. This act of collective security became so costly in blood and treasure that the United Nations did not repeat collective security for nearly 40 years.

The second application of collective security concerned the Iraqi invasion of Kuwait. When this invasion occurred, both the Soviet Union and China restrained their veto, allowing collective security to go forward. The UN coalition forces, based mainly on NATO powers recruited and led by the United States, crushed the Iraqi forces in January 1991 and sent them scurrying home. Again, the United States had a special motive: The Iraqi invasion endangered the supply of oil critical to Western states and Japan. Moreover, this collective security episode took place without even the pretense of a unified UN command or a UN flag flying over the coalition forces.[12]

The United Nations coalition forces have continued enforcement against Iraq since 1991 by establishing "no-fly zones" in northern and southern Iraq to protect, respectively, the Kurdish and Shi'a minorities. The United States and several European allies took this

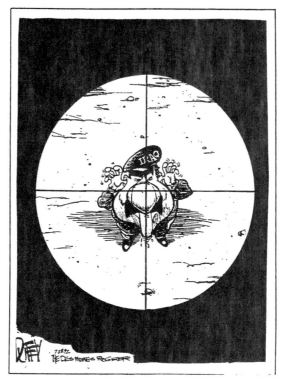

Duffy, *The Des Moines Register*

step of enforcement without the approval of the United Nations.[13] When the United States fired cruise missiles against Iraq in 1996 as a punishment for moving its troops into northern Iraq, the United States acted unilaterally in this episode. In addition, the United Nations has inspected and destroyed dread-weapons facilities in Iraq and refuses to allow Iraq to have normal sales of oil until it complies with all United Nations requirements. Nevertheless, Saddam Hussein is defiant in his attitude toward the United Nations, and no one knows whether the United Nations has discouraged future Iraqi aggression.

During his term as secretary-general, Boutros Boutros-Ghali, optimistic about the role of the United Nations following the Persian Gulf War, proposed that a UN force be at his disposal.[14] After experiencing the surge of requests for United Nations help in the 1990s, then Secretary-General Boutros-Ghali realized that the costs of a standing UN force of adequate size would be prohibitive. The Secretary-General next stressed that member-states maintain "ready reaction forces" at the battalion level in their own countries, forces that could quickly join United Nations missions.[15] Several Scandinavian countries, at least, do maintain ready reaction forces for the use of the United Nations. As another adjustment, Secretary-General Boutros-Ghali became more accepting of peace enforcement by sub-contracting this role to member-states.[16] While the role of the United Nations may not always be decisive in the name of world peace, numerous acts of peacekeeping and two episodes of collective security carry the world well beyond the traditional balance of power system. Decidedly, these developments portend an international society that prefers peace over conflict and war.

EFFORTS AT ECONOMIC PROGRESS

The League of Nations and the United Nations focused on the promotion of peace, but both organizations also encouraged economic and social progress. The League gradually moved toward this undertaking, while the United Nations, from the outset, sought significant economic and social improvements for the world. In this section, we examine efforts at economic progress by the UN system, regional organizations, and INGOs.

Efforts of the United Nations to rebuild the European economy after the Second World War rapidly extended to more and more countries as European colonial empires gave way to the emergence of the Third World. In time, well over 100 countries in Africa, Asia, Latin America, and the Middle East would require economic development. In the Third World live three-fourths of the world's population, most of them poor by Western standards and millions living subsistence lives. As we learned in Chapter Eight, leaders and intellectuals from the Third World blame the rich West for holding these underdeveloped countries in a pattern of global dependency. This dependency allows for an exploitation of these countries that is reminiscent of their colonial past. Asserting a right to economic development, the Third World has used its weight of numbers to steer the United Nations in the direction of economic development. Although the Third World has had political success bringing the North-South struggle into the corridors of the United Nations, it has failed to transfer wealth from the rich to the poor countries.

Clear evidence of a commitment by the United Nations to economic progress was the creation of the Economic and Social Council (ECOSOC) as one of the six original institutions of the UN System. Through multiple agencies created by the General Assembly or autonomous agencies affiliated with ECOSOC, the United Nations has launched thousands of development projects reaching more than 130 countries.[17] The UN System allocates a substantial part of its regular budget to promote socioeconomic progress, and the large majority of the UN System's personnel work in this area. A description of some of the United Nations' activities will illustrate its role in economic development.

We already discussed the roles of the World Bank and the International Monetary Fund (IMF) in Chapters Eight and Nine. Recall that the World Bank makes over $20 billion of loans for development projects and the IMF insists that countries use realistic currency values and operate austere economies before receiving loans. These agencies do put needed money into the Third World, but they do so mainly on the terms of Western bankers.

Central to the UN's development efforts has been the United Nations Development Program (UNDP), which the General Assembly created in 1965 and reports to the ECOSOC. The UNDP provides research, expert advice, and pilot projects for investment and industry to the Third World. Its annual budget, provided by voluntary contributions, amounted to over $1 billion by the mid-1990s. Complementing UNDP's efforts was the optimistic declaration that the 1960s would be the "Development Decade." The fact that future decades received the same appellation is proof that Third World states, after much effort, have still failed to reach the elusive "take-off" point calling for a viable national economy, one no longer in need of outside aid. Other important agencies that help with economic development are the International Fund for Agricultural Development (IFAD) and the Industrial Development Association (IDA).

Smaller and more specialized is the Operational Executive and Administrative Personnel Services (OPEX). OPEX recruits skilled administrators to work in Third World countries and to train local executives while they are in-country. Another interesting project is the UN University created in 1972, a university without a regular faculty or student body. The UN University does have a planning and coordinating center in Tokyo that strengthens scholarly and university activities in the Third World. Its educational foci are in the areas of population, energy, science, and technology.

In addition to institutional apparati and personnel, the UN System offers masses of published data and reports that are critical to economic and social planning by governments, IGOs, INGOs, and scholars around the world. The *World Economic Survey,* the *World Development Report,* the *Statistical Yearbook,* and the *Human Development Report* are among the most frequently used sources of economic data in the world.[18]

Efforts by Regional Organizations

Several regional organizations also contribute to economic development. The more advanced British Commonwealth countries began the Colombo Plan in 1950 and have lent billions of dollars to Asian countries. The European Union (previously the European Economic Community) established the European Development Fund in 1958 for African countries and extended its benefits to Caribbean and Pacific countries in 1975. The United States led in the creation of the Alliance for Progress for Latin American countries in the early 1960s, but that organization petered out by the end of that decade. Regional banks also lend money for development: The Inter-American Bank began operations in 1960 and now loans over $5 billion annually; the African Development Bank started operations in 1965 and loans $2 billion a year; and the Asian Development Bank, started in 1967, loans $5 billion a year.

Efforts by INGOs

Hundreds of INGOs offer help with economic development. CARE is a private organization that began in 1945 in New York City, started up through the cooperation of religious groups, labor unions, and business managers. CARE began with the treasure trove of 2 million large food packages stored up (but unneeded) for the planned invasion of Japan. After sending food packages to Europe during its postwar recovery and then packages of food and various tools to countries threatened by communist takeover in the Cold War of the 1950s, CARE began to emphasize long-term health, educational, agricultural, and environmental projects through its offices scattered around the world.

Another interesting INGO is the Oxford Committee for Famine Relief, or Oxfam. Founded in Great Britain in 1942, Oxfam now has seven autonomous groups in the world, including Oxfam America. Oxfam does not take government money, but it accomplishes much good with the small-scale projects it can afford. Oxfam projects distribute tools and seeds, dig wells for safe drinking water, build irrigation systems, and construct fish hatcheries.

Oxfam is a good example of the mini-aid programs in private hands that operate more efficiently than the public efforts of the UN System and state-to-state bilateral aid programs.

A standard criticism of the UN System is that it operates too many development projects that are applied too thinly around the world. In fairness to the United Nations, its major problem is the scant amount of money available to boost economic development. Then, too, the United Nations is attempting to help governments that will not do enough to help themselves. Frequently Third World governments do not make sufficient efforts to expunge corruption, control population size, downsize the world's "debt bomb," and dampen internal conflict and ethnic strife. At least the United Nations has attempted some reforms, such as setting up five regional Economic Commissions and placing a single coordinator in each country to prevent overlap and waste.

The enormity of the problems confronting economic development creates bleak prospects for impressive economic progress in the near future. Although the world's economy is growing slowly, it cannot outpace the demands of a global population increasing at a rate of nearly 100 million people a year. Nor are there any guarantees that the economic growth occurring will provide an equitable distribution of benefits, according to past Secretary-General Boutros-Ghali in his report *Agenda for Development*.[19] The recently renewed expansion of the world economy is clearly benefiting the rich more than the poor. In 1960, the richest one-fifth of the people on the planet had incomes 30 times greater than the poorest one-fifth; today the richest one-fifth earn 60 times more income.[20]

Although recognizing the world's inequality, Boutros-Ghali, when secretary-general, believed the international marketplace, with its accompanying liberalization of international trade, holds the potential for the economic growth the world needs.[21] His view is consistent with the one American leaders and other Westerners with capitalist orientations have been urging on the world for decades.[22] However, Secretary-General Boutros-Ghali wisely questioned whether the expanding world economy allows for *sustainable development*, meaning the replacement of resources as rapidly as the world consumes them. He correctly observes that it is easy to exploit natural resources for economic gain, but we must, as the previous secretary-general pointed out, manage these resources for long-term development.[23]

EFFORTS AT SOCIAL PROGRESS

Efforts at economic and social progress intertwine and reinforce one another. For instance, when a country advances economically, it will then have the money for population programs. A successful population program, in turn, will prevent overpopulation from undercutting future economic achievement. We divide the two only for descriptive purposes. This discussion of social progress focuses on human rights, slavery, children, women, and refugees.

Human Rights

A major success story of the United Nations is the promotion of human rights as universal standards. Despite Article 2(7) of the UN Charter, which promises respect for the sovereignty of member-states, the United Nations has set norms as to how governments are to treat their peoples, norms gradually distilled into the legal requirements of global and regional human rights treaties.[24] As past Secretary-General Boutros-Ghali once observed, respect for sovereignty remains strong, but the centuries-old doctrine of sovereignty is no longer absolute.[25]

The United Nations set up the UN Commission on Human Rights in 1946 and followed up with the *Universal Declaration of Human Rights* in 1948. A recent and important step in human rights progress was the World Conference on Human Rights held in Vienna, Austria, in 1993. This conference confirmed that human rights will remain a top priority, along with economic development, and, after 40 years of effort, supporters of human rights progress were able to establish the post of UN High Commissioner for Human Rights. The first high commissioner is José Ayala Lasso of Ecuador, who has announced he will focus on the rights of women and children. While this position is a breakthrough development, the high commissioner began his four-year term with a paltry budget of only $1.4 million.[26]

The Vienna Conference also reaffirmed the principle that human rights have universal application, much to the chagrin of Third World leaders and scholars who argue for the principle of "cultural relativism." Scholar Abdullahi Ahmed An-Na'im, recognizing that many regional and local traditions in the Third World are in conflict with universal standards on human rights, calls for a compromise between the two.[27] Ken Booth puts the idea of compromise nicely when he argues for "sensitive universalism," allowing universal human rights concepts to ground in local cultures in varied ways.[28] Yet stronger voices, supporting the "cultural relativism" position, claim that the human rights tradition, including the recent Vienna Conference, represent Western cultural hegemony and nothing more.

In contrast, human rights scholars, supporting universal standards, contend that the cultural argument is a way to dodge respect for rights. Gayle Binion believes that to argue for exceptions in human rights practices for local cultural reasons is to deny the rights. As she observes, all political and social structures, including slavery and the disempowerment of women, are understandable as culture. A cultural status quo, then, can hurt human rights.[29]

It may be true that cultural values have spread because of Western victory in war or through Western colonialism, as cultural relativists have pointed out; yet Western notions of human rights also are widely disseminated because they find a receptive "market" around the world. The appeal of universal human rights is strong enough that non-Western peoples embrace these values and take them as their own.[30]

The caning of an 18-year-old American, Michael P. Fay, in Singapore in 1994 is a good example of a cultural collision over human rights. Caning is not unusual in parts of the Middle East and Asia. Singapore, in fact, canes a thousand people a year. Although the government and courts of Singapore resented Western pressures, including the appeals of President Bill Clinton, the High Court of Singapore cut Fay's sentence from six to three strokes by a martial arts expert. Western countries rarely use corporal punishment and could cite Article Seven of the Covenant on Civil and Political Rights, prohibiting cruel or degrading punishment, as an argument against Singapore's caning punishment.

Is caning cruel or degrading? Here is the cultural problem and the rub for making any final decision about a proper understanding of human rights in Fay's case. At least the practical argument Singaporeans, and some Americans, make, that caning is a deterrent to crime, does not hold up well. Finland, Ireland, and Japan have even lower crime rates than Singapore, and these countries do not cane. Singapore probably has a low crime rate

Toles. © *The Buffalo News*. Reprinted with permission of Universal Press Syndicate. All rights reserved.

because of its Confucian social order as a tightly knit and disciplined society, not because of corporal punishment.

If democracy continues to spread in the world, we can expect better respect for human rights. These two practices tend to invigorate and reinforce each other and contribute to the recipe for domestic and international peace.[31] The advancement of universal human rights, along with democracy, offers much practical value for the world and deserves the celebration held on every December 10 as Human Rights Day. For this reason, many human rights supporters have been disappointed that President Bill Clinton has been reluctant to push China to improve its poor human rights record. Many human rights supporters fail to realize the weak leverage the United States has over China on human rights issues. China is a rising economic superpower with an economy larger than some of the influential G-7 states (called the G-8 by President Bill Clinton because of Russia's deeper involvement marked by the Denver summit in the summer of 1997). The United States now depends on the Chinese market for its exports, especially to buy U.S. farm products, and China can choose from a growing diversity of trade partners. In fact, the expansion of the Chinese economy in the last decade and its world impact are profound.

Slavery

A particularly heinous human rights violation concerns slavery, a practice most people might assume ended in the nineteenth century. Unfortunately, elements of slavery still exist in the world. One hundred million to 200 million people may still live in some form of slavery in spite of the *Slavery Convention* of 1926. Supporting human rights treaties preventing slavery are the activities of IGOs and INGOs. The United Nations Working Group on Contemporary Forms of Slavery and the British-based Anti-Slavery Society, founded in 1839, are the outstanding examples. The Anti-Slavery Society may be the oldest human rights organization still in existence.

Mark Peters/SIPA

Child struggles in indentured
service in Pakistan making Bricks
in hellish fields of mud.

With legal slavery ending in the Arabian peninsula in 1970, the clearest form of *chattel* slavery remaining today is the ownership of African people by Arab people in Mauritania. Arab people in that country sell or trade African people for money or livestock. Also, in Ghana and several neighboring states, the *Trokosi* ("wife of the gods" in the Ewe language) practice involves giving young girls to priests in animist temples where they become concubines of the priests. When cast aside in middle age, these victims are uneducated and unemployable. This practice involves up to 12,000 girls.

Much more common than the outright ownership of people is *debt bondage,* and it occurs in many countries, including the United States. Usually poor, uneducated people work at menial labor, never quite able to pay off their debts. If they are illegal aliens, such workers are equally unable to complain to authorities for fear of deportation. Migrant farm laborers and, more recently, illegal Chinese immigrants have fallen into this trap in the United States. In Brazil, thousands of illegal Bolivian aliens work 16-hour days in the garment industry below minimum wages. A married couple in India worked in a rock quarry to pay off a $46 debt, and eight years later, through interest accumulation, they owed $88.

A hideous tale of slavery that happened during the Second World War but came to light only recently is the case of the "comfort women," victims the media dubbed "sex slaves." The Japanese forced 200,000 women from the Philippines and Korea to serve in Japanese military brothels from Burma to Indonesia. Many of the women were as young as 15 years. After an 18-month investigation in the early 1990s, the Japanese government has admitted to this terrible misconduct. In 1996, Japanese Prime Minister Ryutaro Hashimoto apologized for this terrible treatment of women and, through a private fund in Japan, offered each victim a sum of $18,600 if she chose to accept.

Patrick Robert/SYGMA

Liberian soldier: *Young and obedient.*

Children

Perhaps the most tragic example of modern slavery involves millions of children who toil 12-hour days in rug factories in India, brickyards in Pakistan, the coal mines and cane fields of Latin America, or the sex trade of the Philippines and Thailand. Locked away from society and enjoying little or no education, they work under terrible conditions, receiving beatings and poor food. Arlene Sumampan's supervisor in a Manilia print shop attached clothespins to her ears for miscounting sheets of paper. Iqbal Masih of Pakistan became famous for escaping his indentured service in a rug factory and crusading against child labor. At age 12, he died from a gunshot wound presumably inflicted because of his crusading efforts.

A particularly dangerous misuse of children is their placement in armies. As many as 200,000 children, mostly boys, are soldiers somewhere in the world. The large majority carry weapons in the many African conflicts, but in Myanmar (Burma), in the self-proclaimed Shan state, hundreds of boys also receive training beginning at age 10 and go into combat at age 16.[32]

Many INGOs and IGOs are trying to improve the conditions of children. The Anti-Slavery Society is attempting to end the indentured service of children. The Save the Children Fund of Australia has set up schools in Bangladesh to steer girls away from prostitution, and the Quaker United Nations and the Lutheran World Federation try to keep children out of war's harm.[33]

The best-known IGO in the world looking out for children is the UN International Children's Fund (UNICEF). Although the organization has dropped "Emergency" from its name, it still uses the acronym UNICEF because the acronym is so well known. UNICEF counts on donations as well as money raised by selling Christmas cards in Christian countries and collecting money at Halloween in the United States. UNICEF frequently helps children in refugee camps, most recently in Somalia. Movie star Audrey Hepburn, before her death in 1992, worked for six years as a "personal ambassador" for UNICEF and visited 30 states for UNICEF, the last being Somalia.

UNICEF issues an annual report called *The State of the World's Children* that guides reforms benefiting children. In addition to the problems already mentioned, UNICEF works to end malnutrition and diseases that harm and kill as many as 13 million children a year. Among the many inexpensive yet effective remedies that have saved children are vitamins, iodized salt, immunization, and healthy food. As a result, UNICEF has been able to do much good with its money, but its ability to raise the necessary $60 billion a year is in decline due to donor fatigue.

Women

Another group in need of social progress is the world's women. No country treats its women as well as it does its men, and in some cultures, the lives of women are especially hard. In fundamentalist Muslim societies, women are not able to drive a car, vote, visit a male doctor, show their faces in public, or leave home without a male escort from their families. In Iran, authorities have treated women wearing makeup as prostitutes. Women in Pakistan who experience rape may find their husbands can divorce them for adultery. Druze women, from a Muslim minority in Israel, have sometimes lost their lives to "honor killings," when their families think the victim has brought disgrace to her family. No mistreatment of women infuriates feminists more than female circumcision, which takes place in many African societies and several Middle Eastern countries. Practitioners of female circumcision, an act critics call female mutilation, defend it in "cultural relativism" terms current in the ongoing human rights debate.[34]

Women also experience sexual exploitation in what has become an international network of "sex tours." Travel agencies, hotels, bars, and police join in the booming $4 billion business of bringing clients from well-off countries, such as Australia, Japan, and the United States, to poorer countries, especially Thailand. The subjects of attraction are usually poor, uneducated village girls who, through trickery, wind up in debt and under the control of their managers. Governments of these poor countries do little to intervene because of the foreign income they enjoy.[35]

Aside from directly harmful treatment, women experience unfavorable differentials compared to men. On a worldwide scale, the political differential involves women holding 10 percent of parliamentary seats and 3.5 percent of cabinet seats. In 1995, only nine states—Bangladesh, Dominica, Iceland, Ireland, Nicaragua, Norway, Pakistan, Sri Lanka, and Turkey—had a woman serving as head of government or state.[36]

Regarding the economic differential, women perform two-thirds of the hourly labor, receive 10 percent of the world's labor income, and own 1 percent of the world's private property.[37] Women also receive 40 percent less wages than men for performing the same jobs and have less access to bank credit.[38] Of the 1.3 billion people around the world living in subsistence poverty, 70 percent are women.

The social differentials are no better. Women have half the education and literacy men do. In Africa and Asia, 75 percent of women over age 25 cannot read or write.[39] In China and India, where population pressures are great and families prefer male babies, female fetuses are aborted more often than male fetuses. Male children mean higher

© Tribune Media Services, Inc. All rights reserved. Reprinted with permission.

income when the child grows up, the receipt of a bride's dowry, and the labor and services of a son's wife.

At least legal and promotional efforts have occurred to make the world more equitable for women. We saw in Chapter Eight that economic development experts recognize the central role of women's progress to economic development. Ratified by a majority of the states of the world is the *Convention an All Forms of Discrimination Against Women* of 1979, a veritable bill of rights for women.[40] More recently, a major evaluation of women's standing in the world took place during the *Global Tribunal on Violations of Women's Human Rights,* held at the World Conference on Human Rights in Vienna in 1993.

The United Nations has regularly served as a catalyst for gender equality by sponsoring or contributing to conferences that promote progress for women. Since 1975, a series of specialized conferences has called for the advancement of women. The fourth of these, the World Conference on Women held in Beijing, China, in 1995, became controversial because its Chinese hosts were less than cooperative with the conference. The 6,000 women at the conference site and the 24,000 women at the accompanying forum for INGOs received rough handling and poor, inadequate facilities in many instances.

The demonstrations of such independent-minded women surprised the authoritarian Chinese government. First Lady Hillary Clinton, a guest speaker at the conference, rebuked the Chinese hosts for their treatment of their international guests and criticized China's policies toward women, especially the policy of forced abortions to create one-child families. Other conferences in the 1990s on the environment, economic development, children's welfare, and population matters have stressed that progress in these various areas cannot succeed unless they are in step with progress for women.

Refugees

An area of concern in which the fates of children and women clearly coincide is the misfortunes of refugees. A refugee is a person fleeing persecution because of his or her

Kevin Carter/SYGMA

Tiny refugee barely survives in the Sudan.

ethnic background or political opinion. As many as 80 percent of the world's 16 million refugees and 26 million internally displaced persons are women and children.[41] Africa and the Middle East contain most of the world's refugees today. However, the Bosnian tragedy, with as many as 2 million refugees and displaced persons, evokes memories of the European refugee problems following the First and Second World Wars.

In recent years, more and more people are migrating because of difficult economic conditions, and the distinction between refugee and migrant status is tending to blur.[42] The distinction can be important because many governments are more open to a trickle of political refugees than a flow of economic migrants. Are the Cuban and Haitian "boat people" trying to reach Florida political refugees or economic migrants? The U.S. government, for a time, treated Cubans as refugees fleeing from communism and Haitians as economic migrants. With the end of the Cold War, President Bill Clinton's administration is prone to treat all illegal entries as would-be economic migrants.

The League of Nations appointed the first High Commissioner for Refugees in 1921, a world-famous Norwegian explorer named Fridtjof Nansen, who focused on repatriating Russian POWs. He began the "Nansen passports," which provided international identity papers to refugees enabling them to cross borders in search of a new homeland.[43] The Second World War created a new surge of refugees, resulting in temporary arrangements to handle the refugee problem between 1943 and 1951, until the United Nations created a permanent High Commissioner for Refugees (UNHCR) in 1951. The budget of this office has risen to well over $1 billion a year, with much of the money going to short-term food needs.[44]

In addition, the United Nations created special refugee programs. It began the UN Relief and Works Agency for Palestine Refugees in the Near East (UNRWA) in 1950. UNRWA has stressed food supplies and education. In 1972, the Office of United Nations Disaster Relief Coordinator (UNDRC) came into existence. This office channels the aid of governments, private donors, and other IGOs into a disaster area to help the victims of natural disasters.

Other social problems needing reform abound. The International Labor Organization (ILO), associated with the UN system, began work in 1919 to improve working conditions

AP Photo/United States Coast Guard/PA3 Tyler Johnson

Rescued from the Sea: A tiny Haitian refugee is pulled to freedom by Coast Guard personnel aboard the cutter *Dependable*.

and to defend labor unions' right to organize. The UN Educational, Scientific, and Cultural Organization (UNESCO), also part of the UN System, has sought to protect cultures, those of both antiquity and modern times. UNESCO is the chief sponsor of the UN University in Tokyo, and UNESCO promotes research and scholarship around the world. The best-known program of UNESCO is its struggle to reduce illiteracy in the world. Close to one-fifth of the human population is illiterate, and millions more are functionally illiterate.

WHO strives to rid the world of diseases such as malaria and cholera and has eliminated all cases of smallpox in the world. WHO has fought female circumcision, which threatens 80 million women and girls with the danger of infection.[45] (We will return to WHO activities in Chapter Fourteen, where we look at AIDS as a pandemic experienced by humankind around the world.) The United Nations Population Fund (also called the UN Family Planning Agency [UNFPA]) tries to balance the size of the world's population with environmental limits, and the United Nations sponsored the International Conference on Population and Development in Cairo, Egypt, in 1994. (We discussed population regarding economic development in Chapter Eight, and we will return to this subject in terms of environmental matters in Chapter Thirteen.) Finally, as an example of social progress efforts, the Food and Agricultural Organization (FAO) of the United Nations has promoted the "green revolution." Using hybrid seeds, the FAO has resulted in higher food production. (Food supplies are a subject of Chapter Thirteen as well.)

Overall, international organizations have been up against gargantuan social problems but funded with too few dollars. Sovereign states around the world, though willing to spend a trillion dollars on arms by 1987, have neglected to confront the social problems of their peoples with their full capability. To their credit, IGOs and INGOs have embraced a wide array of these social problems with their meager resources.

IGO COOPERATION IN TECHNICAL AREAS

Political scientists have long surmised that states cooperate more effectively in areas of "low politics" where technical matters hold obvious, mutual benefits, as opposed to the "high politics" of power competition. Craig N. Murphy, maintaining that international organizations are expressions of social forces that invite cooperation at the international level, finds some of the closest cooperation in the world among technically based IGOs.[46] These IGOs provide the regulation and coordination, associated with governance, that guide the interaction of states in technical areas. Such IGOs are among the autonomous agencies linked to the United Nations by treaty.

The International Civil Aviation Organization (ICAO) has promoted air safety by specifying the rules for international airports and flights, including the rule that pilots and air controllers must speak English. A common language in use in international air travel is necessary for safety's sake. Particularly important, the ICAO has the authority to suspend flights to countries harboring skyjackers. The International Maritime Organization (IMO) has a similar set of rules governing use of the seas to provide for mutual safety and convenience.

The World Meteorological Organization (WMO) operates a World Weather Watch program to collect weather information that virtually everyone needs. Few human activities escape the effects of weather, activities that range from growing crops to coping with natural disasters. As mentioned earlier in the chapter, the Universal Postal Union, dating from 1876, arranges for the transborder flow of mail and deals with postage rate and mail weights.

Issues can arise, however, even in technical areas characterized by high levels of cooperation. Economic advantages are sometimes at stake in organizations that manage technical cooperation, and conflict arises particularly along the North-South divide. We saw in Chapter Eight that the World Intellectual Property Organization (WIPO) regulates property rights concerning patents and licenses. The WIPO has difficulty with rapidly industrializing countries because their governments acquiesce in the theft of intellectual property. While these thefts harm the richer trade states wanting protection for intellectual property, poor people can have access to cheaper products such as medicine, and national economies can expand more rapidly if the use of technology and ideas goes without payment.

The organization more closely identified with North-South controversy than any other is the International Telecommunication Union (ITU), also mentioned earlier in this chapter. The ITU is the oldest IGO presently in the UN System, dating back to its management of transborder telegraph services in 1865, when it operated as the International Telegraph Union. At issue today are the "frequency spectrums" and the "slots" left in the geostationary orbit for communication satellites. These "spectrums" and "slots" exist in limited number, and states of the South feel they do not have their fair share. Historically, countries of the North were first in line to grab up these assets because of their technological capabilities. Not only is money at stake, but so is the nature of the information flowing around the world. From television entertainment programs to news services, communications originating in the West carry a "Western" bias to a global audience.[47] At least, non-Western audiences might understandably take this view.

Finally, as we learned in Chapter Ten, the International Atomic Energy Agency (IAEA) has concerned itself with atomic supplies and devices proliferating from atomic powers to nonnuclear states for the making of an atomic bomb. In this case, a regulatory body in a technical field does influence traditional "high politics" by trying to stanch the spread of the world's most powerful weapon.

The extent of cooperation highlights the history of technical organizations; yet neorealists are correct to point out that conflict can occur within the framework of the most extensive cooperation. However, to the chagrin of neorealists, technical organizations not only reflect the ongoing cooperation of states but also can act as change agents to produce new levels of cooperation. The European Telecommunications Standards Institute of the EU, for example, led a patchwork of national telecommunication fiefdoms into an integrated system. The Institute standardized equipment and shared programs to the advantage of the EU countries and their peoples.[48]

UNITED NATIONS VITALITY

Does the United Nations have the capacity for continued useful service to the world? The answer is yes, but with several important qualifications. The United Nations faces at least three types of constraints affecting its vitality: the lack of a dependable process for handling violations of the peace, the absence of an efficient bureaucracy with a reliable budget, and the distraction and division caused by different expectations for the world body.

The first constraint involves not only the large number of peace violations but their changing nature. As mentioned earlier, the number of peacekeeping missions, their costs, and the obdurate nature of some conflicts almost overwhelm the United Nations. Fierce internal conflicts involving ethnic groups are notably troublesome. Also, the management of these missions has operated through a convoluted "command and control" system headed by United Nations officials without adequate military expertise. The United Nations cannot regularly count on enough military forces or the funds to pay for a peacekeeping mission. Further, the United Nations is unsure, in some cases, whether to turn to collective security, peacekeeping, or subcontracting enforcement to states as the world body faces border violations, interstate warfare, and varied internal conflicts. Surely, at least, humanitarian intervention in the midst of continued fighting is a nonviable option based on the Bosnian and Somalian experiences. To the United Nations' credit, it has improvised impressively while working from a Charter that has never completely matched the real world.

A second constraint is the United Nations' image as a bloated, expensive bureaucracy that leads some member-states to withhold dues. The United Nations needs to put its house in order and become more efficient. As President Bill Clinton has put the matter, "The

United Nations simply does not need a separate agency with its own acronym, stationery, and bureaucracy for every problem." In late 1996, the United States owed over $1 billion in dues according to the UN, and other countries' arrears have raised the total amount owed the United Nations to $1.5 to $2 billion. This shortfall in funding is immense on the United Nations scale. The United Nations' regular annual budget is about $1.3 billion, and peacekeeping costs were over $3 billion at one time.[49] Consequently, the United Nations regularly works with a cash flow problem and must constantly scramble to meet payrolls and to pay for peacekeeping.

Some relief may be on the way. In the summer of 1997, with an unprecedented degree of cooperation in recent times, both Republicans and Democrats on the U.S. Senate Foreign Relations Committee called for a foreign policy budget that will provide the UN with $819 million in arrears, two-thirds of what the UN claims the United States owes. The conditions are that the UN will receive the money over three years, the UN must lay off one thousand of its bureaucrats, and the world body has to reduce U.S. dues by one-fifth. Presently the United States pays 25 percent of the UN's basic budget.

Coming to the defense of the United Nations, John Ruggie points out that the UN System is in an odd situation as a bureaucracy. The United Nations contains semiautonomous agencies, has business going on in six languages, a staff that extends around the world, and a large membership of sovereign states, now numbering at least 185.[50] Dealing with its wide array of responsibilities, the United Nations has a core staff of under 10,000 workers, and the whole UN System must perform a multitude of tasks with the services of 52,000 personnel.[51]

In addition to placing a ceiling on growth, the United Nations should reform by hiring on merit instead of geographical distribution; placing more women in senior positions; holding open searches for the secretary-general; establishing an inspector-general position that could do audits and special inspections, as Madeline Albright suggested when she was U.S. ambassador to the United Nations; and finding an independent income for the United Nations, such as an international air travel tax. In regard to the last reform proposal, member-states demand reform, but few want an income for the United Nations that would provide the world body with greater independence from member-states.

The third constraint on the United Nations is the differing expectations of member-states for the UN. The largest divide in expectations is the awkward imbalance between the few Western states that provide most of the money and the large majority of Third World states that exercise their influence through votes. As we discussed in Chapter Eight, the Third World wants the United Nations to channel more of the West's wealth to them, while the West wants the United Nations to guide bootstrap economic development in the Third World along a capitalist pattern.

Differing expectations have shown up in the choices for secretary-general. Although Boutrous Boutrous-Ghali said he would not seek a second term, he did so. The United States has been unhappy with the lack of internal reforms at the United Nations and Boutrous-Ghali's focus on the Third World perspective at the expense of Western priorities. In spite of a major campaign for his job, Boutrous-Ghali finally lost out, though he won the support of the Third World and France. The adamant insistence for another choice by the United States, backed by its threat of a veto, finally led to the selection of Kofi Annan as secretary-general in December 1996, with Boutros-Ghali formally stepping

Iikka Vimonen/SYGMA

down on the first day of January 1997. Annan is a black African from Ghana and is a United Nations insider. He has the advantage of having served as Under-Secretary-General for Peacekeeping, a service that won him a reputation for good money management.

In sum, the UN System clearly has not ground away all the world's woes, but it has taken modest steps to do good by promoting economic development, improving health conditions, encouraging respect for human rights, and stopping at least some conflicts. Whatever its shortcomings, as Nigerian writer Ben Okri has said, "The United Nations remains the only organization still vaguely capable of articulating the notion of one world, a sort of symphony of humanity."[52]

INTERNATIONAL ORGANIZATIONS AND INTERNATIONAL SOCIETY

To gain a sense of perspective about the contribution of international organizations to the formation of an international society, let us review the positions of theorists—namely, realists, neorealists, and transnationalists—on international organizations.

The League's failed efforts at collective security drew realists' attacks in Britain before the Second World War, and after this war, Hans Morgenthau spearheaded attacks by realists in the United States. The Second World War profoundly disillusioned Morgenthau about the prospects for keeping the peace through an international organization, as his *Politics Among Nations,* with its first edition appearing in 1948, bears testimony. For him, the failure of the League was complete and the prospects of the United Nations were doubtful.

The realist message, reduced to its simplest form, was that states must control power with counterpower, not a naive reliance on collective security provided by an international organization. Similarly to other realists, Morgenthau feared that an idealistic preoccupation with international organizations would cause leaders to lose sight of the real "meat" of international politics, power relationships among states. Morgenthau could not foresee more than a modest role for international organizations.[53]

Anthony Boyle, once a student of Morgenthau and an acquaintance of Morgenthau's in his elderly years, recognizes that Morgenthau believed history had repudiated international organization through the occurrence of the Second World War. However, Boyle remembers that later, in 1978, Morgenthau left an audience thunderstruck by embracing the idea that world government might take root through the United Nations and that this development could become a desirable direction for the world. Then, according to Boyle, months before Morgenthau's death in 1980, Morgenthau again grew pessimistic because of the prospects for nuclear war, as he saw the situation.[54] Although Boyle's observations are interesting, it is Morgenthau's *Politics Among Nations* that survives as a realist charge with lance held at full tilt: States may possibly have peace if they deter opponents' power with their own power, but they dare not count on an international organization for security.

Writing several decades after Morgenthau, Kenneth N. Waltz, a major neorealist, gives international organizations short shrift by barely mentioning the United Nations.[55] For Waltz, states should focus on achieving a stable balance of power, and preferably with a bipolar structure. From his point of view, the best efforts of the United States after the Second World War went not into the United Nations but into the Marshall Plan, the Truman Doctrine, the Berlin Airlift, and NATO. These acts served U.S. interests and, at the same time, helped the United States hold up its end of a bipolar power structure.[56]

Writing during the mood of triumphalism after the Persian Gulf War, Ernest W. Lefever warns against a rejuvenated Wilsonian idealism that calls for a world body to manage power and preserve peace. Taking a realist tack, Lefever sees a world driven by the motives of major states, with the role of IGOs being almost incidental. Lefever calls the UN police action in the Korean War a fig leaf to cover the United States policy of stopping the spread of communism. Further, he views the Persian Gulf War as the product of major states protecting a prime source of oil. Lefever has no quarrel with motives based on national interests, but believes covering these motives with a United Nations imprimatur only creates unnecessary complications.[57]

The problem with realists and neorealists views, however, is that they simply fail to explain the extensive network of cooperation among states that is gradually gaining ascendancy over conflict, a development aided by international organizations. To rectify this failure, transnationalists, such as Robert O. Keohane and Joseph S. Nye, hasten to explain why international organizations offer important service to states and to humankind. These scholars observe that many problems exist beyond territorial borders that states and other actors cannot handle alone, and so these actors collaborate over mutually shared problems. Then webs of cooperative ties build up in shared policy areas, reflecting interdependent relations.[58]

More specifically, John G. Ruggie observes that international organizations are a necessary catalyst to develop global policy for the problems of overpopulation, pollution, weapons proliferation, trade problems, and other global concerns. Ruggie recognizes such comprehensive policy responses through international organizations as global governance. This governance, he concludes, is not a transformation of the state system but a rule-governed change to which states accede.[59] Ernest B. Haas, realizing that international life would be more difficult, dreary, and dangerous without international organizations, asserts that these institutions will improve on their progressive role because, as human institutions, they can "adapt" and "learn."[60]

We can sharpen our perspective further by referring to the three abstract models from Chapter One. Our discussion of international relations is relevant to two elements used to form the models. The meetings in the bodies of the UN System and the UN-sponsored conferences continuously seed *international society* with new norms and rules that may become customary or treaty law. At least, on these forums, states and thousands of INGOs forge standards in numerous policy areas to make life better around the world. This governance process raises the *problem-solving level* from the state to the regional and global levels, and the more extensively the actors share in governance, the closer they move together in an international society.

At the same time, the *orientation* of greater cooperation also promotes an international society over the model of *international anarchy,* with its pattern of conflict. Significant discord still characterizes meetings in organizations and conferences, however, demonstrating differences among democratic and nondemocratic states, rich and poor states, and peoples from varied cultures. Agreements on norms and policies on international forums usually represent compromises finally hammered out following arguments and negotiations. The cultural and moral bonds that would provide a common global identity to support an *international community* are not close at hand.

Overall, we can conclude the harms of conflict and disarray are still with humankind, but their presence is at least more local and patchy and less globalized than during the Cold War structure of power. Today it is implausible that major states will pursue the kinds of goals that cause hostile relations and possibly war. Most states, in fact, increasingly realize they can attain many desired goals only by cooperating. Moreover, states work through international organizations because cooperation is inherent to these institutions. While the state may remain the primary actor, the international organization is becoming a more prominent cast player on the world stage.

CHAPTER SUMMARY

The presence of international organizations in the world is a measure of the progress states have made toward cooperation. International organizations come in many forms: public or private, unifunctional or multifunctional, and global or regional. Their history traces mainly from the nineteenth century based on the influences of river commissions, conference diplomacy, and public unions that supervised international mail and telegraph communications. Other historical forces working to energize international organizations are such matters as growth in the number of actors, the rise of technology, and the spread of democracy.

The most important international organizations have been the League of Nations and the United Nations, because they have attempted to institutionalize international society with universal membership for all, or nearly all, states and have offered multiple services. The League ended its institutional life in 1939 but served as the precursor to the United Nations. The United Nations continues to adjust to a changing world, finding ways to be a major role player in international relations. Its primary function has been to guide states toward peaceful relations. When collective security has not been possible or relevant, the United Nations has turned to peacekeeping. When peacekeeping has proven inadequate, the United Nations has arranged for peace enforcement by delegating mission responsibilities to particular member-states.

In addition, the UN System and INGOs work to close the large economic gap between rich and poor states, although needs constantly outpace resources. These same actors also try to improve social conditions that degrade, especially the lives of women and children. The highest level of cooperation, however, is in technical areas. States can easily see their common advantages in matters such as safe international air and sea travel.

An immediate task before the UN System is to convince the world it can reform itself thoroughly and hold on to both respect and funding by member-states. The UN System is the most visible element in the rapid growth of international organizations since the Second World War. Its continued success joins forces with the robust development of international law and a rising level of world trade to deepen cooperative interaction within an international society.

POINTS OF VIEW

It is the law of the jungle, and not the law of the UN, that dominates the "New World Order" in the post–Cold War era.

—CUMHURIYET
ISTANBUL, JUNE 27, 1993

The chief fantasy is that the U.S., indeed the world, can now rely on "collective security" and its agency, the UN, for its safety and security.

—CHARLES KRAUTHAMMER
TIME, JUNE 15, 1992

The United Nations is not and cannot be a political actor in a world of sovereign states.

—ERNEST W. LEFEVER
FOREIGN AFFAIRS, SUMMER 1993

The UN is in need of overhaul—a real cleanup.

—MADELINE ALBRIGHT
U.S. AMBASSADOR TO THE UN
JUNE 1993

. . . the image of the soldier that dominates television screens worldwide is not the soldier as destroyer but the soldier as bringer of hope to the hopeless, of food to the starving, of order to anarchy.

—SINA ODUGBEMI
GUARDIAN
LAGOS, NIGERIA
MARCH 1993

[Comment on a Druze woman leaving her kinsfolk] "She disobeyed our rules, and we were happy to finish her off. Any girl who does a thing like that has to die. Every dog will get what it deserves.

—COUSIN OF THE VICTIM
QUOTED IN THE PRESS, DECEMBER 21, 1995

The UN must win the peace in Yugoslavia. The world peace-keeping body is after all the world's only hope for peace, and not only in the Balkans.

—JAPAN TIMES
TOKYO

REVIEW QUESTIONS

1. What nineteenth-century precedents contributed to the international organization of the twentieth century?
2. How would you evaluate the League's experience with collective security?
3. How comparable are the League and the United Nations in their formal structures?
4. What techniques of peaceful settlement does the United Nations recommend to states in dispute?
5. Why is peacekeeping a major innovation of the United Nations?
6. What do we mean by *preventive diplomacy*?
7. How is collective security different from the traditional balance of power system?
8. Why has humanitarian intervention, as in the cases of Bosnia and Somalia, been complex and dangerous as a peacekeeping operation?
9. Do you think the United Nations should embark on "peace enforcement" in internal conflicts? Why or why not?
10. How successful has the United Nations been in achieving economic and social progress?
11. Why is technological cooperation relatively successful within the UN System?
12. How do realists and transnationalists assess international organizations?

GLOSSARY

collective security The combined power of states to deter or punish an aggressor with economic and/or military sanctions.

conciliation A third-party technique of peaceful settlement, more formal than mediation, that functions through a commission.

good offices A third-party technique of peaceful settlement that involves passing information as a go-between for disputants.

inquiry A third-party technique of peaceful settlement that calls for investigating a dispute to provide information for the disputants.

mediation A third-party technique of peaceful settlement that calls for the third party to recommend settlement terms for the disputants.

peaceful settlement Political negotiation or adjudication methods advocated by the UN Charter for resolving disputes.

peacekeeping A major innovation of the UN to handle conflicts by disengaging disputing parties and placing a UN force between them; substitutes when collective security is inappropriate.

secretariat An international bureaucracy or civil service that serves an international organization.

RECOMMENDED READINGS

Peter R. Baehr and Leon Gordenker. *The United Nations in the 1990s.* New York: St. Martin's Press, 1992.

Dimitris Bourantonis and Jarrod Wiener, ed. *The United Nations in the New World Order: The World Organization at Fifty.* New York: St. Martin's Press, 1996.

Paul F. Diehl, ed. *The Politics of International Organizations: Patterns and Insights.* Chicago: Dorsey Press, 1989.

Paul F. Diehl. *International Peacekeeping.* Baltimore: Johns Hopkins University Press, 1993.

Paul F. Diehl, ed. *The Politics of Global Governance: International Organizations in an Interdependent World.* Boulder, CO: Lynne Rienner Publishers, 1997.

Richard A. Falk, Samuel S. Kim, and Saul H. Mendlovitz, eds. *The United Nations and a Just World Order.* Boulder, CO: Westview Press, 1991.

Martha Finnemore. *National Interests in International Society.* Ithaca, NY: Cornell University Press, 1996.

David P. Forsythe. *The Internationalization of Human Rights.* Lexington, MA: Lexington Books, 1991.

Robert W. Gregg. *About Face? The United States and the United Nations.* Boulder, CO: Lynne Rienner Publishers, 1993.

Ernst B. Haas. *When Knowledge Is Power: Three Models of Change in International Organizations.* Berkeley, CA: University of California Press, 1990.

Christopher C. Joyner, ed. *The United Nations and International Law.* 2nd ed. New York: Cambridge University Press, 1997.

F. T. Liu. *United Nations Peacekeeping and the Non-Use of Force.* Boulder, CO: Lynne Rienner Publishers, 1992.

Gil Loescher. *Beyond Charity: International Cooperation and the Global Refugee Crisis.* New York: Oxford University Press, 1993.

Craig N. Murphy. *International Organization and Industrial Change: Global Governance Since 1850.* New York: Oxford University Press, 1994.

A. H. Robertson and J. G. Merrills. *Human Rights in the World: An Introduction to the Study of the International Protection of Human Rights.* 4th ed. New York: St. Martin's Press, 1996.

James N. Rosenau. *The United Nations in a Turbulent World.* Boulder, CO: Lynne Rienner Publishers, 1992.

The State of the World's Refugees: The Search for Solutions. New York: Oxford University Press, 1995.

Henry J. Steiner. *Diverse Partners: Non-Governmental Organizations in the Human Rights Movement.* Cambridge, MA: Harvard Law School Human Rights Program, 1991.

Nigel White. *The Law of International Organizations.* New York: St. Martin's Press, 1997.

Mark W. Zacher. *Governing Global Networks: International Regimes for Transportation and Communication.* New York: Cambridge University Press, 1996.

ENDNOTES

1. Boutros Boutros-Ghali, *An Agenda for Development 1995* (New York: United Nations, 1995), pp. 76–77.

2. A concise history of these nineteenth-century precedents appears in Inis L. Claude, *Swords Into Plowshares,* 4th ed. (New York: Random House, 1971), Chapter 2.

3. Mark W. Zacher, "The Decaying Pillars of the Westphalian Temple: Implications for International Order and Governance," in *Governance Without*

Government: Order and Change in World Politics, ed. James N. Rosenau and Ernst-Otto Czempiel (New York: Cambridge University Press, 1992), pp. 65–66.
4. Paul F. Diehl, *International Peacekeeping* (Baltimore: Johns Hopkins University Press, 1993).
5. Karen Mingst and Margaret P. Karns, *The United Nations in the Post–Cold War Era* (Boulder, CO: Westview Press, 1995), pp. 93–94.
6. John Keegan, *A History of War* (New York: Alfred A. Knopf, 1993), p. 58.
7. Boutros Boutros-Ghali, *An Agenda for Peace*, 2nd ed. (New York: United Nations, 1995), pp. 28–29.
8. F. T. Liu, *United Nations Peacekeeping and the Non-Use of Force* (Boulder, CO: Lynne Rienner Publishers, 1992), Chapter 3; Marrack Goulding, "The Evolution of United Nations Peacekeeping," *International Affairs*, July 1993, pp. 451–64. On the Suez Canal and Congo crises, see also John G. Stoessinger, *The United Nations and the Superpowers: China, Russia, and America*, 4th ed. (New York: Random House, 1977), pp. 63–120.
9. Michael Renner, *Critical Juncture: The Future of Peacekeeping*, Worldwatch Paper 114 (Washington, D.C.: Worldwatch Institute, 1993), pp. 8–9.
10. Boutros-Ghali, *Agenda for Peace*, p. 43.
11. Ibid., p. 7.
12. The nature of the UN's role in Korea and the Persian Gulf War are described in Bruce Russett and James S. Sutterlin, "The U.N. in a New World Order," *Foreign Affairs*, Spring 1991, pp. 73–75; Peter R. Baehr and Leon Gordenker, *The United Nations in the 1990s* (New York: St. Martin's Press, 1992), pp. 69–79.
13. Robert W. Gregg, *About Face? The United States and the United Nations* (Boulder, CO: Lynne Rienner Publishers, 1993), p. 162.
14. *Changing Concepts of Sovereignty: Can the United Nations Keep the Peace?* (Muscatine, IA: The Stanley Foundation, 1992), p. 25; Andrew Bennett and Joseph Lepgold, "Reinventing Collective Security After the Cold War and Gulf Conflict," *Political Science Quarterly*, Summer 1993, p. 234.
15. Boutros-Ghali, *Agenda for Peace*, p. 18.
16. Ibid., p. 28.
17. Baehr and Gordenker, *The United Nations in the 1990s*, p. 32.
18. Ibid., pp. 134–35.
19. Boutros-Ghali, *Agenda for Development 1995*, p. 26.
20. Erskine Childers, "The UN at 50: Midlife Crisis," *World Policy Review*, June 1995, p. 10.
21. Boutros-Ghali, *Agenda for Development 1995*, p. 29.
22. "Current Policy," No. 763, Bureau of Public Affairs, U.S. State Department, November 6, 1985.
23. Boutros-Ghali, *Agenda for Development 1995*, p. 32.
24. David P. Forsythe, *The Internationalization of Human Rights* (Lexington, MA: Lexington Books, 1991); Antonio Cassese, *Human Rights in a Changing World* (Philadelphia: Temple University Press, 1990); Craig Murphy, "Global Institutions and the Pursuit of Human Needs," in *The Power of Human Needs in World Society*, ed. Roger A. Coate and Jerel A. Rosati (Boulder, CO: Lynne Rienner Publishers, 1988), pp. 205–24.
25. Boutros Boutros-Ghali, "Empowering the United Nations," *Foreign Affairs*, Winter 1992–1993, pp. 89–102; David P. Forsythe and Kelly Kate Pease, "Human Rights, Humanitarian Intervention, and World Politics," *Human Rights Quarterly*, May 1993, pp. 290–314.
26. *The United Nations and Human Rights 1945–1995*, The United Nations Blue Books Series, Volume VII (New York: United Nations, 1995), pp. 92, 94, 109–11.
27. Abdullahi Ahmed An-Na'im, ed., *Human Rights in Cross-Cultural Perspectives: A Quest for Consensus* (Philadelphia: University of Pennsylvania Press, 1992).
28. Ken Booth, "Global Ethics: Human Wrongs and International Relations," *International Affairs*, January 1995, pp. 119–20.
29. Gayle Binion, "Human Rights: A Feminist Perspective," *Human Rights Quarterly*, August 1995, pp. 521–23.
30. Tom J. Farer and Felice Gaer, "The UN and Human Rights: At the End of the Beginning," in *United Nations, Divided World*, 2nd ed., ed. Adam Roberts and Benedict Kingsbury (Oxford: Clarendon Press, 1993), p. 167; Jack Donnelly, "Human Rights in the New World Order," *World Policy Journal*, Spring 1992, pp. 249–77.
31. David P. Forsythe, *Human Rights and Peace* (Lincoln, NE: University of Nebraska Press, 1993), p. 167.

32. *World Press Review,* January 1996, p. 9; *World Press Review,* October 1994, p. 25.
33. *World Press Review,* January 1996, pp. 8–12.
34. *Human Rights Are Women's Rights* (New York: Amnesty International, 1995), pp. 131–35; Alice Walker, *Warrior Marks: Female Genital Mutilation and the Sexual Blinding of Women* (New York: Harcourt Brace, 1993); Alison T. Slack, "Female Circumcision: A Critical Appraisal," *Human Rights Quarterly,* November 1988, pp. 437–86.
35. Alice Leuchta, "Sex Tours: The New Slave Trade," *The Humanist,* March–April 1995, pp. 11–16.
36. Linda Starke, ed., *Vital Signs 1995* (Washington, D.C.: Worldwatch Institute, 1995), p. 134.
37. Binion, "Human Rights: a Feminist Perspective," p. 511.
38. Starke, *Vital Signs,* p. 94.
39. Binion, "Human Rights: A Feminist Perspective," p. 511; *Calypso Log,* August 1995, p. 23.
40. *The Advancement of Women 1945–1995,* The United Nations Blue Books Series, Volume VI (New York: United Nations, 1995), p. 5.
41. *The ZPG Reporter,* July–August 1995, p. 11.
42. Gil Loescher, *Beyond Charity: International Cooperation and the Global Refugee Crisis* (New York: Oxford University Press, 1993), pp. 3–6.
43. Ibid., p. 37.
44. Boutros-Ghali, *Agenda for Peace,* pp. 52–53.
45. The number of women and girls affected by female circumcision is from an AP news story, May 13, 1993. The AI report, *Human Rights Are Women's Rights,* puts the figure even higher at 110 million women and girls affected.
46. Craig N. Murphy, *International Organization and Industrial Change: Global Governance Since 1950* (New York: Oxford University Press, 1994).
47. Stephen D. Krasner, "Global Communications and National Power: Life on the Pareto Frontier," *World Politics,* April 1991, pp. 336–66; Wayne Sandholtz, "Institutions and Collective Action: The New Telecommunications in Western Europe," *World Politics,* January 1993, pp. 242–70.
48. *ISQ Newsletter* 17, no. 5 (1990), p. 21.
49. Paul Kennedy and Bruce Russett, "Reforming the United Nations," *Foreign Affairs,* September–October 1995, p. 68.
50. John Gerard Ruggie, "The United States and the United Nations: Toward a New Realism," in *International Organizations: Patterns and Insights,* ed. Paul F. Diehl (Chicago: Dorsey Press, 1989), pp. 402–4.
51. Childers, "The UN at 50," p. 8.
52. Ibid., p. 8.
53. Hans J. Morgenthau, *Politics Among Nations: The Struggle for Power and Peace,* 5th ed. (New York: Alfred A. Knopf, 1978); Clive Archer, *International Organizations* (London: George Allen & Unwin, 1983), pp. 74–80; Francis Anthony Boyle, *World Politics and International Law* (Durham, NC: Duke University Press, 1985), pp. 11–12.
54. Boyle, *World Politics and International Law,* pp. 16, 70–73.
55. Kenneth N. Waltz, *Theory of International Politics* (Reading, MA: Addison-Wesley, 1979), pp. 42, 164.
56. See, for example, Waltz, ibid., pp. 169, 171, 183.
57. Ernest W. Lefever, "Reining in the U.N.," *Foreign Affairs,* Summer 1993, pp. 18–20.
58. Robert O. Keohane and Joseph S. Nye, *Power and Interdependence,* 2nd ed. (Boston: Scott, Foresman, 1989), p. 240.
59. John G. Ruggie, "On the Problem of 'the Global Problematique': What Roles for International Organizations?" in *The United Nations and a Just World Order,* ed. Richard A. Falk, Samuel S. Kim, and Saul H. Mendlovitz (Boulder, CO: Westview Press, 1991), pp. 447–66.
60. Ernst B. Haas, *When Knowledge Is Power: Three Models of Change in International Organizations* (Berkeley, CA: University of California Press, 1990), pp. 1–3.

PART FOUR

SHARING A PLANET AND PLANETARY EXPERIENCES

CHAPTER 13

ENVIRONMENT OF HUMANKIND: A FUTURE IN JEOPARDY

The world's **environment,** the surrounding physical conditions of the globe, has helped crystallize the idea that humanity has a common, interdependent future more than any other issue has. Only by a major effort, requiring the cooperation of peoples and governments around the world, can humankind hope to survive and prosper within a sustaining environment.

Humankind has occupied planet Earth for thousands of years, but in modern times, human effects on the planet have rapidly accelerated. Incredible developments in technology, a fivefold growth in the world economy since 1950, and a burgeoning population of over 6 billion people have placed enormous demands on the planet's resources in a short time, demands that will grow dramatically as we enter the 21st century. For instance, since 1950, grain needs, water use, and the burning of firewood have tripled. Seafood consumption has risen four times, paper production is up sixfold, and lumber use has more than doubled.[1]

Fearing that an overexploitation of the earth's resources will cause environmental collapse, a worldwide environmental movement now urges humankind to find ways to live in balance with the natural environment. The environmental movement began with citizens at the local level advocating family planning, the recycling of materials, and laws that would protect air and water quality for national communities. In the United States, the celebration of Earth Day on April 22 every year since 1970 is a tribute to environmental action by private citizens.

By the 1990s, the grass-roots environmental movement came to emphasize a transnational approach since many problems, such as acid rain, fail to heed borders and because people around the planet must somehow share the resources of the "global commons," such as the fish catch from the oceans. Multiple actors, including states, international government organizations (IGOs) such as the United Nations, and international nongovernment organizations (INGOs) such as Greenpeace and Worldwatch, are making strides to protect and manage the various elements of the earth's environment. This cooperation converges around regimes, with their norms and rules, to provide environmental governance in the absence of a true global authority. Although various environmental regimes exist, the rhetoric about environmental governance has so far outweighed effective action.[2]

In this chapter, we first explore the nature of human interaction with the natural environment to assess how severely humankind has jeopardized its future. Then we identify and describe the role of the core variables concerning human behavior that are the driving forces behind the degradation of the earth's environment, a degradation that is occurring on an element-by-element basis that includes the atmosphere, water, soil, forests, and wildlife. Next, we examine the evolution of governance for the preservation of the global environment, an evolution propelled by the growth of a civil society that operates transnationally. Finally, we look at how this evolution in turn contributes to the development of an international society.

HUMAN ECOLOGY

All animal and plant species depend on the life support system known as the **biosphere,** the thin layers of soil, ocean, climate, and atmosphere that envelop the planet.[3] The study of species interacting with the biosphere is **ecology.** Thus, when we study the human interaction with the biosphere, we are investigating **human ecology.** This interaction can be a healthy one, with humankind balancing what it takes from the natural environment with what the biosphere can afford to provide. Alternatively, **ecocide** can take place, meaning humans can cause the widespread destruction of the natural environment. Humankind is now at a crossroads, able to overwhelm the planet's support capabilities or to turn matters around and preserve its life-giving qualities for future generations.

Basically, two views exist as to how human ecology should operate. One is the view of the environmentalists, who think humankind must work hard to protect the natural environment before time runs out. Environmentalists reject the view that humankind occupies a special place in nature as the earth's landlord and privileged exploiter.[4] Environmentalists want humankind to practice a *stewardship* of the earth that calls for protecting nature. A stewardship role is not really a new idea, since most cultures and religions since ancient times have appreciated nature's gifts. Environmentalists today only ask people to renew a sense of stewardship of the earth, for instance, in a way similar to that of Native Americans (American Indians). Native Americans have viewed the earth as a "mother," a fertile giver of life, and, in traditional times, lived in harmony with nature.[5]

As a part of stewardship, environmentalists also call for *intergenerational equity,* meaning each generation inherits the natural environment from the previous generation and then holds it in a moral trust for the next generation. To provide a sound environmental future, environmentalists urge that humankind hold its numbers and lifestyles within the **carrying capacity** of the earth; that is, people must live on the rate of resources the planet can generate over time. Otherwise, humankind will surpass the earth's carrying capacity by living off the environmental "capital" instead of the environmental "interest."[6] Unfortunately, according to most environmentalists, many people around the world are still abusing the planet's natural bounty by living for today without planning for tomorrow. If the earth's population were to achieve a long-term, sustainable balance between their use of natural resources and a preserved biosphere, they would be living in a global **steady-state society.**[7]

The most far-reaching argument for protecting the earth's environment is that of scientist James Lovelock. His theoretical notion, named the **Gaia hypothesis** after the ancient Greek goddess who nurtured and cared for earth, views the planet as alive and functioning as one superorganism. Within this superorganism, living species, both flora and fauna, interact with geophysical and chemical processes to maintain conditions suitable for life.

Lovelock's approach is *holistic* in the sense that the earth amounts to an organic whole greater than the sum of its elements. For him, all the elements are interdependent, and so harm to one part of the biosphere can easily spread to other parts.[8] The Gaia hypothesis has inspired a flood of research, and the first major scientific conference based on this hypothesis took place in 1988.

The other view of how human ecology should operate is that of *eco-optimists,* who believe the world's resources are adequate and, as scarcity occurs in a natural resource area, human ingenuity and technology will take care of any problem. For eco-optimists, the earth is so vast and nature so powerful that nothing people can do will have a major or lasting effect on the normal functioning of the biosphere.[9] Eco-optimists frequently are market economists who see the environment as provider of natural resources for conversion into human use. From this perspective, more people in the world simply means more production and consumption take place, developments that are healthy market forces. Overburdening the carrying capacity of the planet hardly enters into their thinking.

Market economists are not worried that human ecology has veered into destructive practices. These economists are confident that the free market economy can provide for all human needs and that economic competition can produce the technology to use resources efficiently. The market economy can postpone indefinitely the problems of scarcity and the subsequent problems of poverty and conflict. Besides, these economists claim, not only is an infinite supply of natural resources available, but "sinks" are available for disposing of various types of wastes made from processing natural resources into products for human use.[10]

The eco-optimists' view is a human-centered one that allows for a predatory relationship with the elements of the biosphere. The eco-optimists had considerable influence in the United States during the Ronald Reagan and George Bush presidencies, as well as in some other countries, and fought a strong rear-guard action in the World Bank before environmental priorities gained favor. In the United States, the election in 1992 of Bill Clinton as president and Al Gore as vice president, with Gore's positive environmental record in the U.S. Senate being well known, marked a renewal of environmental protection as a government priority.

Although it began within national contexts, the environmental movement soon became an international one, as the UN Conference of the Human Environment at Stockholm in 1972 demonstrates. This global movement reached its high-water mark with the UN Conference on Environment and Development of 1992 (UNCED, also known as the Earth Summit) held in Rio de Janeiro. While the global environmental movement does not represent a consensus of opinion or a concerted plan of action, masses of people at the grass-roots level, their national governments, and a variety of international organizations have a growing awareness that cumulative stresses are imperiling the environment. These stresses endanger food supplies, harm human health, and even threaten the much-sought-after economic development of poorer countries.

In spite of growing environmental awareness and thousands of environmental activists organized from the local to the global levels, it is safe to say the world's physical environment continues to deteriorate. The greatest danger is that humankind will set off unchecked degradation that will pass a point of no return, making it impossible to restore a healthy environment. In 1992, 1,600 scientists, including 102 Nobel laureates, issued a "Warning to Humanity." They asserted that we were reaching a dangerous stage regarding the

© Watterson. Dist. by Universal Press Syndicate. Reprinted with permission. All rights reserved.

planet's life support system.[11] As humans move mountains, reverse the flow of rivers, build cities in deserts, burn tropical forests, pollute the atmosphere with smokestacks, and stuff mountains of refuse into the earth, it is becoming increasingly evident that the practice of human ecology is more exploitative of nature than protective. Several examples of environmental abuse will illustrate this point.

Sometimes abuse occurs as a by-product of attempts to accomplish worthy human goals; other times abuse is pure human folly. The Soviet Union built unsafe nuclear reactors throughout the country to produce cheap electricity, but one result was the meltdown of a nuclear energy plant at Chernobyl in the Ukraine in 1986. This accident killed hundreds and caused cancer and birth defects for thousands more. To grow cotton by irrigation methods, the Soviets also diverted huge amounts of water from the Aral Sea, once the fourth largest inland sea in the world. Channeling this sea into irrigation ditches interrupted the restoration process of the sea, leaving large fishing boats at rest on the dry bed of the much reduced Aral Sea. During the Cold War, at least five submarines sank in accidents that deposited nuclear weapons and nuclear reactors on the bottoms of the oceans, where they are now deteriorating and leaking radiation. In addition, people around the world have recklessly sprayed pesticides to save crops from insects, but an unforeseen, major threat to bird life occurred as well.

Often simple human folly has wrought great environmental damage. Because a ship's captain was drinking in his cabin and left an inexperienced pilot in charge, the supertanker *Exxon Valdez* ran aground on rocks off the Alaska coast in 1989. This wreck created the largest oil spill in U.S. history. Thousands of birds, seals, and sea otters perished, and commercial fishing experienced a blow from which it will take many years to recover. In 1991, the Iraqis, after losing the Persian Gulf War, spitefully released oil to foul Saudi Arabia's desalinization plants and set fire to over 600 Kuwaiti oil wells, acts certainly unrelated to military necessity and probably in violation of the international laws of war.

When human ecology results in environmental deterioration, human conflict will almost surely intensify as a result of growing scarcity. In particular, Oran R. Young worries that conflict will derive from a growing human population placing higher demands on the earth's natural systems.[12] Scarcity, of course, intensifies the competition over "who gets what, when, and how," thus contributing to more deadly global quarrels. Scarcity and the

David Turnley/Corbis/Black Star

U.S.S.R. Fishing boats lie marooned far away from the receding waters of the Aral Sea, which has shrunk two-thirds in 30 years.

conflict it spawns are doubtlessly behind some local and regional clashes that now disturb the world's post–Cold War hopes for a more peaceful world order. Some futurists have predicted environmental collapse by the mid-21st century, resulting in nightmarish levels of conflict.[13]

Thomas Homer-Dixon makes the interesting observation that states are more likely to fight over *nonrenewable resources* such as oil and minerals and less likely to fight over *renewable resources* such as fisheries.[14] Pressures for oil supplies on the part of Japan before the Second World War and Western states' fear of losing oil supplies before the Persian Gulf War in 1991 are good examples of conflict over nonrenewable resources. Professor Homer-Dixon does think interstate conflict might occur over the renewable resource of river water as demands on water grow.[15] Nearly 40 percent of the world's people live in river basins shared by two or more countries. Although other issues are present, sharing the Indus River does not improve India's and Pakistan's relationship. Nor will Israel's dependence on the Jordan River, a dependence shared with the two Arab states of Jordan and Syria, ease these states' other problems.[16] Israel has diverted much of the headwaters of the Jordan River for its irrigation needs and siphoned off the aquifer beneath the West Bank, where Palestinian self-rule is at a fledgling stage. The Israelis use five times the water per person allowed to the Palestinians.[17]

Furthermore, environmental degradation encourages migration as overpopulation and soil depletion stir people to move on to a more productive place. Sometimes the migration takes people across international borders. Bengali Muslims from Eastern Pakistan (the independent state of Bangladesh since 1971) crowded into the Indian state of Assam over a period of years, finally provoking an attack by the local Lalung tribal people, who massacred 1,700 Bengalis in 1983. As this case shows, ethnic conflicts can originate from environmental stress that forces two or more groups to compete for the same land and resources.[18] Finally, the migration of El Salvadorians to Honduras, spurred by land stress and the uneven distribution of land, contributed to the so-called Soccer War of 1969 between the two states.[19]

Scarcity within Third World countries, produced by growing numbers of people exercising rising expectations, has pressured governments to deliver social services and goods that are simply unavailable. The inevitable shortfall between what people need and want and what the government can deliver results in instability. Frequently a government with inadequate resources to match people's demands chooses to rely on political repression for control.[20] For instance, Haiti, the poorest country in the Western Hemisphere and one of the world's most dramatic cases of environmental despoilation, experienced repressive, authoritarian rule until the mid-1990s. Historically, a small mulatto elite suppressed the black majority so this elite could seize the limited wealth of Haiti for themselves. Once called the "Pearl of the Antilles," Haiti now stands bare of its forests and experiences worsening erosion problems. Haiti's new democratic government, coping with a population that will double by 2025, may face unsurmountable problems as it tries to regenerate Haiti's economic growth from a ruined resource base. Haiti's environmental degradation may have crossed the threshold of irreversibility, meaning more instability and authoritarian government for the future of this sad country.[21]

THE CORE VARIABLES

We have learned that human interaction with the planet's ecology is harming the environment, sometimes leading to scarcity and conflict. In this section, we will identify the core variables involved in human behavior that are behind most environmental problems. These variables are the size and growth of the human population, economic growth, and the effects of technological developments. The core variables closely intertwine. For example, as the population grows in size, the economy must expand to accommodate more people who need jobs, housing, clothes, and much else. As the economy expands, technology also evolves, sometimes adversely affecting the environment and other times helping to save resources.

Population

If there is a starting point for explaining environmental deterioration, it is human population pressures. The human population has grown at an exponential, or geometric, rate at least since the nineteenth century. From 1 billion people in that century, the world population jumped to 2 billion by 1930 and, in 1975, rose to over 4 billion. In July 1987, the United Nations symbolically declared Matej Gaspar, upon his birth in Zagreb, Yugoslavia, to be the five billionth person in the world. Today over six billion people live on the planet, and the human population could rise anywhere from 9 to 14 billion during the 21st century, depending on what the present generation does about population control. This exponential growth has been possible because of the widespread dispersal of twentieth-century food and medical technologies that allow birth rates to exceed death rates on a regular basis.

Environmentalists have accurately understood the centrality of population's connection to the environment, but awareness by governments and publics in general has lagged far behind. Population growth is a "slow crisis" because it amasses into a problem over decades. Such gradual change does not lend itself to easy perception and has a hard time competing for attention with the threat of nuclear war, the fall of European communism, terrorism, ethnic conflicts, and even the pandemic proportions of AIDS, crises that have appeared on the scene with relative suddenness.

At least some efforts toward world population control have taken place. Although the critical role of population did not receive due attention at the Earth Summit in 1992, the United Nations has sponsored global population conferences every 10 years, the last being the important UN International Conference on Population and Development at Cairo, Egypt, in 1994. The United Nations also has operated the UN Population Fund since 1967, using voluntary funds to assist countries in planning and operating population control programs. At the Cairo conference, despite some fractious opposition by Catholic and Muslim church leaders, 182 countries acceded to the "Program of Action," calling for countries to provide $17 billion by the year 2000 to curb population growth. The Cairo conference set the ambitious target of leveling the world population at 7.8 billion in 2050.[22] The ultimate goal is to achieve **zero population growth,** meaning each couple will have only two children to replace themselves on the planet.

The "Program of Action" focuses on women as a strategy to control population growth. As women's education improves and as women take jobs and start businesses, the population growth rate should decline. Frequently education and careers persuade women to overcome traditional values calling for women to stay home and raise large families. Not only does the environment and economic development benefit from reforms for women, but women also are more likely to achieve gender equality if they have smaller families.

Since it will be decades before the human population stabilizes, the impact on the environment will intensify meanwhile as 100 million new births each year add to the burden of the world's carrying capacity. About 90 percent of this population growth is taking place in Third World countries, where human services are already inadequate. Nor does the smaller population growth in the Western world offer much encouragement, because each Westerner consumes from 10 to 30 times the resources a Third World individual does. Although there can be mitigating circumstances, such as the culture and economic level of the region or country, each person in a population makes some demand on the environment to provide resources and absorb wastes and pollutants.[23]

On the matter of population growth, the United States National Academy of Sciences and the Royal Society of London issued a highly unusual joint statement in 1992 stating that the annual growth of 100 million people in the world is the principal cause of destruction of the world's forests, of global warming, and of the unprecedented pace of extinction of species.[24] Population burdens also contribute to cropland loss, soil erosion, water shortages, and air and ocean pollution, and create mountains of trash.

Finally, not only does the environment suffer from overpopulation but so do the people themselves, because the needs of millions go unfulfilled. While inadequate sources of food and water exist in rural areas, especially in Africa, it is in the mushrooming cities of the Third World where people live in true misery. Only one city of over 5 million people existed in the Third World in 1950, but by the year 2000 there will be 46 such cities.[25] According to the World Bank, several cities, including Bombay, Lagos, Jakarta, Karachi, Sao Paulo, and Shanghai, plus Tokyo in the industrialized world, will have over 20 million people by the year 2015. Such *mega-cities* struggle to achieve and maintain a good quality

POPULATION STABILIZATION
The Real Solution

OVERPOPULATION
The Root of The Problem

Reprinted with permission of Sierra Club.

of life. In the slums of mega-cities, large numbers of dwellers suffer from a lack of clean water and air, must live with open sewers, experience high crime and unemployment rates, and develop a variety of illnesses due to hygiene deficiencies. Human misery may soon worsen because by 2020, more than half of the world's population will live in cities.[26] In 1996, the UN Conference on Human Settlements met in Istanbul, Turkey, to deal with these problems. At this "City Summit," many countries turned in a variety of plans for making burgeoning cities more livable.

Another core variable putting pressure on the natural environment is economic growth. When more people need and want to consume, an economy already operating on a global scale tends to expand. Economic activity causes environmental problems through the extraction, manufacture, distribution, and consumption of natural resources.[27] During the conversion of natural resources for human use, a basic law of nature, the "conservation of matter," is at work. Whatever goes into production and consumption must come out, either as useful goods or as waste materials.

Further, economic growth means the depletion of the stock of nonrenewable resources such as coal, oil, natural gas, and minerals. Economic expansion also can consume renewable resources—for instance, soil, forest products, fish, and water—faster than their renewable rate. Aesthetic properties of nature do not fare well either. Strip-mining levels mountains. Industrial runoff causes polluted, smelly streams. Sales of camping gear, from tents to recreational vehicles, allow growing numbers of visitors to overwhelm national parks.[28]

Unfortunately, the depletion of nonrenewable resources and the slow replenishment of renewable resources do not show up in standard economic measures, such as the GNP or the GNP per capita for a given country. Reports on economic income fail to offer a ledger with a line entry for the loss of natural resources. Leaders typically brag about economic growth and national income as though resources were inexhaustible. Yet a narrow focus on the economic dimension of human activity either ignores legitimate environmental concerns or assumes humankind can circumvent scarcities by shifting to different resources or by improving technology.[29]

A wide-open use of finite natural resources cannot go on forever. At a time when three-fourths of the human population, living in the South, insist on expanding their economies, they face doubtful prospects if they weaken their environmental foundation.[30] The economic development of today can so stress the environment that economic development tomorrow will fall short of what billions more people will need and want. Kenya offers an interesting case. Although Kenya is a country-case Western economists often choose to cite as a success story on the hard-pressed African continent, Kenya's future may be bleak. Kenya enjoyed an average economic growth rate of only 0.3 percent in GNP per capita from 1980 to 1993. In the same period, a high average consumption rate among Kenyans of 4.7 percent growth and a high population growth rate of 3.3 percent diminished their environmental foundation. This foundation increasingly lacks the resilience and potential needed for further economic expansion.[31] Overpopulation in particular causes such problems as the desertification of the country's soil and the poaching of wildlife, the feature attraction of Kenya's lucrative foreign tourist industry. Kenya is a country of 27 million people and will probably reach 45 million by the year 2010.

Proper environmental management does not have to restrict economic growth; in fact, a synergy between the economy and the environment is plausible. Efforts to save the environment create new jobs in research and technology development as industrial enterprises offer such products as electric-powered cars and water-efficient flush toilets. Pressure to save energy has made some countries even more competitive in international trade, as happened for the robust German and Japanese economies of the 1980s.[32] The United States presently has the most competitive national economy in the world and does so with some of the toughest environmental laws and the third largest national population in the world. Casting a shadow over the United States' economic future, however, is a rapid rate of depletion of its national resource base and the addition each year of 2 million more people to the present population, which already is reaching 262 million.

Recognizing the ongoing conflict between most economic activities and the health of the environment, scholars and leaders have turned to the broad approach of **sustainable development,** a concept similar to stewardship but with an economic focus. In 1987, the Bruntland Report, formally titled *Our Common Future,* by the World Commission on Environment and Development popularized the widely accepted definition of sustainable development. This development is humankind's ability to ensure that it meets the economic needs of the present without compromising the ability of future generations to respond to their own needs. The Bruntland Report takes the position that both economic and environmental objectives are achievable if planners use proper technology and social organization.[33] Implicitly, sustainable development requires the replenishment of natural resources at the same rate as people use them.[34] Although the world falls short of practicing sustainable development in renewable resources, the Achilles' heel of this economic/environment approach is nonrenewable resources. Finding energy resources after oil runs out is the most critical issue of the economic/environmental nexus.

Energy is a prerequisite for economic development and a higher standard of living. Since the Industrial Revolution of the eighteenth century, the world has primarily used one or another form of fossil fuel. By the end of the nineteenth century, energy use began to shift from coal to oil, especially after the development of the internal combustion engine. Not only is oil becoming scarce, but burning petroleum, in its various forms, is detrimental to the environment. At its present rate of use, oil can last for about 40 years and natural gas for approximately 60 years. Natural gas also is expensive and difficult to liquefy, a necessary step for its transportation. Coal is still available in copious amounts, but it is a dirty fuel to use and is the chief culprit causing acid rain.[35]

The pressure on oil, as well as the desire for more minerals, has led to demands for mining Antarctica. This continent amounts to 10 percent of the earth's land and water mass, and it is a nearly pristine **ecosystem,** one of the few balanced, healthy environments left in the world. Many countries have agreed to ban military activities under the Antarctica Treaty of 1959 and to refrain from mining as well. Although several countries have not surrendered territorial claims to parts of Antarctica, world opinion increasingly views Antarctica as belonging to the "common heritage" of humankind.

Instead of hoping to find more fossil fuel, industrial scientists should give priority to converting to alternative energies, not only for the environment's sake but so future generations will have sufficient energy available. Research on energy from solar, wind, geothermal, ocean tides, and ethanol sources continues, but an adequate and practical replacement for oil remains elusive. The once expected blessings from splitting the atom for peaceful purposes now mixes with the dangers of accidental meltdowns of nuclear reactors as well as the long-term, problematic storage of spent nuclear fuel.

Humankind, as an intelligent and social animal, can think about the future and recognize that human society, nationally and internationally, requires fundamental reorganization to maintain a healthy environment. Nonetheless, other priorities probably will take precedence over environmental concerns for the foreseeable future. Certainly wealth accumulation still comes first as the North pursues ever-higher standards of living and the South scrambles to catch up through economic development programs. Both work on their respective development goals and strategies, while each blames the other for failing to show restraint for the environment's sake. Together the North and South are hurting the chances for expanding an international economy that is already struggling to provide for billions of people. With the passing of the Cold War, humankind may have escaped the cataclysm of a nuclear holocaust only to face the degradation of human life, as world economic decline must surely follow environmental decline.

The third and last core variable affecting the environment is the role of technology. Technology has not freed humankind from dependence on nature but has allowed us to borrow, transform, consume, and discard the substance of nature as we wish.[36] Technology concerns the tools and processes that change natural resources into something humans use. It would be wonderful if miraculous technological breakthroughs allowed for sustainable development, but the real story of technology is a mixed one at best.

Although technology has a history of depleting stocks of the earth's resources and leaving wastes and pollutants in the wake of economic activities, properly designed technology can use resources sparingly and minimize harm. Efficient drip irrigation, the development of nonwood pulp for paper, hybrid seeds for larger crop yields, recycling of materials, and the use of unleaded gasoline are a few examples of environmental progress through better technology. However, wiser use of technology can only buy time while we bring population growth and consumption rates down to sustainable levels.[37]

The role of computers vividly illustrates the mixed effects of technology. Computers allow artificial testing of the air coefficient of cars, the strength of architectural designs, the flight performance of planes, and many other products before manufacturing begins, thus saving a lot of material resources that would otherwise go into experimental models and production units that would not perform adequately. Computers also keep track of such matters as pollutants, biodiversity, the disappearance of tropical forests, and much else related to the environment. By accounting for many variables, computers can forecast the deterioration of the environment and generally create models of future environmental scenarios.

Computers can cause problems for the environment as well. Computers are a major consumer of electricity, and their human operators sometimes develop carpal tunnel syndrome (inflammation of the wrists), requiring surgery. Moreover, toxic waste results from the manufacture of microchips, including glycol ethers, which have caused miscarriages in their female human makers. Finally, the operation of computers causes a growing demand for paper at the expense of the world's forests.[38] The prediction that computers would put information into electronic storage and thus save paper has not come true. Everyone still wants hardcopy in addition to a computer-stored record.

Multinational corporations (MNCs), as the major innovators and transmitters of technology, quickly spread technology and its mixed effects on a global basis. Fortunately, most MNCs do not seek "pollution havens," where environmental laws are weak or nonexistent, to save money on the new technology needed for environmental protection. The United States, for instance, has tough environmental laws, yet this country attracts many foreign MNCs and ranks first in the world as the recipient for foreign direct investment.[39]

In addition, through modern transportation technology, MNCs carry on the bulk of international trade. Regrettably, this trade contributes to a misperception that countries can exceed their environmental limits. By importing numerous goods and materials, major trade countries may create the illusion that infinite supplies of resources are available. In reality, all imports draw from the natural capital of the one finite planet that we all share.[40]

ELEMENTS OF THE ENVIRONMENT

If population, economic activities, and technology have combined to wreak a hardship on the physical environment of the planet, how much damage to and depletion of the natural elements of the biosphere have occurred? The elements we will focus on are the atmosphere, water, soil, forests, and wildlife.

Atmosphere

Of all the damage occurring to the biosphere, nothing has captured the attention of public opinion, the media, the scientific community, and governments as have concerns over the atmosphere. One concern is *global warming*, or the "greenhouse effect." An accumulating blanket of waste gases are trapping the sun's heat close to the earth's surface. The chief

Scott Willis

culprit is carbon dioxide emitted from burning wood fires and coal and the use of natural gas and petroleum products. The world's factories, power plants, and automobiles pumped 186 billion tons of carbon into the atmosphere between 1945 and 1995, more than three times the amount in all previous history.[41] In an early 1997 visit to China, Vice President Al Gore urged China's leaders to control emissions that are contributing to the greenhouse effect as they expand their huge economy.

The greenhouse effect may be raising the earth's overall temperature by two degrees or more. Although some scientists dispute the greenhouse effect, the 1990s are the warmest decade in history. A variety of long-term, harmful effects could be under way. Animal and plant life may suffer from unnatural temperatures, and coral reefs will "bleach" white from warmer water. The melting of ice in the Arctic and Antarctic and from mountain glaciers will raise ocean levels, thus endangering island countries and countries with low-lying plains meeting their ocean fronts, such as Bangladesh. Recently the remains of a 4,000-year-old man were found in the Alps only because of unusual ice melt in these European mountains.[42]

Another concern is *ozone depletion,* which allows an unnatural degree of ultraviolet solar radiation to reach the earth, causing skin cancer and related deaths. The ozone layer protecting earth has depleted by 30 percent in the last 40 years. This problem became a major concern with the discovery of the "ozone hole" over Antarctica in 1985, a hole the size of Europe in square miles. The release of humanmade chloroflurocarbons (CFCs) into the atmosphere is depleting the ozone layer. The use of CFCs in house and car air conditioning, refrigeration, solvents, and aerosol cans has been the culprit. The CFCs, once free, rise to the stratosphere, where they break up and release chlorine that destroys ozone.[43] The effects on the ozone layer have caused such concern that they have probably brought about the most important environmental treaty to date, the Montreal Protocol of 1987. This treaty and its updates have called for an end of CFC production by the year 2000 and for states to provide $240 million in foreign aid to help developing countries purchase CFC substitutes.[44] The more modern countries have already devised new types of air conditioners and coolants to replace CFCs.

While the ozone layer may repair itself in 50 years, an immediate danger remains. The illegal importation of CFCs from Third World countries, such as India and Mexico, where their manufacture is still allowable, may undermine chances for restoring the ozone layer. The expense of refurbishing older automobile car air conditioners is behind the multimillion-dollar U.S. black market in freon, known as C-12, which the United States stopped making in 1995. In early 1997, the U.S. Justice Department reported that its officers had confiscated 1.5 million pounds of illegal freon, but 20 million pounds probably crossed the U.S. border illegally in 1996.

Water

To many people, the oceans of the world and the powerful rivers that flow into them appear so vast that they should provide an unlimited supply of water and fish and offer a bottomless "sink" for wastes. Oceans and rivers, however, are not limitless. Dumping refuse in the ocean, discharging sewage and industrial waste into rivers, and allowing the runoff from fertilizers and petroleum products from farms and cities to make their way via rivers to coastal wetlands and then on to the oceans cause multiple harms. Animal and marine life become sick and die, recreational use of beaches declines, and fishers' livelihood and the human food supply based on fish diminish.[45] Marine biologists and environmentalists fear that ocean pollution has reached epidemic proportions, and we are only beginning to offer the oceans some protection.

The immediate impact on humankind from a deteriorating ocean environment is the depletion of fisheries. Growing numbers of people have come to count on ocean fish catch as part of their diet, including populations of landlocked countries. Environmental damage to fish life joins the problem of overharvesting the fish stocks of the seas. The worldwide catch climbed fivefold since 1950, but peaked and began to decline in 1989. Further, aquaculture, the raising of fish in ponds, has not made up for the losses in fish catches. The UN Food and Agricultural Organization (FAO) has reported that the 17 major fisheries of the world's oceans have reached or exceeded their natural limits, with 9 of them in especially serious decline.[46]

Over 37,000 high-tech boats, many equipped with sonar gear and freezers, pursue the declining schools of fish. Fishing boats must now range across thousands of miles of ocean to bring home a sufficient catch. As a result, squabbles among fishers operating boats under different national flags are growing, as is the scarcity of fish. All of the poorer fishing countries are hurting their economic futures, as well as their present food supplies, because they are exporting much of their fish catch for foreign income instead of managing sustainable fisheries.[47]

Fresh water is another resource that people easily take for granted. For several generations, humankind has been fouling and exhausting a precious resource necessary for all life on the planet. The use of water worldwide doubled between 1940 and 1980 and will double again by the year 2000.[48] More than 1.2 billion people around the world presently lack readily available, safe drinking water. Millions of women and girls spend hours every day trekking miles to fetch water to their homes.[49] Water shortages force people to drink water tainted by industrial chemicals and limit the amount of crops farmers can grow. Moreover, a scarcity of good water not only is a problem in Third World countries but is almost a

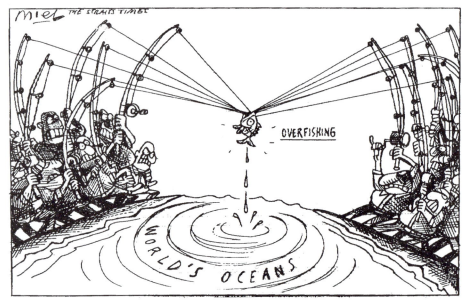

Miel/*Straits Times*/Singapore

universal concern. Insufficient water supplies due to rising population numbers now threaten the Florida Everglades. In the American West, city dwellers fight with ranchers over water to a degree reminiscent of the legendary conflicts among ranchers for water in the last century's Old West.

The development of water treatment plants and drip-water irrigation is a positive step, but technology has yet to preserve aquifers serving farms and cities around the world. Aquifers, such as those under the lower American Midwest, Beijing, and Mexico City, are dropping in water levels at a rate measurable in feet per year.[50] Because new discoveries of water are unlikely and desalinization of ocean water is expensive, humankind must stop polluting the water we have and find the most efficient ways to use water. While water is not finite in the strictest sense, it takes years to clean up surface water in rivers and replenish underground aquifers. Presently, humans are losing the water battle as their numbers multiply.

Soil

Similar to replenishing fresh water, soil rich enough to grow crops can replenish itself, but only over a period of years and through the decay of organic material. However, the global pattern is for soil erosion to overpower topsoil replenishment. The *desertification* of land, the process of turning arable land into a desert through drought or overfarming, is taking place at an alarming rate. A three-year study by 250 scientists located around the world, the *Global Assessment of Soil Degradation,* concluded that 550 million hectares (a hectare is a metric measure equaling 2.471 acres) are losing topsoil or undergoing other forms of degradation.[51] Some authorities estimate the affected soil areas as much larger, but it is safe to say that arable land for supplying food for humans, livestock, and wildlife is definitely in decline.

Between the 1960s and 1980s, the "green revolution"—based on hybrid seeds producing bountiful crop yields, the widespread use of chemical fertilizers and pesticides, and the improvements in farm machinery and technology—promised enough food for the world's population. This development appeared to cheat Thomas Malthus (1766–1834) out of any theoretical credibility.[52] The Malthusian theory claimed population was growing at an exponential, or geometric, rate, while food production advanced at only an arithmetical rate. According to Malthus, food supplies would inevitably fall short of population needs unless war and famine balanced population numbers with food availability.

Nowadays fears are arising again over some form of a Malthusian crisis because food production is plateauing while population growth remains robust. Food returns from high-tech farming are diminishing, with grain production either at a standstill or in decline, depending on the specific grain. Overall, between 1984 and 1993, grain production fell 11 percent per person. Hunger, malnutrition, and rising food prices are the unfortunate outcomes. China in particular is in a position to drive grain market supplies and prices in a way that will mean less grain and higher prices. China shifted from the status of a net grain exporter of 8 million tons in 1994 to a net grain importer of 16 million tons in 1995. China's economic growth rate of 10 percent a year, based on a 1.2 billion population that is still growing, means China will inevitably tighten the world grain market.[53]

Food supplies and population growth by themselves, however, do not explain food shortages. The extent of human generosity with food aid, or its absence, both internationally and domestically, is important too. Because of a maldistribution in global wealth, people in the West are overeating to an unhealthy extent, while the excess food should go to feed hungry Africans. Also, venal elites in many Third World countries live well by charging the masses high food prices and converting cropland to cash crops for the export market. In war, scorched-earth policies, blockades, and the theft of food supplies are common methods of forcing one side's will on the other side, as the world recently witnessed in Bosnia and Somalia. As a result of these influences on food supply, about one billion people in the world are chronically hungry, and many die from causes related to malnourishment.[54]

Forests

Forest destruction has become an urgent worldwide issue. Today forests cover about one-fourth less of the earth's land surface than in 1700, and the disappearance rate today is one-and-one-half acres per second.[55] Rainforests, which gird the earth at the equator, receive the most attention. Rainforests that once covered 16 percent of the earth's surface now cover only 7 percent, a loss involving millions of acres per year.[56] As examples, Africa has lost 60 percent of its forest cover, and Haiti now stands virtually denuded of its forests, as mentioned earlier.[57] Further, the forests of Europe and North America suffer depletion of their hardwoods and pines through overcutting and acid rain. Europe, for instance, has lost 35 percent of its forest cover since the industrial age began.[58]

Clearing forests for cattle ranching, selling timber to industrialized countries, and the widespread burning of firewood in the Third World for warmth and cooking are the chief causes of the depletion of tropical forests. The loss of these forests on a massive scale hurts the environment in several ways. Trees not only hold the soil in place to prevent erosion but

Mauldin, reprinted with permission, *Chicago Sun-Times*, © 1997.

also "scrub" the air by absorbing carbon dioxide and releasing oxygen. Burning forests in Brazil and other countries to make way for ranches not only leaves fewer trees for "scrubbing" the air but adds to the waste gases creating the greenhouse effect.

In addition, when large tracts of forest disappear, so does much of the planet's **biodiversity,** the great variety of animal and plant life involving thousands of species. Not only is aesthetic appreciation at stake, but the many useful products the earth's biodiversity provides are in danger. The drug for childhood leukemia and Hodgkin's disease comes from the rosy periwinkle plant found in tropical forests. When President Reagan fell wounded from an assassin's bullet, doctors stabilized his blood pressure by using a medicine derived from the venom of an Amazonian bush viper.[59] Many of today's prescription drugs contain ingredients found in rainforest regions. If humans can restrain their harmful intrusions, the biodiversity of rainforests can do much for humankind. Much of this biodiversity still awaits discovery if "development" does not destroy it first.

Finally, the rainforests are home to many groups of indigenous peoples, such as the Yanomamo Indians of Brazil and the Penan people living in Malaysian Borneo. While indigenous peoples usually live exemplary lives in balance with their environment, they are highly vulnerable to the interferences of more sophisticated peoples, with their extractive technology for mining and logging. Cutting forests for ranches and mining for gold are literally eliminating the homeland of the Yanomamo, while the logging industry is doing the same to the Penan.

Environmentalists who have urged the preservation of the rainforests have run head on into the economic North-South controversy. The South's cutting and burning of its rainforest, from their perspective, is helping economic development but, as the North sees it, these activities are causing environmental disaster. Leaders in the tropical areas have suggested that the richer countries of the North either reward them with more development aid for

Chapter 13 / Environment of Humankind: A Future in Jeopardy   445

Zero Population Growth,
Jan/Feb 1996.

Seal trapped in plastic net.

preserving the forests or stop meddling in their business. The 1996 Brazil–United States partnership, formed to jointly develop the resources of the tropical forests, indicates somewhat less antagonism along the North-South line of conflict.

Recently, as environmental awareness has risen at home in Brazil and other tropical states, the deforestation process has slowed. The economic advantages of leaving the forests standing are coming into better view as well. Rubber tapping, providing medicines, and the harvesting of fruits, nuts, and resins result from leaving forests standing.[61] While the exploitation of forests still exceeds a sustainable rate, the view that humankind needs to harvest the wealth of the forests as much as the forests themselves is on the rise.

Wildlife

Animals are important for many reasons, not the least of which is aesthetic appreciation of their beauty and fascinating behaviors. Tragically, humankind, supposedly the most intelligent species on earth, frequently interacts with other animal species in ways that cause terrible harm.

The economic motive of humans, involving both legal and illegal means, has led to wanton abuse that threatens some animal species with extinction. Fishing with miles-wide drift nets traps nonfish marine species, often drowning them, and fishers throw the dead sea turtles, porpoises, and dolphins overboard. Environmentalists accuse Japan, South Korea, and Taiwan, the principal users of drift nets, of "strip-mining" the ocean with killer nets. Only a few years ago, harpooners hunted and seriously endangered the large whale species of bluewhale and finback. Until recently, Canadian and Norwegian hunters clubbed to death the pups of harp seals to harvest their white fur. Ironically, their white fur is nature's way of protecting the pups from natural predators.

The poaching of wildlife can bring great economic rewards and thus is difficult to stop completely. Poachers have gone after North American black bears to acquire their bladders, which will sell in Asia as an aphrodisiac for $500 an ounce. Selling rhinoceros horns as dagger handles in Yemen has reduced the black rhino population in Africa from 20,000 in 1970 to 450 today. Elephants have fared little better; in Africa, their numbers have declined from 1.3 million to 625,000 in several decades due to the illegal trade in ivory. The various subspecies of Asian tiger have declined by 95 percent during the twentieth century; today only 5,000 to 7,000 tigers live in the Asian wild. Poachers hunt them for their beautiful fur and to sell their body parts to make traditional Asian medicines. Some tiger species are already extinct, and the remainder are on the endangered list.

In addition to legal and illegal economic motives, ravages of wildlife occur as an unintended by-product of human activities. In the late 1980s, harbor seals in the North Sea of Europe were dying in unusually large numbers as a result of acute pollution. "Plastic pollution" from consumer products causes cruel deaths for marine animals and birds by entangling them in six-pack yokes or when these animals swallow plastic items that they think are food. While picnicking and fishing trips deluge water areas with plastic flotsam, merchant and cruise ships create most of the problem by dumping millions of tons of trash overboard each year.[62] Then, too, many seals and sea lions ensnare themselves in torn and deserted nets. Finally, the gentle manatee of Florida suffer many cuts from the propellers of pleasure craft and are declining in number.

Countering but not halting the decimation of wildlife are protective steps by governments, private groups, and citizens. Governments agreed to the *Convention on International Trade in Endangered Species (CITES)* in 1973 and updated this treaty to place a worldwide ban on ivory trade beginning in 1990.[63] Overall CITES' ban on the ivory trade has slowed elephant poaching considerably. While elephant numbers dropped from 1.3 million in 1979 to 625,000 in 1990, the year of the ban, their numbers have diminished to only 580,000 during the seven years of the ban. Unfortunately for African elephants, the three countries of Botswana, Namibia, and Zimbabwe, in the southern cone of Africa, successfully lobbied CITES in 1997 to renew some trade in ivory. The governments of these three countries hope to gain $8 billion in badly needed revenue by selling ivory mainly to the ivory carvers of Japan. While the southern cone countries can argue persuasively that they are overpopulated with elephants, the danger is that ivory trade will rekindle poaching in the eastern horn of Africa where the elephant is truly endangered.

CITES has not had sufficient success protecting the Asian tigers, though many countries stand ready to use trade sanctions in such cases. Texas ranchers are raising black rhino hoping to preserve the species. As a partial success story, because of consumer and government sanctions, especially from the United States, Asian fishers have developed new fishnets that preserve other marine life such as sea turtles and dolphins.

One of the most successful protective measures is the moratorium on the hunting of whales. Several countries have long histories of whaling, and their populations traditionally have enjoyed eating whale meat. Also, economic motives are present. Several hundred minke whales hunted recently for "scientific purposes" by Japan fetched $200 a pound as a delicacy for Japanese dinner tables. The governments of countries with whaling histories, such as Norway and Japan, argue that whale hunts can operate and leave all whale species at sustainable levels. Whales have drawn major concern from several private organizations within the environmental movement.

Sobol/SIPA

Loretta Swit and one of her furry young friends.

Harp seals too enjoyed a reprieve when actresses Brigitte Bardot and Loretta Swit championed their cause. Pictures of the bludgeoned, bloody, white pups brought an international outcry that the Canadian and Norwegian governments could not ignore. Interestingly, Loretta Swit went to the Gulf of St. Lawrence in 1992 to promote Seal Watch, a wildlife project that brings tourists to see the seals. The intent is to make the harp seal pups worth more alive than dead; yet Norwegian hunters are pushing their government to renew the hunt of seal pups.

Positive steps that save bird life are especially good news because birds are an *indicator species*. Birds are everywhere, are easy to track and study, and respond quickly to environmental change. The bald eagle (the American national symbol) is now only a "threatened" species instead of an "endangered" one. Its numbers were in the tens of thousands in the nineteenth century but declined to 417 pairs in 1963. Today there are more than 4,000 pairs of bald eagles. Also, some environmentalists call the whopping cranes, a bird five feet tall with a seven-foot wing span, the "comeback bird" because 50 years ago only 16 were alive. Now 270 whooping cranes exist, though these birds have not escaped the danger of extinction.[64] Regrettably, the positive steps by humankind illustrated in these examples are not nearly sufficient to undo all the damage humankind has caused the animal kingdom with its encroachment on the animal's share of the biosphere.

We have learned thus far that human ecology is not in a healthy condition as the core variables (population growth, economic activities, and technology) have damaged and depleted important natural elements of the biosphere. Rapacious human behavior toward the atmosphere, water, soil, forests, and wildlife is undermining long-range prospects for the quality of human life. In the next section, we will learn that a growing enlightenment concerning the importance of our environment is producing a global civil society that insists on extensive reform.

PROTECTING THE ENVIRONMENT THROUGH A GLOBAL CIVIL SOCIETY

Important issues are creating a civic spirit among people ready to work for the common good. Today this civic spirit extends from the local to the global level as private individuals and groups link up across borders to improve human rights, prospects for peace, and environmental conditions. Environmental issues are especially salient. People can easily appreciate environmental problems personally by experiencing firsthand poisoned air, contaminated water, and toxic wastes in ways that transcend culture, social status, nationality, and other differences.[65]

Beginning in the 1960s, with scientists and private groups operating within their own countries, a civic spirit arose calling for the protection of the environment for the good of a country. Then national environmental movements quickly merged into the historical development of a **global civil society.** Such a society is a public sphere of private individuals and groups working together internationally for common goals, an interaction that may or may not include coordination with states and their IGOs.[66]

The global civil society is forming because issues important to masses of people around the world span national jurisdictions but do not receive enough attention by states. The fit between a geographical map of states on the one hand and the distribution of resources and dispersion of environmental harms on the other is not even close.[67] Because of environmental concerns, people around the world are nudging toward an identity as the "human species" in spite of much diversity among them. They are at least able to imagine themselves sharing a single society, a "country" without borders.[68] Inspiriting the global civil society is an awareness by the earth's inhabitants that they are biospherically interdependent and share a real danger.[69]

The global civil society is now just a thin layer of cause and identity, but it is growing deeper roots due to the spread of democracy and the growth of modern communications. Established democracies, with their respect for political liberties, already have allowed national civil societies to grow vigorously at home, and the new democracies make available more governments that are sensitive to the needs of people. Moreover, because of more democracies in the world, people are able to travel more freely across borders and link up with one another on issues such as environmental concerns.[70] Complementing the democracy movement are jet planes and modern communication. Conferences of thousands are possible because wide-body jets can descend on a single site from many points around the globe. A high-tech, global communication grid allows individuals and groups, working for the same causes, to coordinate their activities through telephones, faxes, E-mail, and the web sites of the Internet.[71]

States

The global civil society can encompass states, individuals, INGOs, IGOs, and conference activities. Although the environmental movement often ignores or works around states, the state remains both indispensable and inadequate.[72] The state still marshals more authority and power than any other actor, and so any hope for the enforcement of environmental rules and norms depends largely on states' cooperation. Yet states habitually protect their sovereignty and sometimes behave as though they enjoyed environmental insulation instead of facing environmental interdependence.

As a result, the environmental movement has found it necessary to operate both at the *subnational level* as nongovernment organizations (NGOs) and at the *transnational level* as INGOs. These private groups lobby states and IGOs and frequently take direct action such as planting trees and interfering with whaling operations. Gradually, however, more

© 1989 Time, Inc. Reprinted by permission.

states are realizing that they cannot chop up the biosphere into national possessions and draw wantonly from "global commons" such as the oceans. Their sovereignty must give way, to a degree, to protect shared interests.

As they approach the protection of the environment, states have differing starting points. States impose varying costs on the environment, receive different benefits, and reflect a range of environmental commitment. The Western, industrialized states have large scientific communities, numerous concerned NGOs, and the necessary environmental technology. Overall, these states have made dramatic, though uneven, progress in the last 20 years.[73]

After an energetic two decades of cleaning up air and water in the 1960s and 1970s, the United States lapsed in environmental endeavors for more than a decade, as previously mentioned. This country returned to a greater environmental emphasis when President Bill Clinton announced on Earth Day in 1993 that he would sign the *Convention on Biodiversity* of 1992, which protects varieties of animal and plant species from extinction. The U.S. Senate has failed to ratify this treaty, however, though other countries put it into force in 1993. Also, President Clinton promised that the United States would adhere to the Montreal Protocol calling for restricting "greenhouse" waste gases to 1990 levels by the year 2000. The United States carries a special responsibility to the world on environmental matters, since this country, with only 5 percent of the world's population, contributes as much as 25 percent of the world's pollution in some areas and uses about one-third of the world's available energy.[74]

Environmental concerns have risen significantly in Japan, with both the Japanese public and government taking a stronger interest in environmental protection. Japan's rapacious use of marine life has declined substantially as a result; for instance, Japan uses smaller drift nets and has changed their design to allow dolphins and sea turtles to escape. Once a chief importer of ivory, Japan respected the international ban on trade in ivory until CITES reopened the trade in 1997. A huge amount of rainforest timber still flows to Japan, however, and this country maintains its desire for a larger quota allowed for harvested minke whales.

Writing about environmental problems in the former Soviet Union, Professors Murray Feshbach and Alfred Friendly, Jr., titled their book *Ecocide in the USSR: Health and Nature Under Siege*.[75] They found that Soviet leaders and industrialists followed a recipe for environmental distress as they pushed hard to catch up with Western military power and wealth. Dangerous nuclear reactors, unsafe drinking water, rampant air pollution, and saturation levels of pollution in Soviet lakes and rivers were the outcomes. Since the recent transformation of the Soviet Union into a capitalist-democratic Russia, Russian NGOs have spoken out shrilly about their deeply rooted environmental problems, and the new Russian government acts as if it wishes to respond. However, this government lacks the money and technology to make rapid progress on environmental cleanup.[76]

Third World countries also have made a limited response to environmental degradation, although, for the Third World, environmental protection threatens economic development. These poorer countries have resented Western governments and INGOs extolling them to preserve their shares of the biosphere when the aggressive exploitation of their resources brings them badly needed foreign income. We already referred to Brazil's resentment toward the North over the widespread clearance of Brazil's rainforest. Brazil has claimed it needs more ranches and homesteads for its burgeoning population, and profits from timber sales help pay off its elephantine national debt. Today Brazil is experiencing pressures from its own NGOs, is learning to exploit standing forests, and is working more cooperatively with other states. On the whole, the record of environmental protection by Third World countries is spotty, but they are gradually coming to share in global environmental concerns.

INGOs

Private organizations that individuals begin in their own countries but frequently spread across borders create the global civil society more than any other actor. This global civil society, sometimes with state cooperation and other times without, works for a better world by improving the environment as well as promoting human rights and peace. Individuals, such as Chico Mendes, organized the rubber workers in Brazil to save the rainforests from ranchers. Some of these ranchers killed Mendes in 1988 for his efforts. Wangari Matthai organized other Kenyan women into the Greenbelt movement, and they have planted over 8 million trees. Matthai spoke before an assembly of the World Bank in 1993 advocating the "greening" of economic activities.[77]

People living ordinary lives can boycott goods such as hamburgers unless plastic containers give way to cardboard, tuna until companies purchase tuna caught without killing dolphins, or a particular corporation's brand of gasoline if its oil tankers fail to operate safely. Or people can take a more activist role, including acts of civil disobedience such as throwing red dye, symbolizing the blood of animals, on fur coats; ramming whaling boats with other vessels; or chaining themselves to the fence of the embassy of a country testing nuclear bombs.[78]

Sometimes celebrities pitch in to help INGOs or even to form them. Ted Danson founded and is president of the American Ocean Campaign, Richard Chamberlain works with American Rivers, Madonna associates with Conservation International, and Ted Turner of Cable Network News (CNN) recently offered a large monetary prize for a plan to provide a peaceful, sustainable world future. After reviewing 10,000 manuscripts, he could not find a manuscript with a suitable environmental vision.[79]

Boycotts and acts of civil disobedience effectively dramatize the environmental issues, but perhaps more important over the long run are the organizations that educate people around the world about environmental issues and promote cooperation among states and IGOs to preserve the environment. On environmental issues, INGOs hold more expertise and are more sensitive and responsive than the 200 states and the relevant IGOs in the world.[80]

Examples of effective environmental INGOs abound. In 1989, the Coalition for Environmentally Responsible Economies drafted the Valdez principles to guide MNCs' conduct as they interact with the environment. Many MNCs today not only practice good environmental deeds but advertise those deeds to consumers, who are increasingly sharing in the values of the global "green culture." The World Wildlife Fund (WWF), formed in Switzerland in 1961, has since placed offices in 20 countries. The WWF tries to protect wildlife and wildlands, but also tries to make its activities compatible with the economic development of countries. Other prominent INGOs in the environmental field are the Sea Shepherds Conservation Society, Earth First, the Cousteau Society (focusing on marine biology), the Rainforest Action Network, and the Lobayan Save-the-Trees movement, which began in India and then spread to other countries, including European countries.

Perhaps the best-known environmental INGO is Greenpeace. Since the 1960s, Greenpeace activists, sometimes known as "environmental commandos," have obstructed whaling ships, parachuted from smokestacks, plugged up industrial discharge pipes, and occupied French nuclear test sites in French Polynesia. Greenpeace now has 3.1 million dues-paying members around the world, 1,000 full-time staff, a $140 million budget, 43 offices around the globe, and a small fleet of ocean-going ships, including the *Rainbow Warrior II* and the *MV Greenpeace,* which the French seized during the nuclear protests of 1995. Despite internal divisions within the organization and occasional flubs, such as accusing Shell Oil of dumping far more oil into the North Sea in 1995 than it actually did, Greenpeace is an environmental force that states and MNCs cannot afford to take lightly.

Conferences and IGOs

INGOs not only carry out direct actions on behalf of the environment but, because of their technical expertise and monitoring capabilities, serve as a bridge between the peoples of the world and governments meeting in world and regional conferences and in the halls of IGOs. INGOs typically push the policy agenda that conferences and IGOs ultimately embrace and undertake to carry out.

Two environmental conferences especially deserve attention. The UN Conference of the Human Environment, meeting in 1972 in Stockholm, marked the arrival of environmental issues as an important part of the global agenda. The 114 states and numerous INGOs attending educated world opinion about the human ecological impact. A noteworthy accomplishment was the enunciation of 26 principles for protecting the environment; in particular, Principle 21 called for states to take responsibility for the environmental damage they cause. The 1972 Stockholm conference also helped create the United Nations Environment Program (UNEP) intended to reduce ecological deterioration.

The United Nations Conference on Environment and Development, better known as the "Earth Summit," held in 1992 at Rio de Janeiro, has proven to be one of the most important world conferences. Attending the Earth Summit were 150 state delegations, 100 heads of state including President George Bush, 1,400 NGOs, and 8,000 journalists to help the world observe the activities of the conference. The Earth Summit had the ultimate purpose of pulling all organizations, states, and peoples into a cooperative world strategy that would provide for a sustainable future. The Earth Summit served as a quasi-legislature by offering environmental norms and rules for the world to converge around. Coming out of the Earth Summit were sets of environmental principles, including one set calling for the protection of forests and two conventions on climate change and the sharing of the planet's biodiversity that states could ratify as international law.

The United Nations and environmental conferences have taken the next step and created environmental IGOs for permanent monitoring and improvement of the environment. As mentioned, the Stockholm conference led to the UNEP, a comprehensive monitoring system, located in Nairobi, Kenya, with assets close to $1 billion. UNEP launched the Global Environmental System (GEM) in 1975 to collect data on glaciers and air and water pollution, and also has the Earthwatch Program for additional monitoring of elements of the biosphere. Then there is the Global Environment Facility (GEF), created in 1991 as a pilot program to finance investment for preserving the global commons of the atmosphere, biological diversity, and international waterways. The World Bank proposed the GEF in response to an idea suggested by France. The GEF became permanent in 1994, with $2 billion in funding. The GEF draws on the UNEP for expertise, while the World Bank became responsible for investing and managing GEF funds.

Moreover, the Earth Summit created two new bodies that overlap and sometimes confuse what the UNEP does. The Commission on Sustainable Development (CSD) provides a forum to review progress on Earth Summit's Agenda 21, a broad, nonbinding "Plan for Action" to provide protection for the environment and to offer a cost estimate for this protection. The Inter-Agency Committee on Sustainable Development (IACSD) aims to bring coordination among United Nations agencies promoting the environment and sustainable development.

Finally, the World Bank and the International Monetary Fund are increasingly "greening" their policies by working for sustainable economic development. The International Maritime Organization (IMO) regulates what ships dump in the ocean and encourages treaties that protect the seas from pollution. The World Meteorological Organization (WMO), associated with weather study, takes a strong interest in climate matters, particularly the greenhouse problem.[81]

Governance

The interactions of individuals, publics, INGOs, states and their IGOs, and conferences generate a steady flow of rules and norms providing governance for the new age of environmental awareness. This governance offers some order to environmental protection efforts in the absence of a true, central world authority. A quiltwork of these rules and

TABLE 13.1
Selected Environmental Conventions

1946	*International Whaling Convention.* 50 parties. Protects whales from excessive harvesting. All commercial whaling banned in 1982.
1959	*Antarctica Treaty.* 42 parties. Restricts Antarctica to scientific research. 1991 protocol bans mining and development for 50 years.
1972	*London Dumping Convention.* 75 parties. Originally banned the ocean dumping of high-level radioactive and toxic wastes. By mid-1990s banned low-level radioactive wastes and all other industrial wastes.
1973	*Washington Convention on International Trade in Endangered Species of Wild Fauna and Flora (CITES).* 128 parties. Restricts trade in species that are endangered with extinction. Ban on elephant ivory trade took effect under this treaty in 1990.
1973	*Prevention of Pollution from Ships Convention.* 95 parties. Restricts intentional discharges by ships, such as oil and sewage. Particularly effective in preventing discharges near shore.
1982	*Convention on the Law of the Seas.* 75 parties. Broad treaty that covers such matters as 200-mile economic zones, protects living resources of the oceans, and protects the oceans from pollution.
1987	*Montreal Protocol on the Ozone Layer.* 149 parties. With updates, requires the phaseout of CFCs by 1996. Also requires restrictions on a number of other ozone-depleting chemicals.
1989	*Basel Convention.* 88 parties. Controls transborder shipments of hazardous wastes. Updated in 1993 to ban shipment of waste exports to nonindustrialized countries.
1992	*Framework Convention on Climate Change.* 136 parties. Restricts output of carbon dioxide to 1990 levels by the year 2000.
1992	*Convention on Biological Diversity.* 118 parties. Calls for preserving and sharing the benefits of genetic resources.
1994	*Convention on Desertification.* 107 parties. Encourages programs for preserving soil and water.

norms operates through specialized regimes that attempt to regulate such matters as whaling, the atmosphere, and forests. Recall that regimes can be either the hegemonic or cooperative type. Environmental regimes are largely cooperative ones, with first one country and then another frequently taking the lead according to the particular environmental issue. For instance, the United States may have offered the most leadership in negotiations for the Montreal Protocol on the ozone problem, and France has shown more energy in cleaning up the Mediterranean littoral than any other country in that region.[82]

The natural temptation of all states is to use as much of the world's resources as they can so their populations can enjoy the best life possible. Yet states' leaders are gradually joining their scientific communities and environmental INGOs by thinking in terms of Garrett Hardin's famous "tragedy of the commons."[83] In Hardin's metaphor, each herder grazes as many cattle as desired on the village commons, shared by all, without regard for the general effect. Soon the grazing land deteriorates, and all herders suffer a common tragedy of a grass shortage and starving cattle. A quarter-century of environmental activism by the evolving global civil society has conditioned states' leaders to see such matters as the atmosphere, the ocean, and biodiversity as "common-pools" that the world's population holds and uses collectively.[84] All leaders, of course, do not share this view, nor do its supporters adhere to it consistently. Still, *environmental security* is emerging today, alongside national and economic security, as a key dimension of a country's policy.

While it would be difficult to argue persuasively that states now focus on their environmental duties as much as they should, a substantial body of environmental conventions and

AP Photo/Dave Caulkin

Members of Greenpeace demonstrate outside Dublin Castle at the start of the 47th annual meeting of the International Whaling Commission. Conservationists are lobbying delegates to push Japan and Norway to end whale hunting.

regimes have come into existence to regulate use of the environment and move humankind toward sustainable development. Now more than 170 environmental treaties cover everything from the pristine ecology of Antarctica, agreed to by many states, to the mesh of a fishing net accepted by several states sharing the same fishery. The large majority of environmental treaties are bilateral or regional, although a few deal with instances of the "global commons." Examples of the latter are the *Convention on Biological Diversity,* signed by 160 countries and entered into force in 1993, and the *Convention on Climate Change,* which became international law when the fiftieth country ratified it in 1994.[85] The first treaty protects animal and plant species from extinction, as mentioned earlier; the latter treaty intends to reduce greenhouse gas emissions to 1990 levels by the year 2000.

Multiple environmental regimes, with varying degrees of effectiveness, provide some coordination by guiding states and other actors to converge around norms and rules for the protection of a particular element of the biosphere. Several examples of regimes will help clarify this point. The *whaling regime,* for instance, got under way in 1946 when the International Whaling Commission (IWC) formed. The IWC initially regulated whale hunts but took steps in the 1980s to ban commercial whaling and to renew the ban in the 1990s. Some "scientific" harvests allowed the Japanese and Norwegians to hunt a few minke whales. These two countries continue to pressure the IWC to allow commercial hunts of whale species that are not endangered. Without some relaxation of the rules on commercial hunts, the IWC faces desertion by its members. Iceland left the IWC in 1992, and Norway announced in 1993 that it would conduct commercial hunts, much to the vexation of environmental groups.

Until the 1992 Glasgow, Scotland, meeting of the IWC, when demands for commercial hunts intensified, this regime was strong, with some member-states standing ready to use trade sanctions against whale-hunting states. Now the whaling regime may become a regime of only moderate strength. Perhaps the best hope of saving whales from hunters is to convert the whaling industry. The IWC and the World Wildlife Fund have persuaded countries, including Japan, to start whale-watching industries. Some ex-whalers now conduct tours of whale watchers, an industry that involved 4 million people and $300 million per year by the 1990s.[86]

An *atmosphere regime* is fairly successful and regulates a true "global commons." It has been easy for leaders, scientists, and the public around the world to understand that destroying the ozone layer will allow ultraviolet rays from the sun to intensify and threaten everyone with skin cancer. Many scientists and governments also realize that warming the earth's atmosphere by even two degrees will harm crops and flood some island states as glaciers and polar caps melt. The 1987 Montreal Protocol and the Convention on Climate Change proposed at the 1992 Earth Summit have been fairly easy to achieve, as international treaties go, because of the widely perceived atmospheric dangers. In the future, pulling Third World states, especially the newly industrializing countries (NICs) such as India and Mexico, with their stress on economic development priorities, to converge around higher standards regarding CFCs and other waste gases may prove far more difficult.

The *forest regime,* in contrast, is a weak regime. At least states discuss this matter at Group of Seven summits, and states agreed to nonbinding principles to protect forests at the Earth Summit. Unfortunately, Western states, such as Germany and the United States, continue to use large amounts of coal because it is a cheap, abundant source of energy and thus choose to live with the effects of acid rain. Mainly to protect forests, states have agreed to some limits on the waste gases leading to acid rain, but states are not adhering to these limits particularly well. It is the United States and Canada in North America and most of Northern Europe that suffer the worst acid rain effects. Germany's famous Black Forest is especially under threat.

Trying to cajole tropical countries of the South to turn off their chain saws has depended more on economic persuasion about the benefits of standing forests than enforcing adherence to regime rules. Currently, the motives for cutting rainforests are overriding the persuasions for leaving these forests standing.

Overall, multiple environmental regimes, with fairly clear rules and norms but with weak or no enforcement powers, are tempering but not stopping the rapacious use of the world's resources. Concerned actors have a difficult time trying to hold in check the demands of a burgeoning 6 billion people who want richer material lives. The next logical step for the environmental movement is to achieve more coherence in environmental protection. The elements of the biosphere interconnect, and so attempts to regulate the biosphere with multiple uncoordinated regimes is environmentally inefficient. Needed also are treaties that go beyond a standard-setting role to one exercising real enforcement power, such as trade sanctions. Presently, at least some countries use occasional trade sanctions at their discretion. Environmental governance has come a long way in several decades, but if the global civil society cannot push states to act more forcefully in the near future, humankind's environmental jeopardy will deepen.

THE ENVIRONMENT AND INTERNATIONAL SOCIETY

Environmental issues prominently demonstrate that a theoretical perspective that goes beyond that of realists is now necessary. The realist emphasis on the state, involving territorial boundaries and sovereign independence, does not lend itself to the transborder nature of environmental problems. Realists either ignore or misunderstand the role of the environment.[87] Specifically, realists are unable to envision the kind of cooperation among states that environmental progress requires. For realists, states will always be self-interested actors unable to make sacrifices for the common good. Further, a hegemonic state, which some realists believe is necessary to compel cooperation, is not available to support the global environment. Nor would a realist approve the erosion of sovereignty that a growing number of environmental treaties requires or appreciate the rise in importance of environmental INGOs.[88]

Realists have been slow to recognize a new agenda of issues associated with the global commons, such as the oceans and the atmosphere. For them, environmental questions are of marginal importance, and they treat these issues as mere "low politics." Their preoccupation with the pursuit of power by states also leads realists to neglect the United Nations, international law, and the normative aspirations of the global civil society, all of which help to propel the environmental agenda.[89]

Hans Morgenthau, a leading realist offering his views after the Second World War, hardly thought about environmental issues except as natural resources for power: How blessed is a given state in food resources, oil, metals, minerals, and a skilled population of sufficient size? And how successfully can a state channel these resources into a warmaking ability?[90] Of course, in fairness to Morgenthau and other realists, the "greening" of international relations became prevalent to some degree only in the 1970s. As others recognized the importance of environmental issues, they had to find realism theoretically ill equipped to recognize and handle these issues.

Neorealists, such as Kenneth N. Waltz, also worry about natural resources only as they relate to power. Recall that the focus for neorealists is the global structure of power and states' respective shares of the given power distribution. As a later realist, Waltz also concerns himself with the dangers of interdependence that transnationalists claimed were waxing into place in the 1970s. Although Waltz concludes that the state-entangling forces of interdependence are an exaggeration, he does ponder over the United States' need to stockpile, especially oil, a major energy resource.[91] For Waltz, major states depend on one another only to avoid a nuclear war. He appears to be without concern for a healthy environment that requires an extensive and active pattern of cooperation among states for an indefinite time.[92]

Both realists and neorealists could hardly imagine widespread cooperation beyond partnership within alliances or joint steps among opponents to prevent nuclear holocaust. In their perception, the world has been too hostile and anarchy too deep a pattern to permit long-term, widespread cooperation. Yet recent history is reducing the relevance of these earlier theorists. The modern flowering of regimes, based on many issues that include environmental matters, involves more than the mere adjustments of states that Waltz has claimed.[93] Environmental regimes augment the state system in an important way, with states working more closely together because they must have a healthy, sustainable environment for their peoples to survive and to live well.[94] States today grudgingly, but knowingly, acknowledge the mismatch between their limited territorial jurisdictions and a global biosphere.

Perhaps the best example of extensive state cooperation within an environmental regime is the Mediterranean Plan. France and Italy as industrialized democracies, Albania as a communist state at the time of regime formation, and Algeria and Egypt as Third World countries, among the other states of the Mediterranean littoral, all came together to protect and preserve a regional commons at the urging of their respective scientists.[95] The common concern over the environment helped override national particularism for a diverse group of countries, a development unanticipated by realists and neorealists.[96]

By the 1970s and 1980s, transnationalists, such as Robert O. Keohane and Joseph S. Nye, argued that realists' and nonrealists' theoretical efforts could no longer account for many important aspects of international life. These transnsationalists could perceive the emergence of a "global village" experiencing multiple issues that go beyond military security, issues that include environmental concerns. These issues diminish the importance of national borders as governments and people realize their mutual dependence, a condition prompting them to collectively handle problems of regional and global scope. For instance, states and environmentalists call on elements of the UN System concerned with the ocean to help with oil pollution, the survival of whale species, the sustainability of fisheries, and more.[97]

Since Keohane and Nye's important *Power and Interdependence* first appeared, an active global civil society, in development for years but intensified by the end of the Cold War, has burst on the modern international scene. This global civil society of individuals and INGOs now joins the actors of states and IGOs on the global stage.[98]

In addition to appreciating a mixed-actor, multiple-issue world, transnationalists recognize the formation of a true world opinion. With a modern global communication network and the spread of democracy, there is more than an *opinion of states* operating in diplomatic circles. Today an *opinion of people* is a global force, able to raise a variety of values and concerns to a level of importance alongside that of states' traditional interest in guns and dollars.[99] Environmental priorities are prominent among these values and concerns as a global dialogue on saving the planet draws together both state and private actors.

To appreciate the role of the environmental movement, we can turn to our models of analysis from Chapter One. The jeopardized world environment, as much as any *issue*, creates an *orientation* among states that focuses their attention on cooperation. States recognize that the biosphere envelops their national borders and the global commons of the oceans, necessitating unprecedented levels of cooperation for humankind to have a sustainable future. Joining states in important roles in the pursuit of a healthy environmental future are IGOs and INGOs as nonstate *actors*. Environmental concerns almost dismiss *international anarchy* as a plausible model of modern world patterns. A system of interacting states focused on the danger of war has little time to devote to survival of forests or the quality of air. These concerns require at least the recognition of the emergence of a Grotian *international society* with its emphasis on cooperation for the common good.

Furthermore, environmental matters hint at the Kantian world of an *international community*. Similar to Immanuel Kant's views, an evolving world of republics (democracies) is currently producing a civil society that has spread to the international level. Moreover, this prototype community of republics and world citizenry is cosmopolitan in nature because citizens in most countries share commercial and moral values supportive of peace. Unforeseen in Kant's eighteenth-century vision, the shared values of today include the protection of the environment.

CHAPTER SUMMARY

Alongside global concerns over human rights and peace, environmental threats have caught the attention of multiple actors, including both states and INGOs. We can no longer afford to practice a human ecology of reckless exploitation of the earth's resources because we desire the economic rewards of this exploitation. The rising human population, with its economic motives and technological capacity, threatens to undermine the life-sustaining capacity of the planet for future generations.

Although environmentalists may have achieved a higher moral ground than the eco-optimists amid world opinion, the actual practices by humankind still involve a pattern of only partially restrained exploitation. Cleaner air in some Western cities is helpful but is a small victory when set against the bigger battle of saving the ozone layer and checking the greenhouse effect. Rivers and oceans in some places are cleaner, but the fish stock, vital to the world as a food source, is in decline. Soil depletion is far in excess of its replenishment, endangering the agricultural future of humankind. Saving forests to preserve the "world's lungs" and to protect the biodiversity of the planet is a limited success. Rainforests in particular are dangerously in decline. And the fate of wildlife hangs in the balance. Many beautiful, exotic animals may one day exist only in zoos, if that.

Probably more than any other single issue, environmental concerns have inspired a global civil society of concerned world opinion based on hundreds of INGO environmental groups, such as Greenpeace, and millions of private citizens. This transborder civil society insists that states and IGOs, especially the United Nations, undertake the critical mission of protecting all elements of the biosphere. This protection has led to a measure of governance, or regulation, of the environment by states and their IGOs and regimes.

Finally, the concern over humankind's jeopardized environmental future reinforces the formative international society because the degree of cooperation has expanded in a world shared by independent actors. The environmental issues even hint at a prototype international community, since many people scattered about the world share the deeply embedded values of a global "green culture." They have as a common identity a common cause.

POINTS OF VIEW

In the new biospheric age, human beings belong to the earth rather than the Earth belonging to human beings.
—JEREMY RIFKIN
BIOSPHERIC POLITICS

These greenies have nice speeches, but in practice they're pigs.
—RIO GARBAGE COLLECTOR AT THE EARTH SUMMIT

The environment, perhaps more than any other issue, has helped crystalize the notion that humanity has a common future.
—OUR GLOBAL NEIGHBORHOOD

Nearly all human traditions recognize that we, the living, are but sojourners on earth and temporary stewards of its resources.
—EDITH BROWN WEISS IN NAZLI CHOUCRI'S GLOBAL ACCORD

If we don't control the population with justice, humanity, and mercy, it will be done for us by nature—brutally.
—PHYSICIST HENRY KENDALL OF MIT
NOBEL LAUREATE

Nature is still seen as a mine or a dump and is treated accordingly.
—WILLIAM OPHULS
ECOLOGY AND THE POLITICS OF SCARCITY REVISITED

It's important to raise the environment to the same level as national security. If we poison our planet, what is there left to defend?
—ROBERT REDFORD, ACTOR

While overpopulation in poor nations tends to keep them poverty-stricken, overpopulation in rich nations tends to undermine the life-support capacity of the entire planet.
—PAUL R. EHRLICH, BIOLOGIST,
QUOTED IN NATIONAL GEOGRAPHIC MAGAZINE

REVIEW QUESTIONS

1. Contrast the views of environmentalists with those of eco-optimists regarding the human ecology.
2. Why does a declining environment produce conflict?
3. What are the core variables creating hazards for the world's physical environment, and how are these variables interrelated?
4. What is the GAIA hypothesis?
5. Why are rainforests important to sustaining a balanced environment?
6. Why is river water, though a replenishable resource, a potential source of conflict among states?
7. What are some alternative sources of energy to oil, and do we have enough time to develop other sources of energy?
8. What is a global civil society, and why is the environment such an apt illustration of this society?
9. How effective are environmental regimes?
10. How does the global environmental movement contribute to an international society and even hint at a Kantian community?

GLOSSARY

biodiversity   The broad range of variety in both animals and plants and the physical conditions under which they live.

biosphere   The layers of soil, ocean, climate, and air that envelop planet Earth and sustain all animal and plant life.

carrying capacity   The number of people or animals that a given habitat can sustain at a healthy standard of life.

ecocide   The destruction of the natural environment; usually a result of human activity.

ecology   The study of organisms interacting with their natural environment.

ecosystem   A balanced environment in a particular habitat that allows animals and plants to meet their needs and to function successfully.

environment   The combination of surrounding physical conditions, such as air, water, minerals, and other organisms, that affect a particular organism, including human life.

GAIA hypothesis   The theory that the earth is a superorganism made up of interdependent parts that form a greater whole.

global civil society   A public sphere of activity by private individuals and groups interacting for common causes; may or may not include the cooperation of states and their IGOs.

human ecology   The study of human interaction with the biosphere, especially concerning healthy human life while sustaining the physical environment.

steady-state society   A human society that can balance its numbers with the natural resources available, usually by leveling off human numbers and replenishing resources as people use them.

sustainable development   Economic development that provides for the present generation without compromising future generations' needs by overusing and harming the environment.

zero population growth   A fertility level in society that sustains its population at the same number, usually by each couple replacing themselves with two children.

RECOMMENDED READINGS

Lester R. Brown, ed. *State of the World.* New York: W. W. Norton, annual.

Nazli Choucri, ed. *Global Accord: Environmental Challenges and International Responses.* Cambridge, MA: MIT Press, 1993.

Gregg Easterbrook. *A Moment of the Earth: The Coming Age of Environmental Optimism.* New York: Penguin Books, 1996.

Julie Fisher. *The Road from Rio: Sustainable Development and the Nongovernmental Movement in the Third World.* Westport, CT: Praeger, 1993.

Al Gore. *Earth in the Balance: Ecology and the Human Spirit.* New York: Houghton Mifflin, 1992.

Pranay Gupte. *The Crowded Earth: People and Politics of Population.* New York: W. W. Norton, 1984.

Garrett Hardin. *Living Within Limits: Ecology, Economics, and Population Taboos.* New York: Oxford University Press, 1995.

Jim MacNeill, Pieter Winsemius, and Taizo Yakushiji. *Beyond Interdependence: The Meshing of the World's Economy and the Earth's Ecology.* New York: Oxford University Press, 1991.

Norman Myers, ed. *GAIA: An Atlas of Planet Management,* rev. ed. New York: Anchor Books, 1993.

William Ophuls. *Requiem for Modern Politics: The Tragedy of the Enlightenment and the Challenge of the New Millennium.* Boulder, CO: Westview Press, 1997.

William Ophuls and A. Stephen Boyan, Jr. *Ecology and the Politics of Scarcity Revisited: The Unraveling of the American Dream.* New York: W. H. Freeman, 1992.

Elinor Ostrom. *Governing the Commons: The Evolution of Institutions for Collective Action.* New York: Cambridge University Press, 1991.

Dennis Pirages. *Building Sustainable Societies: A Blueprint for a Post-Industrial World.* Armonk, NY: M. E. Sharpe, 1996.

Gareth Porter and Janet Welsh Brown. *Global Environmental Politics.* 2nd ed. Boulder, CO: Westview Press, 1996.

Thomas Princen. *Environmental NGOs in World Politics: Linking the Local with the Global.* New York: Routledge, 1994.

Jeremy Rifkin. *Biosphere Politics: A Cultural Odyssey from the Middle Ages to the New Ages.* New York: HarperCollins, 1992.

Lawrence E. Susskind. *Environmental Diplomacy: Negotiating More Effective Global Agreements.* New York: Oxford University Press, 1994.

Jacqueline Vaughn Switzer. *Environmental Politics: Domestic and Global Dimensions.* New York: St. Martin's Press, 1994.

Edward O. Wilson. *The Diversity of Life.* Cambridge, MA: Harvard University Press, 1992.

ENDNOTES

1. Lester R. Brown, "The Acceleration of History," in *State of the World 1996* (New York: W. W. Norton, 1996), pp. 3–4.
2. Hilary French, "After the Earth Summit: The Future of Environmental Governance," Worldwatch Paper 107 (Washington, D.C.: Worldwatch Institute, 1992), pp. 7, 49.
3. This definition is based on Jeremy Rifkin, *Biosphere Politics* (New York: HarperCollins, 1992), p. 3; Gareth Porter and Janet Welsh Brown, *Global Environmental Politics* (Boulder, CO: Westview Press, 1991), p. 2.
4. Barbara Ward and Rene Dubos, *Only One Earth: The Care and Maintenance of a Small Planet* (New York: W. W. Norton, 1972).
5. Edith Brown Weiss, "International Equity: Toward an International Legal Framework," in *Global Accord: Environmental Challenges and International Responses,* ed. Nazli Choucri (Cambridge, MA: MIT Press, 1993), p. 347; Al Gore, *Earth in the Balance: Ecology and the Human Spirit* (New York: Houghton Mifflin, 1992), pp. 238–65.
6. Porter and Brown, *Global Environmental Politics,* p. 30.
7. William Ophuls and A. Stephen Boyan, Jr., *Ecology and the Politics of Scarcity Revisited: The Unraveling of the American Dream* (New York: W. H. Freeman, 1992), p. 15.
8. Norman Myers, ed. *GAIA: An Atlas of Planet Management,* rev. ed. (New York: Anchor Books, 1993); James Lovelock, *Gaia: A New Look at Life on Earth* (Oxford: Oxford University Press, 1995).
9. Gore, *Earth in the Balance,* p. 6.
10. This description of market economists is from Porter and Brown, *Global Environmental Politics,* pp. 27, 31–32. A positive view of the economy's relationship to the environment can be found in Julian L. Simon, *Theory of Population and Economic Growth* (New York: Basil Blackwell, 1986), and Julian L. Simon, *Population Matters: People, Resources, Environment, and Immigration* (New Brunswick, NJ: Transaction Publishers, 1990).
11. Sandra Postel, "Carrying Capacity: Earth's Bottom Line," in *State of the World 1994* (New York: W. W. Norton, 1994), p. 19.
12. Oran R. Young, *International Cooperation: Building Regimes for Natural Resources and the Environment* (Ithaca, NY: Cornell University Press, 1989), p. 4.
13. David C. Korten, *Getting to the 21st Century: Voluntary Action and the Global Agenda* (West Hartford, CT: Kumarian Press, 1990), pp. 9–11.
14. Thomas F. Homer-Dixon, "Environmental Scarcities and Violent Conflict," *International Security,* Summer 1994, p. 18.
15. Ibid., p. 19.
16. *Calypso Log,* February 1993, pp. 14–16.
17. *World Press Review,* January 1995, p. 38; Homer-Dixon, "Environmental Scarcities," pp. 13–16.

18. Homer-Dixon, "Environmental Scarcities," pp. 21–22.
19. Thomas F. Homer-Dixon, "On the Threshold: Environmental Changes as Causes of Acute Conflict," *International Security,* Fall 1991, p. 82.
20. Conway W. Henderson, "Population Pressures and Political Repression," *Social Science Quarterly,* Summer 1993, pp. 322–33.
21. Homer-Dixon, "Environmental Scarcities," pp. 33–35.
22. *ZPG Reporter,* December 1994, p. 3.
23. Paul C. Stern, Oran R. Young, and Daniel Bruckman, eds., *Global Environmental Change* (Washington, D.C.: National Academy Press, 1992), pp. 76–83.
24. Ramon G. McLeod, "Environmentalists Start to Focus on Overpopulation," *San Francisco Chronicle,* March 22, 1992.
25. Jacqueline Vaughn Switzer, *Environmental Politics: Domestic and Global Dimensions* (New York: St. Martin's Press, 1994), p. 345.
26. *ZPG Reporter,* December 1994, p. 8.
27. Nazli Choucri, "Multinational Corporation and the Global Environment," in *Global Accord,* p. 207.
28. Stern et al., *Global Environmental Change,* p. 80.
29. Homer-Dixon, "On the Threshold," pp. 95–104.
30. Switzer, *Environmental Politics,* p. 35.
31. These data on Kenya are from *World Development Report 1995* (New York: Oxford University Press, 1995).
32. Francisco R. Sagasti and Michael E. Colby, "Eco-Development Perspectives on Global Change from Developing Countries," in *Global Accord,* p. 199.
33. Faye Duchin and Glenn-Marie Lange, *The Future of the Environment: Ecological Economics and Technological Change* (New York: Oxford University Press, 1994), pp. 3–5.
34. Brown, "The Acceleration of History," p. 11.
35. Ophuls and Boyan, *Ecology and the Politics of Scarcity Revisited,* p. 83; Dennis Pirages, *The New Context for International Politics: Global Ecopolitics* (North Scituate, MA: Duxbury Press, 1978), pp. 58–62.
36. This view of technology is from Jeremy Rifkin, *Biosphere Politics* (New York: HarperCollins, 1992), p. 284.
37. Postel, "Carrying Capacity," pp. 15–16.
38. John E. Young, "Using Computers for the Environment," in *State of the World 1994,* pp. 99–116.
39. Choucri, "Multinational Corporations," in *Global Accord,* pp. 208–215.
40. Postel, "Carrying Capacity," pp. 16–20.
41. Hilary F. French, *Partnership for the Planet: An Environmental Agenda for the United Nations* (Washington, D.C.: Worldwatch Institute, 1995), p. 8.
42. French, "After the Earth Summit," pp. 14–15: Gore, *Earth in the Balance,* pp. 104–5.
43. Much of this discussion on global warming and ozone depletion draws on Porter and Brown, *Global Environmental Politics,* pp. 7, 11, 74–78; Pirages, *Global Ecopolitics,* pp. 128–30.
44. French, "After the Earth Summit," pp. 13–14.
45. Porter and Brown, *Global Environmental Politics,* p. 12.
46. Postel, "Carrying Capacity," p. 11.
47. *National Geographic,* November 1995, pp. 2–37; *World Press Review,* June 1995, p. 36.
48. Jim MacNeill, Pieter Winsemius, and Taiozo Yakushiji, *Beyond Interdependence: The Meshing of the World's Economy and the Earth's Ecology* (New York: Oxford University Press, 1991), p. 56; Porter and Brown, *Global Environmental Politics,* p. 144.
49. Postel, "Carrying Capacity," p. 6.
50. Gore, *Earth in the Balance,* p. 11.
51. Postel, "Carrying Capacity," p. 9.
52. Thomas Robert Malthus, *An Essay on the Principle of Population,* ed. Donald Winch (New York: Cambridge University Press, 1992).
53. Brown, "The Acceleration of History," pp. 7–11. Lester R. Brown, "Facing Food Insecurity," in *State of the World 1994,* pp. 177–97.
54. Joseph Collins, "World Hunger: A Scarcity of Food or a Scarcity of Democracy," in *World Security: Challenges for a New Century,* ed. Michael T. Klare and Daniel C. Thomas (New York: St. Martin's Press, 1994), p. 356.
55. Postel, "Carrying Capacity," p. 12; Gore, *Earth in the Balance,* p. 119.
56. Julie Fisher, *The Road from Rio: Sustainable Development and the Nongovernmental Movement in the Third World* (Westport, CT: Praeger, 1993), p. 2.
57. Porter and Brown, *Global Environmental Politics,* p. 14.

58. MacNeill, Winsemius, and Yakushiji, *Beyond Interdependence,* p. 56; Porter and Brown, *Global Environmental Politics,* p. 144.
59. Gore, *Earth in the Balance,* p. 119.
60. Edward O. Wilson, *The Diversity of Life* (Cambridge, MA: Harvard University Press, 1992).
61. Fisher, *The Road from Rio,* p. 16; Sagasti and Colby, "Eco-Development Perspectives," p. 200.
62. Michael Weisskopf, "Plastic Reaps a Grim Harvest in the Oceans of the World," *Smithsonian,* March 1988, pp. 58–67.
63. French, "After the Earth Summit," p. 11.
64. *Calypso Log,* August 1994, pp. 18–21.
65. James N. Rosenau, "Environmental Challenges in a Turbulent World," in *The State and Social Power in Global Environmental Politics,* ed. Ronnie D. Lipschutz and Ken Conca (New York: Columbia University Press, 1993), p. 89; Ronnie D. Lipschutz, "Reconstructing World Politics: The Emergence of Global Civil Society," *Millennium: Journal of International Politics,* Winter 1992, p. 393.
66. Paul Wapner, "Politics Beyond the State: Environmental Activism and World Civic Politics," *World Politics,* April 1995, pp. 311–13; *Our Global Neighbor: The Report of the Commission on Global Governance* (New York: Oxford University Press, 1995), p. 66.
67. Rosenau, "Environmental Challenges," in *The State and Social Power in Global Environmental Politics,* p. 76.
68. Richard Falk, *Explorations at the Edge of Time* (Philadephia: Temple University Press, 1992), pp. 2, 153; Elise Boulding, *Building a Global Civic Culture: Education for an Interdependent World* (New York: Teachers College Press, 1988), pp. 65–66.
69. Daniel Deudney, "Global Environmental Rescue and the Emergence of World Domestic Politics," in *The State and Social Power in Global Environmental Politics,* pp. 300–301.
70. Paul C. Stern, Oran R. Young, and Daniel Druckman, eds., *Global Environmental Change: Understanding the Human Challenge* (Washington, D.C.: National Academy, 1992), p. 82; *Our Global Neighborhood,* p. 62; "The UN System and NGOs: New Relationships for a New Era?" 25th United Nations Issues Conference of 1994, sponsored by the Stanley Foundation, February 18–20, 1994, pp. 6–7.
71. Lipschutz, "Reconstructing World Politics," pp. 411–13; Wapner, "Politics Beyond the State," p. 317.
72. Karen Litfin, "Eco-Regimes: Playing Tug of War with the Nation-State," in *The State and Social Power in Global Environmental Politics,* p. 96.
73. Peter M. Haas, Marc A. Levy, and Edward W. Parson, "Appraising the Earth Summit: How Should We Judge the UNCED's Success?" *Environment,* October 1992, pp. 1–9.
74. Rifkin, *Biosphere Politics,* p. 283.
75. Murray Feshbach and Alfred Friendly, Jr., *Ecocide in the USSR: Health and Nature Under Siege* (New York: Basic Books, 1992).
76. Ibid., pp. 251–67.
77. Postel, "Carrying Capacity," p. 20.
78. Wapner, "Politics Beyond the State," pp. 325–27.
79. Some of these examples are from *ZPG Reporter,* January–February 1996; Switzer, *Environmental Politics,* p. 367.
80. *GAIA Atlas,* p. 236.
81. This discussion on IGOs draws on Hilary F. French, "Partnership for the Planet: An Environmental Agenda for the United Nations," Worldwatch Paper 126 (Washington, D.C.: Worldwatch Institute, 1995).
82. Litfin, "Eco-Regimes."
83. Garret Hardin, "The Tragedy of the Commons," *Science,* December 13, 1968, pp. 1243–48.
84. Ophuls and Boyan, *Ecology and the Politics of Scarcity Revisited,* p. 193.
85. French, "Partnership for the Planet," pp. 9–21.
86. *Calypso Log,* August 1994, pp. 18–21.
87. Homer-Dixon, "On the Threshold," pp. 84–85.
88. Peter M. Haas with Jan Sundgren, "Evolving International Environmental Law: Changing Practices of National Security," in *Global Accord,* pp. 402–3, 411–13, 418–19.
89. Richard Falk, *Explorations at the Edge of Time: The Prospects for World Order* (Philadelphia: Temple University Press, 1992), pp. 225–27.
90. Hans Morgenthau, *Politics Among Nations,* 5th ed. (New York: Alfred A. Knopf, 1978), pp. 120–28, 130–34.
91. Kenneth N. Waltz, *Theory of International Politics* (Reading, MA: Addison-Wesley, 1979), pp. 146, 156.

92. Lipschutz, "Reconstructing World Politics," pp. 401–9.
93. James N. Rosenau, "The Two Worlds of World Politics," in *Classic Readings of International Relations,* ed. Phil Williams, Donald M. Goldstein, and Jay M. Shafritz (Belmont, CA: Wadsworth, 1994), p. 493.
94. Deudney, "Global Environmental Rescue," pp. 286–89.
95. Peter M. Haas, "Making Progress in International Environmental Protection," in *Progress in Post-War International Relations,* ed. Emanuel Adler and Beverly Crawford (New York: Columbia University Press, 1991), pp. 285–305.
96. Deudney, "Global Environmental Rescue," pp. 289–90.
97. Robert O. Keohane and Joseph S. Nye, *Power and Interdependence,* 2nd ed. (Boston: Scott, Foresman, 1989), pp. 3, 24–29, 63–65, 124, 149; see in general Chapters 4, 5, and 6.
98. Dianne Otto, "Nongovernmental Organizations in the United Nations System: The Emerging Role of International Civil Society," *Human Rights Quarterly,* February 1996, pp. 107–41.
99. Christopher Hill, "World Opinion and the Empire of Circumstance," *International Affairs,* January 1996, pp. 109–31.

CHAPTER 14

SHARED EXPERIENCES OF HUMANKIND

Humankind shares not only the biosphere but also social and political forces with global sweep that condition and shape lives around the world. These forces can involve both positive and negative shared experiences. Either way, these experiences are drawing states and peoples closer together as they enjoy the positive and work together to cope with the negative.

This chapter begins with what are basically positive experiences, though some negative reactions to these experiences can occur. We start this chapter by looking at the emergence of a sophisticated global communication system that draws the world together by sharing information. Next, we examine the growing use of English, if only as a second language, that makes the global communication system more useful. Then we take note of a spreading popular culture that helps make for a more cosmopolitan world. A much stronger foundation for the nascent international society of today is the current wave of democracy, the subject of the next section. The rising tide of democracy portends the end of a deep ideological cleavage that has wracked the world for over two centuries.

We then turn to experiences that are negative, beginning with the question of cultural fissures. Do such fissures completely block the development of an international society? Particularly of concern is Islamic revivalism, allegedly energized by the Muslims' perception of Western intrusions in their share of the world. We then look at the clearly negative experiences of spreading diseases and international drug trafficking, which governments and an aroused global civil society are struggling to control. Finally, we assess the growth of the international society.

THE GLOBAL COMMUNICATIONS NETWORK

The modern electronic age creates in its wake the "information age," with information flows doubling and doubling again and able to reach people all over the world with a rapidity unforeseen a few years ago. **Telecommunications,** the electronic transmission of information, take many forms, beginning with transborder telegraph lines in the mid-nineteenth century, telephone lines by the turn of the century, and radio broadcasts by the 1920s. From small beginnings, mostly in Europe, the international communications network has grown in technical sophistication and has expanded into a global network. In addition to undersea cables for telegraph and telephone hook-ups and shortwave broadcast for radio, global communications took a giant leap forward with the development of the communications satellite, which had widespread use by the 1980s.

INTELSAT Global Satellite Network

In practice, INTELSAT needs many satellites to cover the earth's surface with strong television, telephone, and data channels.

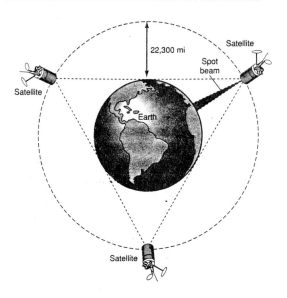

Source: Howard H. Frederick, *Global Communications and International Relations* (Belmont, CA: Wadsworth, 1993), p. 92.

The most useful satellites are **geostationary** satellites, meaning they operate at 22,300 miles in space and can travel with the orbit of the earth. With a combination of geostationary satellites and a set of ground stations spread around the earth, telephone and television signals "multihop" from earth to space and back again almost instantaneously. Millions of people in multiple countries can simultaneously watch the same live soccer match or news broadcast. Satellite communications allow state and private news services to broadcast on a regional or global basis, subsidiaries of multinational corporations (MNCs) to stay in touch with one another, and many international nongovernment organizations (INGOs) of the global civil society to coordinate the activities of their respective groups. For instance, Billy Graham's "Global Mission" became the Christian church's largest outreach in 1995 when his message, broadcast in 102 languages, reached nearly 1 billion people living in 172 countries.

The primary carrier of intercontinental telecommunications is the International Telecommunications Satellite Organization (INTELSAT), founded in 1964. INTELSAT is a consortium of over 100 countries cooperating together to form a network of satellites and earth stations for "multihopping" signals around the globe. Best known for transborder transmissions, INTELSAT does offer domestic transmission service, mostly for Third World countries, beginning with Algeria in 1975. INTELSAT enjoyed a monopoly for years, but, starting with President Ronald Reagan's insistence on deregulation in 1984, an "open skies" approach paved the way for private satellite systems to compete.[1]

Making use of worldwide telephone and satellite links, an "internet" of computers has mushroomed and offers users around the world access to an "information superhighway."

The global Internet is a network of national and local computer systems tied together by telephone lines. Governments, universities, libraries, private citizens, and other users "surf," or browse, through the intersections of the superhighway and can send and receive information on every imaginable subject. A special feature of the Internet is the World Wide Web, with a multimedia capability allowing the transmission of pictures, sounds, and graphics. With the Bill Clinton presidency, the White House acquired its own web site or address. So mammoth is the bulk and types of information moving through the Internet that operators use "web browsers," computer software that allows them to "surf the Net" efficiently.

In the spring of 1997, Bill Gates of Microsoft and a partner began setting up Teledesic Corporation, which will involve a constellation of about 840 close-orbiting satellites 435 miles above earth. This $9 billion investment will allow the Internet to reach the world through tightly synchronized satellites and ground stations. Presently, the Internet system reaches mainly North America and Europe, as they are "hard-wired" through telephone lines.

The modern marvel of the Internet is a major facilitator of the global civil society. Human rights organizations, environmental groups, and peace advocates inform and arouse their memberships to lobby governments and take direct action for their causes. Amnesty International, through its "Urgent Action Network," can receive reports of human rights abuses and, in just hours, prompt the flow of thousands of hardcopy letters toward the abusive governments. Messages can go out to thousands of members of INGOs in an electronic instant. Deposited in their E-mail (electronic mail) "mailboxes," the messages wait only until the members access them on their computers, much as people check their "land" mailboxes daily.

Not only does a huge information flow move constantly around the world, but this information carries values and creates expectations by growing numbers of people. Modern communication has helped break the grip of censors and has exposed millions of people to images of better economic and political lives. Information flows from the West helped to unseat the communist governments of Europe and is doing the same with Third World dictators. Cuba may become more susceptible to democratic and human rights influences in the near future. Since Cuba expelled the Associated Press in 1969, no U.S. news service operated in that country until 1997. Although the U.S. government recently approved 10 news bureaus for opening offices in Cuba, the Cuban government has accepted only Cable News Network (CNN) thus far.

News services, particularly CNN, have made politics planetary in scope by attracting millions of ordinary people to their round-the-clock television broadcasts and encouraging these people to take an interest in events far-flung around the globe. Millions of people, including President George Bush and Saddam Hussain of Iraq, watched live the dramatic events of the Persian Gulf War as they unfolded in 1991. Less dramatic but still important is the role of fax machines, electronic devices for transmitting facsimile (hence the term *fax*) pictures and letters over telephone lines. Millions of fax machines operate around the world to transmit business information, even in the most oppressive countries. Political information, however, transmits equally well from one fax machine to another. As communist governments began to topple in eastern Europe in 1989, Chinese students in America and Europe faxed news stories and pictures to their friends back home past Chinese government censors. These stories and pictures helped to simulate the demonstration for democracy in Tiananmen Square in Beijing, China, in 1989.

Reprinted with special permission of North America Syndicate

The global communications network, created for news and entertainment, is having the unforeseen effect of disseminating information that helps democratize societies. America's technological edge leaves this country well positioned to exercise the formidable *soft power* of its democratic ideology. Western ideals concerning democracy and capitalism easily reach foreign populations literally over the heads of their governments because of satellite communications. Recall from Chapter Four that soft power is the capacity to achieve desired outcomes through attraction rather than coercion.[2] Democracy's appeal in the world is the subject of a later chapter section.

Third World states have objected to the West's near-dominance over global telecommunications not only because of the dissemination of Western ideas but also due to Western ownership of and profiting from telecommunications. Beginning in the 1970s with the Third World's ascent to power within the UN System, these new states called for a New World Information and Communication Order (NWICO). On forums such as the 1976 UNESCO General Conference in Nairobi, Kenya, the Third World claimed the West used telecommunications to threaten its cultural independence and economic development. The West, in turn, accused the Third World of wanting free speech and press curtailed in the name of managing economic development but in reality to protect authoritarian governments. These issues led the United States and Great Britain to leave UNESCO in 1984 and 1985, respectively. Today issues on the North-South line are less ideological and more focused on sharing telecommunications for business reasons.[3]

ENGLISH AS A GLOBAL *LINGUA FRANCA*

Global communication's effectiveness depends partly on the English language, which serves the world as a ***lingua franca***, a language spoken in common by peoples of diverse cultures. This term originally referred to the Frankish language that medieval traders employed in the market centers of Europe. In practice, traders mixed French, Italian, Spanish, and other languages with the Frankish language.

Over 400 years ago, in Shakespeare's time, only 7 million people, on a small island off the European coast, spoke English. Today a billion people speak English, though for half of these people, English is a second language. English followed the expansion of the British Empire and the spread of British influence in commerce. As this empire waned, the English language still grew in importance, due largely to its literary influence, including works of writers ranging from Shakespeare to James Joyce. The rise of the United States, another English-speaking country, to a major power status after the Second World War further propelled the wide acceptance of English.

Other languages might have become global *lingua francas* but did not for different reasons. Chinese is the mother tongue of over a billion people, but Chinese sharply divides into various dialects. Further, Chinese never spread around the world as the communication vehicle for a global empire. French was a major candidate as a *lingua franca,* rivaling if not surpassing English until about the time of the First World War. Until then, French was the language of diplomats and European royal courts. The French also established their language across an intercontinental empire.

Gradually, however, English shouldered French aside, keeping French speakers busy trying to protect the purity of French at home. Periodically, the French Academy of Arts and Sciences, with the support of the French government, screens the French language to expunge foreign terms. In 1993, Culture Minister Jacques Toubon asked for a measure from the French parliament to help "police" the incursion of "franglais," a mix of English and French words, into the French language. A later French culture minister encouraged the development of computer software in French so French users of the Internet will not have to rely on English, which dominates the Internet.

Spanish speakers have begun to complain similarly to the French. In the spring of 1997, the First International Congress on the Spanish Language convened in Zacatecas, Mexico. Those attending and pressing for purity in Spanish in the face of English intrusions included the president of Mexico, the king of Spain, literary figures, and journalists. Spanish purists fear that the 21 Spanish-speaking countries, with a total of 345 million people, will drift to the use of "espanglish," a mixture of Spanish and English words.

A special advantage of English is that it absorbs terms and concepts from other languages aggressively. English has five times as many words as French and almost three times as many words as German. Some unabridged English dictionaries contain a half-million entries. English is a "language bulldozer" because it pulls so many foreign language terms into its lexicon and pushes its own words into foreign languages. Although English is difficult to pronounce for some, holds many exceptions to its rules of grammar, and is replete with idiomatic expressions and jargon, it is increasingly the foreign language of choice around the world.

In many countries, university students take English as a second or third language. Once, when this author was walking in the outskirts of Helsinki, Finland, a young lady stopped her car and asked for directions. In English, I explained that I did not speak Finnish. Without hesitating, she switched to flawless English, got her directions, and drove away. When Chinese students in Tiananmen Square held up signs for the world's TV cameras, the signs were in English so the planet could understand their message.

English is the language that journalists, academics, diplomats, and scientists use most around the globe, and it is the obligatory language for control towers at international

By permission of Johnny Hart and Creators Syndicate, Inc.

airports and for pilots making international flights. At international conferences, such as the "City Summit" at Istanbul, Turkey, in 1996, most publications are in English and attendees speak English more than any other language. Further, English is the language of the global civil society as people around the globe coordinate their missions to promote peace, improve human rights practices, and disarm the world. When an electronic communication system encircles the world in a language understood by a significant portion of the world's population, the metaphor of a "global village" comes closer to reality.

The disadvantage of English's widespread use is that English speakers often do not bother to learn foreign languages. America would have a better chance of retaining its competitive edge in world trade if American trade representatives could speak the languages of their foreign customers. Unfortunately, unlike schools in Europe and Japan, American schools rarely teach fluency in foreign languages, a major asset in a sales-oriented, capitalist world.

A COSMOPOLITAN WORLD?

If the world shared one **culture,** meaning the same behavior and beliefs drawing all peoples together as one social group, conflict could more easily give way to extensive patterns of cooperation. The reality of the world, however, is one of diverse, ancient cultures such as the Buddhist, Christian, Hindu, Islamic, and Jewish value systems that focus on religion. Moreover, the world still contains the varied political systems of communist countries such as China and Cuba, military dictatorships, and a rising number of democracies, with relations among these states sometimes prickly and even antagonistic. Obviously, the marvels of electronic communication and the availability of a *lingua franca* will not easily transform the world's diversity into a world culture, and to think so would be naive.[4] Adda Bozeman, a long-time scholar of multicultural differences, cannot fathom a world culture and believes manifold cultural differences are well entrenched for the indefinite future.[5]

Much of the world, however, does participate in a popular culture of movies, television programs, sports, dances, and foods. Some of the same literature, music, art, and theater plays offer enriching entertainment to millions of people around the world. Since a language can be a "vehicle for culture," the spread of English has enabled the United States to become a "superpower of popular culture," with its outpouring of media products around the world. If the French worry about their language, Canadians worry about their sense of national identity. Taking a critical view of American influence on Canada, Canadian Heritage Minister Sheila Copps denigrated this influence by referring to it as the "American culture vulture" in early 1997. In one effort to stop this influence, the Canadian government placed a tax on American magazines that a panel of the World Trade Organization ruled against as unwarranted protectionism.

What also may be in development is a more **cosmopolitan world** of leaders and significant numbers of citizens who can rise above provincial and nationalistic outlooks to embrace global perspectives. These *cosmolites* appreciate exemplary national models—for instance, Japanese management style, American universities, and Swedish health care—and they embrace a sense of common interests for the world. Such cosmolites are sometimes state leaders, but they also can be leaders and members of the global civil society. These globally aware people share progressive views in the human rights, environmental, and disarmament areas, and, increasingly, in the democratic movement.

If a world culture is in development today, it may involve only altruistic values. Yet such a culture, concerned with human progress, may be rising and bridging gaps among the ancient cultures of the world. After all, new behavior and beliefs can be consistent with old cultures and graft onto them. If we envision a future world culture, it might be one that is modeling, in rough fashion, after the behavior and beliefs of western Europe. On top of their language, religious, and nationalistic diversity, Europeans have accepted extensive economic cooperation, democratic government, respect for human rights, peaceful dispute settlement, and the diminution of the state as they have integrated into the European Union with its highly permeable borders. For decades the UN System, through its policies and norm-setting role, has tried to nudge the world in a direction not unlike Europe's accomplishments. The turn of the 21st century may be watershed years, determining whether an emerging international society can cohere around some form of shared culture.[6]

PROSPECTS FOR A DEMOCRATIC WORLD

The most widely accepted core around which a developing world culture may form is democracy. The end of the Cold War in 1991, accompanied by the collapse of the Soviet Union, heralded a new era in which democracy, for the first time, would be without a major ideological rival. In 1776, American democracy was a radical curiosity in a world of monarchies. When the legitimacy of monarchical power finally perished for most peoples in the ashes of the First World War, communism took hold in 1917 in post-Czarist Russia as an alternative system of rule. However, Nazism and fascism, from the 1920s to 1945, posed the greatest threat to democracy. Soon after the end of the Second World War, the Soviet Union's network of allies and client-states became locked in struggle with the Western democracies, led by the United States. Intense conflict, short of nuclear war, lasted over four decades between two completely incompatible ideological systems.

Understandably, when communism fell in Europe, supporters of democracy felt a sense of triumph. This remarkable development is one that Francis Fukuyama romantically called "the end of history," setting off a clamorous argument among policymakers and scholars. For Fukuyama, the "end of history" did not mean people would stop doing interesting things; rather, he meant the great epic struggle of the twentieth century over contending ideologies was at an end. With the Cold War over and the fall of European

TABLE 14.1
Historical Waves Affecting Democracy

First democratic wave	1828–1926
Reverse wave	1922–1942
Second democratic wave	1943–1962
Reverse wave	1958–1975
Third democratic wave	1974–

communism at hand, he came to believe the field is now clear for democracy to become universal as the final form of human government.[7] Generally, democracy has surged forward since the end of the Cold War, but without guarantees that it will survive in its new host countries or that it will move to yet other countries.

The basic meaning of democracy calls for a political process in which the government is responsive and accountable to the people.[8] There is also a constellation of institutions commonly associated with the democratic form of government, including free elections with competing political parties; an independent judiciary; universal suffrage; a wide range of rights, including free speech and the right of assembly; and the rule of law. In addition, to many minds, especially those newly embracing democracy, this liberal, Western governmental form suggests the material prosperity of free trade and capitalism. Although history has not necessarily bound democracy and capitalism together, the two frequently appear to be jointly in place.

About half of the nearly 200 states in the world today are democracies or near-democracies. Although many of these states are new and fragile as democracies, never in history have so many democracies existed.[9] The most recent historical wave favoring democracy started in the mid-1970s when Portugal and Spain began a change that netted 30 new democracies by 1990.[10] Many of these new democracies were Latin American countries deserting military dictatorship. When the Soviet empire disintegrated, 15 republics emerged from the Soviet Union, several more from Yugoslavia, and numerous democracies in the rest of eastern Europe.

The prosperous Asian Tigers of East Asia govern with "controlled democracy" pioneered by Lee Kuan Yew of Singapore. Controlled democracy allows some freedom and some representation in government, including the use of elections, but elites manage political affairs so that their preferred order is not seriously challenged. Influenced by the current wave of democracy, as many as half of the sub-Saharan African states have held elections, but usually without the complete constellation of practices associated with democracy, including full respect for individual rights.

Future prospects for democracy are good, although democracy is far from consolidated in some of the new democratic states, and setbacks are a real possibility. Especially disturbing is Samuel Huntington's observation that reverse waves usually follow democratic waves. Huntington's history of democratic and reverse waves appears in Table 14.1.[11] A third reverse wave may be unstoppable; yet historical patterns often prove unreliable for predicting the future. For the time being, supporters of democracy can dare to be cautiously optimistic.

Ramirez and Copley News Service

At least a hard core of western European democracies and the so-called Anglo-Saxon democracies of Australia, Canada, New Zealand, and the United States, as well as Japan, will remain firmly in the democratic camp. Latin American countries have already experienced two previous waves of democracy and reversed, with democracy giving way each time to a wave of military dictatorship.[12] Fidel Castro's communist Cuba stubbornly resists the current historical tide of democracy, making this island country an oddity in the Western Hemisphere.

At risk also are Russia and the eastern European democracies. These countries face a tough future of handling organized crime, ethnic conflict, and, most challenging, a painful adjustment to market economies. The reality is daily reports about democracy's ups and downs. Belarus took an authoritarian direction in 1996, and its president, Alexander Lukashenko, favors a centrally planned economy and a political union with Russia. A Bosnian election in 1996 took place only under the watchful eyes of NATO troops. However, Boris Yeltsin won reelection in 1996 as Russia's president, and he continues to push for democratic reforms in spite of Russia's many troubles. Another positive development occurred in January 1997 when Peter Stoyanov became the second democratically elected president of Bulgaria since the fall of communism.

In Asia, the prosperity of the area will probably secure the "controlled democracies" of Singapore, South Korea, and Taiwan, though they may not entirely lose their authoritarian bent. Further, it is in Asia where the three stalwart communist countries of China, North Korea, and Vietnam endure and where Myanmar (Burma) and Indonesia stubbornly remain military dictatorships. Sub-Sahara Africa, as a region, is the most dismal regarding democratic prospects, because the recent elections in some countries may prove to be fig leaves covering "strong-man" rule, and this sad area has the poorest economies and some of the most intense ethnic conflicts.[13] A bright spot on the African record is South Africa, now under the control of a black majority in a democratic system. Northern Africa and the nearby Middle East will, for the most part, probably stay with their authoritarian traditions. The anachronistic Arab monarchies especially will dedicate themselves to ruling far into the 21st century.

If the democratic wave can sustain momentum and spread to more states, important advantages will flow to the world. Larry Diamond, co-editor of the *Journal of Democracy*, has identified the benefits that derive from democracy. Democracies are more peaceful and avoid wars with one another. They are more likely to honor treaties and to obey international law in general. Democracies are safer for foreign investment and encourage international free trade, which brings greater prosperity for more people. These governments are more sensitive to nongovernment organizations (NGOs) on the domestic scene and to INGOs that promote environmental agendas, human rights, and peace objectives of the global civil society.[14] Contrasting the democratic half of the globe with the authoritarian half, one sees a general picture of prosperity and peace as opposed to hardship and conflict. Bearing in mind the goal of human progress, a world of democratic states clearly would be a better foundation for the emerging international society than a mixture of democracies and authoritarian states.

Will democracy, with its liberal order of free trade and respect for human rights, become pervasive in the world? A world of democracies may be in the making, but caution is necessary here, for we cannot assume an irreversible democratic force is at work. Yet John Ikenberry urges us not to underestimate the power of the Western model featuring democracy. He insists that the liberal democratic order was already well established after the Second World War and that the post–Cold War era, with the fall of European communism, is simply an opportunity to extend the liberal democratic order worldwide. Unlike some writers, Ikenberry views the turbulence following the Cold War's end as a normal and temporary time of adjustment as the liberal order extends itself.[15]

Regarding the future dispersion of democracy in the world, pushing and pulling forces are at work. Deciding how much the West should push democracy on the authoritarian world versus allowing this part of the world to pull the attractive Western model to itself will require artful statecraft. After all, the triumph of the Western model has spawned its own opposition. Traditional cultures naturally resist the onrush of new values and lifestyles. Moreover, the mostly authoritarian governments within these cultures already sting with resentment over the maldistribution of wealth and power favoring the West.[16] The push of the West must be gentle for fear authoritarian states will perceive and reject a Western "civilizing mission."

Views similar to those of Immanuel Wallerstein already have some popularity in the traditional, authoritarian areas of the world. Although a Westerner, this scholar discusses Western culture as the construct of the powerful and is critical of the West for setting up its own culture as the apogee of civilization for others to emulate.[17] Backlash to Westernization is already observable in the human rights movement, as discussed in Chapter Twelve on international organization. Authoritarians criticize the West's insistence on universal human rights practices, as well as other elements of the Western model, accusing the West of "cultural imperialism."[18] Authoritarians prefer the loose standard of "cultural relativism," meaning that whatever the practices in authoritarian countries, their way of life is natural to them and is as good as ways of life elsewhere.

The West's degree of push behind its model is gentle, and thus this model, centered on democracy, may have a chance to extend farther in the world. In addition to the content of Western media, with its global reach, Western countries call attention to democracy, human rights, and free trade in public speeches and summit conferences. The United States, for instance, has long operated the United States Information Agency (USIA) and the Voice of America (VOA) radio station, described in Chapter Six on intelligence and propaganda. Then there is America's National Endowment for Democracy (NED), which supports and funds democratic movements in other countries. More recently, President Bill Clinton called for a voluntary "Democracy Corps" to nurture democratic development and promote civic education in countries emerging from communism and authoritarianism.

Western states' push for democracy does not have to be entirely circumspect. Western states have rewards they can use, such as trade opportunities, foreign aid, loans, and other positive means, to encourage authoritarian states to flow with the current democratic wave. Ultimately, however, the diffusion of democracy in the world will depend on nondemocratic countries pulling the Western model to themselves because of its appeal. Democratic elements have cropped up among the populations of countries as diverse as China, Haiti, Kuwait, Mozambique, Nepal, and South Africa.

People such as Aung San Suu Kyi of Myanmar (Burma), the 1991 Nobel Peace Prize winner, are at work for democracy, risking their freedom and even their lives in democratic movements. She is one of several women distinguishing themselves as leaders in the democratic movement. Before her was Corazon Aquino in the Philippines during the 1980s, and now Megawati Sukarnoputri of Indonesia is advancing the democratic cause against authoritarian government. As never before in history, people want freedom and prosperity, and their leaders feel pressure to legitimate their rule by appealing to democratic ideals.[19]

A few scholars believe democracy has a chance to go beyond its state-by-state movement as the government form for domestic societies. Richard Falk thinks the global arenas of decision making, external to states, also may democratize, providing humankind with its best chance for humane governance.[20] On this point, David Held calls for *cosmopolitan democracy,* democratic processes that take hold in the global civil society activities of INGOs, IGOs, and particularly the General Assembly of the United Nations.[21]

To this point in the chapter, we have spoken of shared positive experiences that are encouraging cooperation as the base for an international society. A worldwide communication system carries ideas and images to many people around the world in minutes. English, as a global *lingua franca,* facilitates this communication network. In addition, popular culture and democracy are finding a warm reception in many places around the globe.

However, shared negative experiences also shape international relations. These include radical Islamic fundamentalism, a plague of diseases, and international organized crime. These matters are problems for the formative international society, and they challenge the world to find cooperative solutions.

THE REPUTED "CLASH OF CIVILIZATIONS": THE CASE OF ISLAMIC FUNDAMENTALISM

Before Western triumphalism over communism could subside, Samuel Huntington predicted that world politics would enter a new phase of conflict, with future "battle lines" coinciding with civilization lines in the world. Huntington called this predicted conflict the "clash of civilizations" and quickly provoked a debate among scholars and policy commentators.[22] One critic of Huntington's idea claimed states were still primary and would cross civilization lines to follow national interests, such as when Egypt, Saudi Arabia, Turkey, the United States, and western European states combined forces to defeat the Arab state of Iraq in the Persian Gulf War.[23]

Other critics have observed that the West is a repository of important and desirable values that amount to a formula for successful economic development and freedom that appeals across civilization lines. According to these critics, traditional leaders from other cultures have not found a model that can rival Western appeal with its progressive image.[24] Huntington has responded that his critics have not offered a better explanation of the world that accounts for what he sees as prolonged, violent conflict among peoples of different civilizations.[25]

The civilizations into which the world divides tend to coincide with major religious divisions, divisions prone to sharp conflict since the rise of fundamentalism in the 1970s. Although Christian, Hindu, and Jewish fundamentalism have become political forces, it is the upsurge of Islamic revivalism that has captured the most attention. Religious fundamentalism is partly a counterattack of ideas against Western secularism and modernization, but the situation of Islamic revivalism is more complex.

Although fundamentalists of several religions object to the West's rampant consumerism, crime and divorce rates, nudity in entertainment, and other matters they find offensive, the "clash of civilizations" between the West and some Muslims has a sharper line of conflict. Radical Islamic fundamentalists often direct violent acts at the West because they bitterly object to the West propping up governments the Islamics oppose. Making matters worse, Western governments are prone to accept the rationale for repression by Algerian, Egyptian, and some other governments in Muslim countries: These governments defeat radical revolutions that would otherwise topple governments friendly to the West and form a radical Islamic front across the Middle East. This front would sponsor terrorism and threaten Western interests, particularly oil supplies, according to antifundamentalist governments. Many Westerners regard Islamic revivalism as the newest ideology to threaten them, replacing the nearly defunct communism.

Regrettably, the West's perception of Muslims, derived through its own media, is a crass, distorted stereotype of radical and violent people. The reality is much different. One billion Muslims live mostly in Asia and the Middle East and constitute the second largest religious group in the world after Christians. They are the majority population in 50 countries. Most of these countries have secular governments, though a few, including Iran, Pakistan, Saudi Arabia, and the Sudan, are theocracies built around Islamic law. In addition to the Arab culture, which involves one-fifth of the Muslims in the world, the Islamic faith overlaps the Persian and Turkish cultures and the multiple cultures of Pakistan. Surprising to many Westerners, the largest Muslim country is Indonesia. As Muslims reflect different cultures, histories, and national foreign policies in their countries, they also hold varied religious views within the two Islamic sects of Sunni and Shi'a. Only a tiny minority of Muslim zealots use violence to bring about political change.[26]

The West's distorted view of the Muslim world increased with Iran's Islamic revolution in 1979, which marked a milestone in Islamic revivalism. Radical and violent events by a small minority have peppered the news ever since. For instance, a truck bomb killed 241 U.S. Marines in Lebanon in 1983, and two bombing attacks in Saudi Arabia in 1995 and 1996 took more American lives. Perhaps this problem reached a crescendo with the bombing of the World Trade Center in New York City in 1993, a major attack on American soil.

Upon closer examination, we find that the Islamic fundamentalists direct their anger less at the West than at their own corrupt, unjust rulers. The Gamaa al-Islamiyah bombing of the World Trade Center was a protest of the gift of $2 billion each year by the United States to the Egyptian government of President Husni Mubarak. It is this government the Gamaa al-Islamiyah group holds responsible for Egypt's overpopulation and poverty, and the lack of full democratic participation in Egypt's political process.[27]

In Algeria, as well as in Egypt, governments are repressing the demands for reform by Islamic fundamentalists. The gap between a small elite of rich and a mass of poor in Algeria, added to government corruption, created a large political party, the Islamic Salvation Front (FIS), that demanded reform. This party was on its way to election victory in 1991–1992 until Algerian military leaders blocked the democratic process with a *coup d'état*. The new military regime received support from Western governments, particularly France, further raising the ire of Islamic fundamentalists toward Westerners.[28] Any Westerner is a favorite target of terrorists in Algeria. The conflict in Algeria has taken thousands of Algerian lives and lives of foreigners since 1991.

The fissure along the West-Muslim cultural line may be partly bridgeable, however. Not only can Westerners come to appreciate the motives of fundamentalists better than they do, but there may be more cultural overlap than many realize. For instance, Jill Crystal, a specialist on Arab countries who focuses on human rights, believes the interests of the global human rights movement and Islamic reformers can coincide to some extent. Both want justice, accountability by government to the governed, the end of corruption, and the rule of law. For Islamic fundamentalists, however, the rule of law would derive from the Quran, the Islamic bible.[29]

Islamic fundamentalism is not necessarily a violent, revolutionary threat to a government in the Muslim world or in the West, as the Pakistani case shows. Despite some fundamentalists acting with violence in Pakistan, most have accepted access to government through the political party process, as in the case of the Jama 'at Party. Perhaps a healthy democratic process would prevent radicalization and the kind of violence that occurred in Algeria after the military blocked a majority fundamentalist party from governing.[30] Instead of accepting the suppression of Islamic fundamentalists in Muslim countries, Western governments might be wise to encourage democratic reform in these countries. Democracy would create competition between Islamic parties and the existing governments, obligating both to adopt proposals addressing their citizens' real problems.

INTERNATIONAL HEALTH THREATS

The scourge of disease respects no borders and demonstrates cruelly the vulnerability of all humankind. At the same time, responding to diseases is an excellent opportunity for multiple actors to maximize cooperation for the common good. Fighting the shared negative experiences of disease is positive for everyone, for the promotion of health in one country is the promotion of health everywhere.

In the 1960s and 1970s, confidence grew, especially with the elimination of the last smallpox case in 1977, that the eradication of all diseases was within the foreseeable future. The United Nations sponsored the "Health for All, 2000" accord in 1978. Yet today the world health community speaks of the "plague of plagues." Twenty well-known diseases have resurfaced, and 29 new diseases have appeared since 1973.[31] Some of these diseases are **pandemics,** meaning they spread worldwide and in a short time. Director-General Dr. Hiroshi Nakajima of the World Health Organization (WHO) said for the press in 1996, "We are standing at the brink of a global crisis in infectious diseases."

For instance, tuberculosis (TB) has been around a long time, but it has not died the predicted death. TB now has new energy. Eight million people contract TB each year, and 3 million die from it. TB is the number one killer among diseases in the world. New York City health officials are battling the W-strain of TB, which is especially resistant to drugs and kills half of its victims.[32] Malaria, an ancient disease, takes over 2 million lives a year and causes misery to millions more. Overpopulation has pushed more people into mosquito-infested areas of Africa, the worst-hit region, and mosquitoes have become more spray resistant.

A more recent disease, and probably the most feared in the world, is the human immunodeficiency virus (HIV). With the breakdown of the victim's immunities, HIV progresses to acquired immunodeficiency syndrome (AIDS). HIV has been around for decades but exploded into a pandemic only in the 1980s. WHO estimates that 30 million people in the world currently have HIV, and 1 million die each year from AIDS, the last stage of this disease.[33] Frequently HIV victims die by contracting parasitic diseases, such as TB, because of a weakened immune system. AIDS has so alarmed the world that December 1st is set aside as World AIDS Day to dramatize the danger of the disease and to renew education on how to avoid this dread disease. In addition, the 12th annual International Conference on AIDS will take place in July 1997.

First experienced in 1977, ebola is the newest serious disease threatening to be a pandemic. Humans, moving deeper into the forests of Zaire, recontracted this virus in 1995 from animals, and 245 people quickly died from it. WHO officials, however, believe they have contained ebola in Zaire.

Viruses, as well as bacteria, are capable of endless mutations of kaleidoscopic variety, leaving the medical community trailing behind in the search for appropriate vaccines. And infectious diseases spread easily. A cough can transmit the airborne TB bacillus. Mosquitoes transmit hemorrhagic dengue and malaria from one person's blood to another's. Some diseases are waterborne, making exposure to untreated water through drinking and bathing a major source of disease. Sexual contact and the sharing of "dirty needles" spread HIV from person to person.

Human movement magnifies the problem because diseases make the same journeys people do. In 1334, the plague, or "Black Death," traveled from Constantinople (today's Istanbul) across Europe and also reached large portions of Asia in the other direction. The Black Death killed an estimated 25 million people. More recently, the influenza of 1918–1919 became a true pandemic, costing 22 million people their lives around the world, probably more than the war dead of the First World War. Nearly a billion people contracted the influenza, though most survived.[34] Today a human individual, bitten by a hemorrhagic dengue–bearing mosquito in Africa, can travel to another continent in hours by jet plane, where local mosquitoes wait to bite that person anew, thereby spreading the disease to a whole new human population.

Many infectious diseases begin in the Third World, and then, through modern travel, reach the rest of the world. Disease epicenters form in crowded Third World mega-cities, where, because of squalor and poor health care systems, astronomical transmission of infectious diseases can occur. With a half-billion people boarding airline flights each year, diseases span the globe in days, if not hours. Millions of refugees and illegal immigrants on the move worsen the situation because medical inspections at custom checks may never screen the movements of so many people. Yellow fever, a disease not seen in America since 1905, threatens to invade the United States through illegal immigration. Medical screenings, when they are in use, do not always catch a disease that takes days to incubate, such as ebola. An infected person can pass a medical screening only to infect other people on the other side of the globe days later. Then, too, panic sets in with knowledge of a disease outbreak. News of ebola in Zaire in 1995 and pneumonic plague in India in 1994 set thousands of people fleeing as far away as possible.[35] War also disrupts the "war on diseases," if for no other reason than it makes vaccines difficult to deliver. The resistance to Russian rule in Chechnya led to the outbreak of 152 polio cases among Chechen children in 1995.

Cooperation by multiple actors should be at a premium in the area of disease control because political motives behind the problem of diseases is unusual. The structure of disease control begins with WHO, formed in 1948 as a follow-up to the League of Nations Health Organization established in 1923. WHO is one of the better-funded elements of the UN System and has been fairly successful in leading global campaigns against various diseases, though it has been unable to contain the recent "plague of plagues" mentioned earlier. At least WHO's Rapid Response Team, able to engage its resources with 24 hours' notice, did help stanch the spread of the ebola virus. WHO also has 200 collaborating centers around the world that the Internet wires together.

The amount of cooperation is not as extensive in the global health community as it should be, however. Beneath the global level are national health programs of widely varying effectiveness. Unfortunately, weak national links make for a weak global chain when global health strategies are necessary, as they often are. Occasionally countries deny the world health effort **transparency,** meaning complete disclosure about the presence and effects of a disease. The pneumonic plague cost India $2 billion in sales and travel expenditures as other countries boycotted India to prevent this disease from reaching their citizens. Sometimes countries deliberately hide diseases to protect trade and tourism rather than suffer India's experience.[36] Also, medical researchers have jealously fought over money and credit for medical accomplishments. Finally, the United States has withheld $211 million from WHO in an effort to force managerial reforms on this organization.

Ultimately, will medical technology and human cooperation or the growth of dangerous bacteria and viruses have ascendancy? Although the much ballyhooed supremacy over diseases has not come to pass, the potential of research and the positive role of cooperation can permit humankind to do better in fighting diseases than at present. Ridding the world of lethal and debilitating diseases is a shared negative experience everyone wants to end. Eradication of more diseases extends life, improves the quality of life, and can save billions of dollars in health care.

INTERNATIONAL ORGANIZED CRIME

The tentacles of organized crime, which reach octopuslike around the globe, is another shared negative experience that should invite considerable international cooperation. However, unlike with diseases, a human element is present that profits prodigiously from crime

Ronnen/Israel/Cartoonists & Writers Syndicate

and that ruthlessly and ingeniously confounds international policing efforts. In 1996, Roy Godson of Washington's National Strategy Information Center estimated worldwide crime profits at $1 trillion. International cooperation also falls short of its potential because the North-South conflict makes an appearance in international crime as well as the issue-areas of world trade and the environment.

Nonetheless, substantial cooperation in fighting international organized crime does take place because the pernicious effects of this crime demand attention. Thousands of lives are lost worldwide each year due to illegal drugs, and governments must divert billions of dollars needed for human social services into drug-related law enforcement. Those persons captured in drug-related crimes tie up courts and pack prisons with convicted felons. Large bribes, which drug smugglers can afford to pay, cause widespread corruption in governments, sometimes reaching the highest executive offices. Illegal drugs also destroy families, undermine work productivity and safety, and spread AIDS with the shared use of dirty needles. Other afflictions of internationally organized crime are the hardships of debt-bonded laborers illegally smuggled from Latin America and China. Many sufferers are young women, enticed by criminal organizations into prostitution with money and drugs and then moved by the crime organization from resort city to resort city until their health and beauty diminish. In early 1997, reports became common about thousands of attractive, educated Russian women whom Russian crime organizations lured, with false promises, into many countries as part of the burgeoning international sex trade.

There are several well-known examples of international crime organizations. The most famous is the *Mafia,* which originated in Sicily and became firmly rooted internationally after the Second World War. The Mafia (which incidentally, once meant *courage* and *resistance* in Italian) moved up from protection, gambling, and prostitution rackets in

Sicily to control heroin routes from Asia to Turkey and to Europe and America. The Mafia has ties to New York City's organized crime, sometimes known as *Cosa Nostra* ("our affair"), and has a community of Sicilians living in Colombia who participate in the lucrative cocaine trade to the United States. The Mafia bribes those they can and kills those they cannot. Italian law enforcement has faltered before the power of the Mafia. Four years passed before the 1992 bombing death of Giovanni Falcone, a famous Italian judge, brought the arrest of the Mafia leader responsible.

Better known to Americans are the drug cartels in Colombia. The cartels purchase cocaine processed from coca leaves, which are grown throughout the Andes Mountains, and then smuggle the cocaine through a variety of routes into the United States. The Cali cartel alone probably handles as much as 80 percent of the cocaine trafficking.

Chinese organized crime also has tentacles reaching into Europe and the United States. The Hong Kong–based *Triads* and Chinese American street gangs work together to smuggle and distribute "China White," a nearly pure form of heroin, to American cities. In addition, the Fujian gangs, from the Chinese province of that name, smuggle as many as 100,000 people a year to Europe and the United States. These victims work for years in sweatshops or as prostitutes to free themselves from their debt bondage. This form of international organized crime became widely known when the *Golden Venture,* a cargo ship carrying several hundred illegal Chinese immigrants, beached accidentally near New York City in 1993.

The newest organized criminals with international reach are the *mafiya,* or Russian gangs. These gangs spawned from the relaxed law enforcement atmosphere that followed the dissolution of the Soviet Union. In the changeover from the Soviet command economy to the free play of capitalism, a Russian criminal element became entrepreneurs of the wrong kind, for their methods involved bribery, murder, smuggling, and money laundering. By 1993, according to the Russian Ministry of Internal Affairs, organized crime controlled as much as 40 percent of the country's turnover in goods and services. The *mafiya* are especially vicious and kill hundreds of people a year. In November 1996, an assailant fired 11 bullets into Paul Tatum, a 41-year-old Oklahoma native, in a parking garage in Moscow.

Russian gangs have trafficked in illegal minerals, arms, and drug sales across the porous borders with the ex-republics of the old Soviet Union and now also seek entrance into the nearly borderless European Union. The emigration of Russians to the United States, especially to New York City in the 1980s and 1990s, has provided an opportunity to expand *mafiya* criminal activity across the Atlantic Ocean.[37] Russian gangs also have been active in car-theft rings that have stolen 300,000 American cars for the international black market at a loss of $900 million to American owners.

Criminal organizations traditionally have staked off regional turfs, with the Cali cartel controlling the cocaine trade in the Americas, the Sicilian Mafia the heroin trade from Asia to Europe, and the Triads reaching from Asia to the American Pacific cost. Today international crime organizations have become the criminal equivalent of multinational corporations. They have a nerve center for controlling and coordinating elements of their gangs as they operate in several or more countries and often on two or more continents. Organized crime uses sophisticated technology, including encrypted messages for faxes and cellular phones and computers for their recordkeeping. In minutes, organized criminals can circuitously launder money through a chain of banks by the latest means of telecommunications. In March 1997, the United States, without support from other industrialized democracies, proposed at the

Organization for Economic Cooperation and Development (OECD) that countries require users of the Internet to file their "computer keys," or codes, with national authorities. Then police could inspect the communications for terrorist and criminal activities.

Today organized crime is ascending above regional operations to form global connections. The Cali cartel sells heroin for the Sicilian Mafia in the Americas, while the latter moves Cali cocaine into European and Asian markets. In 1993, Colombian, Israeli, and Russian gangs joined forces to transport one ton of cocaine to St. Petersburg, Russia. So far, the global pattern consists mostly of mutual assistance among gangs rather than control by a single decision-making center.

National and international police units are fighting back, but the rise in organized crime activities suggests law enforcement efforts are not keeping up with new organizational patterns among criminals. To control an estimated $1 trillion in international criminal business, countries have made valiant efforts. The United States spent $14 billion in 1994, and all levels of American government have expended $250 billion in the last 15 years to fight crime, according to Drug Strategies, a Washington-based policy organization. The U.S. government has frozen bank assets of the Cali cartel and blacklisted businesses that front for this drug cartel. Much of the money the United States spends on its antidrug war goes to the countries supplying drugs. The intent of the United States is to help them substitute money-crops for coca plants and opium poppies and to enhance these countries' police and military campaigns against organized crime. In 1989, President George Bush even resorted to using America's armed services to interdict drug smuggling.

Yet, after all the efforts, drug flows of cocaine, heroin, and marijuana to the United States have risen. One major objective of the drug war has been to raise prices of drugs to prohibitive levels, but the prices have fallen with readily available supplies for street sales. The production costs of illegal drugs are so low that the drug market can adjust easily to the market pressures caused by law enforcement. Complete interdiction of the flow of these drugs may be impossible. For instance, a few small planes, slipping under radar nets, can supply the American market with cocaine for a year. Drug policymakers of the United States might do well to shift strategies by emphasizing education and the rehabilitation of addicts.[38]

Other countries also do what they can to suppress the illegal drug trade. They apply the usual techniques of custom searches, drug-sniffing dogs, infiltrating drug gangs, and toughening punishments, including hanging drug traffickers in Malaysia. In addition to turning to their military branches, some countries are enlisting their spy agencies, since these agencies are now less busy due to the end of the Cold War. The CIA and FBI infiltrate and spy on organized crime that reaches across international borders. The British MI-6 recently helped break up an organized crime ring headquartered in London. For the Russians, crime control, even in the case of international crime, must begin at home with laws that will distinguish and protect honest business entrepreneurs from organized crime, especially in the banking and financial areas.[39]

More promising are international coordinated efforts by Interpol (International Police) and now Europol (European Police), formed in 1992, to meet an expected precipitous rise in crime within the open borders of the European Union.[40] Because criminals enjoy advantages from the fragmented law enforcement of multiple national jurisdictions, the burgeoning regional and global crime rings necessitate an equal escalation in organization and cooperation by governments through such agencies as Europol and Interpol.

As enforcement efforts try to match strides with organized crime, especially in the drug enforcement area, the broad conflict between North and South makes another appearance. North-South differences undermine full cooperation in fighting drug smuggling. Principally, the producers of raw materials for drugs are in the poorer South, while the consumers are in the richer North. Each accuses the other of being the problem, as in the issue-areas of trade disagreements and environmental impact. The United States and Europe want Colombia and Peru to eradicate coca cultivation and for Turkey and Afghanistan to halt opium poppy harvests. The South, in turn, wants the North to educate its populations and rehabilitate its addicts. If you do not want the illegal flow of drugs, then end the consumer market, the South is saying to the North. Moreover, the South acquires needed income from drug sales for its national economies, though much of the drug money goes for rampant consumption by dealers and corrupting officials with bribes. The needful peasants who do the harvesting receive only a small share from the drug exports. Thus, governments of the North have been unable to persuade governments of the South to give complete cooperation.

We can see that shared negative experiences occur alongside positive experiences. Fundamentalists in several religious contexts object to "Western decadence," although the perception of Islamic revivalists as ideologically anti-Western is surely an exaggeration. The other negative experiences at least offer opportunities to cooperate for the common good. Stamping out organized crime is more complex than eradicating diseases because of human avarice and even political ill will. Presumably, everyone wants diseases eradicated.

SHARED EXPERIENCES AND INTERNATIONAL SOCIETY

Shared experiences can serve to draw separate peoples and states together. These experiences, especially democracy and communications, are helping to shape an international society whose development is leaning toward the liberal, Western model.

Realist Hans Morgenthau, however, is averse to wispy notions of an international society occupying the minds of scholars or policymakers. For him, these notions, which began in the nineteenth century and that President Woodrow Wilson projected into modern times, depreciate the role of power as immutable and universal in time and place. To stray from power and security as the core interests of states is folly to Morgenthau.[41] Similarly to Morgenthau, other realists have little confidence that a world of democracies can ensure the victory of international harmony and peace. Not only is advancing the democratic cause anathema to realists because it is a diversion from power, but realists assert that it is morally wrong to foist democracy on other sovereign peoples who are already content with their own governments and cultures.[42] That democracy has made significant, recent advances in the world because of its inherent appeal to others does not necessarily faze the tough mind-set of realists. For instance, in his recent book *Diplomacy,* realist Henry Kissinger gives short shrift to America's "soft" power as an exemplar of democracy and capitalism.[43]

Hans Morgenthau does not have a better view of communications helping to create a world society than he does of democracy. Although he wrote the original edition of *Politics Among Nations* in 1948, a time of oceanic cables, shortwave radio, and propeller aircraft, the gist of his writing on communications suggests that intensifying and improving communication would only drive states and peoples farther apart rather than uniting them. Morgenthau could see "one world" technologically, with planes and radio obliterating geography, but, he asserts, people will understand concepts such as democracy and freedom differently because of dissimilar cultures. For Morgenthau, worldwide moral and political spheres cannot correspond to the technological unification of the world.[44]

Neorealists, such as Kenneth N. Waltz, stick to the basic power paradigm and give scant attention to nonsecurity issues. When neorealists do sidestep issues immediately related to national security, they see continuing struggles among states, as when Stephen D. Krasner observes the North-South conflict over controlling wave bands in the telecommunications field.[45] For neorealists, interdependence and the necessity of cooperation in "marginal issues," such as communication, diseases, and crime fighting, mean an extension of the arena of conflict and competition. Neorealists believe it is the inherent nature of states to approach cooperative ventures to maximize their individual advantages, but they think states will desert cooperative tasks when short-term advantages become tempting enough.

Transnationalists, as today's bearers of the liberal, Wilsonian torch, are not naive about power as the realists claim; rather, they wish to tame power. Much as eighteenth-century philosopher Immanuel Kant called for "perpetual peace" through a society of republican states, modern liberal thinkers believe that as democracy spreads throughout the world, it will reduce war, expand global commerce, and develop a world opinion supportive of human progress on a range of nonsecurity issues. They dare to form a hopeful vision of world affairs and to forsake realism's premise of endless cycles of power struggles and war. Transnationalists recognize that the world is only half democratic while the other half is authoritarian, but they also observe that in the democratic half, people are freer, better off materially, and more at peace.[46] For a progressive international society, the worldwide expansion of democracy worldwide is clearly in the interests of all states and their peoples.[47] However, transnationalists realize their hopeful vision may or may not become universal.

As for communications, transnationalists, such as Robert O. Keohane and Joseph S. Nye, would take issue with Hans Morgenthau. The basic pattern of modern communication does not cause conflict and misunderstandings among peoples from different cultures. Instead, Keohane and Nye believe communication is a form of interaction that encourages agreement and cooperation. Common interests are identifiable, and new strategies for coping with international problems are possible because of communications.[48] Effectively handling pandemic diseases and internationally organized crime will require extensive exchanges of strategy ideas and information among states and the helpful nonstate actors of the global civil society.

The world has moved beyond the model of *international anarchy* with its cycles of war among major states and is even clear of the nightmarish stability of the Cold War. This stability depended on the threat of a nuclear Armageddon between superpowers. During the Cold War, the chief hope was for a détente of relaxed antagonism. Today the opportunities for the spread of democracy, and with it improved human rights and material prosperity, are good. In fact, more people than ever before in history share the same vision of human progress.

Anarchical developments, namely disorder and sharp conflict, are not impossibilities, however. Much of the world stubbornly holds onto authoritarian ways, and a few states, such as North Korea, possess dangerous weapons and unpredictable leadership. China remains obstinate and troublesome as a communist state and has a strong sense of its emerging economic and military power in Asia. China flexed its military muscle in 1996 by holding maneuvers around Taiwan to intimidate its neighbor during Taiwan's elections. Russia may be teetering between its new democratic/capitalist present and a resurgent potential as a great power with revanchist goals toward the lost territories of the old Soviet Union.

However, if present patterns hold, with the democratic wave as yet unsubsided and capitalism on the rise, a society will continue to form among peoples and states favoring the Western model. The *international society* of today contains many states with democracy in place and includes authoritarian states with elements of their populations desiring democracy. The fact that democracy is holding sway means there is a growing *consensus* in a world historically fractured by ideological conflict. Moreover, the absence of a great struggle over power and ideology among the leading states of the post–Cold War era has opened the way for an *orientation* of states stressing cooperation. The major states of today are more in agreement about the world order than at any time since the post-Napoleonic concert of European states in the early nineteenth century.

Moreover, below the level of ideological agreement, people are enjoying the same popular culture, wearing jeans, using cellular telephones, and, as transnational tourists, businesspeople, and students, are speaking to one another in English. The modern telecommunications system has the emergent international society hearing the same words and seeing the same pictures daily. Societies also form by dealing with the same *issues*. Adding to a long list, including environmental and peace issues, the world is learning how to cope with internationally organized crime and with pandemic diseases. The global civil society has formed specific organizations to help reduce the problems in these issue-areas as in others.

The evidence of this chapter falls short of strongly encouraging thoughts about an *international community,* although some sharing of values and experiences around the world is taking place. Ample evidence of cooperation across the fading East-West line of conflict contrasts with the North-South conflict that involves crime and health as well as other issues. Raw materials for illegal drugs come from the South, and many diseases begin there too, aggravating already antagonistic trade relations. In addition, it is in the South where Islamic fundamentalist objections arise to some aspects of the West. A common global heritage is not the history of the world, and the chances to build such a heritage, necessary for a world community, depend on overcoming the North-South divide.

CHAPTER SUMMARY

From this chapter, we have learned that sharing experiences and embracing similar values can be a societal building process in the world. Even the negative experiences of disease and crime are opportunities for cooperation if humankind is to control these transborder problems.

The peoples of the world do not live in insulated, domestic societies with little awareness of happenings across borders and around the world. With the telegraph in the nineteenth century and the radio in the early part of the twentieth century, news moved speedily to many parts of the planet. Sophisticated telecommunications, via satellite and computer networks, in the last quarter of the twentieth century have only accelerated the effects of communications. Millions of people around the world now share the same communications as they "multihop" around the world almost instantaneously. The wide use of English by one-fifth of the human population eliminates the need for translations for elites in most academic and scientific fields and for many political leaders.

The world also has become more cosmopolitan in the sense that one part learns from another, whether borrowing technology or organizational systems. Ordinary citizens in most countries frequently partake in the same popular culture of movies and music. More important, at a deeper level of involvement, many people in the world either enjoy democracy, along with capitalism, or they wish to do so. Democracy has triumphed. At least, it is the ideology left standing after other ideological systems have fallen or lost their legitimacy before the world.

Islamic fundamentalism is a belief system some scholars wrongly label the "new ideological challenge" to democracy. In the main, Islamic fundamentalism calls for reform within Muslim countries. The anger and violence of a tiny minority, directed at Western targets, distorts for the West the character of the Islamic revivalist movement. Islamic fundamentalist groups have shown they will work within democratic frameworks when they have the chance to do so.

The negative experience of disease creates positive energy for cooperation among countries and other health community actors such as the WHO. Virtually everyone wants diseases eradicated; unfortunately, cooperation in this area and the intensity of effort have eased. The world's health community became overconfident that, one by one, the diseases in the world would inevitably meet the same desirable fate smallpox did.

Internationally organized crime is tough to deal with because the solution depends not on scientific breakthroughs but on overcoming human greed and addiction. The tendency for the North and South to blame each other over international drug trafficking further complicates solutions that depend largely on the cooperation of many, if not all, countries.

All these experiences are societal builders. People around the planet recognize that they share much in common, and international society is enjoying robust development. Yet it will take a long time and many favorable conditions before the world becomes as tightly integrated as the EU, which comes close to the concept of a community.

POINTS OF VIEW

I am the right man in the right place at the right time. Not me alone, but all the people who think the world can be brought together by telecommunications.
—TED TURNER,
OWNER OF CNN
TIME, JANUARY 6, 1992

It is a remarkable fact that in Britain we have produced the world's most successful language. Yet a great many people today look in dismay at what is happening to that language in the very place where it evolved . . . they wonder what it is about our country and our society that our language has become so impoverished, so sloppy, and so limited—that we have arrived at such a dismal waste and of banality, cliche, and casual obscenity.
—PRINCE CHARLES,
QUOTED IN THE *GUARDIAN*
LONDON

Freedom is a virus for which there is no antidote, and it travels on information networks.
—WALTER WRISTON,
FORMER CHAIRMAN OF CITICORP
NEWSWEEK, DECEMBER 30, 1991

Democracy is the highest state of politics, the stage at which there is nothing left but the withering away of politics itself.
—JACQUES JUILLARD
LE NOUVEL OBSERVATEUR
PARIS

No one pretends that democracy is perfect or all-wise. Indeed, it has been said that democracy is the worst form of government except all those other forms that have been tried from time to time.
—WINSTON CHURCHILL

. . . few Latin American campesinos *will hesitate for long between the income from an acre of coca or poppy and the payment being offered for destroying their crops by their* gringo *cousins.*
—J. P. GENE
LIBERATION
PARIS

REVIEW QUESTIONS

1. What are modern telecommunications, and how are they involved in the transfer of values?
2. How did English become the *lingua franca* of the world, and what advantage does English have in this service to the world?
3. How cosmopolitan is the world? Do you believe a world culture is possible?
4. What are the prospects for the "third wave" of democracy to sustain itself into the 21st century?
5. What are some of the advantages associated with the spread of democracy?
6. How seriously opposed to the West are Islamic fundamentalists?
7. What is the modern "plague of plagues"? What circumstances are hampering complete cooperation in the area of disease control?
8. What is the distinction between HIV and AIDS?
9. How extensive is the pattern of cooperation among organized criminals at the international level?
10. How do you assess the development of international society through democracy and communications?

GLOSSARY

cosmopolitan world Beliefs and behavior shared widely in the world, ranging from popular culture such as movies to fundamental values.

culture Fundamental beliefs and behaviors concerning such matters as politics and religion that historically are particular to regions and countries.

geostationary The position of communications satellites 22,300 miles above earth to allow them to move with the earth's orbit.

lingua franca A language spoken in common by people with diverse language backgrounds.

pandemic A disease prevalent throughout an area or the world.

telecommunications The technology of communicating by electronic impulses, now possible on a global scale through communication satellites and computer networks.

transparency Complete disclosure by countries planning to cooperate with one another, as in the case of disease conditions, trade terms, or other matters.

RECOMMENDED READINGS

Daniele Archibugi and David Held, eds. *Cosmopolitan Democracy: An Agenda for a New World Order.* Cambridge, MA: Polity Press, 1995.

Benjamin R. Barber. *Jihad vs. McWorld.* New York: Times Books, 1995.

Christopher Coker. *The Decline of the West.* Boulder, CO: Westview Press, 1997.

Richard Falk. *On Humane Governance: Toward a New Global Politics.* University Park, PA: Pennsylvania State University Press, 1995.

Howard H. Frederick. *Global Communications and International Relations.* Belmont, CA: Wadsworth, 1993.

Lewis A. Friedland. *Covering the World: International Television News Services.* New York: Twentieth Century Fund Press, 1992.

Graham E. Fuller and Ian O. Lesser. *A Sense of Siege: The Geopolitics of Islam and the West.* Boulder, CO: Westview Press, 1995.

David Held. *Democracy and the Global Order: From the Modern State to Cosmopolitan Governance.* Stanford, CA: Stanford University Press, 1995.

Samuel P. Huntington. *The Third Wave: Democratization in the Late Twentieth Century.* Norman, OK: University of Oklahoma Press, 1991.

Mir Zohair Husain. *Global Islamic Politics.* New York: HarperCollins College Publishers, 1995.

John C. Merrill, ed. *Global Journalism: Survey of International Communication.* 2nd ed. New York: Longman Publishing Group, 1991.

J. M. Mitchell. *International Cultural Relations.* Boston: Allen & Unwin, 1986.

Dorothy Nelkin, David P. Willis, and Scott Parris, eds. *A Disease of Society: Cultural and Institutional Responses to AIDS.* New York: Cambridge University Press, 1991.

Robert Schaeffer. *Understanding Globalization: The Social Consequences of Political and Economic Change.* Lanham, MD: Rowman & Littlefield, 1997.

Michael Schuman. *Towards a Global Village: International Community Development Initiative.* Boulder, CO: Pluto Press, 1994.

Georg Sorensen. *Democracy and Democratization: Processes and Prospects in a Changing World.* Boulder, CO: Westview Press, 1993.

Paul B. Staves. *Global Habit: The Drug Problem in a Borderless World.* Washington, D.C.: Brookings Institution Press, 1996.

ENDNOTES

1. Howard W. Frederick, *Global Communications and International Relations* (Belmont, CA: Wadsworth, 1993), p. 104; Muhammad I. Ayish, "International Communication in the 1990s: Implications for the Third World," *International Affairs,* July 1993, pp. 494–97.
2. Joseph S. Nye, Jr. and William A. Owens, "America's Information Edge," *Foreign Affairs,* March–April 1996, pp. 20–36.
3. Ayish, "International Communication in the 1990s," pp. 487–510.
4. Michael Vlahos, "Culture and Foreign Policy," *Foreign Policy,* Spring 1991, pp. 59–78.
5. Adda Bozeman, "The International Order in a Multicultural World," in Hedley Bull and Adam Watson, eds., *The Expansion of International Society* (New York: Oxford University Press, 1984), pp. 387–406.
6. Robert Gilpin, "Global System," in *Order and Violence,* ed. J. D. B. Miller and R. J. Vincent (Clarendon: Oxford University Press, 1990), pp. 138–39.
7. Francis Fukuyama, "The End of History?" *The National Interest,* Summer 1989, pp. 3–18.
8. Vernon Van Dyke, *Introduction to Politics,* 3rd ed. (Chicago: Nelson-Hall, 1996), p. 4; Robert Wesson, *Democracy: A Worldwide Survey* (New York: Praeger, 1987).
9. Robert A. Dahl, "The Newer Democracies: From the Time of Triumph to the Time of Troubles," in *After Authoritarianism: Democracy or Disorder?,* ed. Daniel N. Nelson (Westport, CT: Praeger, 1995), p. 5.
10. Samuel P. Huntington, *The Third Wave: Democratization in the Late Twentieth Century* (Norman, OK: University of Oklahoma Press, 1991), p. 280.
11. Ibid., p. 16.
12. Tina Rosenberg, "Overcoming the Legacies of Dictatorship," *Foreign Affairs,* May–June 1995, pp. 134–52.
13. Naomi Chazan, "Africa's Democratic Challenge," *World Policy Journal,* Spring 1992, pp. 279–307.
14. Larry Diamond, "Promoting Democracy," *Foreign Policy,* Summer 1992, p. 30.
15. John Ikenberry, "The Myth of Post–Cold War Chaos," *Foreign Affairs,* May–June 1996, pp. 79–91.
16. Graham Fuller, "The Next Ideology," *Foreign Policy,* Spring 1995, pp. 145–58.
17. Immanuel Wallerstein, *Geopolitics and Geoculture: Essays on the World-System* (Cambridge, England: Cambridge University Press, 1991), pp. 158–99.
18. David P. Forsythe, *The Internationalization of Human Rights* (Lexington, MA: Lexington Books, 1991), pp. 2–3.
19. These two paragraphs are based in part on Tony Smith, *America's Mission: The United States and the Worldwide Struggle for Democracy in the Twentieth Century* (Princeton, NJ: Princeton University Press, 1994); Joshua Muravchik, *Exporting Democracy: Fulfilling America's Destiny* (Washington, D.C.: The AEI Press, 1991).
20. Richard Falk, *On Humane Governance: Toward a New Global Politics* (Universal Park, PA: Pennsylvania State University Press, 1995), pp. 106–8.
21. David Held, "Democracy: From City-States to a Cosmopolitan Order?", in *Prospects for Democracy: North, South, East, West,* ed. David Held (Stanford, CA: Stanford University Press, 1993), pp. 13–52. See also David Held, *Democracy and the Global Order: From the Modern State to Cosmopolitan Governance* (Stanford, CA: Stanford University Press, 1995).
22. Samuel P. Huntington, "The Clash of Civilizations?" *Foreign Affairs,* Summer 1993, pp. 22–49.
23. Fouad Ajami, "The Summoning," *Foreign Affairs,* September–October 1993, pp. 2–9.
24. Kishore Mahbubani, "The Dangers of Decadence," *Foreign Affairs,* September–October 1993, pp. 10–14; Robert L. Bartley, "The Case for Optimism," *Foreign Affairs,* September–October 1993, pp. 15–18.
25. Samuel P. Huntington, "If Not Civilizations, What?" *Foreign Affairs,* November–December 1993, pp. 186–94.
26. Mir Zohair Husain, *Global Islamic Politics* (New York: HarperCollins College Publishers, 1995);

Zackary Karabell, "The Wrong Threat: The United States and Islamic Fundamentalism," *World Policy Journal,* Summer 1995, pp. 37–48.
27. Karabell, "The Wrong Threat," pp. 44–45.
28. Andrew J. Pierre and William B. Quandt, "Algeria's War on Itself," *Foreign Policy,* Summer 1995, pp. 131–48.
29. Jill Crystal, "Authoritarianism and Its Adversaries in the Arab World," *World Politics,* January 1994, p. 285.
30. S. V. R. Nasr, "Democracy and Islamic Revivalism," *Political Science Quarterly,* Summer 1995, pp. 261–85.
31. Laurie Garrett, "The Return of Infectious Disease," *Foreign Affairs,* January–February 1996, pp. 68–73.
32. Ibid., p. 76.
33. Ibid., p. 72.
34. A history of influenza appears in Jack Fincher, "America's Deadly Rendezvous with the 'Spanish Lady,' " *Smithsonian,* January 1989, pp. 131–45.
35. Garrett, "The Return of Infectious Disease," pp. 69–73.
36. Ibid., pp. 73–74.
37. Stephen Handelman, "The Russian 'Mafiya,' " *Foreign Affairs,* March–April 1994, pp. 83–96.
38. Mathea Falco, "U.S. Drug Policy: Addicted to Failure," *Foreign Policy,* Spring 1996, pp. 120–33.
39. Handelman, "The Russian 'Mafiya,' " p. 89.
40. *World Press Review,* December 1992, pp. 11–16.
41. Hans Morgenthau, *Politics Among Nations,* 5th ed. (New York: Alfred A. Knopf, 1978), pp. 35–36.
42. Muravchik, *Exporting Democracy,* pp. 24–29.
43. Henry Kissinger, *Diplomacy* (New York: Simon & Schuster, 1994).
44. Morgenthau, *Politics Among Nations,* pp. 267–69.
45. Stephen D. Krasner, "Global Communications and National Power: Life on the Pareto Frontier," *World Politics,* April 1991, pp. 336–66.
46. Stanley Hoffman, "The Crisis of Liberal Internationalism," *Foreign Policy,* Spring 1995, pp. 159–77.
47. Smith, *America's Mission,* pp. 326–38.
48. Robert O. Keohane and Joseph S. Nye, Jr., *Power and Interdependence,* 2nd ed. (Boston: Scott, Foresman, 1989), pp. 39–40, 227–28, 262–63.

PART FIVE

CONCLUSION

CHAPTER 15

CONDITIONS AND TRENDS AT THE TURN OF THE 21ST CENTURY

In this final chapter, we will draw on previous chapters to form a broad view of today's international relations. When we began our intellectual adventure to learn about international relations, we intended to evaluate the world's progress at replacing patterns of conflict with those of cooperation. Specifically, we wished to find out if the international system has moved away from the Hobbesian order of anarchy to a Grotian order of greater peace and cooperation. Furthermore, we have inquired whether signs of an international community, similar to a Kantian order, are in sight.

We can make a final, overall assessment of how cooperative the world has become by returning to the eight basic elements used in Chapter One (see Table 1.1). These elements are authority, actors, orientation, force, interaction, issues, problem-solving level, and consensus. We will also speculate about the trends concerning these elements as they extend into the 21st century. Finally, we will inquire which of the three models of international anarchy, international society, and international community best fits today's world conditions based on these elements collectively.

AUTHORITY

Recall that authority in the world is weak because the international system is a horizontal system inhabited primarily by sovereign states with a diffusion of power among them. As a result, realists focused on the anarchy of the world and, relatedly, the states' all-consuming concern with power and national security. Without the authority of a world government, realists assumed conflict must hold primacy over cooperation in international affairs.

The growing ill fit between realism and the world shows up clearly with respect to the role of authority in the world. Realists have a hard time explaining today's extensive amount of cooperation. Cooperation frequently derives from governance involving actors voluntarily sharing goals and rules rather than the coercion traditionally associated with government. Because of this governance, a measure of order exists in a world that otherwise would be more anarchical.[1] Today's world is still one where "nobody-is-in-charge," but it is not a world where the notion of "everyone-for-themselves" reigns.

International organizations and regimes offer numerous rules and norms that guide actors' behaviors and move actors, if not toward harmony, at least several steps into an international society. Many rules and norms become part of the large and growing body of international law. As part of the international law framework, the three traditional functions of government—rulemaking, rule enforcement, and rule adjudication—take place in some fashion and in the absence of a world government.

Eighteenth-century philosopher Immanuel Kant, whose views went further than most in calling for an international community, saw no essential need for a world government. He feared such a government might be either ineffective or tyrannical. Kant was content to promote the idea of a loose arrangement of democratic states opposed to war. What is, in fact, presently transforming into place is an international society of growing numbers of democratic states that are responsive to rules in multiple issue-areas, with none more important than the rules preventing or limiting war.[2]

Transnationalists had to feel some exhilaration when the UN coalition punished Iraq's aggression against Kuwait. It appeared that with the Cold War over, the world could move beyond the realist balance of power system to collective security for keeping the peace.[3] Further, when wars do occur, as in Bosnia, there is now hope of limiting some types of warring activities through international humanitarian law. The war crimes trial at The Hague, Netherlands, of accused Bosnian war criminals is a statement by international society that moral standards apply even in war. Consequently, killing prisoners and raping women during a time of war can and should result in punishment.[4] Whether these positive developments will repeat themselves with any regularity is a question for the future, but the momentum of these developments may carry into the next century.

Authority through governance will probably increase as the world turns into the 21st century because actors can see a widening array of problem-areas requiring cooperation. We can expect further cooperation over rulemaking and rule adherence because the leading powers are free of deep ideological divisions and competing military alliances and because of tightening interdependence in the world.

ACTORS

Although the realists focused almost entirely on states, the world stage now has an ensemble of multiple kinds of actors. By the 1970s, transnationalists were able to see an increasing variety of actors interacting with states, both influencing states and being influenced by states. Joining the states on the world stage are MNCs, IGOs, INGOs, terrorists, churches, ethnic groups, and individuals. Recall that states form regimes, sometimes thought of as actors, by converging around rules and norms and that regimes often operate from the setting of IGOs. Among this diversity of actors, international law clearly recognizes IGOs and individuals as subjects in addition to states.

A mixed-actor situation has been mostly a healthy response to growing needs and concerns of people. Nonstate actors have had to fill in with services when states, limited to national jurisdictions, cannot handle problems by themselves. INGOs in particular constitute a global civil society of private citizens, able to think and act as a global citizenry. These INGOs advance environmental, peace, and human rights causes for the sake of all humankind. Hundreds of INGOs have established regional and global networks of communication and finance systems that allow them to be influential with states and IGOs and to join in debates at international conferences.[5] The nonstate actors enrich the international society and make it more serviceable to the human universe.

Although the state is no longer the dominant actor it once was, it is still the primary actor in the world regarding authority, wealth, and military power. If the state cannot dominate, it is not replaceable in the foreseeable future. The state remains as an indispensable executive agent serving as the intermediate actor between a national body of citizens and the international level.[6]

Some interesting changes regarding states involve the state system. Their number has grown dramatically to about 200 states, and their variation, based on culture, military strength, economic health, geographical size and location, population size, and other characteristics is kaleidoscopic. Accompanying the rise in the number of states has been a major change in the power distribution of the international system. The end of the Cold War and its bipolar power structure shifted the world toward a multipolar power structure. Although this power structure is forming into place, power divided among multiple states does not necessarily mean an even sharing of power. Making the power structure of the future especially difficult to discern is the role of China. Already expanding into an economic superpower, China, through the development of high-tech weapons, may assume a more prominent role, first in Asia and then at the global level as a military power.

The United States, with its wealth and military power, now enjoys leadership over a coalition of major states that has triumphed ideologically over communism and militarily over Iraqi aggression. Coalition unity and its U.S. leadership, molded by NATO and tempered by the Persian Gulf War, may prove temporary, however. Thus far, coalition unity has a mixed record. The coalition of major states finally agreed on strong action in Bosnia, producing relative peace and elections by the fall of 1996, but the coalition responded weakly to U.S. efforts when this country tried to check the Iraqi Army's advance against the Kurds in northern Iraq, also in the fall of 1996.

As for U.S. leadership of the coalition, international and domestic forces may be undermining what Charles Krauthammer has called America's "unipolar moment" as the world's lone superpower.[7] Internationally, a proliferation of sophisticated weapons is undermining the advantage of the United States. For instance, anti-aircraft missiles, available to many Third World states, can make punitive missions by a United States–led coalition a dangerous undertaking for their warplanes.

Domestically, less perceptible forces are at work. For example, declining education among its citizens will ultimately weaken America's economic competitive edge and its military strength. David Halberstam, well-known writer and critic, argues that the United States must revamp its educational system if it wishes to remain a prominent state. In a fast-moving, technologically oriented world, the average American high school student is receiving weak preparation for the changing world that will be the 21st century. As a consequence, the lack of a competitive educational system will have an insidiously debilitating effect on America's future role in the world. In the meantime, the better educational systems of Europe and Japan will further advance these countries as prominent states.[8]

The world's actors will probably grow in number and variety as humankind strengthens its global civil society to fulfill new needs and to act from a global perspective in the 21st century. States, however, reduced from the dominant actors to primary actors, will remain indispensable for the indefinite future because of their executive capabilities in military and economic areas. The continuance of United States leadership within a coalition of major states has become an uncertainty. Probably different states will

Watterson. Distributed by Universal Press Syndicate.

emerge as leaders in various issue-areas and regions in an increasingly multipolar world of the next century.

ORIENTATION

If one paramount measure is available to gauge change in international relations, it may be a shift in orientation from a basic pattern of conflict to one of cooperation. Conflict, or so realists would tell us, has been the hallmark of international relations and has appeared frequently in history in the lethal form of war. Realists at least agree that states cooperate when it is in their interest to do so. For realists, though, such behavior is occasional, while for transnationalists cooperative behavior is increasingly common.[9]

In recent years, the general decline in international warfare and the absence of war among major states have reoriented the thinking of many scholars about the sharp conflict of war. Most wars today occur inside Third World states as civil wars or revolutions, while at the international level, the large majority of states at least co-exist and frequently cooperate over shared problems. The end of the Cold War and of most ideological division in the world offers rich opportunities for patterns of cooperation to widen and deepen.

Currently, the most prominent conflict among the major states may be the regional bloc orientation in trade. What should be healthy world competition in trade has become a three-way trade conflict among the Asian-Pacific, EU, and NAFTA groups. The worldwide recessionary tendencies of the 1980s made a further extension of free trade terms difficult to achieve. Yet the completion of the Uruguay Round (1986–1994) of the GATT offered encouragement for the expansion of world trade and made possible the creation of the World Trade Organization. So far, trade disagreements have not become so sharp as to undermine faith in the benefits of global free trade. Although major trade states have gone to the brink of trade wars in the 1990s, they have backed off and compromised, realizing the potential for mutual harm. Thus far, the WTO has had a marked success at resolving trade conflicts.

Repeated favorable experiences through cooperation are propelling further cooperation in the late twentieth century. As states and other actors learn that cooperation holds payoffs, they naturally expect extended patterns of cooperation to bring further benefits in the future. Cooperative change, importantly, is not just in the statistics of lowered casualty rates or rising trade and investment flows but in the mind-sets of actors who recognize that bold, basic changes are under way.[10]

Conflict has increasingly given way to greater cooperation among states, and as these actors learn that cooperation produces benefits, we can expect patterns of cooperation to become more prevalent as we enter the 21st century.

FORCE

Traditionally, states have used force as they saw fit, believing that "might makes right." Force, of course, can range from economic pressure to military attack. According to many realists, only a balance of power system can restrain force of the military kind. Under this system, the expectation is that prudence will check the use of force when states and opponents match one another in power or when a goal is not worth the combat costs involved. In the Cold War, the balance became a "balance of terror" based on nuclear weapons. Fortunately, with the end of the Cold War, the danger of a superpower nuclear war, which overshadowed humankind for half a century, has diminished significantly.[11] Today the danger of nuclear weapons occurs less in the deterrence context of major states and more in the area of nuclear proliferation among radical Third World states.[12]

Transnationalists make much of interdependence, but they take note of its presence in security matters as well as in other issue-areas. States are learning that the pursuit of national security in a unilateral way will only generate fear on the part of other states. Arming for self-defense by one state means arming for offense to a neighbor. States have begun to realize their security is indivisible from the security of other states. Mutually disarming, taking part in peacekeeping missions, and supporting collective security against aggressors show that states understand their security depends on one another.

During the twentieth century, attempts to break from the historical pattern of using force to settle issues occurred through bold experiments. These experiments were the League of Nations and the United Nations. Both attempted to restrict the use of force by international law and even to punish aggressors. While the League experiment resulted in ignominious failure, the United Nations has experienced a partial but promising success. That success has been sufficient to establish a widespread perspective that international war is no longer a normal means to a political end in the Clausewitzian sense.[13] War, more than ever before, has become the exception and not the rule. Given present trends, international war could be on its way to obsolescence.

War and more limited uses of force still occur in state practice, however. In addition to current revolutions and civil wars, areas of international conflict exist that could still explode into war. In the Middle East and Asia, arms races involving missiles and ABC dread weapons are disturbing matters that warrant the serious attention of weapons regimes.

Fortunately, recent international wars have not encouraged states to turn to this option. Argentine aggression in 1982 against the Falkland Islands and Iraq's attack on Kuwait in 1990–1991 ended in failure, with much loss of life and war material. The Iranian-Iraqi War of the 1980s was the longest and most expensive war of recent times, yet it ended in stalemate. Moreover, the lesson is not lost on most states that the Soviet Union experienced economic decay in part because of large outlays of its GNP for superpower weaponry. In contrast, Germany and Japan prospered with a small percentage of their countries' GNP going for military capability.[14]

The best hope for leaving lethal force behind in history is to "unlearn" war. It is arguable that the use of force for systematic killing among humankind is unnatural and thus avoidable. After all, killing within a species is a practice peculiar to the human animal. Of course, the causes of war, including learned behavior, remain in dispute. So far, the "zone of peace," where force is absent from state relations, exists among the major states, stretching from Japan and Australia across North America and throughout western Europe, and this zone is expanding. Eastern Europe and Russia have the potential to become firmly established members of the zone of peace, although NATO expansion agitates Russian nationalism.

Eighteenth-century philosopher Immanuel Kant saw war as becoming impossible for Europe because of cultural commonality and an interdependence of interests. In modern times, a similar pattern of conditions could spread to other regions of the world, hence extending the zone of peace.[15] Most states at odds today prefer to use only "soft" power such as diplomatic persuasion or force no greater than economic sanctions. It is a profound historical development that the international system is no longer a war system, at least for a large majority of states.[16]

The use of force has been the constant companion of history. Yet many states in modern times have found that fulfilling many of their interests, including security, is no longer possible through power alone. Further, the legal proscription against war now has much currency in the world. In the coming 21st century, force may become an option only for terrorists and a few Third World states.

INTERACTION

Realists have compared the interactions of states to billiard balls that can roll across a table independently of one another, but clash when they make contact. This picturesque metaphor does not nearly approximate the evolving society of states. The international society of today springs from the growing recognition that states are interdependent, and this situation provides a different picture than clashing billiard balls. States, traditionally proud and defensive over sovereignty, now respond to the pulling force of mutual dependence. More and more, states have to work together to deal effectively with the issues they face. The growing interdependence of the world and the cooperation it encourages have become the central concern of the transnational approach to international relations.

Interdependent interaction leads to the joint management of many issues through cooperative regimes based on accepted rules and norms. Importantly, these regimes work as well as they do because "regimes can learn."[17] That is, policymakers involved in coordinating activities through the regimes draw on the lessons of their experiences to improve cooperation. National leaders, for instance, upon learning that protectionism hurts their national economies while free trade expands them, focus on removing restrictions to trade, such as through the GATT rounds.

The nature of interaction around the world offers some variation, however. Areas of war-threatening conflict persist in a few places, while the process of economic integration is at work to different degrees in Asia, Europe, and North America. The success of the

European Union amounts to the apogee of responding positively to the pulls of interdependence. The EU has managed a level of economic integration among its 15 member-states that requires a supranational type of political coordination. The EU even achieves a degree of common cultural identity associated with the concept of international community. Despite speaking different languages, the multiple nationalities of the European Union share many values concerning democracy, human rights, and capitalism. Regardless of its enviable accomplishments, the EU is unlikely to achieve a common currency and bank within the planned time frame, and controversy, such as Great Britain's problem with "mad cow" disease, can still be disruptive.

A major and deepening trend for the 21st century is likely to be an intensifying interdependence that propels states to cooperate for mutual benefits. Actors are realizing that in order for "us" to have peace, more wealth, better health, and a sustainable environment, "all" must enjoy these values as indivisible interests.

ISSUES

In his 1993 presidential address to the International Studies Association, Charles W. Kegley, Jr., observed that realism, as a paradigm, had become less relevant for understanding international relations. He contends that realism cannot properly address a global agenda that is much broader than security concerns, especially because of new realities of the post–Cold War era.[18] Over much of the history of the state system, national security was the chief concern of the state, and so for a time realism was the appropriate mode of study. For the last several decades, however, multiple issues have produced an evolving global agenda in addition to security. Now the world's agenda includes the sharp competition of world trade, ecological damage to the biosphere, numerous human rights violations, ethnic-driven national disintegration, AIDS, arms proliferation, and drug trafficking, among other concerns.

Many actors view these issues as global in nature and urge the acceptance of global strategies to deal with them. Recognition of these global issues has helped move the world from a national to a more cosmopolitan outlook, helping to give rise to both the global civil society and the transnational approach among scholars.[19] Nevertheless, efforts to find solutions to global issues are halting and irregular, and the outcomes of these issues are unknown.

The issue that may prove the most intractable is the *problematique* concerning the interplay of overpopulation, the finite stock of world resources, and the need for economic growth to meet burgeoning human demands. Unfortunately, the continued population growth undermines the capacity of the environment to support the necessary economic expansion. Without an unprecedented outpouring of human services worldwide, including health care, education, adequate food, housing, jobs, and other human needs, the 10 billion people, and maybe as many as 14 billion, of the 21st century will experience sharp scarcity. An already divided world of "haves" and "have-nots" may then witness worsening poverty. An injustice of such magnitude, with its conflict-prone "politics of scarcity," may militate against the formative international society. Somehow the world must check its population growth, protect its environment, and increase its wealth, all at the same time.

In *Preparing for the Twenty-First Century,* Yale historian Paul Kennedy foresees a grim future for the coming century. Professor Kennedy argues that a technological revolution in the North may sustain the good life there, but the continued population explosion of the South will further impoverish the living standards of the world's majority, which lives in the South. Professor Kennedy worries whether the states and global and regional organizations can tame the forces degrading life on earth.[20]

Jacques Attali's outlook in *Millennium: Winners and Losers in the Coming Order* is more positive than Kennedy's. He believes the world's peoples today hold the power to shape their common future if leadership will be wise enough to look beyond national sovereignty and develop a new perception of global stewardship. Attali believes, however, that improvement will require much long-term cooperation and sharing if we are to close the gap between a rich North and a poor South so all of human posterity can have a better life.[21]

To the international society's credit, combined efforts at policymaking are under way to improve the peace and well-being of the world. These efforts represent much progress over a focus on national security in the more anarchical, war-oriented times of the past. Efforts to reduce problems in multiple issue-areas will probably continue into the 21st century, but the injustice involved in the maldistribution of human wealth and welfare in the world may remain the most obdurate issue of all.

PROBLEM-SOLVING LEVEL

Historically, states have been able to carry out many activities unilaterally. Until modern times, most of their problems existed inside their borders, where they possessed adequate authority and resources to deal with these problems. The chief problem arising outside the state was the danger of war in an anarchical world, a danger that international law and diplomacy only partially moderated.

By the nineteenth century, European states had become increasingly aware that their interests sometimes intertwined with the interests of others, and so these states came to use an occasional conference to reach agreement. The multilateral conference for problem solving became a regular and fundamental part of international relations during the twentieth century. During the last decade of this century, world conferences, with multiple kinds of actors attending, have convened to improve the environment, human rights, population matters, problems of cities, and food shortages. While cooperation does not always follow from conferences, multiple kinds of actors can negotiate and put into place policies for common problems through conference diplomacy. Of course, agreement can fail, or conference participants may achieve only a partial settlement of issues, such as at the Earth Summit in 1992.

The multilateral level for problem solving creates the social interaction needed for an international society and is highly useful for generating norms and rules for this society. Occasionally, the products of multilateral conferences may amount only to high-flown principles as policy guidelines over such matters as economic development or the behavior of MNCs. Yet other multilateral meetings may produce treaties to which states and non-state actors will adhere in the future as international law.

Accelerated changes in technology in the areas of telecommunications and air travel have substantially facilitated meetings at the global and regional levels for all kinds of actors. Still, the more specialized meetings of the major states, as in the cases of the Group of Seven and the UN Security Council, have the most impact by determining global trade terms or responses to threats to the peace. Coordination among the major states has become fairly regular, showing up in the UN coalition during the Persian Gulf War and later in the Bosnian intervention by NATO. Whether this coalition can become a more harmonious concert of states, not only sharing democratic and free market values but achieving coherence over interests as well, remains a question for the future.

The lack of full and unqualified support by coalition states when Bill Clinton retaliated with cruise missiles in response to Iraq's troop movement into northern Iraq in 1996 makes us give pause before assuming an imperturbable harmony is in place among the major states. Had Iraq again committed aggression beyond its borders, perhaps the Persian Gulf War coalition of 1991 would have been quick to reassemble.

Multilateral problem solving is an established part of the emerging international society and will undoubtedly serve into the 21st century. This level of problem solving invites the smaller states and nonstate actors to participate in shaping policy in many areas of concern. However, reaction to some problems, especially the most serious security threats, will remain the prerogative of the major states, continuing a long-standing historical tradition.

CONSENSUS

The focus of realists on power and war delayed appreciation for an evolving societal sharing of values on the international level. These values developed first in Europe and then spread to the rest of the world. Between the Peace of Westphalia, recognizing the sovereignty of European states at mid-seventeenth century, and the height of Europe's colonial domination at the end of the nineteenth century, Europeans came to embrace an appreciable stock of values. In addition to a system of independent states, buttressed by nationalism, Europeans learned to use balance of power techniques, including war, to prevent one state from imposing an empire on the others. Diplomacy provided useful communication and international law the rules to guide trade and the practice of war. In the early nineteenth century, European society took clearer form as these states made use of conference diplomacy to deal with multistate problems and to develop the norm of major states taking responsibility for peace. In the same century, democracy gathered momentum as the appropriate form of government reaching a touchstone status as a model government after the First World War.

The world has become more than a globalized European international society, however. With the end of colonialism, Europe was able to impose values no longer; rather, other parts of the world, to some degree, chose to embrace similar values leading to a worldwide international society. Although Hedley Bull once worried that the diverse multiple cultures of the world would weaken the formative international society stemming from Europe, subsequent events have led Barry Buzan to believe a shared stock of values has managed to encompass most of the world in a positive way and is a remarkable success.[22]

As European colonialism began to break up after the Second World War, the emerging new states could share in international law and democratic values already established, but also could insist on new values according to their preferences. These new states were nonwhite, weak, and poor. As nonwhite states, they insisted that the evolving human rights movement decry racial and ethnic discrimination. As weak states, they especially wanted force to be illegitimate in the affairs of states. And as poor states, they objected to free trade rules if such rules amounted to neocolonialism, and they believed the rich North should perform a welfare service as a moral duty to help raise the South's economic performance. The Law of the Sea conferences from 1973 to 1982 stand out as instances of non-Western states injecting their own interests and perspectives into the stock of values vested in the final treaty, including sharing the rewards of seabed mining.

A global society also has emerged because of the science and technology that have allowed the world to become a "global village" through travel and communication. Outgrowths are the use of English and development of a consumer "culture" around the globe.

Yet the accumulation of a stock of values as a core for forming the international society of today is not without some turbulence. While the Cold War ideological divide has lapsed, a handful of unrepentant, sometimes hostile communist states remain. China has atomic weapons, and North Korea may have one or more atomic bombs. Several rogue states, such as Iran and Iraq, define their foreign policies in mostly anti-Western terms and pursue dread-weapon programs. Resurgent nationalism in Russia, where superpower weapons co-exist with a weak government and economy, remains a concern. Also, gross inequality between North and South creates a divisive "class system" of states. Finally, perhaps most disruptive today is ethnic "tribalism," causing both domestic and international havoc. The cultural particularism of ethnicity can easily take the strident form of rebellion and terrorism.

On balance, the evidence of an international society progressively taking shape outweighs the turbulent hindrances that threaten to pull us backward toward a model of conflict-prone anarchy similar to that offered by Thomas Hobbes. Humankind today is more than a loose system of interacting states that clash if they make contact. We at least live in a norm-governed society where actors recognize the need for and benefits of cooperation that Hugo Grotius described. Nevertheless, we must remain aware that while a shared stock of values is presently accumulating, a deep sense of common interests and identity, a "oneness of humanity" needed for an international community, does not characterize the planet as yet. Probably not even the peoples of the European Union have risen above some nationalistic outlooks and preoccupation with national interests. If Immanuel Kant could review the present world, he might be hopeful that a world sharing extensive trade and working hard for peaceful democracies also might be able to take a more healthy, cosmopolitan view of itself.[23]

The world has gone through a historical transformation, witnessing European society's stock of values spread in the world and mix with the contributions of other regions of the globe. With the downfall of communism, the rising popularity of free trade and democracy provides a good chance for these values to expand into more countries as we move into the 21st century, further embedding a sense of international society among the peoples of the world.

A PARTING WORD

The reader has probably discerned that this textbook is not only a description of international relations but also an argument that the world is in transition from an anarchical order to a societal order. Today there is greater agreement over the goals, rules, and institutions that make up the emerging international society than ever before in history. Of the analytical models that have guided this text, *international society* best fits the real-world situation.

We cannot assume, however, that the world will improve further because of positive, immutable historical forces. Leaders and citizens must act for a better world. People educated in international matters are better able to understand and deal with a global context that affects their lives. If they share a vision of a progressive international society, such people can help shape a better world in which to live. This textbook was written with this kind of education and vision in mind.

POINTS OF VIEW

If anyone tells you something strange about the world, something you had never heard before, do not laugh but listen attentively; make him repeat it, make him explain it; no doubt there is something there worth taking hold of.
—GEORGES DUHAMEL,
FRENCH AUTHOR (1884–1966)

That we live forward while we can think only backward is a perennial condition.
—JOHN LUKACS
THE END OF THE TWENTIETH CENTURY

Our time has taught us that we live in one world, and that peace is possible.
—PIERRE HASSNER
INTERNATIONAL AFFAIRS, 1994

It is the spirit of cooperativeness, not confrontation, that makes the world go round.
—JOHN KEEGAN
A HISTORY OF WARFARE

Peace is not an absence of war, it is a virtue, a state of mind, a disposition for benevolence, confidence, justice.
—BARUCH SPINOZA

Mankind has always lived dangerously. The dangers are no longer the same, but they have not disappeared.
—DAEDALUS, 1966, P. 502

REVIEW QUESTIONS

1. Do you think we will ever have a world government? Do we need one? What about supranational institutions?
2. Do you believe the state is becoming obsolete? What about war?
3. Can you imagine a world more peaceful and cooperative in the future?
4. Do you think the world is better off in the post–Cold War era than before? Why or why not?
5. Can the world follow Europe into deeper integration as an international community? Why or why not?
6. Can you identify any new and different issues the world is likely to confront that this textbook has not covered?
7. What turbulent forces in the world today might undermine the cooperative process that has been made?
8. How does this textbook compare with other texts you have used in your college education?

RECOMMENDED READINGS

Jacques Attali. *Millennium: Winners and Losers in the Coming World Order.* New York: Random House, 1991.

Francis Fukuyama. *The End of History and the Last Man.* New York: The Free Press, 1992.

David Halberstam. *The Next Century.* New York: William Morrow, 1991.

Charles Hauss. *Beyond Confrontation: Transforming the New World Order.* Westport, CT: Praeger, 1996.

Paul Kennedy. *Preparing for the Twenty-First Century.* New York: Random House, 1993.

David C. Korten. *Getting to the 21st Century: Voluntary Action and the Global Agenda.* West Hartford, CT: Kumarian Press, 1990.

John Lukacs. *The End of the Twentieth Century and the End of the Modern Age.* New York: Ticknor & Fields, 1993.

Geir Lundestad and Odd Arne Westad, eds. *Beyond the Cold War: New Dimensions in International Relations.* New York: Scandinavian Press, 1993.

Mihaly Simai. *The Future of Global Governance: Managing Risk and Change in the International System.* Washington, D.C.: United States Institute of Peace Press, 1994.

Max Singer and Aaron Wildavsky. *The Real World Order: Zones of Peace/Zones of Turmoil.* Chatham, NJ: Chatham House, 1993.

ENDNOTES

1. James N. Rosenau, "Governance, Order, and Change in World Politics," in *Governance Without Government: Order and Change in World Politics,* ed. James N. Rosenau and Ernst-Otto Czempiel (New York: Cambridge University Press, 1992), pp. 4–8.
2. Pierre Hassner, "Beyond the Three Traditions: The Philosophy of War and Peace in Historical Perspective," *International Affairs,* October 1994, pp. 745–47.
3. Alexander L. George, "Regional Conflicts in the Post–Cold War Era," in *Beyond the Cold War: New Dimensions in International Relations,* ed. Geir Lundestad and Odd Arne Westad (New York: Scandinavian Press, 1993), pp. 125–26.
4. Geoffrey Best, "Justice, International Relations and Human Rights," *International Affairs,* October 1995, p. 785.
5. David C. Korten, *Getting to the 21st Century: Voluntary Action and the Agenda* (West Hartford, CT: Kumarian Press, 1990), p. 215.
6. Best, "Justice, International Relations and Human Rights," p. 798.
7. Charles Krauthammer, "The Unipolar Moment," *Foreign Affairs,* 70, no. 1 (1991), pp. 23–33.
8. David Halberstam, *The Next Century* (New York: William Morrow, 1991).
9. Arthur A. Stein, *Why Nations Cooperate: Circumstance and Choice in International Relations* (Ithaca, NY: Cornell University Press, 1990), p. 174.
10. Charles Hauss, *Beyond Confrontation: Transforming the New World Order* (Westport, CT: Praeger, 1996), p. 153.
11. Mihaly Simai, *The Future of Global Governance: Managing Risk and Change in the International System* (Washington, D.C.: United States Institute of Peace Press, 1994), p. 340.
12. Hassner, "Beyond the Three Traditions," p. 753.
13. Hauss, *Beyond Confrontation,* pp. 17–18, 143.
14. Michael Howard, "The Control of the Arms Race," in *Beyond the Cold War,* p. 46.
15. Hassner, "Beyond the Three Traditions," p. 748.
16. Chris Brown, "International Theory and International Society: The Viability of the Middle Way?" *Review of International Studies,* April 1995, p. 195.
17. Hauss, *Beyond Confrontation,* p. 223.
18. Charles W. Kegley, Jr., "The Neoidealist Movement in International Studies: Realist Myths and the New International Realities," *International Studies Quarterly,* June 1993, pp. 134, 141.
19. Best, "Justice, International Relations and Human Rights," p. 778; Hassner, "Beyond the Three Traditions," p. 751.
20. Paul Kennedy, *Preparing for the Twenty-First Century* (New York: Random House, 1993).
21. Jacques Attali, *Millennium: Winners and Losers in the Coming Order* (New York: Random House, 1991).
22. Barry Buzan, *People, States and Fear: An Agenda for International Security Studies in the Post–Cold War Era* (Boulder, CO: Lynne Rienner Publishers, 1991), pp. 166–74.
23. This paragraph borrows partly from Brown, "International Theory and International Society," pp. 185–87.

INDEX

ABC (atomic, biological, chemical) weapons, 5, 311; *see also specific types*
Abi-Saab, Georges, 383 n
Accommodation, 69–70
Acid rain, 455
Actors, 16–17, 20, 27, 61–90; *see also specific types*
  dominant, 52, 61
  history of international relations and, 56–57, 494–496
  international government organizations, 74–77
  international nongovernment organizations, 77–87
  levels of analysis and, 24–26
  mixed-actor world, 17, 87–90, 361, 494
  primary, 52, 61
  state, 61–66
  substate, 66–74
Adams, Gerry, 210
Adams, Ian, 58 n
Adelman, Carol C., 381 n
Adid, Mohammed Farrah, 397
Adjudication, 367–370, 381
Adler, Emanuel, 349 n, 463 n
Agee, Philip, 190
Aggarwal, Vinod K., 271 n
Aggression, 133
Agrément, 205, 233
Agriculture, 105, 281–282, 415–416, 441
AIDS/HIV, 8, 478

Ajami, Fouad, 488 n
Akaha, Tsuneo, 162 n
Akhavan, Payam, 382 n
Akrasanee, Narongchai, 306 n
Albert, Prince, 137
Albright, Madeline, 209, 418, 422
Alexander, Yonah, 162 n
Alger, Chadwick F., 66, 72, 93 n
Algeria, 477
Allende, Salvador, 177
Alliances, 108–111, 124
Allies, 328
Allison, Graham T., 29 n, 163 n, 349 n, 382 n
Ambassadors, 202–210, 212–217, 226–227, 233, 371; *see also* Diplomacy
Ames, Aldrich, 170, 179, 194, 213
Amin, Idi, 152
Amir, Yigal, 183
Amnesty International (AI), 9, 17, 56, 77, 356–357, 359, 386, 467
An-Na'im, Abdullahi Ahmed, 408, 424 n
Anarchy, 11–12, 27; *see also* International anarchy model
Anaya, James S., 381 n
Andean Pact, 79, 293, 369
Anderson, Helen, 227
Anderson, Jeffrey J., 306 n
Andrew, Christopher, 197 n, 198 n
Andropov, Yuri, 154, 180
Angell, Norman, 145, 162 n
Annan, Kofi, 418–419

Antiballistic missiles (ABMs), 321, 332
Apartheid, 73–74, 369
Approach, 23–24, 27
Aquino, Corazon, 475
Arafat, Yasser, 210
Arbetman, Marina, 120, 126 n, 138–139, 161 n
Arbitration, 367, 381
Archibugi, Daniele, 487 n
Arend, Anthony Clark, 162 n, 381 n
Argentina, 371
Aristide, Jean-Bertrand, 186, 252
Aristophanes, 145
Arms control, 319, 320–322, 346
Arms limitations, 311–345, 363; *see also* Arms proliferation; Cold War
Arms proliferation, 313–315, 327–337
Arms transfers, 319, 327
Art, Robert J., 59 n, 305 n
Asian Development Bank, 121, 256
Asian Tigers, 251, 259, 297–298, 472
Asmus, Ronald D., 126 n
Assassinations, 176–177, 189
Assimilation, 69, 71
Association of Southeast Asian Nations (ASEAN), 275, 298–300
Asylum, 216–217, 233, 374
Atmosphere, 439–441, 449, 454, 455
Atomic, biological, and chemical (ABC) weapons, 5, 311; *see also specific types*
Attaché, 208, 233

Attali, Jacques, 500, 503 n, 504 n
Atwood, Tanya M., 306 n
Aung San Suu Kyi, 299, 475
Autarky, 247, 270
Authority, 20, 57, 65, 493–494
Autonomy, ethnic group, 67–68, 71
Axelrod, Robert, 28 n, 60 n, 274 n, 307 n, 349 n
Ayala Lasso, José, 408
Ayish, Muhammad I., 488 n
Ayyash, Yehia, 176–177

Baehr, Peter R., 423 n, 424 n
Bainbridge, Michelle, 306 n
Baker, James E., 197 n, 199 n
Balance of power, 38, 42, 114–116, 124
Balance of terror, 114–115, 124
Baldwin, David A., 28 n, 271 n
Ball, Nicole, 347 n
Barber, Benjamin R., 487 n
Bardot, Brigitte, 447
Bargaining, diplomatic, 210–212
Barkin, David, 306 n
Barnet, Richard J., 95 n
Barry, James A., 176, 198 n
Barston, R. P., 235 n
Bartley, Robert L., 488 n
Barton, John H., 382 n
Baselines, 363, 364
Baylis, John, 234 n
Beck, Robert J., 162 n, 381 n
Beer, Francis A., 160 n
Beggar-thy-neighbor policies, 7
Begin, Menachem, 227–228
Beiner, Robert, 29 n
Bennett, LeRoy A., 382 n
Bennett, Andrew, 424 n
Bergsten, Fred C., 306 n
Berry, Nicholas, 235 n
Best, Geoffrey, 381 n, 504 n
Bhasin, Kamla, 136
Bhutto, Zulfikar, 328
Bilateral aid, 256
Binion, Gayle, 408, 424 n
Biodiversity, 444, 449, 454, 459
Biological weapons, 140, 159, 325, 330–331, 338
Biosphere, 430, 459
Bipolar systems, 46, 55, 114–116, 120, 138, 139
Bismark, Otto von, 157
Bittman, Ladislav, 178, 198 n
Black, Ian, 198 n
Black, Shirley Temple, 218, 226
Blacklists, 264, 270

Blackmail, 178
Blake, David H., 272 n
Blechman, Barry M., 162 n, 348 n
Bledsoe, Robert L., 382 n
Blockades, 264–265, 270
Bloomfield, Lincoln P., 383 n
Bobbio, Norberto, 29 n
Boczek, Boleslaw A., 382 n
Bodin, Jean, 35–36
Booth, Ken, 160 n, 408, 424 n
Booth, William James, 29 n
Boren, David L., 198 n
Borgwardt, Elizabeth, 234 n
Bosnia, 187–188, 221, 344, 358–359, 397–399, 494
Boulding, Elise, 462 n
Bourantonis, Dimitris, 423 n
Boutros-Ghali, Boutros, 314, 336, 347 n, 385, 397, 404, 407–408, 418–419, 423 n, 424 n
Boyan, Stephen, Jr., 460 n
Boycotts, 262, 270, 450–451
Boyer, Paul, 25
Boyle, Francis Anthony, 419–420, 425 n
Bozeman, Adda B., 372, 381 n, 383 n, 470, 488 n
Brady, Linda P., 212, 234 n, 235 n, 347 n
Brandt, Willy, 247
Brazil, 444–445, 450
Bretton Woods system, 276–279, 284
Brezhnev, Leonid I., 151
Bribery, 176
Brinton, Crane, 60 n
Brock-Utne, Birgit, 136, 161 n
Brodie, Bernard, 160 n
Brown, Chris, 29 n, 504 n
Brown, Janet Welsh, 460 n
Brown, Lester R., 459 n, 460 n, 461 n
Brown, Ron, 262, 263
Brown, Seyom, 18, 28 n, 30 n, 159 n, 161 n, 268, 305 n, 307 n
Bruckman, Daniel, 461 n
Brzoska, Michael, 312, 346 n, 347 n
Buchan, Alastair, 163 n
Buchanan, Pat, 297
Bueno de Mesquita, Bruce, 126 n, 159 n, 162 n
Bugs, 171, 215
Bull, Hedley, 28 n, 29 n, 30 n, 31 n, 58 n, 59 n, 60 n, 92 n, 155, 162 n, 231, 236 n, 373 n, 380, 381 n, 382 n, 488 n, 501
Burley, Anne-Marie Slaughter, 378, 384 n

Burstein, Stanley M., 347 n
Burton, John, 17, 30 n
Bush, Barbara, 190
Bush, George, 4, 9, 51, 53, 72, 143–144, 150, 178, 191, 203, 204, 215–216, 221, 224, 226, 245, 246, 296–297, 327, 354, 431, 452, 467, 482
Butler, Alison, 273 n
Buzan, Barry, 28 n, 501, 504 n

Cable, Vincent, 92 n
Calingaert, Michael, 304 n
Calley, William, 358
Calvo Clause, 374
Calvo Doctrine, 373–374
Campbell, John Franklin, 226, 235 n
Canada, 108–111, 354; *see also* North American Free Trade Agreement (NAFTA)
Cantor, Mickey, 246
Capitalism, 7, 8, 39, 135, 239–240, 270, 375–376
Caporaso, James A., 59 n, 60 n, 307 n
Carazo, Rodrigo, 345
CARE, 406
Carlisle, Charles R., 305 n
Carlos the Jackal, 81–82, 154–155
Carr, Edward Hallet, 14, 29 n
Carroll, Thomas F., 273 n
Carrying capacity, 430–431, 459
Cartels, 105, 260, 270
Carter, Barry E., 382 n
Carter, Jimmy, 48, 149, 207, 321, 340
Carver, George A., Jr., 198 n
Case overload, 402
Casey, William, 179
Cashman, Greg, 159 n, 347 n
Cassese, Antonio, 69, 93 n, 359, 381 n, 382 n, 424 n
Castaneda, Jorge G., 303
Castro, Fidel, 53, 152, 176, 206, 264, 473
Catherine the Great, 137
Central Intelligence Agency (CIA), 65, 167–171, 176–178, 179, 183, 190–194, 208, 482
Chamberlain, Richard, 450–451
Charlemagne, 34–35, 387–388
Charles, Prince of Wales, 486
Chase-Dunn, Christopher, 272 n
Chazan, Naomi, 93 n, 488 n
Chemical weapons, 140, 159, 314, 325, 330–331, 337, 338–339
Chen, Lung-chu, 381 n, 382 n

Childers, Erskine, 424 n
Children, 365, 411–412
Chiles, James R., 198 n
China, Nationalist; *see* Taiwan
China, People's Republic of, 7, 205–206
  arms limitations and, 321, 325, 328, 329–330, 337, 338
  arms proliferation and, 329–330, 335, 340
  drug trade and, 481
  economic development strategy of, 259, 261–262
  human rights violations, 259, 261–262, 409, 413
  intellectual property rights and, 256
  intelligence agencies of, 181
  Russia and, 224
  socialist law and, 375
  spheres of influence in, 39
  Tiananmen Square uprising, 50, 74, 216
  in tripolar power structure, 113–114
  U.S. rapprochement with, 73
Chirac, Jacques, 288
Chlorofluorocarbons (CFCs), 440–441
Choucri, Nazli, 59 n, 458, 459 n, 460 n, 461 n
Churches, 35, 61, 85–87, 189, 228
Churchill, Winston, 53, 111, 114–115, 486
Cimbala, Stephen J., 198 n, 346 n
Ciphers, 175, 196
Cities, 71–73, 435–436, 478–479
Citizen diplomacy, 71–72, 227
City states, 202
Civil law, 374
Civil war, 142, 159
Clark, Grenville, 145
Clark, Ian, 28 n, 162 n
Class systems, 252
Claude, Inis L., 88, 95 n, 126 n, 423 n
Clausewitz, Carl von, 130–131, 143, 148, 149, 160 n, 221
Cline, Ray S., 102–103, 111, 112 n, 125 n, 162 n
Clinton, Bill, 5, 9, 51, 84, 87, 109, 122, 123, 178, 179, 180, 203, 204, 206, 209, 213, 219, 221, 224, 226, 227, 229, 246, 261, 262, 295–297, 298, 320–321, 324, 325–326, 329–330, 338–339, 354, 361, 375, 409, 414, 417–418, 431, 449, 467, 475, 501

Clinton, Hillary, 257, 413
Coate, Roger A., 30 n, 93 n, 424 n
Codes, 175, 196
Codification, 351–352, 381
Coercion, 69–70
Coercive diplomacy, 221–222, 233
Coffey, Peter, 304 n
Cohen, Benjamin J., 272 n
Cohen, Raymond, 218–219, 234 n, 235 n
Coker, Christopher, 487 n
Colby, Michael E., 461 n
Cold War; *see also* Arms limitations; Arms proliferation; Post-Cold War era
  bipolar power structure of, 114–116, 120
  collapse of Communism and, 48–51
  containment policy, 46–48, 58, 64, 110, 115–116, 378
  crisis management in, 4, 47–48
  diplomacy styles and, 205, 219
  end of, 4, 10, 15, 140–141, 179, 180–181, 474
  penetration operations in, 172, 177
  post-Cold War era, 51–52, 180–181, 191–194
  power relationships in, 101, 139
  propaganda used during, 186, 188
Collective security, 402–405, 422
Collins, Joseph, 461 n
Colombia, 481, 483
Colonial system, 39–40, 65, 202
Combs, Cindy C., 91 n
Command economy, 247–248, 270
Common law, 374
Common market, 285, 304
Commonwealth of Independent States (CIS), 50; *see also* Soviet Union, former
Communism, 4, 7, 15, 43–44, 48–51, 58, 122, 373, 374–375, 471–472
Community, 12–13; *see also* International community model
Compellance, 100
Complete test ban treaty organization (CTBTO), 338
Comprehensive test ban treaty (CTBT), 320–321, 337–338
Compulsory jurisdiction, 367, 381
Computers, 175–176, 439, 467, 469, 481–482
Conca, Ken, 462 n
Concentration of power, 117–118, 124
Conciliation, 394, 422

Conference diplomacy, 388
Confidence and security-building measures (CSBMs), 325–327
Confiscation, 264, 270
Conflict, 149–155, 159, 371; *see also* Ethnic conflict; War
Congo (Zaire), 402
Congress of Vienna (1815), 38, 40–41, 202, 217–218, 353, 388
Consensus, 20, 501–502
Consociational societies, 70, 91
Consulates, 209, 217, 233
Consuls, 209, 217, 233
Containment policy, 46–48, 58, 64, 110, 115–116, 378; *see also* Arms limitations
Contiguous zones, 363, 364
Continuum, 10–19
Conventional war, 140, 159
Conventional weapons, 311, 326–327, 333–336, 340
Conybeare, John A. C., 271 n
Coordinating Committee (CoCom), 263–264
Copernicus, Nicolaus, 24
Copps, Sheila, 471
Corbett, Richard, 306 n
Cordozo, Michael H., 235 n
Cornett, Linda, 307 n
Cornish, Paul, 346 n
Corporatism, 246
Cortwright, David, 234 n, 271 n, 273 n
Cosa Nostra, 480–481
Cosmopolitan world, 470–471, 475, 487
Council for Mutual Economic Assistance (CMEA; COMECON), 247
Counterguerrilla wars, 141, 159
Counterintelligence, 166–167, 170, 171, 182, 189, 192, 193, 196, 213
Coups d'etats, 70–71, 151, 165, 177, 207
Cousteau, Jacques, 268
Covenant on Civil and Political Rights (1976), 360, 365, 370
Covert acts, 176–178, 189, 196, 215–216
Covert intelligence, 167, 196
Craig, Gordon A., 60 n, 234 n
Crawford, Beverly, 273 n, 463 n
Creasy, Edward, 168
Crenshaw, Martha, 94 n
Crisis, 4, 47–48, 58
Crone, Hugh D., 346 n

Cronkite, Walter, 227–228
Cropsey, Seth, 348 n
Crotty, William, 126 n, 272 n
Crystal, Jill, 477, 489 n
Cuba, 7, 48, 101, 206–207, 264, 467
Cuban Missile Crisis of 1962, 115, 221–222, 321
Cultural relativism, 408
Culture, 208–209, 372–376, 470, 487
Cupitt, Richard T., 272 n
Curie, Marie, 89
Currency blocs, 278, 285–286
Customary law, 353–354, 371, 381
Customs unions, 285, 304
Czempiel, Ernst-Otto, 28 n, 29 n, 307 n, 349 n, 383 n, 424 n, 504 n

Dahl, Robert A., 488 n
Dallin, Alexander, 174 n
D'Amato, Anthony, 381 n
Damrosch, Lori F., 381 n, 383 n
Dando, Malcolm, 346 n, 348 n
Danson, Ted, 450
Dark Ages, 34
Darwin, Charles, 136
Dassin, Joan, 95 n
de Gaulle, Charles, 288
Dean, Jonathan, 346 n
Debt, 257–258, 278, 313–314, 407
Declarations, 366, 381
Defectors, 169–170, 177–178
Defectors-in-place (moles), 169, 170
Defensive weapons, 316, 346
Delors, Jacques, 285, 288–289
Democracy, 58
   characteristics of, 42, 43
   ethnic groups and, 70–71
   international law and, 375–376
   military dominance and, 11
   prospects for, 471–475
   and secrecy of penetration operations, 190–191
   spread of, 388
   and state system, 40
Demonstration, 150, 159
Dependency theory, 240–241, 259, 270, 405
Desertification, 442
Dessler, David, 160 n
Détente, 48, 73, 312
Deudney, Daniel, 462 n
Deutch, John, 178, 180, 192
Diamond, Larry, 474, 488 n
Dictatorship, 42–43

Diehl, Paul F., 28 n, 125 n, 160 n, 162 n, 377, 384 n, 423 n, 424 n, 425 n
Dilks, David, 197 n, 198 n
Dinan, Desmond, 273 n, 304 n, 305 n
Dinkins, David, 72
Diplomacy, 40–41, 42, 201–233; *see also* International law
   citizen, 71–72, 227
   coercive, 221–222, 233
   conference, 388
   immunity and, 212–217, 233, 371
   legal setting of, 212–218, 364, 373
   nonstate actors and, 71–72, 227–229
   preventive, 395–396
   protocol in, 217–218, 225–227, 234
   shuttle, 205, 223–224, 234
   styles of, 205, 218–219, 225–227
   summit, 203–205, 223–224, 234
Diplomatic courier, 208, 233
Disarmament, 319–320, 322–325, 346
Disengagement, 319, 325–327, 346
Diversity, of states, 62–64
Divestment, 262, 270
Divine Right, 35, 58
Dixon, William J., 347 n
Doctorow, E. L., 345
Domke, William, 126 n
Donnelly, Jack, 424 n
Double agents, 178, 182
Dougherty, James E., 14, 29 n, 92 n, 160 n, 347 n
Douglas, Sara U., 306 n
Douglas, Stephen A., 306 n
Dowd, Douglas, 239, 272 n
Doyle, Michael W., 29 n, 159 n, 163 n
Driscoll, William, 346 n
Druckman, Daniel, 462 n
Drug trade, 8, 481–483
Drummond, Eric, 391
Dubos, Rene, 460 n
Duchack, Ivo D., 93 n
Duchin, Faye, 461 n
Duhamel, Georges, 503
Dumping, 244, 270
Dunn, David J., 30 n
Dunne, Timothy, 30 n

Earth Summit (1992), 431, 435, 452, 455, 500
Easterbrook, Gregg, 459 n
Ebon, Martin, 197 n, 199 n
Ecocide, 430, 459
Ecology, 192, 430–434, 459

Economic and Monetary Union (EMU), 286, 292
Economic development; *see also* International political economy
   China and, 259, 261–262
   as core variable in economy, 436–438
   and measurement of power, 106–108
   United Nations and, 255, 259, 262–263, 405–407
Economic hegemony, 237, 267–268, 270
Economic integration, 8, 242, 275, 281–282, 283, 284–301, 304
Economic nationalism; *see* Mercantilism
Economic union, 285, 304
Economic warfare, 264, 270
Economy; *see* Economic development; Economic integration; International political economy (IPE)
Ecosystems, 438, 459
Eftimiades, Nicholas, 197 n, 199 n
Egypt, 477
Ehrlich, Paul R., 458
Eichmann, Adolf, 177, 354
Einstein, Albert, 342
Eisenhower, Dwight D., 203, 317, 345
Eland, Ivan, 274 n
Eley, Geoff, 92 n
Elliot, Jeffrey M., 346 n
Elshtain, Jean Bethke, 161 n
Embargo, 262, 271
Embassies, 202, 214–217, 233, 384
Energy, 438
Enigma, 175, 182
Enloe, Cynthia, 93 n, 137, 161 n
Environment, 8–9, 429–459
   Global Environment Facility, 277
   underground testing of nuclear weapons, 318–319, 320–321, 337–338, 341, 342
   for war and war preparation, 314, 322
Epstein, Edward Jay, 197 n
Epstein, Ethan A., 348 n
Esman, Milton J., 93 n
Esty, Daniel C., 273 n, 305 n
Ethnic cleansing, 70–71, 358, 365
Ethnic conflict, 5, 67–71
   civil war and, 142, 159
   penetration operations and, 189–190
   population size and, 104–105

terrorism and, 82–83, 86, 476–477
war crimes and, 70, 354, 358–360, 365, 366
Ethnic groups, 91
  conflict between; *see* Ethnic conflict
  ethnic minorities, 82
  penetration operations of, 189–190
Ethnic nationalism, 67–71, 91
Ethnic-states, 69
Ethnoclasses, 252
Etzioni, Amitai, 92 n
Eurocentrism, 41
European Community (EC), 285
European Currency Unit (ECU), 285–286
European Economic Area, 287
European Free Trade Area (EFTA), 287
European Monetary System (EMS), 285–286
European Union (EU), 498–499
  Community Agricultural Policy (CAP), 281–282
  defense and foreign policy, 287
  economic development and, 8, 406
  formation of, 283, 364
  history of, 285–286
  institutions within, 288–290
  as major trade state, 241, 242, 244–245, 248–249
  political integration and, 287–293
Evans, Peter B., 305 n
Exclusive economic zones, 363, 364
Extradition, 362, 381
Extraterritoriality, 214, 233

Fagan, Stuart I., 92 n
Falco, Mathea, 489 n
Falcone, Giovanni, 481
Falk, Richard A., 18, 28 n, 29 n, 30 n, 349 n, 376, 382 n, 383 n, 423 n, 425 n, 462 n, 475, 487 n, 488 n
Falkland Islands War (1982), 173, 205, 376–377
Farer, Tom J., 424 n
Fascism, 44–45, 58
Fay, Michael P., 408
Federal Bureau of Investigation (FBI), 167, 170, 179, 183, 190, 192, 193, 213, 482
Feltham, R. G., 234 n
Ferguson, Yale H., 59 n, 92 n
Ferraro, Vincent, 273 n
Feshbach, Murray, 450, 462 n

Feudalism, 34, 58
Fincher, Jack, 489 n
Finger, Seymour Maxwell, 235 n
Finnemore, Martha, 423 n
First-strike capacity, 115
First World, 7 n
First World War, 13–14, 21–22, 41, 42–45, 116, 145, 185–186
Fisher, Cathleen S., 348 n
Fisher, Julie, 459 n, 461 n
Fisher, Roger, 234 n, 383 n
Fishing, 441, 445, 454
Fitzmaurice, Malgosia, 382 n, 383 n
Float system, 278
Food and Agricultural Organization (FAO), 415–416, 441
Foran, Virginia, 346 n
Force, 20, 497–498
Forced assimilation, 69
Ford, Gerald, 73, 218, 226
Forde, Steven, 30 n
Foreign aid, 256–257
Foreign direct investment, 242, 258, 271
Foreign Service Officers (FSOs), 225–227
Forests, 443–445, 455
Former Soviet Republics (FSRs), 323–325; *see* Soviet Union, former
Forsberg, Randall, 346 n
Forsythe, David P., 423 n, 424 n, 488 n
Fourteen Points, 42, 224–225
France, 36, 40, 43, 316, 321, 325, 337–338, 469
Franck, Thomas M., 376–377, 383 n
Frank, Isaiah, 94 n
Franklin, Benjamin, 157
Frederick, Howard H., 466 n, 487 n, 488 n
Frederick the Great, 221
Free trade (*laissez-faire*), 39
Free Trade Agreement (1989), 364
Free trade area, 285, 304
Freeman, Chas W., Jr., 234 n
Frei, Eduardo, 297
French, Hilary F., 273 n, 303, 305 n, 460 n, 461 n, 462 n
Freud, Sigmund, 133, 160 n
Frieden, Jeffry A., 272 n, 305 n
Friedland, Lewis A., 487 n
Friedmann, John, 72 n
Friedmann, Wolfgang, 382 n
Friendly, Alfred, 450, 462 n
Fromkin, David, 28 n
Fuchs, Klaus, 169

Fukuyama, Francis, 471–472, 488 n, 503 n
Fuller, Graham E., 487 n, 488 n
Funabashi, Yeichi, 125 n

Gabriel, Jurg Martin, 29 n
Gaddis, John Lewis, 30 n, 59 n, 60 n
Gadhafi, Moammar, 150
Gaer, Felice, 424 n
Gaia hypothesis, 430–431, 459
Gandhi, Indira, 68, 134, 137
Gandhi, Mohandas K., 67
Ganson, Brian, 234 n
Gardner, Gary T., 346 n
Gareau, Frederick H., 31 n
Garnham, David, 306 n
Garrett, Laurie, 489 n
Garten, Jeffrey E., 305 n
Gates, Bill, 467
Gates, Robert, 181, 194
Gavin, Francis J., 305 n
Geldenhuys, Deon, 92 n
Gene, J. P., 486
General Agreement on Tariffs and Trade (GATT), 204, 241, 255, 256, 275, 364–365; *see also* World Trade Organization (WTO)
  conference of 1993, 7, 10–11
  Tokyo Round, 267, 280, 301–302
  Uruguay Round, 238, 244, 246, 267, 275, 279–280, 281, 283, 301–302, 496
Generalized System of Preferences, 255
Genghis Khan, 103
Genocide, 70–71, 354, 358–360, 365, 366
Geography, power and, 103–104
Geopolitics, 104, 124
George, Alexander L., 60 n, 221, 234 n, 235 n, 504 n
George, Susan, 258, 271 n, 273 n
Georgia, Republic of, 213
Geostationary, 466–467, 487
Germ warfare, 140, 159, 325, 330–331, 338
Germany, 4, 5, 45, 47–48, 116, 185–186, 291, 323, 328, 374
Gerner, Deborah J., 69, 91 n, 93 n
Gildenhorn, Joseph, 226
Gilpin, Robert, 43, 55, 59 n, 60 n, 92 n, 94 n, 126n, 138, 161 n, 271 n, 272 n, 488 n
Glahn, Gerhard von, 162 n, 382 n
Glasnost, 49

Glaspie, April, 220
Global civil society, 77, 447–455, 457, 459, 471
Global communication, 9–10, 465–468
Global debt, 257–258
Global warming, 439–440, 449, 454
Globalism, 8, 16–18, 283–284, 304
Globalization, 52–55
Globerman, Steven, 274 n, 304 n, 306 n
Godson, Roy, 480
Goebbels, Joseph, 185–186
Goertz, Gary, 377, 384 n
Goldstein, Donald M., 463 n
Good offices, 394, 423
Goose, Stephen D., 348 n
Gorbachev, Mikhail, 48, 49–50, 53, 54, 73, 108, 122, 195, 204, 224, 318, 319–320, 322, 323, 326
Gordenker, Leon, 423 n, 424 n
Gore, Albert, Jr., 65, 192, 431, 440, 459 n
Goree, Janie, 71
Goulding, Marrack, 424 n
Governance, 17–18, 27, 54, 275, 452–455
Gowa, Joanne, 271 n
Graham, Billy, 466
Grant, Rebecca, 161 n
Graubard, Stephen R., 59 n, 92 n
Gray, Colin S., 312, 346 n, 347 n
Great Britain
    American Revolution and, 36, 40, 43
    arms limitations and, 316, 320, 325, 337
    colonialism and, 40
    First World War and, 116
    human rights and, 360–361
    Industrial Revolution, 39, 41
    intelligence agencies of, 182, 190, 191
    propaganda and, 186–187
    role in European Union, 286, 291
Great Depression, 64
Greece, ancient, 34, 202, 316, 352
Green revolution, 443
Greenhouse effect, 439–440, 449, 454
Greenpeace, 56, 342, 429, 451
Gregg, Robert w., 423 n, 424 n
Grenada, 371
Grieco, Joseph, 267, 271 n, 274 n, 301–302, 307 n
Gries, David, 191, 199 n

GRIT (graduated and reciprocated initiatives in tension reduction), 327
Gross national product (GNP), 101, 106, 107, 111–112, 246, 250–252, 256, 282, 290, 437
Grotius, Hugo, 11, 12, 352–353, 355, 363, 502
Group of Seven (G-7), 51, 84, 100, 120–121, 204, 243, 250, 251, 281–282
Guehenno, Jean-Marie, 91 n
Guerrilla wars, 141, 159
Gunboat diplomacy, 222
Gupte, Pranay, 459 n
Gurr, Ted Robert, 59 n, 66–67, 83, 91 n, 92 n, 93 n, 94 n
Gurutz, Jauregui Bereciartu, 91 n
Guzman, Manual A., 82

Haas, Ernest B., 420, 423 n, 425 n
Haas, Peter M., 462 n, 463 n
Hafiz, Abdul, 171
Haglund, David G., 94 n
Hague Conference of 1899, 40–41, 325, 338, 341, 362, 367, 388
Hague Conference of 1907, 40–41, 325, 362, 367, 388, 389
Haig, Alexander, 205
Haiti, 434
Halberstam, David, 94 n, 495, 503 n, 504 n
Halliday, Fred, 31 n
Halperin, Mortin H., 93 n
Hamilton, Adrian, 231
Hammarskjold, Dag, 396, 402
Handel, Michael I., 159 n, 160 n
Handelman, Stephen, 489 n
Hanink, Dean M., 304 n
Hannum, Hurst, 93 n
Hanson, Eric O., 91 n, 94 n
Hard power, 100
Hardin, Garrett, 453, 459 n, 462 n
Harff, Barbara, 91 n
Harkin, Tom, 123
Harries, Owen, 126 n
Harriman, Pamela, 226
Hartmann, Frederick H., 235 n
Hartung, William D., 348 n
Hashimoto, Ryutaro, 410
Hassner, Pierre, 29 n, 503, 504 n
Hastedt, Glenn, 272 n
Hauchler, Ingomar, 280 n
Hauss, Charles, 93 n, 503 n, 504 n
Hawes, Michael K., 94 n
Head, Ivan L., 273 n

Health, 8–9, 386, 389, 415, 477–479
Hegemon, 116, 124, 237, 240, 267–268
Hegemony, 76, 116, 117–121, 125, 138–139
Heilbroner, Robert, 274 n
Held, David, 475, 487 n, 488 n
Henderson, Conway W., 94 n, 461 n
Henkin, Louis, 377–378, 380, 384 n
Henry VII, 35
Hepburn, Audrey, 412
Herblock, 318 n
Heredia, Carlos, 303
Herman, Michael, 197 n
Herz, John H., 64, 92 n
Herz, Martin F., 234 n
Heseltine, Michael, 268
Higgins, Rosalyn, 382 n, 383 n
Hill, Carla, 246
Hill, Christopher, 463 n
Historical setting of international relations, 33–58
Hitler, Adolf, 45, 69, 87, 103, 108, 134, 182, 185, 315, 360
Hobbes, Thomas, 11–12, 35–36, 502
Hobbs, Heidi H., 92 n, 93 n
Hoffer, Eric, 56, 81, 94 n
Hoffman, Stanley, 31 n, 60 n, 305 n, 306 n, 489 n
Hogan, Michael J., 28 n, 30 n, 59 n
Holbraad, Carsten, 125 n
Holland, Martin, 304 n, 305 n
Hollins, Harry B., 162 n, 347 n, 383 n
Holsti, Kalevi J., 160 n
Holsti, Ole R., 30 n
Holt, Pat M., 194, 197 n, 199 n
Holy Roman Empire, 34–35
Home state, 78
Homer-Dixon, Thomas F., 433, 460 n, 461 n
Horowitz, Donald L., 92 n, 93 n
Host state, 78, 79
Hostages, 364
Hotchkiss, Carolyn, 306 n, 382 n, 383 n
Howard, Michael, 59 n, 130, 160 n, 504 n
Howes, Ruth H., 159 n
Hufbauer, Gary Clyde, 304 n, 305 n, 306 n
Human ecology, 430–434, 459
Human rights, 208
    China and, 259, 261–262, 409, 413
    international law and, 360–361, 365, 369
    United Nations and, 9, 110–111, 372, 397–399, 407–409

Humanitarian intervention, 397–399
HUMINT, 168, 183, 197
Huntington, Samuel P., 472, 475–476, 487 n, 488 n
Huntley, Wade L., 29 n
Husain, Mir Zohair, 487 n, 488 n
Hussein, Saddam, 108, 156, 168, 220, 262–263, 315, 404, 467
Hutchinson, John, 92 n
Hwang Jang Yop, 216–217

Idealism, 13–14, 145
Ideology, 42–46, 58, 62, 82–83, 86, 108, 476–477
Ignatieff, Michael, 123
Ikenberry, John G., 305 n, 474 n, 488 n
Ikle, Fred Charles, 159 n, 211, 234 n, 235 n
Imaging radar, 174
Immunity, diplomatic, 212–217, 233, 371
Imperial Preference System, 279
Import substitution, 258
Inamore, Kazuo, 272 n
Income distribution, 250–252
India, 321, 328
Indigenous peoples, 365
Individuals, 73–74
  as cause of wars, 133–134
  citizen diplomacy and, 71–72, 227
  international law and, 354, 357–361
  as level of analysis, 25
Industrial capability, power and, 106–107
Industrial espionage, 193–194
Industrial Revolution, 39, 41, 438
Industrialization, 253
Infrastructure, 253–254
Inkeles, Alex, 161 n
Inquiry, 423
Intellectual property rights (IPRs), 255–256, 416
Intelligence, 166–176, 175–176, 197
  counterintelligence and, 166–167, 170, 171, 182, 189, 192, 193, 213
  covert, 167, 196
  national intelligence agencies, 178–184; *see also specific agencies*
  overt, 167, 197
  in post-Cold War era, 180–181, 191–194
  secrecy and democracy, 190

Interaction, 20, 498–499
Intercontinental ballistic missiles (ICBMs), 317, 318, 321–324, 326
Interdependence, 7, 16–18, 27, 204, 255–256
Interdisciplinary, 23, 27
Intergovernmentalism, 288
Intermediaries, 211, 212
Intermestic politics, 66, 91
International anarchy model, 11–12, 13–15, 20, 21
  arms limitations and, 344
  diplomacy and, 232
  economic cooperation and, 302
  economic instruments and, 268–269
  environment and, 457
  history of international relations and, 56
  international law and, 378–379
  international organizations and, 421
  international power and, 122–123
  multiple actors and, 89
  penetration operations and, 194
  shared experiences and, 484
  war and, 156
International Atomic Energy Agency (IAEA), 317–319, 329–330, 337, 417
International Bank for Reconstruction and Development (IBRD); *see* World Bank
International Civil Aviation Organization (ICAO), 389, 416
International Committee for the Red Cross (ICRC), 357, 386
International community model, 12–13, 18–19, 20
  arms limitations and, 344
  diplomacy and, 232
  economic cooperation and, 302
  economic instruments and, 269
  environment and, 457
  history of international relations and, 57
  international organizations and, 421
  international power and, 122–123
  multiple actors and, 89–90
  penetration operations and, 195
  shared experiences and, 485
  war and, 157–158
International Court of Justice, 353–355, 368–369, 392
International Development Association (IDA), 277

International Finance Corporation (IFC), 275, 277
International government organizations (IGOs), 74–77, 91, 340–342, 356, 386, 416–417, 429, 448, 451–452; *see also* European Union (EU); Organization of American States (OAS); United Nations (UN)
International law, 40–41, 43, 212–218, 351–380, 381
International Law Commission, 366–367
International legal personality, 355–356, 381
International liberals, 16–18
International Monetary Fund (IMF), 26, 120–121, 204, 241, 248, 257–259, 275, 278–279, 405, 452
International nongovernment organizations (INGOs), 77–87, 91, 386, 388–389; *see also* Multinational corporations (MNCs); Terrorism
  arms limitations and, 340–342
  democracy in, 474
  diplomacy and, 227–229
  economic development and, 406–407
  economic integration and, 298
  environment and, 429, 448, 450–452
  global communication and, 466
  international law and, 356–357
International organizations, 74–77, 91, 385–422, 493–494; *see also* International government organizations (IGOs); International nongovernment organizations (INGOs); *specific organizations*
International policy, 54
International political economy (IPE), 6–8, 237–270, 271, 275–303; *see also* Economic development; North-South relationship; Trade
  interdependence in, 7, 16–18, 27
  international society and, 265–269, 301–302
  negative economic instruments, 260, 263–265
  positive economic instruments, 260, 261–263
  in post-Cold War era, 247–249
  summit diplomacy and, 204–205

International public union, 388
International relations, 3–27, 493–502
International Social Darwinism, 136
International society model, 12, 15–18, 20
  arms limitations and, 343–344
  diplomacy and, 230–232
  economic cooperation and, 301–302
  economic instruments and, 265–269
  environment and, 455–457
  history of international relations and, 55–57
  international law and, 372, 376–379
  international organizations and, 420–421
  international power and, 122–123
  multiple actors and, 87–90
  penetration operations and, 194–195
  political system and, 41
  shared experiences and, 483–485
  war and, 155–158
International Telecommunications Union (ITU), 275, 389, 416–417
International Telephone and Telegraph (ITT), 79, 189
International Trade Organization (ITO), 279
Internet, 467, 469
Intervention, 151–153, 159
Intraregional ballistic missiles (IRBMs), 331–332
Iran, 140
Iraq, 112, 119, 122, 140, 220, 319, 337, 339, 341
Irish Republican Army (IRA), 141–142, 191, 210
Iron Curtain, 49
Irredentism, 69, 91
Isaacson, Walter, 94 n
Isaak, Robert A., 73, 92 n, 93 n, 271 n
Ishihara, Shintaro, 246, 272 n
Islamic religion, 69, 82–83, 86, 375, 475–477
Israel, 86–87, 150–151, 182–184, 189, 190, 191, 210, 228, 264, 321, 328–329, 361, 433
Issues, 20, 499–500
Italy, 44, 45, 316, 341
Ivory trade, 446, 449–450

Jackson, Robert H., 59 n
Jacobs, Francis, 306 n
Jacobson, Harold K., 94 n, 126 n, 161 n, 305 n
Jaggers, Keith, 59 n, 92 n
James, Alan, 59 n
Janis, Mark W., 383 n
Janning, Josef, 28 n
Japan
  arms limitations and, 316, 330, 341
  arms proliferation and, 328
  civil law and, 374
  democracy in, 473
  economic growth and, 8, 297–298
  environmental concerns and, 446, 449–450
  as major trade state, 241, 242–243, 245–246
  neomercantilism of, 238
  power of, 100, 101, 107, 108, 114, 121
  terrorism in, 6, 332–333
  trade ties with United States, 16, 283–284
  women slaves and, 410
Jenkins, Brian M., 94 n
Jensen, Kenneth M., 29 n, 161 n, 236 n
Jervis, Robert, 59 n, 116, 126 n
Jewish religion, 86–87
Johansen, Peter M., 303
John Paul II (Pope), 85
Johnson, Bryan, 95 n
Johnson, Loch K., 176, 197 n, 198 n, 199 n
Johnson, Lyndon, 314
Johnson, Rebecca, 348 n
Jomini, Antoine Henri, 130
Jones, Charles, 28 n
Jones, Walter F., 161 n, 383 n
Jowett, Garth S., 197 n, 199 n
Joyce, James, 469
Joyner, Christopher C., 423 n
Judicial decisions, 355, 381, 394
Juillard, Jacques, 486
Just war, 143–144, 159

Kaczynski, Theodore J., 81
Kagan, Donald, 159 n
Kahler, Miles, 283, 305 n
Kaiser, Robert G., 94 n
Kant, Immanuel, 11, 12–13, 14, 18–19, 157–158, 457, 484, 494, 498, 502
Kantor, Mickey, 297
Kaplan, Stephen S., 162 n

Kapstein, Ethan Barnaby, 271 n, 347 n
Karabell, Zackary, 489 n
Karadzic, Radovan, 359
Karns, Margaret P., 424 n
Katz, Samuel M., 197 n
Kauppi, Mark V., 28 n, 30 n, 126 n
Kayser, Carl, 347 n
Keegan, John, 131, 148, 157, 159 n, 160 n, 161 n, 399, 424 n, 503
Keeley, James F., 94 n
Kegley, Charles W., Jr., 25, 28 n, 30 n, 60 n, 94 n, 125 n, 126 n, 162 n, 377, 384 n, 499, 504 n
Kellogg-Briand Pact (1928), 148, 362
Kelman, Herman C., 93 n
Kendall, Henry, 458
Kennan, George F., 47, 53, 60 n, 110, 231, 378
Kennedy, John F., 48, 101, 152, 221–222
Kennedy, Paul M., 126 n, 280 n, 425 n, 499–500, 503 n, 504 n
Kenya, 437
Keohane, Robert O., 16, 28 n, 30 n, 56, 60 n, 88–89, 94 n, 95 n, 125 n, 127 n, 231–232, 236 n, 242, 267, 272 n, 274 n, 305 n, 306 n, 378, 420, 425 n, 457, 463 n, 484, 489 n
Keylor, William R., 59 n
KGB, 167, 169, 171, 178, 191–192
Khalilzad, Zalmay, 126 n
Khan, Yahya, 134
Khrushchev, Nikita, 48, 101, 157, 203, 221–222
Kidnapping, 177, 189, 354
Kim, Samuel S., 30 n, 423 n, 425 n
Kim, Woosang, 116, 126 n
Kimmel, Paul R., 235 n
King, Martin Luther, Jr., 67
Kingsbury, Benedict, 29 n, 424 n
Kissinger, Henry, 3, 5, 25, 28 n, 56, 73, 114, 205, 225, 247, 483, 489 n
Klare, Michael T., 93 n, 273 n, 347 n, 349 n, 461 n
Klein, Joe, 231
Knightley, Phillip, 197 n
Knippenberg, Joseph M., 29 n
Knutsen, Torbjorn L., 28 n
Koestler, Arthur, 345
Kohl, Helmut, 51, 87
Kondratieff, N. D., 240–241
Kondratieff cycle, 240–241
Korean War, 48, 130, 402, 403, 420

Korten, David C., 460 n, 503 n, 504 n
Krasner, Stephen D., 15, 30 n, 92 n, 94 n, 199 n, 267, 272 n, 301, 307 n, 425 n, 484, 489 n
Krass, Allan S., 347 n
Krauthammer, Charles, 126 n, 268, 422, 495, 504 n
Kremenyuk, Victor A., 234 n
Krepon, Michael, 348 n
Krugman, Paul, 246–247, 272 n
Kugler, Jacek, 126 n
Kugler, Richard L., 125 n, 126 n
Kuhn, Thomas, 31 n
Kuwait, 112, 119, 122, 220

Laden, Osama bin, 83
Lake, Anthony, 180
Lake, David A., 272 n, 305 n
Lalman, David, 126 n, 159 n, 162 n
Lambert, Der, 332 n
Lampert, Donald E., 92 n
Land area, differences among states, 63–64
Land mines, 314, 336–337
Lange, Glenn-Marie, 461 n
Lansing, Robert, 68
Lantos, Tom, 345
Lanyi, George A., 235 n
Larrabee, Stephen F., 126 n
Latin America, 151–152, 373–374; see also names of specific countries
Law, Bonar, 157
Law of the Sea (1982), 363, 364, 376, 502
Law of the Sea Treaty (1994), 229–230, 259–260, 367, 379
Law of Treaties (1969), 370
Lawrence, Robert Z., 305 n
Layne, Christopher, 116, 126 n
League of Nations, 14, 21–22, 40–41, 43, 76, 147–148, 225, 320, 388, 497
   arms limitations and, 341
   Covenant, 147–148, 353, 390, 393
   formation of, 389–390
   international law and, 366, 368
   United Nations versus, 390–394
Lebanon, 153–154
Lee, Yong S., 272 n
Lefever, Ernest W., 420, 422, 425 n
Legal issues; see International law
Leigh, Monroe, 382 n
Lenin, Vladimir I., 44, 46, 135–136, 240

Leo III (Pope), 34
Lepgold, Joseph, 126 n, 424 n
Lesser, Ian O., 487 n
Leuchta, Alice, 425 n
Levchenko, Stanislav, 171, 198 n
Levels of analysis, 24–26, 54
Levi, Werner, 372, 382 n, 383 n
Levy, Jack S., 135, 159 n, 160 n, 161 n
Levy, Marc A., 462 n
Lewis, David W. P., 305 n, 306 n
Leyton-Brown, David, 94 n
Liberalism, 238, 239–240, 241, 271
Liberation theology, 85
Libya, 150, 339
Lieber, Robert J., 161 n
Light weapons, 336–337
Lijphart, Arend, 70, 93 n, 235 n
Lincoln, Edward J., 271 n, 272 n, 306 n
Lingua franca, 468–470, 475, 487
Lipschutz, Ronnie D., 462 n
Litfin, Karen, 462 n
Little, Richard, 28 n, 29 n, 349 n
Litwak, Robert S., 346 n
Liu, F. T., 423 n, 424 n
Loescher, Gil, 423 n, 425 n
Lomperis, Timothy J., 160 n
Lopez, George A., 162 n, 271 n, 273 n
Lord, Mary, 349 n
Lorenz, Konrad, 134, 160 n
Louis XIV, 36
Louis XVI, 36
Lovelock, James, 430–431, 460 n
Low-intensity warfare, 141–142, 159
Lowe, Vaughan, 382 n, 383 n
Luard, Evan, 29 n, 59 n, 125 n, 151, 159 n, 162 n, 163 n, 346 n
Luce, Henry, 120
Lukacs, John, 92 n, 503 n, 503 n
Lukashenko, Alexander, 473
Lumpe, Lora, 348 n
Lundestad, Geir, 503 n, 504 n
Lynn-Jones, Sean M., 126 n
Lyons, Gene M., 31 n
Lysenko, Aleksander, 213

Maastricht Treaty (1992), 245, 285–286, 288, 292, 364, 376
MacArthur, Douglas, 130, 403
McGuire, Michael, 348 n
McGeough, Paul, 89
McGill, Peter, 268
Machiavelli, 14
Mackinder, Halford, 104, 125 n

McKinlay, R. D., 29 n, 349 n
McKinley, William, 135
McLeod, Ramon G., 461 n
McNamara, Kevin J., 199 n
McNamara, Robert S., 347 n
MacNeill, Jim, 459 n, 461 n
McNeill, William H., 59 n
McWilliams, Wilson C., 235 n
Madonna, 451
Mafia, 480–481
Maghroori, Ray, 92 n
Mahan, Alfred Thayer, 125 n
Mahbubani, Kishore, 488 n
Major, John, 83, 142, 210, 288
Makridakis, Spyros G., 306 n
Malthus, Thomas Robert, 443, 461 n
Mandelbaum, Michael, 125 n, 126 n, 328, 348 n
Manifest destiny, 39–40
Mann, Otto, 303
Mansbach, Richard W., 28 n, 59 n, 92 n, 95 n
Mansfield, Edward D., 117–118, 120, 125 n, 126 n, 139, 161 n, 267–268, 271 n, 272 n
Mao Zedong, 141
Maoz, Zeev, 135, 161 n
Maquilladoras, 296
Margulies, Jimmy, 329 n
Marshall Plan, 284
Martin, Lisa L., 271 n, 273 n
Marx, Karl, 43–44, 238, 240
Marxism, 238, 240–241, 271
Masih, Iqbal, 411
Mass, Peter, 198 n
Mass deportation, 70
Mastanduno, Michael, 271 n, 274 n
Matthai, Wangari, 450
Matthiessen, Peter, 199 n
May, Ernest R., 198 n, 349 n
Mazarr, Michael J., 346 n
Mearsheimer, John J., 25
Mediation, 394, 423
Mediterranean Plan, 456
Meehan, Elizabeth, 306 n
Mega, Thomas, 25
Mega-cities, 435–436, 478–479
Melman, Seymour, 146, 162 n
Mendes, Chico, 450
Mendlovitz, Saul H., 423 n, 425 n
Mercantilism, 38–39, 238, 241, 258, 271
Meron, Theodore, 380
Merrill, John C., 487 n
Merrills, J. G., 382 n, 423 n
Merritt, Richard L., 134, 161 n
Methods, 23–24, 27

Mexico, 354; *see also* North American Free Trade Agreement (NAFTA)
Meyer, Herbert E., 197 n
Microloans, 256–257
Middle Ages, 34, 35
Military power, 11, 62, 103–105, 107–108, 115–116, 389
Miller, J. D. B., 28 n, 31 n, 92 n, 162 n, 384 n, 488 n
Miller, Lynn H., 28 n
Miller, Robert Hopkins, 234 n
Miller, Steven E., 126 n
Millot, Marc Dean, 348 n
Milner, Helen, 30 n, 60 n
Mindszenty, Josef, 216
Minehart, Tom, 348 n
Mingst, Karen, 424 n
Minilateral economic cooperation, 281–282
Ministates, 64
Mintz, Alex, 314–315, 347 n
Missiles, 317, 318, 321–324, 326, 331–332, 339–340, 341; *see also* specific types
Mitchell, J. M., 487 n
Mixed-actor world, 17, 87–90, 361, 494
Mkharadge, Gueovgui, 213
Mladic, Ratko, 359
Modern state; *see* State(s)
Modernization process, 67, 258–259
Mohamad, Mahathir, 246, 272 n, 299–300
Moles, 169, 170
Mollemann, Jurgen W., 268
Monarchies, 35–36
Monetary union, 286, 304
Monnet, Jean, 288
Montevideo Convention on Rights and Duties of States of 1933, 356, 362
Montreal Protocol, 449, 453, 455
Montville, Joseph V., 93 n, 236 n
Moon, Bruce E., 304 n, 305 n
Moore, Will H., 59 n, 92 n
Morgenthau, Hans J., 14–15, 29 n, 55, 60 n, 87–88, 95 n, 99, 125 n, 155, 162 n, 194, 199 n, 224, 230, 231, 235 n, 236 n, 265, 274 n, 307 n, 312, 320, 343, 347 n, 377–378, 383 n, 419–420, 425 n, 456, 462 n, 483–
Moro, Aldo, 83
Morris, Benny, 198 n
Morrow, Lance, 67, 93 n

Most favored nation (MFN) status, 271, 279, 356
Mother Teresa, 74
Moynihan, Daniel Patrick, 92 n, 179–180, 382 n
Mubarak, Hosni, 477
Mueller, John, 116, 126 n, 163 n
Muller, Ronald E., 95 n
Multilateralism, 88–89, 201, 229–232, 256–257
Multinational corporations (MNCs), 77–79, 91
  diplomacy and, 228–229
  divestment and, 262
  economic cooperation and, 276, 284
  economic power of U.S. and, 243, 244
  foreign direct investment and, 258
  global communication and, 466
  international law and, 357
  newly industrialized countries and, 253–254
  penetration operations of, 189, 193–194
  technology effects and, 439, 451
Multiple independently targeted reentry vehicles (MIRVs), 321–324
Multipolar systems, 55, 113, 139
Municipal systems, 354, 381
Muravchik, Joshua, 488 n
Murphy, Craig N., 416, 423 n, 424 n, 425 n
Mussolini, Benito, 44, 45
Mutually assured destruction (MAD), 115, 320, 323
Myers, Norman, 460 n

Nagler, Michael N., 29 n
Naim, Moses, 305 n
Nakajima, Hiroshi, 478
Nansen, Fridtjof, 414
Napoleon Bonaparte, 35, 36, 38, 40, 45, 51, 56, 103, 105, 113, 114, 131, 388
Nardin, Terry, 159 n, 382 n
Nasr, S. V. R., 489 n
Nast, Thomas, 222
Nathan, Andrew J., 273 n
Nation-state, 33–34
Nationalism, 36–37, 58, 67–71, 91, 120
Natural law, 352, 381
Nau, Henry, 305 n
Nazih, N. M. Ayubi, 91 n

Nazism, 45, 185–186, 354
Negotiation, diplomatic, 210–212, 394
Nelkin, Dorothy, 487 n
Nelsen, Brent F., 306 n
Nelson, Daniel N., 488 n
Neocolonialism, 240
Neoliberals, 16–18
Neomercantilism, 238
Neorealism, 15–16, 19
  arms limitations and, 343
  diplomacy and, 230–231
  economic instruments and, 265–267
  economic integration and, 294, 301
  economic power and, 242
  environment and, 456
  history and, 55
  international law and, 378
  international organizations and, 420
  international power and, 121
  multiple actors and, 88
  shared experiences and, 484
  war and, 155
Netanyahu, Benjamin, 87, 210
Neumann, Iver B., 28 n
New international economic order (NIEO), 260, 271
New world order, 3, 10–11, 51
Newland, Kathleen, 161 n
Newly industrialized countries (NICs), 241, 250–252, 275, 455; *see also* North-South relationship; Third World
Nicholson, Harold J., 170
Nicolson, Harold, 218, 231, 234 n, 235 n
Nitze, Paul, 47
Nivola, Pietro S., 268
Nixon, Richard, 48, 73, 205, 278, 358
Nobel, Jaap W., 30 n
Nonproliferation Treaty (NPT), 312, 317, 321, 329–330, 337
Nonstate actors, 61; *see also* International nongovernment organizations; Substate actors
  arms limitations and, 340–342
  diplomacy and, 71–72, 227–229
  penetration operations of, 189–190
  as subjects of international law, 355
Nontariff barriers (NTBs), 241, 244, 261, 271
Noriega, Manuel, 152, 217
Normative choices, 24, 27
Norms, 76
Norris, Robert S., 348 n

North, Oliver, 166
North, Robert C., 59 n, 160 n
North American Free Trade
    Agreement (NAFTA), 242, 275,
    283, 293–297, 364
North Atlantic Treaty Organization
    (NATO), 108–111, 287, 311,
    324, 326–327, 335, 359, 387,
    398–399
North Korea, 7, 154, 216–217, 318,
    329–330
North-South relationship, 8, 240–241,
    249–260
    environmental decline and, 438,
        443–445
    organized crime and, 483
    shared experiences and, 484, 485
    technical cooperation and, 416
Nuclear power, 9, 330, 432
Nuclear Test Ban Treaty of 1963,
    312, 341
Nuclear utilization theorists (NUTS),
    115
Nuclear weapons, 140–141, 159; see
    also Arms limitations; Arms
    proliferation
    arms control and, 320–323,
        337–338
    Cold War containment policy and,
        46–48, 58, 64, 110, 115–116,
        378
    disarmament and, 322–325
    obstacles to limitations on,
        317–319
    proliferation of, 327–330
    security risks and, 4, 5
    threshold nuclear powers and, 321,
        328, 337
    underground testing of, 318–319,
        320–321, 337–338, 341, 342
    viability of states and, 64
Nuclear winter, 140, 159
Nye, Joseph S., Jr., 16, 25, 28 n,
    30 n, 56, 60 n, 88–89, 94 n,
    95 n, 100, 119–120, 123, 125 n,
    126 n, 127 n, 231–232, 236 n,
    267, 274 n, 301, 307 n, 343,
    347 n, 420, 425 n, 457, 463 n,
    484, 488 n, 489 n

Obeid, Sheik, 177
O'Donnell, Victoria, 197 n, 199 n
Odugbemi, Sina, 422
Offensive weapons, 316, 346
Ohmae, Kenichi, 305 n
Oil, 105, 258, 260

Okri, Ben, 419
Olson, William Clinton, 30–31 n
Oneal, Frances H., 163 n
Oneal, John R., 163 n
"Open skies" arrangement, 317, 327
Ophuls, William, 458, 460 n
Opium War, 39
Order, 10–11, 27
Organization for Economic
    Cooperation and Development
    (OECD), 266, 281, 481–482
Organization for Strategic Services
    (OSS), 179
Organization of African Unity
    (OAU), 54, 387
Organization of American States
    (OAS), 54, 109, 152, 264, 386,
    387
Organization of Petroleum Exporting
    Countries (OPEC), 105, 258, 260
Organized crime, 5, 479–483
Organski, A. F. K., 120, 126 n,
    138–139, 161 n
Orientation, 20, 496–497
Orphans, 328–329
Ortiz, Guillermo, 296
Ortiz, Irene, 306 n
Ostrom, Elinor, 460 n
Otto, Dianne, 463 n
Outer Space Treaty of 1967, 322,
    341, 363
Overt intelligence, 167, 197
Owens, John, 236 n
Owens, William A., 488 n
Oxford Committee for Famine Relief
    (Oxfam), 406–407
Oye, Kenneth A., 60 n, 307 n
Ozone depletion, 440–441

Paarlberg, Robert L., 305 n
Paine, Thomas, 56
Pakistan, 321, 328–329, 340
Palach, Jan, 74
Palestinian Liberation Organization
    (PLO), 210, 228, 361
Palmer, Norman D., 31 n
Palmieri, Deborah Anne, 273 n
Panama, 152
Pandemic, 478, 487
Papp, Daniel S., 161 n
Paradigm, 23–24, 27
Paret, Peter, 130, 160 n
Parris, Scott, 487 n
Parson, Edward W., 462 n
Paschke, Karl, 360
Patriarchy, war and, 136–137

Peace, 43, 312–315, 363, 394–405
Peace dividend, 315, 334
Peaceful settlement, 394–395, 423
Peacekeeping, 395–402, 423
Pearlstein, Richard M., 81, 94 n
Pearson, Frederic S., 306 n, 312,
    346 n, 347 n, 348 n
Pease, Kelly Kate, 424 n
Peltier, Leonard, 187
Penetration operations, 165–196
    covert acts, 176–178, 189, 196,
        215–216
    against diplomats, 213, 215–216
    intelligence; see Intelligence
    organized crime and, 482
Penn, William, 145
People's Republic of China; see
    China, People's Republic of
Perestroika, 49
Perkins, Edward, 206
Perot, Ross, 296–297
Perry, Mark, 197 n, 199 n
Persian Gulf War, 119, 131, 143–144,
    174–175, 314, 329, 402,
    403–405, 420, 495, 501
Persona non grata, 212–213, 234, 371
Personality, 81–82, 134, 355–356,
    381
Peters, Ralph, 161 n
Peterson, Pete, 206
Peterson, V. Spike, 161 n
Pfaff, William, 59 n, 92 n
Pfaltzgraff, Robert L., Jr., 14, 29 n,
    92 n, 160 n, 347 n
Philby, Kim, 169
PHOINT, 168, 172–173, 197
Physical factors, 62–64, 103–105
Physical quality of life (PQLI), 252,
    290
Pick, Daniel, 160 n
Pierre, Andrew J., 489 n
Pinder, John, 306 n
Piquard, Patrice, 123
Pirages, Dennis, 126 n, 460 n, 461 n
Pitts, Earl E., 170
Plischke, Elmer, 234 n
Poe, Stephen, 273 n
Poland, 48–49, 247
Polarity, 113–117, 125, 137–138
Poles, 113, 125
Political actors, 61, 91
Political capacity, 108
Political integration, 287–293, 304
Political parties, 40
Political repression, 69–70
Political system, 40–42, 108–112,
    137–140

Pollard, Jonathan, 169–170, 171, 183
Pool, John Charles, 305 n
Popular sovereignty, 36, 58
Population size
  as core variable in economy, 434–436
  differences among states, 62–63
  growth of, 389, 434–436, 443
  migration and, 433–434
  overpopulation and, 254
  power and, 104–105
Porter, Bruce D., 59 n, 89, 95 n
Porter, Gareth, 460 n
Positivism, 352–353, 381
Post, Jerrold M., 94 n
Post-Cold War era, 179, 180–181, 191–194, 247–249, 313–315; *see also* Arms limitations; Arms proliferation; Cold War
Postel, Sandra, 460 n
Poulsen, Thomas M., 59 n
Powell, Colin, 157
Powell, Robert, 30 n
Power, 99–124, 125
  balance of, 38, 42, 114–116, 124
  diplomacy and, 220–222
Power ratios, 316, 346
Power structure, 112–118, 125
  bipolar, 46, 55, 114–116, 120, 138, 139
  concentration of power and, 117–118, 124
  multipolar, 55, 113, 139
  unipolar, 116–117, 118–121, 137–138
Power transition, 113, 125
Powers, Averill L., 162 n, 347 n, 383 n
Prebisch, Raul, 240
Predatory elites, 252
Preemptive purchases, 264, 271
Preferential trade system, 280, 304
Premises, 214, 234
Preston, Lee E., 271 n, 272 n
Preston, Lee F., 305 n
Preventive diplomacy, 395–396
Primakov, Yevgeni, 109, 191
Primitive law, 371
Princen, Thomas, 235 n, 460 n
Principles of law, 354–355, 381
Private actors, 73
Problem-solving, 20, 500–501
Propaganda, 184–188, 189, 197, 211, 322
Protectionism, 238, 271
Protestant Reformation, 35
Protocol, 217–218, 225–227, 234

Prowse, Michael, 303
Prussian wars, 38
Psychological warfare, 184, 197
Public actors, 73
Publicists, 355, 381
Puchala, Donald J., 92 n
Putnam, Robert D., 305 n

Quandt, William B., 489 n
Quarles, Charles, 86
Quinpolar power structure, 114
Quotas, 241, 271

Rabb, Theodore K., 161 n
Rabin, Yitzhak, 183, 210
Rajaie-Khorassani, Said, 225
Rajavi, Maryam, 137
Ramaker, Jaap, 348 n
Ramberg, Bennett, 92 n
Ramcharan B. G., 370, 383 n
Rapproachment, 73
Rasler, Karen, 146, 162 n
Rathjens, George W., 347 n
Ray, James Lee, 160 n, 306 n
Raymond, Gregory, 126 n, 162 n, 377, 384 n
Reagan, Ronald, 48, 53, 73–74, 107–108, 150, 179, 203–204, 206, 222, 229, 243, 264, 316, 322, 368, 369, 371, 431, 444, 466
Realism, 14–15, 19, 24
  actors and, 494
  arms limitations and, 343
  authority and, 493
  consensus and, 501
  diplomacy and, 230, 231–232
  economic instruments and, 265
  environment and, 455–456
  history and, 55
  interaction and, 498
  international law and, 377–379
  international organizations and, 419–420
  international power and, 112–113, 117–118, 121, 122
  issues and, 499
  multiple actors and, 87–88, 89
  orientation and, 496
  penetration operations and, 190, 194
  shared experiences and, 483–484
  war and, 155
Rebellion, 142, 159
Reciprocity, 244, 255, 271, 370–371

Redford, Robert, 458
Refugees, 314, 413–416, 479
Regimes, 76, 91
Reginald, Robert, 346 n
Regionalism, 283–301, 304
  Asian-Pacific, 297–301
  European, 8, 281–282, 283, 284–293
  international organizations and, 386–387
  North American, 242, 275, 283, 293–297
  regional courts and, 369
Reich, Walter, 94 n
Reisman, W. Michael, 197 n, 199 n
Reiss, Edward, 346 n
Reiss, Hans, 29 n
Reiss, Mitchell, 346 n
Renaissance, 35
Renan, Ernest, 36, 59 n
Rengger, N. J., 234 n
Renner, Michael G., 347 n, 424 n
Reprisal, 150–151, 159
Republic, 36, 58
Resolutions, 366, 381
Retorsion, 149, 159, 371
Revolution, 142, 159
Rhodes, Carolyn, 271 n, 272 n, 305 n
Rhodes formula, 205
Ricardo, David, 239, 284
Richardson, Lewis F., 132
Richelson, Jeffrey T., 194, 197 n, 198 n, 199 n
Rifkin, Jeremy, 59 n, 348 n, 458, 460 n, 461 n
Rimington, Stella, 191
Riveles, Suzanne, 235 n
River commissions, 387–388
Roberts, Adam, 29 n, 424 n
Roberts, Brad, 126 n, 348 n, 383 n
Robertson, A. H., 423 n
Robinson, J. P. Perry, 348 n
Rogers, Paul, 346 n, 348 n
Rogue states, 154, 156, 192, 329
Roman Catholic Church, 35, 61, 85, 189, 228
Roman Empire, 34, 202, 352
Rommel, Erwin, 175
Roosevelt, Franklin D., 149, 151–152
Rosati, Jerel A., 30 n, 93 n, 424 n
Rosen, Fred, 306 n
Rosenau, James N., 17–18, 28 n, 29 n, 30 n, 54, 60 n, 92 n, 93 n, 307 n, 349 n, 383 n, 423 n, 424 n, 462 n, 463 n, 504 n
Rosenberg, Tina, 488 n
Roskin, Michael, 235 n

Ross, George, 306 n
Rosser, Melissa, 273 n
Rotberg, Robert I., 161 n
Rotblat, Joseph, 342
Rothgeb, John M., Jr., 125 n
Rubin, Robert, 257
Ruggie, John Gerard, 418, 420, 425 n
Ruggiero, Renato, 280
Rules, 76, 368
Rummel, R. J., 161 n
Rush-Bagot Agreement of 1817, 325
Ruskin, John, 56
Russell, Bertrand, 342
Russett, Bruce, 93 n, 135, 161 n, 163 n, 383 n, 424 n, 425 n
Russia; *see also* Soviet Union, former
   arms limitations and, 311, 314, 323–235, 337
   China and, 224
   communism and, 43–44
   democracy in, 473
   intelligence agencies of, 180–181
   North Atlantic Treaty Organization and, 109–110
   October Revolution (1917), 44
   organized crime and, 5, 481
   physical factors in power of, 103–105
   security concerns and, 4–5
Rwanda, 359–360, 399

Sabotage, 178
Sadat, Anwar al-, 227–228
Saddam Hussein, 108, 156, 168, 220, 262–263, 315, 404, 467
Sagasti, Francisco R., 461 n
Samuels, Richard J., 107, 125 n, 126 n
Sanctions, 371
Sandholtz, Wayne, 306 n, 425 n
Santayana, George, 56
Santer, Jacques, 288–289
Satellites, 173–175, 183, 192, 317, 466–467
Scali, John, 212
Scarritt, James R., 93 n
Schaeffer, Robert, 487 n
Scheffer, David J., 93 n, 162 n
Schellenberg, James A., 160 n
Schlagheck, Donna M., 94 n
Schneider, Andrea Kupfer, 234 n
Schoenberg, Harris O., 235 n
Schott, Jeffrey J., 304 n, 305 n, 306 n
Schuman, Michael, 93 n, 487 n
Schuman, Robert, 288
Schwartz, Herman M., 271 n, 272 n
Schweizer, Peter, 193, 199 n
Scientism, 23, 27
Scope, 22–23, 27
Scott, Catherine V., 254, 272 n, 273 n
Sea-launched intercontinental ballistic missiles (SLICBMs), 323
Secchia, Peter, 226
Secession, 67–68, 91
Second-strike capacity, 115
Second World, 7 n
Second World War, 14, 45–46, 54–55, 146, 175, 182, 276–282, 354, 358, 360
Security, 4–6, 325–327, 402–405, 422
Segal, George, 126 n
Seitz, Raymond, 226
Self-determination, 42, 58, 68–71
Self-help, 371, 381
Sen, B., 234 n
Separatist movements, 68
Shackleton, Michael, 306 n
Shafritz, Jay M., 463 n
Shakespeare, William, 56
Shannon, Thomas Richard, 272 n
Shared experiences, 465–486
Sherman, William T., 157
Shulsky, Abram N., 197 n, 198 n
Shultz, George, 222
Shuttle diplomacy, 205, 223–224, 234
SIGINT, 168, 172–173, 182, 183, 197
Silverman, Joy, 226
Simai, Mihaly, 504 n
Simon, Julian L., 460 n
Singapore, 408–409
Singer, J. David, 125 n, 129, 132, 160 n
Singer, Max, 28 n, 163 n, 504 n
Single Europe Act (1986), 285
Sire, H. J. A., 236 n
Situational power, 100–101
Sivard, Ruth Leger, 347 n
Slack, Alison T., 425 n
Slavery, 409–410
Slomanson, William R., 234 n, 382 n
Small, Melvin, 129, 132, 160 n
Small, Patricia L., 93 n
Smist, Frank J., Jr., 197 n, 199 n
Smith, Adam, 39, 41, 239, 241–242, 269, 276
Smith, Anthony D., 92 n, 488 n
Smith, Dale L., 306 n, 347 n
Smith, Russell Jack, 197 n, 198 n
Smoke, Richard, 346 n, 347 n
Smyth, Frank, 348 n
Social Darwinism, 136
Socialism, 8, 374–375
Society, 12; *see also* International society model
Sociobiology, 133–134
Soft power, 100, 468, 483
Sohn, Louis B., 145
Soil, 442–443
Somalia, 9, 397, 398
Sommer, Mark, 347 n, 383 n
Sommers, Harry G., 131
Sommers, Mark, 162 n
Sorensen, Georg, 488
Soroos, Marvin S., 59 n, 60 n, 94 n, 348 n
South Africa, 73–74, 262, 321, 328, 337, 369
South Korea, 330
Sovereignty, 35–36, 58, 353, 354, 381
Soviet Union, former, 213, 323–325;
   see also Arms limitations; Arms proliferation; Cold War
   breakup of, 4, 15, 65, 66, 118, 311, 319–320
   communism and, 4, 15, 43–44, 48–51
   Cuba and, 7, 48, 101, 115, 221–222, 321
   democracy in, 473
   détente and, 48, 73, 312
   economic factors in power of, 106–108
   economic position after Cold War, 247–249
   environmental concerns, 450
   ethnic nationalism in, 68
   intelligence agencies of, 167, 169, 171, 178, 180–181, 191–192, 215–216
   international law and, 373
   intervention by, 151
   organized crime and, 5, 481
   origins of, 44
   physical factors in power of, 103–105
   propaganda and, 187–188, 322
   security concerns and, 4–5
   state-sponsored terrorism and, 154
   in tripolar power structure, 113–114
Spanier, John, 31 n
Special Drawing Rights (SDRs), 278
Spector, Leonard S., 346 n
Spero, Joan Edelman, 79, 94 n
Spiegel, Steven L., 273 n
Spies, 169–171, 178
Spillover, 287–288, 304
Spinoza, Baruch, 503
Spruyt, Hendrik, 59 n

Spy satellites, 173–175, 183, 317
Stalin, Joseph, 44, 45, 46, 168, 219, 247
Stamos, Stephen C., Jr., 305 n
Starke, Linda, 425 n
Starr, Harvey, 93 n, 161 n, 383 n
State(s)
 as actor on international stage, 61–66
 causes of war based on, 134–137
 and classical state system, 37–42
 defined, 33, 58
 diversity and, 62–64
 environmental concerns and, 448–450
 as level of analysis, 25
 origins of modern, 33–37
 proliferation and, 65–66
 rogue, 154, 156, 192, 329
 as subjects of international law, 355, 356
 treaties of, 353, 381
 viability and, 64–65
State-sponsored terrorism, 153–155, 159, 180, 223; *see also* Terrorism
State system, 37–42, 137–140, 352
Staves, Paul B., 487 n
Steady-state society, 430, 459
Steigman, Andrew L., 234 n, 235 n
Stein, Arthur A., 347 n, 504 n
Steiner, Henry J., 423 n
Sterling, Clare, 92 n
Stern, Paul C., 461 n, 462 n
Stevenson, Michael R., 159 n
Stevenson, Randolph T., 314–315, 347 n
Stiles, Kenneth W., 162 n
Stoessinger, John, 134, 160 n, 161 n, 424 n
Stohl, Michael, 162 n
Stoll, Richard J., 93 n, 125 n, 127 n, 161 n, 383 n
Stoyanov, Peter, 473
Strange, Susan, 65, 93 n, 228, 236 n, 273 n
Strategic Arms Limitations Talks (SALT I and SALT II), 321–322
Strategic Arms Reduction Talks (START I and START II), 323–325, 327
Strategic Defense Initiative (SDI; Star Wars), 107–108, 178, 316
Strategic minerals, 105
Strategic weapons, 317, 324, 346
Structural realism; *see* Neorealism

Stubb, Alexander C-G., 306 n
Sturgeon, T. Vance, 162 n
Subjects, of international law, 355–361
Submarines, 331–332
Subnational authority, 65
Substate actors, 26, 66–74, 91
Suez Canal, 40, 396
Sukarnoputri, Megawati, 475
Sullivan, Michael P., 125 n
Sumampan, Arlene, 411
Summers, Harry G., 160 n
Summit diplomacy, 203–205, 223–224, 234
Sun Tsu, 345
Sundgren, Jan, 462 n
Supranationalism, 18–19, 288–290, 304
Susskind, Lawrence E., 460 n
Sustainable development, 407, 437–438, 459
Sutterlin, James, 424 n
Swit, Loretta, 447
Switzer, Jacqueline Vaughn, 460 n, 461 n

Tactical weapons, 327, 346
Tadic, Dusan, 359
Taiwan, 205–206, 328–329
Tariffs, 241, 271
Tatum, Paul, 481
Taylor, Phillip, 92 n
Technology; *see also* Arms limitations; Arms proliferation
 changes in, 389
 computer, 175–176, 439, 467, 469, 481–482
 as core variable in economy, 438–439
 diplomacy and, 223–224
 industrialization and, 39, 41, 253
 intelligence operations and, 175–176
 intergovernmental organizations and, 416–417
 international law and, 363
 as obstacle to arms limitation, 316–319
 power and, 107–108
Telecommunications, 465–468, 485, 487
Television, 9
Terent, George, 180
Terrorism, 79–85, 91
 arms proliferation and, 332–333
 diplomacy and, 222–223

 ethnic conflict and, 82–83, 86, 476–477
 examples of, 6, 80–83, 122, 192, 476–477
 international law and, 362
 penetration operations and, 189, 192
 reprisal and, 150
 security concerns and, 5–6
 state-sponsored, 153–155, 159, 180, 223
Thatcher, Margaret, 288
Thayer, Alfred, 104
Thayer, Charles W., 224, 234 n, 235 n
Theater weapons, 317, 346
Theory, 23, 28
Third World, 7–8, 496
 arms limitations and, 320, 321
 arms spending and, 313
 debt "bomb" and, 257–258, 278, 407
 diplomatic skill and, 225
 drug trade and, 8
 environmental concerns, 450, 455
 global communication and, 468
 health concerns, 478–479
 intelligence operations of, 192
 international law and, 368–369, 373
 International Monetary Fund (IMF) and, 26
 multinational corporations and, 78–79
 North-South relationship and; *see* North-South relationship
 post-Cold War era and, 51–52
 rebellion and revolution in, 142
Thomas, Daniel C., 93 n, 273 n, 347 n, 349 n, 461 n
Thompson, Mike, 328 n
Thompson, W. Scott, 29 n, 161 n, 236 n
Thompson, William A., 272 n
Thompson, William R., 146, 161 n, 162 n
Thucydides, 14
Thurow, Lester C., 246, 272 n
Timmerman, Kenneth R., 348 n
Tobias, Sheila, 161 n
Toffler, Alvin, 65
Toland, John, 160 n
Tolley, Howard, Jr., 94 n
Totalitarian dictatorship, 42–43, 58
Track-two diplomacy, 227–229, 234

Trade; *see also* General Agreement on Tariffs and Trade; North American Free Trade Agreement
  drug, 8, 481–483
  interdependence in, 7, 16–18, 27, 204, 255–256
  international law and, 364–365
  in North-South relationship, 255–256
Transnational actors, 61
Transnational authority, 65, 494
Transnationalism, 16–18, 28
  arms limitations and, 343
  authority and, 65, 494
  diplomacy and, 230, 231–232
  economic instruments and, 266
  economic integration and, 301
  environment and, 457
  force and, 497
  history and, 56
  international law and, 377, 378
  international power and, 121
  multiple actors and, 88–89
  shared experiences and, 484
  war and, 155–156
Transparency, 479, 487
Treaties, 353, 364–365, 370, 381
Treaty of Rome (1957), 364
Treverton, Gregory F., 29 n, 163 n, 349 n, 382 n
Triad systems, 320
Tripolar power structure, 113–114
Truman, Harry, 130, 131, 140, 227, 279, 380, 403
Tucker, Robert W., 125 n
Turner, Stansfield, 193, 199 n
Turner, Ted, 451, 486
Tutu, Desmond, 73–74
Twain, Mark, 65

Ukraine, 328–329
UN System, 385, 457, 479; *see also* United Nations (UN)
UN Educational, Scientific, and Cultural Organization (UNESCO), 415
UN International Children's Fund (UNICEF), 411–412
UN Conference on Trade and Development (UNCTAD), 255, 259
Underground testing, 318–319, 320–321, 337–338, 341, 342
Ungar, Sheldon, 346 n, 347 n
Unilateral actions, 319, 327
Unilateral arms limitations, 319, 327

Unipolar power structure, 116–117, 118–121, 137–138
United Nations (UN), 76, 77, 385, 388, 390–416, 497; *see also* International Court of Justice; International law; International Monetary Fund (IMF)
  arms limitations and, 320, 336–337, 340, 341
  Center on Transnational Corporations, 357
  Charter, 144, 145, 148, 150, 151, 353, 362, 388, 391, 402–403
  economic development and, 255, 259, 262–263, 405–407
  environmental concerns and, 435, 451–452
  ethnic conflict and, 5, 68–69, 397–399
  foreign aid and, 256
  governance and, 17–18
  human rights and, 9, 110–111, 372, 397–399, 407–409
  International Law Commission, 217, 366–367
  League of Nations compared with, 390–394
  legality of war and, 137, 144, 145, 147–149, 362
  penetration operations and, 165
  policymaking roles of ambassadors and, 209
  War Crimes Tribunal, 358–359
  Zionist movement and, 86
United States; *see also* Arms limitations; Arms proliferation; Cold War
  colonial period, 36, 39, 40, 43
  Cuba and, 7, 48, 101
  diplomatic establishment of, 219, 220, 226–227, 229–230
  economic factors in power of, 8, 106–108, 237, 241–242, 243
  as hegemonic power, 117–121, 237, 267–268, 276, 284, 294
  intelligence agencies of, 166–171, 176–178, 179–180, 183, 190, 191, 193–194, 215–216
  intervention by, 151–152
  leadership position of, 495–496
  as major trade state, 241–242, 243, 245, 247
  and North American Free Trade Agreement (NAFTA), 242, 275, 283, 293–297, 364
  North Atlantic Treaty Organization and, 108–111

  organized crime and, 480–483
  physical factors in power of, 104, 105
  propaganda and, 186–187, 188
  role in international relations, 11
  terrorism and, 6, 80, 82–85, 122
  trade ties with Japan, 16, 283–284
  in tripolar power structure, 113–114
  United Nations and, 417–418
  United States Information Agency (USIA), 474–475
U.S. Arms Control and Disarmament Agency, 313, 319
Universal Declaration of Human Rights, 353, 365, 373, 408
Universal military service (UMS), 104
Universal state, 34–35
Upton, Emory, 130
Urwin, Derek W., 306 n
Ury, William L., 163 n

Van Dyke, Vernon, 59 n, 92 n, 199 n, 488 n
Van Moltke, Gebhardt, 126 n
Vasquez, John A., 28 n, 92 n, 95 n, 160 n
Vaubel, Roland, 305 n
Verification, 317, 346
Vernon, Raymond, 88, 95 n
Versailles Treaty (1919), 392
Viability, of states, 64–65
Victoria, Queen of England, 137
Vienna Convention on Consular Relations (1963), 217, 364, 367
Vienna Convention on Diplomatic Relations (1961), 212, 215, 217, 223, 354, 364, 367
Vienna Convention on the Law of Treaties (1969), 353
Vietnam War, 111, 130, 142–143, 225, 313–314, 358, 362–363
Vincent, R. J., 28 n, 31 n, 92 n, 378, 384 n, 488 n
Viotti, Paul R., 28 n, 30 n, 126 n
Vlahos, Michael, 488 n
Vo Nguyen Giap, 141
Voltaire, 35

Walker, John, 171
Walker, Michael, 274 n, 304 n, 306 n
Walker, William, 348 n
Wallerstein, Immanuel, 240–241, 272 n, 474, 488 n

Walters, Robert S., 272 n
Waltz, Kenneth N., 15, 25, 30 n, 31 n, 55, 60 n, 88, 95 n, 133, 139, 155, 160 n, 161 n, 162 n, 230–231, 236 n, 265–266, 274 n, 343, 349 n, 378, 384 n, 420, 425 n, 456, 462 n, 484
Walzer, Michael, 143, 160 n, 161 n
Wapner, Paul, 462 n
War, 129–158, 159; *see also* Arms limitations; Arms proliferation; Conflict
   Correlates of War Project (COW), 102–103, 132
   diplomatic relations and, 212, 220
   economic warfare, 264, 270
   force and, 20, 497–498
   legal status of, 137, 144, 145, 147–149, 362
   and state system, 37–38
War crimes, 70–71, 354, 358–360, 365, 366
Warbrick, Colin, 382 n
Ward, Barbara, 33, 59 n, 460 n
Ward, Michael D., 125 n, 127 n
Warsaw Pact, 108–109, 111, 116, 249, 263–264, 311, 326
Washington, George, 179
Water, 441–442, 450
Watson, Adam, 30 n, 58 n, 59 n, 234 n, 373, 380, 382 n, 488 n
Wayman, Frank W., 28 n, 162 n, 384 n
Wealth, differences among states, 62
Weapons; *see* Arms limitations; Arms proliferation
Webb, Gregory, 346 n
Webster, William, 176
Weintraub, Sidney, 305 n
Weiss, Edith Brown, 458, 460 n
Weisskopf, Thomas E., 273 n, 462 n
Welch, David A., 160 n, 162 n
Welch, Richard, 190
Wells, H. G., 56
Wesson, Robert, 312, 347 n, 383 n, 488 n
Westad, Odd Arne, 503 n, 504 n

Weston, Burns H., 346 n, 377, 382 n, 383 n
Westphalia, Peace of (1648), 35, 41, 68, 143, 352, 365, 501
Whaling, 446, 450, 454–455
Wheeler, Nicholas J., 30 n
White, Nigel, 423 n
Wiener, Jarrod, 423 n
Wieviorka, Michel, 92 n
Wight, Martin, 12, 28 n, 29 n, 155, 162 n
Wildavsky, Aaron, 28 n, 163 n, 504 n
Wildlife, 445–447, 450, 451, 454–455
Wiley, Joyce N., 95 n
Wilhelm, Kaiser, 134
Willett, Thomas D., 305 n
Willetts, Peter, 92 n, 95 n
Williams, Phil, 463 n
Willis, David P., 487 n
Willkie, Wendell L., 273 n
Wilson, Edward O., 133–134, 161 n, 460 n, 462 n
Wilson, James Q., 239, 272 n
Wilson, Woodrow, 14, 42, 68, 224–225, 389, 483
Winch, Donald, 461 n
Windsor, Duane, 271 n, 272 n, 305 n
Winsemius, Pieter, 459 n, 461 n
Wise, David, 170, 194, 197 n, 198 n
Wittkopf, Eugene R., 30 n, 60 n, 162 n
Woito, Robert, 162 n
Wolfenden, Jeremy, 178
Wolkomir, Joyce, 348 n
Wolkomir, Richard, 348 n
Women, 136–137, 254, 277, 341, 410, 412–413, 475, 480
Wood, David M., 305 n
Woods, Lawrence T., 236 n, 305 n, 306 n
Woolsey, James, 179–180, 191–193
World Bank, 256, 367, 405, 431, 450, 452
   history of, 276–278
   International Monetary Fund (IMF), 26, 120–121, 204, 241, 248, 259

World Health Organization (WHO), 386, 389, 415, 478, 479
World Intellectual Property Organization (WIPO), 256, 416
World Meteorological Organization (WMO), 416, 452
World Trade Organization (WTO), 7, 246, 248, 275, 280, 284, 365, 496; *see also* General Agreement on Tariffs and Trade (GATT)
World War I; *see* First World War
World War II; *see* Second World War
World Wide Web, 467
Worldwatch, 429
Wright, Joanne, 92 n
Wright, Quincy, 132, 160 n
Wriston, Walter, 486
Wu Yi, 262, 263

Yakushij, Taizo, 459 n, 461 n
Yeltsin, Boris, 5, 49–50, 54, 109, 123, 180, 187, 204, 248, 323, 324, 325–326, 331, 338, 473
Yesilada, Birol A., 305 n
Yew, Lee Kuan, 472
Yomamoto, Isoroku, 175
Yost, David S., 29 n
Young, Gay, 273 n
Young, John E., 461 n
Young, Oran R., 432, 460 n, 461 n, 462 n

Zacker, Mark W., 383 n, 389, 423 n
Zalewski, Marysia, 161 n
Zangwill, Israel, 56
Zedillo Ponce de Leon, Ernesto, 294–295
Zero population growth, 435, 459
Zimmerman, William, 126 n, 161 n
Zinnes, Dina A., 134, 161 n
Zionist movement, 86–87